Women and Museums

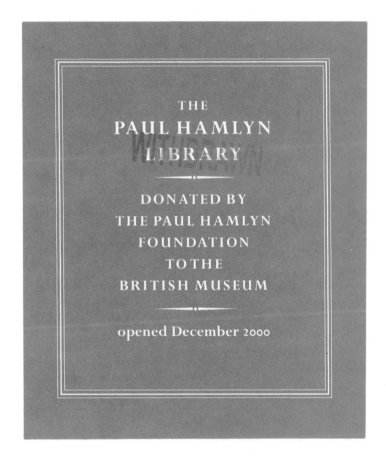

Women and Museums

A Comprehensive Guide

Victor J. Danilov

ALTAMIRA
PRESS

A Division of
ROWMAN & LITTLEFIELD PUBLISHERS, INC.
Lanham • New York • Toronto • Oxford

ALTAMIRA PRESS
A division of Rowman & Littlefield Publishers, Inc.
A wholly owned subsidiary of The Rowman & Littlefield Publishing Group, Inc.
4501 Forbes Boulevard, Suite 200
Lanham, MD 20706
www.altamirapress.com

PO Box 317, Oxford OX2 9RU, UK

Copyright © 2005 by AltaMira Press

British Library Cataloguing in Publication Information Available

Library of Congress Cataloging-in-Publication Data

Danilov, Victor J.
    Women and museums : a comprehensive guide / Victor J. Danilov.
        p.   cm.
    Includes bibliographical references and index.
    ISBN 0-7591-0854-4 (cloth : alk. paper) — ISBN 0-7591-0855-2 (pbk. : alk. paper)
    1. Museums—United States—Directories.   2. Museums and women—United States.
  3. Women—United States.   4. Cultural property—Protection—United States.   5. Popular culture—United States.
  6. United States—Intellectual life—19th century.   7. United States—Intellectual life—20th century.   I. Title.
AM11.D354 2005
069′.025′73—dc22

                                                                                            2005002692

Printed in the United States of America

♾™ The paper used in this publication meets the minimum requirements of American
National Standard for Information Sciences—Permanence of Paper for Printed Library
Materials, ANSI/NISO Z39.48–1992.

Contents

Preface

Women have had a long relationship with museums and museumlike facilities in the United States. They have founded, funded, and/or spearheaded the establishment of numerous museums and related sites; have had many museums and other institutions named for them; and have served as directors, trustees, staff members, donors, and volunteers in the development of a wide range of museums and other such places.

Unfortunately, women's contributions to the American museum movement have not been fully recognized. This study looks at two aspects of the role of women—how they have been influential in the starting and/or naming of many of the nation's museums, galleries, historic houses and sites, botanical gardens, arboretums, aquariums, zoos, and other museumlike institutions; and how an increasing number of museums, galleries, and halls of fame are being devoted to the history, art, and achievements of women in the United States.

Nearly 1,000 of the more than 8,000 museums and related facilities in the nation have been founded by and/or named for women (sometimes with their spouses). Some of these women have been art patrons, philanthropists, civic leaders, community workers, and/or collectors, who have given funds, collections, time, and/or their homes to launch museums and similar institutions, while others have been honored with museums, historic houses, and other types of memorials named for them because of their artistic, literary, scientific, technological, political, or other exemplary work.

This book tells the story of women who have been responsible for the establishment of some of the nation's largest, best-known, and most highly regarded museums, as well as hundreds of smaller community museums and related facilities. It also describes the growing number of American institutions created to trace the history, display the art, and/or honor the accomplishments of women.

The museums and related facilities listed in this book can be classified as devoted to women, art-oriented, historical, science-based, or other types. The greatest number are historical in nature, followed by art institutions and facilities devoted to women. The sites are located in 49 states, with New York, California, Texas, and Massachusetts having the greatest number.

This volume is the first comprehensive overview of the important role of women in the development of American museums and related facilities—combined with descriptions of those institutions devoted specifically to women. It represents a significant step toward recognizing the great influence of women in museums, but it is only the beginning of the study needed to fully demonstrate the enormous impact of women in one of America's most prized cultural fields.

For Toni Dewey,
my beloved wife

Introduction

Susan Armitage

In the 1970s, when the study of women's history was just getting started, those of us in this new field often spoke of the time in the future when our "hidden history" would change the way American history was written. At the time, our belief that we could recover the ignored history of women was more a hope than a confident prediction. Yet here we are today, more than thirty years later, with an example of recovered women's history that does indeed change our understanding of the role of museums in American civic life. As the evidence compiled by Vic Danilov in this volume shows, women have always had a vital part in the founding and functioning of American museums, albeit one that has not been fully appreciated until recently. Just as important as the story of the founding and functioning of museums are the reasons that women have given for their activities. In this introduction, I will place those reasons within the larger context of American women's activism as it has been rediscovered by historians of women, interweaving my account with Danilov's descriptions.

First, though, let me consider one basic question: why were women's museum activities overlooked and underappreciated in the first place? In the nineteenth century, one major reason was the nearly universal opinion that women were domestic and private creatures, while the public realm belonged to men. Because women couldn't vote and had limited legal rights, they could not participate in politics as men did. Historians used to think that women therefore left politics and public life to men, but that answer failed to appreciate

the ways in which women engaged in public life simply by redefining the terms.

The work of organizing political parties, of running for public office, and of voting were all exclusively male activities before national women's suffrage in 1920. But we now know that early in the nineteenth century, women began petition drives, fund-raising, lobbying, projects for young people, and scores of other activities that took them outside the home and into the public arena. Because women were careful to explain their concerns as domestic and supportive, none of these activities were considered political. But when we look at the deep and continuing involvement of women's groups in social reform, we now see that they did everything men did, short of the ballot box. This insight is beginning to change the scope and scale of what historians and political scientists call politics. When we include informal as well as official activity, we see that women have been political participants with men all along, but until well into the twentieth century, women did their politics differently. Perhaps this is why it took so long for men to notice.

This story of different political involvement is tied directly to women's museum activities. From our vantage point today, it is possible to discern three distinct phases of women's involvement in museum activities. First women were preservers, then contributors, and finally founders; these three activities reflect the ways in which women over the course of more than a century gradually took increasingly assertive parts in public life.

PRESERVING WOMEN

Among the public activities that nineteenth-century middle-class women considered a natural part of their family responsibilities was community building, that is, creating and sustaining basic civic institutions such as churches, schools, libraries, and hospitals. In many respects, historic preservation was a logical offshoot of community building. In communities all over the nation, women's groups saved and maintained the historic houses of important men and, rarely, women.

1

There was a crucial national component to this effort: Starting with efforts to preserve and maintain buildings connected with the nation's founders, women's groups took the lead in creating a visible national heritage. As early as the 1850s, the Mount Vernon Ladies' Association took steps to preserve the home of the nation's first president on the banks of the Potomac as a historic house museum. Similarly, the Ladies' Hermitage Association preserved Andrew Jackson's home outside Nashville, Tennessee, while the Monticello-Jefferson Memorial Association performed a rescue mission for Thomas Jefferson's property in Charlottesville, Virginia. In every case, women first raised the money for preservation and later either administered the site directly or provided the support staff for the male administrator who nominally headed the operation.

In 1878, the preservation of General George Washington's headquarters at Valley Forge, near Philadelphia, was begun by women who later became members of the Daughters of the American Revolution (DAR) when the group was organized in 1890. Since then, historic preservation and the erection of historic monuments have been major DAR activities. DAR chapters have preserved several hundred historic houses across the nation. The society also operates a major decorative arts museum, the Daughters of the American Revolution Museum, housed in the 1904 Memorial Continental Hall in Washington, D.C.

The Colonial Dames of America, founded in 1891, also began preserving historic properties at the turn of the twentieth century. The national society and its chapters now own or manage eighty-two sites, including Dumbarton Oaks, the 1800 Federal-style mansion in Georgetown with significant research resources in Byzantine studies, pre-Columbian studies, and landscape architecture on a property that boasts ten acres of formal gardens.

Many other women's organizations have restored and operate historic sites and/or have founded historical and other museums. The Alamo in San Antonio, where Texans battled Mexicans for independence in 1836, has been under the care of the Daughters of the Republic of Texas since 1905. The Daughters of Hawaii have preserved the ca. 1838 Hulihee Palace and the ca. 1847 Queen Emma Summer Palace, while the Daughters of Utah Pioneers have founded and operate 86 historical museums in Utah and twenty in surrounding states.

Local and regional women's garden clubs, medical auxiliaries, and other organizations such as the Junior League have founded or assisted museums, historic houses, botanical gardens, and other museumlike facilities. For example, the Sheldon Museum and Cultural Center in Haines, Alaska, was started by the Haines Women's Club; the Health Adventure in Asheville, North Carolina, was founded as a children's health museum by the Medical Auxiliary of Buncombe County; and the Founders' Memorial Gardens in Athens, Georgia, was established by the Ladies Garden Club of Athens, which later became the Garden Club of Georgia.

The built environment is an important but often underappreciated source of our sense of the past. The preservation work that nineteenth-century groups like the Daughters of the American Revolution accomplished—and the related effort to build monuments to notable events or personages—was essential to building our sense of national heritage and fostering national feeling and patriotism.

It is significant that the sites saved by women's groups were historic *homes*. The association between women and domesticity was absolute in the nineteenth century, and few men objected to women's attention to those particular sites. Then too, it often was the case that women possessed the detailed knowledge of furniture, fabrics, and decorative arts necessary for authentic preservation or replication. What women's groups often lacked was money, but they were skilled fund-raisers and rarely experienced difficulty in getting donations for such worthy and noncontroversial causes.

There are several other aspects of this early work in historic preservation that deserve special mention. First, historic homes, even if they were saved because a great man lived there, preserved a lot of women's history. Indeed, many historic house museums honor famous women—they were, until recently, one of the major ways in which exceptional women were honored. Second, the nineteenth-century preservation efforts by women's groups laid the foundation for today's more controversial historic preservation movement. Today, when preservationists argue with developers about what should be saved, they are able to invoke the nineteenth-century tradition of preservation as an example of enlightened citizenship—no matter now that the women who did the preservation were second-class citizens who were denied the vote and other legal rights as well.

PRESERVING HISTORIC HOUSES

More than half of the nation's 8,000-plus museums and museumlike organizations are historical in nature—and many are historic houses and sites. Some have significant importance in national or regional history. Others were saved and restored because of their age, size, architecture, gardens, past occupants, donors, or other factors. And many have involved women as former residents or as persons who have bequeathed or contributed the homes for use as historic houses or sites for other types of museums.

The ca. 1653 Alden House in Duxbury, Massachusetts, was the last home of Pilgrims John and Priscilla Alden, who crossed the Atlantic on the *Mayflower*. The ca. 1765 Morris-Jumel Mansion, home of the flamboyant and somewhat eccentric Eliza Jumel, was where General George Washington and the British once had their Revolutionary War headquarters in New York City. It also was where Jumel married political leader Aaron Burr in 1833, after the death of her wine merchant husband.

The Betsy Ross House in Philadelphia was the 1773–1786 home of the seamstress of the first American flag. The 1852 Surratt House in Clinton, Maryland, is where Mary Elizabeth Jenkins Surratt, a Confederate sympathizer who was recruited by John Wilkes Booth into a plot to kidnap President Abraham Lincoln, provided weapons and supplies to Booth after the assassination. She later was arrested, convicted in the plot, and hanged.

Among the other early homes, plantations, farms, and other sites involving women that have become historic houses and museums are the Shirley Plantation, Virginia's oldest plantation near Charles City, which was built by Sir Thomas West on 8,000 acres received in a grant from King James of England in 1613 and named for his wife, Lady Cessaeley Shirley; Tudor Place Historic House and Garden, built in 1805–1816 by Martha Parke Custis Peter, granddaughter of Martha Washington, with an $8,000 legacy from her step-grandfather, George Washington, in Washington, D.C.; and the Rokeby Museum, located on a prosperous farm founded by Quaker immigrants Thomas and Jemima Robinson in the 1780s in Ferrisburgh, Vermont, where four generations of women were active abolitionists and noted artists.

Some estates left by wealthy women have become historic museums, such as the Winchester Mystery House, a 160-room Victorian mansion in San Jose, California, that Sarah L. Winchester, a Winchester rifle heiress, began building in 1884 and that occupied the lives of craftsmen until her death 38 years later; the Astors' Beechwood Victorian Living History Museum, housed in an 1857 mansion in Newport, Rhode Island, which was the summer home of Mrs. Caroline Astor, creator of America's first social register; and Hillwood Museum and Gardens, the 25-acre former estate of Marjorie Merriweather Post, prominent businesswoman, collector, and philanthropist, that features a 40-room mansion with collections of Russian and French art and decorative arts in Washington, D.C.

Many historic houses honor famous women, such as those where First Ladies once lived. They include the Abigail Adams Birthplace in Weymouth, Massachusetts, where the wife of the nation's second president, John Adams, and mother of the sixth president, John Quincy Adams, was born in 1744 and spent her first twenty years in the restored 1685 house; Mary Todd Lincoln House, a 14-room Georgian home in Lexington, Kentucky, where the wife of President Abraham Lincoln lived with her parents from 1832 until her marriage in 1842; and Eleanor Roosevelt National Historic Site near Hyde Park, New York, where she had a fieldstone cottage—called Val-Kill—that later was her home from 1945 until her death in 1962.

Other historic houses are the former homes of noted authors, artists, and other women known for their achievements, such as Orchard House, the 1800s home of Louisa May Alcott, author of *Little Women*, in Concord, Massachusetts; Harriet Beecher Stowe Center, where the author of the classic antislavery novel *Uncle Tom's Cabin* and 30 other books lived in Hartford, Connecticut; Georgia O'Keeffe Home and Studio in Abiquiu, New Mexico, home of the artist from 1949 to 1984 and where she painted some of her most famous semiabstract works; and Amelia Earhart Birthplace Museum in Atchison, Kansas, where the world's most famous female aviator was born in 1897 and lived until she was twelve.

A number of women are honored at more than one site. Six New England houses where Mary Baker Eddy, founder of the Christian Science movement, formerly lived are now historic houses operated as branches of the Longyear Museum in Chestnut Hill, Massachusetts. Laura Ingalls Wilder, author of the *Little House on the Prairie* books, is the focus of five midwestern historic

The Harriet Beecher Stowe Center in Hartford, Connecticut, is housed in the former home of the author of the classic antislavery novel Uncle Tom's Cabin. She made her home in the neighborhood of writers and reformers from 1864 until her death in 1896. Courtesy Harriet Beecher Stowe Center.

sites. The Massachusetts birthplace and a national historic site in Maryland both recognize Clara Barton for her work as founder and first president of the American Red Cross, and Nobel Prize–winning author Pearl S. Buck is honored at her birthplace in West Virginia and at a historic home in Pennsylvania. In her Minnesota hometown of Grand Rapids, entertainer Judy Garland is remembered both at her birthplace historic house and at a children's museum bearing her name.

Historic preservation is a civic cause that still attracts the efforts of many women today, and there are few historic house museums across the country that could continue to function without the dedicated work of the women who are their administrators, staff, and volunteers.

CONTRIBUTING WOMEN

By the turn of the twentieth century, the association of women with domesticity was beginning to be less absolute. Women were moving into the public gaze in new ways, as students and faculty in higher education, in the workplace (although most working women were poor and unnoticed), but above all in women's groups with openly public agendas. In Chicago, Jane Addams created the new profession of social work as she directed a largely female group of reformers headquartered at Hull House, the famous settlement house located in the middle of the Chicago slums. Elsewhere, Frances Willard shaped the Women's Christian Temperance Union into a formidable national force for reform in fields far beyond temperance. These new trends in women's lives were epitomized by a short-lived women's museum—the Women's Building at the World Columbian Exposition held in Chicago in 1893. There, collections by state committees from all over the country exhibited materials showing women's accomplishments. The Iowa women's committee, for example, gathered materials by sending out a request for "all articles which illustrate woman's share in the industrial, educational, artistic, religious and philanthropical activities of Iowa to indicate the progress women have made in all these [areas] during the comparatively few years of our state's existence."[1] By all accounts the Women's Building was a huge success, but it was torn down and the collections dispersed at the fair's end. Nevertheless, some women looked for more. Within a decade the moribund women's suffrage movement had sprung to life, and soon hundreds of thousands of women were demanding the right to vote. Some women also sought a greater public role in cultural affairs.

Early in the twentieth century, wealthy women began to donate their collections to museums or were among the founders of the nation's great art museums. Usually we think of money and power as going hand in hand, but in fact wealthy women usually failed to be accorded the recognition that their generous contributions ought to have brought them. According to Kathleen McCarthy, who has closely studied women's philanthropy, this was because wealthy American men took the lead in founding the nation's great cultural institutions, such as the Metropolitan Museum in New York and the Boston Museum of Fine Arts. They did not wish to see their control over culture and philanthropy challenged by women of their own social class. Thus they made sure that wealthy women followed the advice of male connoisseurs when buying art and when deciding whether to donate their collections to museums. And although women were often major financial contributors, their dollars did not give them seats on the governing boards of museums. Generally, they were effusively thanked and then shuffled off to concentrate on lesser collections, such as decorative arts. As late as the 1940s, McCarthy relates, the governing board of the Metropolitan Museum was all male, retaining "the jolly informal stag atmosphere" it had had since its founding.[2]

The Whitney Museum of American Art was started in New York City in 1930 by sculptor Gertrude Vanderbilt Whitney. It now occupies this landmark building designed by noted architects Marcel Breuer and Hamilton Smith in 1963–1966. Courtesy Whitney Museum of American Art and photographer Jerry L. Thompson.

McCarthy tells us that only a few women stood out against this male dominance of high culture. Perhaps not surprisingly, they were among the very wealthiest. While the men were competing to own the Old Masters of Europe, women staked out the avant-garde as their own. For example, while her husband collected medieval and Chinese artifacts, Abby Aldrich Rockefeller and two associates founded the Museum of Modern Art, in 1929. After years as a patron of modern art, Gertrude Vanderbilt Whitney went one step further by founding a museum in her own name. The Whitney Museum of American Art opened in 1931. In a delightful irony, these wealthy women amassed huge collections because contemporary art was so inexpensive, compared with the prices their husbands were paying for scarce Old Masters. McCarthy argues that these women signaled a shift from the charity organizations of the past (which included most of the historic house preservationists) to innovative cultural authority. Because these wealthy women were able to act as patrons of artists on a grand scale, they directly influenced the development of modern art in America. Their predecessors, the preservationists, had shaped the past. These women shaped the future.

Many other women followed in the footsteps of these wealthy women founders, and their generosity took many and diverse forms.

One of the first non-historic house museums founded by women was the Museum of Art at the Rhode Island School of Design in Providence. It was established as part of the school in 1877 by Helen Adelia Rowe Metcalf and the Women's Centennial Committee, with $1,675 left over from the state's participation in the Centennial Exposition in Philadelphia in 1876. Another prominent design museum—the Cooper Union Museum for the Arts of Decoration (now the Cooper-Hewitt National Design Museum of the Smithsonian Institution)—was started by three sisters, Amy, Eleanor, and Sarah Hewitt, in New York City in 1897. They were granddaughters of Peter Cooper, who established the Cooper Union for the Advancement of Science and Art in 1853.

Two leading art museums founded by women also were launched in the 1890s. The Fogg Art Museum at Harvard University in Cambridge, Massachusetts, was founded in 1891 with a $220,000 bequest from Elizabeth Fogg in memory of her husband, "for the enlightenment of the people." In 1903 Isabella Stewart Gardner opened a museum in Boston featuring her exceptional eclectic art collection, housed in a Venetian-style palace that she designed and for which she oversaw construction.

In California, two wealthy women helped start three science museums at the University of California at Berkeley in the early twentieth century. Phoebe A. Hearst, wife of Senator George Hearst and mother of newspaper publisher William Randolph Hearst, generously supported the systematic collecting of archaeologists and ethnologists at the Lowie Museum of Anthropology, which opened in 1901. The museum's name later was changed to the Phoebe A. Hearst Museum of Anthropology, in recognition of her early financial assistance. Naturalist Annie Montague Alexander founded and endowed the Museum of Vertebrate Zoology in 1908 and the Museum of Paleontology in 1921 on the campus. She also had more than fifteen fossils and plant and mammal species named for her as a result of her exploratory work.

Most museums and related institutions established by women are the result of gifts of funds, real estate, and/or collections. The contributions often are monetary, such as the Strybing Arboretum and Botanical Gardens that was made possible in San Francisco in 1937 by donor Helen Strybing; Betty Brinn Children's Museum, founded in Milwaukee in 1995 with financial support from the businesswoman for whom it was named; and Draper Museum of Natural History, which was added as a wing to the Buffalo Bill Historical Center in Cody, Wyoming, in 2002 after a major gift by trustee Nancy-Carroll Draper.

Bequests often initiate museums, as occurred with the Fitchburg Art Museum, founded in Fitchburg, Massachusetts, in 1925 through the expatriate artist Eleanor Norcross's will; Bayly Art Museum (which later became the University Art Museum), which was started in 1935 by Dr. Evelyn May Bayly Tiffany's bequest at the University of Virginia in Charlottesville; and the Degenhart Paperweight and Glass Museum, established in Cambridge, Ohio, in 1978 through the bequest of Elizabeth Degenhart, who had run a glass factory.

This statuary is in the Marie Selby Botanical Gardens in Sarasota, Florida. The tropical gardens and Spanish-style home were bequeathed for public enjoyment by the widow of the founder of the Texaco Oil Company. The gardens cover 8.5 acres and feature rare orchids and bromeliads. Courtesy Marie Selby Botanical Gardens and photographer Stan Pastor.

Many women leave their homes, and sometimes their gardens, to local history and other museums, or to serve as historic houses or sites for new institutions. For instance, the 1730 Elizabeth Perkins House, one of the finest examples of Colonial Revival architecture and interior design in New England, was bequeathed to the historical society in York, Maine, for its home in 1952. Among those places that became museums are Historic Smithfield, a 1775 plantation in Blackburg, Virginia, given by Janie Preston Boulware Lamb, a great-great-granddaughter of the founders, to the Association for the Preservation of Virginia Antiquities in 1959 for operation as a living history site; High Museum of Art, founded in 1926 in the Atlanta home donated by Hattie High, wife of a local merchant; and Marie Shelby Botanical Gardens, featuring a 1921

Spanish-style home and botanical gardens, left by the widow of a cofounder of Texaco in her 1971 will for the enjoyment of the public in Sarasota, Florida.

Sometimes a woman will purchase a building or site for a museum, as occurred with the Clarke Historical Museum, founded in 1960 in a former bank building purchased for the museum by high school teacher Cecile Clarke; Shemer Art Center, housed in an adobe building donated to the city of Phoenix in 1984 by realtor Martha Evvard Shemer to be used as an art gallery and studio for art classes; and Gertrude Herbert Institute of Art, located in an 1818 three-story Federal-style house bought by Olivia Herbert in 1935 and donated to the Augusta Art Club in Georgia as a memorial to her daughter, who died of spinal meningitis.

In addition to providing funds, women frequently will give their collections of art or other objects toward the establishment of a museum. The Colorado Springs Fine Arts Center was opened in Colorado in 1936 by Alice Bemis Taylor, who wanted a place for her extensive collection of southwestern Spanish Colonial folk art and Native American and Hispanic art, as well as a home for visual arts, performing arts theater, art school, art library, and sculpture garden. Businesswoman and philanthropist Julia Shaw Patterson Carnell helped start the Dayton Art Institute in Ohio by donating the first of many artworks and a mansion for its first home in 1919—and later gave $2 million for a new building when the museum outgrew the mansion in 1930. The Museum of International Folk Art—the world's largest folk art museum, in Santa Fe, New Mexico—was founded in 1953 by Florence Dibell Bartlett, a Chicago collector, humanitarian, and philanthropist who lived part-time on her nearby ranch.

Collections sometimes result in the founding of new museums. Naomi Wood, a Philadelphia collector of colonial furniture, decorative arts, and other antiques, left her collection in trust to be exhibited to the public in a historic house for educational purposes. After her death in 1926, the executors of her will restored the 1756 Woodford Mansion to display the collection. The Abby Aldrich Rockefeller Folk Art Museum at Colonial

Williamsburg in Virginia began in 1957 with a core collection of 424 objects from Mrs. John D. Rockefeller Jr., wife of the originator of the historical village. The Marion Steinback Indian Basket Museum in Tahoe City, California, started with nearly 1,000 Native American baskets collected by Steinback, while Nora Eccles Harrison Museum of Art at Utah State University in Logan features the extensive ceramics collection of the donor. Electra Webb, a sugar heiress and a collector, founded the Shelburne Museum in Shelburne, Vermont, in 1947 because she was enthralled with "the beauty of every-day things" and wanted to share them with the public.

Many museums are started by women simply convinced of the need, who contribute primarily their leadership efforts rather than funds or collections. Among such institutions are the Nevada Historical Society, founded in Reno in 1904, largely through the efforts of historian Jean Elizabeth Wier of the University of Nevada; Connecticut Audubon Birdcraft Museum, established in Fairfield in 1914 by pioneer conservationist Mabel Osgood Wright while serving as founding president of the Connecticut Audubon Society; and Arkansas Museum of Science and History, created almost single-handedly by journalist, poet, and author Bernie Babcock in Little Rock in 1927 because the state was being criticized for lacking cultural facilities. Some founders also become the director of the museum. This happened with Ellen S. Quillan, a botanist and teacher who started the Witte Museum in San Antonio, Texas, in 1926 and served as director for 34 years; territorial historian Sharlot Hall at the Old Governor's Mansion—later renamed in her honor—in the frontier town of Prescott, Arizona, in 1927; Berta Calloway, who founded the Great Plains Black Museum in Omaha, Nebraska, in 1975 and still serves as the director; Portia Hamilton Sperr, a Montessori educator who launched the Please Touch Museum for young children in Philadelphia in 1976; and Ruth J. Abram, who initiated the Lower East Side Tenement Museum in New York City in 1988 and has served as president and chief executive officer since.

FOUNDING WOMEN

The most recent stage of women's museum activities is directly connected with the women's movement of the 1960s, the same movement that fostered the flowering of women's history with which this essay began. What has happened is that women have stepped fully into

the spotlight. Some—an increasing number—now enter directly into politics and are elected to public office. Many local and state positions are now held by women, though gains at the national level remain slow. These political women exemplify the ways in which women are now vigorously participating in all aspects of society, although equality is still an elusive goal. Women still earn less than men, and many still carry the burden of the "double day": full-time employment followed by nights and weekends of housework. But one of the most novel and encouraging signs of women's aspirations is the founding of museums by women and about women.

The early museums devoted to women for their accomplishments tended to be historic houses—places where the women were born or once lived. Following the adoption of the 1920 Suffrage Amendment, many more historic houses honoring women were established. One of the first was the Clara Barton Birthplace, an 1818 North Oxford, Massachusetts, house where the founder and first president of the American Red Cross was born in 1821 that became a historic house in 1921. Another was the Sewall-Belmont House, an 1800 historic mansion in Washington, D.C., which was the home and office of Alice Paul, founder of the once-militant National Woman's Party, who organized the 10,000-women suffrage demonstrations in the nation's capital in 1913 and wrote the first Equal Rights Amendment in 1923 (which did not pass).

The Women's Rights National Historical Park in Seneca Falls, New York, celebrates the first women's rights convention, held there in 1848. These figures of some of the organizers and attendees are displayed in the park's visitor center. Courtesy Women's Rights National Historical Park and National Park Service.

The pace of establishing historic houses and other museumlike institutions in recognition of women activists accelerated after World War II—a wartime period when women demonstrated that they could perform many jobs usually held by men. The Susan B. Anthony House, where the legendary leader of women's rights lived in Rochester, New York, from 1866 until her death in 1906, became a historic house museum

in 1946. The Elizabeth Cady Stanton House, where Anthony's longtime suffrage coleader planned the first Women's Rights Convention in 1848, was later included in the Women's Rights National Historical Park, created in Seneca Falls, New York, in 1980. The homes of two other women who had a role in planning the convention—Mary Ann M'Clintock and Jane Hunt—also were added to the federal historical park. Among the other suffrage-related facilities established were the Margaret Brent Garden, named for the nation's first suffragist and Maryland's first female landowner; a part of Historic St. Mary's City, an outdoor living history museum in St. Mary's City, Maryland; and the Harriet Taylor Upton House, the home of a leading suffrage activist in Warren, Ohio, from 1883 to 1931 and the headquarters of the National American Woman Suffrage Association in 1903–1905.

Women activists in other fields, such as abolition, temperance, social work, peace, and civil rights, also became the focus of historic houses and museums. The Willard House, which became a historic house in Evanston, Illinois, in 1946, is where Frances Willard lived and spearheaded the national temperance movement in the late 1800s. In 1950, the Carry A. Nation Home Memorial was opened in her 1890–1903 residence in Medicine Lodge, Kansas, where the temperance crusader began her hatchet-wielding career of saloon smashing during Prohibition.

The 1960s women's movement that stressed equal pay and opportunities for women resulted in Congress passing the Equal Rights Amendment, which failed to win ratification in 1972. However, the battle against sexual discrimination intensified interest in honoring women activists and others for their accomplishments. Among the historic houses and other museums established to memorialize activists were the Nicholas House Museum, founded in 1961 at the Boston home of Rose Standish Nichols, a noted landscape architect and lifelong pacifist who was a founding member of the Women's International League for Peace and Freedom in 1915; Jane Addams Hull-House Museum, which began in Chicago in 1967 at the social-welfare pioneer and peace advocate's settlement house where she lived and worked at the turn of the twentieth century; and Mary McLeod Bethune Council House National Historic Site, created in 1979 at an 1876 Victorian row house in Washington, D.C., that was the home of the noted African American educator and activist.

Many other historic houses and museums have been established to recognize outstanding women since World War II and the 1960s women's movement. They include such sites as Ivy Green, Birthplace of Helen Keller in Tuscumbia, Alabama, where the noted blind and deaf woman was born and spent her childhood (founded in 1952); Dickinson Homestead in Amherst, Massachusetts, home of poet Emily Dickinson, who lived all but fifteen years of her life in the house in the nineteenth century (1965); Babe Didrikson Zaharias Museum in Beaumont, Texas, dedicated to one of the nation's greatest female athletes (1976); and Margaret Chase Smith Library in Skowhegan, Maine, a library/archive/museum honoring the life and career of the first woman elected to both houses of Congress, who served more than three decades (1982).

One of the earliest specific women's facilities was the Women's Archives, a research library on women established at Radcliffe College in Cambridge, Massachusetts, in 1943 when alumna Maud Wood Park donated papers, books, and memorabilia documenting the 1848–1920 suffrage movement and women's political and reform work after 1920. In 1967 the resource was renamed the Arthur and Elizabeth Schlesinger Library in recognition of the couple's support and dedication to women's history and the archives. The library, which presents changing museumlike exhibitions on women's history and issues, now is part of the Radcliffe Institute for Advanced Studies at Harvard University.

Two women's historical museums were founded in the 1950s. The U.S. Army Women's Museum, featuring the role of women in the army and the history of the Women's Army Corps (WAC), was started in 1955 at Fort McClellan near Anniston, Alabama, and was later moved to Fort Lee, Virginia. In 1958 the Pioneer Woman Museum in Ponca City, Oklahoma, was dedicated to the state's pioneering women homesteaders, as well as to female pioneers in such fields as aviation, civil rights, public service, and the arts.

The Artemisia Gallery, a woman-run cooperative in Chicago, opened in 1973 to provide a professional space for emerging and mid-career women artists to explore and display their artworks. In 1992 a second Chicago gallery—the Woman Made Gallery—sought to support women in the arts largely through thematic exhibitions.

The Women's Rights National Historical Park—devoted to the history of the women's rights movement and its founders—was established in 1980 in Seneca Falls, New York, site of the first women's rights movement convention, in 1848. The following year, the National Museum of Women in the Arts was founded in Washington, D.C. It became the first museum dedicated solely to the diverse artistic achievements of women. Another specialty women's museum that began in the 1980s was the International Women's Air and Space Museum, featuring exhibits and memorabilia of women aviators and astronauts. Founded in 1976, it opened in 1986 in Centerville, Ohio, and moved to Cleveland in 1998.

Numerous other women's museums were launched in the 1990s. They include the Women's History Museum, a mobile museum housed in a school bus that tells about outstanding historic women, in West Liberty, West Virginia (1990); First Ladies National Historic Site, containing information and memorabilia on the lives and works of the wives of the nation's presidents, in Canton, Ohio (1998); 99s Museum of Women Pilots, with exhibits on women in aviation, in Oklahoma City (1998); and the Women's Museum: An Institute for the Future, dealing with the history and contributions of women in American life, in Dallas (founded in 1998 and opened in 2000). Among the others in various stages of development are the National Women's History Museum, Washington, D.C.; International Museum of Women, San Francisco; and Mabel Strickland Cowgirl Museum in Cheyenne, Wyoming.

Sometimes museums honoring women take the form of halls of fame. One of the oldest and most prominent such facilities is the National Women's Hall of Fame in Seneca Falls, New York, where the nation's women's suffrage movement began. Founded in 1969, the hall enshrines women who have made significant national contributions to art, athletics, business, government, philanthropy, humanities, science, and education. Some halls of fame are more specialized, such as the National Cowgirl Museum and Hall of Fame, which honors women who have distinguished themselves while personifying the pioneer spirit of the American West. The museum/hall of fame began in Hereford, Texas, in 1975, and reopened in a new $21 million home in Fort Worth in 2002.

Because they are so recent, it is too soon to fully assess the meaning and impact of these women's museums. But one theme is apparent. Women have founded museums about women because they felt a strong need to recover their hidden history and to fully consider their lives. As the founding statement for the Women of the West Museum put it, "To cast a shadow, women must stand in the light." These museums thus exemplify the hopes of women's historians that understanding women's lives will contribute to a fuller version of American history. This fuller version of American history is now readily available at the nation's universities and in contemporary historical scholarship, but relatively little of it has "trickled down" into popular understanding. Reaching large audiences with appealing and novel information about women is an important way to change the public image of American history. There is every reason to hope that women's museums will flourish and grow. They have much to tell us.

CONCLUSION

The recent founding of women's museums is only the latest and perhaps most visible chapter in the history of women's museum activities in the United States, but as this brief survey has shown, women have always been active, first as preservers and later as contributors and founders. The material compiled by Vic Danilov and presented in this volume goes a long way toward documenting a past that most of us had not known existed, and for whose recovery we should all be grateful. It is a vital first step toward the fuller story of American history still to be told.

NOTES
1. Jeanne Madeline Weimann, *The Fair Women* (Chicago: Academy Chicago, 1981), 129.
2. Kathleen D. McCarthy, *Women's Culture: American Philanthropy and Art, 1830–1930* (Chicago: University of Chicago Press, 1991).

Directory of Museums and Related Facilities Founded by, Named for, and/or Devoted to Women

Museums and Related Facilities Devoted to Women

WOMEN'S MUSEUMS, GALLERIES, AND HALLS OF FAME

See also Historic House Museums; Memorials to Women; Museums Honoring Exceptional Women; Museums Founded and/or Operated by Women's Organizations; Shrines to Women.

Alabama

ALABAMA WOMEN'S HALL OF FAME. Sixty-five notable women are enshrined in the Alabama Women's Hall of Fame in A. Howard Bean Hall at Judson College in Marion, Alabama. Exhibits describe the achievements of such honorees as Dr. Hallie Farmer, educator and activist who urged women to run for office; Annie Rowan Forney Daugetter, designer of the state's seal; and Dixie Bibb Graves, the first and only Alabama woman in the U.S. Senate (she served for four months in 1937 when Senator Hugo Black was appointed to the Supreme Court).

Alabama Women's Hall of Fame, Judson College, A. Howard Bean Hall, Lafayette and Bibb Sts., Marion, AL 36756. **Phone:** 334/683-5184. **Fax:** 334/683-5188. **Website:** www.ci.marion.al.us/judson. **Hours:** 8-4 Mon.-Fri.; closed Sat.-Sun. and major holidays. **Admission:** free.

Arizona

ARIZONA WOMEN'S HALL OF FAME. Founded in 1979, the Arizona Women's Hall of Fame is now part of the broad-based Arizona Hall of Fame Museum, which was opened in the 1908 Carnegie Library Building in Phoenix in 1987 and is operated by the Arizona Department of Library, Archives, and Public Records.

The women's hall of fame has recognized 102 outstanding women who settled the Arizona frontier and/or contributed to the state's development and progress. It presents changing exhibitions on such women as Sharlot Hall, poet, historian, and museum founder; Mary Velasquez Riley, tribal leader who lobbied Congress on Native American issues; Lorna Lockwood, chief justice of the state supreme court and first woman in any state to hold that position; Vernell Myers Coleman, community advocate and political

organizer; Nellie T. Bush, the state's first licensed riverboat pilot; and Anna Moore Shaw, a Pima Indian author who sought to preserve the tribe's language and culture with her books.

Arizona Women's Hall of Fame, Arizona Hall of Fame Museum, 1101 W. Washington St., Phoenix, AZ 85007. **Phone:** 602/255-5110. **Fax:** 602/255-3314. **E-mail:** capmus @lib.az.us. **Website:** www.dlapr.lib.az.us. **Hours:** 8-5 Mon.-Fri.; closed Sat.-Sun. and major holidays. **Admission:** free.

California

BURLESQUE HALL OF FAME AND MUSEUM. One of the most flamboyant theatrical and entertainment eras in America's history is celebrated at the Burlesque Hall of Fame and Museum—also known as the Exotic World—on a 40-acre ranch near Helendale, California. The hall of fame/museum, which was founded in 1962 in San Pedro by exotic dancer Jeanie Lee and is now operated by Dixie Evans, pays tribute to approximately 200 stripteasers and exotic dancers, such as Gypsy Rose Lee, Josephine Baker, Sally Rand, Lili St. Cyr, Tempest Storm, Blaze Starr, and Georgia Southern. It features one of the largest collections of burlesque costumes, photographs, posters, and memorabilia.

Burlesque Hall of Fame and Museum, 29053 Wild Rd., Helendale, CA 92342. **Phone:** 760/243-5261. **Website:** www.exoticworld.org. **Hours:** 9-5 daily. **Admission:** donation.

INTERNATIONAL MUSEUM OF WOMEN. The International Museum of Women in San Francisco is engaged in a $120 million campaign to build a 120,000-square-foot building along the city's waterfront. Groundbreaking is planned for 2006, with the museum opening in 2008.

The museum, which began as the Women's Heritage Museum in Palo Alto in 1985, now has its office in San Francisco and operates as a "museum without walls," presenting changing exhibitions, public programs, and an annual book fair; providing teacher resources for Women's History Month; honoring women in local history; and recreating historic events.

When the new building opens, the museum will have exhibits that chronicle international women's history and examine contemporary issues and future possibilities. Changing exhibitions will feature explorations of women's lives, work, and creativity. Interactive technology and the Website will enable visitors worldwide to view the displays and engage in educational programs. The museum also will offer seminars, lectures, performances, and tours, and will have special programs for school groups, a children's learning gallery, a teachers' resource center, a teen center, and a visiting scholars' program.

Until the museum building opens, the museum is presenting changing temporary exhibitions at its office and at other sites, such as "Celebrating Women All Over the World," in the Steuart Tower Lobby at One Market Concourse in late 2004.

International Museum of Women, PO Box 190038, San Francisco, CA 94119-0038. **Phone:** 415/543-4669. **Fax:** 415/543-4668. **E-mail:** infor@imow.org. **Website:** www.imow.org. **Hours:** 9-5 Wed. and Fri.; closed remainder of the week. **Admission:** free.

District of Columbia

The National Museum of Women in the Arts in Washington, D.C., is the first and only museum dedicated solely to the diverse artistic achievements of women. Founded by Wilhelmina Cole Holladay, it contains over 2,700 works from the sixteenth century to the present by over 800 artists. Courtesy National Museum of Women in the Arts.

NATIONAL MUSEUM OF WOMEN IN THE ARTS. The National Museum of Women in the Arts in Washington, D.C., is the first and only museum dedicated solely to celebrating the diverse artistic achievements of women.

The museum was founded in 1981 by Wilhelmina Cole Holladay, who began collecting art with her husband, Wallace F. Holladay, in the 1960s—just as scholars were starting to address the underrepresentation of women in museum collections and major art exhibitions. The Holladays, who became committed to collecting artwork by women, gave their extensive collection and art library to the museum, which opened in 1987 in a 1907 Renaissance Revival building that was formerly a Masonic temple. The museum collection has increased substantially since then, through acquisitions and gifts.

The museum was established with the goal of reforming traditional histories of art, discovering and making known those women artists who have been overlooked and unacknowledged, and assuring the place of women in contemporary art.

The museum now contains approximately 3,000 works of art from the sixteenth century to the present—created by nearly 900 artists, including Judith Leyster, Maria Sibylla Merian, Mary Cassatt, Camille Claudel, Georgia O'Keeffe, Frida Kahlo, Elizabeth Catlett, Lee Krasner, Helen Frankenthaler, and Louise Bourgeois. It also has special collections of eighteenth-century silver tableware and botanical and zoological prints, and it operates a library and research center relating to the study of women artists.

National Museum of Women in the Arts, 1250 New York Ave. N.W., Washington, DC 20005. **Phone:** 202/783-5000. **Fax:** 202/393-3235. **Website:** www.nmwa.org. **Hours:** 10-5 Mon.-Sat., 12-5 Sun.; closed New Year's Day, Thanksgiving, and Christmas. **Admission:** suggested donations—adults, $5; seniors and children, $3.

NATIONAL WOMEN'S HISTORY MUSEUM. A fundraising campaign is underway to develop a National Women's History Museum near the Mall in Washington, D.C. The primary focus will be on the documentation, study, and interpretation of the history of American women, but it will also include the role of women worldwide.

The museum project, which was started by psychologist Karen Staser of Alexandria, Virginia, hopes to open by 2005. It will have exhibits and programs on women in such fields as technology, politics, business, labor, education, medicine, sports, and the arts, as well as outreach and online programs, traveling exhibitions, a research center, and a repository for artifacts, films, photographs, and other materials relating to women.

The museum currently operates the CyberMuseum, with the initial virtual exhibit being *Motherhood, Social Service, and Political Reform: Political Culture and Imagery of American Woman Suffrage*. It develops traveling exhibitions, such as *Rights for Women*; presents lectures, plays, and conferences on women; and sponsors an awards program, titled "Women Making History Awards."

National Women's History Museum, PO Box 1296, Annandale, VA 22003. **Phone:** 703/813-6209. **Fax:** 703/813-6210. **E-mail:** info@nwhm.org. **Website:** www.nwhm.org. **Hours:** 10-6 Mon.-Fri.; closed Sat.-Sun. and major holidays. **Admission:** free.

Florida

LADIES PROFESSIONAL GOLF ASSOCIATION HALL OF FAME. Such leading women golfers as Patty Berg, Betty Jameson, Nancy Lopez, Betsy Rawls, Louise Suggs, and Mildred "Babe" Didrikson Zaharias are among the twenty enshrined in the Ladies Professional Golf Association Hall of Fame, part of the World Golf Hall of Fame in St. Augustine, Florida.

The World Golf Hall of Fame, centerpiece of the World Golf Village, also houses the Professional Golfers' Association of America Hall of Fame and the PGA Tour Hall of Fame. In addition to tributes to the 100 inductees in the various halls of fame, the exhibits contain photographs, trophies, artifacts, memorabilia, films, videos, and interactive units.

Ladies Professional Golf Association Hall of Fame, World Golf Hall of Fame, World Golf Village, 1 World Golf Place, St. Augustine, FL 32092. **Phones:** 904/940-4000 and 904/940-4123. **Fax:** 904/940-4399. **Website:** www.wgv.com. **Hours:** 10-6 daily; closed New Year's Day and Christmas. **Admission:** adults, $10; seniors and children 13-18, $9; children 5-12, $5; children under 5, free.

Illinois

ARTEMISIA GALLERY. The Artemisia Gallery in Chicago was founded in 1973 as a woman-run cooperative to provide emerging and mid-career artists with a professional environment to explore and display their artwork and to reach greater audiences.

The nonprofit organization, located in the River West Gallery District, has five galleries to show work in all media. It also has lectures, guided tours, and a mentorship program for professional women artists. Goals of the nonprofit gallery include expanding the

The Woman Made Gallery in Chicago specializes in promoting and displaying artworks by women. The nonprofit gallery seeks to support women in the arts mainly through solo and group shows, which raise public awareness and recognition of women's cultural contributions. Courtesy Woman Made Gallery and photographer Tom Van Eynde.

role of women in the arts, encouraging innovative and experimental art that would otherwise not be seen in commercial galleries, and providing a forum for the exchange of ideas.

Artemisia Gallery, 700 N. Carpenter St., 3rd floor, Chicago, IL 60622. **Phone:** 312/226-7323. **Fax:** 312/226-7756. **E-mail:** artemisia@enteract.com. **Website:** www.enteract.com/~artemisia. **Hours:** 11-5 Tues.-Sat.; closed Sun.-Mon. **Admission:** free.

WOMAN MADE GALLERY. The Woman Made Gallery in Chicago seeks to support women in the arts by providing opportunities, awareness, and advocacy—largely through monthly thematic exhibitions. The nonprofit gallery, which recently moved into the Acme Artist Community complex just northwest of downtown, was founded in 1992 to enable women artists to exhibit, perform, publish, and sell their work and to offer a place for support and community.

The gallery holds eight juried group exhibitions and six solo shows a year; presents slide lectures, workshops, and poetry readings; and operates a slide registry, online artists' registry, and research library. More than 3,000 women artists from the United States and other countries have participated in exhibits on themes ranging from domestic violence and prejudice issues to such stylistic themes as still life and surrealism.

Woman Made Gallery, 2418 W. Bloomington Ave., Chicago, IL 60647. **Phone:** 312/328-0038. **Fax:** 312/328-1108. **E-mail:** gallery@womanmade.org. **Website:** www.womanmade.org. **Hours:** 12-7 Wed.-Fri., 12-4 Sat.-Sun.; closed Mon.-Tues. and holidays. **Admission:** free.

Louisiana

ELIZABETH BASS COLLECTION ON WOMEN AND MEDICINE. The Elizabeth Bass Collection on Women and Medicine at the Rudolph Matas Medical Library at Tulane University Medical Center in New Orleans documents the obstacles women had to overcome to become physicians. The collection includes newspaper clippings, medical school catalogs, magic-lantern slides, photographs, and other historical materials relating to the difficulties experienced by Dr. Bass, her sister Edith Ballard, and other women in being admitted to medical schools and practicing medicine.

Dr. Bass and her sister enrolled at the Woman's Medical College in Philadelphia when southern schools would not accept women. When New Orleans hospitals would not admit women as physicians, she helped establish a free dispensary that later became Sara Mayo Hospital. In 1911 the sisters became the first women on the Tulane medical faculty. Dr. Bass campaigned for suffrage and steadily worked her way up the medical professional ladder—becoming the first woman in the Orleans Parish Medical Society, the first to chair a section (pathology) of the Southern Medical Association, and the 1953 winner of the American Medical Women's Association Elizabeth Blackwell Centennial Medal.

Elizabeth Bass Collection on Women and Medicine, Rudolph Matas Medical Library, Tulane University Medical Center, 1430 Tulane Ave., New Orleans, LA 70112. **Phone:** 504/588-5155. **Fax:** 504/587-7417. **E-mail:** kopeland@tulane.edu. **Website:** www.medlib.tulane.edu. **Hours:** 8:30-4:30 Mon.-Fri.; closed Sat.-Sun. and university holidays. **Admission:** free.

Massachusetts

ARTHUR AND ELIZABETH SCHLESINGER LIBRARY. The nation's largest collection of books, papers, photographs, and memorabilia on women's history is located at the Arthur and Elizabeth Schlesinger Library at the Radcliffe Institute for Advanced Studies at Harvard University in Cambridge, Massachusetts.

The library was established in 1943, when alumna Maud Wood Park gave Radcliffe College the papers, books, and memorabilia documenting the 1848–1920 suffrage movement and women's political and reform work after 1920. It became the nucleus of Radcliffe's research library on women, first called the Women's Archives, and in 1967 was renamed for Elizabeth Bancroft and Arthur M. Schlesinger Sr. in recognition of their dedication to women's history and the archives.

The Schlesinger Library has more than 60,000 books, a similar amount of photographs, over 2,000 manuscripts, oral histories, and thousands of personal papers and memorabilia relating the experiences and activities of women from the nineteenth century to the present. Among the collections are such items as the diaries of suffrage leader Susan B. Anthony, papers of author Harriet Beecher Stowe, letters to Jane Addams of Hull House, and the lace cap of feminist Julia Ward Howe, author of the *Battle Hymn of the Republic*. The library also presents changing exhibitions.

Arthur and Elizabeth Schlesinger Library, Radcliffe Institute for Advanced Studies, Harvard University, 10 Garden St., Cambridge, MA 02138. **Phone:** 617/495-8647. **Fax:** 617/496-8340. **E-mail:** slref@radcliffe.edu. **Website:** www.radcliffe.edu/schles/index.html. **Hours:** 9-5 Mon.-Fri.; closed Sat.-Sun. and major holidays. **Admission:** free.

Michigan

MICHIGAN WOMEN'S HISTORICAL CENTER AND HALL OF FAME. The Michigan Women's Historical Center and Hall of Fame in Lansing has exhibits on the lives, achievements, and history of Michigan women, including members of the Michigan Women's Hall of Fame, as well as changing displays of art and photography by women of the state.

The center, which opened in 1987, is a project of the Michigan Women's Studies Association, founded in 1973 to improve what is taught and thought about women in Michigan schools, colleges, and universities. It is located in the restored Cooley-Haze House in the center of downtown Lansing, the state capital.

The Michigan Women's Hall of Fame, which inducted its first members in 1983, has enshrined over 170 women, including Laura Smith Haviland, known as the "Superintendent of the Underground Railroad"; Roberta A. Griffith, who devoted her life to the blind and prevention of blindness; Mabel Holmes, credited with inventing jiffy biscuit mix; "Big Annie" Clemenc, a courageous supporter of striking copper miners in 1913; and Dora Hall Stockman, the first woman elected to a Michigan state office (Board of Agriculture).

Michigan Women's Historical Center and Hall of Fame, 213 W. Main St., Lansing, MI 48933-2315. **Phone:** 517/484-1880. **Hours:** 12-5 Wed.-Fri., 2-4 Sun.; closed Mon.-Tues., Sat., and major holidays. **Admission:** adults, $2.50; seniors, $2; children 5-14, $1; children under 5, free.

Missouri

WOMEN'S INTERNATIONAL BOWLING CONGRESS HALL OF FAME. The Women's International Bowling Congress Hall of Fame in St. Louis honors more than 140 women in two sections—performers and contributors. The amateur women's hall of fame began in 1953 and became part of the International Bowling Museum and Hall of Fame when it opened in 1984.

The museum also houses three other bowling halls of fame—those of the American Bowling Congress, Professional Bowlers Association, and Bowling Propri-

etors Association of America—and the St. Louis Cardinals Hall of Fame, formerly located at Busch Stadium across the street.

The International Bowling Congress Hall of Fame traces the 5,000-year history of bowling, contains other exhibits, offers opportunities for free bowling on old-time and modern computerized lanes, and has separate galleries for the various halls of fame. The women's hall of fame features oil portraits of outstanding amateur women bowlers and contributors.

Women's International Bowling Congress Hall of Fame, International Bowling Congress Hall of Fame, 111 Stadium Plaza, St. Louis, MO 63102. **Phone:** 314/231-6340. **Fax:** 314/231-4054. **E-mail:** bowling@anet-stl.com. **Website:** www.bowlingmuseum.com. **Hours:** Apr.-Sept.— 9-5:30 Mon.-Sat., 11-5:30 Sun.; remainder of year—11-4 daily; closed New Year's Eve and Day, Thanksgiving, and Christmas Eve and Day. **Admission:** adults, $6; children 6-12, $4; children under 6, free.

New York

INTERNATIONAL WOMEN'S SPORTS HALL OF FAME. The outstanding female athletes and coaches in the world are honored in the International Women's Sports Hall of Fame at the Women's Sports Foundation's headquarters in Eisenhower Park in East Meadow, New York.

The foundation has display cases with trophies, clothing, equipment, photographs, and other materials related to the inductees. Among the 106 athletes and eighteen coaches enshrined are such sports figures as tennis standouts Althea Gibson and Billie Jean King, track star Wilma Rudolph, golfer Patty Berg, gymnast Mary Lou Retton, and all-around athlete Mildred "Babe" Didrikson Zaharias.

The hall of fame was founded in 1980. A $4 million campaign to build a home for the hall of fame adjacent to the Women's Sports Foundation is now underway, with construction expected to begin in several years.

International Women's Sports Hall of Fame, Women's Sports Foundation, Eisenhower Park, East Meadow, NY 11554. **Phones:** 516/542-4700 and 800/227-3988. **Fax:** 516/542-4176. **E-mail:** wosport@aol.com. **Website:** womensportsfoundation.org. **Hours:** 9-5 Mon.-Fri.; closed Sat.-Sun. and major holidays. **Admission:** free.

NATIONAL WOMEN'S HALL OF FAME. The National Women's Hall of Fame, located in Seneca Falls, New

York, where the nation's women's suffrage movement began, has honored 217 women who have made significant national contributions to art, athletics, business, government, philanthropy, humanities, science, and education.

The hall of fame, founded in 1969, is part of the Seneca Falls Historic District, where the first women's rights convention was held in 1884. A "Declaration of Sentiments" was adopted by the approximately 300 women and men attending the convention, which stated that "it is the duty of the women of this country to secure to themselves their sacred right to the elective franchise."

Twenty women were enshrined in the hall of fame in its first induction in 1973, including Elizabeth Cady Stanton, an early women's rights proponent and one of the principal organizers of the first convention, and Susan B. Anthony, the suffrage movement leader.

Among the others in the hall of fame are Margaret Chase Smith, U.S. senator from Maine; Marian Anderson, singer; Jane Addams, social worker; Mary McLeod Bethune, educator; Rachel Carson, biologist and author; Emily Dickinson, poet; Amelia Earhart, aviator; Margaret Mead, anthropologist; Helen Hayes, actress; Georgia O'Keeffe, artist; Rosa Parks, civil rights activist; Eleanor Roosevelt, author, diplomat, and humanitarian; Sally Ride, astronaut; and Mildred Didrikson Zaharias, athlete.

The National Women's Hall of Fame, housed in a historic 1916 former bank building, features large panels with biographies, photographs, and artifacts of the women honored—arranged in groupings according to areas of achievement.

National Women's Hall of Fame, 76 Fall St., PO Box 335, Seneca Falls, NY 13148. Phone: 315/568-8060. Fax: 315/568-2976. E-mail: womenshall@aol.com. Website: www.greatwomen.org. Hours: May-Oct.—9:30-5 Mon.-Sat., 12-4 Sun.; remainder of year—10-4 Wed.-Sat., 12-4 Sun.; closed Mon.-Tues., New Year's Day, Thanksgiving, and Christmas. Admission: adults, $3; seniors and students, $1.50; children under 6, free; families, $7.

WOMEN'S RIGHTS NATIONAL HISTORICAL PARK. The history of the women's rights movement and its founders is the focus of the Women's Rights National Historical Park, located at the site where the first women's rights movement convention was held in 1848 in Seneca Falls, New York.

More than 300 women and men attended the first women's rights convention at Wesleyan Chapel, "to discuss the social, civil, and religious condition and rights of a woman." The convention was called because five local women—Elizabeth Cady Stanton, Lucretia Mott, Jane Hunt, Mary Ann M'Clintock, and Martha Wright—felt the need to publicly address the grievances of women who resented men's freedom while they were confined to "the woman's sphere" to care for the children and manage the home.

The women drafted a "Declaration of Sentiments"—modeled after the Declaration of Independence—which declared that "all men and women are created equal" and called for the right of women to vote and seventeen other rights. The declaration was signed by 68 women and 32 men at the convention, although some participants refused to approve such extreme provisions as the right to vote.

The park includes the restored Wesleyan Chapel, Stanton's 1836 home (where the first planning meeting was held), the M'Clintock and Hunt houses, and a visitor center with changing exhibitions and nineteen life-size bronze sculptures of the prime convention movers and attendees. Interpretive talks and walking tours are given by National Park Service rangers in June through September.

Women's Rights National Historical Park, 136 Fall St., Seneca Falls, NY 13148. Phone: 315/568-2991. Fax: 315/568-3414. Website: www.nps.gov/wori. Hours: visitor center—9-5 daily; Stanton house—June-Sept.: 9-5 daily; remainder of year—12-4 daily; closed major holidays. Admission: adults and children over 16, $3; with tour of Stanton house, additional $1; children under 17, free.

Ohio

FIRST LADIES NATIONAL HISTORIC SITE. The First Ladies National Historic Site in Canton, Ohio, was founded in 1998 to honor and provide a central repository of information and memorabilia on the lives and works of the nation's 44 wives of presidents.

The library/museum, located in the former home of President William McKinley and his wife, Ida Saxton McKinley, was started by Mary Regula, the wife of Congressman Ralph Regula, who was distressed to find relatively little bibliographical and other information available on the first ladies while preparing to give a talk on Mary Todd Lincoln. She organized a group of thirteen influential Ohio women, who raised the necessary funds to establish the center.

Mrs. Regula wanted the public to know that first ladies are involved in more than social events—and to make the information readily available both at the restored mid-1800s Victorian site and online. A bibliography has been assembled with all the books, writings, articles, and manuscripts written by and about America's first ladies, as well as displays of books, letters, photographs, campaign buttons, and other memorabilia relating to them. The third-floor ballroom of the house features a complete collection of reproduced paintings and photos of all the first ladies. The facility also presents "First Ladies Salute First Women" awards, which honors other women who have had a great influence on American society.

First Ladies National Historic Site, 331 Market Ave. South, Canton, OH 44702-2107. **Phone:** 330/452-0876. **Fax:** 330/456-3414. **E-mail:** pkrider@firstladies.org. **Website:** www.firstladies.org. **Hours:** June-Aug.—10-2 Mon., Wed., and Sat. by reservation; remainder of year—10-2 Wed. and Sat. by reservation; closed remainder of week and major holidays. **Admission:** adults, $5; seniors and students, $4.

The history of women in aviation and space is presented at the International Women's Air and Space Museum in Cleveland. The museum, which began in Centerville, Ohio, is now located at Burke Lakefront Airport. It features memorabilia and exhibits on women aviators and astronauts. Courtesy International Women's Air and Space Museum.

INTERNATIONAL WOMEN'S AIR AND SPACE MUSEUM. The history of women in aviation and space is preserved and displayed at the International Women's Air and Space Museum at Burke Lakefront Airport in Cleveland. It features memorabilia of pioneering women aviators and astronauts and exhibits about women who have made exceptional achievements in the aeronautical and space fields.

Founded in 1976, the museum first opened in 1986 in the historic 1806 home of Asahel Wright, the great-uncle of aviation pioneers Orville, Wilbur, and Katharine Wright, in the Dayton suburb of Centerville. In 1998 the museum moved to its present site on Cleveland's lakefront. It contains the personal papers, clothing, trophies, military uniforms, art, posters, photographs, and biographical information of the leading women in aviation and space, as well as a research library.

International Women's Air and Space Museum, Burke Lakefront Airport, 1501 N. Marginal Rd., Cleveland, OH 44114. **Phone:** 216/623-1111. **Fax:** 216/623-1113. **E-mail:** jhrube@iwasm.org. **Website:** www.iwasm.org. **Hours:** 10-4 Mon.-Fri. (but exhibits accessible at all times in the airport terminal); closed Sat.-Sun. and major holidays, except for Labor Day. **Admission:** free.

OHIO WOMEN'S HALL OF FAME. The Ohio Women's Hall of Fame, housed in the Ohio Department of Job and Family Services headquarters in Columbus, was established to honor Ohio women who have made significant contributions to the growth and progress of the state and nation.

Among the more than 300 women inducted are Rita Dove, U.S. poet laureate; Maya Lin, Vietnam Memorial designer; Judith Resnik, space shuttle astronaut; Millie Benson, Nancy Drew mystery writer; and Gloria Steinem, feminist activist and founder of *Ms.* magazine.

The hall of fame contains photographs and biographies of recent inductees and a 20-minute video chronicling the evolving role of Ohio women from pioneer times to the present. Regional displays have also been installed at the Ohio Department of Job and Family Services local offices in Athens, Canton, Cincinnati, Mount Vernon, Toledo, and Xenia.

Ohio Women's Hall of Fame, 145 S. Front St., Columbus, OH 43215 (contact: Women's Section, Ohio Dept. of Job and Family Services, 145 S. Front St., Columbus, OH 43215). **Phone:** 614/466-4496. **E-mail:** hammonn@odjfs.state.oh.us. **Website:** www.state.oh.us/odjfs/women. **Hours:** 8-5 Mon.-Fri.; closed Sat.-Sun. and major holidays. **Admission:** free.

Oklahoma

99s MUSEUM OF WOMEN PILOTS. The 99s Museum of Women Pilots is a museum about women in aviation at the Ninety-Nines headquarters in Oklahoma City. It features memorabilia and exhibits about such topics as early women pilots, Amelia Earhart, the 1929 women's air derby, World War II women pilots, women in the space program, air racing and racers of today, and aviation careers for women.

The Ninety-Nines, Inc., an international organization of women pilots, was founded in 1929. It was called the Ninety-Nines when 99 women pilots came for the first organizational meeting at Curtiss Field in Valley Stream, New York. Amelia Earhart was elected the first president of the group. The organization now has over 6,500 member pilots in 35 countries.

99s Museum of Women Pilots, Ninety-Nines, Inc., 4300 Amelia Earhart Lane, Oklahoma City, OK 73159 (postal address: 7100 Terminal Dr., Box 965, Oklahoma City, OK 73159). Phone: 405/685-9990. Fax: 405/685-7985. E-mail: ihq99s@cs.com. Website: www.ninety-nines.org. Hours: 10-4 Tues.-Sat.; closed Sun.-Mon. and major holidays. Admission: adults, $5; seniors, $4; children 6-14, $2; children under 6, free.

PIONEER WOMAN MUSEUM. The Pioneer Woman Museum in Ponca City, Oklahoma, is dedicated to the state's pioneering women homesteaders, as well as female pioneers in such fields as aviation, civil rights, public service, and the arts. A 17-foot bronze statue of a sunbonneted pioneer woman holding her son by the hand welcomes visitors at the entrance (see Memorials to Women).

The statue by sculptor Bryant Baker was conceived and financed by oilman and philanthropist Ernest W. Marland, who served as congressman and governor and wanted to create a memorial to pioneer women. It was unveiled in 1930, with the museum being added in 1958. The museum, now operated by the Oklahoma Historical Society, contains artifacts and memorabilia relating to Oklahoma's pioneer women and displays on some of the more recent accomplishments of women.

Pioneer Woman Museum, 701 Monument Rd., Ponca City, OK 74604-3910. Phone: 580/765-6108. Fax: 580/762-2498. E-mail: piown@ok-history.mus.ok.us. Website: www.ok-history.mus.ok.us. Hours: 9-5 Tues.-Sat., 1-5 Sun.; closed Mon. and state holidays. Admission: adults, $3; seniors, $2.50; children 6-18, $1; children under 6, free.

Pennsylvania

UNITED STATES FIELD HOCKEY ASSOCIATION HALL OF FAME. The United States Field Hockey Association has a hall of fame at Ursinus College in Collegeville,

Pennsylvania. Opened in 1988 and recently relocated from Hellfferich Hall to the new Floy Lewis Bakes Fieldhouse, it contains exhibits with information and photographs on 29 enshrined women, as well as artifacts, memorabilia, and a history of field hockey in the United States. Field hockey was introduced to this country from England in 1901.

U.S. Field Hockey Assn. Hall of Fame, Ursinus College, Floy Lewis Bakes Fieldhouse, Collegeville, PA 19428. Phone: 610/409-3606. Fax: 610/409-3620. Hours: 8:30-5 Mon.-Fri.; closed Sat.-Sun. and major holidays. Admission: free.

Tennessee

WOMEN'S BASKETBALL HALL OF FAME. Sixty-eight women and eleven men have been inducted into the Women's Basketball Hall of Fame, which opened in 1999 in Knoxville, Tennessee. They include such players as Nancy Lieberman-Cline and Cheryl Miller and such coaches as Tara VanDerveer and Pat Head Summitt.

A Hall of Honor contains plaques devoted to the lives and careers of the inductees. The museum also has a Ring of Honor, with more than 100 jerseys representing the year's high school and collegiate all-Americans; a Winner's Wall, featuring past national team champions; a Players of the Year exhibit, containing memorabilia and artifacts of past high school, collegiate, and professional players of the year; and a collection of memorabilia highlighting extraordinary players, coaches, programs, officials, and international competition.

Other offerings include a lifelike animatronic figure of Senda Berenson, "the mother of women's basketball," sharing her thoughts on the game; displays on two early women's basketball efforts—the All American Red Heads and the Amateur Athletic Union teams; and "Hoopful of Hope," a film on the history of more than 100 years of women's basketball.

Women's Basketball Hall of Fame, 700 Hall of Fame Dr., Knoxville, TN 37915. Phone: 865/633-9000. Fax: 865/633-9294. Website: www.wbhof.com. Hours: 10 a.m.-7 p.m. Mon.-Sat., 1-6 Sun.; closed Easter, Thanksgiving, and Christmas. Admission: adults, $7.95; seniors and children 6-15, $5.95; children under 6, free.

Texas

DAR MUSEUM/FIRST LADIES OF TEXAS HISTORIC COSTUMES COLLECTION. See Museums Founded and/or Operated by Women's Organizations.

The newly opened Women's Basketball Hall of Fame in Knoxville, Tennessee, honors outstanding women basketball players and coaches from throughout the world. It also traces the history of women's basketball and contains numerous artifacts and equipment of prominent players. Courtesy Women's Basketball Hall of Fame.

NATIONAL COWGIRL MUSEUM AND HALL OF FAME.

The National Cowgirl Museum and Hall of Fame, which began in Hereford, Texas, in 1975, moved into a new $21 million home in the cultural district in Fort Worth in 2002. It honors women who have distinguished themselves while personifying the pioneer spirit of the American West.

The new 33,000-square-foot building has four galleries and a hands-on children's area, multipurpose theater, research library, and store. Past and current hall of fame inductees are featured in the rotunda. They include women pioneers, artists, writers, entertainers, humanitarians, businesswomen, educators, ranchers, and rodeo cowgirls.

Among the approximately 170 honorees are Sacajawea, Shoshone guide and interpreter for the Lewis and Clark Expedition; Lucille Mulhall, considered the first "cowgirl"; Wilma Mankiller, first woman chief of the Cherokee Nation; sharpshooter Annie Oakley; western movie star Dale Evans; artist Georgia O'Keeffe, and Willa Cather, Mari Sandoz, and Laura Ingalls Wilder, early authors of frontier life.

The museum's galleries are "Into the Arena," featuring the difficulties and accomplishments of rodeo cowgirls; "Kinship with the Land," highlighting the life of pioneer and ranch women; "Claiming the Spotlight,"

This 33,000-square-foot building is the new home of the National Cowgirl Museum and Hall of Fame in Fort Worth, Texas. The museum/hall of fame, which began in the basement of the county library in Hereford, Texas, in 1975, moved into the new $21 million facility in Fort Worth's Cultural District in 2002. Courtesy National Cowgirl Museum and Hall of Fame and photographer Rhonda Hole.

focusing on the cowgirl's influence on popular culture; and a changing exhibition gallery.

National Cowgirl Museum and Hall of Fame, 1720 Gendy St., Fort Worth, TX 76107. **Phone:** 817/336-4475. **Fax:** 817/336-2470. **E-mail:** cowgirl@startext.net. **Website:** www.cowgirl.net. **Hours:** 10-5 Tues.-Sat. (also to 8 p.m. Tues.), 12-5 Sun.; closed Mon. and major holidays.

Admission: adults, $6; seniors and students 6-18, $5; children under 6, free.

RANGERETTE SHOWCASE MUSEUM. The Rangerette Showcase Museum at Kilgore College in Kilgore, Texas, is devoted to the history and travels of the famed Kilgore Rangerettes drill-dance team. The Rangerettes, organized in 1940 by Gussie Nell Davis, have performed at football games and other special events throughout the world.

Rangerette Showcase Museum, Kilgore College, Physical Education Complex, Ross St. and Broadway, Kilgore, TX 25662 (postal address: 1100 Broadway, Kilgore, TX, 25662-3299). **Phone:** 903/983-8650. **Fax:** 903/983-8255. **E-mail:** wylied @kilgore.cc.tx.us. **Website:** www.kilgore.cc.tx.us. **Hours:** 9-4 Mon.-Fri., 10-4 Sat.; closed Sun. and major holidays. **Admission:** free.

This is the entrance to the Women's Museum: An Institution for the Future, located at Fair Park in Dallas. The nation's most comprehensive women's history museum has exhibits on the lives and accomplishments of more than 3,000 American women. Courtesy Women's Museum: An Institution for the Future.

THE WOMEN'S MUSEUM: AN INSTITUTE FOR THE FUTURE. One of the newest, largest, and most compre-

hensive women's museums is the Women's Museum: An Institute for the Future, located in the renovated 1910 former Texas State Fair Coliseum building in Fair Park in Dallas.

The $27 million, 70,000-square-foot museum was founded in 1998 and opened in 2000 by the Foundation for Women's Resources, an international educational nonprofit based in Austin, with the assistance of a $10 million contribution from SBC Corporation—the largest corporate gift ever to any women's project.

The three-story museum is dedicated to the history and contributions of women to American life, highlighting achievements from the earliest settlers to modern-day astronauts. The exhibits feature interactive displays about women in sports, politics, arts, science, and other fields. Among the highlights are "Milestones in Women's History," celebrating historic events in women's history; "Electronic Quilt," a 30-foot-high display with 35 cubes and video screens with photographs, quotes, and moving images; and "Funny Women," which uses images from movies, television, and stand-up routines to show how women have used humor to challenge traditions.

Other exhibits include "Unforgettable Women," featuring 38 outstanding women who have changed American life and society; "It's Amazing," which challenges old and new ideas about what it means to be a woman; and "Finding Our Voices, Finding Our History," a video presentation by four mentors—former Texas Governor Ann Richards, newswoman Connie Chung, actress Maria Conchita Alonzo, and singer Gladys Knight. The museum also provides educational and enrichment programs through the Ronya Kozmetsky Institute for the Future, including specialized curricula in math, science, computer, and Internet technology for middle school girls.

The Women's Museum: An Institute for the Future, 3800 Parry Ave., Dallas, TX 75226 (postal address: PO Box 150381, Dallas, TX 75315-0381). **Phone:** 214/915-0887. **Fax:** 214/915-0870. **Website:** www.thewomensmuseum.org. **Hours:** 10-5 Tues.-Sun.; closed Mon. and major holidays. **Admission:** adults, $5; seniors and students 13-18, $4; children 5-12, $3; children under 5, free.

Virginia

U.S. ARMY WOMEN'S MUSEUM. The roles women have played in the army and the history of the Women's Army Corps (WAC) are presented at the U.S. Army Women's Museum at Fort Lee, Virginia.

The museum, which was founded in 1955, was originally located at Fort McClellan near Anniston, Alabama.

The WACs were formed during World War II and were merged with the army in 1978. The museum has exhibits, films, and archives that trace the history and role of women in the army and interpret the training, barracks life, duties, traditions, and contributions of army servicewomen. Among the objects on display are uniforms, memorabilia, art, flags, photographs, and other historical items relating to women in the army.

U.S. Army Women's Museum, A Ave. and 22nd St., Fort Lee, VA 23801 (postal address: Mifflin Hall, Rm. 103B, 1201 22 D St., Fort Lee, VA 23801-1601). **E-mail:** burgessj@lee.army.mil. **Website:** www.awm.lee.army.mil. **Hours:** 10-5 Tues.-Fri., 11-5 Sat.-Sun.; closed Mon. and major holidays. **Admission:** free.

West Virginia

A converted school bus houses the Women's History Museum, the nation's only mobile women's museum. The West Liberty, West Virginia, museum, which circulates in the region, has memorabilia, artifacts, and displays on more than 20 historic women. Courtesy Women's History Museum and photographer Robert W. Schramm.

WOMEN'S HISTORY MUSEUM. The Women's History Museum in West Liberty, West Virginia, is the nation's only mobile women's museum. Housed in a school bus, the museum travels around the region to schools, colleges, festivals, and conventions to tell about historic women who have made a difference.

Founded in 1990, the self-contained bus museum has artifacts, letters, documents, autographs, photographs, and other historical materials associated with more than 20 women activists, reformers, and pioneers in such fields as women's rights, social work, prison reform, abolition, mental health, peace, temperance, and help for the disabled.

Among the women represented are suffrage leaders Susan B. Anthony, Elizabeth Cady Stanton, and Anna Howard Shaw; temperance organizer Frances Willard; social worker and peace advocate Jane Addams; prison reformer Elizabeth Fry; American Red Cross founder Clara Barton; author Harriet Beecher Stowe; Planned Parenthood founder Margaret Sanger; human rights spokesperson Eleanor Roosevelt; and Helen Keller, who overcame being blind, deaf, and mute to fight for better treatment of the disabled.

Women's History Museum, 108 Walnut St., West Liberty, WV 26074 (postal address: JR Enterprises, PO Box 209, West Liberty, WV 26074). **Phone:** 304/336-7159. **Fax:** 304/336-7893. **Hours:** by appointment. **Admission:** adults and children over 12, $2; children under 13, $1.

Wyoming

MABEL STRICKLAND COWGIRL MUSEUM. The Mabel Strickland Cowgirl Museum is being developed in Cheyenne, Wyoming, to showcase the contributions and the "lives, thrills, heart breaks, and injuries" of rodeo cowgirls.

The museum is named for Mabel Strickland, an early cowgirl saddle bronc rider, steer roper, relay racer, and trick rider who won numerous championships and has been inducted into several western halls of fame. Her husband, Hugh Strickland, was also a champion rodeo performer, specializing in bronc riding.

According to president Margie E. Earlywine, the purpose of the museum will be to ignite a new interest in the early cowgirls' rodeo history. She points out that these early cowgirls defied social standards by competing in rodeo events, created new clothing styles, pioneered the western way of life, and were the first women athletes to compete in any sport. The museum is collecting the artifacts, memorabilia, and records of rodeo cowgirls, which are being used in temporary and traveling exhibitions until the museum opens.

Mabel Strickland Cowgirl Museum, PO Box 293, Cheyenne, WY 82003. **Phone:** 307/632-8022. **Fax:** 307/632-8022. **Hours and Admission:** to be determined.

OTHER HALLS OF FAME

California

TELEVISION ACADEMY HALL OF FAME. The Academy of Television Arts and Sciences has a hall of fame that honors individuals and programs for their outstanding contributions to television in an outdoor plaza adjacent to its headquarters in North Hollywood, California. The achievements of many of the approximately 100 individual inductees—15 percent of which are women—are celebrated with bas-reliefs, bronze busts, and life-size and miniature statues. The honorees include television actors, newscasters, talk show hosts, producers, directors, writers, executives, and others in the industry. Lucille Ball is among those recognized with life-size statues, while Carol Burnett is honored with a small statue. Gracie Allen is memorialized with a bas-relief, and Joyce Hall and others are recognized with bronze busts. Other women enshrined include Mary Tyler Moore, Dinah Shore, Angela Lansbury, Barbara Walters, and Oprah Winfrey. The only TV program honored is the *I Love Lucy* series.

Colorado

WORLD FIGURE SKATING MUSEUM AND HALL OF FAME. The World Figure Skating Museum and Hall of Fame in Colorado Springs, Colorado, is actually the site of two halls of fame—one national and the other international in scope. In addition to the World Figure Skating Hall of Fame, the U.S. Figure Skating Hall of Fame occupies a portion of the museum building. The world hall of fame has 87 inductees, and the U.S. hall of fame has honored 103. Among the many women enshrined are Sonja Henie of Norway, Barbara Ann Scott of Canada, Katarina Witt of Germany, Dianne Towler of Great Britain, and Peggy Fleming, Dorothy Hamill, Janet Lynn, and Jojo Starbuck of the United States. Each inductee has a plaque with a photograph and a description of his or her skating accomplishments. Other exhibits include ice skates, costumes, posters, programs, photographs, films, and other historical materials related to ice-skating.

District of Columbia

NATIONAL STATUARY HALL. Statues of six women—Frances E. Willard, Maria L. Sanford, Dr. Florence R. Sabin, Esther H. Morris, Mother Joseph, and Sakakawea (often spelled Sacagawea)—are among the 98 figures from 50 states in National Statuary Hall in the U.S. Capitol in Washington, D.C. Statuary Hall was established in 1864 by Congress to honor those "illustrious for their historic renown or for distinguished civic or military services." Each state can contribute two statues. The first woman in Statuary Hall was Willard, a famed feminist and temperance movement leader, installed by Illinois in 1905. She was the only woman represented in the hall for over 50 years. Then came five others—Sanford, an innovative educator and civic leader, Minnesota, 1958; Dr. Sabin, a noted medical researcher and the first woman elected to the National Academy of Sciences, Colorado, 1959; Morris, a suffrage pioneer who was the first woman to hold a political office (justice of peace) in the nation, Wyoming, 1960; Mother Joseph (Esther Parlseau), a nun who founded numerous hospitals, schools, and orphanages, Washington, 1980; and Sakakawea, the Native American guide/interpreter for the Lewis and Clark Expedition, North Dakota, 2003.

Florida

INTERNATIONAL SWIMMING HALL OF FAME. Of the more than 600 aquatic greats in the International Swimming Hall of Fame in Fort Lauderdale, Florida, 200 are women (more than half from the United States). Among the notable women swimmers enshrined are Dawn Fraser, Eleanor Holm, Pat McCormick, Katherine Rawls, and Esther Williams. In addition to museum exhibits related to the inductees and swimming, the complex has an art gallery, library and archives, two Olympic-size pools, diving pool, teaching pool, and swimming flume.

Indiana

QUILTERS HALL OF FAME. Thirty women and four men have been inducted into the Quilters Hall of Fame in Marion, Indiana. Founded in 1979, the hall of fame honors those who have made outstanding contributions to quilting, preserves the nation's quilting heritage, and celebrates quilt making as an art form. Among those enshrined are Marie Webster, designer, entrepreneur, and author of the first quilt book;

Sally Garoutte, founder of the American Quilt Study Group; Joyce Gross, pioneering quilt historian; and Karey Breshhan, founder of Quilts, Inc., and director of the International Quilt Festival.

Michigan

NATIONAL SKI HALL OF FAME AND MUSEUM. The National Ski Hall of Fame and Museum in Ishpeming, Michigan, has inducted more than 330 athletes and ski sport builders, including over 50 women, since it was opened in 1954. Plaques with each honoree's photograph and a brief biography are displayed among the exhibits, which also feature skiing pioneers, modern Olympic medalists, the U.S. Army 10th Mountain Division, skiing trophies, and historical information about skiing equipment, clothing, and other areas.

New York

DANCE HALL OF FAME. See National Museum of Dance in Other Museums.

HALL OF FAME FOR GREAT AMERICANS. The Hall of Fame for Great Americans was America's first hall of fame. It was founded in 1901 by New York University in a 630-foot open-air colonnade that is now part of Bronx Community College of the City University of New York. The hall of fame was established to encourage a deeper appreciation of noteworthy individuals who have made significant contributions to the American experience. The granite colonnade, designed by architect Stanford White and considered one of New York's architectural treasures, contains bronze busts of 98 of the 102 distinguished Americans, including eleven women, who have been named to the hall of fame. Four busts remain to be made and installed. The last selections for the hall were made in 1976. Among the women honored are Susan B. Anthony, suffrage leader; Clara Barton, American Red Cross founder; Harriet Beecher Stowe, writer and reformer; Mary Lyon, educator and early feminist; Maria Mitchell, self-taught astronomer; and Charlotte Cushman, nineteenth-century actress.

Ohio

ROCK AND ROLL HALL OF FAME AND MUSEUM. The Rock and Roll Hall of Fame and Museum, which occupies a stunning building designed by I. M. Pei on Cleveland's lakefront, honors musicians, singers, and industry leaders who have had a great impact on the art form of rock and roll. Opened in 1995, the museum has a gallery devoted to Rock and Roll Hall of Fame inductees, including such women as Aretha Franklin, Madonna, Tina Turner, Ruth Brown, Gladys Knight, and the Supremes. The hall of fame was established in 1983. It has four categories—performers, nonperformers, early influences, and lifetime achievement. Other exhibits in the museum deal with rock and roll's early influences, its relationship to fashion and media, leading performers, and other aspects of the field.

Oklahoma

INTERNATIONAL GYMNASTICS HALL OF FAME. The International Gymnastics Hall of Fame, which began in 1987 in Oceanside, California, and moved to Oklahoma City in 1997, has inducted over 30 gymnasts and coaches, including more than a dozen women. Among the women honored are Olga Korbut of Russia, Nadia Comaneci of Rumania, and Mary Lou Retton of the United States. The hall of fame is housed temporarily in a downtown underground mall while plans are being made for a permanent home.

NATIONAL HALL OF FAME FOR FAMOUS AMERICAN INDIANS. Four women—Pocahontas, Sacajawea, Alice Brown Davis, and Roberta Campbell Lawson—are among the 41 Native Americans honored in the National Hall of Fame for Famous American Indians in Anadarko, Oklahoma. Bronze busts of the honorees are displayed in an outdoor sculpture garden. Pocahontas was a chieftain's daughter known for saving the life of Captain John Smith, leader of the Virginia colony, in 1608; Sacajawea was the Shoshone woman who served as a guide and interpreter for the Lewis and Clark Expedition in 1804–1806; Alice Brown Davis was an activist superintendent of a mission school for Native American girls in Wewoka, Oklahoma, in 1908; and Roberta Campbell Lawson, the great-granddaughter of Delaware Sally Journeycake, had a distinguished public service career, including serving as president of the General Federation of Women's Clubs in 1935–1938.

Rhode Island

INTERNATIONAL TENNIS HALL OF FAME MUSEUM. Such outstanding tennis players as Helen Wills Moody Roark, Alice Marble, Billie Jean King, Chris Everett, and Hana Mandlikova are among the 186 men and women enshrined in the International Tennis Hall of Fame in Newport, Rhode Island. The hall of fame museum is housed in one of America's architectural masterpieces—the 1880 Newport Casino, site of the first U.S. National Lawn Tennis Championships (now the U.S. Open) in 1881. Designed by noted architect Stanford White, the Newport Casino was originally a social and recreational club for summer residents. It was converted into a museum in 1955 and now features tributes to tennis legends in the hall of fame (started in 1954) and exhibits of trophies, equipment, photographs, art, videos, and memorabilia.

Wisconsin

NATIONAL FRESH WATER FISHING HALL OF FAME. The National Fresh Water Fishing Hall of Fame, which began as a community promotional project in Hayward, Wisconsin, in 1960, was initiated by fishing resort and restaurant operator Bob Kutz, who later became comanager of the museum with his wife and business partner, Fannie Kutz. They developed it into the largest fishing museum in the world. The facility's famous building—shaped like a leaping muskellunge with its open jaws serving as an observation platform (covering half a block and four and a half stories tall)—was constructed in 1975. Since then, five other buildings have been added to display early lures, rods, reels, fishing accessories, outboard motors, more than 400 mounts of nearly 200 fish species, and a hall of fame recognizing outstanding men and women anglers.

MUSEUMS HONORING EXCEPTIONAL WOMEN

See also Historic House Museums; Other Types of Museums and Sites; Memorials to Women; Shrines to Women.

Alabama

IVY GREEN, BIRTHPLACE OF HELEN KELLER. Ivy Green is a simple, white clapboard 1820 home in Tuscumbia, Alabama, where Helen Adams Keller was born in 1880 and spent her childhood. It is now a shrine to the remarkable woman who was stricken with a severe illness that left her blind and deaf at the age of 18 months but succeeded in learning things that unimpaired children learn, graduated cum laude from Radcliffe College in 1904, and devoted her life to improving conditions for the blind and deaf-blind around the world.

At the age of six, Keller was taken by her parents, Arthur H. and Kate Adams Keller, to see Alexander Graham Bell, who put her in touch with a young teacher, Anne Mansfield Sullivan. One day in 1887, Sullivan was able to make a miraculous breakthrough by pumping cool water into one of the girl's hands while repeatedly tapping out an alphabet code of five letters in the other. The world of silence was broken when young Helen finally realized that the signals had meaning. By nightfall she had learned 30 words.

Keller proved so gifted that she soon learned the finger-tip alphabet and how to write. In six months she knew 625 words. By the age of ten, Keller had mastered Braille as well as the manual alphabet and even learned to use the typewriter. She soon could speak well enough to go to preparatory school and college. Sullivan stayed with her through those years, interpreting lectures and class discussions, and became regarded as a "miracle worker." Keller went on to author books and give talks in more than 25 countries on five continents, bringing encouragement to millions of blind people.

Ivy Green has been maintained in its original state, with its surrounding buildings, manicured landscape, and gardens. It was placed on the National Register of Historic Places in 1954.

Ivy Green, Birthplace of Helen Keller, 300 W. North Commons, Tuscumbia, AL 35674. **Phone:** 256/383-4066. **Fax:** 256/383-4068. **Website:** www.helenkellerbirthplace.org. **Hours:** 8:30-4 Mon.-Sat., 1-4 Sun.; closed major holidays. **Admission:** adults, $5; seniors, $4; children 5-18, $2; children under 5, free.

SCOTT AND ZELDA FITZGERALD MUSEUM. See Historic House Museums.

WEEDEN HOUSE MUSEUM (Maria Howard Weeden). The Weeden House in Huntsville, Alabama, is where Maria Howard Weeden, an early poet and painter of portraits of African Americans, lived her entire life, except for three years during the Civil War when it was occupied by Union soldiers. She was born in the house in 1846 and died there in 1905. Her poetry and paintings are displayed throughout the house.

Weeden House Museum, 300 Gates Ave., Huntsville, AL 35801 (postal address: PO Box 2239, Huntsville, AL 35804). Phone and Fax: 256/536-7718. Hours: 11-4 Mon.-Fri.; closed Sat.-Sun. and major holidays. Admission: adults, $4; seniors, students, and children, $2.

Arizona

SHARLOT HALL MUSEUM. Sharlot Macbridth Hall was a most unusual woman for her time on the Arizona frontier. Born in 1870, she was a largely self-educated, highly literate child who became a poet, territorial historian, and founder of a museum in Prescott that was later named for her.

Hall collected historical documents and artifacts during much of her life. In 1927 she agreed to move her extensive collection to the Old Governor's Mansion in Prescott and open it as a museum. After her death in 1943, a historical society continued her efforts and changed the name to the Sharlot Hall Museum.

The museum now contains major collections of early tools, furniture, clothing, and buildings from pre-statehood Arizona; extensive prehistoric Prescott-region materials and Yavapai Indian baskets; and gardens ranging from an 1870s kitchen garden to a pioneer herb garden, ethnobotanical garden, and Territorial Women's Memorial rose garden.

Among the historic structures on the site are the 1863–1864 Fort Misery log trading post; 1864 Governor's Mansion; 1875 former home of Territorial Governor Charles Frémont and his wife, Jessie Benton; 1877 Victorian house of William and Louise Bashford; 1885 iron turbine windmill; and 1930s ranch house. Other buildings include a museum center, exhibit building, transportation exhibit building, amphitheater, gazebo, and replica of an early schoolhouse.

Sharlot Hall Museum, 415 W. Gurley St., Prescott, AZ 86301. Phone: 520/445-3122. Fax: 520/776-9053. E-mail: sharlot @sharlothall.lib.az.us. Website: www.sharlot.org. Hours: 10-5 Mon.-Sat., 1-5 Sun.; closed New Year's Day, Thanksgiving, and Christmas. Admission: donation.

The 1864 Territorial Governor's Mansion and 1875 Frémont House (at left) are among the historic structures at the Sharlot Hall Museum in Prescott, Arizona. The history museum was founded in 1928 by Hall, a poet, historian, and independent thinker. Courtesy Sharlot Hall Museum.

Arkansas

CARRY A. NATION HOUSE. See Other Historic Houses.

California

ARDEN-THE HELENA MODJESKA HISTORIC HOUSE AND GARDENS. Helena Modjeska was a leading Polish actress who immigrated to southern California in 1876 with her husband, Charles Bozenta Chlapowski (known as Count Bozenta), and a small group of friends, including future novelist and Nobel laureate Henryk Sienkiewicz. They formed an agricultural colony in the pioneer town of Anaheim, which was a financial failure in the drought and depression of 1877.

However, Modjeska learned some of her former stage roles in English and made a successful debut in San Francisco that summer, launching an American dramatic career that covered 30 years. She played in the great theaters of New York, London, and other large cities, as well as in makeshift halls and so-called "opera houses" of the American West and elsewhere. She became one of America's most distinguished Shakespearean actresses of the 1880s and 1890s.

Arden, Modjeska's 1888 shingled rambling cottage that was named for Shakespeare's forest in *As You Like It*, still sits in a grove along the Santiago Creek in the foothills of the Santa Ana Mountains, near the community of Lake Forest. Modjeska and her husband sold Arden in 1906, just before her final theatrical tour. The house is now owned by Orange County and contains exhibits and some of Modjeska's furniture and personal belongings.

Arden-The Helena Modjeska Historic House and Gardens, 29042 Modjeska Canyon Rd., Modjeska Canyon, CA 92676. **Phone:** 949/855-2028. **Fax:** 949/855-6321. **Website:** www.helenamodjeska.net. **Hours:** Jan.-Nov.—by appointment 1st and 3rd Tues. and 2nd and 4th Sat. of month; closed remainder of month and Dec. **Admission:** adults, $5; children, $2.

GRACE HUDSON MUSEUM AND SUN HOUSE. The Grace Hudson Museum and Sun House in Ukiah, California, features two facilities—a museum devoted to the artist and her Native American paintings and the 1911 Craftsman bungalow that she and her ethnologist husband, John Hudson, occupied until they died in the 1930s.

Grace Carpenter Hudson was nationally known for her paintings of local Pomo Indians. A city-operated museum built in her honor in 1986 traces her life and career, displays over 60 of her works, and contains the manuscripts and correspondence of her husband. The adjacent house, where she and her husband lived and she had her studio, has many of the Hudsons' furnishings, memorabilia, and artworks. The Hopi sun sign, symbol of eternal life, was the Hudson family emblem and is perpetuated as the museum logo.

Grace Hudson Museum and Sun House, 431 S. Main St., Ukiah, CA 95482. **Phone:** 707/467-2836. **Fax:** 707/467-2835. **E-mail:** gracehudson@pacific.net. **Website:** www.gracehudsonmuseum.org. **Hours:** 10-4:30 Wed.-Sat., 12-4:30 Sun.; closed Mon.-Tues. and major holidays. **Admission:** suggested donations—$2 per person; $5 per family.

Colorado

BETTY FORD ALPINE GARDENS. See Botanical Gardens and Arboretums.

GOLDA MEIR MUSEUM. A small brick duplex in which Golda Meir, Israel's future prime minister, lived in Denver in 1913–1914 houses a museum in her name on the Auraria Higher Education Center campus. The house was moved to the campus when it was threatened with demolition in the 1980s.

Meir, whose home was in Milwaukee, lived with her sister, Shayna Korngold, for nearly two years while she attended high school and worked part-time as a presser in her brother-in-law's dry-cleaning shop. Although her stay was brief, it apparently greatly influenced her life. The Korngold house was a social and intellectual haven for numerous Russian-Jewish immigrants and an environment in which she discussed politics, met her future husband, and started to develop her future political philosophy. She later became deeply involved in Zionism and immigrated to Israel in 1921.

The modest duplex's kitchen and bathroom have been restored to reflect their appearance when Meir lived there, while the living room and bedroom contain exhibits and objects pertaining to her stay and her life. The building is also used as a conference center and serves as the site of the Golda Meir Center for Political Leadership, a program of the Metropolitan State College, which shares the campus with the Community College of Denver and the University of Colorado at Denver.

Golda Meir Museum, Auraria Higher Education Center, 1146 9th St., Campus Box A, PO Box 173361, Denver,

CO 80217-3361. **Phone:** 303/556-3291. **Fax:** 303/556-4403. **E-mail:** vadenb@ahec.edu. **Website:** www.goldameircenter .org. **Hours:** June-Aug.—10-2 Mon.-Wed.; remainder of week and year—by appointment. **Admission:** free.

MOLLY BROWN HOUSE MUSEUM. Margaret "Unsinkable Molly" Brown acquired her nickname when she rowed hysterical passengers to safety aboard a lifeboat during the sinking of the *Titanic* in 1912. Her former home in Denver is now the Molly Brown House Museum.

Molly and her husband, James Joseph Brown, bought the 1889 lavastone house in 1894 after he struck it rich mining in Leadville. Although the Browns did not live in the house long (it was leased to others and then became a rooming house), it remained in the family until Molly's death in 1932. The house has been restored to its 1910 appearance by Historic Denver, Inc., and features period furnishings and decorative arts—including many possessions of the Brown family.

Molly Brown House Museum, 1340 Pennsylvania St., Denver, CO 80203. **Phone:** 303/832-4092. **Fax:** 303/832-2340. **E-mail:** admin@mollybrown.org. **Website:** www .mollybrown.org. **Hours:** June-Aug.—10-4 Mon.-Sat., 12-4 Sun.; remainder of year—10-4 Tues.-Sat., 12-4 Sun.; closed Mon. and major holidays. **Admission:** adults, $6.50; seniors, $4.50; children 6-12, $2.50; children under 6, free.

Connecticut

HARRIET BEECHER STOWE CENTER. Harriet Beecher Stowe, author of the classic antislavery novel *Uncle Tom's Cabin* and 30 other books, lived in this 1871 home in Hartford, Connecticut, that now serves as a memorial and center devoted to her life, work, and commitment to social justice.

Stowe lived in the house from 1873 until her death in 1896. Her home in Hartford's Nook Farm area was a neighborhood of writers and reformers, including Samuel Clemens (better known as Mark Twain) and women's rights advocate Isabella Beecher Hooker.

In addition to the collections, exhibits, and programs in the Stowe house, the center has a visitor center and a library, located in the adjacent Katharine Seymour Day House. Many of the center's collections and programs also pertain to nineteenth-century women's history, especially the suffrage movement.

Harriet Beecher Stowe Center, 77 Forest St., Hartford, CT 06105. **Phone:** 860/522-9258. **Fax:** 860/ 522-9259. **E-mail:** stowelib@hartnet.org. **Website:** www. harrietbeecherstowecenter.org. **Hours:** 9:30-4:30 Tues.-Sat., 12-4:30 Sun.; closed Mon., major holidays, and Columbus Day through Memorial Day, except for Dec. **Admission:** adults, $6.75; seniors, $6; children 6-16, $2.75; children under 6, free.

WHITNEY MUSEUM OF AMERICAN ART AT CHAMPION PLAZA. (Gertrude Vanderbilt Whitney). See Art Museums.

District of Columbia

MARY McLEOD BETHUNE COUNCIL HOUSE NATIONAL HISTORIC SITE. An 1876 three-story brick Victorian row house in Washington, D.C., memorializes Mary McLeod Bethune, a noted African American educator and activist. The building, known as the Council House, was her home from 1943 to 1950.

Bethune, one of seventeen children born to former slaves in South Carolina in 1885, founded and was the first president of the National Council of Negro Women; started an African American girls school that became part of the combined Bethune-Cookman College, of which she became president; and served as director of the Division of Negro Affairs in the National Youth Administration, minority adviser to President Franklin D. Roosevelt, and vice president of the National Association for the Advancement of Colored People.

The house, now maintained by the National Park Service, features changing exhibitions on various aspects of African American women's history. The nineteenth-century carriage house at the rear serves as home to the National Archives for Black Women's History, containing Bethune's papers and those of other African American women leaders; the early files of the National Council of Negro Women; and other materials documenting the history of African American women in the United States.

Mary McLeod Bethune Council House National Historic Site, 1318 Vermont Ave. N.W., Washington, DC 20005. **Phone:** 202/673-2402. **Fax:** 202/673-2414. **Website:** www.nps.gov/mamc. **Hours:** 10-4 Mon.-Sat.; closed Sun. and federal holidays. **Admission:** free.

SEWALL-BELMONT HOUSE. The Sewall-Belmont House, a historic three-story brick mansion in Washington, D.C., was the home and office of Alice Paul, founder of the once-militant National Woman's

Party, who was responsible for the 10,000-woman suffrage demonstration in the nation's capital in 1913 and wrote the first Equal Rights Amendment in 1923.

The house was built in 1800, incorporating a ca. 1750 structure, by Robert Sewall, who rented it to Secretary of Treasury Albert Gallatin. Financial details of the Louisiana Purchase were reportedly negotiated there. Gallatin remained a tenant until 1813. During the War of 1812, the house was damaged by British troops. The house, which the Sewall family owned for 123 years, became a lively social center late in the 1800s when Sewall's granddaughter married Senator John Strode Barbour of Virginia. In 1921 the house was purchased by Vermont Senator Porter Dale, who restored it and the gardens.

The National Woman's Party, which was founded in 1913 as the Congressional Union for Woman Suffrage, bought the property in 1929 and renamed it the Alva Belmont House in honor of its major benefactor. The party was headed by Alice Paul, a fiery Quaker lawyer from New Jersey who had been jailed in England during suffrage demonstrations, which influenced her suffrage strategy in America. She later founded the World Party for Equal Rights of Women and was instrumental in including an affirmation of the equal rights of women and men in the preamble to the charter of the United Nations. By the time of her death in 1977, Alice Paul was considered the elder stateswoman of the feminist movement.

The historic house, jointly managed by the National Woman's Party and National Park Service, now contains a collection of suffrage and equal rights memorabilia, portraits and Adelaide Johnson's marble busts of women suffrage leaders, Alva Belmont's living room furniture and china, a rolltop desk once owned by Susan B. Anthony, Elizabeth Cady Stanton's upholstered chair, Alice Paul's four-poster bed and drop-leaf desk, and a painting of Inez Milholland on her white horse leading the 1913 suffrage parade.

Sewall-Belmont House, 144 Constitution Ave. N.E., Washington, DC 20002. **Phone:** 202/546-1210. **Fax:** 202/546-3997. **E-mail:** nwpweb@starpower.net. **Website:** www.natwomanparty.org. **Hours:** 11-3 Tues.-Fri., 12-4 Sat.; closed Sun.-Mon. and major holidays. **Admission:** suggested donation—$3 per person.

Florida

MARJORIE KINNAN RAWLINGS HISTORIC STATE PARK. See Historic Parks and Sites.

ZORA NEALE HURSTON MEMORIAL PARK. See Historic Parks and Sites.

Georgia

JULIETTE LOW BIRTHPLACE. The birthplace of Juliette Gordon Low, founder of the Girl Scouts of the U.S.A., is an 1818–1821 Regency-style townhouse that has been restored to the late-1800s period in Savannah, Georgia.

Low was born in the Wayne-Gordon family home in 1860 and lived there until her marriage to William Mackay Low, a wealthy Englishman, in 1886. The couple moved to England, but she returned to Savannah after her husband's death and after meeting Sir Robert Baden Powell, founder of the Boy Scouts and Girl Guides. She became interested in the youth movement and organized the first troop of the American Girl Guides in 1912. The name of the organization was changed to the Girl Scouts the following year.

In developing the Girl Scout movement in the United States, Low brought girls of all backgrounds into the outdoors, emphasizing self-reliance and resourcefulness. Approximately 3.6 million girls now participate in Girl Scouting in this country annually, making it the world's largest nonprofit organization for girls.

The home was purchased from the Gordon family in 1953 by the Girl Scouts of the U.S.A. It contains many of the family's memorabilia, furnishings, outbuildings, and a Victorian garden, and tells the story of Juliette Low and the early history of the Girl Scouts.

Juliette Low Birthplace, 10 E. Oglethorpe Ave., Savannah, GA 31401-3723. **Phone:** 912/233-4501. **Fax:** 912/236-3871. **E-mail:** birthplace@girlscouts.org. **Website:** www.girlscouts.org/birthplace. **Hours:** 10-4 Mon.-Tues., Thurs.-Sat.; 12:30-4:30 Sun.; closed Wed., some Sun. in Dec.-Jan., and major holidays. **Admission:** adults, $8; children under 18, $6 ($5 for Girl Scouts).

MARGARET MITCHELL HOUSE AND MUSEUM. The house where Margaret Mitchell wrote *Gone With the Wind* in the 1920s is part of the Margaret Mitchell House and Museum in midtown Atlanta. The 1936 Pulitzer Prize–winning novel, which was made into a blockbuster motion picture, has become the world's second best-selling book, surpassed only by the Bible.

Mitchell and her husband, John Marsh, lived in an apartment in the house in 1925–1932. The house, built in 1899, is a two-story, single-family home that was converted into a 10-unit apartment building in 1919.

The Mitchell apartment is the only interior space of the restored house that has been preserved as an apartment.

The two-block site also contains an adjacent visitor center with a small theater and photography exhibit gallery and a museum in a nearby renovated bank building that features memorabilia, films, and other materials from the *Gone With the Wind* movie.

Margaret Mitchell House and Museum, 990 Peachtree St., Atlanta, GA (postal address: Suite 775, 999 Peachtree St., Atlanta, GA 30309-3964). **Phone:** 404/249-7012. **Fax:** 404/249-9388. **E-mail:** mary-rosetaylor@gwtw.org. **Website:** www.gwtw.org. **Hours:** 9:30-5 daily; closed major holidays. **Admission:** adults, $10; seniors and students over 17, $8; children 6-17, $5; children under 6, free.

OAK HILL AND THE MARTHA BERRY MUSEUM. See Historic House Museums.

Hawaii

'IOLANI PALACE (Queen Lili'uokalani). 'Iolani Palace in Honolulu was the last official residence of the kings and queens who ruled Hawaii as a united kingdom for a century, and earlier as separate kingdoms for a thousand years. The 1882 palace was the residence of King Kalakaua until his death in 1891 and then the home of his sister, Queen Lili'uokalani, until the overthrow of the Hawaiian monarchy in 1893.

The 140- by 100-foot building features a wide hall that runs the entire width of the palace, with portraits of ten Hawaiian kings and queens; the Throne Room, scene of royal audiences, balls, receptions, and the 1895 trial of Queen Lili'uokalani, who was accused of knowing about a rebellion mounted by supporters to restore the monarchy; the Blue Room, where informal audiences and small receptions took place; and the State Dining Room, containing portraits of German, French, Russian, and British rulers and leaders and three massive sideboards made in Boston. When the palace served as the Republic of Hawaii capitol, the Throne Room was used by the House of Representatives and the State Dining Room served as the Senate chamber.

A curved staircase leads from the hallway to the royal family's living quarters on the second floor, which has an upper hallway used as a private dining room and parlor and for occasional displays; the King's Suite, with Gothic-style furniture; a library; a music room; the Queen's Bedroom; and two guest rooms. In 1895 Queen Lili'uokalani was imprisoned in the front room for eight months following her trial by the Republic of Hawaii.

'Iolani Palace, King and Richards Sts., Honolulu, Hawaii (postal address: Friends of 'Iolani Palace, PO Box 2259, Honolulu, HI 96804). **Phone:** 808/522-0822. **Fax:** 808/532-1051. **E-mail:** miuraa@hawaii.edu. **Website:** www.openstudio.hawaii.edu/iolani/. **Hours:** galleries—9-4 Tues.-Sat.; guided tours—9-2:15 Tues.-Sat.; closed Mon. and Sun., except for 1st Sun. of month (not May). **Admission:** galleries—adults and children over 12, $10; children 5-12, $5; children under 5, free; tours—adults and children over 12, $15; children 5-12, $5; no children under 5 admitted.

Illinois

JANE ADDAMS HULL-HOUSE MUSEUM. The Jane Addams Hull-House Museum on the University of Illinois at Chicago campus commemorates the social welfare pioneer and peace advocate, her settlement house associates and programs, and the neighborhood served from 1889 until her death in 1935.

Addams lived and worked in the Hull Mansion built by the Charles J. Hull family in 1856. It is where she, Ellen Gates Starr, and others began their social settlement work in 1889 among the many immigrants in the residential and industrial neighborhood on Chicago's west side. They provided such services as kindergarten and day-care facilities for children of working mothers, an employment bureau, libraries, music and art classes, and an art gallery. By 1900, Hull-House activities were expanded to include a cooperative residence for working women, the first little theater in America, a labor museum, and a meeting place for trade union groups. Hull-House grew to include thirteen buildings around the original site and a summer campground near Lake Geneva, Wisconsin.

The Hull-House residents and their supporters spearheaded a powerful reform movement—launching an immigrants' protective league, a juvenile protective association, the first juvenile court in the nation, and a juvenile psychopathic clinic. They also worked to enact Illinois protective legislation for women and children, a compulsory education law, and state and federal child labor laws.

Addams wrote and spoke widely about Hull-House activities and played an important role in many settlement, neighborhood, women's, civil rights, and peace organizations, receiving the Nobel Peace Prize in 1931.

The Jane Addams Hull-House Museum, which includes the Residents' Dining Hall that was added in

1905, contains original furnishings, paintings, and photographs and exhibits that re-create the history of the settlement and the work of Addams and her associates.

Jane Addams Hull-House Museum, University of Illinois at Chicago, 800 S. Halsted St., Chicago, IL 60607-7017. **Phone:** 312/413-5353. **Fax:** 312/413-2092. **E-mail:** jahh@uic.edu. **Website:** www.uic.edu/jaddams/hull/. **Hours:** 10-4 Mon.-Fri., 12-5 Sun.; closed Sat. and major holidays. **Admission:** free.

LINCOLN HOME NATIONAL HISTORIC SITE (Mary Todd Lincoln). See Historic Parks and Sites.

WILLARD HOUSE. The Willard House in Evanston, Illinois, is where Frances Willard lived and spearheaded the national temperance movement in the late 1800s. The house has been restored with her furnishings and mementos and is now on the grounds of the national Woman's Christian Temperance Union (WCTU).

Willard, who was from Janesville, Wisconsin, graduated from North Western Female College in Evanston, where a town ordinance prohibited the sale of alcohol, in 1859. She then taught school for several years before returning to Evanston in 1871 as president of the new Evanston College for Ladies, which had financial difficulties and was absorbed by Northwestern University two years later. She became dean of women and professor of English and art at Northwestern, but she resigned in 1874 after constant conflicts with the university president, Charles H. Fowler, to whom she had been engaged in 1861.

It was at that time that the so-called "Woman's Crusade," an anti-liquor movement, was underway, and she was invited to become president of a Chicago temperance organization. That began a series of temperance positions, leading to her election as president of the national Woman's Christian Temperance Union in 1879—a position she held until her death in 1898. It was under her leadership that the WCTU became a well-organized movement of public education and political pressure, linking temperance and suffrage. The organization also worked for labor legislation and programs of social health and hygiene, prison reform, international peace, and world drug control.

Willard House, National Woman's Christian Temperance Union, 1730 Chicago Ave., Evanston, IL 60201-4585. **Phone:** 847/864-1397. **Fax:** 847/864-9497. **Hours:** 1-4 1st Sun. of month, unless a holiday, then 2nd Sun.; other times by appointment. **Admission:** $3 per person.

Iowa

LAURA INGALLS WILDER PARK AND MUSEUM. The Laura Ingalls Wilder Park and Museum in Burr Oak, Iowa, honors the *Little House on the Prairie* author. It features the hotel in which Wilder and her family lived and worked in 1876–1877 before returning to Walnut Grove, Minnesota. The 11-room building has been restored with period furniture. (See also Laura Ingalls Wilder Museum in Walnut Grove, Minnesota; Laura Ingalls Wilder Home and Museum near Mansfield, Missouri; Surveyors' House and Ingalls Home and Museum in De Smet, South Dakota; and Laura Ingalls Wilder Wayside near Pepin, Wisconsin).

Laura Ingalls Wilder Park and Museum, 3603 236 Ave., Burr Oak, IA 52131. **Phone:** 319/735-5916. **Website:** www.bluffcountry.com/liwbo.htm. **Hours:** May-Sept.—9-5 daily; closed remainder of year. **Admission:** adults, $4; seniors, $3.50; students and children, $2.50; families, $12.

MAMIE DOUD EISENHOWER BIRTHPLACE. The Mamie Doud Eisenhower Birthplace in Boone, Iowa, is where the wife of President Dwight D. Eisenhower was born in 1896. The restored Victorian home contains family furniture, memorabilia, and photographs and exhibits on the lives of the Doud and Eisenhower families.

Mamie Doud Eisenhower Birthplace, 709 Carroll St., PO Box 55, Boone, IA 50036. **Phone:** 515/432-1896. **Fax:** 515/432-2571. **Website:** www.mamiesbirthplace .homestead.com/mamie~ns4.html. **Hours:** June-Oct.—10-5 daily; Apr.-May—1-5 Tues.-Sun.; other times by appointment; closed major holidays. **Admission:** adults, $3; children 6-17, $1; children under 6, free.

Kansas

AMELIA EARHART BIRTHPLACE MUSEUM. The 1861 Gothic Revival cottage where Amelia Earhart, the world's most famous female aviator, was born in 1897 and lived until she was twelve is the site of a museum in her honor in Atchison, Kansas.

Earhart learned to fly in 1920–1921 and was chosen by publisher and promoter George Palmer Putnam (whom she married in 1951) to be the standby pilot on a transatlantic flight in 1928, becoming the first woman to fly across the Atlantic. In 1932 Earhart was the first woman to fly across the Atlantic solo, and she then made the first solo flight from Honolulu to the United States mainland and the initial Mexico City to New

York flight in 1935. But in 1937 her plane disappeared over the Pacific while attempting a round-the-world flight with Frederick J. Noonan as navigator. No trace of the plane was ever found.

The Amelia Earhart Birthplace Museum is owned and operated by the Ninety-Nines, Inc., an international organization of women pilots founded by Earhart and 98 other women. It contains period furnishings, memorabilia, and exhibits on Earhart and other women pilots. Life-size statues of Earhart are also located in downtown Atchison and a memorial park (see Memorials to Women).

Amelia Earhart Birthplace Museum, 223 N. Terrace St., Atchinson, KS 66002 (postal address: 117 S.W. Winterpark Lane, Lee's Summit, MO 64081). Phones: 816/554-2567 and 913/367-4217. Fax: 816/554-3239. Hours: May-Oct.—9-4 Mon.-Sat., 1-4 Sun.; remainder of year 1-4 daily; closed New Year's Day and Christmas. Admission: free.

CARRY A. NATION HOME MEMORIAL. The Carry A. Nation Home Memorial in Medicine Lodge, Kansas, is where the temperance crusader began her hatchet-wielding career of saloon smashing during Prohibition. She lived in the 1886 brick house in 1890–1903 with her second husband, David Nation, a journalist and sometime lawyer and minister (who divorced her for desertion in 1901 after one of her barroom raids).

Mrs. Nation was originally married to Charles Gloyd, an alcoholic who resisted her efforts to reform him (see also Carry A. Nation House in Other Historic Houses). After moving to Medicine Lodge with her second husband, she organized a chapter of the Woman's Christian Temperance Union in 1892. Although Kansas had been a "dry" state since 1880, Prohibition had been openly flouted and opposition forces sought to repeal the law in 1890.

Alone or with hymn-singing supporters, she first sought to convince saloon occupants to stop drinking. Starting in 1899, the saloon visits turned into hatchet-swinging missions. She felt that since selling liquor was illegal, the saloons were outside the law. She was frequently arrested for disturbing the peace and paid her fines from lecture fees, contributions, and the sale of souvenir hatchet pins. For a time, she was much in demand as a speaker in her deaconess's clothing, holding a hatchet. She died in 1911 from declining health, which may have been due in part to the physical assaults sometimes received in barroom encounters.

The Carry Nation house, which became a city museum in 1950, features her antique pump organ,

writing desk, cupboard, bed, and other period furnishings. A glass case also displays her valise, hat, purse, and a hatchet pin she sold to help pay her fines. Admission includes the adjacent Stockade Museum.

Carry A. Nation Home Memorial, 211 W. Fowler Ave, Medicine Lodge, KS 67104 (postal address: 317 W. Kansas Ave., Medicine Lodge, KS 67104). Phone: 316/886-3553. Fax: 316/886-5978. Hours: 10:30-5 daily; closed New Year's Day, Easter, and Christmas. Admission: adults, $4; seniors, $3.50; children 6-17, $3; children under 6, free.

MARTIN AND OSA JOHNSON SAFARI MUSEUM. Martin Johnson and his wife, Osa Johnson, were explorers, documentary filmmakers, and authors who traveled the South Seas and Africa from 1917 to 1936, a time when relatively few Americans ventured into those wildernesses. They captured the public's imagination with their films, lectures, and books about wild animals, native peoples, and adventures in distant exotic lands.

The Martin and Osa Johnson Safari Museum, located in a historic train depot in their hometown of Chanute, Kansas, is devoted to their lives and adventures, African cultures, and changing themes. The museum was founded in their memory in 1961 by Mrs. Johnson's mother, Belle Leighty, and civic leaders. The museum contains the largest collection of the Johnsons' films, photographs, writings, and personal items. The main permanent exhibit traces the Johnsons' lives, with an emphasis on their documentary work in Africa, Borneo, and the South Pacific.

Martin and Osa Johnson Safari Museum, 111 N. Lincoln Ave., Chanute, KS 66720. Phone: 620/431-2730. Fax: 620/431-3848. E-mail: osajohnson@safarimuseum.com. Website: www.safarimuseum.com. Hours: 10-5 Mon.-Sat., 1-5 Sun.; closed New Year's Day, Easter, Fourth of July, Thanksgiving, and Christmas. Admission: adults, $4; seniors and students 13-18, $3; children 6-12, $2; children under 6, free.

SALTER MUSEUM (Susanna Medora Salter). See Historic House Museums.

Kentucky

MARY TODD LINCOLN HOUSE. The Mary Todd Lincoln House in Lexington, Kentucky, is a 14-room Georgian home where the wife of President Abraham Lincoln lived with her parents from 1832 until the marriage in 1842. Mrs. Lincoln was born in Lexington in 1818 and spent her formative years in the city. The house later became the first site restored in America to honor a First Lady (see also Lincoln Home National Historic Site in Springfield, Illinois).

Built as a tavern in 1803–1806, the house was renovated in the early 1830s by Mary's father, Robert Todd, an influential banker and legislator. Gracious and well educated, she participated in many of the political discussions that took place in the upper-class family home with such illustrious guests as Henry Clay. However, life in Washington was not everything she expected. She found herself attacked by both sides during the Civil War. She was considered a traitor by southerners and a southern spy by northerners. After seeing Lincoln shot and killed in 1865, she became a recluse and was later put on trial for insanity by her only surviving son.

The house contains period furniture and family portraits, furnishings, and belongings of the Todds and the Lincolns. A recently added garden reflects the charm of the original.

Mary Todd Lincoln House, 578 W. Main St., PO Box 132, Lexington, KY 40588. **Phone:** 859/233-9999. **Fax:** 859/252-2269. **E-mail:** mtlhouse@iglou.com. **Website:** www .mtlhouse.org. **Hours:** Mar. 15-Nov. 15—10-4 Mon.-Sat.; closed Sun., major holidays, and remainder of year. **Admission:** adults and children over 12, $7; children 4-12, $4; children under 6, free.

Louisiana

BEAUREGARD-KEYES HOUSE (Frances Parkinson Keyes). The Beauregard-Keyes House in the French Quarter is one of the best known of the many historic houses in New Orleans. Built in 1826, it is named for Confederate General Pierre G. T. Beauregard, who lived there for only 18 months, and novelist Frances Parkinson Keyes, who restored the house and wrote a number of her books while spending her winters there in 1944–1970.

The Greek Revival–style house, originally constructed by Joseph Le Carpentier, a well-to-do auctioneer, had many owners over the years, including the Swiss consul John A. Merle and his wife, Anais, who added a formal garden. But the house came to be known for General Beauregard, who returned to Louisiana after the Civil War, and Keyes, who first rented and eventually took over the house from a patriotic women's group, which raised funds and saved the house after it became dilapidated and was about to be demolished and replaced by a macaroni factory in 1925. In 1948

Keyes set up the Keyes Foundation and entrusted the house to its care.

The stately restored house, which is a Louisiana raised cottage, is where Keyes wrote such books as *Dinner at Antoine's, Chess Player*, and *Blue Camellia*. It now features heirloom furniture that once belonged to Beauregard and his family; Keyes's collections of dolls, *veilleuses* (tea warmers), costumes, furniture, and books; and a lovely restored courtyard and garden. Tours are offered on the hour.

Beauregard-Keyes House, 1113 Chartres St., New Orleans, LA 70116. **Phone** and **Fax:** 504/523-7257. **Hours:** 10-3 Mon.-Sat.; closed Sun. and major holidays. **Admission:** adults, $5; seniors, $4; children 6-12, $2; children under 6, free.

KATE CHOPIN HOUSE AND BAYOU FOLK MUSEUM. The 1809 two-story Louisiana-style house in Cloutierville, Louisiana, in which Creole writer Kate Chopin lived with her husband, Oscar Chopin, and six children in 1880–1884 became the Kate Chopin House and Bayou Folk Museum in 1965.

After her husband's death, Kate Chopin returned to St. Louis, where she was born and reared, and began writing of her experiences in the South. She became a frequent contributor to children's magazines and literary journals and published several collections and novels, including *The Awakening*, which describes a young mother's growing awareness of her sexuality and artistic nature. She was known for her intriguing plots, vivid descriptions of Louisiana scenes, and realistic portrayals of Creole and Cajun characters and society.

The house, which contains items that belonged to Kate Chopin, is devoted primarily to artifacts of the educational, religious, social, and economic life of the bayou country. Agricultural equipment, a doctor's office, and a blacksmith shop are located behind the house.

Kate Chopin House and Bayou Folk Museum, 243 State Hwy. 495, Cloutierville, LA 71416. **Phone:** 318/379-2233. **Fax:** 318/379-0055. **Hours:** 10-5 Mon.-Sat., 1-5 Sun.; closed major holidays. **Admission:** adults, $5; students over 12, $3; children 6-12, $2; children under 6, free.

Maine

MARGARET CHASE SMITH LIBRARY. The Margaret Chase Smith Library in Skowhegan, Maine, is a library/archive/museum honoring the life and career of Margaret Chase Smith, who served in the U.S. House of Representatives and Senate for more than three decades.

Chase was the first woman elected to both houses of Congress, serving in the House of Representatives in 1940–1949 and the Senate in 1949–1973. She was also the first woman to have her name placed in nomination for the presidency (at the 1964 Republican Convention in San Francisco). It was through her efforts that women were granted permanent status in the armed services. She also was known as a guardian of individual rights and protector of freedom of speech, and she was one of the few senators to condemn McCarthyism in the 1950s.

The research library, which is affiliated with Northwood University, is located in an extension of Smith's home in Skowhegan. It contains more than 300,000 documents, as well as photographs, recordings, scrapbooks, artifacts, memorabilia, and 50 bound volumes of the senator's speeches, news releases, and general statements that reflect Smith's long career in public service.

Margaret Chase Smith Library, 54 Norridgewock Ave., Skowhegan, ME 04976. **Phone:** 207/474-7133. **Fax:** 207/474-8878. **E-mail:** mcsl@somtel.com. **Website:** www .mcslibrary.org. **Hours:** 10-4 Mon.-Fri.; closed Sat.-Sun. and between Christmas and New Year's Day. **Admission:** free.

NORDICA HOMESTEAD (Lillian Norton). The ca. 1840 Nordica Homestead near Farmington, Maine, was the birthplace of opera singer Lillian Norton, who was also known as Madame Nordica. The farmhouse is devoted to the life of the famous diva and contains some of her original furniture, gowns, stage jewelry, china, photographs, and gifts from admirers.

Nordica Homestead, 116 Nordica Lane, Farmington, ME 04938 (postal address: Nordica Memorial Assn., c/o Franklin County Savings Bank, Farmington, ME 04938). **Phone:** 207/778-2042. **Hours:** June-Labor Day—10-12 and 1-5 Tues.-Sat., closed Sun.-Mon.; day after Labor Day-mid-Oct.—by appointment; closed remainder of year. **Admission:** adults, $2; children 5-16, $1; children under 5, free.

SARAH ORNE JEWETT HOUSE. The Sarah Orne Jewett House in South Berwick, Maine, is the stately 1774 Georgian house where the prominent regional author Sarah Orne Jewett was born in 1849 and lived her life. It focuses on Jewett's life, her artistic and literary circles, the Colonial Revival movement, and the changing role of women in the nineteenth century. The author's bedroom/study is furnished as she left it.

Sarah Orne Jewett House, 5 Portland St., South Berwick, ME 03908 (postal address: Society for the Preservation of New England Antiquities, 141 Cambridge St., Boston, MA 02114). **Phone:** 617/227-3956. **Fax:** 617/227-9204. **E-mail:** ezopes@spnea.org. **Website:** www.spnea.org. **Phone:** 207/384-2454. **Fax:** 207/384-8192. **Hours:** June-Oct. 15—11-5 Wed.-Sun.; closed remainder of week and year. **Admission:** adults, $5; seniors, $4; children 6-12, $2; children under 6, free.

Maryland

CLARA BARTON NATIONAL HISTORIC SITE. The Clara Barton National Historic Site in Glen Echo, Maryland, was the 1897–1912 home of the humanitarian and founder of the American Red Cross. She lived there for the last fifteen years of her life.

Born in Massachusetts in 1821, Barton taught school, founded one of the first free schools in New Jersey, served as a Patent Office clerk, aided the wounded during the Civil War, and searched for the postwar missing U.S. Army servicemen (see also Clara Barton Birthplace in North Oxford, Massachusetts). After the Civil War, she began to speak her opinions and convictions, promoting the enfranchisement of former slaves, becoming a staunch supporter of the growing feminist movement, and lobbying the government for adoption of the Treaty of Geneva, which established the red cross as a symbol of neutral aid.

After suffering a nervous breakdown in 1868, she traveled to Europe for rest, which is when she first heard of the International Red Cross. In 1870–1871, during the Franco-Prussian War, she worked for the Red Cross, helping war-stricken civilians of France and Germany. She was so impressed with the Red Cross that she became determined to establish a similar service in the United States. She founded the American Red Cross in 1881 and served as its first president, from 1882 until 1904. At the age of 77, Barton went to war again, directing relief from the battlefields of Cuba during the Spanish-American War. In 1905 she established the National First Aid Association of America.

The 35-room historic house was first used as the Red Cross headquarters and warehouse. In 1897 it was modified for living quarters and offices. It now contains many of the items that once belonged to Barton, as well as Red Cross supplies.

Clara Barton National Historic Site, 5801 Oxford Rd., Glen Echo, MD 20812. **Phone:** 301/492-6245. **Fax:** 301/492-5384. **E-mail:** clara_barton_nhs@nps.gov. **Website:** www.nps.gov/clba. **Hours:** 10-4 daily; closed New Year's Day, Thanksgiving, and Christmas. **Admission:** free.

Massachusetts

ABIGAIL ADAMS BIRTHPLACE. Abigail Smith Adams, wife of John Adams, the second president of the United States, and mother of John Quincy Adams, the sixth U.S. president, was born in 1744 and spent her first twenty years in this restored 1685 house in Weymouth, Massachusetts.

The house, which has been moved several hundred feet from its original location, features a blue-paneled parlor with a table set for tea, a tiny bedroom that Abigail shared with her sisters (with a fireplace rebuilt with bricks donated by various presidents' wives), and a study where the Reverend William Smith schooled his daughters and developed their interest in literature and where Abigail began her extraordinary letter writing (she later became one of the nation's most celebrated correspondents). Abigail left the house in 1764 after marrying lawyer John Adams and moving to Quincy (see also Adams National Historical Park in Historic Parks and Sites).

The historic house has period furniture, including some original Smith family furnishings, and tells of the early life of Abigail Adams and everyday life in colonial America.

Abigail Adams Birthplace, 180 Norton St., Weymouth, MA 02191 (postal address: Abigail Adams Historical Society, PO Box 350, Weymouth, MA 02188). **Phone:** 781/335-4205. **Hours:** July-Labor Day—1-4 Tues.-Sun.; closed Mon.; June and day after Labor Day-Oct. 15—by appointment; closed remainder of year. **Admission:** adults and children over 12, $1; children under 13, 25¢.

ADAMS NATIONAL HISTORICAL PARK (Abigail Adams). See Historic Parks and Sites.

BORDERLAND STATE PARK (Blanche Ames). See Historic Parks and Sites.

CLARA BARTON BIRTHPLACE. Clara Barton, the founder and first president of the American Red Cross, was born on Christmas Day in 1821 in this 1818 New England Cape house in North Oxford, Massachusetts. The house contains Barton family furnishings and memorabilia and tells about Clara Barton's

accomplishments as a teacher, Civil War humanitarian, and Red Cross leader (see also Clara Barton National Historic Site in Glen Echo, Maryland).

Clara Barton Birthplace, 68 Clara Barton Rd., PO Box 356, North Oxford, MA 01537. **Phone:** 508/987-5375. **Hours:** summer—11-5 Wed.-Sun.; closed Mon.-Tues.; fall—11-5 Sat.-Sun.; closed Mon.-Fri.; remainder of year—by appointment. **Admission:** adults, $2.50; children, $1.

DICKINSON HOMESTEAD (Emily Dickinson). Emily Dickinson, one of America's foremost poets, lived all but fifteen years of her life in the Dickinson Homestead in Amherst, Massachusetts. She was born in the family home in 1830, lived there until 1840, and returned permanently in 1855. She died in the ca. 1813 Federal-style brick house in 1886.

Dickinson, the daughter of a prominent lawyer who was later a congressman and treasurer of Amherst College, was lively and outgoing as a girl, but she became increasingly reclusive in adulthood and disliked being away from home. She never married, although she had several emotional involvements. She began writing poems in the 1850s, showing them to only a few people outside her family circle. Of the nearly 1,800 poems she wrote, only seven were published in her lifetime. It wasn't until after her death that her sister, Lavinia, discovered hundreds of her poems in a dresser drawer and sought to have them published.

The 16-room Dickinson house, which was built by Emily's grandfather, Samuel Fowler Dickinson, a lawyer and principal founder of Amherst College, also had a barn, orchards, several small gardens, and 11 acres of hay fields. Today the homestead grounds cover only 1.5 acres but are filled with a variety of flowers, many of which were popular in the 1800s. The homestead is owned by Amherst College, which offers tours of seven rooms, including the bedroom in which Emily wrote most of her poems, and an exhibit on her life and publication history.

Dickinson Homestead, Amherst College, 280 Main St., Amherst, MA 01002. **Phone:** 413/542-8161. **E-mail:** csdickinson@amherst.edu. **Website:** www.dickinsonhomestead.org. **Hours:** grounds—10-5 daily; house tours—June-Aug.: 1-5 Wed.-Fri. and Sun., 10:30-12:30 Sat.; Mar.-May and Sept.-early Dec.: 1-4 Wed.-Sat. (also first Sun. in Oct.); closed Mon.-Tues. and early Dec.-Feb. **Admission:** adults, $5; seniors and students, $4; children 6-18, $3; children under 6, free.

FITCHBURG ART MUSEUM (Eleanor Norcross). See Art Museums.

This is the interior courtyard of the Isabella Stewart Gardner Museum in Boston. The art museum was founded in 1903 by Mrs. Gardner, who designed the building in the style of a fifteenth-century Venetian palace. Courtesy Isabella Stewart Gardner Museum.

ISABELLA STEWART GARDNER MUSEUM. The Isabella Stewart Gardner Museum in Boston is a monument to a remarkable woman who formed an exceptional eclectic art collection, designed and oversaw the construction of her Venetian-style palace, and opened the museum to the public in 1903.

Gardner was a New Yorker who married into an old Boston family and shocked and dazzled her adopted city. She initially began collecting rare editions, but she switched to art after a visit to John Singer Sargent's London studio, where she saw his famous *Portrait of Madame X*. She then began collecting art, with the assistance of Bernard Berenson, a recent Harvard graduate who eventually became a world authority on early Italian and Renaissance art.

To accommodate her growing collection, she built a house—which she called Fenway Court—based on Venetian palaces of the fifteenth and sixteenth centuries, with an inner courtyard that still features fresh flowers and three floors of exhibits. Although she opened her home as a museum, Gardner continued to live in the building until her death in 1924.

She believed that works of art should be displayed in a setting that fires the imagination. Therefore, her arrangement of the collection is not organized chronologically or by country, but is arranged purely to enhance the objects. The museum's collection is composed of approximately 2,500 works, representing many cultures and spanning 30 centuries. They include paintings, sculpture, drawings, prints, furniture, textiles, ceramics, and other objects—not including collections of rare books, manuscripts, and correspondence.

The museum is particularly rich in Italian Renaissance paintings, with works of Botticelli, Raphael, and Titian. It also has art by later French, German, and Dutch masters, including Rembrandt; works by such artists as Degas, Matisse, Sargent, and Whistler; and such other objects as Greco-Roman marbles, medieval polychromed wood figures, tapestries, stained glass, and metal works.

Following a tradition established by Gardner, the museum offers more than 125 concerts each year. Among these who have performed in the musical series are Isaac Stern, Eileen Farrell, and Glenn Gould.

Isabella Stewart Gardner Museum, 280 The Fenway, Boston, MA 02115 (postal address: 2 Palace Rd., Boston, MA 02115). **Phone:** 617/566-1701. **Fax:** 617/278-5125. **E-mail:** information@isgm.org. **Website:** www.gardnermuseum.org. **Hours:** 11-5 Tues.-Sun.; closed Mon., New Year's Day, Thanksgiving, and Christmas. **Admission:** adults, $10 ($11 on Sat.-Sun.); seniors, $7; college students, $5; children under 18, free.

MARIA MITCHELL BIRTHPLACE HOUSE. The Maria Mitchell Birthplace House in Nantucket, Massachusetts, is where America's first woman astronomer was born in 1818. It is a 1790 typical Nantucket Quaker house that became a historical museum and memorial to Maria Mitchell in 1902.

Mitchell, who was educated at home by her parents, took an early interest in astronomy. She assisted her father in observing an annular eclipse of the sun when she was twelve, and by the time she was fourteen, sea captains had trusted her to rate their chronometers for their whaling voyages. She became a schoolteacher and librarian, and in 1847 she observed and plotted the course of a comet through her Dolland telescope, which is still on display in the Mitchell house. The discovery led to many awards and honors.

In 1848 she was the first woman elected to the American Academy of Arts and Sciences; this was followed by election to the American Association for the

Advancement of Science. This led to her being invited to become the first professor of astronomy at the newly founded Vassar College—and probably the first American woman to make her living as a scientist. During the 23 years she taught at Vassar, Mitchell founded and served as president of the American Association for the Advancement of Women.

The restored Mitchell house contains family furniture, portraits, and artifacts; many of Mitchell's personal belongings; and exhibits on her life and discoveries. The Maria Mitchell Association, which owns the house, also built an observatory with her 5-inch Alvan Clark telescope adjacent to the house and operates a natural science museum, science library, and aquarium in Nantucket.

Maria Mitchell Birthplace House, 1 Vestal St., Nantucket, MA 02554. **Phone:** 508/228-2896. **Fax:** 508/228-1031. **E-mail:** ahunt@mmo.org. **Website:** www.mmo.org. **Hours:** mid-June-Labor Day—10-4 Tues.-Sat.; closed Sun.-Mon.; Sept. weekends-Columbus Day—hours vary; closed remainder of year. **Admission:** adults, $5; seniors and children under 18, $3; combination ticket with natural history museum and aquarium—adults, $7; seniors, $5; and children under 14, $4.

MARY BAKER EDDY HISTORIC HOUSES. Mary Baker Eddy, founder of the Christian Science movement, lived in numerous houses in New England as she sought help for her frail health and clarified her thoughts on health, religion, and reality. Most of these sites are now historic house museums in her memory.

Mary Baker Eddy, who was born in Bow, New Hampshire, in 1821, was subject to seizures and nervous disorders and later suffered from the effects of a severe fall. She sought help from many types of healing, and after an exhaustive trial of physical methods she turned to mental healing. In 1862 she was assisted by and became a student of Phineas P. Quimby, a mental healer in Portland, Maine. She then turned to the Bible and discovered the spiritual and metaphysical system known as Christian Science.

In 1870, while living in Lynn, Massachusetts, she began her career of divine healing and teaching based on the actions and sayings of Jesus as she interpreted them. She denied the reality of the material world and argued that sin and illness are illusions to be overcome by the mind. Therefore, medical help should be refused in fighting sickness.

In 1879 she chartered the Church of Christ, Scientist, which was followed by the chartering of the Massachusetts Metaphysical College in 1881—the year

both were moved to Boston. It was there that the "Mother Church" and later the larger dome "Church Extension" were built, publications were produced, and students departed to spread Christian Science beliefs across the nation. Over the years, Christian Science branches and membership multiplied. Despite her declining health, Eddy retained control of the church until her death in 1910 in Chestnut Hill, Massachusetts, where she had moved two years earlier.

Eddy was married three times—the last in 1877 to Asa G. Eddy, one of her followers. She lived in at least a dozen houses throughout her life: in childhood, with her various husbands, in her search for healing, and in the development of the Christian Science movement. Six of the houses—in Amesbury, Stoughton, and Swampscott, Massachusetts, and Concord, North Groton, and Rumney, New Hampshire— are now operated as branches of the Longyear Museum in Chestnut Hill and open to the public. The Longyear Museum, governed by the Longyear Foundation, features artifacts, manuscripts, letters, portraits, paintings, photographs, and books pertaining to the life and achievements of Mary Baker Eddy and her followers.

Longyear Museum, 1125 Boylston St., Chestnut Hill, MA 02467. **Phone:** 617/278-9000. **Fax:** 617/278-9003. **E-mail:** letters@longyear.org. **Website:** www.longyear.org. Exhibits at the Longyear Museum are temporarily closed. **Three of the historic houses have scheduled hours:** Swampscott, MA (23 Paradise Rd.)—May-Oct.: 10-5 Mon.-Sat., 2-5 Sun.; remainder of year: 1-4 Tues.-Sun.; North Groton, NH (Hall's Brook Rd.)—May-Oct.: 10-5 Tues.-Sat., 2-5 Sun.; Rumney, NH (Stinson Lake Rd.)—10-5 Tues.-Sat., 2-5 Sun.; all closed national holidays. **Admission:** adults, $3; seniors and students, $1.50; children under 12, free. Call other historic houses for hours and admission.

THE MOUNT (Edith Wharton). The Mount, a 1902 Classical Revival mansion in Lenox, Massachusetts, was designed and built by author Edith Wharton, the first woman to receive the Pulitzer Prize for fiction. She and her niece, landscape architect Beatrix Farrand, also designed the landscaping and formal gardens of the 150-acre estate.

Wharton, who lived in the house in 1902–1911, based the house on the precepts of her first book, *The Decoration of Houses,* a collaboration with architect Ogden Codman Jr. The author of more than 50 books, she wrote her first best-selling novel, *The House of Mirth,* at the Mount. Her most famous work was *Ethan Frome,* a 1911 novella of simple New England people unhappy to live within the walls of convention. *The Age of*

Innocence, a 1920 novel, won the Pulitzer Prize and was considered her best work.

The house, which is undergoing restoration, has several floors open for guided tours that interpret Wharton's life and work, life in the Gilded Age, and the mansion and garden design and restoration. The house also has some of her furniture, personal items, first-edition books, and photographs.

The Mount, 2 Plunkett St., PO Box 974, Lenox, MA 01240. **Phone:** 413/637-1899. **Fax:** 413/637-0619. **E-mail:** admin@edithwharton.org. **Website:** www.edithwharton.org. **Hours:** Memorial Day weekend-Oct.—9-5 daily; closed remainder of year. **Admission:** adults, $7.50; seniors, $7; children 13-18, $5; children 6-12, $3; children under 6, free.

ORCHARD HOUSE (Louisa May Alcott). Orchard House in Concord, Massachusetts, was the home of Louisa May Alcott, author of the acclaimed *Little Women*, and the Alcott family (on whom the book was largely based).

The house is a brown clapboard structure that was originally built in 1700 and was modified in 1858 and 1877. Also located on the site is the 1880 building that housed the Concord School of Philosophy, the coeducational summer school operated by Louisa's father, A. Bronson Alcott.

Louisa May Alcott began publishing poems, stories, and sketches in periodicals in 1851 to help her family financially. Her first book, *Flower Fables*, appeared in 1854, and her first successful book, *Hospital Sketches*, based on her experiences as a volunteer nurse in Civil War hospitals in Washington, D.C., was published in 1863. She became the editor of a children's magazine in 1867 and was urged by the publisher to write a novel for young girls. The result was *Little Women*, which was published in two parts in 1868–1869 and became an immediate success. It was followed by a stream of other books before her death in 1888.

Orchard House contains Alcott family furniture, clothing, and memorabilia; May Alcott's original artwork; and information about the family's contributions and Louisa May Alcott's life and writings.

Orchard House, 399 Lexington Rd., PO Box 343, Concord, MA 01742. **Phones:** 978/369-5617 and 978/369-2290. **Fax:** 978/369-1367. **E-mail:** louisa@acunet.net. **Website:** www.louisamayalcott.org. **Hours:** Apr.-Oct.—10-4:30 Mon.-Sat., 1-4:30 Sun.; remainder of year—11-3 Mon.-Fri., 10-4:30 Sat., 1-4:30 Sun.; closed Jan.1-15, Easter, Thanksgiving, and Christmas. **Admission:** adults, $7; seniors, $6; children 6-17, $3.50; and children under 6, free.

Michigan

ROCHESTER HILLS MUSEUM AT VAN HOOSEN FARM (Dr. Bertha Van Hoosen). See Historic Farms and Ranches.

Minnesota

JUDY GARLAND BIRTHPLACE HISTORIC HOUSE. The 1892 house in which singer and movie star Judy Garland was born and spent her formative years (1922–1926) has been restored as part of the Judy Garland Birthplace Historic House in Grand Rapids, Minnesota. The 1,700-square-foot, two-story house, which has been restored to its 1925 appearance, features period furniture, Garland memorabilia, and an adjacent memorial garden—with a "Wizard of Oz" theme. A $1 million addition containing Garland memorabilia was opened in 2003. A children's museum in Grand Rapids is also named for Garland, who changed her name from Frances Gumm when she went into the entertainment industry (see also Judy Garland Children's Museum).

Judy Garland Birthplace Historic House, 2727 U.S. Hwy. 169 South, PO Box 724, Grand Rapids, MN 55744-0724. **Phones:** 218/327-9276 and 800/664-5839. **Fax:** 218/326-1935. **E-mail:** jgarland@uslink.net. **Website:** www.judygarlandmuseum.com. **Hours:** mid-May-mid-Oct.—10-5 daily; remainder of year—by appointment; closed New Year's Day and Christmas. **Admission:** adults and children, $3; children under 1, free; combination ticket with children's museum, $5.

JUDY GARLAND CHILDREN'S MUSEUM. The Judy Garland Children's Museum is located in the singer and actor's hometown of Grand Rapids, Minnesota—where her birthplace is also a historic house (see also Judy Garland Birthplace Historic House). The museum features costumes and other memorabilia from Garland's films, interactive units on music and art, and environmental exhibits.

Judy Garland Children's Museum, 19 N.E. 4th St., PO Box 724, Grand Rapids, MN 55744-0724. **Phone:** 218/326-1900. **Fax:** 218/326-1935. **E-mail:** jgarland@uslink.net. **Website:** www.judygarlandmuseum.com. **Hours:** mid-May-Oct.—10-5 daily; remainder of year—10-5 Tues.-Sun.; closed Mon. and major holidays. **Admission:** adults and children, $3; children under 1, free; combination ticket with historic house, $5.

LAURA INGALLS WILDER MUSEUM. The Laura Ingalls Wilder Museum, a general museum housed in a ca. 1894 railroad station in Walnut Grove, Minnesota, is named for the author of the *Little House on the Prairie* books, who was the town's most renowned resident. The museum contains memorabilia pertaining to the life of Laura Ingalls Wilder and her family, as well as artifacts and other historical materials relating to the early history of Walnut Grove. Also on the site is the 1890s Grandma's House, with approximately 300 dolls. (See also Laura Ingalls Wilder Home and Museum near Mansfield, Missouri; Surveyors' House and Ingalls Home and Museum in De Smet, South Dakota; Laura Ingalls Wilder Park and Museum in Burr Oak, Iowa; and Laura Ingalls Wilder Wayside near Pepin, Wisconsin.)

Laura Ingalls Wilder Museum and Tourist Center, 330 8th St., Walnut Grove, MN 56180-1114. **Phones:** 507/859-2358 and 507/859-2155. **Website:** www.walnutgrove.org. **Hours:** June-Aug.—10-6 daily; Apr. and Oct.—10-4 Mon.-Sat., 12-4 Sun.; May and Sept.—10-6 Mon.-Sat., 12-5 Sun.; remainder of year—by appointment. **Admission:** adults, $3; children 6-12, $1; children under 6, free.

Missouri

BONNIEBROOK (Rosie O'Neill). Bonniebrook is an Ozarks mansion in a park near Branson, Missouri, that was the favorite retreat of Rose O'Neill, artist, illustrator, author, poet, and creator of the impish little characters known as "Kewpie" dolls. She began building the 14-room house on her parents' property in approximately 1898, completed the last phase around 1910, and lived in the house sporadically until her death in 1944.

The original Bonniebrook was destroyed in a fire in 1947, but it was rebuilt in 1990–1993 by the Bonniebrook Historical Society and is now a national historic site. The house has been furnished with some of O'Neill's original furniture and other period furniture, and an adjacent museum contains originals of her works in art, books, illustrations, poems, and factory doll molds, as well as hundreds of Kewpie dolls.

Bonniebrook, 485 Rose O'Neill Rd., PO Box 263, Branson, MO 65615. **Phone:** 800/539-7437. **Hours:** Apr.-Dec. 22—9-4 Mon.-Sat.; closed Sun., Thanksgiving, remainder of Dec., and Jan.-Mar. **Admission:** adults, $6; seniors, $5; children 6-18, $3; children under 6, free.

LAURA INGALLS WILDER HOME AND MUSEUM. Laura Ingalls Wilder wrote all nine of the popular *Little House on the Prairie* books about pioneering life on the prairie in the 1870s–1890s at the Rocky Ridge Farm

where she lived with her husband, Almanzo Wilder, and their daughter, Rose Wilder, near Mansfield, Missouri. The site is now known as the Laura Ingalls Wilder Home and Museum.

The Wilders settled on the farm in 1894, building their home and establishing a successful farm. Laura published the first of her books in 1932. When their daughter grew up, she married and became the well-known author, journalist, and world traveler Rose Wilder Lane.

The Wilder home is as Laura left it at her death in 1957. Located adjacent to the house is the Laura Ingalls Wilder-Rose Wilder Lane Museum, which features items spanning over a century of the family's history. They include handwritten manuscripts of Laura's *Little House* books, her needlework, tools and other articles made by Almanzo, manuscripts and other materials of Rose, and keepsakes of the Ingalls and Wilder families. (See also Laura Ingalls Wilder Museum in Walnut Grove, Minnesota; Surveyors' House and Ingalls Home and Museum in De Smet, South Dakota; Laura Ingalls Wilder Park and Museum in Burr Oak, Iowa; and Laura Ingalls Wilder Wayside near Pepin, Wisconsin).

Laura Ingalls Wilder Home and Museum, 3068 County Hwy. A., Mansfield, MO 65704. **Phone:** 417/924-3626. **Fax:** 417/924-8580. **E-mail:** liwhome@windo.missouri.org. **Website:** lauraingallswilderhome.com. **Hours:** June-Aug.—9-5:30 Mon.-Sat., 12:30-5:30 Sun.; Mar.-May and Sept.-Oct.—9-5 Mon.-Sat., 12:30-5:30 Sun.; closed Nov.-Feb. and Easter. **Admission:** adults, $6; seniors, $5; children 6-18, $3; children under 6, free.

ROY ROGERS-DALE EVANS MUSEUM. The Roy Rogers-Dale Evans Museum in Branson, Missouri, contains personal and professional memorabilia of western movie stars Roy Rogers and his wife, Dale Evans, and other materials relating to the cowboy days and western films. They include such things as costumes, saddles, guns, mounted figures of the entertainers' horses, and awards. It also has a "Happy Trails Theater" with live western and country music. The museum moved to the new 29,000-square-foot site from Victorville, California, in 2003.

Roy Rogers-Dale Evans Museum, 3950 Green Mountain Dr., Branson, MO 65616. **Phone:** 417/339-1900. **E-mail:** administrator@royrogers.com. **Website:** www.royrogers.com. **Hours:** museum—9-6 daily; closed Easter, Thanksgiving, and Christmas; theater—June-mid-Dec.—10 and 2, Tues.-Sat.; closed Sun.-Mon., Easter, Thanksgiving, and Christmas. **Admission:** museum—adults, $14.40; children 6-12, $8.90; children under 6, free; theater—adults, $21.08;

children 6-12, $15.51; children under 6, free; combination ticket—adults, $31.98; children 6-12, $21.97; children under 6, free.

Montana

JEANNETTE RANKIN PARK. See Historic Parks and Sites.

Nebraska

BESS STREETER ALDRICH HOUSE. Author Bess Streeter Aldrich, who wrote 160 short stories and articles and nine novels emphasizing family values and pioneer history, lived in this 1922 stucco and brick house in Elmwood, Nebraska, in 1922–1945. A foundation formed in her honor has restored the historic house and opened a nearby museum, the Bess Streeter Aldrich Museum, in her memory.

Aldrich, who began writing as a child, won her first writing prize when at age fourteen. She began writing professionally after a story she wrote while her baby napped was selected as one of the winners in a magazine contest in 1911. Two of her later works—*Miss Bishop* and *A Lantern in Her Hand*—became motion pictures, and a short story, *The Silent Stars Go By*, was made into a television film. She also served as a movie writer and consultant for Paramount Pictures.

Bess Streeter Aldrich House, 204 E. F St., PO Box 167. Elmwood, NE 68349. **Phone:** 402/994-3855. **E-mail:** marceeb@hotmail.com. **Website:** www.lincolnne.com/nonprofit/bsaf. **Hours:** 2-5 Wed.-Thurs. and Sat.-Sun.; closed Mon.-Tues, Fri., and major holidays. **Admission:** adults and children over 12, $3; children 6-12, $2; children under 6, free; families, $10.

MARI SANDOZ HIGH PLAINS HERITAGE CENTER. The Mari Sandoz High Plains Heritage Center opened in 2002 in a renovated former library building on the Chadron State College campus in Chadron, Nebraska. The center contains manuscripts, memorabilia, and archives of Sandoz, who authored such popular western works as *Old Jules, Cheyenne Autumn,* and *Crazy Horse: Strange Man of the Oglalas.* Born in Nebraska in 1896, she wrote mainly about the early days on the High Plains (see also Mari Sandoz Room in Gordon, Nebraska).

Mari Sandoz High Plains Heritage Center, Chadron State College, 1000 Main St., Chadron, NE 69337. **Phone:** 308/432-6276. **Fax:** 308/432-6464. **E-mail:** dgreen@cscl.csc.edu. **Website:** www.csc.edu. **Hours:** to be determined. **Admission:** free.

MARI SANDOZ ROOM. Personal items, photographs, press clippings, and other materials pertaining to the life and writing career of author Mari Sandoz are featured in the Mari Sandoz Room in her hometown of Gordon, Nebraska. Sandoz, who is best known for such works as *Old Jules, Cheyenne Autumn,* and *Crazy Horse: Strange Man of the Oglalas,* grew up in the Gordon area and is buried there. The memorial room is located in a building shared with the Gordon Tourist Information Office (see also Mari Sandoz High Plains Heritage Center in Chadron, Nebraska).

Mari Sandoz Room, 117 N. Main St., PO Box 237, Gordon, NE 69343. **Phone and Fax:** 308/282-9972. **E-mail:** msbooks@gpcom.net. **Website:** www.sandozlit.com. **Hours:** 9-5 Mon.-Fri., 9-12 Sat. (9-4 in June-Aug.); closed Sun. and major holidays. **Admission:** free.

WILLA CATHER STATE HISTORIC SITE. The Willa Cather State Historic Site in Red Cloud, Nebraska, honors the Pulitzer Prize–winning novelist who spent her formative years in Red Cloud and based many of her works on the frontier area, including *O Pioneers!, My Antonia,* and *The Story of the Lark.*

The historic site includes the ca. 1879 house in which Cather lived in 1884–1904, from the age of ten until she went away to college. It has been restored and furnished with period furniture. A Cather museum, art gallery, library, and archives are located in the 1871 Farmers' and Merchants' Bank Building, restored by the Willa Cather Pioneer Memorial and Education Foundation, which offers tours of the house, bank building, and three other historic buildings. The museum contains artifacts, letters, and history related to Cather's life and career.

Willa Cather State Historic Site, 326 N. Webster St., Red Cloud, NE 68970. **Phone:** 402/746-2653. **Fax:** 402/746-2652. **E-mail:** wcpm@gpcom.net. **Website:** www.willacather.org. **Hours:** 8-5 Mon.-Sat., 1-5 Sun.; closed New Year's Day, Easter, Thanksgiving, and Christmas. **Admission (includes museum and tour):** adults and children over 12, $5; children under 13, $2.

New Hampshire

CHRISTA McAULIFFE PLANETARIUM. Sharon Christa McAuliffe was a New Hampshire social sciences teacher who was the first civilian in space and who died in 1986 when the space shuttle *Challenger* exploded shortly after its launch at Cape Canaveral, Florida. The Christa McAuliffe Planetarium in Concord was established in her memory in 1990 by the state of New Hampshire. It presents sky shows and has exhibits about McAuliffe, astronomy, and the space program.

Christa McAuliffe Planetarium, 3 Institute Dr., Concord, NH 03301. **Phone:** 603/271-7831. **Fax:** 603/271-7832. **Website:** www.starhop.com. **Hours:** early Sept.-late June—9-2 Mon.-Wed., 9-5 Thurs.-Fri., 10-5 Sat., 12-5 Sun.; closed major holidays; late June-early Sept.—10-5 Tues.-Sat., 12-5 Sun.; closed Mon. **Admission:** free; planetarium shows—adults, $8; seniors, students, and children under 18, $5.

New Mexico

GEORGIA O'KEEFFE HOME AND STUDIO. The Georgia O'Keeffe Home and Studio in Abiquiu, New Mexico, is where the acclaimed artist lived from 1949 until 1984 and painted some of her most famous semiabstract works of desert landscapes and bleached animal skulls.

O'Keeffe's breakthrough came in 1916 after some of her paintings were shown to famed photographer Alfred Stieglitz, whom she married in 1924. She became enchanted with New Mexico during a visit in 1929 and returned to live there after Stieglitz's death in 1946. She bought the ca. 1760–1860 Pueblo/Spanish Colonial building in late 1945, spent the next three years rebuilding and renovating before moving to the site in 1949, and lived there until two years before her death in Santa Fe in 1986 (see also Georgia O'Keeffe Museum in Santa Fe).

The home/studio was closed to the public until the Georgia O'Keeffe Foundation reopened the site on a limited basis. It can now be seen on guided tours from mid-April through late November. The building remains much as O'Keeffe left it in 1984. Many of her best-known works were inspired by the house and its surrounding views, such as the patio and black door, cottonwood trees along the Chama River, and the road to Santa Fe.

Georgia O'Keeffe Home and Studio, PO Box 140, Abiquiu, NM 87510. **Phone:** 505/685-4539. **Fax:** 505/685-4428. **Hours:** mid-Apr.-late Nov.—9:30-3:30 Tues., Thurs., and Fri. by reservation; closed remainder of week and year. **Admission:** $22 per person.

GEORGIA O'KEEFFE MUSEUM. The extraordinary landscape and brilliant light of New Mexico captured the heart and inspired the artworks of Georgia O'Keeffe from her first visit to New Mexico in 1917. She then made frequent visits before settling in the state in 1949. O'Keeffe lived in a renovated old adobe home in the

The Georgia O'Keeffe Museum in Santa Fe, New Mexico, is housed in this classic adobe-style building. It features the world's largest permanent collection of works by O'Keeffe, a pioneering modernist and a leading proponent of abstraction. Courtesy Georgia O'Keeffe Museum.

village of Abiquiu for nearly four decades, and then moved to Santa Fe a few years before her death in 1986 at the age of 98 (see also Georgia O'Keeffe Home and Studio in Abiquiu, New Mexico).

The Georgia O'Keeffe Museum, located in Santa Fe, contains the largest permanent collection of her work—featuring drawings, paintings, pastels, sculptures, and watercolors of the pioneering modernist and proponent of abstraction. The museum's collection ranges from the artist's iconic flowers and bleached desert bones to abstractions, nudes, landscapes, cityscapes, and still lifes.

Georgia O'Keeffe Museum, 217 Johnson St., Santa Fe, NM 87501. **Phone:** 505/946-1000. **Fax:** 505/946-1091. **E-mail:** main@okeeffemuseum.org. **Website:** www.okeeffemuseum.org. **Hours:** Nov.-June—10-5 Thurs.-Tues. (also to 8 p.m. Fri.); closed Wed., New Year's Day, Easter, Thanksgiving, and Christmas; July-Oct.—10-5 daily (also to 8 p.m. Fri.). **Admission:** adults, $8; seniors and New Mexico residents, $4; children under 17, free.

MABEL DODGE LUHAN HOUSE. See Historic House Museums.

MARY AUSTIN HOUSE. See Other Historic Houses.

SAN ILDEFONSO PUEBLO MUSEUM (Maria Martinez). See Cultural Art and History Museums.

New York

ALICE AUSTEN HOUSE MUSEUM. The Alice Austen House Museum on Staten Island in New York City is located in the restored former home of photographer

Alice Austen, who was one of the first and most accomplished American female documentary photographers. The house was the home of her grandparents when Alice Austen and her mother moved into the family home in 1866, after being abandoned by Alice's father. She continued to live there until 1945, when financial problems and illness forced her to move.

Alice's grandfather, businessman John Haggerty Austen, purchased the ca. 1690 house in 1844 and transformed the simple Dutch farmhouse into a Victorian Gothic cottage, called "Clear Comfort," with extensive additions and embellishments. It overlooks New York Harbor and offers a panoramic view of the metropolitan area. After Alice Austen left, the house fell into decay until a group of concerned citizens convinced New York City officials to provide over $1 million to renovate it in 1984–1985. The Friends of Alice Austen House now operates the house and extensive garden as a historic house museum. The site became a national historic landmark in 1993. The house museum features Victorian furniture and furnishings and photographs by Austen.

Alice Austen House Museum, 2 Hylan Blvd., Staten Island, NY 10305. Phone: 718/816-4506. Fax: 718/815-3959. E-mail: eaausten@aol.com. Website: www.aliceausten.org. Hours: Mar-Dec.—12-5 Thurs.-Sun.; closed Mon.-Wed., Jan.-Feb., and major holidays. Admission: adults and children over 6, $2; children under 7, free.

ELEANOR ROOSEVELT NATIONAL HISTORIC SITE. The Eleanor Roosevelt National Historic Site near Hyde Park, New York, honors the humanitarian and stateswoman first lady at "Val-Kill," where she had a fieldstone cottage (that later became her home from 1945 until her death in 1962) and once established a workshop with friends for unemployed local craftsmen.

The wife of President Franklin D. Roosevelt never felt comfortable in her husband's Hyde Park family home, which was dominated by his mother, Sara Delano Roosevelt (see Home of Franklin D. Roosevelt National Historic Site in Historic Parks and Sites). She wanted her own place to relax and be with friends. In 1925, with Mr. Roosevelt's assistance, she built the retreat two miles east of the main house to share with friends Nancy Cook and Marion Dickerman. The following year the three women joined with Caroline O'Day to open a small workroom to reproduce early American furniture (and later weaving). Val-Kill Industries thrived until it became a victim of the Depression and was closed in 1936. After her husband's death in 1945, Mrs. Roosevelt lived much of her life in the cottage, which has become a two-story stucco structure with approximately twenty rooms with many of her furnishings and belongings. The grounds also include outbuildings, gardens, woodland trails, a stream, and a pond.

Eleanor Roosevelt National Historic Site, 4097 Albany Post Rd., Hyde Park, NY 12538. Phones: 845/229-9115 and 845/229-9116. Fax: 845/229-0739. E-mail: rova-superintendent@nps.gov. Website: www.nps.gov/elro/. Hours: May-Oct.—9-5 daily; Mar.-Apr. and Nov.-Dec.—9-5 Sat.-Sun.; closed Jan.-Feb., New Year's Eve and Day, Thanksgiving, and Christmas. Admission: adults, $5; children under 17, free; combination ticket with Home of Franklin D. Roosevelt National Historic Site, Franklin D. Roosevelt Library and Museum, and Vanderbilt Mansion National Historic Site, $18.

ELIZABETH CADY STANTON HOUSE. The Elizabeth Cady Stanton House in Seneca Falls, New York, has been restored to the way it was when the suffragist, abolitionist, and temperance leader planned the first Women's Rights Convention in 1848. The 1830 Greek Revival house is now part of the Women's Rights National Historical Park, with tours offered from the visitor center (see also Women's Museums, Galleries, and Halls of Fame).

In 1840 she married Henry Brewster Stanton, a prominent abolitionist. Later that year she attended the World's Anti-Slavery Convention in London and was outraged when Lucretia C. Mott and several other women delegates were denied official recognition because of their sex. The Stantons moved from Johnstown, New York, to Boston, where Mrs. Stanton associated with leading liberals of the period, and then to Seneca Falls in 1847. It was there that she spoke frequently about women's rights and circulated petitions that helped convince the New York legislature in 1848 to pass a bill granting property rights to married women.

In July 1848 Mrs. Stanton and Mrs. Mott, who was visiting nearby, organized and called for a women's rights convention in Seneca Falls, which effectively launched the women's rights movement. Here, Stanton introduced her "Declaration of Sentiments," modeled after the Declaration of Independence, which described the inferior status of women and called for extensive reforms. She also offered a resolution calling for woman suffrage, which was adopted. Beginning in

1851, Stanton worked closely with Susan B. Anthony—campaigning for suffrage for a half century. In 1878 she drafted a federal suffrage amendment, which was introduced in every Congress and was substantially adopted in 1919—seventeen years after her death.

The homes of two other Seneca Falls women who had a role in planning the first Women's Rights Convention—Mary Ann M'Clintock and Jane Hunt—are also part of the Women's Rights National Historical Park. Both women attended the initial planning meeting at the Stanton home. The second meeting, at the M'Clintock House, is where many of the women's grievances were drafted for the Declaration of Sentiments. The M'Clintock House can also be toured, but the Hunt House is not currently open to visitors.

Elizabeth Cady Stanton House, 32 Washington St., Seneca Falls, NY (contact: Women's Rights National Historical Park, 136 Fall St., Seneca Falls, NY 13148). **Phone:** 315/568-0024. **Fax:** 315/568-2141. **E-mail:** davic_molone@nos.gov. **Website:** www.nps.gov/wori. **Hours:** park—9-5 daily; house tours—May-Labor Day—10-4 daily; remainder of year—11:15-2:15 daily; closed major holidays. **Admission:** park—adults and children over 16, $3; children under 17, free; house tours—adults and children over 16, $1 additional; children under 17, free.

HARRIET TUBMAN HOME. The Harriet Tubman Home in Auburn, New York, is a two-story clapboard house that once belonged to a former slave who led some 300 fugitive slaves to freedom on the Underground Railroad to Canada. She became the Underground Railroad network's most famous "conductor" and was called the "Moses of her people."

Born a slave on a Maryland plantation in 1820, she fled to Philadelphia in 1849 and then made her way to Baltimore, from where she led her sister and two children to freedom. Over the next decade she helped hundreds of slaves to escape. As a result, rewards totaling $40,000 were offered. She bought a small farm near Auburn for her aged parents, whom she also helped to freedom.

During the Civil War, Tubman served as a laundress, nurse, scout, and spy for Union forces. After the war she settled in Auburn and began taking in orphans and the elderly, which led to the establishment of the Harriet Tubman Home for Indigent Aged Negroes by the A.M.E. Zion Church, which now operates the Harriet Tubman Home. Tours of her home and the home for the aged are offered.

Harriet Tubman Home, 180 South St., Auburn, NY 13021. **Phones:** 315/252-2081 and 315/255-1553. **Hours:** Feb.- Oct.—11-4 Tues.-Fri., Sat. and remainder of year by appointment; closed Sun.-Mon. and major holidays. **Admission:** donation.

HOME OF FRANKLIN D. ROOSEVELT NATIONAL HISTORIC SITE (Eleanor Roosevelt). See Historic Parks and Sites.

LUCY-DESI MUSEUM (Lucille Ball). The Lucy-Desi Museum in Jamestown, New York, celebrates the lives and entertainment careers of Lucille Ball, who was born in Jamestown, and her husband, Desi Arnaz. The museum contains some memorabilia and exhibits on the couple and their impact on television. Ball's childhood home, where she lived from age eight until midway through high school, when she left to attend drama school in New York, still exists in neighboring Celoron, New York.

Lucy-Desi Museum, 212 Pine St., Jamestown, NY 14701. **Phone:** 716/484-7070. **Hours:** May-Sept.—10-5:30 Mon.-Sat., 1-5 Sun.; remainder of year—10-5:30 Sat., 1-5 Sun.; closed Mon.-Fri., New Year's Day, Easter, and Christmas. **Admission:** adults, $5; seniors and children 6-18, $3.50; children under 6, free.

MARCELLA SEMBRICH OPERA MUSEUM. The Marcella Sembrich Opera Museum in Bolton Landing, New York, features operatic memorabilia of singer and voice teacher Marcella Sembrich in the former teaching studio of her summer residence along Lake George.

Sembrich, who was born Marcella Kochanska in Poland in 1858 (and adopted her mother's family name), was a reigning star at the Metropolitan Opera and at many opera houses in Europe, from 1883 until her farewell performance in New York in 1909. She also founded and directed the vocal departments at the Juilliard School in New York and the Curtis Institute in Philadelphia, and was a leading teacher of singing in America for 25 years. During the summers she brought students to her studio at Lake George for instruction.

The museum, which is open for two months every summer, displays such operatic memorabilia as costumes, portraits, autographed scores, art objects, commemorative wreaths, trophies, and photographs of the singer and her colleagues in the world of music and art.

Marcella Sembrich Opera Museum, 4800 Lake Shore Dr., PO Box 417, Bolton Landing, NY 12814-0417. **Phone:** 518/644-2492. **Fax:** 518/644-2191. **E-mail:** sembrich@webtv.net. **Website:** www.operamuseum.org. **Hours:** June 15-Sept. 15—10-12:30 and 2-5:30 daily; closed remainder of year.

Admission: adults and children over 9, $2; children under 10, free.

NARCISSA PRENTISS HOUSE. Narcissa Prentiss Whitman, a missionary who was one of the first two white women to cross the Rocky Mountains in 1836, was born in this white clapboard house in Prattsburgh, New York, in 1808. The restored house, which is furnished typically for the period, tells of the Whitman-Spalding mission to the Oregon Territory and related historical-religious matters.

Narcissa Prentiss, who was unable to travel on missionary service because she was an unmarried female, married Dr. Marcus Whitman, another missionary, in 1836 and then set out almost immediately for the American West with another missionary couple, Henry and Eliza Hart Spalding. The Spaldings went to Idaho, while the Whitmans established their mission in the Walla Walla, Washington, area, to serve the Cayuse people. Both Whitmans were killed, however, when revengeful Native American warriors burned their mission in 1847.

Narcissa Prentiss House, 7226 Mill Pond Rd., PO Box 384, Prattsburgh, NY 14873. **Phone:** 607/522-4537. **Hours:** mid-June-Sept.—1-5 Sun.; other times by appointment. **Admission:** free.

SAGAMORE HILL NATIONAL HISTORIC SITE (Edith Roosevelt). See Historic Parks and Sites.

SUSAN B. ANTHONY HOUSE. The Susan B. Anthony House in Rochester, New York, was the home of the legendary women's rights leader from 1866 until her death in 1906. It was here that she organized and wrote about woman suffrage when not crossing the country campaigning for women's rights.

Anthony was born in Adams, Massachusetts, in 1820 and was reared in the Quaker tradition. She became a teacher, then returned to the family farm near Rochester, where she met many leading abolitionists, including Frederick Douglass, William Henry Channing, and William Lloyd Garrison. She became interested in the cause of temperance, and her meetings with Amelia Bloomer and Elizabeth Cady Stanton focused her efforts on woman suffrage.

When she was rebuffed in her attempt to speak at a temperance meeting in Albany in 1852, she organized the Woman's New York State Temperance Society, of which Stanton became president. As a result of the experience, she became more active in women's rights advocacy. In a short time Anthony had become one of the most zealous activists. In the years that followed, she became the chief state agent for the American Anti-Slavery Society; helped change New York's laws to give married women property rights; assisted in organizing the Women's Loyal National League in support of emancipation; campaigned unsuccessfully to change the Fourteenth Amendment to include women as well as "Negro" suffrage; became corresponding secretary of the newly formed American Equal Rights Association; founded and represented the Working Women's Association of New York; and became publisher of the new periodical *New Revolution*, resigning in 1870 and embarking on a lecture tour to pay off the publication's debts.

In 1869 Anthony organized a woman suffrage convention in Washington, D.C., and then formed the National Woman Suffrage Association with Stanton. Although some of the association members later left to join the more conservative American Woman Suffrage Association, she continued to be the principal leader of the original organization. The two associations merged in 1890, and she was chosen president of the combined organization in 1892.

Anthony became the center of a celebrated political court case when she sought to test the legality of the suffrage provision of the Fourteenth Amendment by voting in the 1872 presidential election in Rochester. She was arrested, convicted by the judge's directed verdict, and fined. The case was dropped, however, when she refused to pay the fine.

She traveled constantly, often with Stanton, in support of efforts by women's groups to pass suffrage in various states, and was instrumental in founding the International Council of Women in 1888. She also wrote the *History of Woman Suffrage* with Stanton and Matilda J. Gage (published in four volumes in 1881, 1882, and 1902). At the age of 80 in 1900, she retired as president of the merged National American Woman Suffrage Association. Once scorned, Susan B. Anthony was being hailed as a national heroine by the time she died in 1906. It was not until 1919, however, that woman suffrage was finally enacted by Congress.

Today, the Anthony red brick house, which she shared with her sister, Mary, is a national historic landmark filled with memorabilia, Victorian furniture, and artifacts related to the events of the woman suffrage movement, including photographs and writings of Anthony and other women associated with the movement.

Susan B. Anthony House, 17 Madison St., Rochester, NY 14608. **Phone:** 716/235-6124. **Fax:** 716/235-6212.

E-mail: information@susanbanthonyhouse.org. **Website:** www.susanbanthonyhouse.org. **Hours:** Memorial Day-Labor Day—11-5 Tues.-Sun.; closed Mon.; remainder of year—11-4 Wed.-Sun.; closed Mon.-Tues. and major holidays. **Admission:** adults, $6; seniors, $4.50; students over 12, $3; children under 13, $2.

The Leonard and Evelyn Lauder Gallery at the Whitney Museum of American Art in New York City features the works of Robert Henri, Gaston Lachaise, Maurice Prendergast, George Bellows, and Gertrude Vanderbilt Whitney, founder of the museum. Courtesy Whitney Museum of American Art and photographer Jerry L. Thompson.

WHITNEY MUSEUM OF AMERICAN ART (Gertrude Vanderbilt Whitney). The Whitney Museum of American Art was founded in New York City in 1930 by art patron and sculptor Gertrude Vanderbilt Whitney to present exhibitions by living American artists, whose work had been largely disregarded by traditional museums.

Whitney was a leading supporter of American art from the turn of the twentieth century, when it was almost impossible for artists with new ideas to exhibit or sell their work. She continued to assist such artists by purchasing and showing their work until her death in 1942.

The Whitney Museum, which had its beginnings as showings in Whitney's studio in Greenwich Village in 1914, opened in 1931 with her personal collection of 600 works as the basis for the founding collection. She continued adding to the collection until she died. The museum began accepting other gifts in 1948, including approximately 2,000 artworks by Edward Hopper that were bequeathed by his widow, Josephine, in 1970. The museum now has more than 11,000 paintings, sculptures, prints, drawings, and photographs by over 1,700 artists. It also has more than 30,000 volumes and extensive historical archives, primarily on American art.

As the premier institution devoted to the art of the United States, the Whitney Museum presents the full range of twentieth-century American art, with a special focus on the works of living artists. It has permanent collections and displays and interprets the works of such artists as Hopper, Thomas Hart Benton, George Bellows, Maurice Prendergast, Jasper Johns, Georgia O'Keeffe, Alexander Calder, and others. It also presents the popular Biennial Exhibition, an invitational show of work produced in America every two years. First introduced by Whitney in 1932, it is the only continuous series of exhibitions in the nation to survey recent developments in American art.

The Whitney Museum makes its home in a 1966 building designed by Marcel Breuer and Hamilton Smith and is in the process of developing a major expansion. It was also the first museum to take its exhibitions and programming beyond its walls by establishing corporate-funded branch facilities. The museum currently has branch galleries in the Philip Morris, Inc., building in New York City and the Champion International Corporation headquarters in Stamford, Connecticut (see separate listings).

Whitney Museum of American Art, 945 Madison Ave., New York, NY 10021. **Phone:** 212/570-3600. **Fax:** 212/570-1807. **E-mail:** feedback@whitney.org. **Website:** www.whitney.org. **Hours:** 11-6 Tues.-Sun. (also to 9 p.m. Fri.); closed Mon. and major holidays. **Admission:** adults, $12; seniors and students, $9.50; children under 12, free; pay what visitors wish at 6-9 p.m. Fri.

WHITNEY MUSEUM OF AMERICAN ART AT PHILIP MORRIS (Gertrude Vanderbilt Whitney). See Art Museums.

North Carolina

CHARLOTTE HAWKINS BROWN MEMORIAL STATE HISTORIC SITE. The former Alice Freeman Palmer Memorial Institute, a boarding school for African Americans founded by Charlotte Hawkins Brown in 1902, is now a state historic site in Sedalia, North Carolina. Twelve buildings still remain from the school, and the institution's history and Dr. Brown's contributions to African American education are described in exhibits and audiovisual presentations.

Charlotte Hawkins Brown Memorial State Historic Site, 6136 Burlington Rd., Drawer B, Sedalia, NC 27342. **Phone:** 336/449-4846. **Fax:** 336/449-0176. **Website:** www .ah.der.state.nc.us/hs/chb/chb.htm. **Hours:** Apr.-Oct.—9-5

Mon.-Sat., 1-5 Sun.; remainder of year—10-4 Tues.-Sat., 1-4 Sun.; closed Mon. and major holidays. **Admission:** free.

Ohio

ANNIE OAKLEY MEMORIAL PARK. See Historic Parks and Sites.

HARRIET BEECHER STOWE HOUSE. See Other Historic Houses.

LUCY HAYES HERITAGE CENTER. The Lucy Hayes Heritage Center in Chillicothe, Ohio, is located in the restored birthplace of Lucy Hayes, wife of Rutherford B. Hayes, the nineteenth president of the United States. The historic house contains furniture, letters, photographs, copies of speeches, and other personal belongings of the Hayes family.

Lucy Hayes Heritage Center, 90 W. 6th St., PO Box 1790, Chillicothe, OH 45601. **Phones:** 740/642-5333 and 740/775-1780. **Website:** www.ohiotourism.com. **Hours:** Apr.-Oct.— 1-4 Fri.-Sat. and by appointment; closed Good Friday, Memorial Day weekend, and remainder of year. **Admission:** adults and students over 12, $2; children under 13, free.

Pennsylvania

BETSY ROSS HOUSE. The Betsy Ross House in Philadelphia was the 1773–1786 home of the seamstress of the first American flag. She was renting a room and storefront space in the house when she was approached by George Washington, Robert Morris, and George Ross, members of the Continental Congress flag committee, in 1776 to make a flag for the new country about to declare its independence.

Legend has it that Elizabeth Griscom Ross, who took over her husband John's upholstering business after he died earlier in the year, suggested the five-pointed star instead of the six-pointed star favored by Washington. The proposed stars-and-stripes flag was adopted by the Continental Congress in 1777.

Also in 1777, Ross married Joseph Ashburn, who died in a British prison in 1782. She married for a third time in 1783, to John Claypoole. She continued running the upholstering business, which became quite successful, until 1827, when she turned it over to her daughter.

The historic house has been restored to show how a young, middle-class, widowed shopkeeper of the eighteenth century would have lived. It also tells the Betsy Ross story and features a number of her objects (such as her spectacles, chairs, walnut chest, and family Bible), craftsman's tools, and a restored eighteenth-century upholstery shop.

Betsy Ross House, 239 Arch St., Philadelphia, PA 19106. **Phone:** 215/686-1252. **Fax:** 215/686-1256. **E-mail:** eileenvig @aol.com. **Website:** www.ushistory.org/betsy. **Hours:** Memorial Day-Labor Day—10-5 daily; remainder of year— 10-5 Tues.-Sun.; closed Mon., New Year's Day, Thanksgiving, and Christmas. **Admission:** $2 suggested donation.

DOROTHEA DIX MUSEUM. The Dorothea Dix Museum at the Harrisburg State Hospital in Harrisburg, Pennsylvania, is named for the crusading educator, reformer, and philanthropist who was instrumental in founding the hospital in 1851 and gave the funds for a library/reading room for female patients, which also included a museum, in 1853. Dix helped found 32 mental hospitals in America and two in Japan during her 40-year career.

The library/reading room, which was restored in 1985, now contains exhibits with historic letters, records, furniture, clothing, medical equipment, art, photographs, and items made by inmates that show how the hospital has served more than 300,000 mentally ill patients in Pennsylvania since the mid-1800s. Today, the hospital has fifteen buildings on 125 acres and provides in-patient psychiatric services to over 300 persons.

Dorothea Dix Museum, Harrisburg State Hospital, Cameron and Maclay Sts., Harrisburg, PA 17105. **Phone:** 717/772-7561. **Fax:** 717/772-6015. **E-mail:** jleopold@state.pa.us. **Website:** www.paheritage.com/dadix.html. **Hours:** by appointment. **Admission:** free.

MARIAN ANDERSON BIRTHPLACE AND MARIAN ANDERSON RESIDENCE/MUSEUM. Marian Anderson, the great contralto, is honored at two historic houses— the Marian Anderson Birthplace and Marian Anderson Residence/Museum—in a historic district named for her in Philadelphia.

She was the first African American to become a permanent member of the Metropolitan Opera Company in 1955, and the first African American to perform in the White House. She also served as an alternate delegate to the United Nations in 1958.

Anderson was born in 1897 in the small house that now features a room with information and memorabilia from her childhood. She lived from 1924 to 1990 in the residence museum house, which contains photographs, memorabilia, music, newspaper clippings, and other materials about her life and career. The site was opened in 1998 by the Marian Anderson Historical Society.

Marian Anderson Birthplace, 1833 Marian Anderson Pl., and **Marian Anderson Residence/Museum,** Marian Anderson Way, Philadelphia, PA 19146-1822. **Phone:** 215/732-9505. **Fax:** 215/732-1247. Website: www.marian anderson.org. **Hours:** by appointment. **Admission:** adults, $10; seniors and children under 12, $5.

PEARL S. BUCK HISTORIC SITE.

The 1835 stone farmhouse where author Pearl S. Buck spent the last 40 years of her life is the centerpiece of the Pearl S. Buck Historic Site in Perkasie, Pennsylvania (see also Pearl S. Buck Birthplace Museum in Hillsboro, West Virginia).

The historic house is where Buck, the first American woman to win a Nobel Prize for literature in 1938, lived with her many adopted and foster children, and where the foundation she started in 1964 to help abandoned and neglected American children is still headquartered.

Buck lived and wrote many of her novels in the house from 1936 until she died in 1973. The daughter of Presbyterian missionary parents, she spent much of her childhood in China and returned to teach at Chinese universities in 1925–1930 after marrying and divorcing missionary John L. Buck.

She began writing magazine articles on Chinese life in 1922 and published her first novel, *East Wind, West Wind,* in 1930. The following year she authored *The Good Earth,* which in 1932 made her the first American woman to receive a Pulitzer Prize. In addition to Chinese themes, her subsequent books dealt with such subjects as childbirth and abortion, women's rights, and racism.

Her great interest in cultural understanding and children led her to found the East-West Association in 1941, Welcome House in 1949, and the Pearl S. Buck Foundation (now International) in 1964, and to adopt and serve as foster mother for a number of unwanted children.

Pearl S. Buck International, which seeks to improve the quality of life and opportunities for children, still has its offices at the site; provides tours of Buck's house, grave site, and 60-acre grounds; and operates a cultural center in a renovated 1827 barn. The Buck house contains a rich collection of Pennsylvania country furniture, Chinese decorative screens and other objects, Oriental rugs, Pennsylvania pottery and artworks, and the handcrafted Chinese desk (with her handwritten documents and drafts) at which Buck wrote *The Good Earth.*

Pearl S. Buck Historic Site, 520 Dublin Rd., PO Box 181, Perkasie, PA 18944-3000. **Phones:** 215/249-0100 and 800/220-2825. **Fax:** 215/249-9657. **E-mail:** info@pearl-s-buck.org. **Website:** www.pearl-s-buck.org. **Hours:** Mar.-Dec.—11-2 Tues.-Sat., 1-2 Sun.; closed Mon., Jan.-Feb., and major holidays. **Admission:** adults, $6; seniors and students, $5; children under 6, free; families, $15.

RACHEL CARSON HOMESTEAD.

The Rachel Carson Homestead in Springdale, Pennsylvania, is the birthplace and childhood home of ecologist Rachel Carson, author of the groundbreaking 1962 book, *Silent Spring,* which demonstrated that the indiscriminate use of chemical pesticides and herbicides posed great danger to upsetting the natural ecological balance of the world.

While working as an aquatic biologist and later publications editor for the U.S. Bureau of Fisheries (which became the U.S. Fish and Wildlife Service) in 1936–1952, she wrote her first book, *Under the Sea Wind,* in 1941, and then *The Sea Around Us* in 1951. Both were highly praised for their scientific accuracy and lyrical prose. The latter became a best-seller and won a National Book Award. They were followed by two other best-sellers—*The Edge of the Sea* in 1955 and *Silent Spring* in 1962. *Silent Spring* became controversial, raising public fears and resulting in government inquiries into the ecological problem. She received numerous awards for her scientific investigative work.

The 1870 Carson home, which contains many of the Carson family's personal and period materials, traces Rachel's childhood and professional career.

Rachel Carson Homestead, 613 Marion Ave., Springdale, PA 15144-1242. **Phone:** 724/274-5459. **Fax:** 724/275-1259. **Website:** www.rachelcarson.org. **Hours:** by appointment; closed Christmas. **Admission:** adults, $4; seniors, $3; children, $2.50.

TODD HOUSE (Dolley Payne Todd Madison).

The 1791–1793 Todd House, now part of the Independence National Historical Park in Philadelphia, was the home of Dolley Payne Todd before she became the wife of James Madison, the fourth president of the United States. The restored middle-class home is furnished as it was when the Todd family lived in it. It can now be toured by obtaining tickets at the park's visitor center.

Todd House, 4th and Walnut Sts., Philadelphia, PA (contact: Independence National Historical Park, 313 Walnut St., Philadelphia, PA 19106). **Phone:** 215/597-9373. **Fax:** 215/597-5556. **E-mail:** inde_curatorial@nps.gov. **Website:**

www.nps.gov/inde. **Hours:** 10-3 daily; closed Christmas. **Admission:** adults and children over 16, $2; children under 17, free.

South Dakota

SURVEYORS' HOUSE AND INGALLS HOME AND MU-SEUM (Laura Ingalls Wilder). Two childhood homes of *Little House on the Prairie* author Laura Ingalls Wilder and her family are historic house museums in De Smet, South Dakota. They are the Surveyors' House, originally a surveyors' shanty, and the Ingalls Home and Museum, built in 1887 by Laura's father, Charles Ingalls.

The Ingalls family homesteaded near De Smet in 1880 and then moved into town. Seven sites in De Smet are mentioned in Laura's novels for children based on her life on the frontier, including *Little Town on the Prairie* (which was a reference to De Smet).

The Surveyors' House has been refurbished according to the author's descriptions in her book *By the Shores of Silver Lake*. It now contains the largest collection of artifacts and memorabilia of the Ingalls family. The 1887 Ingalls house, which was occupied by the family until 1928, features many of the family furnishings and items crafted by Charles Ingalls. Tours of the two houses are offered during the summer by the Laura Ingalls Wilder Memorial Society, with a Laura Ingalls Pageant being presented on three of the weekends. (See also Laura Ingalls Wilder Home and Museum near Mansfield, Missouri; Laura Ingalls Wilder Museum in Walnut Grove, Minnesota; Laura Ingalls Wilder Park and Museum in Burr Oak, Iowa; and Laura Ingalls Wilder Wayside near Pepin, Wisconsin).

Surveyors' House, 101 Olivet Ave., and **Ingalls Home and Museum,** 210 3rd St. S.W., De Smet, SD 57231 (postal address: Laura Ingalls Wilder Memorial Society, PO Box 426, De Smet, SD 57231-0426). **Phones:** 605/854-3383 and 800/880-3383. **Fax:** 605/854-3064. **E-mail:** liwms@iw.net. **Website:** www.liwms.com. **Hours:** June-Aug.—9 a.m.-7 p.m. daily; Sept.—9-4 Mon.-Sat., 12-4 Sun.; Apr.-May and Oct.—9-4 Mon.-Sat.; closed Sun.; remainder of year—9-4 Mon.-Fri.; closed Sat.-Sun. **Admission:** adults and children over 12, $5; children 5-12, $2; children under 5, free.

Tennessee

CHATTANOOGA AFRICAN MUSEUM/BESSIE SMITH HALL. Bessie Smith, who was born in Chattanooga, Tennessee, in the 1890s, was one of the nation's great blues singers. Her memory is celebrated today at the Chattanooga African Museum/Bessie Smith Hall, which is devoted to African American history and features exhibits on local artists.

Chattanooga African Museum/Bessie Smith Hall, 200 E. Martin Luther King Blvd., PO Box 11493, Chattanooga, TN 37401. **Phone:** 423/267-1628. **Fax:** 423/267-1076. **E-mail:** chamie@bellsouth.net. **Website:** www.caamhistory.com. **Hours:** 10-5 Mon.-Fri., 12-4 Sat.; closed Sun. and major holidays. **Admission:** adults, $5; seniors and students, $3; children 6-12, $2; children under 6, free.

COAL MINER'S DAUGHTER MUSEUM (Loretta Lynn). The Coal Miner's Daughter Museum in Hurricane Mills, Tennessee, is devoted to the life and career of country-western singer Loretta Lynn. It is located on her ranch, which can also be toured. The museum contains country-western memorabilia, costumes, and other materials relating to the singer, who still lives on the ranch. Tours are offered of Lynn's former plantation home, a replica of the Butcher Holler house in which she was born, a simulated coal mine, and the museum. Concerts also are presented during the summer.

Coal Miner's Daughter Museum, 1877 Hurricane Mills Rd., Hurricane Mills, TN 37078. **Phone:** 931/296-1840. **Fax:** 931/296-1839. **Website:** www.lorettalynn.com. **Hours:** Apr.-Oct.—9-5 daily; remainder of year—9-5 Sat.-Sun. **Admission:** museum—adults, $10; children 6-12, $5; children under 6, free; ranch tour—adults and children over 5, $12.50 plus tax; children under 6, free.

DOLLY PARTON'S "RAGS TO RICHES" MUSEUM. The life story of entertainer Dolly Parton is told at the Dolly Parton's "Rags to Riches" Museum at the Dollywood Entertainment Park in Pigeon Forge, Tennessee. Approximately 2.3 million people visit the theme park each year—with many coming to the museum to see the costumes, awards, and other personal items of the singer featured in movies and on television. The museum is included in the park admission.

Dolly Parton's "Rags to Riches" Museum, Dollywood Entertainment Park, 1020 Dollywood Lane, Pigeon Forge, TN 37863-4101. **Website:** www.dollywood.com. **Hours:** vary considerably with seasons, usually 9-6 or 9-8 when open; closed Dec. 31-Mar. 31 and some Tues. and Thurs. in off-season. Admission (included in Dollywood admission): adults, $32 plus tax; seniors, $27 plus tax; children 4-11, $23 plus tax; children under 4, free.

MARY WALKER MEMORIAL MUSEUM. The Mary Walker Memorial Museum in Chattanooga, Tennessee, memorializes Mary Walker, a former slave who became known as the nation's "oldest student." She was 117 years old when she learned reading, writing, and arithmetic in the Chattanooga-area literacy movement in 1964. She died at the age of 121. The museum is located in a replica plantation house that also has a re-created slave quarters. The museum tells Mary Walker's story and has exhibits on the contributions of African Americans during and after the Civil War and on the literacy and civil rights movements.

Mary Walker Memorial Museum, 3031 Wilcox Blvd., Chattanooga, TN 37411. **Phone:** 423/629-7651. **Fax:** 423/267-2414. **Hours:** by appointment. **Admission:** donation.

Texas

BABE DIDRIKSON ZAHARIAS MUSEUM. The Babe Didrikson Zaharias Museum in Beaumont, Texas, is dedicated to one of the nation's greatest female athletes, Mildred "Babe" Didrikson Zaharias.

Zaharias was an all-American basketball star and a 1932 Olympic gold medalist in track and field who excelled in every sport she tried, including organized baseball, tennis, diving, boxing, skating, and especially golf, winning 82 major tournaments. She was named "Woman Athlete of the Year" six times by the Associated Press—a feat never equaled by men or women.

The memorial is set in a landscaped garden in the shape of the five symbolic rings of the Olympics. It contains many of her medals, trophies, equipment, photographs, and personal items.

Babe Didrikson Zaharias Museum, 10 W. MLK Blvd., PO Box 3827, Beaumont, TX 77704. **Phones:** 409/880-3749 and 409/833-4622. **Fax:** 409/880-3750. **E-mail:** bmtcub@sat.net. **Website:** www.beaumontcub.com. **Hours:** 9-5 daily; closed Christmas. **Admission:** free.

LADY BIRD JOHNSON WILDFLOWER CENTER. See Botanical Gardens and Arboretums.

MARION KOOGLER McNAY ART MUSEUM. The Spanish-Mediterranean home, priceless collection of paintings and sculpture, and bulk of the estate of artist Marion Koogler McNay went to form a San Antonio, Texas, art museum named for her after her death in 1950. In addition to her watercolors, the museum has collections of modern art; sculpture; graphic arts; nineteenth- and twentieth-century European and American paintings; Gothic and medieval art; arts and

crafts of New Mexico; and a theater arts collection relating to opera, ballet, and the musical stage.

Marion Koogler McNay Art Museum, 6000 N. New Braunfels Ave., PO Box 6069, San Antonio, TX 78209-0069. **Phone:** 210/824-5368. **Fax:** 210/824-0218. **E-mail:** sbailey @mcnayart.org. **Website:** www.mcnayart.org. **Hours:** 10-5 Tues.-Sat., 12-5 Sun.; closed Mon. and major holidays. **Admission:** free.

The Menil Collection in Houston is one of the nation's leading private art museums. It was founded in 1980 by Dominique de Menil and features approximately 15,000 paintings, sculptures, prints, drawings, photographs, and rare books. Courtesy Menil Collection and architects Hickey-Robertson, Houston.

THE MENIL COLLECTION (Dominique de Menil). The Menil Collection, one of the nation's most important private art museums, was founded in Houston in 1980 and opened in 1987 by Dominique de Menil, a Texas philanthropist and art collector. The founding collection of artworks was assembled by Mrs. de Menil and her husband, John de Menil, an oil-field equipment executive who died in 1973.

The Menil Collection contains approximately 15,000 paintings, sculptures, prints, drawings, photographs, and rare books. Among its holdings are masterpieces from antiquity, the Byzantine and medieval worlds, the twentieth century, and tribal cultures of Africa, Oceania, and the American Pacific Northwest. It is also known for its surrealist works, which are considered among the foremost collections of their kind.

The museum has two specialized galleries in separate buildings—the Cy Twombey Gallery, containing more than 30 paintings, sculpture, and works on paper by the contemporary artist, and Richmond Hall, which houses the penultimate work of minimalist sculptor Dan Flavin. Also within walking distance are two related independent institutions—the Rothko Chapel, a nondenominational space with fourteen huge abstract paintings by Mark Rothko funded by the de Menils, and the Byzantine Fresco Chapel Museum, with two thirteenth-century Byzantine frescoes ransomed from art thieves by the Menil Foundation.

The Menil Collection, 1515 Sul Ross St., Houston, TX 77006 (postal address: 1511 Branard St., Houston, TX 77006). **Phone:** 713/525-9400. **Fax:** 713/525-9444. **E-mail:** menil@neosoft.com. **Website:** www.menil.org. **Hours:** 11-7 Wed.-Sun.; closed Mon.-Tues. and major holidays. **Admission:** free.

Virginia

ANNE SPENCER MEMORIAL. Anne Spencer, an acclaimed African American poet of the Harlem Renaissance period of the 1920s, lived in this house in Lynchburg, Virginia, for 72 years. The gardens behind the house were built by her husband, Edward Spencer, as inspiration for her poetry. The house contains Victorian furnishings, examples of Spencer's writings, photographs, and other family materials.

Anne Spencer Memorial, 1313 Pierce St., Lynchburg, VA 24501. **Phone:** 804/845-1313. **Hours:** by appointment. **Admission:** adults, $5; seniors, $4; students, $3; children, $2.

MAGGIE L. WALKER NATIONAL HISTORIC SITE. In 1901, businesswoman and community leader Maggie Lena Walker, the daughter of a kitchen slave, said that the African American community in Richmond, Virginia, needed a savings bank founded and operated by themselves to achieve economic empowerment. Two years later she established the St. Luke Penny Savings Bank—the first chartered bank in the United States founded and headed by a woman. Today, the bank thrives as the Consolidated Bank and Trust Company, the oldest continually operated African American bank in the nation.

Walker served as president and then chairperson of the bank until her death in 1934, despite being a paraplegic confined to a wheelchair during the last twenty years of her life. The 28-room, red brick house where she and her family lived from 1904 to 1934 is now the Maggie L. Walker National Historic Site. The house—which Walker expanded several times to accommodate the families of her sons—is furnished with its original pieces and contains many of her personal belongings. A nearby visitor center at 600 N. 2nd Street features a short video and exhibits on Walker's life, the

bank, the fraternal Order of St. Luke where she worked previously, and the Jackson Ward historic neighborhood, which was one of the nation's most prosperous African American communities in the late nineteenth and early twentieth centuries.

Maggie L. Walker National Historic Site, $110\frac{1}{2}$ E. Leigh St., Richmond, VA (postal address: 3215 E. Broad St., Richmond, VA 23223). **Phone:** 804/771-2017. **Fax:** 804/771-8522. **E-mail:** mawa@nps.gov. **Website:** www.nps.gov/malw/. **Hours:** 9-5 Mon.-Sat.; closed Sun., New Year's Day, Thanksgiving, and Christmas. **Admission:** free.

MARY BALL WASHINGTON MUSEUM. See History Museums.

MARY WASHINGTON HOUSE. The Mary Washington House in Fredericksburg, Virginia, was the 1772–1789 home of Mary Ball Washington, mother of George Washington, who bought the house and insisted that she move into town from her nearby farm. She lived in the 1750 Colonial house until her death a few months before her son was inaugurated as president of the United States.

The house contains period furnishings and a few items that belonged to Mrs. Washington, and it interprets her life and times. The Mary Washington Monument is located nearby, and the Mary Ball Washington Museum, a local history museum, can be seen in Lancaster (see separate listings).

Mary Washington House, Assn. for the Preservation of Virginia Antiquities, 1200 Charles St., Fredericksburg, VA 22401. **Phone and Fax:** 540/373-1569. **Website:** www.apva.org. **Hours:** Mar.-Nov.—9-5 Mon.-Sat., 11-5 Sun.; remainder of year—10-4 Mon.-Sat., 12-4 Sun.; closed New Year's Eve and Day, Thanksgiving, and Christmas Eve and Day. **Admission:** adults, $4; children 6-18, $1.50; children under 6, free.

MOUNT VERNON ESTATE AND GARDENS (Martha Washington). See Museums Founded and/or Operated by Women's Organizations.

Washington

SACAJAWEA STATE PARK. See Historic Parks and Sites.

WHITMAN MISSION NATIONAL HISTORIC SITE (Narcissa Prentiss Whitman). See Historic Parks and Sites.

West Virginia

PEARL S. BUCK BIRTHPLACE MUSEUM. The Pearl S. Buck Birthplace Museum near Hillsboro, West Virginia, is located in the 1875 European-style house where the prizewinning author was born in 1892 as Pearl Comfort Sydenstricker. The site was the childhood home of her mother, Caroline Stulting Sydenstricker, whose father built the house on a 16-acre farm after emigrating from Holland in 1847. The house contains some of the family's original furniture and memorabilia and books of Buck, the only American woman to receive both the Nobel Prize and the Pulitzer Prize for literature (see also Pearl S. Buck Historic Site in Perkasie, Pennsylvania).

Pearl S. Buck Birthplace Museum, U.S. Hwy. 219 (1/2 mile N. of Hillsboro), PO Box 126, Hillsboro, WV 24946. **Phone:** 304/653-4430. **Website:** www.wvnet.edu:80/~omb00996/. **Hours:** May-Oct.—9-4:30 Mon.-Sat.; closed Sun., major holidays, and remainder of year. **Admission:** adults, $6; seniors, $5; students, $1; children under 6, free.

Wisconsin

DR. KATE MUSEUM (Dr. Kate Pelham Newcomb). The Dr. Kate Museum in Woodruff, Wisconsin, is devoted to country doctor Kate Pelham Newcomb, who delivered over 3,000 babies, sparked the building of the local hospital, and was known as "the angel on snowshoes" for her dedication in reaching patients when winter roads were impassable.

"Dr. Kate," as Dr. Newcomb was called, spearheaded an unusual "penny" campaign to build a hospital in the small Northwoods community. She and schoolchildren collected a million pennies—many from throughout the nation and the world—in a drive that captured the imagination of the public. The museum tells the story of Dr. Newcomb and the penny campaign.

Dr. Kate Museum, 923 2nd Ave., PO Box 851, Woodruff, WI 54568. **Phone:** 715/356-6896. **Fax:** 715/358-5038. **Hours:** mid-June-Labor Day—11-4 Mon.-Fri.; closed Sat.-Sun. and remainder of year. **Admission:** free.

LAURA INGALLS WILDER WAYSIDE. See Other Historic Houses.

Wyoming

WHITNEY GALLERY OF WESTERN ART (Gertrude Vanderbilt Whitney). See Art Museums.

MEMORIALS TO WOMEN

District of Columbia

SUFFRAGE MONUMENT. The nation's first statue devoted to women's service to women is the Suffrage Monument—formally the Portrait Monument to Lucretia Mott, Elizabeth Cady Stanton, and Susan B. Anthony—in the U.S. Capitol in Washington, D.C. It was dedicated in 1921 on suffrage leader Anthony's birthday—a year after the suffrage amendment was passed to give women the right to vote. Sculptor Adelaide Johnson's eight-ton marble block with portrait heads of suffrage pioneers Anthony, Stanton, and Mott was located in a remote area of the Capitol until 1997, when it was moved to the Capitol Rotunda near the Statuary Hall (see Other Halls of Fame).

Suffrage Monument, U.S. Capitol, Washington, DC 20515. **Phone:** 202/228-1222. **Fax:** 202/228-4602. **Website:** www.aoc.gov. **Hours:** 9-4:30 daily; closed New Year's Day, Thanksgiving, and Christmas. **Admission:** free.

VIETNAM WOMEN'S MEMORIAL. The Vietnam Women's Memorial, located near the Vietnam Veterans Memorial on the Mall in Washington, D.C.—is a tribute to the 11,000 women who were stationed in Vietnam and the more than 265,000 women who served during the war years. The project, started by former army nurse Diane Carlson Evans and featuring a sculpture by Glenna Goodacre, shows four figures on a base of sculpted sandbags—a nurse cradling a wounded serviceman, an African American woman looking skyward, and a kneeling figure holding an empty helmet.

Vietnam Women's Memorial, The Mall, Washington, DC (contact: National Park Service, 900 Ohio Dr. S.W., Washington, DC 20242). **Phone:** 202/426-6841. **Fax:** 202/724-0764. **Website:** www.nps.gov/vive. **Hours:** open 24 hours. **Admission:** free.

Hawaii

QUEEN LILI'UOKALANI STATUE. The Queen Lili'uokalani Statue at the entrance to the state capitol in Honolulu is an eight-foot likeness of Hawaii's last queen. The statue, by sculptor Marianne Pineda, has the regal queen extending her right hand in friendship and holding two items in her left hand—the 1893 constitution, which ultimately cost her the throne, and a page from the traditional Hawaiian farewell song, *Aloha Oe*, which she wrote.

Queen Lili'uokalani Statue, State Capitol Grounds, Honolulu, HI (contact: Hawaii Visitors and Convention Bureau, 2270 Kalakaua Ave., Suite 700, Honolulu, HI 96815). **Phone:** 808/923-1811. **Website:** www.gohawaii.com. **Hours:** open 24 hours. **Admission:** free.

Illinois

MONUMENT TO WOMEN STATUE GARDEN. The Monument to Women Statue Garden, located outside the LDS Visitors' Center in historic Nauvoo, Illinois, features thirteen statues that celebrate the various stages and roles of womanhood. The Mormon center contains exhibits, artifacts, documents, an audiovisual presentation, and a 15-foot scale model of Nauvoo in 1846.

Nauvoo, which was settled in 1839 by Mormon prophet Joseph Smith and his followers, became the religious, governmental, and cultural center of the Church of Jesus Christ of Latter-day Saints. But when Smith was murdered by a mob and the Mormons faced increasing hostility, Brigham Young led the Mormons to Utah in 1846. Many buildings of the period have been restored in the historic community.

Monument to Women Statue Garden, LDS Visitors' Center, Young and Main Sts., PO Box 215, Nauvoo, IL 62354. **Phones:** 217/453-2233 and 800/453-0022. **Fax:** 217/453-6348. **E-mail:** nripa@nauvoo.net. **Hours:** open 24 hours. **Admission:** free.

Kansas

STATUES OF AMELIA EARHART. Two life-size statues of aviation pioneer Amelia Earhart are located in Atchison, Kansas, where she was born in 1897. The original is in a downtown pedestrian mall, and a duplicate is at the International Forest of Friendship at Warnoc Lake. She is depicted with her leather flight jacket, scarf, slacks, and wind-tousled hair.

In 1928 Earhart was the first woman to cross the Atlantic Ocean in an airplane, and in 1932, the first to cross the Atlantic solo. She was also the first person to fly solo from Hawaii to the mainland and to make the flight from Mexico City to New York in 1935. She

was lost at sea in 1937 while attempting an around-the-world flight.

The International Forest of Friendship is a memorial park dedicated in 1976 by the Ninety-Nines, Inc., a women pilots' organization, to those women who have contributed to aviation. In addition to the Earhart statue, it contains trees from every state and approximately 40 countries and honors more than 650 women. The Ninety-Nines also stage an annual fly-in at the Amelia Earhart Memorial Airport in Atchison on her birthday in July. Earhart's birthplace in Atchison has become a historic house museum (see Museums Honoring Exceptional Women).

Earhart memorials are also located in North Hollywood, California, where she lived at the height of her fame, and Meeteetse, Wyoming, where she was building a summer home when she disappeared over the Pacific Ocean.

Statues of Amelia Earhart, Atchison Mall between 6th and 7th St. and Warnoc Lake, Atchison, KS (contact: Atchison Convention and Visitors Bureau, 200 S. 10th St., PO Box 126, Atchison, KS 66002). **Phones:** 913/367-2427 and 800/234-1854. **Fax:** 913/367-2485. **Website:** www.atchison.org. **Hours:** open 24 hours. **Admission:** free.

Massachusetts

HOMAGE TO WOMEN SCULPTURE. The larger-than-life Homage to Women Sculpture in downtown Lowell, Massachusetts, is a tribute to the "mill girls" who worked in Lowell's nineteenth-century textile mills. The 1984 bronze and granite sculpture of five intertwined figures also celebrates the contributions made by women throughout time.

Homage to Women Sculpture, Market Mills Park, Market and Palmer Sts., Lowell, MA (contact: Lowell National Historical Park Visitor Center, 246 Market St., Lowell, MA 01852). **Phone:** 978/970-5000. **Fax:** 978/275-1762. **Website:** www.nps.gov/lowe. **Hours:** open 24 hours. **Admission:** free.

SALEM WITCH TRIALS MEMORIAL AND WITCHCRAFT VICTIMS' MEMORIAL. The victims of witchcraft trials in the Salem, Massachusetts, area in the late seventeenth century are memorialized at two sites in the area.

The fourteen women and five men hanged and tortured to death as "witches" in Salem in 1692 are remembered with stone slabs along a weathered granite wall at the Salem Witch Trials Memorial in a small park next to the Charter Street Cemetery in Salem. In neighboring Danvers (formerly Salem Village), a large granite sculpture—representing a Colonial pulpit on a broken chain of shackles—and an eight-foot-high triptych with the names of the 25 persons condemned as witches (including five who died in jail) can be seen at the Witchcraft Victims' Memorial. Salem also has a historic house and three museums dealing with witches and witchcraft—the Witch House, Salem Witch Museum, Witch Dungeon Museum, and Witch History Museum (see separate listings).

Salem Witch Trials Memorial, Charter and Liberty Sts., Salem, MA (contact: National Park Service Regional Visitor Center, 2 New Liberty St., Salem, MA 01970). Phone: 978/740-1650. Fax: 978/740-1655. Website: www.nps.gov/sama. Hours: open 24 hours. Admission: free.

Witchcraft Victims' Memorial, 176 Hobart St., Danvers, MA (contact: Danvers Archival Center, 15 Sylvan St., Danvers, MA 09123). Phones: 978/774-0554 and 978/777-0001 (Town Hall). Fax: 978/762-0251. Website: www.etext.virginia.edu/salem/witchcraft/archives (shared with University of Virginia). Hours: open 24 hours. Admission: free.

New York

ELEANOR ROOSEVELT STATUE. An eight-foot bronze statue of Eleanor Roosevelt is located in Riverside Park in New York City. Unveiled in 1994, it is the first public statue of a first lady in the nation. The wife of President Franklin D. Roosevelt was known for her independence and social and political activism. She wrote a nationwide newspaper column, walked picket lines, lobbied for civil rights legislation, held nearly 400 press conferences, and served as the first female U.S. representative to the United Nations. In the latter role, she chaired the UN's Commission on Human Rights and spearheaded the General Assembly's adoption of the groundbreaking Universal Declaration of Human Rights and the Human Rights Covenant.

Eleanor Roosevelt Statue, Riverside Park, Riverside Dr. at 72nd St., New York City, NY 10023. Phone: 212/496-2006. Fax: 212/496-2103. Website: www.parks@nyc.com. Hours: open 24 hours. Admission: free.

STATUE OF LIBERTY AND ANNIE MOORE STATUE. Two statues featuring women—the Statue of Liberty and the Annie Moore Statue—are located in the harbor of New York City.

The Statue of Liberty, an 1886 gift from France, is probably the most famous statue of a woman in the world, welcoming immigrants and visitors to America. The figure was allegedly modeled by its creator (Bartholdi) after his mother.

The Annie Moore Statue on nearby Ellis Island depicts a 15-year-old Irish girl, who was the first immigrant to pass through the processing station when it opened in 1892. The bronze statue was installed on the second floor of the Ellis Island museum in 1993—several months after a statue of Annie and her two younger brothers was dedicated at the starting point of their voyage in Ireland.

Statue of Liberty and Annie Moore Statue, Liberty Island and Ellis Island, New York Harbor, New York, NY (contact: National Park Service, Liberty Island, New York City, NY 10004). Phone: 212/363-3200. Fax: 212/363-8347. Website: www.nps.gov/stli. Hours: 9-5 daily; closed Christmas. Admission: free.

North Dakota

STATUE OF SAKAKAWEA. The statue of Sakakawea on the state capitol grounds in Bismarck, North Dakota, honors the "Bird Woman" of the Shoshone tribe who was a guide and interpreter for the Lewis and Clark Expedition in 1804–1806. Sakakawea (usually spelled Sacajawea) was the wife of French-Canadian trader Jean Baptiste Charbonneau and joined the expedition with her husband near Stanton, North Dakota. She is memorialized with statues at a number of other sites, including Fort Benton, Montana; Portland, Oregon; Mobridge, South Dakota; Charlottesville, Virginia; and Fort Washakie, Wyoming.

Statue of Sakakawea, State Capitol Grounds, Bismarck, ND (contact: Bismarck-Mandan Convention and Visitors Bureau, 107 W. Main Ave., PO Box 2274, Bismarck, ND 58501). Phones: 701/222-4308 and 800/767-3555. Website: www.bismarck-mandancvb.org. Hours: open 24 hours. Admission: free.

Ohio

ANNIE OAKLEY STATUE. See Annie Oakley Memorial Park in Historic Parks and Sites.

MADONNA OF THE TRAIL MONUMENT. The first of a dozen Madonna of the Trail monuments—honoring pioneer women who crossed the frontier to the American West in the mid-nineteenth century—was erected in Springfield, Ohio, in 1928. Within a year, similar sculptures were installed in Wheeling, West Virginia; Council Grove, Kansas; Lexington, Missouri;

Lamar, Colorado; Albuquerque, New Mexico; Springerville, Arizona; Vandalia, Illinois; Richmond, Indiana; Washington, Pennsylvania; Upland, California; and Bethesda, Maryland.

The statue, showing a pioneer woman clutching a child to her breast while another clings to her skirts, was conceived by the Daughters of the American Revolution and designed by sculptor August Leimbach to symbolize the courage of women in making the difficult and often dangerous transcontinental trip. Springfield became known as the "town at the end of the National Pike" after a national road connected it to eastern industrial cities in 1838.

Madonna of the Trail Monument, U.S. Hwy. 40, Springfield, OH (contact: Springfield Area Convention and Visitors Bureau, 333 N. Limestone St., Suite 201, Springfield, OH 45503). **Phone:** 937/325-7621. **Fax:** 937/325-8765. **Website:** springfieldnet.com. **Hours:** open 24 hours. **Admission:** free.

Oklahoma

The statue of Pioneer Woman welcomes visitors to the Pioneer Woman Museum in Ponca City, Oklahoma. The museum interprets the history of women in Oklahoma and their influence on the development of the state and the nation. Courtesy Pioneer Woman Museum of the Oklahoma Historical Society.

PIONEER WOMAN STATUE. The Pioneer Woman Statue—a 17-foot bronze statue of a sunbonneted pioneer mother leading her young son by the hand—stands at the entrance to the Pioneer Woman Museum in Ponca City, Oklahoma. The monument and the museum are located on a quarter section of land homesteaded in 1893 that was part of the last free land in the United States.

The statue, dedicated to the nation's pioneer women, carries the following inscription: "In appreciation of the heroic character of the women who braved the dangers and endured the hardships incident to the daily life of the pioneer and homesteader in this country."

The monument was conceived and financed by Ernest Marland, an oilman, philanthropist, congressman, and the tenth governor of Oklahoma, and created by sculptor Bryant Baker. Approximately 40,000 people attended the unveiling in 1930. The museum, which is devoted to Oklahoma's pioneering women and pioneers in aviation, civil rights, public services, and the arts, opened in 1958 (see Women's Museums, Galleries, and Halls of Fame).

Pioneer Woman Statue, Pioneer Woman Museum, 701 Monument Rd., Ponca City, OK 74604-3910. **Phone:** 580/765-6108. **Fax:** 580/762-2498. **E-mail:** piowen@ok-history.mus.ok.us. **Website:** www.ok-history.mus.ok.us. **Hours:** 9-5 Tues.-Sat., 1-5 Sun.; closed Mon. and state holidays. **Admission:** adults, $3; seniors, $2.50; children 6-18, $1; children under 6, free.

Texas

WASP MEMORIAL. The WASP Memorial at Texas State Technical College in Sweetwater, Texas, is a tribute to the Women's Airforce Service pilots who trained at what was the only all-woman military flying school, operated at the site in 1943–1944 under the leadership of noted pilot Jacqueline Cochran. The monument is a life-size statue of a woman in a flight suit, sculpted by Dorothy Swain Lewis, and has an adjacent walk of honor. The school trained 1,076 women who later served as test pilots, ferried bombers across the ocean, and flew target missions to train gunners.

WASP Memorial, Texas State Technical College, 300 College Dr., Sweetwater, TX 79556. **Phone:** 915/235-7300. **Fax:** 915/225-7416. **Website:** www.tstc.org. **Hours:** open 24 hours. **Admission:** free.

Virginia

JANE DELANO MEMORIAL. The Jane Delano Memorial at Arlington National Cemetery in Arlington, Virginia, is a stylized marble statue honoring the famed organizer of the Red Cross nursing corps. It oversees that section of the cemetery occupied by nurses who served the country in World War I. An idealistic Jane Delano Monument is also located in the garden behind the American Red Cross buildings in Washington, D.C.

Delano was chairperson of the National Committee on Red Cross Nursing Services in 1909–1919; superintendent of the Army Nurse Corps in 1909–1912; director of the American Red Cross Department of Nursing in 1918–1919; and directed the mobilization of approximately 20,000 nurses for overseas service in World War I.

Jane Delano Memorial, Arlington National Cemetery, Section 21, Memorial Dr. and McPherson Ave., Arlington, VA 22211-5003. **Phone:** 703/697-2131. **Fax:** 703/614-6339. **Website:** www.arlingtoncemetery.org. **Hours:** Apr.-Sept.—8-7 daily; remainder of year—8-5 daily. **Admission:** free.

MARY WASHINGTON MONUMENT. The Mary Washington Monument in Fredericksburg, Virginia, is a 40-foot granite shaft that stands on the site where George Washington's mother meditated and prayed and is now buried. Andrew Jackson laid the cornerstone for a marble monument in 1833, but the monument was never finished and was later badly damaged by shellfire in 1862, during the Civil War. As a result, it was replaced by the present granite monument, which was dedicated in 1894 by President Grover Cleveland.

Mary Washington Monument, Washington Ave. at Pitt St., Fredericksburg, VA (contact: Fredericksburg Visitor Center, 706 Caroline St., Fredericksburg, VA 22401). **Phones:** 540/373-1776 and 800/678-4748. **Fax:** 540/372-6587. **Website:** www.fredericksburgva.com. **Hours:** open 24 hours. **Admission:** free.

POCAHONTAS STATUE. A statue of Pocahontas, the daughter of Chief Powhatan who befriended the English colonists and saved Captain John Smith from execution in the early 1600s, is near the Old Church Tower at the Jamestown National Historic Site in Jamestown, Virginia. As a child Pocahontas brought food to the ill-prepared colonists after they arrived in 1607, and she later intervened on their behalf during tensions between Native Americans and settlers. She became a friend of Smith, who taught her English and gave her small presents. When he was about to be killed by Chief Powhatan, she stepped forward to save his life. Her father was so impressed by the gesture that he spared Smith and later adopted him into the tribe with Pocahontas as his life guardian.

Pocahontas married settler John Rolfe in 1614 and died three years later in England, where she is buried. The statue in Jamestown was erected in her honor in 1922. A memorial plaque inside the St. George's Church in Gravesend, England, reads: "Gentle and humane, she was the friend of the earliest struggling English colonists whom she nobly rescued, protected and helped."

Pocahontas Statue, Jamestown National Historic Site, Old Church Tower, Jamestown, VA 23081 (contact: National Park Service or Assn. for the Preservation of Virginia Antiquities, 204 W. Franklin St., Richmond, VA 23220). **Phones:** NPS—757/229-1733; APVA—804/648-1889. **Faxes:** NPS—757/229-4273; APVA—804/775-0802. **Websites:** NPS—www.mps.gov/colo; APVA—804/775-0802. **Hours:** mid-June-mid-Aug.—8:30-5:30 daily; remainder of year—9-5 daily; closed Christmas. **Admission:** adults, $5; children under 17, free.

WOMEN IN MILITARY SERVICE FOR AMERICA MEMORIAL. The Women in Military Service for America Memorial—better known as simply the Women's Memorial—honors more than 1.8 million women who have served or are serving in the armed forces, beginning with the American Revolution.

The memorial, located at the ceremonial entrance to Arlington National Cemetery in Arlington, Virginia, consists of an arc of glass panels with quotations from and about servicewomen, a reflecting pool, a Court of Valor, and an Education Center, with a Hall of Honor, exhibit gallery, theater, and computer register, where visitors can access information and photographs about women who have served in the military.

Women in Military Service for America Memorial, Arlington National Cemetery, Arlington, VA (contact: Women in Military Service for America Memorial Foundation, 5510 Columbia Pike, Suite 302, Arlington, VA 22204). **Phones:** 703/533-1155 and 800/222-2294. **Fax:** 703/931-4208. **E-mail:** wimsa@aol.com. **Website:** www.womensmemorial.org. **Hours:** 8-5 daily; closed Christmas. **Admission:** free.

OTHER MEMORIALS

Alabama

EMMA SANSOM MONUMENT. The Emma Sansom Monument in Gadsden, Alabama, is a memorial to a fifteen-year-old girl who guided Confederate General Nathan Bedford Forrest in his pursuit and capture of nearly 2,000 Union troops in 1863. It is a marble statue showing Sansom pointing the way to a shortcut across Black Creek, which enabled Forrest to make the capture.

JULIA TUTWILER MEMORIAL. A large plaque in the Alabama Department of Archives and History Building in Montgomery honors Julia Tutwiler, a teacher, poet, prison reformer, and crusader for industrial and university education for women.

MARY A. CAHALAN MONUMENT. The Mary A. Cahalan Monument, a life-size marble statue in Woodrow Wilson Park in Birmingham, Alabama, is dedicated to an admired teacher and principal at Powell Public School from 1883 until her death in 1906.

MURPHREE SISTERS MEMORIAL. A historical maker on Highway 26 east of Blountsville, Alabama, commemorates the heroics of Celia Murphree and her sister, Winnie Mae Murphree, during the Civil War in 1863 when they duped and captured three Union soldiers who raided the house where they were babysitting.

Alaska

STATUE OF MOLLIE WALSH. The Statue of Mollie Walsh in City Park in Skagway, Alaska, honors a popular young woman who operated a grub tent for hungry mining prospectors in the 1897–1898 gold rush and was shot to death by her husband in 1902. The statue was erected later by another miner, who had loved her but lost out after they quarreled.

California

AMELIA EARHART STATUE. A seven-foot gold-leaf statue of daring aviator Amelia Earhart is located at Magnolia Boulevard and Tujunga Avenue in North Hollywood, where she lived at the height of her fame.

Two statues of the record-setting pilot can also be seen in her hometown of Atchison, Kansas (also see Memorials to Women).

COIT MEMORIAL TOWER. The Coit Memorial Tower on Telegraph Hill and the Volunteer Firemen's Monument in Washington Square in San Francisco were funded in the will of Lillie Hitchcock Coit, who was the mascot of Knickerbocker Company No. 5 as a teenager and inherited a fortune from her husband, B. Howard Coit.

DONNER LAKE MEMORIAL. A heroic-size statue of a pioneer man and woman with a child at their feet stands along Interstate 80 in Truckee, California, honoring the 90 members of the ill-fated Donner party trapped by snow in the nearby mountains as they headed for California in 1847. More than half the men died, while 25 of the 35 women survived the suffering, cannibalism, and death.

ELIZABETH ANN SETON STATUES. At least twelve statues of Elizabeth Ann Seton, the first American-born saint and founder of the Sisters of Charity order, are located at hospitals, convents, and schools across the nation, including the University of San Diego in California. She was canonized as a saint in 1975.

FLORENCE NIGHTINGALE STATUES. Florence Nightingale, the English founder of modern nursing, is honored with statues in San Francisco and Los Angeles. They were installed in the late 1930s as part of the Federal Arts Project in conjunction with local hospital and nurses' associations.

LOTTA'S FOUNTAIN. Lotta Crabtree was a lovable young dancer whose performances in San Francisco sometimes brought out the army to quell her enthusiastic fans. In 1875 a fountain with cast-iron columns and jutting drinking spigots was dedicated in her honor at Geary and Kearny streets.

REBECCA H. LAMBERT MEMORIAL. The founder of the Ladies Seamen's Friend Society is honored with a 25-foot bronze monument near the fifteenth hole of the Lincoln Park Municipal Golf Park in San Francisco.

WOMEN OF THE MORMON BATTALION MEMORIAL. This large granite marker in Presidio Park in San Diego honors the 38 women who accompanied their husbands and families in the Mormon Battalion from Council Bluffs, Iowa, to Santa Fe, New Mexico, during the Mexican-American War. Four of the women then continued on to San Diego in 1847.

Colorado

STATUE OF DR. FLORENCE SABIN. This replica of the bronze statue in National Statuary Hall in the Capitol in Washington, D.C., honors Dr. Florence Sabin, a pioneering physician and researcher. It is located in the Colorado Department of Health building in Denver. After a distinguished medical career in the East, she returned to Colorado to work for public health legislation. Many of her bills were passed as "Sabin's health laws."

THE LADY DOCTOR. This statue at a light-rail station in Denver honors Dr. Justina Ford, Colorado's first African American female licensed physician, who served the city from 1902 to 1952. The memorial shows her cradling an infant. It was dedicated in 1998 as part of the "Art at the Stations" project.

Connecticut

ALICE COGSWELL STATUE. Alice Cogswell was the first student at the nation's first school for the deaf, founded in Hartford, Connecticut, in 1821 and located in Washington, D.C., since 1921. This statue in Hartford shows her being sheltered in the huge hands of her teacher, Thomas Hopkins Gallaudet, for whom the school is now named. A statue of Cogswell with Gallaudet is also in Washington (see Statue of Alice Cogswell).

District of Columbia

JANE DELANO MONUMENT. The founder of the American Red Cross Nursing Service is honored with an idealistic statue representing all nurses in the garden behind the Red Cross buildings in Washington, D.C. A Jane Delano Memorial also overlooks the nurses' section of Arlington National Cemetery in Arlington, Virginia (see Memorials to Women).

MARIAN ADAMS MONUMENT. A hooded bronze figure seated against the wall of an outdoor sanctuary was commissioned by Henry Adams for his wife, Marian Adams, a pioneering photographer and hostess of cultural salons in Boston and Washington, D.C., who committed suicide at the age of 42 in 1885. The memorial, commonly known as *Grief*, is located at Rock Creek Church Road and Webster Street in Washington.

MARY McLEOD BETHUNE MEMORIAL. The Mary McLeod Bethune Memorial honors a distinguished African American educator in Lincoln Park at 13th and East Capitol streets in Washington, D.C. Located across the park from a statue of Abraham Lincoln with a freed slave, the 17-foot statue shows Bethune with an outstretched hand passing her legacy to two young children.

NUNS OF THE BATTLEFIELD MONUMENT. A bronze relief panel set in stone at Rhode Island Avenue and M Street in Washington, D.C., is a tribute to nurses who served on battlefields and in hospitals during the Civil War. Featuring twelve nurses from as many orders, it was erected in 1924 by the Ladies Auxiliary of the Ancient Order of Hibernians, an Irish group that wanted to identify with peace and patriotism and further the image of religious women in public space and history.

STATUE OF ALICE COGSWELL. This statue shows Alice Cogswell, the first student enrolled at the first school for the deaf in the United States, with her teacher, Thomas Hopkins Gallaudet, for whom the school is named. It is located at Gallaudet University in Washington, D.C. A statue of Cogswell sheltered in the giant hands of Gallaudet is also in Hartford, Connecticut, where the school began (see Alice Cogswell Statue).

STATUE OF JOAN OF ARC. The women of France presented this bronze statue of Joan of Arc, the heroine of Orléans, to the women of America in 1922. The statue, a replica of the original at Rheims Cathedral in France, is in Meridian Hill Park at 16th Street and Florida Avenue in Washington, D.C. A statue of Joan of Arc riding a horse is also in New York City (see Joan of Arc Statue).

Georgia

ALICE McLELLAN BIRNEY MEMORIAL. This monument, which features a sundial and stones from every state, honors Alice McLellan Birney, one of the founders of the National Congress of Parents and

Teachers (PTA). It is located on the high school grounds in Marietta, Georgia, her hometown.

CLARA BARTON MEMORIAL. This memorial at the Andersonville National Cemetery near Americus, Georgia, honors Clara Barton, who became known as the "Angel of the Battlefield" and later founded the American Red Cross. In addition to being a nurse in army camps and on battlefields, she helped to identify the missing and dead during the Civil War and marked nearly 13,000 graves with identifying headboards at the Andersonville prison burial ground. She also participated in the Franco-Prussian War and the Spanish-American War. The memorial, located at the former Andersonville prison site, was the first in a national cemetery to honor a civilian not interred there. A Clara Barton Memorial is also located at the Antietam National Battlefield in Maryland.

MONUMENT TO WOMEN OF THE CONFEDERACY. The Monument to Women of the Confederacy at Poplar Street Park in Macon, Georgia, honors the women of the South during the Civil War. It consists of a tall obelisk flanked by two sculptures depicting a woman giving water to a soldier and a woman at a sewing machine protecting a child.

THE WAVING GIRL STATUE. For 44 years, Florence Martus lived on Elba Island near Savannah, Georgia, with her brother, who was the lighthouse keeper. During that time (1887–1931), she waved a handkerchief by day and a lantern at night at all ships arriving or departing Savannah. In return, the ships looked for and saluted the woman. She also once helped with the rescue of 30 men from a burning dredge in a predawn fire. In tribute to her, the Georgia Historical Commission erected the Waving Girl Statue at Savannah Beach Park on Tybee Island.

Illinois

ANNIE LOUISE KELLER MONUMENT. On April 19, 1927, a powerful tornado swept through the Carrollton, Illinois, area. Annie Louise Keller was a 25-year-old teacher at the nearby Centerville country school. When she saw the tornado coming through the schoolhouse window, she had all the children duck under their desks. The tornado struck the schoolhouse, tearing off a large part of the building and killing the teacher, but all the children survived. A marble sculpture honoring Keller in Whiteside Park in White Hall, Illinois, depicts a woman protecting a schoolchild.

MARY ANN BICKERDYKE STATUE. "Mother" Mary Ann Bickerdyke was one of the best-known relief workers in the Union Army during the Civil War. She spent four years at battlefields and camps helping soldiers—cooking, washing clothes, delivering supplies, and even dressing wounds. The Mary Ann Bickerdyke Statue in Courthouse Square in Galesburg, Illinois, shows her giving a wounded soldier a drink of water.

Iowa

SUFFRAGE MEMORIAL. A bas-relief sculpture of goddesslike figures in draped garments in the Iowa State Capitol in Des Moines honors the "Pioneer Suffragists and the long procession of workers who helped to secure the final enfranchisement of women."

Kansas

GRACE BEDELL BILLINGS MONUMENT. A marble monument in the Town Square of Delphos, Kansas, pays tribute to eleven-year-old Grace Bedell, who wrote to candidate Abraham Lincoln, saying his chin was too scrawny and that he would look better with a beard. Lincoln wrote back saying he was concerned that "people would call it a piece of silly affectation if I were to begin it now," but shortly thereafter he let the familiar whiskers grow. The monument features bronze reproductions of the letters.

SARAH AND JOHN M. DAVIS MEMORIAL. A marble and granite monument in Mount Hope Cemetery in Hiawatha, Kansas, was erected by retired farmer John Davis in memory of his wonderful marriage with Sarah Davis. It contains eleven life-size figures depicting various stages of their 50 years together. The scenes begin with the young couple sitting on a love seat and end with John as an old man in an armchair beside an empty chair.

Louisiana

EVANGELINE STATUE. The Evangeline Statue in St. Martinsville, Louisiana, is in the town where Emmeline Labiche is buried. Her life may have been the basis for Longfellow's poem that told of the Acadians being driven from Nova Scotia to Louisiana by the British in 1755. The statue was donated in 1931 by movie star Delores Del Rio, who was featured in the 1929 film *Evangeline.*

GORDON SISTERS MEMORIAL. Jean and Kate Gordon spearheaded an 1899 New Orleans campaign for a water and sewerage system that paved the way for full suffrage for women in Louisiana. Kate was president of the newly formed Woman's League for Sewerage and Drainage, and—assisted by her sister and prominent local suffrage leaders—took advantage of the only voting right that New Orleans women had then (taxpaying women could vote on tax matters). Jean, who was also instrumental in a drive to pass child labor laws and in assisting mentally disturbed children, became the city's first factory inspector in 1906. Kate helped with her sister's reform work and took an active role in establishing a tuberculosis hospital in 1926. A 1919 plaque honoring the work of the sisters and the Era Club (for Equal Rights Association) is in the New Orleans Sewerage and Water Board offices in City Hall. A stained-glass window in the First Unitarian Church also pays tribute to the philanthropic work of Jean and Kate Gordon.

MARGARET HAUGHERY STATUE. The Margaret Haughery Statue in Margaret Place in New Orleans is a tribute to an Irish immigrant who ran a successful baking business and devoted much of her wealth to founding institutions for orphans and poor women. It was dedicated in 1884.

MOLLY MARINE STATUE. The Molly Marine Statue at Canal Street and Elks Place Park in New Orleans was originally a 1940 cement statue of a uniformed woman with a pedestal saying "Free a Marine to Fight." In 1966 some marines who recognized the value of women in the military converted the statue to bronze, with a marble pedestal stating "In honor of women Marines who served their country in keeping with the highest tradition of the United States Marine Corps." Another monument, a block away on Elks Place, features a globe and a dove of peace and honors women who served in all the armed forces.

Maine

SAMANTHA REED SMITH STATUE. During the Cold War in 1982, ten-year-old Samantha Reed Smith of Hallowell, Maine, wrote a letter to Soviet Premier Yuri Andropov, saying "I have been worrying about the Soviet Union and the United States getting into a nuclear war. Are you going to vote to have a war or not? If you aren't please tell me how you are going to help not have a war." Much to everyone's surprise, the letter got to Andropov, and Samantha was invited to visit the Soviet Union the following summer. Samantha became a goodwill ambassador and toured the country for two weeks and focused world attention on the issue. But two years later she was killed in a plane crash near the Augusta-Lewiston airport. A statue honoring Samantha was placed on the state capitol grounds in Augusta, and her mother founded the Samantha Smith Center in Hallowell to foster youth exchanges at a nearby summer camp.

Maryland

CLARA BARTON MEMORIAL. The Clara Barton Memorial at the Antietam National Battlefield in Maryland honors the courageous Civil War nurse and founder of the American Red Cross. A rough-hewn marble slab with a small red cross made of bricks from her birthplace in North Oxford, Massachusetts, is located at the 1862 battlefield, where 23,000 men were killed or wounded and where Barton assisted the wounded and dying. A memorial at the Andersonville National Cemetery in Georgia also pays tribute to Barton, who was known as the "Angel of the Battlefield."

LIZETTE WOODWORTH REESE MEMORIAL. A pink marble monument at Lake Clifton Eastern High School in Baltimore honors poet Lizette Woodworth Reese. The memorial, showing a benevolent shepherd with a cluster of sheep, is inscribed with words from one of Reese's poems, *With a Book of Hymns*, which inspired the sculpture.

Massachusetts

ANNE HUTCHINSON MEMORIAL. A statue of Anne Hutchinson, a religious leader who was expelled from the Massachusetts Bay Colony as a heretic in 1637 for speaking out, was the first outdoor statue of a woman in Boston. It was donated to the State House in 1922 by the Massachusetts State Federation of Women's Clubs and the Anne Hutchinson Memorial Committee. Hutchinson is depicted as a woman looking skyward, holding a Bible and with her daughter at her side.

ANNE SULLIVAN AND HELEN KELLER STATUE. A bronze sculpture of Anne Sullivan teaching the blind, deaf, and mute Helen Keller is located on the Revolutionary War parade grounds in Agawam, Massachusetts. Sullivan, who was born in Agawam, was nearly blinded by a childhood disease. However, an operation restored her sight and she began teaching six-year-old Helen Keller, who later achieved fame as an author and lecturer.

DEBORAH SAMPSON GANNETT MONUMENT. One wing of the memorial to the war dead in Rockridge Cemetery in Sharon, Massachusetts, is dedicated to Deborah Sampson Gannett, a young woman who dressed and represented herself as a man when she enlisted in the Continental Army during the Revolutionary War under the name of Robert Shurtleff. She fought and was wounded in several battles, and her sex was not discovered until a physician treated her for fever. She was honorably discharged in 1783 and was given a $4 monthly pension by Congress in 1805.

ELLEN SWALLOW RICHARDS MEMORIAL. A bronze plaque on the first floor of the Massachusetts Institute of Technology's chemistry building in Cambridge honors scientist Ellen Henrietta Swallow Richards, MIT's first female graduate, who became a leader in the field of public health and a pioneer in home economics.

KATHARINE LEE BATES STATUE. A statue on the grounds of the public library in Falmouth, Massachusetts, depicts Katharine Lee Bates on Pikes Peak, where she was inspired to write *America the Beautiful*. Born in Falmouth in 1859, she became a professor of English at Wellesley College and was vacationing in Colorado when she wrote the poem that was later converted into a patriotic musical score.

MARGARET FULLER MEMORIAL. The Margaret Fuller Memorial in Cambridge, Massachusetts, honors the noted literature and art critic and social reformer who was lost—with her husband and two-year-old child— in an 1850 shipwreck in a storm off Fire Island, New York. The memorial is a bas-relief of Fuller's head with a bronze plaque describing her life.

MILL GIRL MONUMENT. Louisa M. Wells was one of the original workers of the Lawrence Manufacturing Company in Lowell, Massachusetts. When she died in 1886, her will called for a monument to be erected to her career as a textile mill worker. The result was a large marble monolith with carved figures in Lowell Cemetery that became known as the Mill Girl Monument.

STATUES OF ANNE HUTCHINSON and MARY DYER. Anne Hutchinson and Mary Dyer were considered heretics and were excommunicated and banished for challenging the religious hierarchy of the Massachusetts Bay Colony in 1638. They moved to Roger Williams's colony in Rhode Island, and Hutchinson then settled in the Bronx in New York City, while Dyer converted to the new Quaker faith, her beliefs leading to further harassment, arrest, and being hanged. The two exponents of civil liberty and religious freedom are now remembered with statues on the Massachusetts State House grounds in Boston.

STEP ON BOARD STATUE. The *Step on Board* statue in Harriet Tubman Square in Boston shows abolitionist Tubman leading a group of men and women to freedom as part of the Underground Railroad. The square also contains another statue, *Emancipation*, which was created in 1913 and was restored to be placed in the park with the Tubman statue. The two monuments were installed in 1999.

THE PILGRIM MOTHER AND THE PILGRIM MAIDEN STATUE. As part of a 1921 tercentenary observance, the Daughters of the American Revolution erected a statue, titled *The Pilgrim Mother*, in Plymouth, Massachusetts, to honor the women who came over on the *Mayflower*. A similar statue, called *The Pilgrim Maiden*, was placed in Plymouth by the National Society of New England Women.

Michigan

ANNA HOWARD SHAW MONUMENT. This monument in Frayer Halladay Park in Ashton, Michigan, marks the remote frontier farm where Anna Howard Shaw began her career as a Methodist minister, physician, and suffragist. In 1887 she turned to the professional lecture circuit, with temperance and woman suffrage as her principal themes, and quickly became the most eloquent and moving orator in the suffrage cause. She served as president of the American Woman Suffrage Association in 1904–1915 and as chairperson of the

Woman's Committee of the U.S. Council of National Defense during World War I.

JEANNETTE PICCARD MONUMENT. The Jeannette Piccard Monument on the William B. Stout Junior High School grounds in Dearborn, Michigan, honors the first woman to pilot a balloon into the stratosphere. Dr. Piccard made the ascent in 1934 in a 175-foot-high hydrogen-filled balloon from the old Ford Airport nearby, soaring to an altitude of 57,559 feet before landing in Cadiz, Ohio.

LAURA HAVILAND STATUE. A statue of Laura Smith Haviland, the Quaker abolitionist, educator, and social reformer, is located in front of City Hall in Adrian, Michigan. In 1837 she and her husband founded the Raisin Institute, a school for African Americans and whites and a center for fugitive slaves. She became known as the "Superintendent of the Underground" for her work in helping slaves escape from the South. After her husband died in 1845, she continued to run the school and assist fugitive slaves until the Civil War, when she helped tend the wounded. The memorial was erected in 1909 by the local chapter of the Women's Christian Temperance Union.

ROSE HARTWICK THORPE MONUMENT. Sixteen-year-old Rose Hartwick Thorpe, who wrote the poem *Curfew Must Not Ring Tonight* in 1867, is honored with an eight-foot fieldstone/cement monument with a bell along State Highway 99 in Litchfield, Michigan. She wrote the poem after reading the historical account of an English schoolgirl who tried to stop the ringing of a curfew bell—with bleeding hands—that would result in the execution of her lover at sundown during the days of Oliver Cromwell. The poem, which Thorpe traded for a Detroit newspaper subscription, has been adapted in numerous dramas since then.

SOJOURNER TRUTH STATUE. A 12-foot statue honors Sojourner Truth, an 1800s fighter for African American freedom and women's rights, in Battle Creek, Michigan, where she lived for the last 25 years of her life. The monument to the former slave who became an evangelist, reformer, and crusader was erected in 1999.

Minnesota

MARY RICHARDS STATUE. Mary Richards, a symbol of women's liberation on the *Mary Tyler Moore Show* on television in the 1970s, was immortalized in 2002 with the unveiling of an eight-foot bronze statue at a downtown corner in Minneapolis where Richards (Moore) tossed her tam into the air in a sign of exuberance during one of the programs in the series. The sitcom about a Minneapolis TV news station won 30 Emmy awards during its seven-year run. The statue was installed by a cable station dedicated to classic television programs as part of a TV landmarks project.

STATUE OF EDITH GRAHAM MAYO. A statue of Edith Graham Mayo, a nurse and wife of the Mayo Clinic co-founded by Horace Mayo, can be seen at St. Mary's Hospital in Rochester, Minnesota. Mrs. Mayo instructed the Catholic Sisters of St. Francis, a teaching order, in nursing. The hospital, now part of the Mayo Foundation, was founded by the order in 1889 and was where the Mayo brothers first applied many of their medical and surgical techniques. It also has memorials to Sister Alfred, who urged the formation of the hospital, and Sister Mary Joseph, administrator of St. Mary's for nearly a half century.

STATUE OF WE-NO-NAH. The city of Winona, Minnesota, is named for We-no-nah, a Sioux maiden who allegedly leaped into nearby Lake Pepin rather than marry a warrior of her father's choice. A statue of We-no-nah was originally located downtown but was moved to Windom Park as part of an urban renewal program.

Mississippi

MONUMENT TO WOMEN OF THE CONFEDERACY. A heroic Monument to Women of the Confederacy by sculptor Belle Kinney is located on the new capitol grounds in Jackson, Mississippi. It is virtually a duplicate of Kinney's sculpture of Fame, Victory, and a dying soldier at the War Memorial Building in Nashville, Tennessee.

PHILLIS WHEATLEY MEMORIAL. A bronze statue of Phillis Wheatley, who authored the first book by an African American in 1773, is located in the H. T. Sampson Library at Jackson State University in Jackson, Mississippi. Born in Africa, she was kidnapped as a young girl, brought to Boston on a slave ship in 1761, and purchased by a tailor, John Wheatley, as a personal servant to his wife. She was treated as a member of the family, taught English by Mrs. Wheatley and her daughters, and learned Greek and Latin. From the age of thirteen, she began to write poetry and books, including the initial *Poems on Various Subjects, Religious and Moral*. Her work was cited frequently by abolitionists to combat the charge of innate intellectual inferiority among African Americans and to further educational opportunities for them.

Missouri

STATUE OF BEATRICE CENCI. Because of her sex, sculptor Harriet Hosmer was not permitted to study anatomy in the eastern United States in the first half of the nineteenth century. However, her benefactor, Wayman Crow, obtained her admission to anatomical classes at Missouri Medical College and helped support her studies in Italy. In 1856 this statue of a robed woman by Hosmer was presented to the St. Louis Mercantile Library as a gift of Crow.

Montana

LEWIS AND CLARK STATE MEMORIAL. The official state of Montana memorial to the 1804–1806 Lewis and Clark Expedition is in Fort Benton. The bronze sculpture shows Meriwether Lewis and William Clark with Sacajawea and her child, Jean Baptiste, on her back.

OUR LADY OF THE ROCKIES STATUE. A 90-foot statue titled *Our Lady of the Rockies*, on a mountain overlooking Butte, Montana, honors mothers. It was erected in 1985.

New Hampshire

HANNAH DUSTON MONUMENT. On the night of March 30, 1697, Hannah Duston, her nurse, and a fourteen-year-old boy massacred ten sleeping Native Americans who had captured her and brutally killed her six-day-old baby in Haverhill, Massachusetts. A controversial statue of Duston with a tomahawk and a handful of scalps now stands on a small island at the confluence of the Merrimack and Contoocook rivers in Boscawen, New Hampshire. Erected in 1874, it is said to be the first permanent monument to a woman in America. A similar memorial was dedicated in the Grand Army of the Republic Park in Haverhill, Massachusetts, in 1879.

LA DAME DE NOTRE RENAISSANCE FRANÇAISE. The Franco-American community in Nashua, New Hampshire, erected the first monument honoring that ethnic group in New England. Titled *La Dame de Notre Renaissance Française*, the statue shows a nineteenth-century working woman with a boy holding a book.

MEMORIAL BELL TOWER. All American women who have died in war service are honored at this huge stone tower at the Cathedral of the Pines in Rindge, New Hampshire. The tower has murals on its sides depicting the service of women, including those in the armed services, a pioneer woman with a rifle guarding her home, nurse Clara Barton helping a wounded soldier, Sisters of Charity in the War of 1812, Salvation Army women, riveters, entertainers, and war correspondents.

New York

ANGEL OF THE WATERS STATUE. A sculpture of four female figures—Purity, Health, Peace, and Temperance—shows them frolicking in the waters of the Bethesda Fountain in Central Park in New York City. The statue by Emma Stebbins was made in Paris and installed in the park in 1873.

ELIZABETH BLACKWELL STATUE. A statue of Dr. Elizabeth Blackwell, one of the first women to receive a medical degree in the United States, is located on the campus quadrangle of Hobart and William Smith College in Geneva, New York.

ELLA FITZGERALD STATUE. A statue of jazz singer Ella Fitzgerald was dedicated in 1996 in Yonkers, New York, as part of the city's "Art on Main Street" project.

GERTRUDE STEIN STATUE. A 33-inch bronze sculpture of author Gertrude Stein is in Bryant Park behind the New York Public Library in Manhattan. The sculpture, which shows Stein sitting in a buddhalike position, was created by Jo Davidson in 1923 but not cast until 1991. It was installed in 1992.

JOAN OF ARC STATUE. Joan of Arc, the French saint and national heroine known as the "Maid of Orléans," is shown riding a horse in Riverside Park in New York City. Dedicated to goodwill between the French and American people in 1915, it was sculpted in bronze by Anna Vaughn Hyatt (who also went under her married name of Anna Hyatt Huntington). A replica of the statue is in Blois, France, where Joan was imprisoned. A statue of Joan of Arc is also in Washington, D.C.

STATUE OF EMMA WILLARD. When Emma Willard could not obtain public funds for a proposed school in Middlebury, Vermont, she raised $4,000 from the residents of Troy, New York, to establish the Troy Female Seminary, the first endowed institution for the education of women, in 1821. The seminary, now called the Emma Willard School, offered a bold new curriculum and became the forerunner of many future boarding and normal schools. In 1895 a committee of Willard's pupils and friends erected a statue of her, sitting with a book in her right hand, on Second Street in Troy. Also see Vermont for a memorial in her honor.

STATUE OF MARY JEMISON. Mary Jemison was captured by Native Americans as a child, married a Delaware chief and then a Seneca warrior, and later chose to maintain her Native American ways rather than return to white culture. At the age of 80 in 1824, she wrote a popular account of her life, *The Life of Mary Jemison.* A bronze statue of the "White Woman of the Genesee," as Jemison was sometimes called, was erected in 1910 in Letchworth State Park on State Highway 19A near Castile, New York, to mark where she is buried.

STATUE OF SYBIL LUDINGTON. Sixteen-year-old Sybil Ludington was called the "Female Paul Revere" because of her gallant nighttime ride to warn of approaching British troops in 1777. Alerted that the British were raiding nearby Danbury, Connecticut, she rode cross-country from her hometown—now renamed Ludington, New York—to call out volunteer militiamen commanded by her father. Covering twice the distance traveled by Revere, she roused enough volunteers to drive off the British. A bronze statue of a young woman on horseback now commemorates the ride along Highway 52 in Carmel, New York.

WHEN ANTHONY MET STANTON STATUE. In addition to the nineteen life-size bronze statues of the key figures of the first women's rights movement convention in 1848 at the Women's Rights National Historical Park (see Women's Museums, Galleries, and Halls of Fame), another women's rights statue is located in Seneca Falls, New York. Titled *When Anthony Met Stanton,* the sculpture that overlooks the river shows activist Amelia Bloomer introducing Susan B. Anthony and Elizabeth Cady Stanton, who became long-term partners in the women's suffrage struggle.

North Carolina

HEROIC WOMEN OF THE LOWER CAPE FEAR MONUMENT. This statue of a young woman wearing a toga and a laurel wreath and looking at the grave of Polly Slocumb and her husband, Ezekiel Slocumb, is located on the highest hill of the Moores Creek National Battlefield in Currie, North Carolina. The monument is dedicated to women who have demonstrated their devotion and self-sacrifice to their country. Legend has it that Polly Slocumb had a dream on the eve of the historic Battle of Moores Creek Bridge in 1776 in which she saw her husband among the dead and wounded at the battlefield. She leaped out of bed, saddled her horse, and galloped 60 miles from her home to Goldsboro to the battlefield and found her wounded husband.

MEMORIAL TO TABITHA A. HOLTON. A marker on the courthouse grounds in Dobson, North Carolina, is a memorial to Tabitha A. Holton, the first woman licensed to practice law in the state in 1878.

STATUE OF VIRGINIA DARE. A marble statue of Virginia Dare, the first English child to be born in America in 1587, is located in the Elizabethan Garden at the Fort Raleigh National Historic Site along U.S. Highway 64 near Manteo, North Carolina. The colony disappeared three years after being founded, but Virginia has lived on in poems, novels, and plays dealing with her life. The controversial statue of a half-nude maiden clad in a fishnet was sculpted by Maria Louisa Lander in Italy and willed to the state of North Carolina. It was first put on display in 1926.

Ohio

MEMORIAL TO SHARON LANE. A seven-foot bronze statue at Aultman Hospital in Canton, Ohio, honors Sharon Lane, the only U.S. Army nurse killed by enemy fire during the Vietnam War. It also honors more than 100 people from Stark County who died in the war.

Oklahoma

MILLY FRANCIS MEMORIAL. Milly Francis, a Creek woman known as "Oklahoma's Pocahontas," saved the life of a Georgia militiaman from a band of Seminoles in 1817 when the fifteen-year-old and her family were living in Spanish Florida. The militiaman, Captain Duncan McKrimmon, later offered to marry Francis, but she said she did not save his life to wed him. A granite marker in front of the Atloa Lodge Museum at Bacone College in Muskogee, Oklahoma, pays tribute to her.

Oregon

STATUE OF SACAJAWEA. A statue of Sacajawea, the Shoshone guide and interpreter of the Lewis and Clark Expedition of 1804–1806, is in Washington Park in Portland, Oregon. It was dedicated in 1905 when many suffrage leaders, including speakers Susan B. Anthony and Abigail Scott Duniway, were attending a national suffrage convention in Portland.

Pennsylvania

BAS-RELIEF OF FIGURES AROUND A WOMAN PHYSICIAN. A large bas-relief of a group of women around a woman physician hangs in the main entrance of the Medical College of Pennsylvania, which began as the nation's first medical school for women (Female Medical College of Pennsylvania and then Woman's Medical College) in 1850 in Philadelphia. The sculpture by Clara Hill was presented by Dr. Rosalie Slaughter Morton to her alma mater. It reads "Daughter of Science, Pioneer. Thy Tenderness Hath Banished Fear . . . "

KATE SMITH STATUE. A statue outside the Spectrum sports arena in Philadelphia honors Kate Smith, the popular 1930s–1950s singer who frequently sang *God Bless America* (in person or on tape) before hockey games.

STONE AGE IN AMERICA STATUE. An 1888 statue titled *Stone Age in America*, in Philadelphia's Fairmont Park, depicts a Native American woman holding a hatchet while her two children cling to her and a dead bear lies at her feet. It represents a romantic view of fierce protective motherhood.

THE MOTHER'S MEMORIAL. This seven-foot statue in Ashland, Pennsylvania, is based on the famous painting *Whistler's Mother*. The tribute to mothers was erected in 1938 by the local boys' association.

Rhode Island

ELIZABETH ALDEN PABODIE MEMORIAL. A granite monument on the Common in Little Compton, Rhode Island, commemorates the first white girl born in New England in 1623. Elizabeth, who lived to be 94, was the daughter of John and Priscilla Alden, the famous lovers in Pilgrim history. The monument was erected by Sarah Soule Wilbour, known for paying taxes under protest because women did not have the right to vote.

WINNIE DAVIS MEMORIAL. A stained-glass window at the St. Peter's-by-the-Sea Church in Narragansett, Rhode Island, honors Varina "Winnie" Davis, the daughter of Confederacy President Jefferson Davis and Varina Howell Davis, who died of malaria while vacationing at the seashore resort in 1898. It was looked upon as a shrine by many southerners.

South Carolina

EMILY GEIGER MEMORIAL. A memorial tablet in Geiger Cemetery in Lexington, South Carolina, honors Emily Geiger, a farm girl who volunteered to take a message over 100 miles from General Nathanael Greene to General Thomas Sumter through Tory enemy lines in 1781 during the Revolutionary War. The message enabled Greene and Sumter to join forces and eventually drive the British out of the Carolinas. The actual site of Geiger's grave is not known.

MONUMENT TO THE WOMEN OF THE CONFEDERACY. A monument at the South Carolina State House in Columbia honors the women of South Carolina during the Civil War.

South Dakota

ALICE GOSSAGE MEMORIAL. Alice Gossage, a newspaperwoman who was called the "South Dakota Sunshine Lady," is honored with a sundial in her memory in Sioux Park in Rapid City. When her husband, who owned the *Rapid City Journal*, became ill in 1890, she took over the management of the paper and became known for her editorials calling for suffrage, temperance, and community service.

ANNIE TALLENT MONUMENT. Forty-six-year-old Annie Tallent, the first white woman to enter and settle in the Black Hills, is memorialized with a towering granite spire at the Gordon Stockade in Custer, South Dakota. With dreams of gold, she made the trek from the

Missouri River with her husband, young son, and 25 other men and settled on the banks of the French Creek in 1874.

CITADEL STATUE. This statue at the north entrance to the South Dakota State Capitol in Pierre honors the pioneering women of South Dakota. It was erected in 1991 by Ed Duling in memory of his wife, Darleen Duling.

MEMORIAL AND STATUE OF ELIZABETH HAZELTON SHERRARD. Elizabeth Hazelton Sherrard, founder of the South Dakota Children's Home Society, is honored at two sites—a bronze bas-relief of Sherrard with two babies and a little blind boy in the state capitol in Pierre and a statue of Sherrard surrounded by children at the Black Hills Children's Home in Rapid City. She nurtured more than 1,400 orphaned babies, many of them physically and/or mentally handicapped.

MONUMENT TO SAKAKAWEA. A cement shaft at the Dakota Memorial Park in Mobridge, South Dakota, marks the burial home of Sacajawea (spelled Sakakawea here), the Shoshone guide and interpreter of the Lewis and Clark Expedition, who is believed to have died at Fort Manuel in 1812. The chief clerk at the fort recorded her death at the time, but the Wind River Reservation at Fort Washakie, Wyoming, claims that Sacajawea did not die until 1884 and is buried there. The Mobridge monument was made possible by funds donated by schoolchildren.

Tennessee

MONUMENT TO WOMEN OF THE CONFEDERACY. The Monument to Women of the Confederacy at the War Memorial Building in Nashville, Tennessee, was the work of local sculptor Belle Kinney, who also designed a nearly identical memorial in Jackson, Mississippi. It is a heroic sculpture of Fame, Victory, and a dying soldier.

Texas

ANN WHITNEY MEMORIAL. This memorial on the courthouse grounds in Hamilton, Texas, honors Ann Whitney, who sacrificed her life to save her students during a Comanche raid in 1867. During the attack, the 230-pound teacher pushed the children through a small back window of the log schoolhouse to safety while she remained behind.

PIONEER WOMAN MONUMENT. A 13-foot marble monument on the Texas Woman's University campus in Denton is dedicated to the courageous pioneer women.

TEXAS WALK STATUES. Three Texas women—Congresswoman Barbara Jordan, writer Katharine Anne Porter, and athlete Mildred "Babe" Didrikson Zaharias—are among the fifteen historical figures honored with life-size bronze statues in the "Texas Walk" outdoor sculpture garden at the Sea World theme park in San Antonio.

Utah

ELIZA R. SNOW STATUE. Eliza R. Snow, who was first married to Joseph Smith, the original Mormon prophet, and after his death to Mormon leader Brigham Young "in name only," is considered the mother of Mormonism. A bronze statue on the grounds of the Daughters of Utah Pioneers Memorial Museum in Salt Lake City shows her holding the pencil with which she wrote the poem that became the Mormon hymn *O My Father*. A monument containing the bronzed hymn can also be seen at her grave in Brigham Young's private cemetery.

EMMELINE B. WELLS BUST. Emmeline B. Wells was a Mormon religious leader and feminist who founded the Woman Suffrage Association of Utah and was instrumental in obtaining the vote for women and statehood for Utah in 1896. She was the seventh wife of Daniel H. Wells, a high Mormon officer. A bust of Mrs. Wells honors her in the Utah State Capitol in Salt Lake City.

MARY DILWORTH HAMMOND MONUMENT. Mary Dilworth was Utah's first schoolteacher—and later considered one of the finest. She was a Pennsylvania Quaker who converted to Mormonism and first taught in Salt Lake City in 1847. She later began teaching in Huntsville in 1865. She is honored on the Huntsville public school grounds with a slab of red stone containing a plaque depicting the teacher with two children, a tent, and a Conestoga wagon recalling her transcontinental journey.

MARY HEATHMAN SMITH MEMORIAL. A nine-foot concrete shaft in the public square in Huntsville, Utah, honors Dr. Mary Heathman Smith, affectionately known as "Granny Smith." The English-born physician, surgeon, midwife, and nurse came to Utah in 1862 and administered to the medical needs of Ogden Valley for 30 years.

PIONEER MOTHER MONUMENT. The Pioneer Mother Monument in City Park in Springville, Utah, is a tribute to "the noble women who braved the wilderness." The bronze monument shows a sunbonneted woman with a wagon train.

THIS IS THE PLACE MONUMENT. Three women—Clarissa Decker Young, Ellen Saunders Kimball, and Harriet Page Wheeler Decker Young—were among the Mormon party that first arrived in Salt Lake City with Brigham Young on July 24, 1847. A bronze monument in Pioneer Trail State Park honors the women, shown walking alongside the wagons with two children.

Vermont

EMMA WILLARD MEMORIAL. A relief carving on marble in Middlebury, Vermont, was erected in 1941 in honor of Emma Willard for her pioneering efforts in furthering education for women. When Willard could not raise public funds for a proposed school with a bold new curriculum in Middlebury, she established a female seminary in Troy, New York, in 1821. Also see New York for a statue in her honor.

Virginia

CHALLENGER MONUMENT. Two women—astronaut Judy Resnik and teacher Christa McAuliffe—were aboard the ill-fated *Challenger* spacecraft that exploded in 1986, killing all aboard. A bronze relief of the seven crew members and the space shuttle now stands opposite the Tomb of the Unknown Soldier in Arlington National Cemetery in Arlington, Virginia.

ELIZABETH BENNETT YOUNG MEMORIAL. A plaque on a large round table in the old courthouse's visitor center in Smithfield, Virginia, honors Elizabeth Bennett Young, who saved the Isle of Wight County records from the British during the Revolutionary War. While her husband, the deputy county clerk, was away during the war, Mrs. Young hid the records to prevent

their capture by raiding British forces. As a result, the county now has some of the oldest records in the state, going back as far as 1629.

LEWIS AND CLARK AND SACAJAWEA MEMORIAL. A statue of western explorers Meriwether Lewis and William Clark with Sacajawea, their Native American guide and interpreter, is displayed in Midway Park in Charlottesville, Virginia. Lewis and George Rogers Clark, William Clark's brother, were born near Charlottesville.

MARY DRAPER INGLES MONUMENT. An obelisk constructed from stones of the chimney from her house honor Mary Draper Ingles in the West End Cemetery in Radford, Virginia. In 1755 Ingles, her two small sons, and several members of the Drapers' Meadow settlement were captured by the Shawnee in a massacre of the village. She escaped while digging for salt near present-day Cincinnati, Ohio, and wandered in the wilderness for more than 800 miles before being found.

STATUE OF 'THE NORWEGIAN LADY'. In 1891 the Norwegian ship *The Diktator* sank off the coast of Virginia. The captain's wife and son were drowned. Citizens of the ship's home port of Moss, Norway, placed a nine-foot bronze statue of the woman in their harbor and gave a duplicate to Virginia Beach, Virginia. The latter—called "The Norwegian Lady"—is at 25th and Oceanfront streets.

Washington

ESTHER SHORT STATUE. See Esther Short Park in Historic Parks and Sites.

STATUE OF MOTHER JOSEPH. This statue of Mother Joseph in City Hall in Vancouver, Washington, is a small replica of the bronze statue in National Statuary Hall in the Capitol in Washington, D.C. Mother Joseph, who established more than two dozen hospitals, schools, and orphanages, was also an accomplished carpenter and architect and was the first nun and the fifth woman to be honored in Statuary Hall.

West Virginia

ELIZABETH BOZARTH MEMORIAL. A marker along Highway 7 near Core, West Virginia, tells of how

Elizabeth Bozarth, who had been widowed by Native American raids in 1778, fought off a band of intruders with an ax the following year. She killed three of the intruders and chased off the others.

Wisconsin

ELLA WHEELER WILCOX MONUMENT. Ella Wheeler Wilcox, one of Wisconsin's most famous poets, spent part of her childhood on a farm near Westport, Wisconsin. A marker at Easy and I streets now recalls how "Her poetry had a sentimental appeal that touched millions of hearts."

LUCY STONE MEMORIAL. A memorial tablet is located on North Rock Avenue in Viroqua, Wisconsin, where reformer, suffragist, and publisher Lucy Stone gave the first women's rights address and antislavery speech by a woman in the early Northwest in 1857. She was one of the founders of the American Woman Suffrage Association and later edited the *Woman's Journal* with her husband. When the schism in the suffrage movement healed in 1890, she also served as chairperson of the executive board of the merged National American Woman Suffrage Association.

MARY BELLE AUSTIN JACOBS STATUE. This statue in Kosciuszko Park in Milwaukee honors Mary Belle Austin Jacobs for founding organized social work in Wisconsin. She and her husband, Herbert Jacobs, operated a settlement house, helped establish a working-man's camp, promoted home-nursing branch libraries, and were instrumental in other early social efforts in the area.

Wyoming

AMELIA EARHART MEMORIAL. A memorial along State Highway 120 in Meeteetse, Wyoming, pays tribute to aviator Amelia Earhart, who was constructing a summer home nearby when she disappeared in the South Pacific while attempting an around-the-world flight in 1937.

HISTORIC WOMAN MONUMENT. A concrete pillar at 603 Ivinson Avenue in Laramie, Wyoming, honors Louisa Ann Swain for being the first woman to cast a vote anywhere in the world on September 6, 1870, and a number of other Wyoming women for their accomplishments—the first women jurors in the world

in 1870; Mary Godat Bellamy, the first woman elected to the Wyoming Legislature in 1911; and Martha Symons-Boies, the first jurors' bailiff.

MONUMENT TO ELIZA SPALDING AND NARCISSA WHITMAN. On the summit of South Pass at South Pass City, Wyoming, a monument points out that missionaries Eliza Spalding and Narcissa Whitman were the first white women to cross the pass in 1836. They were on their way, with their husbands, to mission work in Spalding, Idaho, and Walla Walla, Washington (see Nez Percé National Historical Park and Whitman Mission National Historic Site).

SACAJAWEA GRAVE AND MONUMENT. The Wind River Reservation of the Arapaho and Shoshone peoples in Wyoming claims that Sacajawea, the Shoshone guide and interpreter for the 1804–1806 Lewis and Clark Expedition, died and was buried there in 1884. She is remembered with a large monument on a hill at Fort Washakie. However, there is debate over where and when she died and is buried. The chief clerk at Fort Manuel in Mobridge, South Dakota, recorded that she died there in 1812, and a monument to her can be seen in the Dakota Memorial Park. Part of the confusion can be attributed to Sacajawea's husband, Jean Baptiste Charbonneau, who had two wives. An argument can be made that Otter Woman, Charbonneau's other wife, may have died in 1812 and been mistaken for Sacajawea. However, that would mean that the Sacajawea buried in Wyoming was approximately 100 years old when she died.

STATUE OF ESTHER MORRIS. Esther H. Morris is known as the heroine of the Wyoming suffrage movement. It was reported for many years that she gave a tea party in 1869 for candidates for the Wyoming Legislature, where she extracted a promise from both Democrats and Republicans to give women the right to vote (which occurred later that year). But historians in the 1990s concluded that Morris never held a party. However, she did become the first woman to hold a political office in the United States, when she was appointed justice of the peace by county commissioners in 1870. A statue of Morris was erected in her honor in 1963 at the entrance to the state capitol in Cheyenne—a larger version is also in National Statuary Hall in Washington, D.C. (see Women's Museums, Galleries, and Halls of Fame).

SHRINES TO WOMEN

Kansas

ST. PHILIPPINE DUCHESNE SHRINE. The St. Philippine Duchesne Shrine in rural Linn County near Pleasanton, Kansas, honors a French Catholic nun who became a saint for her work among Native Americans in the mid-1800s. It is located in a 168-acre park that preserves the site of a Pottawatomie settlement founded with the help of Jesuit priests and nuns, and contains several memorials, historical markers, and Native American burial grounds.

Sister Rose Philippine Duchesne, who was known by Native Americans as Quah-Kah-Ka-Num-Ad (The Woman Who Prays Always), came to the area in the 1830s from St. Charles, Missouri, to teach the Pottawatomie children (see also shrine in Other Shrines). She was canonized as a saint in 1988 for her work.

The park is located at the site of a settlement that was called St. Mary's of Sugar Creek. A massive altar and cross have been erected where the church once stood. The remnants of the foundations of the buildings that housed the priests and nuns are adjacent to the church site, and nearby is a seven-cross memorial with the names of over 600 baptized Native Americans buried there.

St. Philippine Duchesne Shrine, off State Hwy. 7 (16 miles northwest of Pleasanton), Pleasanton, KS (postal address: 8039 Metcalf St., Overland Park, KS 66204). **Phone:** 913/649-8200. **Fax:** 913/901-8199. **Hours:** dawn-dusk daily. **Admission:** free.

Maryland

NATIONAL SHRINE OF ST. ELIZABETH ANN SETON. Elizabeth Ann Seton, the first native-born American saint, founded the first women's religious order (Sisters of Charity) and first free parochial school in the United States. She is now honored at the National Shrine of St. Elizabeth Ann Seton in Emmitsburg, Maryland, where she did most of her work (see also New York City shrine in Other Shrines).

Mother Seton was born in New York City in 1774, married at age nineteen, and was widowed in poverty with five children after nine years of married life. She became a Catholic in 1805 and then went to Baltimore and started a school. She inspired other women to assist in her work and formed a small religious community with her as superioress. In 1809 the group moved to Emmitsburg and established a larger religious community that resulted in the formation of the Sisters of Charity and the free parochial school. She was canonized as a saint in 1975.

In 1991 the shrine chapel was designated a minor basilica. The remains of St. Elizabeth Ann Seton are beneath the altar in the north bay of the basilica. The Emmitsburg site also contains some of the original buildings, an orientation center, and a museum.

National Shrine of St. Elizabeth Ann Seton, 333 S. Seton Ave., Emmitsburg, MD 21727-9298. **Phone:** 301/447-6606. **Fax:** 301/447-6061. **E-mail:** office@setonshrine.org. **Website:** www.setonshrine.org. **Hours:** 10-4:30 Wed.-Sun.; closed Mon.-Tues., New Year's Day, Easter, Thanksgiving, and Christmas. **Admission:** free.

New York

ST. FRANCES CABRINI SHRINE. The St. Frances Cabrini Shrine in New York City is dedicated to an Italian Catholic immigrant, who became the first American citizen to be canonized in 1946. She was made the patron saint of immigrants, and her name was placed at the base of the Statue of Liberty and on the wall of honor on Ellis Island.

Mother Cabrini was originally rejected from religious life in Italy because of her frail health. Instead, she became a teacher in a public school and then at an orphanage, where she befriended many of the girls. In 1880 seven of the orphan girls joined her in establishing the religious community known as the Missionary Sisters of the Sacred Heart of Jesus.

In 1889 she was asked to come to New York City to work with Italian immigrants, particularly children. She and three of her missionary sisters crossed the Atlantic and opened the Sacred Heart Villa boarding school for Italian girls at the shrine site on Fort Washington Avenue along the Hudson River. The property also served as a reception house for orphans before being moved to other sites. In the years that followed, Mother Cabrini was involved in establishing 67 schools, hospitals, and other institutions of the Missionary Sisters of the Sacred Heart in America and abroad. Her first hospital was Columbus Hospital, now known as the Cabrini Medical Center, in New York City. Her work also took her to many parts of the United States, including Colorado, where she opened a school, orphanage, and summer camp for orphans and which now also has a Cabrini Shrine (see shrine in Other Shrines).

Mother Cabrini never learned to speak English fluently, but she became an American citizen in 1909. She died from a fever in a Chicago hospital in 1917, and her remains were reburied in the library (formerly the chapel) of Mother Cabrini High School, which opened at the original New York site in 1930. Only the wooden bench where Mother Cabrini prayed remains from the original structures at the site. Each year the Feast of Mother Cabrini is celebrated at the school's new chapel in mid-November.

St. Frances Cabrini Shrine, 701 Fort Washington Ave., New York, NY 10040. **Phone:** 212/923-3536. **Fax:** 212/923-1871. **E-mail:** cabrinishrineny@worldnet.att.net. **Website:** www.cabrinishrineny.org. **Hours:** Memorial Day-Labor Day—9-6 daily; remainder of year—9-4:30 daily; closed major holidays. **Admission:** free.

NATIONAL SHRINE OF BLESSED KATERI TEKAKWITHA.
The National Shrine of Blessed Kateri Tekakwitha near Fonda, New York, honors the first Native American to be beatified and to become eligible for sainthood. It is located where she was baptized a Catholic and lived for almost half of her 24 years.

Tekakwitha was born in 1656 in Auriesville and was baptized in 1676 in a little chapel in a nearby village then called Caughnewaga, despite the violent opposition of her family. Unwilling to forgo her faith, she fled by canoe to a friendly Christian settlement in Canada, where she became known as "Lily of the Mohawks." She lived a deeply religious life until she died of fever four years later. It is said that the smallpox scars on her face disappeared at the moment of death. Her beatification came in 1980.

The shrine site now features a Mohawk-style chapel, shrine, and museum, as well as a reconstruction of the Mohawk village in which she lived and an excavated seventeenth-century Native American village.

National Shrine of Blessed Kateri Tekakwitha, State Hwy. 5, PO Box 12068, Fonda, NY 12068. **Phone:** 518/853-3646. **Fax:** 518/853-3371. **E-mail:** kateri_s@yahoo.com. **Hours:** May-Oct.—9-4 daily; closed remainder of year. **Admission:** free.

Pennsylvania

ST. KATHARINE DREXEL SHRINE. Katharine Mary Drexel, who was born into a wealthy Philadelphia family in 1858, devoted her life to the Catholic Church and used most of her $20 million inheritance to benefit Native Americans and African Americans.

As a young woman she was deeply distressed by the poverty and hopeless conditions endured by many Native Americans and African Americans. She began to devote her fortune to missionary and educational work among the poorest members of society, became a nun in 1889, and then founded the Congregation of the Sisters of the Blessed Sacrament in 1891 to work among Native Americans and African Americans. For her work, she was canonized as Saint Katharine in 2000.

A convent of Spanish Mission–style buildings was built in Bensalem, Pennsylvania, and the missionary work included the opening of boarding and day schools in the East, Midwest, and rural and urban areas of the South and Southwest, as well as a school to prepare teachers, which later became Xavier University of New Orleans.

Saint Katharine died in 1955 and was interred in the crypt of the Motherhouse Chapel in Bensalem. Also located at the Saint Katharine Drexel Shrine are many of her artifacts, and those of Native Americans, African Americans, and Haitians (a mission was opened in Haiti in 1990).

St. Katharine Drexel Shrine, 1663 Bristol Pike, Bensalem, PA 19020-8502. **Phone:** 215/639-7878. **Fax:** 215/639-1154. **E-mail:** kathdrexel@aol.com. **Website:** www.katharinedrexel.org. **Hours:** 10-5 daily. **Admission:** free.

OTHER SHRINES

Colorado

MOTHER CABRINI SHRINE. The Mother Cabrini Shrine on Lookout Mountain in Golden, Colorado, honors the first U.S. saint (canonized in 1946) with a 22-foot statue of Christ and a complex of buildings with a chapel, convent, building for prayer and meetings, and 1915 stone house and barn. The Italian-born founder of the Missionary Sisters of the Sacred Heart of Jesus came to New York City in 1889 to assist Italian immigrants. Among the 67 schools, hospitals, and other institutions she helped establish were a school and orphanage in Denver in the early 1900s. She also purchased the property on which the shrine is located as a summer camp for orphans. The site is now a place of prayer and devotion. A St. Frances Cabrini

Shrine is also located in New York City (see Shrines to Women).

Illinois

NATIONAL SHRINE OF OUR LADY OF THE SNOWS. The National Shrine of Our Lady of the Snows on State Highway 15 west of Belleville, Illinois, is a 200-acre religious center operated by the Missionary Oblates of Mary Immaculate. The center has a replica of the Lourdes Grotto, prayer gardens, chapels, and a 2,400-seat amphitheater.

Missouri

BLACK MADONNA SHRINE AND GROTTOS. The Black Madonna Shrine and Grottos on County Road FF, south of Eureka, Missouri, is Franciscan Brother Bronislaus's tribute to the Virgin Mary and the Black Madonna Shrine in his native Poland. It consists of an open-air chapel and seven grottos of Missouri barite embedded with costume jewelry, rocks, and seashells.

NATIONAL SHRINE OF OUR LADY OF THE MIRACULOUS MEDAL. Religious scenes and the history of the Vincentian Order can be seen on the walls and ceiling of St. Mary's of the Barrens Church at the National Shrine of Our Lady of the Miraculous Medal on County Road T near Perryville, Missouri. The shrine's museum contains porcelain figurines, Chinese art, paperweights, Chinese and Louis XV furniture, memorabilia from foreign missions, and rare books.

SHRINE OF ST. PHILIPPINE DUCHESNE. The French-born Mother Rose Philippine Duchesne spent much of her life living and working for the pioneers and Native Americans of Missouri and Kansas. She and four sisters founded the first Sacred Heart convent and school for girls in St. Charles, Missouri, in 1818. She then opened a female Native American seminary in Florissant, Missouri, in 1825, and went to the Pleasanton, Kansas, area in the 1830s to work with the Pottawatomie people (see also Shrines to Women for another shrine). She later returned to St. Charles, where she died at the age of 83 in 1852. Her remains are interred at the shrine. The Academy of the Sacred Heart, which has become co-educational, has a room where Mother Duchesne lived and still contains some of her personal items. She was canonized in 1988.

New Jersey

BLUE ARMY SHRINE OF THE IMMACULATE HEART OF MARY. The Blue Army Shrine of the Immaculate Heart of Mary, on Mountain View Road near Washington, New Jersey, contains the Blessed Sacrament Chapel; Rosary Garden; Outdoor Way of the Cross; Holy House U.S.A.; and replicas of the chapel at Fatima, Portugal, and the Holy House of Loretto, Italy.

New York

NATIONAL SHRINE BASILICA OF OUR LADY OF FATIMA. An outdoor cathedral with over 100 life-size statues, a giant rosary, and a translucent domed chapel with an observation deck on top are featured at the National Shrine Basilica of Our Lady of Fatima, on Swan Road, northeast of Lewiston, New York.

ST. ELIZABETH ANN SETON SHRINE. The St. Elizabeth Ann Seton Shrine in New York City's Battery Park is where the founder of the Sisters of Charity, the first American religious sisterhood, lived in 1801–1804. A statue of Mother Seton stands over the doorway of the Catholic church, and a large stained-glass window over the altar traces the steps of her life that led to canonization in 1975 (see also another shrine in Emmitsburg, Maryland, in Shrines to Women).

SHRINE OF OUR LADY OF THE ISLAND. The Shrine of Our Lady of the Island, on a 40-acre site on Eastport Manor Road in Eastport, New York, has Stations of the Cross, gardens, statues, chapels, and wooded walkways.

Ohio

BASILICA AND NATIONAL SHRINE OF OUR LADY OF CONSOLATION. The Basilica and National Shrine of Our Lady of Consolation, in Carey, Ohio, has a statue of the Virgin Mary brought from Luxembourg in 1875 in the basilica and a memorial altar and Stations of the Cross in a nearby 23-acre park.

NATIONAL SHRINE OF OUR LADY OF LOURDES. The National Shrine of Our Lady of Lourdes, at 21281 Chardon Road, near Cleveland, is a grotto in the hillside that resembles the original in France. In addition to shrines and woods, the site has a chapel and Way of the Cross.

NATIONAL SHRINE OF ST. DYMPHNA. The National Shrine of St. Dymphna, located on the grounds of the Massillon Psychiatric Center at 3000 Erie Street near Massillon, Ohio, is a memorial to the patroness of those afflicted with mental and nervous disorders. It has a chapel and outdoor shrine.

SORROWFUL MOTHER SHRINE. The Sorrowful Mother Shrine on State Highway 269, south of Bellevue, Ohio, features statues, grottos, and colorful flowers on 140 wooded acres.

Pennsylvania

NATIONAL SHRINE OF OUR LADY OF CZESTOCHOWA. Stained-glass windows depicting 1,000 years of Polish Christianity are in the upper church of a monastery at the National Shrine of Our Lady of Czestochowa, on Ferry Road northwest of Doylestown, Pennsylvania. The church also has the sculpture *The Holy Trinity* above the altar and a copy of the painting *Our Lady of Czestochowa* below the sculpture.

West Virginia

INTERNATIONAL MOTHER'S DAY SHRINE. Anna M. Jarvis started a Mothers Friendship Day in 1868 to help ease tensions after the Civil War, and when she died in 1905 she hoped that someone would establish a national day as a tribute to mothers everywhere. Three years later, 400 people came to the Andrews Methodist Episcopal Church in Grafton, West Virginia, to honor their mothers, and Mrs. Jarvis's daughter, Anna, gave out hundreds of white carnations. Devoted to her mother's cause, Anna Jarvis continued to work for six more years, lecturing and writing thousands of letters in support of a national Mother's Day. Finally, in 1914, President Woodrow Wilson proclaimed the second Sunday of May as Mother's Day. In 1962 the Grafton church also became the International Mother's Day Shrine.

ART MUSEUMS

See also Art and History Museums; Art Galleries; Arts Centers; Cultural Art and History Museums; Decorative Arts Museums; Folk Art Museums; Museums Honoring Exceptional Women; Sculpture Gardens.

Alabama

WEEDEN HOUSE MUSEUM. See Museums Honoring Exceptional Women.

Arizona

FLEISCHER MUSEUM. Donna and Mort Fleischer's private collection of American Impressionism, California School 1890–1930s, is featured at the Fleischer Museum in Scottsdale, Arizona. The collection included more than 80 artists whose works were characterized by *plein air* painting, with canvases depicting an abundance of sunlight and brilliantly colored landscapes. The museum has also added some examples of Russian and Soviet Impressionism from the Cold War era.

Fleischer Museum, 17207 N. Perimeter Dr., Scottsdale, AZ 85255. **Phone:** 480/585-3108. **Fax:** 480/563-6192. **E-mail:** jhoeffel@ffca.com. **Website:** www.fleischer.org. **Hours:** 10-4 daily; closed major holidays. **Admission:** free.

California

CALIFORNIA PALACE OF THE LEGION OF HONOR. The California Palace of the Legion of Honor—now part of the Fine Arts Museums of San Francisco—was a gift to the city from Adolph B. and Alma DeBretteville Spreckels, whose idea it was to duplicate the Palais de la Légion d'Honneur in Paris and dedicate it to the memory of Californians who died in World War I.

The museum, which opened in 1924, is dedicated largely to French art. Noted French sculptor Auguste Rodin helped Mrs. Spreckels select many of his works now displayed in the central sculpture court. The museum also has exceptional collections of French decorative arts, prints, furniture, tapestries, and paintings

The neoclassical building of the California Palace of the Legion of Honor—part of the Fine Arts Museums of San Francisco—was funded by Adolph B. Spreckles and his wife, Alma DeBretteville Spreckles. It honors Californians who died in World War I and features works covering 4,000 years of ancient and European art. Courtesy California Palace of the Legion of Honor (The Fine Arts Museums of San Francisco).

by such artists as El Greco, Rembrandt, Monet, Renoir, and Picasso.

California Palace of the Legion of Honor, Fine Arts Museums of San Francisco, 100 34th Ave., San Francisco, CA 94121 (postal address: 233 Post St., 6th Fl., San Francisco, CA 94108). **Phone:** 415/863-3330. **Fax:** 415/750-7686. **Website:** www.thinker.org. **Hours:** 9:30-5 Tues.-Sun.; closed Mon. **Admission:** adults, $8; seniors, $6; children 12-17, $5;

children under 12 and school students, free; free 2nd Wed. of month.

GRACE HUDSON MUSEUM AND SUN HOUSE. See Historic House Museums.

IRIS & B. GERALD CANTOR CENTER FOR VISUAL ARTS. The 1989 California earthquake severely damaged Stanford University's art museum, causing it to close for ten years. When the museum reopened in 1999, it had new and restored facilities and collections and a new name—the Iris & B. Gerald Cantor Center for Visual Arts—thanks largely to a $10 million gift from the philanthropic couple in 1994.

The center was preceded by the Leland Stanford Junior Museum, which was founded, along with the university, by Jane and Leland Stanford in 1891 as a memorial to their only child. The museum opened in 1894, but more than two-thirds of the building and collections were destroyed in the 1906 earthquake. The museum never fully recovered, and it finally closed in 1945. The museum reopened in 1963, and the galleries were refurbished, the collections strengthened, and the exhibition programs and educational services improved and expanded over the next 25 years.

In 1985 the B. Gerald Cantor Rodin Sculpture Garden was established on the campus, mainly through the gifts of the Cantors. Before his death in 1996, the founder and chairman of the Cantor Fitzgerald securities firm and his wife, who is now vice chairman of the company and president of the Iris and B. Gerald Cantor Foundation, donated 185 Rodin sculptures in bronze, plaster, terra cotta, ceramics, and stone to the Stanford museum, as well as manuscripts, drawings, photographs, and memorabilia from Rodin's lifetime; other bibliographical materials; and support for the Rodin studies and research program in the Department of Art. The Cantors have given more than 450 Rodin works to over 70 institutions, endowed several galleries, and sponsored numerous exhibitions.

The new visual arts center has 27 galleries with paintings, sculpture, sketches, decorative arts, and photographs in addition to the Rodin sculpture garden. The artworks from America, Europe, Asia, and Africa range from ancient times to the early twentieth century. Among the works are paintings and sculpture by Edgar Degas; paintings by Georgia O'Keeffe; pop art sculpture by Andy Warhol; photographs by Ansel Adams; arts and crafts by Native Americans; and such

The Rodin Garden is adjacent to the Iris & B. Gerald Cantor Center for Visual Arts at Stanford University. Funding from the Cantors and others made it possible to restore and reopen the museum after it was severely damaged by the 1989 California earthquake. Courtesy Iris & B. Gerald Cantor Center for Visual Arts, Stanford University.

well-known Rodin sculptures as *The Thinker, Age of Bronze, The Kiss,* and *Adam and Eve at the Gates of Hell.*

Iris & B. Gerald Cantor Center for Visual Arts, Stanford University, Lomita Dr. and Museum Way, Stanford, CA 94305-5060. **Phone:** 650/725-0462. **Fax:** 650/725-0464. **Website:** www.stanford.edu/dept/suma/homepage.html. **Hours:** 11-5 Wed.-Sun. (also to 8 p.m. Thurs.); closed Mon.-Tues. **Admission:** free.

JANET TURNER PRINT COLLECTION AND GALLERY. Art professor and printmaker Janet Turner, at California State University in Chico, gave her print collection and endowment to the university to establish the Janet Turner Print Collection and Gallery in 1981. The collection, which numbered approximately 2,000 student, professional, and global prints from over 40 countries, has been expanded by nearly 1,000 prints since its founding. The gallery presents seven exhibitions each year and hosts the biannual National Juried Printmaking Competition and Exhibition.

Janet Turner Print Collection and Gallery, California State University, 400 W. 1st St., Chico, CA 95929-0820. **Phone:** 530/898-4476. **Fax:** 530/898-5581. **E-mail:** csullivan @exchange.csuchico.edu. **Website:** www.csuchico.edu/art/galleries/turnergallery.html. **Hours:** Sept.-May—11-4 Mon.-Fri.; closed Sat.-Sun., June-Aug., and university holidays and breaks. **Admission:** free.

MONTGOMERY ART CENTER AND POMONA COLLEGE MUSEUM OF ART. The Montgomery Art Center at Pomona College in Claremont, California, is the home of the Pomona College Museum of Art (formerly the Montgomery Gallery). The center was built by Victor Montgomery in 1958 in honor of his wife, Gladys K. Montgomery, a civic leader and the chair of the college's board of trustees at the time. It contained the Montgomery Gallery, lecture room, sculpture studio, art offices, and storage rooms.

The center was enlarged in 1968 and again in 1973, through the generosity of Mrs. Montgomery. With the growth of the college's collections of the Kress Foundation's Renaissance and medieval paintings, other American and European paintings, prints, drawings, photographs, and Native American works, the name of the Montgomery Gallery was changed in 2001 to the Pomona College Museum of Art to better reflect its expanded holdings, exhibits, and programs.

Pomona College Museum of Art, 330 N. College Ave., Claremont, CA 91711 (postal address: 3333 N. College Way, Claremont, CA 91711). **Phone:** 909/621-8283. **Fax:** 909/621-8989. **E-mail:** mharth@pomona.edu. **Website:** www.pomona.edu/museum. **Hours:** late Aug.-mid-May—12-5 Tues.-Fri., 1-5 Sat.-Sun.; closed Mon., mid-May-late Aug., and college holidays and breaks. **Admission:** free.

MUSEUM OF CONTEMPORARY ART, SAN DIEGO. In 1937 a group of local artists displayed their works in the 1913 Mission-style former home of Ellen Browning Scripps, the noted journalist, publisher, and philanthropist, in La Jolla, California. Four years later the Scripps house became the home of La Jolla's first art center, which evolved into the La Jolla Museum of Contemporary Art and then the Museum of Contemporary Art, San Diego.

The Museum of Contemporary Art is still located at the site, but the original building has been renovated and expanded several times and a sculpture garden added—with architect Robert Venturi completing a major expansion in 1996. In 1993 a branch museum was opened in downtown San Diego. The museum now functions as a cultural center—serving as an art museum preserving, presenting, and interpreting today's art; a forum for the exploration of contemporary art and ideas; and a research laboratory for artists and audiences.

The museum has more than 3,000 works of art created since 1950, including major examples of minimal, conceptual, site/installation, and California art of recent decades. In addition to representative art from many premier contemporary artists, the museum contains works by unrecognized and promising emerging artists.

Museum of Contemporary Art, San Diego, 700 Prospect St., La Jolla, CA 92037. **Phone:** 858/454-3541. **Fax:** 858/454-6985. **E-mail:** info@mcasandiego.org. **Website:** www.mcasandiego.org. **Hours:** June-Aug.—11-8 Mon.-Tues. and Thurs.-Fri.; 11-5 Sat.-Sun.; remainder of year—11-5 Mon.-Tues. and Thurs.-Sun. (also open to 8 p.m. Thurs.); closed Wed., Thanksgiving, and Christmas. **Admission:** museum—adults, $4; seniors, students, and military, $2; children under 12, free; branch—adults, $2; seniors, students, and military, $1; children under 12, free.

MUSEUM OF NEON ART. The Museum of Neon Art—which collects, restores, and exhibits neon, electric, and kinetic art—was founded in 1981 by neon artists Lili Lakich and Richard Jenkins in Lakich's studio space in a converted warehouse in Los Angeles. It moved to the Universal City mall in 1993, and then to the Renaissance Tower apartment complex in 1996.

The museum focuses on art that shares the common bond of electricity and motion. Some of the artworks are rare old neon signs, while others are new neon and mechanical works created by contemporary artists. They take many forms—from abstract geometric shapes and unusual optical effects to mechanical sculptures that move and make strange sounds. The history and technology of neon signage and art is also presented.

Museum of Neon Art, Renaissance Tower, 501 W. Olympic Blvd., Los Angeles, CA 90015. **Phone:** 213/489-9918. **Fax:** 213/489-9932. **E-mail:** info@neonmona.org. **Website:** www.neonmona.org. **Hours:** 11-5 Wed.-Sat. (also to 8 p.m. 2nd Thurs. of month), 12-5 Sun.; closed Mon.-Tues. and major holidays. **Admission:** adults, $5; seniors and students 13-22, $3.50; children under 13, free; free 5-8 p.m. 2nd Thurs. of month.

PASADENA MUSEUM OF CALIFORNIA ART. The Pasadena Museum of California Art was opened in 2002 in Pasadena by businessman Robert Oltman and his wife, Arlene Oltman, and specializes in California art and design. The Oltmans, who are art collectors and philanthropists, live in the penthouse above the new $5 million museum.

Pasadena Museum of California Art, 490 E. Union St., Pasadena, CA 91101. **Phone:** 626/568-3665. **Fax:** 626/568-3674. **Website:** www.pmeaonline.org. **Hours:** 10-5 Wed.-Sun. (also to 8 p.m. Fri.); closed Mon.-Tues. and major holidays. **Admission:** adults, $6; seniors and students above 12, $4; children under 13, free.

PETTERSON MUSEUM OF INTERCULTURAL ART. See Cultural Art and History Museums.

TRITON MUSEUM OF ART. The Triton Museum of Art was founded in San Jose, California, in 1965 by rancher, lawyer, and art patron W. Robert Morgan and his wife, June Morgan. In less than two years, however, the museum had moved to Santa Clara to serve the growing population. It now occupies a new 22,000-square-foot building. The museum has collections of early and contemporary American paintings, drawings, and prints and Native American art and artifacts, and displays selections from the collections and elsewhere in changing exhibitions. It also functions as a community art center with art classes, lectures, films, dance and music performances, and an outreach program to schools and senior centers.

Triton Museum of Art, 1505 Warburton Ave., Santa Clara, CA 95050. **Phone:** 408/247-3754. **Fax:** 408/247-3796. **E-mail:** tritonmusart@aol.com. **Website:** www.tritonmuseum.org. **Hours:** 10-5 Tues.-Sun. (also to 9 p.m. Tues.); closed Mon. and national holidays. **Admission:** free.

USC FISHER GALLERY. Elizabeth Holmes Fisher, a Los Angeles art collector and the first woman member of the University of Southern California board of trustees, founded the USC Fisher Gallery at the university in 1939. She gave the funds to build the museum and its core collection of 70 paintings that included works by the Dutch masters, American landscapes, British portraits, and French Barbizon landscapes.

The Fisher Gallery has approximately 1,800 works, predominantly paintings, prints, miniatures, and photographs. They are largely European and American collections and include the Armand Hammer Collection of Old Masters as well as the Fisher Collection. All types of art from the collections and elsewhere are presented in changing exhibitions.

USC Fisher Gallery, University of Southern California, University Park, 823 Exposition Blvd., Los Angeles, CA 90089-0292. **Phone:** 213/740-4561. **Fax:** 213/740-7676. **Website:** www.usc.edu/fisher gallery. **Hours:** Sept.-mid-May—12-5 Tues.-Sat.; closed Sun.-Mon., mid-May-Aug., Labor Day, Thanksgiving weekend, and Christmas. **Admission:** free.

Colorado

COLORADO SPRINGS FINE ARTS CENTER. The Colorado Springs Fine Arts Center, which opened in 1936 in Colorado Springs, Colorado, was conceived by Alice Bemis Taylor, who wanted a place to house her extensive collection of southwestern Spanish Colonial folk art and Native American and Hispanic art, and to serve as a home for visual arts, performing arts theater, art school, art library, and sculpture garden. It was one of the nation's first institutions to include all these arts in the same facility.

The Native American and Hispanic art and artifacts in the collection are displayed in galleries known as the Taylor Museum of Southwest Studies. Nineteenth- and twentieth-century American paintings, graphics, and sculptures by such artists as Georgia O'Keeffe, John James Audubon, and John Singer Sargent comprise the fine arts permanent collection. The center also displays Charles M. Russell sculptures and memorabilia in the galleries and traditional, contemporary, and Native American sculptures in an outdoor courtyard. It also has a tactile gallery and changing exhibitions.

Colorado Springs Fine Arts Center, 30 W. Dale St., Colorado Springs, CO 80903. **Phone:** 719/634-5581. **Fax:** 719/634-0570. **E-mail:** dturner@csfineartscenter.org. **Hours:** 9-5 Tues.-Fri., 10-5 Sat., 1-5 Sun.; closed Mon. and national holidays. **Admission:** adults, $4; seniors and student 13-21, $2; children 6-12, $1; children under 6, free.

Connecticut

BUSH-HOLLEY HISTORIC SITE. See Historic House Museums.

FLORENCE GRISWOLD MUSEUM. See Art and History Museums.

HILL-STEAD MUSEUM. The Hill-Stead Museum, an art museum featuring Impressionist etchings and paintings, is located in a 1901 Colonial Revival house designed and built by Theodate Pope Riddle, one of the nation's first woman architects, in Farmington, Connecticut.

The 33,000-square-foot country home, of which nineteen of its 36 period rooms are now decorated and open to the public, contains the works of such artists as Monet, Degas, Manet, Cassatt, and Whistler and collections of furniture, ceramics, prints, photographs, books, and archival documents. The 152-acre site also has a sunken garden, trails, and a summerlong poetry festival.

Although acclaimed during her lifetime, Theodate Pope faced discrimination as an early woman architect—including being left out of a book about prominent New York architects because she was female. In 1916 she married career diplomat John Wallace Riddle, and they and their three foster children became the chief occupants of the Hill-Stead mansion, now a national historic landmark.

Hill-Stead Museum, 35 Mountain Rd., Farmington, CT 06032-2304. **Phone:** 860/677-4787. **Fax:** 860/677-0174. **E-mail:** hillstead@juno.com. **Website:** www.hillstead.org. **Hours:** May-Oct.—10-5 Tues.-Sun.; remainder of year—11-4 Tues.-Sun.; closed Mon. and major holidays. **Admission:** adults and children over 12, $7; seniors, $6; children 6-12, $4; children under 6, free.

LYMAN ALLYN MUSEUM OF ART AT CONNECTICUT COLLEGE. The Lyman Allyn Museum of Art, in the seafaring town of New London, Connecticut, was founded in 1926 by a bequest from Harriet U. Allyn in memory of her father, who had been a captain of a whaling ship in the first half of the nineteenth century. The museum

opened in 1932 in a neoclassical building with thirteen art objects, mostly decorative arts. It is now part of Connecticut College and has over 15,000 works, including American and European paintings; master drawings; Asian, Greek, and Roman art; and Colonial New England paintings, furniture, and silver. It also displays contemporary art by local artists.

Lyman Allyn Museum of Art at Connecticut College, 625 Williams St., New London, CT 06320. **Phone:** 860/443-2545. **Fax:** 860/442-1280. **Website:** www.lymanallyn.conncoll.edu. **Hours:** 10-5 Tues.-Sat., 1-5 Sun.; closed Mon. and major holidays. **Admission:** adults, $4; seniors and students, $3; children under 6, free.

WHITNEY MUSEUM OF AMERICAN ART AT CHAMPION PLAZA. The Whitney Museum of American Art at Champion Plaza in Stamford, Connecticut, is one of two branches of the Whitney Museum of American Art, founded by art patron and sculptor Gertrude Vanderbilt Whitney in New York City in 1930 (see also Museums Honoring Exceptional Women). The Stamford branch presents changing exhibitions of American art from the Whitney's collections.

Whitney Museum of American Art at Champion Plaza, Champion International Corp., 1 Champion Plaza, Stamford, CT 06904. **Phone:** 203/358-7652. **Fax:** 203/358-2975. **Hours:** 11-5 Tues.-Sat.; closed Sun.-Mon. and major holidays. **Admission:** free.

District of Columbia

KREEGER MUSEUM. The Kreeger Museum, housed in the former residence of philanthropist David Lloyd Kreeger and his wife, Carmen Kreeger, in Washington, D.C., showcases the Kreegers' personal art collection of nineteenth- and twentieth-century European and American paintings and sculpture and traditional African and Native American art. The impressive travertine structure, designed by Philip Johnson, features the works of such artists as Monet, Picasso, Braque, Miró, Kandinsky, Dubuffet, and Moore. Visits are by tour and by reservation.

Kreeger Museum, 2401 Foxhall Rd. N.W., Washington, DC 20007. **Phone:** 202/337-3050. **Fax:** 202/337-3051. **E-mail:** publicrelations@kreegermuseum.com. **Website:** www.kreegermuseum.com. **Hours:** Sept.-July—tours at 10:30 and 1:30 Tues.-Sat.; closed Sun.-Mon., Aug., and major holidays. **Admission:** suggested donations—adults, $8; seniors and students, $5; children under 12 not permitted.

NATIONAL MUSEUM OF WOMEN IN THE ARTS. See Women's Museums, Galleries, and Halls of Fame.

Florida

APPLETON MUSEUM OF ART. The Appleton Museum of Art—jointly owned and operated by Florida State University and Central Florida Community College in Ocala, Florida—was founded in 1986 by retired businessman Arthur I. Appleton and his family. His sister, Edith-Marie Appleton, gave $2 million toward the construction of a 22,000-square-foot museum wing and endowed a similar amount for programs and exhibitions in 1996. The 67,000-square-foot museum has collections and exhibitions of pre-Columbian, Asian, African, European, and contemporary art and works by Florida artists.

Appleton Museum of Art, Florida State University and Central Florida Community College, 4333 N.E. Silver Springs Blvd., PO Box 3190, Ocala, FL 34478-3190. **Phone:** 352/236-7100. **Fax:** 352/236-7136. **E-mail:** jgonzale@appleton.fsu.edu. **Website:** www.appletonmuseum.org. **Hours:** 10-6 daily; closed New Year's Day and Christmas. **Admission:** adults, $6; seniors, $4; students over 17, $2; children under 18, free.

BASS MUSEUM OF ART. An art museum in a 1934 former public-library building in Miami Beach, Florida, was renovated and renamed the Bass Museum of Art in 1963, after receiving the John and Johanna Bass collection of paintings, sculpture, tapestries, and vestments. The museum features works by French Impressionists, Rembrandt, Rubens, Botticelli, and contemporary artists.

Bass Museum of Art, 2121 Park Ave., Miami Beach, FL 33139. **Phone:** 305/673-7530. **Fax:** 305/673-7062. **E-mail:** bassmus@bellsouth.net. **Website:** www.bassmuseum.net. **Hours:** 10-5 Tues.-Sat. (also to 9 p.m. 2nd and 4th Wed. of month), 1-5 Sun.; closed Mon. and major holidays. **Admission:** adults, $5; seniors and students, $3; children under 6, free.

CUMMER MUSEUM OF ART AND GARDENS. Art collector Ninah May Holden Cummer of Jacksonville, Florida, bequeathed her collection and the bulk of her estate to a foundation for the creation of an art museum—which became the Cummer Museum of Art and Gardens. Founded in 1958 and opened three years later, the museum is located in a neoclassical building overlooking formal gardens and the St. Johns River, at the site of Mrs. Cummer's former home. From an initial collection of approximately 65 paintings and art objects, the museum's holdings have grown to include paintings by American and European masters, sculpture, prints, furniture, graphics, porcelain, decorative arts, and Asian art and objects.

Cummer Museum of Art and Gardens, 829 Riverside Ave., Jacksonville, FL 32204. **Phone:** 904/356-6857. **Fax:** 904/353-4101. **E-mail:** info@cummer.org. **Website:** www.cummer.org. **Hours:** 10-5 Tues.-Sat. (also to 9 p.m. Tues. and Thurs.), 12-5 Sun.; closed Mon. and national holidays. **Admission:** adults, $6; seniors and military, $4; students, $3; children 1-5, $1; children under 1, free; free 4-9 p.m. Tues.

GEORGE D. AND HARRIET W. CORNELL FINE ARTS MUSEUM. Alumnus George D. Cornell and his wife, Harriet W. Cornell, who became an honorary graduate, gave a major gift to Rollins College in Winter Park, Florida, in 1976 to expand the college art museum. Because of the support, the museum was named the George D. and Harriet W. Cornell Fine Arts Museum. The museum has a collection of over 6,000 objects, with holdings of European and American paintings, sculpture, and decorative arts.

George D. and Harriet W. Cornell Fine Arts Museum, Rollins College, 1000 Holt Ave., Winter Park, FL 32789-4499. **Phone:** 407/646-2526. **Fax:** 407/646-2524. **E-mail:** ablumenthal@rollins.edu. **Website:** www.rollins.edu/cfa/. **Hours:** 10-5 Tues.-Fri., 1-5 Sat.-Sun.; closed Mon. and major holidays. **Admission:** free.

HIBEL MUSEUM OF ART. The Hibel Museum of Art in Lake Worth, Florida, is devoted to the paintings, lithographs, porcelains, and limited-edition plates of artist Edna Hibel. The museum was founded in Palm Beach in 1977, moved to Lake Worth in 1999, and became part of Florida Atlantic University in Jupiter in 2002.

Hibel Museum of Art, 701 Lake Ave., Lake Worth, FL 33460. **Phone:** 561/622-1380. **Fax:** 561/622-3475. **Website:** www.hibel.org. **Hours:** 10-5 Tues.-Sat., 1-5 Sun.; closed Mon., New Year's Day, Thanksgiving, and Christmas. **Admission:** free.

JOHN AND MABLE RINGLING MUSEUM OF ART. The John and Mable Ringling Museum of Art, founded and built by the couple with funds from the nation's largest circus (Ringling Bros. and Barnum & Bailey), is housed in an Italian Renaissance–style palace in Sarasota, Florida, and features one of the nation's finest Baroque collections.

John Ringling, the youngest of five brothers, became interested in real estate and developing an art museum after Sarasota became the winter quarters for the circus in the 1920s. In 1930 he and his wife opened the grandiose museum, featuring wings that enclosed a long formal garden court and an 18-foot bronze replica of Michelangelo's *David*.

When Ringling died in 1936, the museum underwent ten years of litigation before the estate was settled and the museum reopened in 1947. It was then transformed into a major public art museum under the direction of A. Everett Austin, former head of the Wadsworth Atheneum in Hartford, Connecticut. It now features large canvases of Baroque painters—mostly of religious, mythological, and historical subjects—reminiscent of European museums. The museum also has collections of other European and American paintings, sculpture, prints, drawings, decorative arts, and photographs and archaeological materials from Cyprus and the ancient Mediterranean region.

Museum admission also includes entrance to Cà d'Zan, a 30-room mansion resembling a Venetian palace on Sarasota Bay that was the Ringlings' winter residence, and the Museum of the Circus, consisting of gilded parade wagons, calliopes, costumes, posters, photographs, circus memorabilia, and changing exhibitions.

John and Mable Ringling Museum of Art, 5401 Bay Shore Rd., Sarasota, FL 34243. Phone: 941/359-5700. Fax: 941/359-5745. E-mail: info@ringling.org. Website: www.ringling.org. Hours: 10-5:30 daily; closed New Year's Day, Thanksgiving, and Christmas. Admission: grounds—free; museum (including Cà d'Zan and Museum of the Circus)—adults, $15; seniors, $12; children under 12, free.

NAPLES MUSEUM OF ART. Myra Janco Daniels, the chairperson, president, and chief executive officer of the Philharmonic Center for the Arts in Naples, Florida, is the founder of the organization's subsidiary Naples Museum of Art and holds the same positions with it. Opened in 2000 on the center's campus, the three-story museum is the only full-scale art museum in southwest Florida. It has collections of 1900–1950 American modern art, Chinese art and artifacts, and photography; a sculpture garden; and fifteen galleries with permanent exhibits and changing exhibitions. The museum furthers the Philharmonic Center's mission of presenting visual and performing arts in a single complex.

Naples Museum of Art, Philharmonic Center for the Arts, 5833 Pelican Bay Blvd., Naples, FL 34108. Phone: 941/597-1900. Fax: 941/597-8163. E-mail: museum@naplesphilcenter.org. Website: www.naplesphilcenter.org. Hours: Oct.-June—10-4 Tues.-Sat., 1-4 Sun.; closed Mon. and remainder of year. Admission: adults, $6; students, $3.

NORTON MUSEUM OF ART. The Norton Museum of Art in West Palm Beach, Florida, was founded in 1940 by Ralph Norton and his wife, Elizabeth Calhoun Norton, a retired Chicago couple who wanted to provide their new community with important cultural access.

The Nortons commissioned architect Marion Wyeth to design a museum building in a parklike setting, and sculptor Paul Manship to create a frieze across the main facade and great bronze sculptures of *Diana* and *Actaeon*. The Nortons' gift also included major works of art by Impressionist and modern masters, and pieces by leading American artists and sculptors.

Among the artists now represented in the museum's collections and exhibits are Gauguin, Picasso, Cézanne, Matisse, Monet, DeChirico, Brancusi, Chagall, O'Keeffe, Bellows, Hassam, Motherwell, Hooper, and Henri. Other works at the museum include Asian art, Renaissance and Baroque art, eighteenth-century English portraits, contemporary art, watercolors, drawings, and photographs. Works by Picasso and Degas are among those in the sculpture patio.

Norton Museum of Art, 1451 S. Olive Ave., West Palm Beach, FL 33401. Phone: 561/832-5196. Fax: 561/832-6529. E-mail: wattickj@norton.org. Website: www.norton.org. Hours: 10-5 Mon.-Sat., 1-5 Sun.; closed Mon. in summer and major holidays. Admission: adults, $6; students 13-21, $2; children under 13, free; free 1:30-5 Wed.

SALVADOR DALI MUSEUM. The Salvador Dali Museum in St. Petersburg, Florida, was initially founded by business executive A. Reynolds Morse and his wife, Eleanor Reese Morse, who donated their comprehensive collection of the Spanish artist's works.

The museum began in Cleveland, Ohio, in 1971 in a wing of Mr. Morse's firm, the IMS Company, which supplied custom accessory equipment to the plastic injection molding industry. In 1980 the collection was given to the state of Florida, and the museum was established a second time in 1982. It is now operated in St. Petersburg by a nonprofit organization. The 34,000-square-foot museum has one of the largest collections of Dali works, including his early Impressionist-style paintings and melting clocks, double images and other paintings, sculptures, holograms, and art glass.

Salvador Dali Museum, 1000 3rd St. S., St. Petersburg, FL 33701-4925. Phone: 727/823-3767. Fax: 727/823-8532. E-mail: info@salvadordalimuseum.org. Website: www.salvadordalimuseum.org. Hours: 9:30-5:30 Mon.-Sat. (also to 8 p.m. Thurs.); 12-5:30 Sun.; closed Thanksgiving and Christmas. Admission: adults, $10; seniors, $7; students, $5; children under 10, free.

Georgia

HIGH MUSEUM OF ART. The High Museum of Art in Atlanta, Georgia, was founded in 1926 in the home donated by Hattie High, wife of merchant Joseph Madison High, to the Atlanta Art Association. The museum now occupies a four-story building and is part of the Robert W. Woodruff Arts Center.

Paintings by American artists highlight the museum's collections, which include western art from the early Renaissance to the present, eighteenth- to early-twentieth-century American decorative arts, eighteenth-century European ceramics, graphics, sculpture, and sub-Saharan and African-style objects. Among the exhibits are fourteenth- through eighteenth-century Italian art, nineteenth-century French art, nineteenth-century through contemporary American art, African art, decorative arts, prints, and photographs.

The museum also operates the High Museum of Art: Folk Art and Photography Galleries, a satellite facility in the Georgia Pacific Building, which presents changing folk art and photography exhibitions.

High Museum of Art, 1280 Peachtree St. N.E., Atlanta, GA 30309. Phones: 404/733-4400 and 404/733-4444. Fax: 404/733-4538. Website: www.high.org. Hours: 10-5 Tues.-Sat., 12-5 Sun.; closed Mon., New Year's Day, Fourth of July, Thanksgiving, and Christmas. Admission: adults, $8; seniors, $6; children 6-17, $4; children under 6, free; free 1-5 Thurs.

Hawaii

TENNENT ART FOUNDATION GALLERY. The Tennant Art Foundation Gallery in Honolulu, Hawaii, houses the oils, watercolors, and drawings of Madge Tennent, a longtime resident known for her portrayal of Hawaiian women.

Tennant Art Foundation Gallery, 203 Prospect St., Honolulu, HI 96813. Phone: 808/531-1987. Hours: 10-12 Tues.-Sat., 2-4 Sun.; other times by appointment; closed Thanksgiving and Christmas. Admission: free.

Illinois

KRANNERT ART MUSEUM. The Krannert Art Museum at the University of Illinois at Urbana-Champaign is named for Indianapolis industrialist Herman Krannert and his wife, Ellnora Krannert, who gave the funds for the founding building and made a $1 million gift for art purchases for the museum, which opened in 1961.

The university began its art collections in 1872 by buying plaster casts of ancient statuary in Paris. It was followed by contemporary paintings and Beau Arts sculpture in the 1920s. But the impetus for a "fine arts" museum came in 1937, when Merle and Emily Trees, a Chicago businessman and his wife, gave the university an important group of Old Masters paintings—the first in a series of gifts. Many other traditional and contemporary artworks were added before the opening of the museum and in the years that followed. In the late 1980s William S. Kinkead donated a collection of graphic art by Henri de Toulouse-Lautrec and an addition called the Kinkead Pavilion.

The 48,000-square-foot museum now houses more than 8,000 works from 4000 B.C. to the present, including early art from Greece, Iran, and Egypt; European and American paintings from the late fifteenth to early twentieth centuries; medieval and Near Eastern paintings; Asian art; contemporary art; and sculpture, prints, drawings, glassware, ceramics, and photographs.

Krannert Art Museum, University of Illinois at Urbana-Champaign, 500 E. Peabody Dr., Champaign, IL 61820. Phone: 217/333-1861. Fax: 217/333-0883. Website: www.art.uiuc.edu/kam/. Hours: Sept.-May—10-5 Mon.-Sat. (also to 8 p.m. Wed.), 2-5 Sun.; June-Aug.—10-5 Mon.-Sat., 2-5 Sun.; closed major holidays. Admission: free.

MARY AND LEIGH BLOCK MUSEUM OF ART. The Mary and Leigh Block Museum of Art at Northwestern University in Evanston, Illinois, evolved from the Mary and Leigh Block Gallery founded by the Chicago couple in 1980. The museum, which began with a wide range of experimental and educational visual art exhibitions, has collections of fifteenth- to twentieth-century European prints and drawings, contemporary prints and photographs, and architectural drawings, and an outdoor sculpture garden with monumental works by such modernists as Jean Arp, Joan Miró, Henry Moore, Barbara Hepworth, and Jacques Lipchitz.

Mary and Leigh Block Museum of Art, Northwestern University, 1967 S. Campus Dr., Evanston, IL 60208-2410. **Phone:** 847/491-4001. **Fax:** 847/491-2261. **E-mail:** blockmuseum@nwu.edu. **Website:** www.nwu.edu/museum. **Hours:** Sept.-May—12-5 Tues.-Sun. (also to 8 p.m. Thurs.-Sun.); closed Mon. and major holidays; June-Aug.—12-4 Tues.-Sat.; closed Sun.-Mon. **Admission:** free.

ROCKFORD ART MUSEUM. The Rockford Art Museum in Riverfront Park in Rockford, Illinois, was formerly the Harry and Della Burpee Art Gallery, started by a local undertaker and his wife, who also founded the Burpee Museum of Natural History (see Natural History Museums). The museum has collections of nineteenth- and twentieth-century American and European paintings; works by American Impressionists and the Taos Society of Artists; African American folk art; sculpture; graphics; decorative arts; and photographs.

Rockford Art Museum, 711 N. Main St., Rockford, IL 61103-6999. **Phone:** 815/968-2787. **Fax:** 815/968-0164. **E-mail:** staff@rockfordartmuseum.com. **Website:** www.rockfordartmuseum.com. **Hours:** 11-5 Tues.-Fri., 10-5 Sat., 12-5 Sun.; closed Mon. and national holidays. **Admission:** free.

Iowa

BLANDEN MEMORIAL ART MUSEUM. The Blanden Memorial Art Museum in Fort Dodge, Iowa, is dedicated to the late Elizabeth Mills Blanden, a popular high school teacher. The memorial was created in 1930 by her husband, former mayor Charles Granger Blanden, who also donated the first 26 artworks for the museum. The city museum's collections and exhibits now include American and European paintings and sculpture, Japanese prints, Asian art, pre-Columbian and African artifacts, and contemporary works from the Midwest.

Blanden Memorial Art Museum, 920 3rd St. S., Fort Dodge, IA 50501. **Phone:** 515/573-2316. **Fax:** 515/573-2317. **E-mail:** blanden@dodgenet.com. **Website:** www.dodgenet.com/blanden. **Hours:** 10-5 Tues.-Fri. (also to 8:30 p.m. Thurs.), 1-5 Sat.-Sun.; closed Mon. and major holidays. **Admission:** free.

BRUNNIER ART MUSEUM. The Brunnier Art Museum at Iowa State University in Ames began in 1975, following the gift of more than 10,000 decorative arts and dolls from Ann Brunnier and her husband, Henry J. Brunnier, an alumnus and noted civil engineer. The museum, now part of the University Museums system, has collections of glassware, ceramics, enamels, snuffboxes, carved ivories, jade figurines and bowls, and dolls from throughout the world, as well as paintings by leading Iowa artists and Japanese prints from the nineteenth and twentieth centuries.

Brunnier Art Museum, Iowa State University, 290 Scheman Bldg., Ames, IA 50011. **Phone:** 515/294-3342. **Fax:** 515/294-7070. **E-mail:** museum@adp.iastate.edu. **Website:** www.museums.iastate.edu. **Hours:** 11-4 Mon.-Fri., 1-4 Sat.-Sun.; closed major holidays. **Admission:** free.

MUSCATINE ART CENTER. The Muscatine Art Center in Muscatine, Iowa, consists of two parts—the Laura Musser Museum, featuring decorative arts from the former Musser Home and selections from a permanent art collection, and the Stanley Gallery, which houses changing exhibitions and studio art classes.

The 1908 Edwardian-style Musser home was established as a museum in a 1965 gift from Laura Musser's daughters and heirs, Mary Catherine McWhirter and Mary Musser Gilmore, who also donated a major art collection. The Stanley Gallery was added in 1976 by C. Maxwell and Elizabeth Stanley.

The decorative arts collection includes paperweights, oriental carpets, American art pottery, and furniture, while the artworks range from works by Grant Wood, Mauricio Lasansky, John Mix Stanley, Georgia O'Keeffe, and Allan Houser, to such European masters as Matisse, Degas, Boudin, Chagall, and Renoir. The art center also has a collection of paintings, drawings, prints, and maps documenting the Mississippi River.

Muscatine Art Center, 1314 Mulberry Ave., Muscatine, IA 52761. **Phone:** 319/263-8282. **Fax:** 319/263-4702. **E-mail:** art@muscanet.com. **Website:** www.muscatineartcenter.org. **Hours:** 10-5 Tues.-Fri. (also 7-9 p.m. Thurs.); 1-5 Sat.-Sun.; closed Mon. and major holidays. **Admission:** free.

Kansas

MARIANNA KISTLER BEACH MUSEUM OF ART. In commemoration of their fiftieth wedding anniversary, Ross Beach, an alumnus, businessman, and philanthropist, gave the lead gift on behalf of the couple for the Marianna Kistler Beach Museum, named in his wife's honor, at Kansas State University in

Manhattan. Mrs. Beach is also a graduate of the university.

The 28,000-square-foot museum, opened in 1996, consolidated the university's collection of art, previously displayed throughout the campus. The collection features twentieth-century prints and other artworks by artists in Kansas and the Mountain-Plains region, including the works of such artists as Thomas Hart Benton, John Steuart Curray, Birger Sandzen, and Grant Wood.

Marianna Kistler Beach Museum of Art, Kansas State University, 701 Beach Lane, Manhattan, KS 66506. **Phone:** 785/532-7718. **Fax:** 785/532-7498. **E-mail:** 1render @ksu.edu. **Website:** www.ksu.edu/bma. **Hours:** 10-5 Tues.-Sat. (also to 8:30 p.m. Thurs.), 1-5 Sun; closed Mon. and major holidays. **Admission:** free.

SPENCER MUSEUM OF ART. The University of Kansas Museum of Art in Lawrence began in Spooner Hall in 1928—ten years after Sallie Casey Thayer, an art collector who had gathered paintings and decorative arts from throughout the world, gave her eclectic collection of approximately 9,000 objects to the university. A half century later, it was renamed the Spencer Museum of Art for Helen Foresman Spencer, who provided the major funding for a new neoclassical building.

Spencer and her husband, Kenneth, were Kansas City alumni who became generous supporters of the university. The Kenneth Spencer Research Library, a separate facility, is named for him. The museum building also houses the art history department and a 90,000-volume library of art and architecture.

The museum's collections include medieval sculpture, early Renaissance paintings, German and Austrian Baroque works, nineteenth-century paintings, Old Masters prints, decorative arts, textiles, Japanese Edo-period works, Japanese woodblock prints, modern Chinese paintings, Korean ceramics, and contemporary art. In addition to showing selections from the collections, the museum presents changing exhibitions of prints, drawings, and photographs.

Spencer Museum of Art, University of Kansas, 1301 Mississippi St., Lawrence, KS 60045-7500. **Phone:** 785/864-4710. **Fax:** 785/864-3112. **E-mail:** spencerart@ku.edu. **Website:** www.ukans.edu/~sma. **Hours:** 10-5 Tues.-Sat. (also to 9 p.m. Thurs.), 12-5 Sun.; closed Mon., New Year's Day, Fourth of July, Thanksgiving and following day, and Christmas Eve and Day. **Admission:** suggested donation—$3.

Kentucky

YEISER ART CENTER. The Yeiser Art Center in Paducah, Kentucky, is named for Mary Yeiser, a local artist and art teacher who founded the Paducah Art Guild in 1957. The guild found a permanent home for its exhibitions and other activities in 1963 at the 1905 Market House, which was built by Yeiser's grandfather. In 1990 the guild changed its name to the Yeiser Art Center to honor its founder and to better reflect its mission—to present exhibitions, lectures, classes, films, and gallery talks about the creation, appreciation, and preservation of the visual arts.

Yeiser Art Center, 200 Broadway, Paducah, KY 42001-0732. **Phone:** 270/442-2453. **E-mail:** yacenter@apex.net. **Website:** www.yeiser.org. **Hours:** 10-4 Tues.-Sat.; closed Sun.-Mon. and major holidays. **Admission:** $1 per person.

Maine

PORTLAND MUSEUM OF ART. The Portland Museum of Art, Maine's largest public museum, was founded in 1882 by the former Portland Society of Art, but it received an early impetus from writer Margaret Jane Mussey Sweat at the turn of the twentieth century. In 1911 the museum moved into the McLellan House, a Federal-era mansion donated by Sweat, who also provided funds for a Beaux-Arts gallery dedicated to her husband, Lorenzo de Medici Sweat, a Maine senator during the Civil War era.

The museum is currently housed in a new building, but the recently restored 1800 mansion—now known as the McLellan-Sweat House—is attached and is still used to display art, as is the memorial gallery. Among Mrs. Sweat's writings is *Ethel's Love Life*, which has been called the nation's "first sapphic novel" by Folger Library. The museum features the Joan Whitney Payson Collection of Renoir, Degas, Monet, and Picasso works; Maine art by Homer, Wyeth, and Harley; and eighteenth- and nineteenth-century European and American artworks.

Portland Museum of Art, 7 Congress Sq., Portland, ME 04101. **Phone:** 207/775-6148. **Fax:** 207/773-7324. **E-mail:** pma@maine.it.com. **Website:** www.portlandmuseum.org. **Hours:** 10-5 Tues.-Sun. (also to 9 p.m. Thurs.-Fri.); closed Mon. (but open 10-5 Mon. from Memorial Day to Columbus Day), New Year's Day, Thanksgiving, and Christmas. **Admission:** adults, $10; seniors and students under 18, $9; children 5-18, $6; children under 5, free.

Maryland

AMERICAN VISIONARY ART MUSEUM. The American Visionary Art Museum, dedicated to self-taught, intuitive art, was conceived by Rebecca Hoffberger, who still serves as the museum's president. Opened in 1995, the museum is located in a combination 1913 former paint company building and new structure at Baltimore's Inner Harbor. It has approximately 4,000 works in its collections, ranging from mixed media assemblages, textiles, and works on paper to the 55-foot-high *Whirligig* in an outdoor plaza. It presents changing exhibitions from the collections.

American Visionary Art Museum, 800 Key Hwy., Baltimore, MD 21230. **Phone:** 410/244-1900. **Fax:** 410/244-5858. **Website:** www.avam.org/stuff/whois.html. **Hours:** 10-6 Tues.-Sun.; closed Mon., Thanksgiving, and Christmas. **Admission:** adults, $6; seniors and children 5-17, $4; children under 5, free.

Massachusetts

ART COMPLEX MUSEUM. The Art Complex Museum in Duxbury, Massachusetts, opened in 1971 as a center for regional arts and a home for the copious collection of founders Carl A. Weyerhaeuser and his wife, Edith G. Weyerhaeuser. Mr. Weyerhaeuser, grandson of the founder of the lumber company of the same name, did most of the collecting, but it was Mrs. Weyerhaeuser who initiated and saw that the museum was completed. The current museum director is their son, Charles A. Weyerhaeuser.

The couple began collecting American and European prints and then branched out to Shaker furniture, American paintings, and Asian art. The museum still has strong collections in those areas, as well as contemporary regional art. The complex also features a Japanese teahouse, in which a tea ceremony is presented in the summer, and Sunday afternoon concerts, workshops, and other special events throughout the year.

Art Complex Museum, 189 Alden St., PO Box 2814, Duxbury, MA 02331. **Phone:** 781/934-6634. **Fax:** 781/934-5117. **Website:** www.artcomplex.org. **Hours:** 1-4 Wed.-Sun.; closed Mon.-Tues. and national holidays. **Admission:** free.

DANFORTH MUSEUM OF ART. The Danforth Museum of Art, housed in a restored 1907 former high school in Framingham, Massachusetts, was founded in 1973 under the leadership of a local couple, Paul and Elaine

Marks. It became a reality with the assistance of government officials, political leaders, and Framingham State College administrators. The Danforth name was chosen to symbolize the range of area residents, who lived on what was once a huge plantation owned by Thomas Danforth. The museum largely collects and displays American art of the nineteenth through twentieth centuries.

Danforth Museum of Art, 123 Union Ave., Framingham, MA 01702. **Phone:** 508/620-0050. **Fax:** 508/872-5542. **Hours:** 12-5 Wed.-Sun.; closed Mon.-Tues. and major holidays. **Admission:** adults, $3; seniors and students, $2; children under 12, free.

FITCHBURG ART MUSEUM. Eleanor Norcross, daughter of the first mayor of Fitchburg, Massachusetts, was an artist, collector, and philanthropist who sought to inspire, educate, and improve society through cultural enrichment in the late nineteenth and early twentieth centuries.

Norcross, who was an expatriate artist in Paris for more than 30 years, initially focused on portraits, interiors, and still lifes, then shifted to works more closely related to her ideas for social betterment. The latter included making copies of works by the Old Masters and collecting art objects for a possible museum for the enlightenment of the people of Fitchburg and America—realizing that many would never have the opportunity to travel abroad.

Norcross died in 1923, but her will provided for the 1925 founding of the Fitchburg Art Museum, where her paintings and copies of the Old Masters were later featured. The will named two women friends as trustees, and they hired a firm of women architects to convert a French Provincial–style brick stable into an art museum. It now occupies three buildings and has collections of eighteenth- to twentieth-century European and American paintings, drawings, prints, and photographs; fifteenth- to twentieth-century illustrated books; pre-Columbian, ancient, Asian, and African art; and decorative arts.

Fitchburg Art Museum, 185 Elm St., Fitchburg, MA 01420. **Phone:** 978/345-4207. **Fax:** 978/345-2319. **Hours:** 12-4 Tues.-Sun.; closed Mon. and major holidays. **Admission:** adults, $5; seniors, $3; students and children, free.

FOGG ART MUSEUM. The Fogg Art Museum, the oldest of three museums that are part of the Harvard University Art Museums in Cambridge, Massachusetts, was founded in 1891 after an unexpected bequest of $220,000 from Elizabeth Fogg, who wanted to establish a museum in memory of her husband, William Hayes Fogg, "for enlightenment of the people."

When the Fogg Art Museum opened in 1895, it housed mostly reproductions. But its collections, its role at the university, and its relationship to the world at large changed over the years. Edward W. Forbes and Paul J. Sachs, known as the spiritual founders of the art museums, enunciated the ideal of the Fogg as a "laboratory for the Fine Arts" and advocated using "original art works of the highest quality" for teaching the young about art. Their three-part program included the training of professionals in the new field of art museum administration, providing resources for the teaching of college and university teachers in art history, and exposing undergraduates to the importance of art in all human cultures.

In 1927 the museum moved to its present location, a neo-Georgian building with an interior courtyard modeled on a sixteenth-century Italian palazzo. Today, the Fogg contains significant European and American art from the Middle Ages to the present, with particular strengths in Italian, British, and French art. Its collections are part of the more than 150,000 objects in all media in the Harvard University Art Museums, which also include the Busch-Reisinger Museum and Arthur M. Sackler Museum, comprising one of the leading art centers in the world.

The Fogg Art Museum also houses the Fine Arts Library, which has a major research collection and more than 1 million photographs and slides of works of art; the Straus Center for Conservation, founded in 1928 and now the oldest fine arts conservation treatment, research, and training facility in the nation; and the Agnes Mongan Center for the Study of Prints, Drawings, and Photographs, which opened in 1994 and has approximately 60,000 prints, 12,000 drawings, and 8,000 photographs from the fourteenth century to the present. The latter, coincident with the Philip and Lynn Straus Gallery for works of art on paper, reemphasizes the Fogg's original purpose of bringing academic, curatorial, and library resources within close proximity in the service of art historical research.

Fogg Art Museum, Harvard University Art Museums, 32 Quincy St., Cambridge, MA 02138. **Phone:** 717/495-9400. **Fax:** 617/495-9936. **E-mail:** huam@harvard.edu. **Website:** www.artmuseum.harvard.edu. **Hours:** 10-5 Mon.-Sat., 1-5 Sun.; closed national holidays. **Admission:** adults, $5; seniors, $4; college students, $3; Harvard students and children under 18, free; free Wed. and 10-12 Sat.

ISABELLA STEWART GARDNER MUSEUM. See Museums Honoring Exceptional Women.

LONGWELL MUSEUM. See Art and History Museums.

ROSE ART MUSEUM. The Rose Art Museum at Brandeis University in Waltham, Massachusetts, was a 1960 gift of mattress manufacturer Edward Rose and his wife, Bertha Rose. A glass and concrete building was built to house artworks that had been accumulating at the university since it opened in 1948. Twentieth-century American and European paintings and sculpture are now featured among the more than 9,000 works in the museum's collections, which also include Tibetan, Oceanic, Japanese, pre-Columbian, African, Native American, and other art. The museum is also responsible for sculptures throughout the university grounds.

Rose Art Museum, Brandeis University, 415 South St., PO Box 9110, Mail Stop 069, Waltham, MA 02254-9110. **Phone:** 781/736-3434. **Fax:** 781/736-3439. **Website:** www.brandeis.edu/rose. **Hours:** 12-5 Tues.-Sun. (also to 9 p.m. Thurs.); closed Mon. and major holidays. **Admission:** free.

STERLING AND FRANCINE CLARK ART INSTITUTE. The Sterling and Francine Clark Art Institute in Williamstown, Massachusetts, was opened in 1955 by sewing machine heir Robert Sterling Clark and his French-born wife, Francine Clark. The museum was built upon the couple's personal collection of French Impressionist art, nineteenth-century American paintings, Italian and Northern Renaissance masterpieces, and other works.

The museum has more than 30 paintings by Pierre-Auguste Renoir, as well as works by such other Impressionists as Claude Monet, Edgar Degas, and Camille Pisarro. Among its American paintings are works by Winslow Homer, John Singer Sargent, Frederic Remington, and Mary Cassatt. The museum also has European portraits and landscapes, salon paintings and sculptures, exceptional decorative arts, and changing exhibitions of prints, drawings, pastels, watercolors, and photography.

The Clark Art Institute is also an international center for research and discussion on all aspects of the visual arts. It has a library of over 200,000 volumes and extensive multimedia resources and brings together leading figures to present their ideas about the theory, history, and interpretation of art in fellowships, conferences, symposia, and lectures.

Sterling and Francine Clark Art Institute, 225 South St., PO Box 8, Williamstown, MA 01267. **Phone:** 413/458-9545. **Fax:** 413/458-2318. **E-mail:** info@clark.williams.edu. **Website:** www.clark.williams.edu. **Hours:** Sept.-June—10-5 Tues.-Sun.; closed Mon., New Year's Day, Thanksgiving, and Christmas; July-Aug.—10-5 Sun.-Fri., 10-7 Sat. **Admission:** adults, $10; children under 18, free.

Michigan

CRANBROOK ART MUSEUM. The Cranbrook Art Museum in Bloomfield Hills, Michigan, is part of the Cranbrook Educational Community founded by newspaper publisher George G. Booth and his wife, Ellen Scripps Booth. The museum is an affiliate of the Cranbrook Academy of Art. The unique educational community also includes lower, middle, and upper schools and the Cranbrook Institute of Science (see Natural History Museums). The Booths' 1908 historic home and gardens are also on the grounds (see Historic House Museums).

Founded in 1927, the Cranbrook Art Museum is a contemporary art museum that depicts Cranbrook's influence on the worlds of twentieth-century art, architecture, and design through the work of its faculty and student artists, and presents changing exhibitions that are a continuing commentary on society and the world. The museum's collections include nineteenth- and twentieth-century prints and ceramics and twentieth-century architectural drawings, ceramics, furniture, metalwork, paintings, sculpture, and textiles.

Also located on the grounds are the bronze sculptures of Swedish sculptor Carl Milles and the 1930 home and studio of noted Finnish architect Eliel Saarinen and his wife, Loja. Saarinen designed many of the Cranbrook buildings and was the first president of the Cranbrook Academy of Art, in 1932–1948.

Cranbrook Art Museum, 39221 N. Woodward Ave., PO Box 801, Bloomfield Hills, MI 48303-0801. **Phone:** 248/645-3361. **Fax:** 248/645-3324. **E-mail:** artmuseum@cranbrook.edu. **Website:** www.cranbrook.edu. **Hours:** Sept.-May—11-5 Tues.-Sun. (also to 8 p.m. Thurs.); June-Aug.—11-5 Tues.-Sun. (also to 10 p.m. Fri.); closed Mon. and major holidays. **Admission:** adults, $7; seniors and students, $5; children under 8, free.

KALAMAZOO INSTITUTE OF ARTS. The Kalamazoo Institute of Arts in Kalamazoo, Michigan, is housed in a 1961 building funded by donors Genevieve and Donald Gilmore that was remodeled and expanded in 1998. Founded in 1924, the museum has an art school and collections of nineteenth- and twentieth-century American art, twentieth-century European art, and fifteenth- to twentieth-century graphics, as well as works on paper, ceramics, sculpture, and photography. Selections from the collections are displayed in half of the museum's ten galleries, with changing exhibitions in the others.

Kalamazoo Institute of Arts, 314 S. Park St., Kalamazoo, MI 49007-5102. **Phone:** 616/349-7775. **Fax:** 616/349-9313. **E-mail:** kiadev@iserv.net. **Website:** www.kiarts.org. **Hours:** 10-5 Tues.-Sat. (also to 8 p.m. Thurs.), 12-5 Sun.; closed Mon. and major holidays. **Admission:** free.

Minnesota

TWEED MUSEUM OF ART. The Tweed Museum of Art at the University of Minnesota at Duluth was founded by businessman George P. Tweed and his wife, Alice Tweed, in 1950. Mrs. Tweed's foundation—the Alice Tweed Tuohy Foundation—continues to provide support for the museum. The museum began as the Tweed Gallery in the Tweed mansion and then moved into its present building, which was constructed in three stages in 1958, 1965, and 1977. The building and a major portion of the permanent collection were gifts of the Tweed family. The museum has a large number of French Barbizon paintings, as well as collections of nineteenth- and twentieth-century American paintings, prints, and sculpture; modern and contemporary works; and paintings and illustrations of the Royal Canadian Mounted Police.

Tweed Museum of Art, University of Minnesota, Duluth, 10 University Dr., Duluth, MN 55812. **Phones:** 218/726-8222 and 218/726-7823. **Fax:** 218/726-8503. **E-mail:** tma@d.umn.edu. **Website:** www.d.umn.edu/tma/. **Hours:** 9-4:30 Tues.-Fri. (also to 8 p.m. Tues.), 1-5 Sat.-Sun.; closed Mon. and national holidays. **Admission:** suggested donations—adults, $3; children, $1; families, $5.

Mississippi

KATE FREEMAN CLARK ART GALLERY. The Kate Freeman Clark Art Gallery in Holly Springs, Mississippi, has one of the largest collections of paintings by a single artist. Approximately 1,500 works by the late 1800s–early 1900s American Impressionist are housed in the museum adjacent to her 1837 former home.

Kate Freeman Clark Art Gallery, 300 E. College Ave., Holly Springs, MS 38635. **Phone:** 662/252-4211. **E-mail:** bgreen@dixie-net.com. **Hours:** by appointment. **Admission:** $2 donation.

OHR-O'KEEFE MUSEUM OF ART. The Ohr-O'Keefe Museum of Art in Biloxi, Mississippi, is named for George E. Ohr, an eccentric local potter, and Annette O'Keefe, the late wife of Jerry O'Keefe, the museum's leading benefactor. The museum, founded in 1989 and renamed in 1994, features the largest public collection of Ohr's wonderful and sometimes odd ceramic pots from the second half of the nineteenth century.

Ohr-O'Keefe Museum of Art, 136 G. E. Ohr St., Biloxi, MS 39530. **Phone:** 228/374-5547. **Fax:** 228/432-0422. **E-mail:** mgowdy@datasyn.com. **Website:** www.georgeohe.com. **Hours:** 9-5 Mon.-Sat.; closed Sun., New Year's Day, Fourth of July, Thanksgiving, and Christmas. **Admission:** adults, $3; seniors, $2; children under 12, free.

Missouri

KEMPER MUSEUM OF CONTEMPORARY ART. The Kemper Museum of Contemporary Art in Kansas City, Missouri, resulted from a 1990 gift of $6.6 million to the Kansas City Art Institute, an art and design school with which the museum is affiliated, by banker R. Crosby Kemper and his wife, Bebe, through the Kemper family foundations.

Mr. Kemper, chairman and chief executive officer of UMB Financial Corporation, also helped establish the Charlotte Crosby Kemper Gallery in honor of his mother, together with her other sons and grandson, at the art institute in 1963. She was an avid art collector who was instrumental in bringing visiting artists to the school. The gallery presented the works of significant contemporary artists for more than 30 years.

The Kemper Museum of Contemporary Art has a permanent collection of more than 700 works, including paintings, sculpture, drawings, prints, photographs, textiles, ceramics, videos, designs, and illustration. The core of the collection is the Bebe and Crosby Kemper Collection, with works by such artists as Jasper Johns, Georgia O'Keeffe, Helen Frankenthaler, Robert Rauschenberg, David Hockney, Frank Stella, and Robert Motherwell.

Kemper Museum of Contemporary Art, 4420 Warwick Blvd., Kansas City, MO 64111. **Phone:** 816/753-5784.

Fax: 816/753-5806. **E-mail:** info@kemperart.org. **Website:** www.kemperart.org. **Hours:** 10-4 Tues.-Fri. (also to 9 p.m. Fri.), 10-9 Sat., 11-5 Sun.; closed Mon., New Year's Day, Fourth of July, Thanksgiving, and Christmas. **Admission:** free.

MARGARET HARWELL ART MUSEUM. Margaret Harwell, a businesswoman, amateur artist, and civic leader in Poplar Bluff, Missouri, died in 1977, leaving part of her estate to the city to establish an art center for classes and exhibitions. The city formed an advisory committee, purchased an 1883 historic mansion, and opened the Margaret Harwell Art Museum in 1981. The museum has collections of mid-nineteenth-century costumes and textiles and contemporary art and presents changing exhibitions by regional and national artists.

Margaret Harwell Art Museum, 421 N. Main St., Poplar Bluff, MO 63901. **Phone:** 573/686-8002. **Fax:** 573/686-8017. **E-mail:** tina@mham.org. **Web site:** www.mham.org. **Hours:** 12-4 Tues.-Fri., 1-4 Sat.-Sun.; closed Mon. and national holidays. **Admission:** free.

NELSON-ATKINS MUSEUM OF ART. William Rockhill Nelson, the flamboyant owner of the *Kansas City Star*, sought to bring significant works of art to the people of the region. His fortune endowed the collection of the Nelson-Atkins Museum of Art, and his family built its neoclassical building with the estate of Mary McAfee Atkins, who died in 1911 and left $300,000 for the erection of a museum of fine arts.

The museum, which opened in 1933 as the William Rockhill Nelson Gallery of Art and Atkins Museum of Fine Arts, shortened its name in 1982. Nelson family members who contributed to the construction of the building included Laura Nelson Kirkwood, $1.2 million; Ida Houston Nelson, $850,000; and Irwin Kirkwood, $250,000. Frank F. Rozzelle, the Nelson family lawyer, also bequeathed $150,000 for the planned museum when he died in 1923. Atkins was a former schoolteacher and the widow of a wealthy Kansas City real estate speculator who became interested in funding a fine arts museum after visiting many of the art treasures in Europe.

The Nelson-Atkins Museum of Art has more than 20,000 works in its collections, 58 galleries, 11 period rooms, and a 17-acre outdoor sculpture garden, featuring 12 monumental bronzes by English sculptor Henry Moore. The museum is best known for its outstanding Asian collection but also has prestigious collections of

European and American art, as well as galleries devoted to such areas as furniture, porcelain, scroll paintings, sculpture, glazed T'ang dynasty tomb figures, contemporary art, and the arts of Africa, Oceania, and the Americas. Among the European paintings in the collection are Northern Renaissance works, early Italian Renaissance art, Venetian paintings, French works, and English art, supplemented by a Georgian period room. The Americas galleries are also adjoined by a series of period rooms.

Nelson-Atkins Museum of Art, 4525 Oak St., Kansas City, MO 64111. **Phone:** 816/561-4000. **Fax:** 816/561-7154. **Website:** www.nelson-atkins.org. **Hours:** 10-4 Tues.-Fri. (also to 9 p.m. Fri.), 10-5 Sat., 12-5 Sun.; closed Mon. and major holidays. **Admission:** free.

The Pulitzer Foundation for the Arts in St. Louis is housed in this striking building designed by Japanese architect Tadao Ando. The facility is a combination art museum and study center founded by Emily Rauh Pulitzer, widow of newspaper publisher Joseph R. Pulitzer Jr. Courtesy Pulitzer Foundation for the Arts and photographer Robert Pettus.

PULITZER FOUNDATION FOR THE ARTS. The Pulitzer Foundation for the Arts—primarily a study center for art and architecture students rather than a museum—houses a collection of modern and contemporary art on loan from founder Emily Rauh Pulitzer and her late husband, Joseph R. Pulitzer Jr. of the Pulitzer newspaper family.

The foundation owns only three works of art—one each by Ellsworth Kelly, Richard Serra, and Doris Salcedo—and has no plans to acquire more. Among the pieces from the Pulitzer collection on display are works ranging from Monet, Picasso, Braque, and Maillol to Mark Rothko, Philip Guston, Andy Warhol, and Roy Lichtenstein. None of the works have labels. The galleries, which are free, are open only on Wednesdays and Saturdays. Reservations are required for groups of five or more.

Pulitzer Foundation for the Arts, 3716 Washington Blvd., St. Louis, MO 36108. **Phones:** 314/754-1850 and 314/754-1848. **Fax:** 314/754-1851. **E-mail:** info@pulitzerarts.org. **Website:** www.pulitzerarts.org. **Hours:** 1-7 Wed. and 11-4 Sat.; closed Sun.-Tues., Thurs.-Fri., and major holidays. **Admission:** free.

Nebraska

GREAT PLAINS ART COLLECTION. The Great Plains Art Collection at the University of Nebraska in Lincoln began in 1981 after Dr. John M. Christlieb and his wife, Elizabeth B. Christlieb, of Bellevue donated their collection of western art, a library of western Americana, and an endowment to care for the collection.

The collection—part of the Center for Great Plains Studies—has more than 1,400 paintings, sculptures, graphics, and photographs pertaining to the art and artists of the Great Plains region. The Christlieb gift of 175 bronzes, 160 paintings, 300 works of art on paper, and a 2,000-volume library forms the core of the collection, which has been enhanced by other contributions.

The collection now has the largest known collections of bronzes by Charles M. Russell (74) and Carl Kauba (17), as well as others by such artists as Frederic Remington, Charles Schreyvogel, Gutzon Borglum, and contemporary sculptor Harry Jackson. The paintings and works on paper encompass works by such artists as Albert Bierstadt, Karl Bodmer, George Catlin, John Clymer, Frank Tenney Johnson, and Olaf Wieghorst. A large number of photographs by William Henry Jackson are also in the collection.

Great Plains Art Collection, University of Nebraska, Center for Great Plains Studies, 1155 Q St., Lincoln, NE 68588-0214. **Phone:** 402/472-6220. **Fax:** 402/472-2960. **E-mail:** asharong@unlserve.ul.edu. **Website:** www.unl.edu/plains. **Hours:** 10-5 Tues.-Sat., 1:30-5 Sun.; closed Mon. and major holidays. **Admission:** free.

JOSLYN ART MUSEUM. In 1928 Sarah H. Joslyn, widow of George A. Joslyn, businessman, civic leader, and the wealthiest man in Nebraska, gave over $3 million in his memory to found the Joslyn Art Museum in Omaha. Located in a stunning Art Deco building, the museum opened in 1931 and was expanded in 1994 to 213,000 square feet—making it the largest art museum in the region.

The museum is noted for its outstanding collection of art from the American West. It features Swiss artist Karl Bodmer's watercolors and prints, which document his 1832–1834 journey to the Missouri River frontier with German naturalist Prince Maximilian (whose three-volume diary on the expedition is also at the museum); a significant body of work by Alfred Jacob Miller that portrays his experiences in the West in the 1830s; and paintings, sculpture, and photographs by George Catlin, George Caleb Bingham, Frederic Remington, Edward S. Curtis, and William Robinson Leigh. The museum also has highly regarded collections of European, American, Asian, ancient, and twentieth-century art.

Joslyn Art Museum, 2200 Dodge St., Omaha, NE 68102-1292. **Phone:** 402/342-3300. **Fax:** 402/342-2376. **E-mail:** info@joslyn.org. **Website:** www.joslyn.org. **Hours:** 10-4 Tues.-Sat., 12-4 Sun.; closed Mon. and major holidays. **Admission:** adults, $6; seniors and college students, $4; children 5-17, $3.50; children under 5, free; free 10-12 Sat.

New Jersey

JANE VOORHEES ZIMMERLI ART MUSEUM. Two women have played important roles in the recent history of the art museum at Rutgers University in New Brunswick, New Jersey. In 1982 the state university's museum was named for Jane Voorhees Zimmerli after her sons, Ralph and Alan Voorhees, made a major contribution for a new museum building. The building was expanded in 2000 with a $7 million gift from Norton and Nancy Dodge, who had earlier given the museum their collection of Soviet and Russian nonconformist art—the largest in the world, with approximately 20,000 pieces. The museum, which was founded in 1966, also has collections and exhibits of paintings, sculpture, French and other graphics, Japanese works, and illustrations for children's literature.

Jane Voorhees Zimmerli Art Museum, Rutgers University, 71 Hamilton St., New Brunswick, NJ 08901-1248. **Phone:** 732/932-7237. **Fax:** 732/932-8201. **E-mail:** cate@rci.rutgers.edu. **Website:** www.rci.rutgers.edu/zamuseum/. **Hours:** Sept.-July—10-4:30 Tues.-Fri., 12-5 Sat.-Sun.; closed Mon., Aug., and major holidays. **Admission:** adults, $3; children under 18, free.

New Mexico

GEORGIA O'KEEFFE MUSEUM. See Museums Honoring Exceptional Women.

The Agnes Martin Gallery is the newest addition to the University of New Mexico's Harwood Museum of Art in Taos. The museum, which honors artist Burt Harwood, was founded in 1923 by his wife, Elizabeth Harwood; members of the Taos Society of Artists; and others. Courtesy Harwood Museum of Art, University of New Mexico, and photographer Andrew Flack, Buzz, Inc.

HARWOOD MUSEUM OF ART OF THE UNIVERSITY OF NEW MEXICO. The Harwood Museum of Art of the University of New Mexico in Taos was founded in 1923 by Elizabeth Harwood—joined by Victor Higgins and Bert G. Phillips of the Taos Society of Artists and others—in memory of her artist husband, Burt Harwood.

Burt Harwood was a member of the now-famous Taos Society of Artists, an art colony formed in 1915 by a group of artists who were drawn to the area by New Mexico's landscape and light and the traditional Native American and Hispanic cultures of the region.

The Harwood Museum is located in the expanded former adobe home of Burt and Elizabeth Harwood. The Harwood complex was at the forefront of the Pueblo/Spanish revival and restoration movement in New Mexico, and it served as a library, museum, and educational center for Taos after Harwood's death and the establishment of the foundation.

In 1935 the Harwood Museum was given to the University of New Mexico and functioned as a base for university operations in the area. The Harwood house was renovated and expanded in 1937 and again in 1977, 1981, and 1997, during which time a library, auditorium, and additional gallery space were added. The site now has galleries devoted to the Taos Society of

Artists and early-twentieth-century artists who came to the area; a gallery and art by prominent local artist Agnes Martin; works from the mid- and late twentieth century; Hispanic traditions; prints, drawings, and photographs; and changing exhibitions.

Harwood Museum of Art of the University of New Mexico, 238 Ledoux St., Box 4080 NDCBU, Taos, NM 87571-6004. **Phone:** 505/758-9826. **Fax:** 505/758-1475. **E-mail:** harwood@unm.edu. **Website:** www.nmculture.org. **Hours:** 10-5 Tues.-Sat., 12-5 Sun.; closed Mon. and major holidays. **Admission:** adults and children over 11, $5; children under 12, free; free Sun. to New Mexico residents.

TAOS ART MUSEUM AT FECHIN HOUSE. The Taos Art Museum at Fechin House in Taos, New Mexico, began as the Van Vechten-Lineberry Taos Art Museum, a memorial to artist Duane Van Vechten and the art and artists of the Taos Society of Artists of the early twentieth century. The museum, which opened in 1994, was founded by contractor-developer Edwin C. Lineberry and his second wife, Novella Lineberry, to display the works of Lineberry's first wife, Duane Van Vechten (named after her grandfather), and the early artists who founded the Taos art colony. The museum, originally located in an addition to Van Vechten's studio and 1929 home, now occupies the home and studio of Russian-born artist Nicolai Fechin. It features more than 300 works by members of the Taos Society of Artists and artists who came to Taos in the twentieth century.

Taos Art Museum at Fechin House, 227 Paseo del Pueblo North, PO Box 1848, Taos, NM 87571. **Phone:** 505/758-2690. **Fax:** 505/758-7320. **E-mail:** museum@taosartmuseum.org. **Website:** www.taosartmuseum.org. **Hours:** Memorial Day-Labor Day—10-5 Tues.-Sun.; remainder of year—10-4 Tues.-Sun.; closed Mon. and major holidays. **Admission:** adults, $6; children 6-16, $3; children under 6, free.

New York

EVERSON MUSEUM OF ART. The Syracuse Museum of Art, founded in 1896 in Syracuse, New York, was renamed for art patron Helen Everson, who left a bequest to the city in 1941 for a museum dedicated to art appreciation and education. In 1965 the Everson Museum of Art building by noted architect I. M. Pei opened. It was Pei's first museum design, which won critical praise and was honored by the American Institute of Arts and the New York State Council on the Arts.

The 55,000-square-foot museum has the nation's most comprehensive collection of American ceramic art—which began in 1916 with the first of several purchases of porcelains from world-famous potter Adelaide Alsop Robineau of Syracuse. The museum was also one of the first to have a video art collection in the United States. In addition, it has other ceramics of America and the world; eighteenth- to twentieth-century paintings, sculpture, drawings, and graphics; study collections of Asian, African, and Oceanic art and artifacts; and photographs.

Everson Museum of Art, 401 Harrison St., Syracuse, NY 13202. **Phone:** 315/474-6064. **Fax:** 315/474-6943. **E-mail:** eversonadmin@everson.org. **Website:** www.everson.org. **Hours:** 12-5 Tues.-Fri. (also to 7:30 p.m. on 1st Thurs. of month) and Sun., 10-5 Sat.; closed Mon. and national holidays. **Admission:** free.

FRANCES GODWIN AND JOSEPH TERNBACH MUSEUM. The art museum at Queens College of City University of New York in Flushing is named for longtime art history professor Frances Godwin and art conservator and collector Joseph Ternbach, whose collection was the core when the museum was founded in 1957. The museum now has collections of Near Eastern, Asian, Western, and contemporary art, as well as other paintings, prints, graphics, glass, and sculpture.

Frances Godwin and Joseph Ternbach Museum, Queens College, City University of New York, 65-30 Kissena Blvd., Flushing, NY 11367. **Phone:** 718/997-4747. **Fax:** 718/997-5493. **E-mail:** a_winter@qc.edu. **Hours:** 11-7 Mon.-Thurs.; closed Fri.-Sun. and college holidays and breaks. **Admission:** free.

FRANCES LEHMAN LOEB ART CENTER. Vassar College in Poughkeepsie, New York, was the first college in the nation to have an art museum for display of its teaching collection. It was established in 1864 by the college founder, Matthew Vassar, after the purchase of the Elias Lyman Magoon Collection.

The museum was known as the Vassar College Art Gallery until 1993, when it was replaced by the Frances Lehman Loeb Art Center, a 59,700-square-foot facility named for the alumna donor. The center, which includes approximately 20,000 square feet of art galleries, also has a sculpture garden, classrooms, and related spaces. About half of the center incorporates the renovated space of the former art gallery. The museum has more than 12,500 paintings, sculptures, prints, drawings, and photographs that span the history of art, from ancient Egyptian to contemporary American art.

Frances Lehman Loeb Art Center, Vassar College, 124 Raymond Ave., PO Box 703, Poughkeepsie, NY 12604-0703. **Phone:** 845/437-5237. **Fax:** 845/437-7304. **E-mail:** jamundy@vassar.edu. **Website:** www.departments.vassar.edu/~fllac/. **Hours:** 8-5 Tues.-Fri.; 10-5 Sat.; 1-5 Sun.; closed Mon., New Year's Day, Thanksgiving, and from Christmas Eve to New Year's Day. **Admission:** free.

FREDERIC REMINGTON ART MUSEUM. Two women were instrumental in establishing the Frederic Remington Art Museum, a memorial to the noted western artist in Ogdensburg, New York. They were the artist's widow, Eva Caten Remington, and his sister-in-law, Emma Caten, who provided their Remington holdings to the museum.

The sisters' materials included Remington paintings, bronzes, sketches, drawings, and family records, archival materials, furniture, and other items. The museum also has other Remington-related materials, such as sculptures by Sally James Farnham, whom Remington introduced to modeling. It also presents changing exhibitions of contemporary western art and children's works.

Frederic Remington Art Museum, 303 Washington St., Ogdensburg, NY 13669. **Phone:** 315/393-2425. **Fax:** 315/393-4464. **E-mail:** info@remington-museum.org. **Website:** fredericremington.org. **Hours:** May-Oct.—9-5 Mon.-Sat., 1-5 Sun.; remainder of year—11-5 Wed.-Sat., 1-5 Sun.; closed Mon.-Tues., New Year's Day, Easter, Thanksgiving, and Christmas. **Admission:** adults, $4; seniors and students 6-22, $3; children under 6, free.

GREY ART GALLERY. The Grey Art Gallery, located in the Main Building of New York University in New York City, was founded in 1975 with donor Abby Weed Grey's extensive collection of contemporary Asian and Middle Eastern art. The museum also has nineteenth- and twentieth-century paintings, sculpture, and graphics in its collections and galleries.

Grey Art Gallery, New York University, 100 Washington Sq. East, New York, NY 10003. **Phone:** 212/998-6780. **Fax:** 212/995-4024. **E-mail:** greygallery@nyu.edu. **Website:** www.nyu.edu/greyart. **Hours:** Sept.-July—11-6 Tues.-Fri. (also to 8 p.m. Wed.), 11-5 Sat.; closed Sun.-Mon., Aug., and major holidays. **Admission:** suggested donation—$2.50.

HILLWOOD ART MUSEUM. The Hillwood Art Museum on the C. W. Post Campus of Long Island University in Brookville, New York, is housed in the former home of cereal heiress and philanthropist Marjorie Merriweather Post, who donated the land for the campus in the 1950s. The museum, founded in 1973, has an eclectic collection and exhibit program that include works ranging from pre-Columbian to contemporary art (see also Hillwood Museum and Gardens in Historic House Museums).

Hillwood Art Museum, Long Island University, C. W. Post Campus, 720 Northern Blvd., Brookville, NY 11548. **Phone:** 516/299-4073. **Fax:** 516/299-2707. **E-mail:** museum@hornet.liu.edu. **Website:** www.liu.edu/museum. **Hours:** Sept.-May—9:30-4:30 Mon.-Fri. (also to 7:30 p.m. Tues.); 11-3 Sat.-Sun.; closed major holidays; June-Aug.—9:30-4:30 Mon.-Fri.; closed Sat.-Sun. **Admission:** free.

HOFSTRA MUSEUM. The Hofstra Museum at Hofstra University in Hempstead, New York, was launched in 1963 with the addition of a gallery wing funded by the Emily and Joe Lowe Foundation, which also donated a number of paintings by Emily Lowe. In addition to collections of nineteenth- and twentieth-century artworks, the museum has 65 works of sculpture—many by leading twentieth-century sculptors—throughout the 240-acre campus.

Hofstra Museum, 112 Hofstra University, Hempstead, NY 11549-1120. **Phones:** 516/463-5671, 5672, and 5673. **Fax:** 516/463-4743. **E-mail:** elgmbw@hofstra.edu. **Website:** www.hofstra.edu/museum. **Hours:** Sept.-May—10-5 Tues.-Fri., 1-5 Sat.-Sun.; closed Mon. and major holidays; June-Aug.—10-4 Tues.-Fri.; closed Sat.-Mon. **Admission:** free.

JOE AND EMILY LOWE ART GALLERY. See Art Galleries.

MUSEUM OF MODERN ART. The Museum of Modern Art in New York City came into being in 1929 because three influential women collectors—Lillie P. Bliss, Mary Quinn Sullivan, and Abby Aldrich Rockefeller—were prepared to challenge the conservative policies of traditional museums and to establish an institution devoted exclusively to modern art.

Bliss, the daughter of a textile manufacturer who served as Secretary of the Interior under President William McKinley, was a collector of post-Impressionist and contemporary art; Sullivan, the wife of attorney Cornelius J. Sullivan, was a tireless proponent of the cause of modern art; and Rockefeller, the daughter of Senator Nelson W. Aldrich of Rhode Island and wife of John D. Rockefeller Jr., was an avid collector of European art who later acquired a taste for modern art and became convinced that America should have a museum devoted to recent art, and especially that of living artists.

The three women seriously began to exchange ideas on forming a museum of modern art in the winter of 1928–1929. Rockefeller and Bliss met by chance while touring in Egypt, and on the return crossing. Rockefeller discovered a fellow enthusiast in Sullivan, who was an acquaintance of Bliss. They soon launched their bold scheme, asking A. Conger Goodyear, a collector and former army officer and president of the Albright Art Gallery in Buffalo, to become the chair of a committee to form the museum in May 1929. Goodyear had been forced off the Albright board after borrowing a portion of Katherine Dreier's avant-garde collection and purchasing a Picasso painting for the museum despite opposition from other trustees to modern art.

Goodyear became one of the founding trustees of the Museum of Modern Art and recruited three others to increase the board to seven. The others were Mrs. W. Murray Crane, who helped finance the Dalton School, considered New York's most progressive educational experiment at the time; Frank Crowninshield, editor of the art-conscious *Vanity Fair* magazine; and Professor Paul J. Sachs, who ran the museum connoisseurship course at Harvard University's Fogg Art Museum and had trained a generation of museum curators and directors. On Sachs's recommendation, Alfred H. Barr Jr., a 27-year-old former student, was hired as director of the new museum. And it was Barr who launched the museum on its rise to its preeminent position in the world of modern art during his fourteen years of service.

From an initial gift of eight prints and one drawing, the museum's collection has grown to more than 100,000 paintings, sculptures, drawings, prints, photographs, architectural models and drawings, and design objects, as well as over 14,000 films, 4 million film stills, and 200,000 books, artist books, and periodicals.

MoMA, as the museum is known, is home to many of the most important and best-known works of modern art created since the 1880s, ranging from iconic paintings by Vincent van Gogh and Claude Monet to the latest video and installation art. The museum's sculpture garden is named in honor of Abby Aldrich Rockefeller, one of the founders, who donated her collection of approximately 2,000 works to the museum. The Abby Aldrich Rockefeller Folk Art Museum at Colonial Williamsburg also is named for her, because of her gift of the core folk art collection to the historical village in 1939 (see Folk Art Museums).

The Museum of Modern Art recently finished its most ambitious building project—a development that began in 1996 and was completed in late 2004. Designed by Yoshio Taniguchi, the $650 million project enlarged the exhibition space; added new education, research, and retail facilities; and restored historic elements of the existing building, including the sculpture garden and building facade. Because of the construction, the museum's exhibition program was temporarily relocated in 2002 to its branch facility—called MoMA Queens—at 33rd Street and Queens Boulevard in Long Island City, Queens. Fifteen of its best-known twentieth-century sculptures were moved temporarily to the New York Botanical Garden and displayed near the Enid Haupt Conservatory.

Museum of Modern Art, 11 W. 53rd St., New York, NY 10019. **Phone:** 212/708-9400. **Fax:** 212/708-9889. **E-mail:** comments@moma.org. **Website:** www.moma.org. **Hours:** 10:30-5:30 Wed.-Mon. (also to 8 p.m. Fri.); closed Tues., Thanksgiving, and Christmas. **Admission:** adults, $20; seniors, $16; full-time students, $14; children under 16 accompanied by adult, free; free 4-8 Fri.

WHITNEY MUSEUM OF AMERICAN ART (Gertrude Vanderbilt Whitney). See Museums Honoring Exceptional Women.

WHITNEY MUSEUM OF AMERICAN ART AT PHILIP MORRIS. Changing exhibitions are presented at the Whitney Museum of American Art at Philip Morris, one of two corporate-funded branches of the Whitney Museum, which was founded in New York City in 1930 by art patron and sculptor Gertrude Vanderbilt Whitney (see also Museums Honoring Exceptional Women). The gallery and a sculpture court are located on the ground floor of the Philip Morris, Inc., building.

Whitney Museum of American Art at Philip Morris, Philip Morris, Inc., 120 Park Ave., New York, NY 10017. **Phone:** 212/878-2453. **Hours:** gallery—11-6 Mon.-Fri. (also to 7:30 p.m. Thurs.), closed Sat.-Sun. and major holidays; sculpture court—7:30 a.m.-9:30 p.m. Mon.-Sat., 11 a.m.-7 p.m. Sun. **Admission:** free.

North Carolina

LOUISE WELLS CAMERON ART MUSEUM. The St. John's Museum of Art, founded in 1962 in Wilmington, North Carolina, was renamed the Louise Wells Cameron Art Museum in 2001 in memory of the daughter of a benefactor family. The museum contains

The 1917 mansion built by tobacco magnate Richard J. Reynolds and his wife, Katharine Smith Reynolds, is now the home of Reynolda House, Museum of American Art, in Winston-Salem, North Carolina. This interior view shows some of the museum's extensive American art and artifact collections. Courtesy Reynolda House, Museum of American Art, and photographer Ken Bennett, Wake Forest University.

collections of North Carolina paintings, sculpture, decorative arts, and works on paper from the eighteenth to twentieth centuries.

Louise Wells Cameron Art Museum, 3201 S. 17th St., Wilmington, NC 28412 (postal address: 114 Orange St., Wilmington, NC 28401). **Phone:** 910/763-0281. **Fax:** 910/341-7981. **E-mail:** info@cameronartmuseum.com. **Website:** www.cameronartmuseum.com/. **Hours:** 10-5 Tues.-Sat., 12-4 Sun.; closed Mon. and major holidays. **Admission:** adults, $5; children 6-18, $2; children under 6, free.

REYNOLDA HOUSE, MUSEUM OF AMERICAN ART.
The 1917 Reynolda House—built by Richard Joshua Reynolds, founder of the R. J. Reynolds Tobacco Company, and his wife, Katharine Smith Reynolds—became a combination historic house and art museum in Winston-Salem, North Carolina, largely through the efforts of their granddaughter, Barbara Babcock Millhouse.

Millhouse grew up in the 40,000-square-foot mansion, which Charles H. Babcock Sr., her father and the son-in-law of the original occupants, donated along

with 20 surrounding acres to Winston-Salem as a nonprofit institution dedicated to the arts and education. She became the president and spearheaded its development as Reynolda House, Museum of American Art, now listed on the National Register of Historic Places.

Reynolda House, which contains the family's early furnishings, clothing, and art, reflects American art history from 1755 to the present. It features works of such American artists as Mary Cassatt, John Singleton Copley, Frederic Church, Thomas Eakins, Gilbert Stuart, Jacob Lawrence, Andrew Wyeth, Georgia O'Keeffe, and Jasper Johns. Much of the art collection was assembled after 1966 with contributions from the Mary Reynolds Babcock Foundation, the Z. Smith Reynolds Foundation, the Arca Foundation, and Anne Cannon Forsyth.

The mansion's spacious living room is the heart of the 64-room building, with original furnishings providing a relaxed ambiance for the enjoyment of American masterworks. The largest and most expensive feature of the house is an Aeolian organ with

2,566 pipes in chambers around the reception hall. Also on view in the house are such vintage family clothing items as Mrs. Reynolds's handsewed wedding dress and the Paris gowns purchased on her honeymoon, as well as children's clothes and toys.

The Reynolds estate, which once covered 1,067 acres, has two separate adjoining sections—the gardens created by Mrs. Reynolds, which have become the Reynolda Gardens of Wake Forest University (see separate listing in Botanical Gardens and Arboretums), and Reynolda Village, where the country home's outbuildings have been converted into a shipping center.

Reynolda House, Museum of American Art, 2250 Reynolda Rd., PO Box 11765, Winston-Salem, NC 27116-1765. Phones: 336/725-5325 and 888/663-1149. Fax: 336/721-0991. E-mail: reynolda@reynoldahouse.org. Website: www.reynoldahouse.org. Hours: grounds—7:30-5 daily; house—9:30-4:30 Tues.-Sat., 1:30-4:30 Sun.; closed Mon., New Year's Day, Thanksgiving, and Christmas. Admission: grounds—free; house—adults, $6; seniors, $5; children, $3; students under 22, free.

North Dakota

LILLIAN AND COLEMAN TAUBE MUSEUM OF ART. The Lillian and Coleman Taube Museum of Art in Minot, North Dakota, was named for a business couple who owned a dress shop after their son, Stan M. Taube, made a major gift in their memory to the Minot Art Association. The association's museum, which occupies a renovated bank building, has collections and showings of paintings, sculpture, and photographs—largely of a contemporary nature.

Lillian and Coleman Taube Museum of Art, 2 N. Main St., PO Box 325, Minot, ND 58702. Phone: 701/838-4445. Fax: 701/839-7225. E-mail: taube@ndfk.net. Hours: 2-5 Tues.-Fri., 12-3 Sat.; closed Sun.-Mon. and major holidays. Admission: donation.

Ohio

DAYTON ART INSTITUTE. Julia Shaw Patterson Carnell, businesswoman, philanthropist, and widow of one of the founders of the National Cash Register Company, played a significant role in the history of the Dayton Art Institute in Dayton, Ohio. Carnell helped start the museum by donating the first of many artworks and a mansion for its first home in 1919. When the museum outgrew the mansion, she gave the museum $2 million to build a new structure resembling a sixteenth-century Italian palazzo, which opened in 1930. She continued

to be supportive of the museum until her death in 1944.

Two other women and their families also made important contributions to the museum. They were Virginia Kettering, who with her husband, Eugene, gave more than 1,200 gifts of art—largely Asian works—to the museum, beginning in 1950, and Virginia Rike Haswell, who donated numerous artworks and whose family foundation, the Rike Family Foundation, funded a new wing—dedicated in memory of Susanne Rike MacDonald—for the museum in 1965.

The Dayton Art Institute is best known for its American and European collections of paintings, sculpture, and prints and Asian works that began with Carnell and were greatly enhanced by Kettering. The museum also has pre-Columbian, Native American, African, and Oceanic works, as well as decorative arts, graphics, and photography. Its annual attendance exceeds 400,000.

Dayton Art Institute, 456 Belmonte Park N., Dayton, OH 45405-4700. Phone: 937/223-5277. Fax: 937/223-3140. E-mail: info@daytonartinstitute.org. Website: www.daytonartinstitute.org. Hours: 10-5 daily (also to 9 p.m. Thurs.). Admission: free.

EDWIN L. AND RUTH E. KENNEDY MUSEUM OF ART. The Edwin L. and Ruth E. Kennedy Museum of Art at Ohio University in Athens was named in 1996 for the couple who provided funds to restore a historic building for the museum's site and gave their collection of Southwest Native American weavings, jewelry, and other works to the museum. In addition to the seventeenth- to twentieth-century Navajo, Hopi, and other Native American works, the museum has collections of American paintings, prints, and ceramics, and photographs. Mr. Kennedy, who is an alumnus, was vice president of a major financial firm.

Edwin L. and Ruth E. Kennedy Museum of Art, Ohio University, Lin Hall, Athens, OH 45701-2979. Phone: 740/593-0955. Fax: 740/593-1305. E-mail: kenmus@www.cats.ohiou.edu. Website: www.ohiou.edu/museum. Hours: 12-5 Tues.-Fri. (also to 8 p.m. Thurs.), 1-5 Sat.-Sun.; closed Mon. and university holidays.

TAFT MUSEUM OF ART. The Taft Museum of Art in Cincinnati, Ohio, was founded in 1932 by Charles Phelps Taft and his wife, Anna Sinton Taft, in their 1820 Baum-Longworth-Taft House. The Tafts inherited the Federal-style home in 1900, when they began assembling their highly regarded art collection.

The museum, now operated by the Cincinnati Institute of Fine Arts, has twelve rooms that display Old Masters paintings, French Renaissance enamels, Chinese Imperial porcelains, Renaissance and Baroque decorative arts, Duncan Phyfe furniture, and jewelry and watches from many countries. The collection includes works by Rembrandt, Goya, Gainsborough, Whistler, Turner, and Corot. Formal gardens are also located on the grounds.

Taft Museum of Art, 316 Pike St., Cincinnati, OH 45202-4293. **Phone:** 513/241-0343. **Fax:** 513/241-2266. **E-mail:** djohnson@taftmuseum.org. **Website:** www.taft museum.org. **Hours:** 10-5 Mon.-Sat., 1-5 Sun. and some holidays; closed New Year's Day, Thanksgiving, and Christmas. **Admission:** adults, $4; seniors and students, $2; children under 19, free; free Wed. and Sun.

Oregon

HALLIE FORD MUSEUM OF ART. The Hallie Ford Museum of Art at Willamette University in Salem, Oregon, is named for a trustee and benefactor who gave a major gift through her foundation—the Ford Family Foundation—to purchase and renovate the museum's building and provided funds to seed an endowment fund. Another important trustee and donor is Maribeth Collins, who also gave funds to help renovate the interior of the museum's 1965 former telephone building in 1997–1998, endowed the director's position, and made an endowment gift that enables the museum to commission a work of art each year for its permanent collection. She also provides funds annually to acquire artworks for the collection. The museum features collections and exhibitions devoted to European, Asian, American, Native American, and contemporary regional art.

Hallie Ford Museum of Art, Willamette University, 700 State St., Salem, OR 97301 (postal address: 900 State St., Salem, OR 97301). **Phone:** 503/370-65855. **Fax:** 503/375-5458. **E-mail:** museum-art@willamette.edu. **Website:** www.willamette.edu/museum_of_art/. **Hours:** 10-5 Tues.-Sat.; closed Sun.-Mon. and major holidays. **Admission:** adults, $3; seniors and children over 12, $2; children under 13, free.

MAUDE KERNS ART CENTER. The Maude Kerns Art Center in Eugene, Oregon, is named for a noted nonobjective artist and art educator who gave a small house in 1958 for the first permanent home of the Eugene Art Center, which was renamed in her honor. The property was sold in 1963, and the center was moved to its present location in an 1895 historic church building.

Kerns painted for 75 years, experimenting with a variety of media and styles. Her work evolved from realistic landscapes and portraits to nonrepresentational oil paintings. She was head of art education at the University of Oregon for 26 years. Her gift of the house for the art center was to "provide broader opportunities for the people of Lane County to be active in the creation and exhibition of art." The center now features her work and that of other artists and offers arts and crafts instructional programs.

Maude Kerns Art Center, 1910 E. 15th Ave., Eugene, OR 97403. **Phone:** 541/345-1571. **Fax:** 541/345-6248. **E-mail:** mkart@pond.net. **Website:** www.mkartcenter.org. **Hours:** 10-5:30 Mon.-Fri., 12-4 Sat.; closed Sun. **Admission:** suggested donations—individual, $2; family, $5.

SCHNEIDER MUSEUM OF ART. In 1983, William and Florence Schneider, owners of a private school in Tucson, Arizona, made a major gift to Southern Oregon University in Ashland for a campus art museum. They also gave artworks by Waldo Peirce, a former Southern Oregon University student, who had developed a relationship with the Schneiders. In appreciation, the university named the museum for Mr. Schneider's parents, Samuel and May Schneider. The museum's collections focus on paper and ceramics, while the exhibitions feature contemporary art and other periods and styles.

Schneider Museum of Art, Southern Oregon University, 1250 Siskiyou, Blvd., Ashland, OR 97520. **E-mail:** schneider_museum@sou.edu. **Website:** www.sou.edu/sma. **Hours:** 10-4 Tues.-Sat.; closed Sun.-Mon. and state holidays. **Admission:** suggested donation—$2.

Pennsylvania

PALMER MUSEUM OF ART. Pennsylvania State University's art museum, which was founded on the University Park campus in 1972, was renovated, expanded, and renamed the Palmer Museum of Art in 1993 for James R. Palmer and his wife, Barbara R. Palmer.

The Palmers donated $3.5 million to the university in 1986, with $2 million being designated for the museum. Mr. Palmer was the chief executive officer of C-COR, a manufacturer of electronic equipment for data communications and cable television systems. The museum's ten galleries contain selections from a permanent collection covering 35 centuries of paintings, sculpture, ceramics, and works on paper from the United States, Europe, Asia, and South America. The museum also has large-scale contemporary sculpture in an adjacent outdoor garden.

Palmer Museum of Art, Pennsylvania State University, Curtin Rd., University Park, PA 16802. **Phone:** 814/865-7672. **Fax:** 814/863-8608. **E-mail:** pjml9@psu.edu. **Website:** www.psu.edu/dept/palmermuseum/. **Hours:** 10-4:30 Tues.-Sat., 12-4 Sun.; closed Mon., Christmas through New Year's Day, and major holidays. **Admission:** free.

PHILIP AND MURIEL BERMAN MUSEUM OF ART AT URSINUS COLLEGE. Philip and Muriel Berman, department store owners who became prominent art collectors, were interested in establishing a museum at an academic institution to further the integration of the visual arts in a cross-disciplinary environment. In 1987 they decided on Mr. Berman's alma mater, Ursinus College in Collegeville, Pennsylvania, making a gift of $1 million to endow the directorship and donating over 1,500 works of art from their collection.

Mr. Berman was president and Mrs. Berman vice president of the Hess department store chain of 40 stores from 1968 to 1985, when they sold the business. Over the years the couple assumed a highly regarded art collection of works by Rembrandt, Peale, Matisse, Miró, Renoir, Cassatt, Picasso, Degas, Gauguin, Chadwick, Moore, Chagall, Pollock, and others.

The Berman Museum's collections include nineteenth- and early-twentieth-century American paintings, prints, and watercolors; eighteenth- and nineteenth-century European portraits; Old Masters and contemporary Japanese woodcut prints, scrolls, and artifacts; 1950–1990 American paintings and graphics; eastern European paintings; and contemporary sculptures—including 40 outdoor pieces across the campus. Exhibitions are presented from the collections, as well as of contemporary regional artists and other works from elsewhere.

Philip and Muriel Berman Museum of Art at Ursinus College, 601 E. Main St., PO Box 1000, Collegeville, PA 19426-1000. **Phone:** 610/409-3500. **Fax:** 610/409-3664. **E-mail:** 1hanover@ursinus.edu. **Website:** www.ursinus.edu. **Hours:** 10-4 Tues.-Fri., 12-4:30 Sat.-Sun.; closed Mon., Dec. 24-Jan. 2, and college holidays. **Admission:** free.

TROUT GALLERY. Two sisters—Ruth and Helen Trout—established the Trout Gallery at Dickinson College in Carlisle, Pennsylvania, in 1983 in memory of their father, Brook Trout. The art museum, with

exhibits covering virtually all periods of art history, has more than 6,000 works in its collections, including Old Masters, prints, decorative arts, and African art.

Trout Gallery, Dickinson College, Weiss Center for the Arts, PO Box 1773, Carlisle, PA 17013-2986. **Phone:** 717/249-7610. **Fax:** 717/258-9332. **Website:** www.dickinson.edu/departments/trout. **Hours:** late Aug.-mid June—10-4 Tues.-Sat.; closed Sun.-Mon. and national holidays; late-June-mid-Aug.—1-4 Wed.; closed remainder of week. **Admission:** free.

Rhode Island

ANNMARY BROWN MEMORIAL. The Annmary Brown Memorial at Brown University in Providence, Rhode Island, is a mausoleum, library, and museum named for the daughter of the founder of the university. Annmary and her husband, General Rush Christopher Hawkins, are buried in the 1905 memorial building that also contains nineteenth- and twentieth-century European and American paintings, 1700–1900 British swords, Brown family heirlooms and correspondence, and books and Civil War mementos of General Hawkins.

Annmary Brown Memorial, Brown University, 21 Brown St., Box 1905, Providence, RI 02912. **Phone:** 401/863-1994. **E-mail:** carol_cramer@brown.edu. **Hours:** 1-5 Mon.-Fri.; closed Sat.-Sun. and national holidays. **Admission:** free.

RHODE ISLAND SCHOOL OF DESIGN MUSEUM OF ART. The Museum of Art at the Rhode Island School of Design in Providence was founded as part of the school in 1877, by Helen Adelia Rowe Metcalf and the Women's Centennial Committee, with $1,675 left over from the Centennial Exposition in Philadelphia in 1876.

The school, established to train artisans and art students and to further public art education, has since grown to be one of the nation's leading schools of art and design, while the museum has become one of the most comprehensive in its field. Located in a four-building, six-story complex, the museum has nearly 80,000 works of art and 45 galleries for permanent displays and changing exhibitions. It has the earliest example of an American wing in Pendleton House, which features a major collection of eighteenth-century American furniture, silver, painting, and decorative arts in period rooms constructed in 1906.

Among the museum's diverse collections are costumes and textiles; American furniture, silver, china, and decorative arts of the eighteenth and nineteenth centuries; Asian art; eighteenth-century European porcelain; fifteenth- to twentieth-century paintings, sculpture, and decorative arts; twentieth-century American art; modern Latin American art; classical, medieval, and ethnographic art; and prints, drawings, and photographs.

Rhode Island School of Design Museum of Art, 224 Benefit St., Providence, RI 02903-2723. **Phone:** 401/454-6500. **Fax:** 401/454-6556. **E-mail:** museum@risd.edu. **Website:** www.risd.edu/museum. **Hours:** 10-5 Tues.-Sun. (also to 9 p.m. 3rd Thurs. of month); closed Mon. and major holidays. **Admission:** adults, $6; seniors, $5; college students, $3; children 5-18, $2; children under 5, free; by donation on Sat.

South Carolina

STUDIO-MUSEUM OF ELIZABETH O'NEILL VERNER. The seventeenth-century house in Charleston, South Carolina, where artist Elizabeth O'Neill Verner created her etchings, prints, and pastels is now the Studio-Museum of Elizabeth O'Neill Verner, featuring her artwork. She was a 42-year-old widow with two children who also used her studio as a nursery.

Studio-Museum of Elizabeth O'Neill Verner, 38 Tradd St., Charleston, SC 29401. **Phone:** 803/722-4246. **E-mail:** info@vernergallery.com. **Website:** www.vernergallery.com. **Hours:** 9-5 Mon.-Sat.; closed Sun., Thanksgiving, and Christmas. **Admission:** free.

Tennessee

DIXON GALLERY AND GARDENS. The Dixon Gallery and Gardens in Memphis, Tennessee, came about through the bequests of philanthropists and community leaders Hugo Norton Dixon and his wife, Margaret Oates Dixon. They left their 1941 Georgian-style mansion, 17-acre garden, and collection of paintings for the enjoyment and education of future generations.

Mr. Dixon was a prominent cotton marketer who served as president of the Memphis Brooks Museum of Art, the Memphis branch of the English Speaking Union, the Cotton Carnival Association, and the Cotton Council International. Mrs. Dixon was an amateur artist, founder and first president of the Memphis College of Arts, and an active board member of several community organizations.

The couple formed the Dixon Foundation in 1958 so that their estate would remain intact for the benefit of the community. Both died in 1974—she in February and he in an auto accident in November. Their foundation now helps support the Dixon Gallery and Gardens.

The art museum's collections include French and American Impressionist and post-Impressionist paintings, with works by Monet, Cézanne, Renoir, Rodin, Gauguin, and Cassatt; eighteenth-century German porcelain; and American and European pewter. Special exhibitions from other private and public collections are also presented. The gardens—landscaped in the English manner—feature open vistas, a series of formal garden spaces, a rose display, a conservatory, and greenhouses.

Dixon Gallery and Gardens, 4339 Park Ave., Memphis, TN 38117. **Phone:** 901/761-5250. **Fax:** 901/682-0943. **E-mail:** jkamm@dixon.org. **Website:** www.dixon.org. **Hours:** 10-5 Tues.-Sat., 1-5 Sun.; closed Mon. and major holidays. **Admission:** adults and children over 11, $5; seniors, $4; children 5-11, $1; children under 5, free.

Texas

AUSTIN MUSEUM OF ART-LAGUNA GLORIA. The Laguna Gloria branch of the Austin Museum of Art in Austin, Texas, is housed in the 1916 Mediterranean villa donated in 1943 by Clara Driscoll, who became known as the "Savior of the Alamo" for devoting nearly twenty years and almost $100,000 to preserving the historic old chapel. Driscoll and her late husband, Henry Sevier, built the villa. She gave the villa and grounds to the Texas Fine Arts Association with the stipulation that the property be used as an art museum. The site later became the Laguna Gloria Art Museum and then the Austin Museum of Art-Laguna Gloria. In addition to the historic house and art collections and exhibitions, it has an art school, gardens, and outdoor amphitheater. The villa is now undergoing restoration.

Austin Museum of Art-Laguna Gloria, 3809 W. 35th St., PO Box 5568, Austin, TX 78763. **Phone:** 512/496-9224. **Fax:** 512/495-9029. **E-mail:** info@amoa.org. **Website:** www.amoa.org. **Hours:** 10-5 Tues.-Sat. (also to 8 p.m. Thurs.), 12-5 Sun.; closed Mon. and major holidays. **Admission:** adults, $3; seniors and college students, $2; children under 13, free; $1 on Thurs.

BAYOU BEND COLLECTION AND GARDENS. The former mansion of Ima Hogg, daughter of a Texas governor who made a fortune in oil and real estate, is the home of the Bayou Bend Collection and Gardens, a branch of the Museum of Fine Arts in Houston.

Miss Ima, as she was lovingly called, collected precious things up until her death at the age of 93 in 1975 and gave generously to many causes. She was one of the founders of Houston's Symphony Society, established the Child Guidance Center and Hogg Foundation for Mental Health and Hygiene, was active in historical presentation and restoration, gave her home to the art museum in 1958, and had much of her land, including the Varner-Hogg Plantation, become part of the Texas parks system.

The 28 rooms of the 1927 Latin Colonial–style house feature selections of early paintings, decorative arts, and furniture from the collection's more than 4,800 works that trace the evolution of American style from the Colonial period to the mid-nineteenth century. The site also has eight formal gardens with native and imported plants and 14 acres of woodlands.

Bayou Bend Collection and Gardens, Museum of Fine Arts, 1 Westcott Dr., PO Box 6826, Houston, TX 77265. **Phone:** 713/639-7750. **Fax:** 713/639-7770. **E-mail:** hirsch@mfah.org. **Website:** www.mfah.org. **Hours:** 10-5 Tues.-Sat., 1-5 Sun.; closed Mon., New Year's Day, Fourth of July, Thanksgiving, and Christmas. **Admission:** adults and children over 9, $3; children under 10, free, but not permitted in house except during open house; guided tours—house and gardens: adults, $10; seniors and students, $8.50; children 10-18, $5; gardens—adults, $7; seniors and students, $6; children 10-18, $5; children under 10, free; first floor of house and gardens free on 3rd Sun. of month.

ELLEN NOËL ART MUSEUM OF THE PERMIAN BASIN.

Philanthropist and amateur artist Ellen Witwer Noël, widow of the late industrialist W. D. Noël, has been called the "guardian angel" of the art museum founded in Odessa, Texas, in 1985. She always seemed to provide the necessary financial help in a time of need.

In 1998 Mrs. Noël established and nurtured "The Connoisseurs," a donor group that assisted in supporting the exhibition program. When the museum ran a serious deficit in 1990, she gave a major gift to the museum. And in 1996, Mrs. Noël made a donation for a needed new collections storage wing, state-of-the-art climate control system, and loading dock. The contribution was also leveraged to fund the addition of a gallery and a multipurpose room.

In appreciation for her generous support, the Art Institute for the Permian Basin was renamed for Mrs. Noël in 1996—and is now the Ellen Noël Art Museum of the Permian Basin. The museum features collections and exhibits, primarily of American art from 1850 to the present, and the George and Milly Rhodus Sculpture Garden, which includes sculptures and a sensory garden.

Ellen Noël Art Museum of the Permian Basin, 4909 E. University Blvd., Odessa, TX 79762. **Phone:** 915/550-9696. **Fax:** 915/550-9226. **E-mail:** info@noelartmuseum.org. **Website:** www.noelartmuseum.org/. **Hours:** 10-5 Tues.-Sat., 2-5 Sun.; closed Mon. and national holidays. **Admission:** free.

MARION KOOGLER McNAY ART MUSEUM. See Museums Honoring Exceptional Women.

THE MENIL COLLECTION (Dominique de Menil). See Museums Honoring Exceptional Women.

SARAH CAMPBELL BLAFFER FOUNDATION GALLERIES.

The Sarah Campbell Blaffer Foundation, founded in 1964 by the late Texas philanthropist and art collector, has a collection of over 560 paintings and prints—selections of which are displayed in the foundation's five galleries in the recent building addition to the Museum of Fine Arts in Houston. The collection includes Old Masters paintings; fourteenth- to eighteenth-century European graphic art; William Hogarth prints; Francisco Goya etchings; and modern European works.

Sarah Campbell Blaffer Foundation Galleries, Museum of Fine Arts, 5601 Main St., PO Box 6826, Houston, TX 77265-6826. **Phone:** 713/639-7741. **E-mail:** jclifton@mfah.org. **Website:** www.rice.edu/projects/Blaffer/. **Hours:** 10-7 Tues.-Sat. and Mon. holidays (also to 9 p.m. Thurs.-Fri.); 12:15-7 Sun.; closed Mon., Thanksgiving, and Christmas. **Admission:** adults, $5; seniors and children 6-18, $2.50; children under 6, free; free on Thurs.

STARK MUSEUM OF ART.

Nelda C. Stark was instrumental in the founding of the Stark Museum of Art in Orange, Texas, in 1974, which honors her late husband, H. J. Lutcher Stark, and features art of the American West that they collected. She served as chairperson of the Nelda C. and H. J. Lutcher Stark Foundation board, which operates the museum, until her death in 1999.

The museum's collection—which largely reflects the Stark family's interest in the people, land, and wildlife of the American West—began in the 1890s when Miriam Lutcher started to collect art, primarily by European artists and craftsmen. Her son, H. J. Lutcher Stark, also became a collector, but with an emphasis on American art of the frontier. He was later joined in the effort by his wife, Nelda.

The collection includes paintings, sculpture, prints, ceramics, and artifacts emphasizing the art and history of the American West in the nineteenth and twentieth centuries. It contains works by such artists as Alfred Jacob Miller, J. M. Stanley, Paul Kane, Albert Bierstadt, Frederic Remington, Charles M. Russell, and John James Audubon, as well as the art and artifacts of Native American peoples of the Great Plains and the Southwest.

Stark Museum of Art, 712 Green Ave., PO Box 1897, Orange, TX 77630-1897. **Phone:** 409/883-6661. **Fax:** 409/883-6361. **E-mail:** starkart@exp.net. **Website:** www.starkmuseumofart. org. **Hours:** 10-5 Tues.-Sat.; closed Sun.-Mon. and major holidays. **Admission:** free.

TRAMMEL AND MARGARET CROW COLLECTION OF ASIAN ART. A 12,000-square-foot space adjacent to the Trammel Crow Center in downtown Dallas is devoted to four galleries of Asian art collected by real estate developer Trammel Crow and his wife, Margaret Crow, and operated by the Crow Family Foundation. Among the works on display are Japanese scrolls, screens, and objects in rock crystal, lacquer, ceramics, and bronze; carved jades of China's Ming dynasty and Chinese paintings, sculptures, porcelains, and decorative and ritual items; and the arts of India, Southeast Asia, Tibet, and Nepal. Many of the works in the collection represent deities from various religions, such as Buddhism, Confucianism, Daoism, Hinduism, and Jainism.

Trammel and Margaret Crow Collection of Asian Art, 2010 Flora St., Dallas, TX 75201-2335. **Phone:** 214/979-6430. **Fax:** 214/979-6439. **E-mail:** clifto@crowcollection.com. **Website:** www.crowcollection.com. **Hours:** 10-5 Tues.-Sun. (also to 9 p.m. Thurs.); closed Mon. and major holidays. **Admission:** free.

Utah

NORA ECCLES HARRISON MUSEUM OF ART. The Nora Eccles Harrison Museum of Art at Utah State University in Logan is named for its donor, an arts patron and potter who also gave her extensive ceramics collection to the museum. Founded in 1982, the museum has collections of Hopi, Navajo, and other Southwest and Northwest Native American arts and twentieth-century American paintings, sculpture, ceramics, and drawings, and is known for its contempo-

rary art collections and exhibitions by artists who have lived or worked in the western region from 1900 to the present.

Nora Eccles Harrison Museum of Art, Utah State University, 650 North 1100 East, Logan, UT 84322-4020. **Phone:** 435/797-1414. **Fax:** 435/797-3423. **E-mail:** swros@cc.usu. edu. **Hours:** 10:30-4:30 Tues.-Fri. (also to 8 p.m. Wed.), 2-5 Sat.-Sun.; closed Mon. and major holidays. **Admission:** free.

Vermont

SHELBURNE MUSEUM. See Art and History Museums.

Virginia

JOSEPH AND MARGARET MUSCARELLE MUSEUM OF ART. The College of William and Mary in Williamsburg, Virginia, has been collecting artworks since the early eighteenth century. But it was not until 1983 that a building was constructed to house the artworks and changing loan exhibitions. It was expanded in 1987, and the museum was renamed the Joseph and Margaret Muscarelle Museum of Art for its prime benefactors.

The museum's collection of over 3,000 works includes English and American portraits of the seventeenth to nineteenth centuries; American abstract expressionist paintings, drawings, and watercolors; a survey collection of European, Asian, and American prints and drawings from the fifteenth to twentieth centuries; and Native American, Asian, Islamic, and African collections. The museum is also known for what is called "the world's first solar painting"—a 65-by 13-foot passive solar wall on the south facade of its building. It contains 124 fiberglass tubes that collect energy by day and glow as colorful stripes at night.

Joseph and Margaret Muscarelle Museum of Art, College of William and Mary, PO Box 8795, Williamsburg, VA 23187-8795. **Phone:** 757/221-2710. **Fax:** 757/221-2711. **Website:** www.wm.edu/muscarelle. **Hours:** 10-4:45 Mon.-Fri., 12-4 Sat.-Sun.; closed major holidays. **Admission:** free.

MAIER MUSEUM OF ART. Collecting art at the Randolph-Macon Woman's College in Lynchburg, Virginia, dates to 1907 when the senior class commissioned a portrait of the college's first president, William Waugh Smith. But it was not until Louise Jordan Smith, the first professor of art at the college and a cousin of President Smith, began to develop the collection that a formal permanent collection was conceived. She fervently believed that the firsthand study of art was essential to a liberal arts education, and she established an annual exhibition of American contemporary art in 1911 and introduced a course on American painting and sculpture in 1915.

In 1928, after Professor Smith's death, the college received her bequest for an endowed acquisition fund, which greatly expanded the college's art collection over the years. The collection was exhibited throughout the campus until 1977, when the major paintings and works on paper were installed in the current museum building, then known as the Art Gallery.

In 1981 Mr. and Mrs. William Thoresen donated funds for a new large exhibition gallery, and the following year a major grant was received from the Sarah and Pauline Maier Scholarship Foundation to fund crucial improvements in the building. It was then that the name was changed to the Maier Museum of Art in honor of the foundation's founder, William J. Maier Jr.

The museum's collection is focused exclusively on American art, featuring paintings, works on paper, and photographs from the nineteenth and twentieth centuries, with the major strength being in American Impressionism. It includes works by such artists as Gilbert Stuart, George Bellows, Childe Hassam, Mary Cassatt, Georgia O'Keeffe, Thomas Cole, Winslow Homer, Thomas Eakins, Edward Hopper, James McNeill Whistler, and Arthur B. Davies.

Maier Museum of Art, Randolph-Macon Woman's College, 1 Quinlan St., Lynchburg, VA 24503 (postal address: 2500 Rivermont Ave., Lynchburg, VA 24503-1526). Phone: 804/947-8136. Fax: 804/947-8726. E-mail: klawson @rmw.edu. Website: www.rmwc.edu/maier. Hours: mid-Aug.-May—1-5 Tues.-Sun.; closed Mon. and college holidays. June-mid-Aug.—1-4 Wed.-Sun.; closed Mon.-Tues. Admission: free.

REEVES CENTER FOR RESEARCH AND EXHIBITION OF PORCELAIN AND PAINTINGS. The Reeves Center for Research and Exhibition of Porcelain and Paintings at Washington & Lee University in Lexington, Virginia, began in 1982 following a gift of porcelain, ceramics, and paintings from artist Louise Herreshoff Reeves and her husband, Euchlin D. Reeves. The collection was supplemented by contributions from others.

The Reeves Center, which presents exhibits in a restored 1840 Greek Revival house and the Palladian-style Watson Pavilion for Asian Arts, has more than 4,000 items in its collections, including paintings and watercolors by Mrs. Reeves, who signed her works with her maiden name of Louise Herreshoff. The holdings are especially rich in Chinese export porcelain and also contain European and Japanese ceramics and nineteenth- and twentieth-century paintings.

Reeves Center for Research and Exhibition of Porcelain and Paintings, Washington & Lee University, Lexington, VA 24450. Phone: 540/463-8744. Fax: 540/463-8741. Hours: 9-4:30 Mon.-Fri.; Sun. by appointment; closed Sat., New Year's Eve and Day, Thanksgiving, and Christmas Eve and Day. Admission: free.

UNIVERSITY ART MUSEUM. The University Art Museum (formerly the Bayly Art Museum) at the University of Virginia in Charlottesville was founded in 1935 as a result of a 1929 bequest from Evelyn May Bayly Tiffany, a Baltimore physician. Of the bequest, $100,000 was designated for an art museum named in honor of her father, Thomas Henry Bayly, one of the university's first graduates, who became a lawyer and member of Virginia's General Assembly.

The name of the Bayly Art Museum was recently changed to the University Art Museum, but the museum still occupies the Bayly Building, constructed largely with funds from the bequest. The museum's collections now include European paintings from the late eighteenth and early nineteenth centuries; Old Masters prints; modern and contemporary American paintings and sculpture; Asian paintings and ceramics; pre-Columbian ceramics; contemporary graphics; and photographs.

University Art Museum, University of Virginia, 155 Rugby Rd., PO Box 400119, Charlottesville, VA 22904-4119. Phone: 804/924-3592. Fax: 804/924-6321. E-mail: cjh6r .virginia.edu. Website: www.virginia.edu/~bayly/. Hours: 1-5 Tues.-Sun.; closed Mon. and major holidays. Admission: free.

Washington

FRYE ART MUSEUM. Charles and Emma Frye left their collection of paintings and the bulk of their estate to establish the Frye Art Museum, which opened in Seattle in 1952. Mr. Frye, a successful farmer turned merchant, was enamored of nineteenth-century German and French academic paintings. The museum contains nineteenth- and twentieth-century European and American paintings and contemporary, figurative, and representational art, and has examples of the works of such artists as John Singleton Copley, Grant Wood,

Everett Shinn, George Luks, and three generations of Wyeths.

Frye Art Museum, 704 Terry Ave., Seattle, WA 98104. **Phone:** 206/622-9250. **Fax:** 206/223-1707. **E-mail:** fryeart@aol.com. **Website:** www.fryeart.org. **Hours:** 10-5 Tues.-Sat. (also to 9 p.m. Thurs.), 12-5 Sun.; closed Mon., New Year's Day, Thanksgiving, and Christmas. **Admission:** free.

MARYHILL MUSEUM OF ART. Sam Hill, an eccentric lawyer and road and monument builder, named his estate and museum of art near Goldendale, Washington, for his daughter, Mary Mendenhall Hill. Three other women also played important roles in the history of the Maryhill Museum of Art—avant-garde dancer Loïe Fuller, sugar heiress Alma de Bretteville Spreckels, and Queen Marie of Romania.

In 1907 Hill purchased 7,000 acres along the Columbia River to start a planned utopian farm community. Construction of his chateaulike mansion began in 1914, as Hill's business and diplomatic travels took him all over the world. It was during this period that he developed lasting friendships with the three women.

When the farm town failed to materialize, Fuller convinced Hill to convert his unfinished house into an art museum. Queen Marie dedicated the museum in 1926 and gave many of her possessions to it. And it was through the committed efforts of Alma Spreckels, the museum's first trustee, that the museum opened to the public in 1940.

The museum now contains such diverse works as the queen's royal furnishings, Auguste Rodin sculptures and watercolors, eighteenth-century Russian icons, French sculptures and theater sets, European and American paintings, early weapons, and rare chess sets. The grounds also feature a sculpture garden.

Maryhill Museum of Art, 35 Maryhill Museum Dr., Goldendale, WA 98620. **Phone:** 509/773-3733. **Fax:** 509/773-6138. **E-mail:** maryhill@gorge.net. **Website:** www.maryhillmuseum.org. **Hours:** mid-Mar.-mid-Nov.—9-5 daily; closed remainder of year. **Admission:** adults, $7; seniors, $6.50; children 6-12, $1.50; children under 6, free.

SEATTLE ART MUSEUM AND SEATTLE ASIAN ART MUSEUM. Members of the Fuller family were sophisticated world travelers and art collectors who were instrumental in the founding of two art museums in Seattle. When they moved to Seattle from New York City in 1923, they brought a collection of Asian art. In the early 1930s, Margaret E. MacTavish Fuller and her son, Dr. Richard E. Fuller, commissioned the construction of a museum in Volunteer Park to house the collection (named in memory of Mrs. Fuller's husband, Dr. Eugene Fuller, who died in 1930), and then made it a gift to the city upon completion in 1933.

The building and collection became the Seattle Art Museum (together with the collection of the Art Institute of Seattle, founded in 1917). The museum later had three expansions—including a 1965 annex in the former United Kingdom Pavilion at the Seattle World's Fair—before moving to its present downtown location. The Volunteer Park building was revitalized and reopened as a branch, becoming the Seattle Asian Art Museum in 1994.

Mrs. Fuller continued to be an active collector until her death in 1953, leaving a substantial endowment to the Seattle Art Museum—with part of the gift being used to form a collection purchase fund in her name. Dr. Fuller, who was previously the president of the Art Institute of Seattle, served as Seattle Art Museum president and director until his retirement in 1973.

In addition to its superb collection of Asian art, the Seattle Art Museum is now also known for its African and Northwest Coast Native American art. The museum also has collections of pre-Columbian and Oceanic art; European and American modern and contemporary paintings, prints, sculpture, and photography; European and American decorative arts; Near Eastern, Egyptian, Greek, Roman, medieval, Renaissance, and Baroque paintings; textiles; and numismatics. The Seattle Asian Art Museum has become one of the nation's leading museums in Asian art, with comprehensive collections of Chinese, Japanese, Korean, Indian, and Southeast Asian art.

Seattle Art Museum, 100 University St., PO Box 22000, Seattle, WA 98122-9700. **Phone:** 206/625-8900. **Fax:** 206/654-3135. **E-mail:** webmaster@seattleartmuseum.org. **Website:** www.seattleartmuseum.org. **Hours:** 10-5 Tues.-Sun. (also to 9 p.m. Thurs.); closed Mon., New Year's Day, Thanksgiving, and Christmas. **Suggested admission:** adults, $7; seniors, students, and children over 12, $5; children under 13, free; free 1st Thurs. of month.

Seattle Asian Art Museum, Volunteer Park, 1400 E. Prospect St., Seattle, WA 98112-3303 (postal address: PO Box 22000, Seattle, WA 98122-9700). **Phone:** 206/625-8900. **Fax:** 206/654-3191. **E-mail:** webmaster@seattleartmuseum.org. **Website:** www.seattleartmuseum.org. **Hours:** 10-5 Tues.-Sun. (also to 9 p.m. Thurs.); closed Mon., New Year's Day, Thanksgiving, and Christmas. **Suggested admission:** $3 per person; combination ticket with Seattle Art Museum, $7; free 1st Thurs. and Sat. of month.

Wisconsin

The Leigh Yawkey Woodson Art Museum in Wausau, Wisconsin, was founded in 1973 in honor of a local philanthropist by her three daughters. Located in this Tudor-style house, it features gardens, a collection focusing on birds, and a sculpture garden. Courtesy Leigh Yawkey Woodson Art Museum.

LEIGH YAWKEY WOODSON ART MUSEUM. The Leigh Yawkey Woodson Art Museum in Wausau, Wisconsin, was founded in 1973 by three daughters—Alice Woodson Forester, Nancy Leigh Woodson Spire, and Margaret Woodson Fisher—in memory of their mother. The museum project was spearheaded by Alice and John E. Forester, and the museum is housed in the Foresters' former residence, a historic Tudor-style house that has been expanded.

The museum features wildlife paintings and sculpture, with an emphasis on birds. It also has decorative art and the 1.5-acre Margaret Woodson Fisher Sculpture Garden, and it presents changing exhibitions by national and international artists. An annual highlight is the Birds in Art exhibition in the fall, which is recognized as one of the best of its type.

Leigh Yawkey Woodson Art Museum, 700 N. 12th St., Wausau, WI 54403-5007. **Phone:** 715/845-7010. **Fax:** 715/845-7103. **E-mail:** museum@lywam.org. **Hours:** 9-4 Tues.-Fri., 12-5 Sat.-Sun.; closed Mon. and national holidays. **Admission:** free.

PAINE ART CENTER AND GARDENS. An exquisite 1920s Tudor Revival mansion, donated by lumber baron Nathan Paine and his wife, Jessie Kimberly Paine, is the home of the Paine Art Center and Gardens in Oshkosh, Wisconsin. The Paines also gave the building's contents, including an exceptional collection of paintings, sculpture, and furniture.

The Paines' legacy includes works by French Barbizon masters such as Corot and Rousseau, American paintings by Inness and Homer, etchings by Whisler and Dürer, and sculptures by Frederic Remington and Helen Farnsworth. Representative works from the art center's collection and changing exhibitions are presented in the main gallery, and specialized works are featured in three other galleries. The English tradition in furniture can be seen throughout the center, while a sunken garden emulates the Pond Garden at Hampton Court in England. Native Wisconsin plants and trees and exotic specimens from elsewhere dominate the arboretum.

Paine Art Center and Gardens, 1410 Algoma Blvd., Oshkosh, WI 54901-2719. **Phone:** 920/235-6903. **Fax:** 920/235-6303. **E-mail:** paca@vbe.com. **Website:** www.paineartcenter.com. **Hours:** 11-4 Tues.-Sun.; closed Mon. and major holidays. **Admission:** adults, $5; seniors, $3; students 13-18, $2; children under 13, free.

PATRICK AND BEATRICE HAGGERTY MUSEUM OF ART. The Patrick and Beatrice Haggerty Museum of Art at Marquette University in Milwaukee was founded and named for its donors, electronic pioneer Patrick Haggerty and his wife, Beatrice Haggerty, in 1984. Mr. Haggerty, an alumnus, was the founder of Texas Instruments.

The museum, which succeeded a library gallery founded in 1955, has more than 4,000 works of art, including European and American paintings from the fifteenth to twentieth centuries; modern paintings, prints, drawings, and photography; works by major twentieth-century artists; decorative arts; and Asian and African art. Many of the works are religious in nature.

Patrick and Beatrice Haggerty Museum of Art, Marquette University, 13th and Clybourne Sts., Milwaukee, WI 53233 (postal address: PO Box 1881, Milwaukee, WI 53201-1881). **Phone:** 414/288-7290. **Fax:** 414/288-5415. **E-mail:** haggertym@vms.csd.mu.edu. **Website:** www.mu.edu/haggerty. **Hours:** 10-4:30 Mon.-Sat. (also to 8 p.m. Thurs.), 12-5 Sun.; closed New Year's Day, Easter, Thanksgiving, and Christmas. **Admission:** free.

Wyoming

WHITNEY GALLERY OF WESTERN ART. The Whitney Gallery of Western Art, one of five museums at the Buffalo Bill Historical Center in Cody, Wyoming, was opened in 1959 in memory of Gertrude Vanderbilt Whitney, sculptor and art patron, who created a monumental bronze sculpture of William F. "Buffalo Bill" Cody in 1922–1924 and donated 40 acres of land for the site of the historical center (she also founded the Whitney Museum of American Art in New York City). Funds for the Whitney Gallery were provided by Whitney's son, Cornelius Vanderbilt Whitney.

In 1969 the Buffalo Bill Museum moved from a log cabin into a new wing linked to the Whitney Gallery. Other additions followed over the years, to comprise the current Buffalo Bill Historical Center, which now also includes the Plains Indian Museum, the Cody Firearms Museum, the McCracken Research Library, and the new Draper Museum of Natural History (see Natural History Museums).

The historical center has one of the most significant collections of western art, featuring the works of such artists as George Catlin, Alfred Jacob Miller, Albert Bierstadt, Frederic Remington, Charles M. Russell, William R. Leigh, and N. C. Wyeth.

Whitney Gallery of Western Art, Buffalo Bill Historical Center, 720 Sheridan Ave., Cody, WY 82414. **Phone:** 307/587-4771. **Fax:** 307/587-5714. **E-mail:** thomb@bbhc.org. **Website:** www.bbhc.org. **Hours:** Apr.—10-5 daily; May—8 a.m.-8 p.m. daily; June-mid-Sept.—7 a.m.-8 p.m. daily; mid-Sept.-Oct.—8-5 daily; Nov.-Mar.—10-3 Tues.-Sun.; closed Mon. **Admission:** adults, $15; seniors, $13; college students, $6; children 6-17, $4; children under 6, free.

ART GALLERIES

Alabama

SARAH MOODY GALLERY OF ART. The Sarah Moody Gallery of Art at the University of Alabama at Tuscaloosa is named for arts patron Sarah Moody McCorkley, who funded the refurbishing of the gallery in 1980. Later, her daughter, Farley Moody Galbraith, established an exhibition endowment, and her granddaughter, Farley Moody Galbraith II, provided funds for the acquisition of new artworks. The gallery displays contemporary works by regional and national artists.

Sarah Moody Gallery of Art, University of Alabama, 103 Garland Hall, PO Box 870270, Tuscaloosa, AL 35487-0270. **Phones:** 205/348-1890 and 205/348-5967. **Fax:** 205/348-0287. **E-mail:** wdooley@woodsquad.as.ua.edu. **Website:** www.as.us.edu/art/indexart.html. **Hours:** mid-Aug.-mid-June—9-4:30 Mon.-Fri., 2-5 Sun.; closed Sat. and university holidays and breaks; mid-June-mid-Aug.—10-12 and 2-4 Mon.-Fri.; closed Sat.-Sun. **Admission:** free.

Arizona

SHEMER ART CENTER. See Arts Centers.

California

ELOISE PICKARD SMITH GALLERY AND MARY PORTER SESNON ART GALLERY. The University of California at Santa Cruz has two art galleries named for women—the Eloise Pickard Smith Gallery in Cowell College and the Mary Porter Sesnon Art Gallery in Porter College. Eloise Pickard Smith was an art activist and the wife of the university's first provost, historian Page Smith. She worked to convert a table-tennis room into an art gallery, which opened in 1965 and now features art of the Monterey Bay region. Mary Porter Sesnon was an artist whose daughter, Barbara Sesnon Cartan, established a gallery and music room in her memory in 1971. Porter College was named for Sesnon's father, Benjamin Franklin Porter. Her three children also gave a 67-acre plot of land to the university. The gallery is devoted to American contemporary art.

Eloise Pickard Smith Gallery, University of California at Santa Cruz, Cowell College, Santa Cruz, CA 95064. **Phone:** 831/459-2953. **Fax:** 831/459-2166. **E-mail:** lapope@aol.com. **Hours:** Sept.-June—10:30-4:30 Tues.-Sun.; closed Mon., July-Aug., and university holidays and breaks. **Admission:** free.

Mary Porter Sesnon Gallery, University of California at Santa Cruz, Porter College, Santa Cruz, CA 95064. **Phones:** 831/459-3606 and 831/459-2314. **Fax:** 831/459-3535. **E-mail:** sgraham@cats.ucsc.edu. **Website:** www.arts.ucsc.edu/sesnon. **Hours:** Sept.-June—12-5 Tues.-Sun., closed Mon., July-Aug., and university holidays and breaks. **Admission:** free.

HELEN LINDHURST FINE ARTS GALLERY AND HELEN LINDHURST ARCHITECTURE GALLERY. Two galleries in Watt Hall on the University of Southern California in Los Angeles were founded in the mid-1980s as a result of the generosity of philanthropist Helen Lindhurst, who had a great interest in fine arts and architecture. The Helen Lindhurst Fine Arts Gallery presents thematic exhibitions of new works by fine arts students, faculty, and guest artists that span all media—from sculpture and painting to ceramics and digital media. It also hosts an annual exhibit of works by high school students. The Helen Lindhurst Architecture Gallery has juried exhibitions of architectural works ranging from the classic to the futuristic, including drawings, photographs, models, and three-dimensional installations.

Helen Lindhurst Fine Arts Gallery and Helen Lindhurst Architecture Gallery, University of Southern California, Watt Hall, University Park Campus, 850 W. 37th St., Los Angeles, CA 90089. **Fine Arts Gallery—Phone:** 213/740-2787. **Website:** www.usc.edu/dept/finearts. **Hours:** Sept.-May—9-4 Mon.-Fri.; closed Sat.-Sun. and university holidays and breaks; June-Aug.—varies with exhibitions. **Admission:** free. **Architecture Gallery—Phone:** 213/740-2723. **Website:** www.usc.edu/dept/architecture. **Hours:** Sept.-May—10-6 Mon.-Fri., 12-5 Sat.; closed Sun. and university holidays and breaks; June-Aug.—varies with exhibitions. **Admission:** free.

HYDE GALLERY. The Hyde Gallery at Grossmont College in El Cajon, California, honors Marjorie Hyde, an artist and founding head of the Department of Art. The contemporary art gallery presents exhibitions of paintings, prints, ceramics, sculpture, and photographs.

Hyde Gallery, Grossmont College, 8800 Grossmont College Dr., El Cajon, CA 92020. **Phone:** 619/644-7299. **Fax:** 619/461-3396. **E-mail:** charlene.engel@gcccd.net. **Hours:** Sept.-May—10-6:30 Mon.-Thurs. (also to 8 p.m. Thurs.); 10-2 Fri.; closed Sat.-Sun., June-Aug., and college holidays and breaks. **Admission:** free.

LaBAND ART GALLERY. The LaBand Art Gallery, founded in 1985 at Loyola Marymount University in Los Angeles, was a gift of French philanthropists Walter and Francine LaBand. The gallery, which is part of the Fritz B. Burns Fine Arts Center, features thematic exhibitions pertaining to traditional and nontraditional spirituality, social and political issues, and ethnological and anthropological subjects.

LaBand Art Gallery, Loyola Marymount University, 7900 Loyola Blvd., Los Angeles, CA 90045-8345. **Phone:** 310/338-2880. **Fax:** 310/338-6024. **E-mail:** gfuglie@popmail.lmu.edu. **Website:** www.lmu.edu/colleges/cfa/art/laband. **Hours:** mid-Aug.-mid-May—11-4 Wed.-Fri., 12-4 Sat.; closed Sun.-Tues., June-mid-Aug., and university holidays and breaks. **Admission:** free.

PEPPERS ART GALLERY. The Peppers Art Gallery at the University of Redlands in Redlands, California, resulted from an art building gift from art patron Ann Peppers after she was an adult art student at the university. The gallery mounts six shows a year—featuring the works of students and faculty and four exhibitions of contemporary art by southern California artists.

Peppers Art Gallery, University of Redlands, 1200 E. Colton Ave., PO Box 3080, Redlands, CA 92373-0999. **Phone:** 909/793-2121. **Fax:** 909/748-6293. **Website:** www.redlands.edu. **Hours:** Sept.-May—1-5 Tues.-Fri., 2-5 Sat.-Sun.; closed Mon., June-Aug., and university holidays and breaks. **Admission:** free.

RUTH CHANDLER WILLIAMSON GALLERY. Family members of alumna and newspaper heiress Ruth Chandler Williamson contributed and raised funds to build an art gallery in her honor at Scripps College in Claremont, California, in 1993–1994. Among its collections are American paintings; contemporary American, British, Korean, Mexican, and Japanese ceramics; Japanese prints; cloisonné; and African sculpture. The gallery presents the nation's oldest and largest annual ceramics show.

Ruth Chandler Williamson Gallery, Scripps College, 1030 Columbia Ave., Claremont, CA 91711-3948. **Phone:** 909/607-4690. **Fax:** 909/607-4691. **E-mail:** mmacnaug @scrippscol.edu. **Website:** www.scrippscol.edu/~dept/ gallery/wwwgallery/homepg.html. **Hours:** Sept.-May—1-5 Wed.-Sun.; closed Mon.-Tues., June-Aug., and college holidays and breaks. **Admission:** free.

Colorado

CLARA HATTON GALLERY. The Clara Hatton Gallery at Colorado State University in Fort Collins honors the founding faculty member and chairperson of the Art Department. Founded in 1970, the gallery presents changing exhibitions of contemporary prints, posters, and other works in the Visual Arts Building.

Clara Hatton Gallery, Colorado State University, Dept. of Art, Visual Arts Bldg., Fort Collins, CO 80523-1770. **Phone:** 970/491-7634. **Fax:** 970/491-0505. **E-mail:** lfrickman@vines.colostate.edu. **Hours:** 8-12 and 1-4:30 Mon.-Fri. (also 1-4 Sat. in Sept.-May); closed university holidays and breaks. **Admission:** free.

Connecticut

EZRA AND CECILE ZILKHA GALLERY. The Ezra and Cecile Zilkha Gallery in the Center for the Arts at Wesleyan University in Middletown, Connecticut, was founded in 1973 with donated funds from the art patrons for whom the gallery is named. The gallery presents changing contemporary art exhibitions.

Ezra and Cecile Zilkha Gallery, Wesleyan University, Center for the Arts, Middletown, CT 06450-0442 (postal address: Wesleyan University, 283 Washington Terrace, Middletown, CT 06459). **Phone:** 860/685-2695. **Fax:** 860/685-2061. **E-mail:** parnold@wesleyan.edu. **Website:** www.wesleyan.edu/cfa/zilkha/home/html. **Hours:** Sept.-May—12-4 Tues.-Sun.; closed Mon. and university holidays and breaks; June-Aug.—varies with showings. **Admission:** free.

District of Columbia

GEORGE WASHINGTON UNIVERSITY ART GALLERY. The George Washington University Art Gallery in Washington, D.C., is a continuation of more than 30 years of service by the Dimock Gallery, named for Susan Dimock Catalini, deceased daughter of Susan Whitney Dimock, who donated funds and a collection of paintings, decorative arts, and furnishings. Founded in 1966, the gallery was renamed and relocated in 2001 from the lower level of Lisner Auditorium to the second floor of a new and more accessible Media and Public Affairs Building across the street. It has a collection of largely American art and presents changing exhibitions of works from the collection, students, faculty, alumni, and other artists—often of a historical nature.

George Washington University Art Gallery, Media and Public Affairs Bldg., 805 21st St. N.W., Washington, DC 20052. **Phone:** 202/994-1525. **Fax:** 202/994-1632. **E-mail:** ldmiller@gwu.edu. **Hours:** 10-5 Tues.-Fri.; closed Sat.-Mon. and national holidays. **Admission:** free.

Florida

POPE AND MARGARET DUNCAN GALLERY OF ART. The Sampson Hall Art Gallery at Stetson University in DeLand, Florida, was renamed in 1991 in honor of Pope and Margaret Duncan, who had served as president and first lady of the university from 1977 to 1987. Founded in 1965, the gallery emphasizes contemporary art of the Southeast.

Pope and Margaret Duncan Gallery of Art, Stetson University, Sampson Hall, Campus Box 8252, 421 N. Woodland Blvd., DeLand, FL 32720-3756. **Phone:** 904/822-7266. **Fax:** 904/822-7268. **E-mail:** cnelson@stetson.edu. **Website:** www.stetson.edu/department/art. **Hours:** Sept.-May—10-4 Mon.-Fri., 1-4 Sat.-Sun.; closed university holidays and breaks; June-Aug.—varies with occasional shows. **Admission:** free.

SELBY GALLERY. The Selby Gallery at the Ringling School of Art and Design in Sarasota, Florida, is named for William and Marie Selby, whose foundation was a major donor in the gallery's founding in 1986. Mr. Selby was an oil executive who cofounded Texaco, and Mrs. Selby left their Sarasota home in her will for the Marie Selby Botanical Gardens (see Botanical Gardens and Arboretums). The 3,000-square-foot gallery offers changing exhibitions of contemporary art and design.

Selby Gallery, Ringling School of Art and Design, 2700 N. Tamiami Trail, Sarasota, FL 34234. **Phone:** 941/359-7563. **Fax:** 941/359-7517. **E-mail:** kdean@rsad.edu. **Website:** www.rsad.edu/. **Hours:** 10-4 Mon.-Sat. (also to 7 p.m. Tues.); closed Mon. and school holidays and breaks. **Admission:** free.

Georgia

GERTRUDE HERBERT INSTITUTE OF ART. See Arts Centers.

Illinois

ARTEMISIA GALLERY. See Women's Museums, Galleries, and Halls of Fame.

BETTY RYMER GALLERY. The Betty Rymer Gallery at the School of the Art Institute of Chicago resulted from a gift by Barry Rymer, a governing board member, in honor of his wife. The gallery presents exhibitions by nationally known artists.

Betty Rymer Gallery, School of the Art Institute of Chicago, 280 S. Columbus Dr., Chicago, IL 60603. **Phone:** 312/443-3703. **Fax:** 312/443-1493. **Website:** www.artic.edu/bettyrymer. **Hours:** 10-5 Mon.-Sat. (also to 8 p.m. Thurs.); closed Sun., mid-July-mid-Aug., and major holidays. **Admission:** free.

LAURA A. SPRAGUE ART GALLERY. The Laura A. Sprague Art Gallery was founded at Joliet Junior College in Joliet, Illinois, in 1978 with funds donated by Sprague's daughter, Laura Kingsbury, and matched by the college foundation. The gallery displays artworks in all media by local, regional, and national artists.

Laura A. Sprague Art Gallery, Joliet Junior College, 1215 Houbolt Ave., Joliet, IL 60431. **Phone:** 815/729-9020. **Fax:** 815/280-6739. **Website:** www.jjc.cc.il.us. **Hours:** Sept.-May—8-8 Mon.-Fri., closed Sat.-Sun. and college holidays and breaks; June-Aug.—varies with occasional shows. **Admission:** free.

RENAISSANCE SOCIETY AT THE UNIVERSITY OF CHICAGO. The Renaissance Society at the University of Chicago has been located since 1979 in Bergman

Gallery on the fourth floor of Cobb Hall. The site was originally funded by art patrons Edwin and Lindy Bergman to house the undergraduate studio art program and an annual exhibition of works by fine arts graduate students. Founded in 1915, the Renaissance Society is the oldest continuously operated gallery in Chicago devoted exclusively to temporary exhibitions of avant-garde art.

Renaissance Society of the University of Chicago, Cobb Hall, 5811 S. Ellis Ave., Chicago, IL 60637. **Phone:** 773/702-8670. **Fax:** 773/702-9669. **Website:** www.renaissancesociety.org. **Hours:** Oct.-June—10-5 Tues.-Fri., 12-5 Sat.-Sun.; closed Mon., July-Sept., and national holidays. **Admission:** free.

WOMAN MADE GALLERY. See Women's Museums, Galleries, and Halls of Fame.

Iowa

ARMSTRONG GALLERY. The Armstrong Hall of Fine Arts and its Armstrong Gallery at Cornell College in Mount Vernon, Iowa, were established in 1937 through the bequest of Blanche Swingley Armstrong, an alumna, amateur painter, and philanthropist. The gallery has collections of paintings, prints, and drawings and presents changing exhibitions of student, faculty, and a range of other art. In addition to the gallery, the fine arts building also contains the art, music, and theater departments and related facilities.

Armstrong Gallery, Cornell College, 600 1st St. W., Mount Vernon, IA 52314-1098. **Phone:** 319/895-4491. **Fax:** 319/895-5296. **E-mail:** scoleman@cornell-iowa.edu. **Website:** www.cornell-iowa.edu. **Hours:** Sept.-May—9-4 Mon.-Fri., 2-4 Sun.; closed Sat., June-Aug., and college holidays and breaks. **Admission:** free.

FARNHAM GALLERIES. The art galleries at Simpson College in Indianola, Iowa, were renamed for alumni John and Dorothy Farnham following their 1990s gift for the renovation of the 1982 exhibition space. Changing showings of contemporary art, largely by regional artists, are presented in the galleries.

Farnham Galleries, Simpson College, 701 N. C St., Indianola, IA 50125. **Phone:** 515/961-1561. **Fax:** 515/961-1498. **E-mail:** heinicke@storm.simpson.edu. **Hours:** Sept.-May—8:30-4:30 Mon.-Fri.; closed Sat.-Sun., June-Aug., and college holidays and breaks. **Admission:** free.

Kansas

ALICE C. SABATINI GALLERY. One of the Topeka and Shawnee County Public Library's two art galleries in Topeka, Kansas, was renamed for artist Alice C. Sabatini and opened in early 2002. The name change for the 1975 gallery came after her husband, banker Frank Sabatini, and family and friends endowed an annual children's exhibition in memory of Mrs. Sabatini. Changing historical and contemporary art exhibitions are presented in the newly expanded gallery.

Alice C. Sabatini Gallery, Topeka and Shawnee County Public Library, 1515 W. 10th St., Topeka, KS 66660-1374. **Phone:** 785/580-4516. **Fax:** 785/580-4496. **E-mail:** lpeters@tscpl.lib.ks.us. **Website:** www.tscpl.org. **Hours:** 10-9 Mon.-Fri., 10-6 Sat., 1-9 Sun.; closed major holidays.

Kentucky

CLARA M. EAGLE GALLERY. The Clara M. Eagle Gallery, named for an early art-faculty member, is one of three galleries that are part of the University Art Galleries at Murray State University in Murray, Kentucky. Regional and traveling contemporary art exhibitions are featured in the gallery at the Price Doyle Fine Arts Center.

Clara M. Eagle Gallery, Murray State University, 604 Price Doyle Fine Arts Center, 15th and Olive Sts., Murray, KY 42071-3342. **Phone:** 270/762-3052. **Fax:** 270/762-3920. **E-mail:** jim.bryant@murraystate.edu. **Hours:** Sept.-May—8-5 Mon.-Fri., 1-4 Sat.-Sun.; closed university holidays and breaks; June-Aug.—9-4 Mon.-Fri.; closed Sat.-Sun. **Admission:** free.

DORIS ULMANN GALLERIES. Freelance photographer Doris Ulmann gave the seed money and 5,000 of her photographs to the Art Department at Berea College in Berea, Kentucky, to create the Doris Ulmann Galleries in 1975. The photos included many of her highly regarded images of Appalachian people and craftsmen. The galleries—which consist of three separate halls—also contain paintings, prints, crafts, textiles, sculpture, and ceramics.

Doris Ulmann Galleries, Berea College, Art. Dept., Chestnut and Elipse Sts., CPO 2342, Berea, KY 40404. **Phones:** 859/985-3000 and 859/985-3544. **E-mail:** robert_boyce@berea.edu. **Website:** www.berea.edu. **Hours:** Sept.-May—8 a.m.-9 p.m. Mon.-Thurs., 8-5 Fri., 1-5 Sun.; closed Sat., June-Aug., and college holidays and breaks. **Admission:** free.

Maine

ETHEL H. BLUM ART GALLERY. The Ethel H. Blum Art Gallery at the College of the Atlantic in Bar Harbor, Maine, was founded in 1993 with a gift from a Boston-area artist and art patron who summered on Mt. Desert Island in Maine. The gallery, located in the Thomas S. Gates Jr. Community Center, mounts exhibitions of works by students, faculty, and regional artists.

Ethel H. Blum Art Gallery, College of the Atlantic, 105 Eden St., Bar Harbor, ME 04609-1105. **Phone:** 207/288-5015. **Hours:** Sept.-May—9-5 Mon.-Fri.; closed Sat.-Sun. and college holidays and breaks; June-Aug.—10-4 Tues.-Sat.; closed Sun.-Mon. **Admission:** free.

Maryland

ELIZABETH MYERS MITCHELL GALLERY. The Elizabeth Myers Mitchell Gallery at St. John's College in Annapolis, Maryland, resulted from a gift by philanthropist and art collector Elizabeth Myers Mitchell, who was a member of the college's board. The gallery, established in 1989, presents changing exhibitions of historical and regional interest and seeks to further connections between the visual arts and liberal arts.

Elizabeth Myers Mitchell Gallery, St. John's College, 60 College Ave., PO Box 2800, Annapolis, MD 21404-2800. **Phone:** 410/626-2556. **Website:** www.sjca.edu. **Hours:** late Aug.-mid-May—12-5 Tues.-Sun.; closed Mon., mid-May-late Aug., and college holidays and breaks. **Admission:** free.

ROSENBERG GALLERY. The Rosenberg Gallery at Goucher College in Baltimore was founded in 1981 in memory of Ruth Blaustein Rosenberg, an alumna and trustee, by her son, Henry Rosenberg. The gallery, located in the lobby of Kraushaar Auditorium, largely features contemporary art by regional artists.

Rosenberg Gallery, Goucher College, 1021 Dulaney Rd., Baltimore, MD 21204. **Phone:** 410/337-6333. **Fax:** 410/337-6405. **E-mail:** lburns@goucher.edu. **Website:** www.goucher.edu/rosenberg/. **Hours:** Sept.-May—9-5 daily (also evenings for auditorium performances); closed Christmas to mid-Jan. and other college holidays and breaks. **Admission:** free.

Massachusetts

IRIS AND B. GERALD CANTOR ART GALLERY. The Iris and B. Gerald Cantor Art Gallery at the College of the Holy Cross in Worcester, Massachusetts, was

proposed and underwritten by the donors for whom it was named. Opened in 1983, the gallery occupies a renovated space in a late-nineteenth-century building that also houses the central administration and some academic departments. It has ten Rodin sculptures in its collections and presents changing exhibitions dealing with art history, contemporary art, and social issues.

Iris and B. Gerald Cantor Art Gallery, College of the Holy Cross, 1 College St., Worcester, MA 01610. **Phone:** 508/793-3356. **Fax:** 508/793-3030. **E-mail:** cantor@holycross.edu. **Website:** www.holycross.edu/departments/cantor/website/cantor.html. **Hours:** Sept.-May—11-4 Mon.-Fri., 2-5 Sat.-Sun.; closed June-Aug. and college holidays and breaks. **Admission:** free.

MIT-LIST VISUAL ARTS CENTER. See Arts Centers.

MOLL ART CENTER. The Moll Art Center in Anna Maria College in Paxton, Massachusetts, is named for Corrin Moll (Sister Louis Arthur), who was the first chair of the Art Department at the college founded by the Sisters of St. Anne. The art gallery presents changing exhibitions of local, regional, and national artworks.

Moll Art Center, 50 Sunset Lane, Paxton, MA 01612. **Phone:** 508/849-3442. **Fax:** 508/849-3408. **Website:** www.annamaria.edu. **Hours:** Sept.-May—9-4 Mon.-Fri.; closed Sat.-Sun., major holidays, and college breaks. **Admission:** free.

WATSON GALLERY. The Watson Fine Arts Center and its Watson Gallery at Wheaton College in Norton, Massachusetts, are named for their donor, Jeanette Kittredge Watson, a 1902 alumna and the wife of Thomas J. Watson, founder of the IBM Corporation. The gallery, which opened in 1962, has collections of American and European paintings, prints, and drawings from the fifteenth to twentieth centuries, as well as antique bronzes, decorative arts, sculpture, Native American baskets, and other works. The gallery presents changing historical and contemporary exhibitions from its collections and elsewhere. The fine arts center also houses the art, music, and theater departments. Plans are underway to double the gallery space in another building.

Watson Gallery, Wheaton College, Watson Fine Arts Center, E. Main St., Norton, MA 02766. **Phones:** 508/286-3578 and 508/286-3570. **Fax:** 508/286-3565. **E-mail:** amurray@wheatonma.edu. **Website:** www.wheatonma.edu/academic/watson/home.html. **Hours:** Sept.-May—

12:30-4:30 daily; closed June-Aug. and college holidays and breaks. **Admission:** free.

Michigan

MEADOW BROOK ART GALLERY. The Meadow Brook Art Gallery at Oakland University in Rochester, Michigan, is named for the estate of Matilda Dodge Wilson, who donated her land for the site of the university. The gallery, located in Wilson Hall, focuses on contemporary art and local emerging artists. Wilson's home on the campus is also a historic house museum (see Historic House Museums). She was the widow of automobile pioneer John Dodge and her second husband, Alfred Wilson, a lumber broker.

Meadow Brook Art Gallery, Oakland University, 208 Wilson Hall, Rochester, MI 48309-4401. **Phone:** 248/370-3005. **Fax:** 248/370-4208. **E-mail:** goody@oakland.edu. **Hours:** Sept.-mid-May—12-5 Tues.-Fri., 1-5:30 Sat.-Sun. (also for theater performances—6:30 p.m. to first intermission Tues.-Fri. and 5:30 p.m. to first intermission Sat.-Sun.); closed Mon., mid-May-Aug., and university holidays and breaks. **Admission:** free.

Minnesota

CATHERINE G. MURPHY GALLERY. Alumna Catherine G. Murphy made a $500,000 contribution to the College of St. Catherine in St. Paul, Minnesota, in 1979 for the visual arts center and the contemporary art gallery named for her.

Catherine G. Murphy Gallery, College of St. Catherine, 2004 Randolph Ave., St. Paul, MN 55105. **Phone:** 651/690-6644. **Fax:** 651/690-6024. **E-mail:** kmdaniels@stkate.edu. **Website:** www.stkate.edu/gallery. **Hours:** Sept.-May—8-8 Mon.-Fri., 12-6 Sat.-Sun.; closed Jan., June-Aug., Thanksgiving, and Christmas. **Admission:** free.

KATHERINE NASH GALLERY. Katherine Nash, an art faculty member and sculptor, was the founder of the Art Department gallery named in her honor at the University of Minnesota in Minneapolis. The gallery, founded in 1973 and located on the lower concourse of Willey Hall, is tied closely to the art curriculum and emphasizes local and regional artists.

Katherine Nash Gallery, University of Minnesota, Willey Hall, 225 19th Ave., Minneapolis, MN 55455 (postal address: 208 Art Bldg., 216 21st Ave. S., Minneapolis, MN 55455). **Phone:** 612/624-6518. **Fax:** 612/625-0152. **E-mail:** nash@tc.umn.edu. **Website:** www.artdept.umn.edu. **Hours:** 10-4 Tues.-Fri. (also to 8 p.m. Thurs.), 11-5 Sat.; closed

Sun.-Mon., Aug., and university holidays and breaks; mid-June-July—sometimes open same hours for special showings. **Admission:** free.

Missouri

NELLIE STRATTON DAVIS ART GALLERY. A donation by Nellie Stratton Davis, an alumna of Stephens College, established an art gallery in her name at the college in Columbia, Missouri. Opened in 1965, the gallery features contemporary and regional art, with an emphasis on women artists.

Nellie Stratton Davis Art Gallery Stephens College, Walnut and Ripley Sts., PO Box 2012, Columbia, MO 65215. **Phone:** 573/876-7267. **Fax:** 573/876-7248. **Website:** www.stephens.edu. **Hours:** Sept.-May—10-4 Mon.-Fri.; closed Sat.-Sun., June-Aug., and college holidays and breaks. **Admission:** free.

Montana

HELEN E. COPELAND GALLERY. The 1974 Haynes Fine Arts Gallery at the Montana State University's School of Art in Bozeman was renamed in 1996 for benefactor Helen E. Copeland, an alumna and artist. It has a collection of prints, ceramics, and crafts and presents contemporary art exhibitions.

Helen E. Copeland Gallery, Montana State University, School of Art, 213 Haynes Hall, Box 173680, Bozeman, MT 59717. **Phone:** 406/994-2562. **Fax:** 406/994-3680. **E-mail:** edungan@montana.edu. **Website:** www.montana.edu/wwwart. **Hours:** Sept.-May—8-5 Mon.-Fri.; closed Sat.-Sun., June-Aug., and university holidays and breaks. **Admission:** free.

Nebraska

ELDER ART GALLERY. The Elder Art Gallery in the Rogers Center for Fine Arts at Nebraska Wesleyan University in Lincoln is named for Edith Dimmit Elder, an alumna, artist, and major donor to the university. Among her contributions was a bequest for the speech building.

Elder Art Gallery, Nebraska Wesleyan University, Rogers Center for Fine Arts, 50th St. and Huntington Ave., Lincoln, NE 68504-2230 (contact: Art Dept., Nebraska Wesleyan University, 5000 St. Paul Ave., Lincoln, NE 68504-2796). **Phones:** 402/466-2371, 402/465-2230, and 402/465-2273. **Fax:** 402/465-2179. **E-mail:** dp@nebrwesleyan.edu. **Hours:** Sept.-mid-May—10-4 Tues.-Fri., 1-4 Sat.-Sun.; closed Mon., mid-May-Aug., and university holidays and breaks. **Admission:** free.

Nevada

DONNA BEAM FINE ART GALLERY. The Donna Beam Fine Arts Gallery, started in 1960 at the University of Nevada at Las Vegas, was renamed in 1987 for the daughter of businessman Thomas Beam, who funded the remodeling of the art center. Contemporary art in all media can be seen in the gallery's changing exhibitions.

Donna Beam Fine Art Gallery, University of Nevada at Las Vegas, 4505 Maryland Pkwy., Las Vegas, NV 89154-5002. **Phone:** 702/895-3893. **Fax:** 702/895-3751. **E-mail:** schefcij@ccmail.nevada.edu. **Website:** www.unlv.edu/main/museums.html. **Hours:** 9-5 Mon.-Fri., 10-2 Sat.; closed Sun. and university holidays. **Admission:** free.

New Hampshire

THORNE-SAGENDORPH ART GALLERY. The Thorne-Sagendorph Art Gallery at Keene State College in Keene, New Hampshire, was founded in 1965 with a gift from artist beaTrix Sagendorph in memory of her mother, Louise E. Thorne. In 1976 the gallery became the Thorne-Sagendorph Art Gallery, when a new wing was dedicated to beaTrix's husband, Robb Sagendorph, founder and publisher of *Yankee* magazine. The gallery's collection includes works by both artists who flourished around Mt. Monadnock at the turn of the twentieth century and more contemporary artists, while the changing exhibitions feature local, regional, national, and international art.

Thorne-Sagendorph Art Gallery, Keene State College, Wyman Way, Keene, NH 03435 (postal address: 229 Main St., Keene, NH 03435-3501). **Phone:** 603/358-2720. **Fax:** 603/358-2238. **E-mail:** mahern@keene.edu. **Website:** www.keene.edu/tsag. **Hours:** Sept.-May—12-4 Mon.-Fri. (also to 7 p.m. Thurs. and Fri.), 12-4 Sat.-Sun.; June-Aug.—12-4 Sat.-Wed. (also to 6 p.m. Tues. and Wed.); closed Thurs.-Fri., major holidays, and college breaks. **Admission:** free.

New York

BERTHA V. B. LEDERER FINE ARTS GALLERY. The art gallery at the State University of New York at Geneseo was renamed in 1982 for Bertha V. B. Lederer, the longtime fine arts department chairperson. The gallery, which was established in 1967, has collections of paintings, sculpture, graphics, ceramics, and furniture, and primarily presents exhibitions of contemporary art.

Bertha V. B. Lederer Fine Arts Gallery, State University of New York at Geneseo, Fine Arts Bldg., 1 College Circle, Geneseo, NY 14454. **Phone:** 716/245-5814. **Fax:** 716/245-5815. **E-mail:** shanahan@geneseo.edu. **Website:** www.geneseo.edu. **Hours:** Sept.-May—2-5 daily (also to 8 p.m. Thurs.); June-Aug.—1-4 Mon.-Fri. when show scheduled; closed Sat.-Sun. **Admission:** free.

JOE AND EMILY LOWE ART GALLERY. The Joe and Emily Lowe Art Gallery at Syracuse University in Syracuse, New York, was established in 1952 following a gift of $150,000 toward the construction of the School of Art building and a $250,000 endowment from the New York City philanthropists to maintain the building. Mr. Lowe was the president of a manufacturing company and an importing firm, while Mrs. Lowe was an artist.

After the art building became too small to house all the departments of the School of Art in 1975, the Lowe Art Center was moved to expanded space in Sims Hall and renamed the Lowe Art Gallery. To assist with the move, the Joe and Emily Lowe Foundation made a $110,000 grant toward the completion of the gallery and its exhibition and teaching programs. The gallery presents changing exhibitions from the University Art Collection and elsewhere on nineteenth- and twentieth-century American paintings, sculpture, and graphics; African and Indian sculpture, textiles, and decorative arts; photography; and other artworks.

Joe and Emily Lowe Art Gallery, Syracuse University, Sims Hall, Shaffer Art Bldg., Syracuse, NY 13244-1230. **Phone:** 315/443-4098. **Fax:** 315/443-1303. **E-mail:** jnhart@syr.edu. **Website:** www.vpa.syr.edu/events/exhibits.cfm. **Hours:** Sept.-May—12-5 Tues.-Sun. (also to 8 p.m. Wed.); closed Mon. and national holidays; June-Aug.—1:30-4 Tues.-Thurs., closed Fri.-Mon. **Admission:** free.

MIRIAM AND IRA D. WALLACH ART GALLERY. Philanthropists Miriam and Ira D. Wallach provided the funds for a research-oriented art gallery in their names at Columbia University in New York City. The Miriam and Ira D. Wallach Art Gallery, which opened in 1986 in Schermerhorn Hall, presents art exhibitions resulting from student and faculty research studies.

Miriam and Ira D. Wallach Art Gallery, Columbia University, 826 Schermerhorn Hall, MC 5517, 1190 Amsterdam Ave., New York, NY 10027. **Phone:** 212/854-2877. **Fax:** 212/854-7800. **Website:** www.columbia.edu/cu/wallach. **Hours:**

Sept.-May—1-5 Wed.-Sat.; closed Sun.-Tues., June-Aug., and major holidays. **Admission:** free.

PICKER ART GALLERY. The Picker Art Gallery in the Charles A. Dana Arts Center at Colgate University in Hamilton, New York, is named for Evelyn Picker, who was involved in government and international affairs and whose son, Dr. Harvey Picker, was the primary fund-raiser for the arts center. The gallery, established in 1966 to provide "visual and intellectual evidence of the world's creative potential," has over 10,000 works of art and exhibition areas devoted to antiquity, pre-Columbian, Asian, African, Old Masters, modern, and contemporary art in all media.

Picker Art Gallery, Colgate University, Charles A. Dana Arts Center, 13 Oak Dr., Hamilton, NY 13346-1398. **Phone:** 315/228-7634. **Fax:** 315/228-7935. **E-mail:** pickerart@mail.colgate.edu. **Website:** www.picker.colgate.edu. **Hours:** 10-5 Mon.-Fri.; closed Sat.-Sun. and national holidays; during academic recesses—9-12 Sat., 1-4 Sun.; closed Mon.-Fri. and national holidays. **Admission:** free.

RUBELLE AND NORMAN SCHAFLER GALLERY. When art patron Rubelle Schafler donated the funds to renovate the Pratt Institute's gallery in Brooklyn, New York, the gallery was renamed for her and her husband, Norman Schafler. The Schafler Gallery and the Pratt Manhattan Gallery in New York City present exhibitions on broad topics or issues of concern in contemporary fine arts, design, and architecture, and survey shows by students, faculty, or alumni.

Rubelle and Norman Schafler Gallery, Pratt Institute, 200 Willoughby Ave., Brooklyn, NY 11205. **Phone:** 718/636-3517. **Fax:** 718/636-3785. **E-mail:** exhibits@pratt.edu. **Website:** www.pratt.edu/exhibitions. **Hours:** Sept.-May—9-5 Mon.-Fri.; June-Aug.—9-4 Mon.-Fri.; closed Sat.-Sun. and major holidays. **Admission:** free.

SCHICK ART GALLERY. The Schick Art Gallery at Skidmore College in Saratoga Springs, New York, is named for Pam Schick Kelsey, a 1970 alumna who made a major gift to the college's art program. Founded in 1926, the gallery has collections of paintings, graphics, ceramics, and sculpture and primarily presents contemporary art exhibitions, group and theme shows, and faculty and student work.

Schick Art Gallery, Skidmore College, 815 N. Broadway, Saratoga Springs, NY 12866-1632. **Phone:** 518/580-5049. **Fax:** 518/580-5029. **E-mail:** damiller@skidmore.edu. **Hours:** Sept.-May—9-5 Mon.-Fri., 1-4 Sat.-Sun.; closed college

holidays and breaks; June-Aug.—9-4 Mon.-Fri., 1-4 Sat.; closed Sun. **Admission:** free.

North Carolina

IRENE CULLIS GALLERY. The Irene Cullis Gallery at Greensboro College in Greensboro, North Carolina, is named for the longtime chairperson of the Art Department. It presents the works of students, faculty, and regional contemporary artists.

Irene Cullis Gallery, Greensboro College, 815 W. Market St., Greensboro, NC 27401-1875. **Phone:** 236-272-7102, Ext. 301. **Fax:** 336/271-6634. **Hours:** Sept.-Apr.—10-4 Mon.-Fri., 2-5 Sun.; closed Sat., May-Aug., and college holidays and breaks. **Admission:** free.

Ohio

DOROTHY UBER BRYAN GALLERY. The Dorothy Uber Bryan Gallery—one of three galleries in the Fine Arts Center at Bowling Green State University in Bowling Green, Ohio—was made possible by a donation from an art alumna. The gallery has collections of prints and student and faculty works and largely presents exhibitions of contemporary art.

Dorothy Uber Bryan Gallery, Bowling Green State University, Fine Arts Center, Bowling Green, OH 43403-0211. **Phone:** 419/372-2786. **Fax:** 419/372-2544. **E-mail:** jnathan@bgnet.bgsu.edu. **Website:** www.bgsu.edu/departments/art/gallery/index.html. **Hours:** Sept.-early May—10-4 Tues.-Sat., 1-4 Sun.; closed Mon. and university holidays; mid May-Aug.—varies with occasional showings. **Admission:** free.

EMILY DAVIS GALLERY. The Emily Davis Gallery at the University of Akron in Akron, Ohio, honors a former Art Department chairperson and artist. It features exhibitions of contemporary works.

Emily Davis Gallery, University of Akron, 150 E. Exchange St., Akron, OH 44325-7801. **Phone:** 330/972-5950. **Fax:** 330/972-5960. **Website:** www.uakron.edu/art. **Hours:** Sept.-May—10-5 Mon.-Sat. (also to 9 p.m. Wed.-Thurs.); closed Sun. and university holidays and breaks; June-Aug.—10-4:30 Mon.-Fri.; closed Sat.-Sun. **Admission:** free.

MAZZA COLLECTION GALLERIA and VIRGINIA B. GARDNER FINE ARTS PAVILION. The Mazza Collection Galleria houses a collection of over 1,800 pieces of original artwork from children's books in the Virginia B. Gardner Fine Arts Pavilion at the University of

Findlay in Findlay, Ohio. The Mazza Collection was established by alumni August C. Mazza and his wife, Aleda Pfost Mazza, in 1982, while the fine arts pavilion was named for Virginia B. Gardner, a community supporter of the arts.

Mazza Collection Galleria, Virginia B. Gardner Fine Arts Pavilion, 1000 N. Main St., Findlay, OH 45840. Phone: 419/424-4689. Fax: 419/424-6480. E-mail: mazza @findlay.edu. Website: www.mazzacollection.org. Hours: 12-5 Wed.-Fri., 1-4 Sun.; closed Mon.-Tues., Sat., and major holidays. Admission: free.

Oklahoma

GARDINER ART GALLERY. Gardiner Art Gallery at Oklahoma State University in Stillwater was named in 1970 for Maude Gardiner, the first dean of women at the university. The gallery, which began in 1965, is located in Barlett Center, which also houses the Art Department. It displays student, faculty, and other contemporary art.

Gardiner Art Gallery, Oklahoma State University, 108 Barlett Center, Stillwater, OK 74078. Phone: 405/744-6016. Fax: 405/744-5767. Hours: Oct.-Apr.—8-5 Mon.-Fri., 9-1 Sat., 12-5 Sun.; closed national holidays and university breaks; May-Sept.—8-5 Mon.-Fri.; closed Sat.-Sun. and national holidays. Admission: free.

Pennsylvania

ESTHER M. KLEIN ART GALLERY. The University City Science Center's Esther M. Klein Art Gallery in Philadelphia is a multicultural community-based gallery dedicated to raising the cultural awareness of its diverse audience. It is named for a major patron of arts and cultural activities in the city, who has written several books on the arts and history of the city, has shown special interest in the education of Philadelphia's youth, and was an active supporter of the 1976 gallery when it was known as the University City Science Center Art Gallery.

The science center, established in 1963, is the nation's first and largest urban university-related research park, a consortium of 28 educational and scientific institutions dedicated to improving the quality of life and fostering economic development. The gallery features art-in-science projects, multicultural exhibitions, works of emerging artists, and student workshops and exhibitions.

Esther M. Klein Art Gallery, University City Science Center, 3600 Market St., Philadelphia, PA 19104 (postal address: 3624 Market St., Philadelphia, PA 19104). Phone: 215/387-2262. Fax: 215/382-0056. E-mail: kleinart@ucsc.org. Website: www.ucsc.org/klein/gallery.html. Hours: 9-5 Mon.-Sat.; closed Sun. and major holidays. Admission: free.

FREEDMAN GALLERY. Doris Chanin Freedman, an alumna, arts patron, and administrator, gave the lead gift for the art gallery named in her honor at Albright College in Reading, Pennsylvania. Founded in 1976, the gallery features collections and exhibitions by contemporary American artists.

Freedman Gallery, Albright College, 1621 N. 13th St., PO Box 15234, Reading, PA 19612-5234. Phones: 610/921-7541 and 610/921-7715. Fax: 610/921-7768. Website: www.albright.edu. Hours: Sept.-May—12-6 Tues.-Fri. (also to 8 p.m. Tues.), 12-4 Sat.-Sun.; closed Mon., July-Aug., major holidays, and college breaks; June—12-4 Wed.-Sun. when show scheduled; closed Mon.-Tues. Admission: free.

LORE DEGENSTEIN GALLERY. The Lore Degenstein Gallery at Susquehanna University in Selinsgrove, Pennsylvania, is named for the wife of donor Charles B. Degenstein, the grocery chain executive who funded the building. Found in 1993, the gallery has a collection of central Pennsylvania art and presents traveling and other exhibitions on a variety of subjects.

Lore Degenstein Gallery, Susquehanna University, 514 University Ave., Selinsgrove, PA 17870-1001. Phone: 570/374-4291. Fax: 570/372-2775. E-mail: livingst@susqu.edu. Website: www.susqu.edu. Hours: Sept.-June—1-4 Tues.-Sun. (also 7-9 p.m. Wed.); closed Mon., Dec. 10-Jan. 21, and university holidays and breaks. Admission: free.

South Carolina

CECELIA COKER BELL GALLERY. The Cecelia Coker Bell Gallery at Coker College in Hartsville, South Carolina, is named in memory of the great-granddaughter of the founder of the college, Major James Lide Coker. She died tragically a year after graduating from college. Opened in 1983, the teaching gallery is housed in the Gladys Coker Fort Building and presents student and visiting artist exhibitions.

Cecelia Coker Bell Gallery, Coker College, Art. Dept., 300 E. College Ave., Hartsville, SC 29550. Phones: 843/383-8156 and 843/383-8150. Fax: 843/383-8048. E-mail: lmerriman@pascal.coker.edu. Website: www.coker.edu/art/index.html. Hours: Sept.-mid May—10-4:30 Mon.-Fri.;

closed Sat.-Sun., mid-May-Aug., and major holidays. **Admission:** free.

SUMTER GALLERY OF ART. The Sumter Gallery of Art in Sumter, South Carolina, has been located since 1977 in the historic Greek Revival–style cottage of Elizabeth White, a noted regional artist whose works are featured in the gallery. The gallery also contains touchable art for blind and visually impaired audiences, and two galleries for changing exhibitions.

Sumter Gallery of Art, 421 N. Main St., PO Box 1316, Sumter, SC 29151-1316. **Phone:** 803/773-9452. **Fax:** 803/778-2787. **E-mail:** sumtergallery@sumter.net. **Hours:** 12-5 Tues.-Fri.; 2-5 Sat.-Sun.; closed Mon., July, and major holidays. **Admission:** free.

Tennessee

EDITH DAVIS GALLERY. The Edith Davis Gallery at the Rose Center in Morristown, Tennessee, was funded by the family of the artist and art patron in 1982. The cultural center, housed in an 1892 former high school building, also has local historical exhibits; art, dance, music, and craft facilities; arts festivals; and educational programs.

Edith Davis Gallery, Rose Center, 442 W. 2nd St. N., PO Box 1976, Morristown, TN 37816. **Phone:** 423/586-6205. **Fax:** 423/581-4307. **E-mail:** rosecent@usit.net. **Website:** www.rosecenter.org. **Hours:** 9-5 Mon.-Fri., 9-1 Sat.; closed Sun. and major holidays. **Admission:** free.

MARGARET FORT TRAHERN AND MABEL LARSON FINE ARTS GALLERIES. Austin Peay State University in Clarksville, Tennessee, has two art galleries named for women—the Margaret Fort Trahern Gallery, honoring the university's first art faculty member, and the Mabel Larson Fine Arts Gallery, named for a local art patron who established the university's major contemporary drawing collection. The Trahern Gallery presents changing exhibitions of contemporary art in all media by regional artists, while the Larson Gallery features drawings and other works from the university's art collection.

Margaret Fort Trahern and Mabel Larson Fine Arts Galleries, Austin Peay State University, PO Box 4677, Clarksville, TN 37044. **Phone:** 931/221-7333. **Fax:** 931/221-7432. **E-mail:** holteb@apsu.edu. **Hours:** Trahern Gallery—Sept.-May: 9-4 Mon.-Fri., 10-2 Sat., 1-4 Sun.; June-Aug.: 9-12 and 1-3 Mon.-Fri.; closed Sat.-Sun.; Larson Gallery—8-4 Mon.-Fri.; closed Sat.-Sun.; both galleries closed university holidays and breaks. **Admission:** free.

Texas

BLAFFER GALLERY, THE ART MUSEUM OF THE UNIVERSITY OF HOUSTON. The Blaffer Gallery at the University of Houston in Houston, Texas, was established in 1973 with the gift of artworks from philanthropist and art patron Sarah Campbell Blaffer. Since then, however, it has become a noncollecting gallery that presents changing exhibitions of art from the last 100 years.

Blaffer Gallery, The Art Museum of the University of Houston, University of Houston, 120 Fine Arts Bldg., Houston, TX 77204-4018. **Phone:** 713/743-9521. **Fax:** 713/743-9525. **Website:** www.blaffergallery.org. **Hours:** 10-5 Tues.-Fri., 1-5 Sat.-Sun.; closed Mon. and university holidays. **Admission:** free.

CORA STAFFORD GALLERY. The University of North Texas in Denton has three art galleries—one of which is named for Cora Stafford, the first chairperson of the Art Department. A gallery in Oak Street Hall was renamed in her honor in 1992. It displays student, faculty, and other art.

Cora Stafford Gallery, University of North Texas, Oak Street Hall, Oak and Ponder Sts., Denton, TX 76203 (postal address: School of Visual Arts, PO Box 305100, Denton, TX 76203-5100). **Phones:** 940/565-4005 and 940/565-4001. **Fax:** 940/565-4717. **Hours:** Sept.-May—2-5 Mon.-Fri.; closed Sat.-Sun., June-Aug., and university holidays and breaks. **Admission:** free.

Virginia

DuPONT GALLERY. The DuPont Gallery at Washington & Lee University in Lexington, Virginia, was a 1952 gift of philanthropist Jessie Ball duPont, the first woman trustee of the university. In addition, the contribution covered the cost of the building, which also houses the art and music departments. The gallery, which opened in 1954, largely presents contemporary art by regional artists.

DuPont Gallery, Washington & Lee University, Lexington, VA 24450-0303. **Phones:** 540/463-8861 and 540/463-8859. **Fax:** 540/463-8104. **E-mail:** psimpson@wlu.edu. **Website:** www.wlu.edu. **Hours:** Sept.-May—9-5 Mon.-Fri.; closed Sat.-Sun., June-Aug., and university holidays and breaks. **Admission:** free.

HUNT GALLERY. The Hunt Gallery at Mary Baldwin College in Staunton, Virginia, is named for Lyda Bunker Hunt, a trustee from 1939 until her death in 1955. The gallery is located in the Lyda Bunker

Hunt Dining Hall building, a gift of Hunt's six children, which also contains a dining space, multipurpose lounge, and lecture hall. The gallery has twentieth-century paintings, drawings, prints, and photographs, as well as contemporary art.

Hunt Gallery, Mary Baldwin College, Lyda Bunker Hunt Dining Hall, Market and Vine Sts., Staunton, VA 24401. Phone: 540/887-7196. Hours: Sept.-May—9-5 Mon.-Fri.; closed Sat.-Sun., June-Aug., and college holidays and breaks. Admission: free.

RIDDERHOF MARTIN GALLERY. The Ridderhof Martin Gallery—one of two galleries that comprise the Mary Washington College Galleries in Fredericksburg, Virginia—was established in 1992 as a gift from Phyllis Ridderhof Martin, a California artist who is an alumna. Two large bodies of works in the galleries' collections are by two women—Phyllis Ridderhof Martin and Margaret Sutton, also an alumna. Selections from the collections, as well as artworks from other sources, are shown in changing exhibitions in the galleries.

Ridderhof Martin Gallery, Mary Washington College, College Ave. at Seacobeck St., Fredericksburg, VA 22401-5358. Phone: 540/654-1013. Fax: 540/654-1171. E-mail: gallery@mwe.edu. Website: www.mwc.edu/. Hours: Sept.-May—10-4 Mon., Wed., Fri., 1-4 Sat.-Sun.; closed Tues., Thurs., June-Aug., major holidays, and college breaks. Admission: free.

Wisconsin

CARLSON GALLERY. The Carlson Gallery in the Fine Arts Center at the University of Wisconsin-Stevens Point is named for Edna Carlson, a longtime art faculty member (1923–1961). Founded in 1971, the gallery features contemporary art.

Carlson Gallery, University of Wisconsin-Stevens Point, Fine Arts Center, Stevens Point, WI 54481. Phone: 715/346-4797. Fax: 715/346-2718. Website: www.uwsp.edu/art-design-carlson/. Hours: Sept.-May—10-4 Mon.-Fri. (also 7-9 p.m. Thurs.), 1-4 Sat.-Sun.; closed June-Aug. and university holidays and breaks. Admission: free.

CROSSMAN GALLERY. The Crossman Gallery at the University of Wisconsin-Whitewater is named for Kathleen Crossman, a noted weaver and former art faculty member. Founded in 1970, the gallery is located in the Center of the Arts building; emphasizes contemporary American art; and hosts annual faculty, invitational, ceramics, and fiber shows.

Crossman Gallery, University of Wisconsin-Whitewater, 800 W. Main St., Whitewater, WI 53190. Phone: 262/472-1207. Fax: 262/272-2808. E-mail: flanagan@uwwvax.uuw.edu. Website: www.uww.edu. Hours: Sept.-May—10-5 Mon.-Fri. (also 6-8 p.m. Mon.-Thurs.), 1-4 Sat.; closed Sun., June-mid-July, mid-Dec.-mid-Jan.; and major holidays; mid-July-mid-Aug.—10-5 Mon.-Fri.; closed Sat.-Sun. Admission: free.

ARTS CENTERS
See also Art Galleries; Art Museums.

Alabama

ISABEL ANDERSON COMER MUSEUM AND ARTS CENTER. See Art and History Museums.

Arizona

SHEMER ART CENTER. In 1984, Arizona realtor Martha Evvard Shemer bought a Santa Fe Mission–style house and gave it to the city of Phoenix to use as an art gallery and studio for art classes. The adobe building was the first house built in the Arcadia section of the city. The center presents changing exhibitions of fine arts and crafts, offers art instruction, and has both an outdoor sculpture garden with 34 pieces and orchards on its landscaped grounds.

Shemer Art Center, 5005 E. Camelback Rd., Phoenix, AZ 85018. Phone: 602/262-4727. Fax: 602/262-1605. Website: www.ci.phoenix.az.us/parks/shemer.html. Hours: 10-5 Mon.-Fri. (also to 9 p.m. Tues.), 9-1 Sat.; closed Sun. and major holidays. Admission: free.

California

TRITON MUSEUM OF ART. See Art Museums.

Colorado

COLORADO SPRINGS FINE ARTS CENTER. See Art Museums.

SANGRE DE CRISTO ARTS CENTER. In the late 1960s, two politically active women—Kathy Farley and

Patricia Kelly—saw the need for an arts center in Pueblo, Colorado, and successfully applied for several grants to establish the Sangre de Cristo Arts Center, which opened in 1972. Farley later became a city council member, and Kelly was elected county commissioner. The arts center complex consists of three buildings—one with four art galleries (one devoted to a western art collection and three for changing exhibitions); a children's museum (Buell Children's Museum); and a 7,000-square-foot conference center.

Sangre de Cristo Arts Center, 210 N. Santa Fe Ave., Pueblo, CO 81003. Phone: 719/543-0130. Fax: 719/543-0134. E-mail: artctr@ris.net. Website: www.chieftain.com/artscenter. Hours: 11-4 Mon.-Sat.; closed Sun. and major holidays. Admission: adults, $4; children over 11, $3; children under 12, free.

Florida

ROBERT AND MARY MONTGOMERY ARMORY ART CENTER. The Robert and Mary Montgomery Armory Art Center in West Palm Beach, Florida, was made possible by funding from attorney Robert Montgomery and his wife, Mary, art collectors and philanthropists. The art center is housed in the former Palm Beach County National Guard Armory, a 1939 Art Deco–style building. It contains 5,200 square feet of exhibit space, studio classrooms, and a library.

Robert and Mary Montgomery Armory Art Center, 1703 Lake Ave., West Palm Beach, FL 33401. Phone: 561/832-1776. Fax: 561/832-0191. E-mail: armory@bellsouth.net. Website: www.armoryart.org. Hours: 9-5 Mon.-Fri., 10-2 Sat.; closed Sun. and major holidays. Admission: free.

Georgia

GERTRUDE HERBERT INSTITUTE OF ART. The three-story Federal-style house built by Georgia legislator Nicholas Ware in 1818 was purchased by Olivia Herbert in 1935 and donated to the Augusta Art Club as a memorial to her daughter, Gertrude Herbert Dunn, who had died of spinal meningitis.

The structure became known as "Ware's Folly" because of the cost of construction (said to be $40,000). Herbert spent approximately the same amount to renovate the house, now the home of the Gertrude Herbert Institute of Art. She also set up an endowment to help finance the operations of the art center. Herbert vacationed in the area with her husband, a prominent New York lawyer and judge, who was an avid golfer and assisted with the funding of a local sporting venture

that became the famed Augusta National Golf Club. The art institute displays works by local and nationally known artists and has workshops and studios for artists, sculptors, and potters.

Gertrude Herbert Institute of Art, 506 Telfair St., Augusta, GA 30901. Phone: 706/722-5495. Fax: 706/722-3670. E-mail: ghia@ghia.org. Website: www.ghia.org. Hours: 8:30-5 Tues.-Fri., 1-2 Sat.; closed Sun.-Mon. and major holidays. Admission: free.

JACQUELINE CASEY HUDGENS CENTER FOR THE ARTS. The Jacqueline Casey Hudgens Center for the Arts in Duluth, Georgia, was named for the wife of real estate developer Scott Hudgens, who provided funds for the arts center's building and later an adjoining Children's Arts Museum. The center features the works of noted Georgia artists since 1920, as well as representative artworks by Picasso, Kandinsky, Lichtenstein, Miró, and Rauschenberg. In addition to the Children's Art Museum, the center also has a botanical and sculpture garden.

Jacqueline Casey Hudgens Center for the Arts, 6400 Sugarloaf Pkwy., Bldg. 300, Duluth, GA 30097. Phone: 770/623-6002. Fax: 770/623-3555. E-mail: calmes @hudgens.org. Website: www.hudgenscenter.org. Hours: 10-5 Tues.-Sat., 1-5 Sun.; closed Mon. and major holidays. Admission: suggested donations—adults and children over 3, $5; children under 4, free.

Iowa

JAMES AND MERYL HEARST CENTER FOR THE ARTS. James Hearst was a poet and faculty member at the University of Northern Iowa, and his wife, Meryl Norton Hearst, was a nurse in Cedar Falls, Iowa. When they died, they left their home and funds for a city arts center that was named in their honor. Since the center was founded in 1989, it has been expanded to three times its original size. The center presents art exhibitions, concerts, dance recitals, lectures, arts festivals, and educational programs.

James and Meryl Hearst Center for the Arts, 304 W. Seerley Blvd., Cedar Falls, IA 50613. Phone: 319/273-8641. Fax: 319/273-8659. E-mail: huberm@ci.cedar-falls.ia.us. Website: www.hearstartscenter.com. Hours: 8-5 Tues.-Fri. (also to 9 Tues. and Thurs.); 1-4 Sat.-Sun.; closed Mon. and major holidays. Admission: free.

MUSCATINE ART CENTER. See Art Museums.

Kentucky

YEISER ART CENTER. See Art Museums.

Massachusetts

ART COMPLEX MUSEUM. See Art Museums.

MIT-LIST VISUAL ARTS CENTER. When art collectors and philanthropists Vera and Albert List made a major gift to the endowment of the MIT Visual Arts Center at the Massachusetts Institute of Technology in Cambridge in the mid-1980s, the name of the center was changed to incorporate their name. The center, which was founded in 1950, has collections of sculpture, paintings, drawings, works on paper, and photographs, and presents changing exhibitions and programs of contemporary art in all media.

MIT-List Visual Arts Center, Massachusetts Institute of Technology, 20 Ames St., Wiesner Bldg., E15-109, Cambridge, MA 02139. **Phones:** 617/253-4680 and 617/253-4400. **Fax:** 617/258-7265. **Website:** www.web.mit.edu/lvac/. **Hours:** Oct.-June—12-6 Tues.-Sun. (also to 8 Fri.); closed Mon., July-Aug., and major holidays. **Admission:** free.

MOLL ART CENTER. See Art Museums.

Missouri

MARGARET HARTWELL ART MUSEUM. See Art Museums.

New Jersey

PERKINS CENTER FOR THE ARTS. The Perkins Center for the Arts in Moorestown, New Jersey, is housed in the historic Perkins Memorial—a 1910 Tudor Revival–style manor house donated by philanthropist Mabel D'Olier in memory of her sister, Alice Perkins, and her husband, Dudley, who lived in the house designed by noted architect Herbert C. Wise, the first editor of *House & Garden* magazine.

The arts center seeks to provide a wide range of creative opportunities for people of all ages and every level of artistic development. Its programs include visual and performing arts classes, exhibitions, music and dance performances, workshops, outreach programs, and visiting artists' residencies.

Perkins Center for the Arts, 395 Kings Hwy., Moorestown, NJ 08035. **Phone:** 856/235-6488. **Fax:** 856/235-6624. **E-mail:** create@perkinscenter.org. **Website:** www.perkinscenter.org. **Hours (gallery):** 10-4 Thurs.-Fri.; 12-4 Sat.-Sun., closed remainder of week. **Admission:** free.

Oregon

MAUDE KERNS ART CENTER. See Art Museums.

Pennsylvania

ESTHER M. KLEIN ART GALLERY. See Art Galleries.

Tennessee

EDITH DAVIS GALLERY. See Art Galleries.

Vermont

HELEN DAY ART CENTER. Helen Day Montanari of Stowe, Vermont, left a $40,000 trust fund that resulted in the founding of the Helen Day Art Center and the Stowe Free Library, which share the same 1861 Greek Revival building that had been used as a school for 100 years. The center, which opened in 1981, offers changing exhibitions of local and national artists.

Helen Day Art Center, School St., PO Box 411, Stowe, VT 05672. **Phone:** 802/253-8358. **Fax:** 802/253-2703. **E-mail:** helenday@stowe.nu. **Website:** www.gostowe.com/saa/helenday. **Hours:** 12-5 Tues.-Sun.; closed Mon. and major holidays. **Admission:** adults, $3; seniors, $1; students and children, 50¢.

DECORATIVE ARTS MUSEUMS
See also Art Museums; Folk Art Museums.

Arkansas

DECORATIVE ARTS MUSEUM. The Arkansas Arts Center in Little Rock operates a branch Decorative Arts Museum in the former home of U.S. Senator David Terry and his wife, Adolfine Fletcher Terry, which was the site of the Arkansas Female College in the 1870s.

Mrs. Terry, who devoted her life to civic and humanitarian affairs, was a leader in fighting segregation in Arkansas. When Governor Orval Faubus ordered the schools closed after NAACP President Daisy Bates led nine African American children into Little Rock's Central High School in 1957, she organized the Women's Emergency Committee to Open Our Schools and worked to defeat segregationist politicians and further public education causes.

Mrs. Terry donated the house to the city with the wish that it be "alive and enjoyed by the people of Arkansas." After her death in 1976, it became the Decorative Arts Museum. The names of the more than 1,000 women who were members of her emergency committee are now etched on the conservatory glass attached to the home.

Decorative Arts Museum, Arkansas Arts Center, 411 E. 7th St., PO Box 2137, Little Rock, AR 72203-2137. Phone: 501/372-4000. Fax: 501/375-8053. E-mail: adubois @arkarts.org. Website: www.arkarts.com. Hours: 10-5 Mon.-Sat., 12-5 Sun.; closed Christmas. Admission: free.

District of Columbia

HILLWOOD MUSEUM AND GARDENS. See Historic House Museums.

Illinois

BIRKS MUSEUM AT MILLIKIN UNIVERSITY. The Birks Museum at Millikin University in Decatur, Illinois, was dedicated in 1981 to honor two sisters whose love of the decorative arts and their alma mater made the museum possible.

Jenna and Florence Birks began their extensive collection of fine glassware, china, and porcelain as tourists in England. During the next half century, they spent hours studying and learning the history of the pieces they would come to collect. Jenna was an ordained minister of the Disciples of Christ and spent most of her career working with the Young Women's Christian Association, while Florence was a home economics teacher in Indiana and Ohio high schools. In addition to donating their collection, they provided an endowment for the museum.

The Birks Museum collection now consists of over 1,000 pieces, primarily of European, Asian, and American ceramics and glassware—some from the fifteenth and sixteenth centuries, with the majority from

the eighteenth, nineteenth, and twentieth centuries. The museum has also become the repository for a number of other university collections, including a collection of largely Chinese art objects from Mr. and Mrs. Guy N. Scovill.

Birks Museum at Millikin University, Gorin Hall, 1184 W. Main St., Decatur, IL 62522. Phone: 217/424-6337. Fax: 217/424-3993. E-mail: ewalker@mail.millikin.edu. Website: www.millikin.edu/state/birks/index/html. Hours: June–Aug.—by appointment; remainder of year—1-4 daily; closed major holidays and when university not in session. Admission: free.

Iowa

BRUNNIER ART MUSEUM. See Art Museums.

MUSCATINE ART CENTER. See Art Museums.

Kansas

STAUTH MEMORIAL MUSEUM. Claude Stauth and his wife, Donalda Stauth, successful investors and farm owners from Montezuma, Kansas, traveled to 95 countries on six continents from 1941 to 1979. During their travels, the couple collected decorative art, woodcarvings, sculpture, ivory carvings, musical instruments, jewelry, real and ceremonial weapons, and other items from distant lands. Just before Mrs. Stauth died in 1993, she set in motion the founding of the Stauth Memorial Museum, a largely decorative arts museum featuring many of their collections, which opened in 1996.

Stauth Memorial Museum, 111 N. Aztec St., PO Box 396, Montezuma, KS 67867. Phone: 316/846-2527. Fax: 316/846-2810. E-mail: stauthm@ucom.net. Hours: 9-12 and 1-4:30 Tues.-Sat., 1:30-4:30 Sun.; closed Mon. and major holidays. Admission: free.

Maine

ELIZABETH PERKINS HOUSE. See Historic House Museums.

JONES MUSEUM OF GLASS AND CERAMICS. The Jones Museum of Glass and Ceramics, founded in 1978 by collector Dorothy-Lee Jones Ward and named for her family, is located close to the summit of Douglas Mountain, near Sebago, Maine. It has an exceptional collection of more than 10,000 pieces of glass, earthenware, stoneware, and porcelain, dating from 1200 B.C.

to the present. The collection includes such diverse works as Sandwich glass, Chinese porcelain, majolica, American art glass, English porcelain, and Baccarat paperweights. It also has four special exhibitions each year and contains the impressive Edward W. Tinney Library, with more than 10,000 volumes on glass and ceramic decorative arts.

Jones Museum of Glass and Ceramics, 35 Douglas Mountain Rd., PO Box 129, Sebago, ME 04029. **Phone:** 207/787-3370. **Fax:** 207/787-2800. **Hours:** mid-May-mid-Nov.—10-5 Mon.-Sat., 1-5 Sun.; remainder of year—by appointment. **Admission:** adults, $5; seniors, $3.75; students, $3; children under 12, free.

Maryland

EVERGREEN HOUSE. See Historic House Museums.

Mississippi

OHR-O'KEEFE MUSEUM OF ART. See Art Museums.

Ohio

DEGENHART PAPERWEIGHT AND GLASS MUSEUM. The Degenhart Paperweight and Glass Museum in Cambridge, Ohio, was established in 1978 through the bequest of Elizabeth Degenhart, who was known as the "first lady of glass" in Ohio. Degenhart ran a glass factory with her husband, John, beginning in 1947. When Mr. Degenhart died in 1964, Mrs. Degenhart operated the factory until she passed away in 1978. The factory was then closed, and it was followed by

the opening of the museum dedicated to the history and exhibition of glassware produced in Ohio, western Pennsylvania, and northern West Virginia. The exhibits focus on glassmaking techniques, midwestern pattern glass, paperweights, Degenhart crystal art glass, Cambridge Glass Company wares, and related topics.

Degenhart Paperweight and Glass Museum, 65323 Highland Hill Rd., PO Box 186, Cambridge, OH 43725. **Phone:** 614/432-2626. **Hours:** Apr.-Dec.—9-5 Mon.-Sat., 1-5 Sun.; remainder of year—10-5 Mon.-Fri.; closed Sat.-Sun. and major holidays. **Admission:** adults, $1.50; seniors, $1; children under 19, free.

Tennessee

HOUSTON MUSEUM OF DECORATIVE ARTS. The decorative arts collection of eccentric antiques dealer Anna Safley Houston is housed in an 1890 Victorian structure in Chattanooga, Tennessee. She left her priceless collection to the people of Chattanooga when she died in 1951. The museum is best known for its antique art glass and early American pressed glass, including thousands of pitchers. But it also has fine china, antique furniture, music boxes, early firearms, lamps, woven coverlets, pewter, silver, early prints, and other glass and ceramics.

Houston Museum of Decorative Arts, 201 High St., Chattanooga, TN 37403. **Phone:** 423/267-7176. **Website:** www.houston@chattanooga.net. **Hours:** June-Sept.—9:30-4 Mon.-Sat., 12-4 Sun.; remainder of year—9:30-4 Mon.-Sat.; closed Sun. and major holidays. **Admission:** adults, $6; children over 11, $3; children under 12, free.

FOLK ART MUSEUMS

See also Art Galleries; Art Museums; Arts Centers; Cultural Art and History Museums.

Georgia

HIGH MUSEUM OF ART. See Art Museums.

Louisiana

KATE CHOPIN HOUSE AND BAYOU FOLK MUSEUM. See Museums Honoring Exceptional Women.

MADAME JOHN'S LEGACY. See Other Historic Houses.

Maryland

JULIA A. PURNELL MUSEUM. See Art and History Museums.

New Mexico

MUSEUM OF INTERNATIONAL FOLK ART. The Museum of International Folk Art in Santa Fe, New Mexico—the world's largest folk art museum, with over 125,000 objects—was founded by Florence

The Museum of International Folk Art was founded in Santa Fe, New Mexico, in 1953 by Florence Dibell Bartlett. The museum has the largest collection of international folk art in the world, with more than 125,000 objects from over 100 countries. This photo shows some of the exhibits in the Girard Wing. Courtesy Museum of International Folk Art and photographer Art Taylor.

Dibell Bartlett, a Chicago collector, humanitarian, and philanthropist who lived part-time on her nearby ranch.

Bartlett traveled extensively and was concerned by what she viewed as the decline of folk art around the world due to mass manufacturing. She developed a collection of folk art from 37 countries that included costumes, pottery, metalwork, carvings, and paintings. They were everyday utilitarian objects as well as some rare pieces of great value. She built the museum, donated her collection to the state of New Mexico, and left approximately $1.5 million to the International Folk Art Foundation.

The 86,967-square-foot museum, which opened in 1953 and is a branch of the Museum of New Mexico, seeks to promote international goodwill and global understanding through the folk arts, defined as an artistic expression shared by members of a community and passed on to future generations by oral tradition and example.

The museum's most significant collections are of ethnic textiles and costumes, Latin American folk art, and Hispanic folk art. However, more than 100 countries are represented with such diverse objects as baskets, jewelry, tinwork, ceramics, silver, furniture, toys, woodcarvings, tools, religious items, and household objects.

Museum of International Folk Art, Camino Lejo, off Old Santa Fe Trail, PO Box 2087, Santa Fe, NM 87504-2087. **Phone:** 505/476-1200. **Fax:** 505/476-1300. **E-mail:** info@moifa.org. **Website:** www.moifa.org. **Hours:** 10-5 Tues.-Sun.; closed Mon. and major holidays. **Admission:** adults, $5; children under 16, free; four-day pass to all four New Mexico museums, $10.

North Carolina

BLUE RIDGE PARKWAY'S FOLK ART CENTER. Allanstand, the nation's first weaving cooperative and craft shop, was started in North Carolina in 1895 by Frances

Goodrich. In 1930 she gave it to the newly formed Southern Highland Craft Guild, and it is now part of the guild's Blue Ridge Parkway's Folk Art Center near Asheville.

The Southern Highland Craft Guild was founded to offer a network and market for mountain craftspeople in nine southeastern states. It has an active juried membership of over 700 craftspeople who make pottery, wood, glass, fiber, metal, jewelry, and other works in the mountain counties. The guild exhibits a portion of its permanent collection dating back to the turn of the twentieth century at the Folk Art Center; hosts a wide range of special exhibitions; and presents craft demonstrations, fairs, and special events. It has 350,000 visitors annually.

Blue Ridge Parkway's Folk Art Center, Milepost 382, Blue Ridge Pkwy., PO Box 9545, Asheville, NC 28815. **Phone:** 828/298-7928. **Fax:** 828/298-7962. **E-mail:** sheg@buncombe .main.nc.us. **Website:** www.southernhighlandguild.org. **Hours:** Apr.-Dec.—9-6 daily; remainder of year—9-5 daily; closed New Year's Day, Thanksgiving, and Christmas. **Admission:** free.

Vermont

SHELBURNE MUSEUM. See Art and History Museums.

Virginia

ABBY ALDRICH ROCKEFELLER FOLK ART MUSEUM. The Abby Aldrich Rockefeller Folk Art Museum—located at Colonial Williamsburg in Virginia—is named for Mrs. John D. Rockefeller Jr., who gave the core collection of 424 objects to the historical village in 1939 and whose husband made possible the restoration of eighteenth-century Williamsburg.

The museum, which opened in 1957, now has approximately 3,000 items and is often called the nation's finest collection of American folk art. It is said to be the country's oldest institution devoted exclusively to collecting, exhibiting, and researching American folk art.

The collections represent many cultural traditions and geographical areas and range from the 1720s to the present. The folk art—which mirrors many aspects of American life—includes such diverse works as paintings, sculpture, toys, pottery, quilts, weather vanes, decoys, shop signs, needlework, painted furniture, and various other decorated utilitarian objects. The annual attendance is nearly 200,000.

Mrs. Rockefeller, who was one of the earliest to recognize the value and beauty of American folk art, was also one of the founders of the Museum of Modern Art in New York City (see Art Museums).

Abby Aldrich Rockefeller Folk Art Center, Colonial Williamsburg, 307 S. England St., PO Box 1776, Williamsburg, VA 23187-1776. **Phone:** 757/220-7670. **Fax:** 757/565-8915. **E-mail:** cweekly@cwf.org. **Website:** www. colonialwilliamsburg.org. **Hours:** mid-Mar.-Dec.—10-5 daily; remainder of year—11-5 daily. **Admission:** adults, $8; children 6-17, $4; children under 6, free.

DESIGN, TEXTILE, AND COSTUME MUSEUMS

See also Art Museums.

California

THE LACE MUSEUM. The Lace Museum, featuring a collection of family lace heirlooms, was cofounded in Sunnyvale, California, in 1981 by Gracie Larsen and Cherie Helm. The museum also has collections of lace-trimmed clothing, decorative lace, lace costumes, old and recent laces, lace patterns from the late 1800s, and lace-making tools. It also offers classes in all facets of lace making.

The Lace Museum, 552 S. Murphy Ave., Sunnyvale, CA 94022. **Phone and Fax:** 408/730-4695. **E-mail:** sherrigid@ thelacemuseum.org. **Website:** www.thelacemuseum.org. **Hours:** 11-4 Tues.-Sat.; closed Sun.-Mon., 1st week in July, Thanksgiving, and between Christmas and New Year's Day. **Admission:** free.

Colorado

GUSTAFSON GALLERY AND HISTORIC COSTUME AND TEXTILES COLLECTION. The Gustafson Gallery at Colorado State University in Fort Collins is named for Dagmar Gustafson, former department head, who began the Historic Costume and Textiles Collection in the Department of Design and Merchandising in the mid-1950s.

The gallery, which opened in 1986, presents selections from the historical collection, which consists of approximately 7,000 historical costumes, 500 textile pieces, and clothing accessories and sewing-related notions, as well as special and traveling exhibitions. The collection includes women's dresses, lingerie, children's wear, ethnic costumes, quilts, flat textiles, and such accessories as jewelry, hankies, handbags, scarves, hats, and shoes. Among the most exquisite items are gowns from the late 1800s and beaded dresses from the 1920s. The oldest piece is a ca. 1450 shirt, and the most valuable is a maharaja's wedding robe with silver ornaments.

Gustafson Gallery and Historic Costume and Textiles Collection, Colorado State University, 145 and 316 Gifford Bldg., Fort Collins, CO 80523 (postal address: Dept. of Design and Merchandising, 314A Gifford Bldg., Fort Collins, CO 80523). **Phone:** 970/491-1983. **Fax:** 970/491-4376. **E-mail:** carlson@cahs.colostate.edu. **Website:** www.colostate.edu/depts/dm. **Hours:** Sept.-May—9-5 Mon.-Fri.; closed Sat.-Sun. and national holidays; June-Aug.—by appointment. **Admission:** free.

ROCKY MOUNTAIN QUILT MUSEUM. The Rocky Mountain Quilt Museum, which opened in Golden, Colorado, in 1990 for the preservation and promotion of the art and history of American quilts and quilt making, started with the donation of a collection of 100 quilts from quilter Eugenia Mitchell. The museum now has more than 250 antique and contemporary quilts, focusing largely on the Rocky Mountain region, and presents five changing exhibitions each year.

Rocky Mountain Quilt Museum, 1111 Washington Ave., Golden, CO 80401. **Phone:** 303/277-0377. **Fax:** 303/215-1636. **E-mail:** rmqm@att.net. **Website:** www.rmqm.org. **Hours:** 10-4 Tues.-Sat.; closed Sun.-Mon., New Year's Day, Thanksgiving, and Christmas. **Admission:** adults, $4; seniors, $2.50; children 6-12, $1; children under 6, free.

Connecticut

WINDHAM TEXTILE AND HISTORY MUSEUM. See History Museums.

Florida

SELBY GALLERY. See Art Galleries.

Indiana

ELIZABETH SAGE HISTORIC COSTUME COLLECTION. Elizabeth Sage, the first professor of clothing and textiles at Indiana University in Bloomington, founded the Elizabeth Sage Historic Costume Collection at the university in 1937. She began teaching at Indiana University in 1913 and donated her personal collection to the university in the year she retired.

The collection, which amounts to a social history of fashion in the nineteenth and twentieth centuries, has more than 15,000 objects, including an extensive contemporary designer component. However, it is not limited to high fashion. It focuses on clothing of the United States and includes such diverse items as athletic uniforms, military clothing, dress of the common person as well as the elite, and nineteenth- and twentieth-century fashion publications, prints, plates, and videos. In 1992 the Department of Apparel, Merchandising, and Interior Design collection was moved from its original location in Wylie Hall, and it is now being stored temporarily in a warehouse.

Elizabeth Sage Historic Costume Collection, Indiana University, 1430 N. Willis Dr., Bloomington, IN (postal address: 232 Memorial Hall East, 1021 E. 3rd St., Indiana University, Bloomington, IN 47405-2201). **Phone:** 812/855-4627. **Fax:** 812/855-0362. **E-mail:** rowold@indiana.edu. **Hours:** by appointment; closed university holidays. **Admission:** free.

QUILTERS HALL OF FAME. See Other Halls of Fame.

Iowa

KALONA HISTORICAL VILLAGE QUILT AND TEXTILE MUSEUM. Marilyn Woodin, owner of a quilt and antiques shop in Kalona, Iowa, started the Kalona Quilt and Textile Museum for her extensive quilt and textile collection in 1989. Ten years later she gave a collection of 32 quilts from 1830 to 1940 to the Kalona Historical Village to establish a replacement museum—if adequate space and care could be provided. In 2000 the historical village opened a new visitor center with a portion devoted to the Kalona Historical Village Quilt and Textile Museum—with Woodin serving as the volunteer curator and presenting changing exhibitions from an expanded collection and elsewhere.

The historical village is also the site of two other museums—the Mennonite Museum and Archives and the Wahl Museum, featuring historical materials—and a collection of historic buildings clustered around an 1879 railroad depot with railroad memorabilia. Among the other buildings are an 1867 church, log house, turn-of-the-twentieth-century store, Victorian house, one-room schoolhouse, and agricultural building with early farm implements.

Kalona Historical Village Quilt and Textile Museum, Visitor Center, 415 D Ave., Kalona, IA 52247. **Phone:** 319/656-3232. **Hours:** Apr.-Oct.—9:30-4 Mon.-Sat.; remainder of year—11-3 Mon.-Sat.; closed Sun., Thanksgiving, and Christmas. **Admission:** adults and children over 12, $6; children 7-12, $2.50; children under 7, free; families, $20.

Kentucky

MUSEUM OF THE AMERICAN QUILTER'S SOCIETY. The world's largest quilt museum—the Museum of the American Quilter's Society in Paducah, Kentucky—was opened in 1991 by Meredith Schroeder and her husband, Bill Schroeder, who were also cofounders of the American Quilter's Society. Mrs. Schroeder is now president of the society and of the museum.

The 27,000-square-foot museum, dedicated to honoring contemporary quilters, has approximately 200 quilts in its collection. Selections from the collection, as well as temporary exhibitions on loan, are displayed in three galleries. The museum also has a lobby and conference room with eight stained-glass windows based on quilts by American quilt makers.

Museum of the American Quilter's Society, 215 Jefferson St., PO Box 1540, Paducah, KY 42002-1540. **Phone:** 270/442-8856. **Fax:** 270/442-5448. **E-mail:** info@quiltmuseum.org. **Website:** www.quiltmuseum.org. **Hours:** Apr.-Oct.—10-5 Mon.-Sat., 1-5 Sun.; remainder of year—10-5 Mon.-Sat.; closed Sun., New Year's Day, Easter, Thanksgiving, and Christmas Eve and Day. **Admission:** adults, $5; students, $3; children under 12, free.

Massachusetts

HELEN GEIER FLYNT TEXTILE MUSEUM. Early coverlets, needlework, clothing, and textiles are featured at the Helen Geier Flynt Textile Museum at Historic Deerfield, a complex of fourteen historic structures from the eighteenth and nineteenth centuries in Deerfield, Massachusetts. The textile museum, which is housed in an 1872 building, is named for a member of the family who founded the historic complex in 1952. The Flynt Center of Early New England Life, containing decorative arts, furniture, and changing exhibitions, is also named for the family.

Helen Geier Flynt Textile Museum, Historic Deerfield, The Street, PO Box 321, Deerfield, MA 01342. **Phone:** 413/774-5581. **Fax:** 413/775-7220. **E-mail:** tours@historic-deerfield.org. **Website:** www.historic-deerfield.org. **Hours:** 9:30-4:30 daily; closed Thanksgiving and Christmas Eve and Day. **Admission:** adults, $12; children 6-17, $5; children under 6, free.

NEW ENGLAND QUILT MUSEUM. The New England Quilt Museum in Lowell, Massachusetts, was founded in 1987 by the New England Quilters Guild, composed mostly of women—with its collection of 150 quilts, beginning with a gift of 35 quilts from quilter and collector Gail Binney Stiles. Housed in a restored ca. 1845 savings building, the museum is dedicated to the preservation and exhibition of quilts and to education on the history, art, and craft of quilt making. Its collections focus on New England quilts and are particularly strong in quilts from 1830 through the nineteenth century. Traditional and contemporary quilts are presented in changing exhibitions.

New England Quilt Museum, 18 Shattuck St., Lowell, MA 01852. **Phone:** 978/452-4207. **Fax:** 978/452-5405. **E-mail:** nequiltmuseum@erols.com. **Website:** www.nequiltmuseum.org. **Hours:** May-Dec.—10-4 Tues.-Sat., 12-4 Sun.; closed Mon.; remainder of year—10-4 Tues.-Sat.; closed Sun.-Mon., major holidays, and between exhibitions. **Admission:** adults, $4; seniors, college students, and children over 5, $3; children under 6, free.

Minnesota

THE GOLDSTEIN: A MUSEUM OF DESIGN. "Art in Everyday Life," the concept that inspired Professors Harriet and Vetta Goldstein more than a half century ago, still drives The Goldstein: A Museum of Design, which bears their name in the Department of Design, Housing, and Apparel at the University of Minnesota in St. Paul. The museum—formerly called the Goldstein Gallery—collects, preserves, documents, and exhibits clothing, textiles, and decorative and graphic arts, with an emphasis on objects of the late nineteenth and twentieth centuries. It started with the personal collections of the Goldstein sisters, but it expanded rapidly through the generosity of others. The museum now has more than 12,000 garments and accessories (historic and ethnic costumes and designer fashions), over 1,500 decorative arts, approximately 2,000 textile pieces, and a growing graphic and interior design archive.

The Goldstein: A Museum of Design, Dept. of Design, Housing, and Apparel, University of Minnesota, 244 McNeal Hall, 1985 Buford Ave., St. Paul, MN 55108. **Phone:** 612/624-7434. **Fax:** 612/624-9243. **E-mail:** mlarson@che.umn.edu. **Website:** goldstein.che.umn.edu. **Hours:** 10-4 Mon.-Fri. (also to 8 p.m. Thurs.), 1:30-4:30 Sat.-Sun.; closed when changing exhibitions. **Admission:** free.

New York

ALLING COVERLET MUSEUM. The Alling Coverlet Museum in Palmyra, New York, features the nation's largest collection of handwoven American coverlets—largely a gift of Merle Alling, who collected coverlets for 30 years. The museum contains 425 coverlets—including approximately 200 from Alling, with about 50 being displayed at a time. It also has exhibits of quilts and framed rug samples illustrating a wide variety of techniques used in early America.

Alling Coverlet Museum, 122 William St., PO Box 96, Palmyra, NY 14522. **Phone:** 315/597-6737. **E-mail:** bjfhpinc@aol.com. **Hours:** June-mid-Sept.—1-4 daily; closed remainder of year. **Admission:** free.

COOPER-HEWITT NATIONAL DESIGN MUSEUM. The Smithsonian Institution's Cooper-Hewitt National Design Museum in New York City was founded as the Cooper-Union Museum for the Arts of Decoration in 1897 by three sisters—Amy, Eleanor, and Sarah Hewitt. They were granddaughters of Peter Cooper, who had established the Cooper Union for the Advancement of Science and Art, a tuition-free school of art, architecture, and engineering, in 1853. Cooper had envisioned that his institution would include a museum, in order to enrich the educational experience, but it was delayed for nearly a half century.

The Hewitt sisters acquired textiles, laces, prints, drawings, and decorative objects of the highest quality to form the core of the initial collections. As the museum evolved, it became a working laboratory of design aimed at educating and inspiring artisans, architects, designers, scholars, and the general public.

By the early 1960s, however, the Cooper Union was hard-pressed to fund the educational programs, and in 1963 it was decided to close the museum. In 1967 the collections were transferred to the Smithsonian, and then the Carnegie Corporation donated the Andrew Carnegie landmark mansion, which included an adjacent townhouse, garden, and terrace. The museum was reborn in 1976 as the Cooper-Hewitt Museum, the Smithsonian Institution's National Museum of Design (later changed to the present name). Another contiguous townhouse was acquired in 1989, and the three disparate buildings became a unified museum complex in the 1990s.

Today, the Cooper-Hewitt is one of the world's great design centers and the only American museum dedicated solely to the study of historical and contemporary design. It presents a wide range of exhibitions and educational programs and has a world-renowned study and reference collection of artifacts spanning 3,000 years of design history. It now covers such diverse areas as architectural and ornamental drawings, prints, textiles, ceramics, wallpapers, jewelry, metalwork, woodwork, and specialized materials.

Cooper-Hewitt National Design Museum, Smithsonian Institution, 2 E. 91st St., New York, NY 10128-0669. **Phone:** 212/849-8404. **Fax:** 212/849-8401. **Website:** www.si.edu/ndm. **Hours:** 10-5 Tues.-Sat. (also to 9 p.m. Tues.), 12-5 Sun.; closed Mon. and federal holidays. **Admission:** adults, $8; seniors and students, $5; children under 12, free; also free after 5 p.m. Tues.

North Carolina

BELLAMY MANSION MUSEUM OF HISTORY AND DESIGN ARTS. See Historic House Museums.

Ohio

GLADYS KELLER SNOWDEN GALLERY AND HISTORIC COSTUME AND TEXTILES COLLECTION. The Historic Costume and Textiles Collection at Ohio State University in Columbus was founded in the 1940s by a group of women faculty members. Selections from the collection—which features clothing from the mid-1800s to the present and textiles from pre-Columbian fabrics to contemporary materials—are displayed in the Gladys Keller Snowden Gallery, named for its donor, in Campbell Hall.

Gladys Keller Snowden Gallery and Historic Costume and Textiles Collection, Ohio State University, Consumer and Textile Sciences Dept., Campbell Hall, 1787 Neil Ave., Columbus, OH 43210-1295. **Phone:** 614/292-3090. **Fax:** 614/688-8133. **E-mail:** costume@osu.edu. **Website:** costume.osu.edu/snowden.htm. **Hours:** 11-4 Wed.-Sat.; closed Sun.-Tues. and university holidays. **Admission:** free.

Oregon

LATIMER QUILT AND TEXTILE CENTER. In 1989 Clara Fairfield, an employee of the Tillamook County Pioneer Museum in Tillamook, Oregon, obtained an inexpensive lease on a 1930s schoolhouse on the museum property and led the restoration of the building, which opened as the Latimer Quilt and Textile Center in 1991. The fiber arts center is named for the Latimer family, which donated the property to the

Pioneer Museum in memory of their grandparents and great-grandparents, James and Permelia Latimer, who originally provided the land for a school in 1892. The school was built in 1900 and was replaced by the current building in the 1930s. The center now preserves and displays quilts, woven items, tapestry, and other needle arts. It also gives weaving and spinning demonstrations, offers classes, and conducts fiber arts research and restoration.

Latimer Quilt and Textile Center, 2105 Wilson River Loop Rd., Tillamook, OR 97141. Phone: 503/843-8622. Fax: 503/842-8692. E-mail: latimertextile@oregoncoast.com. Website: www.oregoncoast.com/latimertextile. Hours: Mar.-Nov.—10-4 Tues.-Sat., 12-4 Sun.; closed Mon., winter Suns., remainder of year, and major holidays. Admission: adults, $2.50; seniors, $2; children 12-17, $1; children under 12, free.

Pennsylvania

PALEY DESIGN CENTER AT PHILADELPHIA UNIVERSITY. The Paley Design Center at Philadelphia University (formerly the Philadelphia College of Textiles and Science) is housed in the donated home of socialite and philanthropist Goldie Paley in Philadelphia. The center, which was established in 1978, has more than 400,000 textiles, costumes, and swatches in its collections. They include international textiles dating from the fourth century to the present and collections of costumes, fashions, clothing accessories, interior fabrics, quilts, lace, historic textiles, color swatch cards, and textile artifacts and implements.

Paley Design Center at Philadelphia University, 4200 Henry Ave., Philadelphia, PA 19144. Phone: 215/951-2860. Fax: 215/951-2662. Website: www.philau.edu/paley. Hours: 10-4 Tues.-Fri., 12-4 Sat.-Sun.; closed Mon. and university and major holidays. Admission: free.

Rhode Island

RHODE ISLAND SCHOOL OF DESIGN MUSEUM OF ART. See Art Museums.

Texas

DAR MUSEUM/FIRST LADIES OF TEXAS HISTORIC COSTUMES COLLECTION. See Museums Founded and/or Operated by Women's Organizations.

TEXAS FASHION COLLECTION. The Texas Fashion Collection, which features more than 12,000 costumes and accessories from 1820 to the present at the University of North Texas in Denton, began in 1938 when brothers Stanley and Edward Marcus assembled a collection in honor of their aunt, Carrie Marcus, co-founder of Neiman Marcus department store, who was known as the arbiter of fashion taste and style for the store.

After her death in 1953, the collection was maintained by the Carrie Marcus Neiman Foundation. In the early 1960s the Dallas Fashion Group showed an interest in starting a fashion collection, and this motivated a group of volunteers to open an exhibition space in the Apparel Mart. The collection was supplemented by donations of clothing from Dallas women. In 1972 the collection was moved to the University of North Texas and became the Dallas Museum of Fashion. Stanley Marcus later turned over the Carrie Marcus Neiman collection and archives to the museum, which was renamed the Texas Fashion Collection, as part of the School of Visual Arts.

Texas Fashion Collection, University of North Texas, School of Visual Arts, Scoular Hall, UNT Box 305100, Denton, TX 76203. Phone: 940/565-2732. Fax: 940/565-4717. E-mail: walker@unt.com. Website: www.art.unt.edu/tfc. Hours: by appointment. Admission: $5 per person; University of North Texas students, free.

Virginia

VIRGINIA QUILT MUSEUM. The Virginia Quilt Museum in Harrisonburg was established by a group of women to display antique and contemporary quilts. It is housed in the 1856 Warren-Sipe House.

Virginia Quilt Museum, 301 S. Main St., Harrisonburg, VA 22801. **Phone and Fax:** 540/433-3818. Hours: 10-4 Mon. and Thurs.-Sat., 1-4 Sun.; closed Tues.-Wed. and major holidays. Admission: adults, $4; seniors, $3; children 6-12, $2; children under 6, free.

Wisconsin

GALLERY OF DESIGN AND HELEN LOUISE ALLEN TEXTILE COLLECTION. Professor Helen Louise Allen taught at the University of Wisconsin-Madison from 1927 to 1968. During her 41 years at the university, she amassed a major private textile collection to support her teaching and research. She gave the collection to the university, and it became the basis for the Helen Louise Allen Textile Collection in 1968.

The collection, which consists of over 10,000 textiles and costumes representing many different eras, places, and techniques, is now an integral part of the academic program of the School of Family Resources and Consumer Sciences. Exhibitions are presented each year in the Gallery of Design. In addition to the exhibitions, the collection brings leading textile scholars to the university through its sponsorship of the annual Ruth Ketterer Harris Memorial Lecture, which honors the first curator of the collection.

Gallery of Design and Helen Louise Allen Textile Collection, University of Wisconsin-Madison, 1300 Linden Dr., Madison, WI 53706-1575. **Phone:** 608/262-1162. **Fax:** 608/265-5099. **Website:** www.sohe.wisc.edu/hlatc/. **Hours:** 9-5 Mon.-Tues., 9-1 Wed.—by appointment; closed Thurs.-Sun. and university holidays. **Admission:** free.

HISTORIC COSTUME COLLECTION. The Historic Costume Collection at Mount Mary College in Milwaukee was started in 1965 by Sister Aloyse Hessburg. The Fashion Department collection, which has representative costumes shown at several locations on the campus, consists of more than 7,000 items dating from 1800 to the present, with an emphasis on American and European designers.

Historic Costume Collection, Mount Mary College, Fashion Dept., 2900 N. Menomonee River Pkwy., Milwaukee, WI 53222-4545. **Phone:** 414/256-1255, Ext. 422. **Fax:** 414/256-0172. **E-mail:** gastone@mtmary.edu. **Website:** www.mtmary.edu. **Hours:** Sept.-mid-May—8:30-4:30 Mon.-Fri.; closed Sat.-Sun., mid-May-Aug., and college holidays. **Admission:** free.

CULTURAL ART AND HISTORY MUSEUMS

See also Archaeology, Anthropology, and Ethnology Museums; Ethnic Museums; History Museums.

Arizona

This is the new Spanish Colonial–style entrance to the Heard Museum in Phoenix. The native cultures and art museum was founded in 1929 by Dwight and Maie Heard, collectors of Native American art and artifacts of prehistoric and living tribes of the Southwest. Courtesy Heard Museum.

HEARD MUSEUM. The Heard Museum, which has one of the nation's richest collections of indigenous art and artifacts, was founded in Phoenix in 1929 by Dwight Heard and his wife, Maie Heard, who moved to Arizona from Chicago in 1895 and began collecting Native American art and artifacts representative of prehistoric and living peoples of the Southwest. They later added to their collections while traveling to South America and Africa.

The 130,000-square-foot museum has more than 32,000 works of art and ethnographic objects and operates a branch in North Scottsdale. Its ten galleries feature traditional and contemporary indigenous art, with sculpture being displayed in outdoor courtyards. The museum has been a leader in promoting the work of contemporary Native American artists and craftspeople. It also hosts three major festivals annually—the Guild Indian Fair and Market, the World Championship Hoop Dance Contest, and the Festival for Children and Spanish Market.

Heard Museum, 2301 N. Central Ave., Phoenix, AZ 85004. **Phones:** 602/252-8840 and 602/252-8848. **Fax:** 602/252-9757. **Website:** www.heard.org. **Hours:** 9:30-5 daily; closed major holidays. **Admission:** adults and children over 12, $7; seniors, $6; children 4-12, $3; children under 4 and Native Americans (with tribal cards), free.

MUSEUM OF NORTHERN ARIZONA. See General Museums.

SYLVIA PLOTKIN JUDAICA MUSEUM. See Ethnic Museums.

California

ANTELOPE VALLEY INDIAN MUSEUM. The Antelope Valley Indian Museum near Lancaster, California, is located in an unusual building that was constructed by artist Howard Arden Edwards, purchased and developed into a museum by anthropology buff Grace Wilcox Oliver, and finally acquired by the state of

California as one of the state's regional Native American museums.

The museum building, nestled among the rock formations of the Mojave Desert on Piute Butte, was originally a house built by Edwards in 1928, with the upper level being used to display his collection of prehistoric and historic Native American artifacts. It was then bought by Oliver, who remodeled the house, expanded the facilities, added her own Native American art and artifacts, and opened the structure as the Antelope Valley Indian Museum in the early 1940s. In 1979 the state of California obtained the property, with Oliver donating all of her art and artifacts. Visitors now actually climb over the building's interior granite boulders to view the collections and exhibits, which emphasize the Southwest, California, and Great Basin peoples.

Antelope Valley Indian Museum, 15701 E. Ave. M., Lancaster, CA 93535 (postal address: Mojave Desert Sector, California State Dept. of Parks and Recreation, 43779 15th St. West, Lancaster, CA 93534). E-mail: emoore@calparkmojave.com. Website: www.avim.av.org. Hours: public—mid-Sept.-mid-June—11-4 Sat.-Sun.; prescheduled group tours—10-12 Tues.-Thurs.; closed remainder of week and year and weekend prior to Christmas. Admission: adults and children over 12, $3; children 6-12, $1.50; school groups, free; other group tours, $25.

BOWERS MUSEUM OF CULTURAL ART. The Bowers Museum of Cultural Art in Santa Ana, California, resulted from the bequests of history buffs Charles Bowers and his wife, Ada Bowers. They left the land and funds to the city for a cultural arts museum that opened in 1936. The museum, which occupies a Mission-style building with a bell tower and open courtyard, features traditional arts of North and South American indigenous cultures, historical and cultural objects from southern California, and cultural arts of the Pacific Rim, Africa, Asia, Southeast Asia, and the Oceanic area. It also has collections of pre-Columbian ceramics, nineteenth- and twentieth-century American decorative arts, and California Impressionism paintings.

Bowers Museum of Cultural Art, 2002 N. Main St., Santa Ana, CA 92706. Phones: 714/567-3600 and 714/567-3968. Fax: 714/567-3603. E-mail: pkeller@bowers.org. Website: www.cowers.org. Hours: 10-4 Tues.-Sun.; closed Mon., New Year's Day, Thanksgiving, and Christmas. Admission: adults, $10; seniors and students, $8; children 5-12, $6; children under 5, free.

CLARKE HISTORICAL MUSEUM. See History Museums.

MARION STEINBACK INDIAN BASKET MUSEUM. The Marion Steinback Indian Basket Museum, which occupies a wing of the Gatekeeper's Museum in Tahoe City, California, features nearly 1,000 Native American baskets collected by Marion Steinback, whose lifelong interest in Native American art and culture led to the study and collecting of representative baskets and artifacts.

By the time of her death in 1991, Steinback had gathered rare and diverse baskets from over 85 tribes, as well as dolls, pottery, and other artifacts. The woven works range in size from highly detailed miniatures as small as one-quarter inch in diameter to burden baskets measuring nearly three feet across. She also developed an extensive Native American research library.

The North Lake Tahoe Historical Society operates both the Steinback Museum and the Gatekeeper's Museum, a local historical museum in a 1981 hand-carved log cabin, on the same foundation as the 1913 original cabin used by Lake Tahoe's gatekeeper, which was destroyed by fire in 1978.

Marion Steinback Indian Basket Museum, Gatekeeper's Museum, 130 W. Lake Blvd., PO Box 6141, Tahoe City, CA 96145. Phone: 530/583-1762. Fax: 530/583-8992. Hours: May-mid-June and Labor Day-Oct. 1—11-5 Wed.-Sun.; closed Mon.-Tues.; mid-June-Labor Day—11-5 daily; closed remainder of year. Admission: adults and children over 12, $2; seniors, $1.50; children under 13, free.

PETTERSON MUSEUM OF INTERCULTURAL ART. For twenty years Florence Lerrigo, head of public relations at Pilgrim Place, a religious-oriented retirement community in Claremont, California, thought about an international art show because of the many exceptional arts and crafts brought back by missionaries and the large number of accomplished potters, painters, weavers, sculptors, musicians, singers, and dancers at the facility.

In 1967 she invited a group of Claremont women interested in international arts to brainstorm the idea. Out of the discussion came a support group and an annual spring international arts celebration, featuring a different country each year. One of the women attending was Alice Petterson, a local artist whose husband, Richard, was professor of art and a noted ceramist at Scripps College. She became artistic coordinator for the project.

So many international art objects were donated, including many pieces from the Pettersons, that a museum was established in 1983. It was named the Petterson Museum of Intercultural Art to recognize the extensive work and art contributions of the couple. The museum's collections now include such diverse works as Chinese bronzes and imperial court robes, Latin American textiles, African masks and woodcarvings, and intercultural costumes and puppets.

Petterson Museum of Intercultural Art, Pilgrim Place, 730 Plymouth Rd., Claremont, CA 91711 (postal address: 660 Avery Rd., Claremont, CA 91711). **Phone:** 909/399-5544. **Fax:** 909/399-5508. **Website:** www.plymouthplace.org. **Hours:** 2-4 Fri.-Sun. (guided tours); closed Mon.-Thurs., New Year's Day, Easter, Thanksgiving, and Christmas. **Admission:** free.

Colorado

UTE INDIAN MUSEUM. See History Museums.

District of Columbia

LILLIAN AND ALBERT SMALL JEWISH MUSEUM. See Ethnic Museums.

Georgia

TUBMAN AFRICAN-AMERICAN MUSEUM. See Ethnic Museums.

Hawaii

BISHOP MUSEUM. See Archaeology, Anthropology, and Ethnology Museums.

Illinois

DuSABLE MUSEUM OF AFRICAN-AMERICAN HISTORY. See Ethnic Museums.

MITCHELL MUSEUM OF THE AMERICAN INDIAN. The Mitchell Museum of the American Indian at Kendall College in Evanston, Illinois, resulted from a 1977 gift of an extensive collection of Native American art and ethnographic materials from realtor/businessman John M. Mitchell and his wife, Betty Seabury Mitchell. They amassed the collection over 60 years. It has been supplemented by other contributions and purchases.

The museum has permanent exhibits on Illinois prehistory and modern lifeways of four Native American cultural areas—the western Great Lakes, the Plains region, and the Navajo and Pueblo cultures of the Southwest. In interpreting the cultures, the displays make use of such objects as pottery, basketry, clothing, textiles, beadwork, quillwork, jewelry, musical instruments,

toys, dolls, carvings, and paintings. The museum also presents special exhibitions based on a single theme or subject.

Mitchell Museum of the American Indian, Kendall College, 2600 Central Park, Evanston, IL 60201. **Phone:** 847/495-1030. **Fax:** 847/495-0911. **Website:** www.mitchellmuseum.org. **Hours:** 10-5 Tues.-Sat. (also to 8 p.m. Thurs.), 12-4 Sun.; closed Mon., last 2 weeks of Aug., and college holidays. **Admission:** adults, $5; seniors and children, $2.50; families, $10.

SCHINGOETHE CENTER FOR NATIVE AMERICAN CULTURES. Herbert Schingoethe and his wife, Martha Dunham Schingoethe, were collectors of Native American cultural artifacts who wanted others to learn about America's original inhabitants. In 1989 they gave their collection to Aurora University in Aurora, Illinois, for a museum in their name, and they also funded the construction of the Dunham Hall (named in honor of Mrs. Schingoethe's family) to house the Schingoethe Center for Native American Cultures.

The museum's collections and exhibits are based largely on the Schingoethe collection, which features southwestern Native American art and artifacts. However, other donors and the museum have expanded the offerings to include other Native American cultural areas. The museum also holds an annual Powwow on Memorial Day weekend with Native American dancers from across the country.

Schingoethe Center for Native American Cultures, Aurora University, Dunham Hall, 1400 Marseillaise Place, Aurora, IL 60506 (postal address: 347 S. Gladstone Ave., Aurora, IL 60506-4892). **Phone:** 630/841-5402. **Fax:** 630/844-8884. **Website:** www.aurora.edu/museum. **Hours:** 10-4 Tues.-Fri., 1-4 Sun.; closed Mon., Sat., Jan., and national holidays. **Admission:** free.

SPURLOCK MUSEUM. The former World Heritage Museum at the University of Illinois at Urbana-Champaign reopened in a new building in 2002 as the Spurlock Museum, named for pharmaceutical executive William R. Spurlock and his wife, Clarice V. Spurlock, an Indianapolis couple who made a major contribution to the new 53,000-square-foot building. It had been closed for three years during construction.

The museum, which began as separate museums of classical and European culture in 1911, has more than 45,000 artifacts, including the world's most complete cast of the Parthenon frieze, an extensive collection of Merovingian bronzes, nearly 2,000 cuneiform tablets dating back to the third millennium B.C., a renowned collection of Canelos Quechua ceramics, a seminal collection of cultural materials from the Plains people, and the nation's largest collection of Amazonian bark cloth.

The new building also has three walk-through historical environments—an Egyptian mastaba tomb in the African Gallery, a classical Greek temple in the Ancient Mediterranean Gallery, and a Gothic chapel in the European Gallery.

Spurlock Museum, University of Illinois at Urbana-Champaign, 600 S. Gregory St., Urbana, IL 61801. **Phone:** 217/244-3355. **Fax:** 217/244-9419. **E-mail:** ksheanan@uiuc.edu. **Website:** www.spurlock.uiuc.edu. **Hours:** 9-5 Tues.-Fri. (also to 8 p.m. Tues.), 10-5 Sun.; closed Mon. and university holidays and breaks. **Admission:** free.

Nebraska

LENTZ CENTER FOR ASIAN CULTURE. The Lentz Center for Asian Culture at the University of Nebraska at Lincoln was established with a gift from Don Lentz, a former music faculty member, and his pianist wife, Velma Lentz. The museum features Asian art and artifacts that include ceramic, ivory, jade, and lacquer objects; prints and musical instruments; and Tibetan ritual and secular art.

Lentz Center for Asian Culture, University of Nebraska at Lincoln, 1155 Q St., Lincoln, NE 68588-0252. **Phone:** 402/472-5841. **Fax:** 402/472-8899. **E-mail:** bbanks@unl.edu. **Hours:** 10-5 Tues.-Sat., 1:30-4 Sun.; closed Mon., Easter, Fourth of July, and Christmas to New Year's Day. **Admission:** free.

New Mexico

MILLICENT ROGERS MUSEUM OF NORTHERN NEW MEXICO. The Millicent Rogers Museum of Northern New Mexico in Taos was founded in 1953 by family members in memory of the woman who assembled one of the foremost collections of southwestern art and design.

Millicent A. Rogers was born to a prominent New York family, was educated abroad, and spent much of her life in Europe. She came to Taos for a short visit in 1948 and became enamored with the landscape, the people, and the area's history. She decided to make her home in New Mexico and became interested in preserving Native American and Spanish Colonial art, both of which were rapidly disappearing. In the few short years

before her death in 1953, she assumed a vast collection of jewelry, textiles, baskets, pottery, furniture, kachinas, santos, paintings, and other such objects of the region.

Under the leadership of one of her sons, Paul Peralta-Ramos, the family opened a museum in her honor devoted to the art and material culture of the Native American and Hispanic peoples of the Southwest, with a focus on northern New Mexico.

Millicent Rogers Museum of Northern New Mexico, 1504 Millicent Rogers Rd., PO Box A, Taos, NM 87571. **Phone:** 505/758-2462. **Fax:** 505/758-5751. **E-mail:** mrm@newmex.com. **Website:** www.millicentrogers.org. **Hours:** 10-5 daily; closed Mon., Nov.-Mar., and major holidays. **Admission:** adults, $6; seniors and students, $5; children under 17, $1; families, $12.

SAN ILDEFONSO PUEBLO MUSEUM. The San Ildefonso Pueblo Museum at the tribal pueblo near Santa Fe, New Mexico, is dedicated to Maria Martinez, the leading Native American potter of matte black-on-black-style pottery she perfected with her husband, Julian Martinez, in the early 1900s.

Maria Martinez taught her people as well as her family the famous style of pottery making. Her four sisters—Maxmilliana, Desideria, Juanita, and Clara—did much of their pottery work as a team, with one shaping the pot and another decorating it. Among the other San Ildefonso artisans who became well known for their pottery are Carmelita and Carlos Dunlap; Santana and Adam Martinez; Maria Poveka; Barbara Gonzales; and Maria, Popovi, and Tony Da. Maria Martinez and many of the other potters are represented in the museum, which is devoted to tribal history and pottery making.

San Ildefonso Pueblo Museum, off State Hwy. 502, Rural Rte. 5, Box 315-A, San Ildefonso Pueblo, Santa Fe, NM 87506. **Phone:** 505/455-3549. **Hours:** 8-4 Mon.-Fri.; closed Sat.-Sun., major holidays, and ceremonial dances. **Pueblo admission:** $3 per private vehicle (includes museum).

WHEELWRIGHT MUSEUM OF THE AMERICAN INDIAN. Mary Cabot Wheelwright, a Boston aristocrat who found the Southwest beautiful and liberating and the Navajos of great interest, cofounded—with Navajo medicine man Hastin Klah—a museum in Santa Fe, New Mexico, dedicated to Navajo ceremonial art in 1937. In the mid-1970s the focus of the museum was amended to concentrate on contemporary Native American artists, and the name was changed to the Wheelwright Museum of the American Indian.

The museum now has collections of historic and contemporary Native American art, with exhibits devoted primarily to historic collections and individual artists. The museum possesses textiles, jewelry, pottery, baskets, fetishes, sculpture, and other objects, as well as archival information on Mary Cabot Wheelwright, anthropologists Washington Matthews and John Adair, and textile scholar Kate Peck Kent.

Wheelwright Museum of the American Indian, 704 Camino Lejo, PO Box 5153, Santa Fe, NM 87505. Phone: 505/982-4636. Fax: 505/989-7386. E-mail: wheelwright@ wheelwright.org. Website: www.wheelwright.org. Hours: 10-5 Mon.-Sat., 1-5 Sun.; closed New Year's Day, Thanksgiving, and Christmas. Admission: free.

New York

HERBERT AND EILEEN BERNARD MUSEUM. See Ethnic Museums.

North Carolina

MATTYE REED AFRICAN HERITAGE CENTER. See Ethnic Museums.

Oklahoma

ATALOA LODGE MUSEUM. Mary Stone McLendon, a Chickasaw whose Native American name was Ataloa (Little Song), taught at Bacone College in Muskogee, Oklahoma, in 1927–1935, when it was the only Native American college in the nation. She also served as field secretary for the college and collected many material culture items for her dream—a Native American museum at the institution. The dream became a reality in 1932, incorporating many of her artifacts, and was named in her honor after her death in 1967.

The Ataloa Lodge Museum, which has more than 20,000 items in its collections, is one of the nation's finest privately owned collections of traditional and contemporary Native American art and artifacts. It includes pottery, paintings, baskets, clothing, blankets, rugs, kachinas, quillwork, moose-hair embroidery, ceremonial items, decorative materials, weapons, canoes, contemporary art, and other such materials—some which date back thousands of years.

A number of objects in the collections came from the families of such Native American leaders as Geronimo, Chief Joseph, and Pleasant Porter. The holdings also include some materials pertaining to the Civil War, European and Asian influence, Colonial and early American furniture, prehistoric fossils, and historic documents by President Abraham Lincoln, Chief John Ross, and others. The museum's stone-and-log building features a fireplace made of rocks and stones provided by numerous Native American peoples from the lands where they lived.

Ataloa Lodge Museum, Bacone College, 2299 Old Bacone Rd., Muskogee, OK 74403-1597. Phone: 918/683-4581, Ext. 283. Fax: 918/687-5913. Hours: 10-12 and 1-4 Mon.-Fri.; other times by appointment; closed national holidays. Admission: adults, $2; children, free.

Virginia

LOIS E. WOODS MUSEUM. See Ethnic Museums.

ART AND HISTORY MUSEUMS

See also Art Museums; Arts Centers; Cultural Art and History Museums; History Museums.

Alabama

ISABEL ANDERSON COMER MUSEUM AND ARTS CENTER. The Isabel Anderson Comer Museum and Arts Center in Sylacauga, Alabama, is named for the woman who spearheaded the drive and helped fund the renovation of a former library building to house the facility in 1982. The art and history museum has examples of fine art, mixed media, marble sculpture, Native American artifacts, period furnishings, and a replica and documentation of the Hodges meteorite.

Isabel Anderson Comer Museum and Arts Center, 711 N. Broadway, PO Box 245, Sylacauga, AL 35150. Phone: 256/245-4016. Fax: 256/245-4612. Hours: 10-5 Tues.-Fri.; closed Sat.-Mon. and major holidays. Admission: free.

California

DE SAISSET MUSEUM. The de Saisset Museum at Santa Clara University in Santa Clara, California, resulted from a bequest by Isabel de Saisset in memory of her artist brother, Ernest. The museum is located in a building constructed adjacent to the Mission Santa Clara and houses paintings by Ernest de Saisset and artworks of many eras and styles, as well as exhibits and collections on California history.

De Saisset Museum, Santa Clara University, 500 El Camino Real, Santa Clara, CA 95053-0550. **Phone:** 408/554-4528. **Fax:** 408/554-7840. **E-mail:** rschapp@scu.edu. Website: www.scu.edu/desaisset. **Hours:** 11-4 Tues.-Sun.; closed Mon., major holidays, and between exhibitions. **Admission:** free.

HAGGIN MUSEUM. The Haggin Museum in Stockton, California, began as the Pioneer Museum in 1928 and changed its name to the Pioneer Museum and Haggin Galleries after a gift of approximately 180 paintings by Eila Haggin McKee, who inherited the works from her father. The name was later shortened to simply the Haggin Museum. The history and art museum contains artifacts and exhibits on California's Central Valley, including Native American basketry; nineteenth-century French and American paintings; American, European, and Asian decorative arts; and folk art.

Haggin Museum, 1201 N. Persing Ave., Stockton, CA 95203. **Phone:** 209/940-6300. **Fax:** 209/462-1404. **E-mail:** hagginmuseum@earthlink.net. Website: www.haggin museum.org. **Hours:** 1:30-5 Tues.-Sun.; closed Mon., New Year's Day, Thanksgiving, and Christmas. **Admission:** free.

MUSEUM OF THE AMERICAN WEST. The history and culture of the real and mythical American West are presented at the Museum of the American West (formerly the Autry Museum of Western Heritage), founded by singing cowboy movie star Gene Autry and his wife, Jackie Autry, in Los Angeles in 1984 with a $54 million gift from the Autry Foundation.

The 148,000-square-foot museum, which opened in 1988 in Griffith Park, uses artifacts, art, audiovisual materials, and other exhibit techniques to tell the story of the Old West in seven permanent galleries, two special exhibition halls, and a hands-on children's gallery. Most of the exhibits feature historical objects and art from the museum's collection of such historical items as saddles, firearms, clothing, maps, manuscripts, films, posters, photographs, and western artworks by such artists as Albert Bierstadt, Thomas Moran, John Mix Stanley, Frederic Remington, and Charles Russell.

Museum of the American West, 4700 Western Heritage Way, Los Angeles, CA 90027-1462. **Phone:** 323/667-2000. **Fax:** 323/660-5721. **E-mail:** autry@autry-museum.org. Website: www.autry-museum.org. **Hours:** 10-5 Tues.-Sun. (also to 8 p.m. Thurs.) and Mon. holidays; closed Mon., Thanksgiving, and Christmas. **Admission:** adults, $7.50; seniors and children 13-18, $5; children 2-12, $3; children under 2, free.

Connecticut

FLORENCE GRISWOLD MUSEUM. The 1817 home of Florence Griswold in Old Lyme, Connecticut, interprets the Lyme Art Colony and its significance as a center of America's Impressionism and re-creates historical aspects of the region's past.

The national historic landmark—now the Florence Griswold Museum—features an exceptional collection of paintings, drawings, and watercolors by artists associated with the art colony. Griswold opened her home to some of the nation's most accomplished artists in 1899. Such artists as Childe Hassam, Willard Metcalf, and Henry Ward Ranger lived and worked at the Griswold House, where they created many significant works. In addition to historic period rooms, the museum has an "old-fashioned" garden, the restored studio of Impressionist William Chadwick, and the ca. 1794 Huntley-Brown House on its 11 acres.

Florence Griswold Museum, 96 Lyme St., Old Lyme, CT 06371. **Phone:** 860/434-5542. **Fax:** 860/434-9778. **E-mail:** jeff@flogris.org. Website: www.flogris.org. **Hours:** June-Oct.—10-5 Tues.-Sat., 1-5 Sun.; closed Mon.; remainder of year—1-5 Wed.-Sun.; closed Mon.-Tues. **Admission:** adults, $5; seniors and students, $4; children under 13, free.

Florida

CORNELL MUSEUM OF ART AND HISTORY. The Cornell Museum of Art and History in Delray Beach, Florida, is named for philanthropists George Cornell and his wife, Harriet Cornell, who made a major donation to the conversion of a 1913 former elementary school into a home for the museum. The museum, founded in 1990, is part of the Old School Square complex that also includes a historic theater and gymnasium.

Cornell Museum of Art and History, 51 N. Swinton Ave., Delray Beach, FL 33444. **Phone:** 561/243-7922. **Fax:** 561/243-7018. **E-mail:** museum@oldschool.org. Website: www.oldschool.org/oldschool. **Hours:** 11-4 Tues.-Sat. (also 1-4 Sun. in Jan.-May and Nov.-Dec.); closed Mon. and major holidays. **Admission:** adults, $3; children 6-12, $1; children under 6, free.

Maryland

JULIA A. PURNELL MUSEUM. The Julia A. Purnell Museum in Snow Hill, Maryland, honors a local folk and needle artist who lived in the community for 100 years (1843–1943). It was founded in 1942 by her son,

William Purnell, as a gallery of her artwork, but gradually evolved into a museum of regional art and history. Housed in an 1891 former Catholic church building, the museum has collections and exhibits on the history of Worcester County and the Pocomoke people in the region, as well as needlework and other art from the area.

Julia A. Purnell Museum, 208 W. Market St., Snow Hill, MD 21863. **Phone and Fax:** 410/632-0515. **E-mail:** purnellmuseum@dmv.com. **Website:** www.intercom.net/local.snowhill/snowhill.html. **Hours:** Apr.-Oct.—10-4 Tues.-Sat., 1-4 Sun.; closed Mon. and remainder of year. **Admission:** adults, $2; children 5-17, 50¢; children under 5, free.

Michigan

ELLA SHARP MUSEUM. Ella Merriman Sharp, an activist for forests, civic improvements, and women's issues, left her 530-acre property and Victorian home to the city of Jackson, Michigan, in 1912 for a park and museum. The Ella Sharp Park opened in 1916, followed by the Ella Sharp Museum in 1965. The art and history museum features Sharp's elegantly furnished nineteenth-century home, exhibits of art and Jackson's history, three hands-on discovery areas for families, a collection of carriages, a one-room schoolhouse, a woodworking shop, and several other early buildings used for educational purposes.

Ella Sharp Museum, 3225 4th St., Jackson, MI 49203. **Phone:** 517/787-2320. **Fax:** 517/787-2933. **Hours:** 10-4 Tues.-Fri., 11-4 Sat.-Sun.; closed Mon. and major holidays. **Admission:** adults, $4; seniors and students, $3; children 5-15, $2; children under 5, free; families, $10.

Missouri

LONGWELL MUSEUM. The Museum of Arts and Sciences at Crowder College in Neosho, Missouri, was renamed the Longwell Museum in 1970 after Mary Longwell donated the art collection that she and her recently deceased husband, Dan Longwell, had assembled over the years. He was a retired editor of *Life* magazine. The museum contains oil paintings by Ozark artist Daisy Cook; original prints by such artists as Birger Sandzen, Grant Wood, Peter Hurd, and Thomas Hart Benton; Japanese woodblock prints; Chinese paper cuts; and historical materials related to Camp Crowder, an Army Signal Corps post once located in the area.

Longwell Museum, Crowder College, 601 La Clede Ave., Neosho, MO 64850. **Phone:** 417/451-3223, Ext. 201. **Fax:** 417/451-4280. **Website:** www.crowdercollege.net. **Hours:** 10-4 Mon.-Fri.; closed Sat.-Sun. and college holidays. **Admission:** free.

Oklahoma

WOOLAROC MUSEUM. Frank Phillips, founder of the Phillips Petroleum Company, grew up during the last days of the Old West and was intrigued with cowboys, Native Americans, outlaws, and the untamed spirit of the American West. He and his wife, Jane Phillips, sought to share these memories with the public by founding the Woolaroc Museum on their 3,600-acre rustic ranch near Bartlesville, Oklahoma, in 1929.

The museum—called "a living monument to the American West"—has five large exhibit halls with a wide range of western history and art—each devoted to a specific era or time period—as well as a Native American Heritage Center, historic log lodge, wildlife refuge, nature trails, and other facilities. Mr. and Mrs. Phillips and their son, John, are buried in the family mausoleum on the property.

Woolaroc Museum, State Hwy. 123, Rte. 3, Box 2100, Bartlesville, OK 74003. **Phone:** 918/336-0307. **Fax:** 918/336-0084. **E-mail:** woolarocl@aol.com. **Website:** www.woolaroc.org. **Hours:** 10-5 Tues.-Sun.; closed Mon., Thanksgiving, and Christmas. **Admission:** adults and children over 11, $5; seniors, $4; children under 12, free.

Vermont

SHELBURNE MUSEUM. Electra Havemeyer Webb, a sugarcane heiress, was a collector for 53 years. In 1947 she founded the Shelburne Museum in Shelburne, Vermont, to house what had grown into an extremely large and diverse array of folk art; American paintings of the eighteenth, nineteenth, and twentieth centuries; decorative arts and furniture; quilts, samplers, and textiles; tools, toys, and carousel figures; horse-drawn carriages; railroad cars; and the 220-foot Lake Champlain steamboat *Ticonderoga*, a national historic landmark.

Webb, who was enthralled with "the beauty of everyday things," was the daughter of the great Impressionist painting collectors H. O. and Louisine Havemeyer of New York City. Though inspired by her parents' tastes, she charted her own course. Equally consumed with New England architecture as with art and artifacts, she brought to the museum's 45 acres such historic structures as seven eighteenth- and nineteenth-century houses, a general store, a covered bridge, an 1840 meeting house, and an 1890 slate jailhouse.

The Shelburne Museum now has 39 historic structures—most of which have been moved to the site from throughout the Northeast. An arboretum, an orchard, and flower, herb, and heritage vegetable gardens are also located on the grounds. And each year new exhibitions of significant aspects of American art, history, and culture are presented at the museum.

Shelburne Museum, 5555 Shelburne Rd., PO Box 10, Shelburne, VT 05482. **Phone:** 802/985-3346. **Fax:** 802/985-2331. **E-mail:** info@shelburnemuseum.org. **Website:** www.shelburnemuseum.org. **Hours:** late May-mid-Oct.—10-5 daily; mid-Apr.-late May—1-4 daily; closed remainder of year. **Admission:** late May-mid-Oct.—adults, $17.50; children 6-14, $7; children under 6, free; mid-Apr.-late May (only ten buildings open)—adults, $10; children 6-14, $4; children under 6, free.

SCULPTURE GARDENS

See also Art Museums.

Arizona

SHEMER ART CENTER. See Art Centers.

California

IRIS & B. GERALD CANTOR CENTER FOR VISUAL ARTS. See Art Museums.

MUSEUM OF CONTEMPORARY ART, SAN DIEGO. See Art Museums.

Colorado

COLORADO SPRINGS FINE ARTS CENTER. See Art Museums.

Florida

JOHN AND MABLE RINGLING MUSEUM OF ART. See Art Museums.

NAPLES MUSEUM OF ART. See Art Museums.

NORTON MUSEUM OF ART. See Art Museums.

Georgia

JACQUELINE CASEY HUDGENS CENTER FOR THE ARTS. See Arts Centers.

Illinois

MARY AND LEIGH BLOCK MUSEUM OF ART. See Art Museums.

VERA AND A. D. ELDEN SCULPTURE GARDEN. The Vera and A. D. Elden Sculpture Garden at the David

and Alfred Smart Museum of Art at the University of Chicago was created in 1974 when the museum was built. It was named for the Eldens in 1988 in recognition of an endowment grant from the Smart Family Foundation. Mrs. Elden was the sister of Smart brothers for whom the museum is named. The courtyard garden contains works by such sculptors as Scott Burton, Anthony Caro, Joel Shapiro, Jene Highstein, and Arnaldo Pomodoro.

Vera and A. D. Elden Sculpture Garden, David and Alfred Smart Museum of Art, University of Chicago, 5550 S. Greenwood Ave., Chicago, IL 60637. **Phone:** 773/702-0200. **Fax:** 773/702-3121. **E-mail:** smartmuseum@uchicago.edu. **Website:** www.smartmuseum.uchicago.edu. **Hours:** 10-4 Tues.-Fri. (also to 9 p.m. Thurs.), 12-6 Sat.-Sun.; closed Mon. and major holidays. **Admission:** free.

Massachusetts

ROSE ART MUSEUM. See Art Museums.

Michigan

CRANBROOK ART MUSEUM. See Art Museums.

Missouri

NELSON-ATKINS MUSEUM OF ART. See Art Museums.

New York

FRANCES LEHMAN LOEB ART CENTER. See Art Museums.

HOFSTRA MUSEUM. See Art Museums.

MUSEUM OF MODERN ART. See Art Museums.

WHITNEY MUSEUM OF AMERICAN ART AT PHILIP MORRIS. See Art Museums.

Pennsylvania

MURIEL AND PHILIP BERMAN SCULPTURE GARDENS. The Lehigh University Art Galleries in Bethlehem, Pennsylvania, include the Muriel and Philip Berman Sculpture Gardens, endowed by the couple known for their philanthropic work in the art field. The contemporary sculpture collection is located mainly in the campus courtyard surrounded by the Mudd, Mart, Whitaker, and Sinclair buildings. Other works are also at the Murray H. Goodman and Mountaintop campuses.

Muriel and Philip Berman Sculpture Gardens, Lehigh University, Bethlehem, PA 18015 (contact: Lehigh University Art Galleries, Zoellner Arts Center, 420 E. Packer Ave., Bethlehem, PA 18015). **Phone:** 610/758-3615. **Fax:** 610/758-4580. **E-mail:** rv02@lehigh.edu. **Website:** www.lehigh.edu/~inluag. **Hours:** open 24 hours. **Admission:** free.

PALMER MUSEUM OF ART. See Art Museums.

PHILIP AND MURIEL BERMAN MUSEUM OF ART AT URSINUS COLLEGE. See Art Museums.

South Carolina

BROOKGREEN GARDENS. See Botanical Gardens and Arboretums.

Texas

ELLEN NOËL ART MUSEUM OF THE PERMIAN BASIN. See Art Museums.

Washington

MARYHILL MUSEUM OF ART. See Art Museums.

Wisconsin

LEIGH YAWKEY WOODSON ART MUSEUM. See Art Museums.

Historical Museums, Houses, and Sites

HISTORY MUSEUMS

See also Art and History Museums; Cultural Art and History Museums; Historic Farms and Ranches; Historic House Museums; Historic Opera Houses; Museums Founded and/or Operated by Women's Organizations; Women's Museums, Galleries, and Halls of Fame; Museums Honoring Exceptional Women; Re-created Pioneer Villages.

Alabama

ALABAMA WOMEN'S HALL OF FAME. See Women's Museums, Galleries, and Halls of Fame.

ISABEL ANDERSON COMER MUSEUM AND ARTS CENTER. See Art and History Museums.

Alaska

CARRIE M. McLAIN MEMORIAL MUSEUM. The Nome Museum, a one-room regional history museum founded as part of Alaska's 1967 centennial celebration of the purchase of Alaska from Russia, was renamed in 1973 for a pioneer resident who helped preserve the area's rapidly changing history and culture.

Carrie McLain, who arrived in Nome with her parents in 1905 when she was ten years old, was a teacher, switchboard operator, city clerk, and mother of five who collected photographs and artifacts of the area and gave lectures on the history of the Bering Strait region. The museum is dedicated to collecting, preserving, and interpreting materials related to the Alaska gold rush, indigenous peoples, history and culture of Nome, Bering Strait region, and Alaska.

Carrie M. McLain Memorial Museum, 223 Front St., PO Box 53, Nome, AK 99762. **Phone:** 907/443-6630. **Fax:** 907/443-7955. **E-mail:** museum@ci.nome.ak.us. **Website:** www.nome.alaska.org. **Hours:** June-Sept.—9-5:30 daily; remainder of year—12-6 Tues.-Sat.; closed Sun.-Mon. and major holidays. **Admission:** suggested donations—adults, $1; children 50¢.

DOROTHY G. PAGE MUSEUM. The Dorothy G. Page Museum in Wasilla, Alaska, is named for a former mayor who founded the museum and the cross-country Iditarod dogsled race and saved many of the town's historic buildings. The museum, which also serves as a visitor center, is housed in the 1931 log Wasilla Community Hall adjacent to the old Wasilla town site, which contains Wasilla's first schoolhouse, two early log cabins, a blacksmith's shop, and the town's first public bath. The museum features the region's history of mining, homesteading, farming, native culture, dog mushing, and the Iditarod trail and race.

Dorothy G. Page Museum, 323 Main St., Wasilla, AK 99654. **Phone:** 907/373-9071. **Fax:** 907/373-9072. **E-mail:** museum@ci.wasilla.ak.us. **Hours:** June-Aug.: 9-5 Tues.-Sat.; closed Sun.-Mon.; remainder of year—9-5 Mon.-Fri.; closed Sat.-Sun. and major holidays. **Admission:** adults, $3; seniors, $2.50; children under 13, free.

ISABEL MILLER MUSEUM. The Sitka Historical Society's Isabel Miller Museum in Sitka, Alaska, is named for a missionary, social worker, teacher, and museum volunteer who was instrumental in the early years of the museum, which was founded in 1957. The museum has collections and exhibits on the city's history; its fishing, timber, and tourism industries; and Tlingit basketry and wood carvings.

Isabel Miller Museum, 330 Harbor Dr., Sitka, AK 99835. **Phone:** 907/747-6455. **Fax:** 907/747-6588. **E-mail:** sitkahis@ptialaska.net. **Website:** www.sitka.org/historicalmuseum. **Hours:** May-mid-Sept.—8-5 daily; remainder of year—10-12 and 1-4 Mon.-Sat.; closed Sun. in winter and major holidays. **Admission:** donation.

Arizona

ARIZONA WOMEN'S HALL OF FAME. See Women's Museums, Galleries, and Halls of Fame.

SHARLOT HALL MUSEUM. See Museums Honoring Exceptional Women.

Arkansas

ARKANSAS MUSEUM OF SCIENCE AND HISTORY. See Natural History Museums.

California

BURLESQUE HALL OF FAME AND MUSEUM. See Women's Museums, Galleries, and Halls of Fame.

CLARKE HISTORICAL MUSEUM. In 1959, high school teacher Cecile Clarke purchased a 1911–1912 Italian Renaissance–style former bank building and founded the Clarke Historical Museum in Eureka, California, the following year. The regional history museum—located in the heart of Eureka's Old Town—was originally established as a memorial to Clarke's parents, but was later changed to also honor Cecile, who was a teacher for over 40 years.

The museum is known for its Native American basketry and other artifacts, especially its collections of Hupa, Yurok, and Karuk dance regalia, stonework, and intricately woven baskets. It also has Victorian furniture, glass, and china; firearms; textiles; photographs; and materials from the area's lumbering and maritime past.

Clarke Historical Museum, 240 E St., Eureka, CA 95501. **Phone:** 707/443-1947. **Fax:** 707/443-0290. **Hours:** 12-4 Tues.-Sat.; closed Sun.-Mon. and major holidays. **Admission:** free.

DE SAISSET MUSEUM. See Art and History Museums.

HAGGIN MUSEUM. See Art and History Museums.

FLORENCE GRISWOLD MUSEUM. See Art and History Museums.

INTERNATIONAL MUSEUM OF WOMEN. See Women's Museums, Galleries, and Halls of Fame.

MUSEUM OF THE AMERICAN WEST. See Art and History Museums.

ROY ROGERS-DALE EVANS MUSEUM. See Museums Honoring Exceptional Women.

Colorado

BLACK AMERICAN WEST MUSEUM AND HERITAGE CENTER. See Ethnic Museums.

FOUR MILE HISTORIC PARK. See Historic Parks and Sites.

LUCRETIA VAILE MUSEUM. The Lucretia Vaile Museum in Palmer Lake, Colorado, is named for a Denver librarian who spent many of her summers since childhood in the mountain town and was interested in the cultural development of the community.

When she died in 1977, Vaile left a bequest that made it possible—with additional funds from El Paso County—to build a combination museum and library in Palmer Lake. She also donated her Palmer Lake home to the town's Little Art Group in 1968 to serve as the home for an art gallery—now known as the Vaile Hill Art Gallery.

Two other women—Marian McIntyre McDonaough and Lena Royse—also played important roles in the history of the Palmer Lake Historical Society and its museum and library. McDonaough, a pioneer resident and author, was instrumental in founding the historical society, museum, and library, and Royse, a longtime community service leader, left her estate to the society, enabling it to build an addition to the museum in 1995.

The historical museum features a time line from 1873 to the present and contains artifacts, photographs, manuscripts, and other historical materials.

Lucretia Vaile Museum, 66 Valley Crescent St., PO Box 662, Palmer Lake, CO 80133. **E-mail:** plhist@aol.com. **Website:** www.ci.palmer-lake.co.us/plhs/index.html. **Hours:** June-Aug.—1-4 Wed., 10-2 Sat.; closed remainder of week; remainder of year—10-2 Sat.; closed remainder of week. **Admission:** free.

PRICE PIONEER MUSEUM. Charles Price and his wife, Velma Price, collected a wide range of historical materials from the Florence, Colorado, area over the years, and then opened a museum in 1964 and gave it to the city later that year. The museum, now called the Price Pioneer Museum, is housed in an 1894 former lodge building with an adjacent 1875 structure that was the first city jail. The museum features pioneer, Native American, industrial, and other artifacts, as well as minerals, documents, and other materials from the area.

Price Pioneer Museum, Pikes Peak Ave. and Front St., PO Box 87, Florence, CO 81226. **Phone:** 719/385-5990. **Hours:** mid-May–mid-Sept.—1-4 daily; closed remainder of year. **Admission:** free.

UTE INDIAN MUSEUM. The Ute Indian Museum in Montrose, Colorado, is devoted to the Ute people and their Chief Ouray and his influential wife, Chipeta, whose advice was frequently sought and who was invited to participate in tribal council meetings. The museum, operated by the Colorado Historical Society, contains collections and exhibits about the Ute people of Colorado and Chief Ouray and Chipeta, while the grounds include Chipeta's grave, Ouray Memorial Park; a native plants garden; and an outdoor display on the 1776 Dominguez-Escalante Expedition in the region.

Ute Indian Museum, Colorado Historical Society, 17253 Chipeta Rd., Montrose, CO 81401. **Phone:** 970/240-3098. **Fax:** 303/252-8741. **E-mail:** cjbradford@state.co.us. **Hours:** May-Oct.—9-4:30 Mon.-Sat., 11-4:30 Sun.; remainder of year—9-4:30 Mon.-Sat.; closed Sun., New Year's Day, and Christmas. **Admission:** adults, $3; seniors, $2.50; children 6-16, $1.50; children under 6, free.

Connecticut

WINDHAM TEXTILE AND HISTORY MUSEUM. The Windham Textile and History Museum, located in the 1877 store, library, and store warehouse of what was once the world's largest textile mill, in Willimantic, Connecticut, was founded in 1989 by a group that included Laura Knott Twine, a weaver devoted to preserving and interpreting the role of women in producing textiles.

The Willimantic Linen Company was started in 1854 by Austin Dunham. His son and successor, Austin Cornelius Dunham, was a friend of inventor Thomas Edison. This association led to the Willimantic mills becoming the first to be illuminated by electricity, in 1879. Dunham hired an engineer and social visionary, William Eliot Barrows, who built the company store and library in 1877 and then designed and constructed an 840-foot by 168-foot textile mill, the world's largest mill and the first textile mill to be built entirely on one level, in 1880. Tragically, the building burned to the ground in 1995. Barrows also built a row of workers' cottages in 1880, which captured the imagination of industrialists and social reformers.

The museum, known as the Mill Museum, tells the story of the mill's history and the fire that consumed it, as well as the role of women in the factory and at home during the late 1800s and early 1900s. Visitors can also tour a re-created nineteenth-century textile mill and experience life in a mill worker's home and a mill owner's mansion.

Windham Textile and History Museum, Main St., Willimantic, CT 06226 (postal address: 157 Union St., Willimantic, CT 06226). **Phone and Fax:** 860/456-2178. **Website:** www.millmuseum.org. **Hours:** Memorial Day-Columbus Day—1-4:30 Thurs.-Sun. and by appointment; remainder of year—1-4 Fri.-Sun. and by appointment; closed New Year's Day, Easter, and Christmas. **Admission:** adults, $4; seniors and children over 5, $2.50; children under 6, free.

District of Columbia

LILLIAN AND ALBERT SMALL JEWISH MUSEUM. See Ethnic Museums.

NATIONAL WOMEN'S HISTORY MUSEUM. See Women's Museums, Galleries, and Halls of Fame.

Florida

CORNELL MUSEUM OF ART AND HISTORY. See Art and History Museums.

LADIES PROFESSIONAL GOLF ASSOCIATION HALL OF FAME. See Women's Museums, Galleries, and Halls of Fame.

Georgia

LUCY CRAFT LANEY MUSEUM OF BLACK HISTORY. See Ethnic Museums.

Hawaii

KAMUELA MUSEUM. The Kamuela Museum in Waimea (also called Kamuela) on the island of Hawaii is operated by Albert T. Solomon Sr. and his wife, Harriet M. Solomon, who built their 1963 home to house the historical museum. It features a wide collection of Hawaiian artifacts and other historical materials. The museum, located at a site that was predicted by Mr. Solomon's grandmother in 1913, contains Hawaiian objects collected by the couple over the years. They include such items as early stone and wood implements, a 60-pound stone ram used by Kamehameha's warriors against enemy war canoes, an 1843 English-Hawaiian Bible, a clock given to Queen Liliuokalani by Queen

Victoria of England, original furniture brought from New England, and European and Asian art.

Kamuela Museum, State Hwy. 19 at State Hwy. 250, PO Box 507, Kamuela (Island of Hawaii), HI 96743. Phone: 808/885-4724. Hours: 8-5 daily. Admission: adults, $5; children 5-12, $2; children under 5, free.

LYMAN HOUSE MEMORIAL MUSEUM. The story of Hawaii and its people is told at the Lyman House Memorial Museum in an 1839 mission house built by Protestant missionaries David and Sarah Lyman, who lived in the New England–style house until their deaths in the early 1880s. The house has been restored and contains many of the Lymans' furnishings. It is configured to reflect life in Hawaii in the 1860s. The site also has a museum building with five galleries devoted to Hawaii's social and cultural history, art of the nineteenth and early twentieth centuries, and other Hawaiian historical artifacts and natural specimens.

Lyman House Memorial Museum, 276 Haili St., Hilo, HI 96720. Phone: 808/935-5021. Fax: 808/969-7685. E-mail: lymanwks@interpac.net. Website: www.lymanmuseum.org. Hours: 9-4:30 Mon.-Sat.; closed Sun., New Year's Day, Fourth of July, Thanksgiving, and Christmas. Admission: adults, $7; seniors, $5; children 6-17, $3; children under 6, free; families, $12.

Idaho

FORT HALL REPLICA. Fort Hall was a trading post built by Nathaniel Wyeth in 1834 on the banks of the Snake River, where the Oregon Trail passes through southeastern Idaho near Pocatello. It served thousands of trail emigrants and indigenous peoples, but was abandoned in 1856 largely because of Native American hostilities. A flood eight years later demolished most of the fort, and the remains were used to help build a stage station in 1863.

All traces of the trading post were lost. However, a 1916 search party led by Ezra Meeker found fragments of pottery and metallic objects at the site after a member of the party, Joseph Rainey, an interpreter and scout for the army and later for the nearby Native American reservation, remembered seeing materials moved from the fort as a young adult. Another member of the search party was Dr. Minnie Howard, who tried for over 40 years to restore the old fort or build a replica. However, it was not until 1962 that the Bannock County Centennial Committee, headed by Jack Alvord, began building a replica as part of Idaho's 1963 territorial centennial celebration. After Alvord's death his widow,

Laura, dedicated the rest of her life to finding artifacts for the replica displays.

Although the original fort site was eight miles north of Pocatello on the Fort Hall Indian Reservation, the replica trading post was built in a sheltered bend of the Snake River in Ross Park in Pocatello. The fort was rebuilt based on the dimensions in the possession of the Hudson's Bay Company, which bought the trading post in 1837 and operated it until it was closed. Its exhibits trace the history and early life of the fort and feature Native American artifacts. Admission includes visits to two other sites—the Bannock County Historical Museum and Pocatello Junction.

Fort Hall Replica, Alvord Loop (upper Ross Park), PO Box 4169, Pocatello, ID 83205. Phone: 208/234-6238. Fax: 208/234-6578. E-mail: jacdau2@aol.com. Website: www.poky.interspeed.net/fort hall. Hours: mid-Apr.-day before Memorial Day—10-2 Tues.-Sat.; closed Sun.-Mon.; Memorial Day-Labor Day—10-6 daily; day after Labor Day-Sept.—10-2 daily; closed remainder of year. Combination Admission: adults, $2.50; seniors, $1.75; children 6-18, $1.50; children 3-5, 50¢; children under 3, free.

HISTORICAL MUSEUM AT ST. GERTRUDE'S. Sister Alfreda Elsensohn, a Benedictine nun, founded the Historical Museum at St. Gertrude's on the monastery grounds near Cottonwood, Idaho, in 1931 to house pioneer, Native American, and other artifacts and books of the area. The museum now also contains art, minerals, textiles, military accoutrements, medical equipment, and exhibits devoted to Polly Bemis, a Chinese woman believed to have been sold into the mines of Idaho, and Winifred Rhoades Emmanuel, a concert organist whose fingers were once insured for $1 million.

Historical Museum at St. Gertrude's, HC3, Box 121, Cottonwood, ID 83522-9408. E-mail: museum@camasnet.com. Website: www.camasnet.com/~museum/. Hours: 9:30-4:30 Tues.-Sat., 1:30-4:30 Sun.; closed Mon., New Year's Day, Thanksgiving, and Christmas. Admission: adults, $4; children 7-17, $1; children under 7, free.

Illinois

DuSABLE MUSEUM OF AFRICAN-AMERICAN HISTORY. See Ethnic Museums.

Indiana

LOUIS H. AND LENA FIRN GROVER MUSEUM. The Shelby County Historical Society's museum in

Shelbyville, Indiana, is named for a local farm couple, Louis H. Grover and his wife, Lena Firn Grover. Mrs. Grover left their 80-acre farm to the historical society in her will. The farm was then sold in 1950, and the proceeds were used to buy the Elks Lodge building to provide a home for the museum. The museum contains local historical materials and exhibits and features 28 reconstructed storefronts from the 1900–1910 period.

Louis H. and Lena Firn Grover Museum, 52 W. Broadway, Shelbyville, IN 46176. **Phone:** 317/392-4634. **E-mail:** grover@shelbynet.net. **Hours:** 1-4 Fri.-Sun.; closed remainder of week and major holidays. **Admission:** free.

Kansas

HILLSBORO HISTORICAL MUSEUM. The Hillsboro Historical Museum in Hillsboro, Kansas, is housed in the 1876 pioneer Mennonite adobe house built by Peter Loewen and his wife, Anna Loewen. The seven-room whitewashed house was occupied by the Loewen family and others in Hoffnungathal (Hope Valley) until 1956, and then was moved and restored in Hillsboro Heritage Park. Other structures in the park include the Loewens' attached barn and shed, an 1886 one-room schoolhouse, a replica of an 1876 pioneer mill, and a visitor center.

Hillsboro Historical Museum, 501 S. Ash St., Hillsboro, KS 67063. **Phone:** 316/947-3775. **Hours:** Mar.-Dec.—10-12 and 1:30-4 Tues.-Fri., 2-4 Sat.-Sun.; closed Mon., Jan.-Feb., Thanksgiving, and Christmas. **Admission:** adults, $2; students, $1.

Maine

MARY MEEKER CRAMER MUSEUM. See Old Conway Homestead and Museum in Historic Farms and Ranches.

NORLANDS LIVING HISTORY CENTER. The Norlands Living History Center in Livermore, Maine, began in 1974 when the Washburn family left its estate to Billie Gammon, a teacher who worked as a librarian at the site. Gammon converted the property into a museum with historic buildings, exhibits, and programs re-creating pioneer life in the 1790s and 1870s. The center has five buildings—a 1790 house, one-room schoolhouse, church, library, and a mansion with an attached farmhouse and barn. It offers public and school programs that enable visitors to live and work as pioneers did in the 1790s and 1870s.

Norlands Living History Center, 290 Norlands Rd., Livermore, ME 04253. **Phone:** 207/897-4366. **Fax:** 207/897-4963. **E-mail:** norlands@ctel.net. **Website:** www.norlands.org. **Hours:** June-Labor Day—10-4 daily; remainder of year—school groups by appointment; closed major holidays. **Admission:** adults and children over 14, $6; children 2-14, $3; children under 2, free.

STANLEY MUSEUM. Businesswoman Susan G. Davis was part of a community movement to save a 1903 schoolhouse in Kingfield, Maine, which was designed by F. E. Stanley, coinventor of the "Stanley Steamer," who was born in the town. In the process of saving the building, Davis became fascinated with the history of steam-powered cars and the Stanley family, and founded the Stanley Museum in the restored schoolhouse in 1981.

The museum is devoted largely to the technology of steam cars and the technical, artistic, social, and economic achievements of the Stanley family. It features three operating steam cars and has paintings, photographs, violins, and other historical materials documenting the inventions of Stanley and his twin brother, F. O. Stanley, and the photography of their sister, Chansonetta Stanley Emmons.

The Stanley brothers invented a photographic dry plate process in 1883 and operated a platemaking firm in 1883–1905 before developing a steam car in 1897 and starting the Stanley Motor Company to produce Stanley Steamers in 1902–1917. They also developed Stanley violins, while Chansonetta became known for her photos of life in rural America at the turn of the twentieth century. Davis also operates a similar branch museum at the landmark Stanley Hotel and Conference Center in Estes Park, Colorado.

Stanley Museum, 40 School St., PO Box 77, Kingfield, ME 04947. **Phone:** 207/265-2729. **Fax:** 207/265-4700. **E-mail:** maine@stanleymuseum.org. **Website:** www .stanleymuseum.org. **Hours:** May-Oct.—1-4 Tues.-Sun.; closed Mon.; remainder of year—8-5 Mon.-Fri.; closed Sat.-Sun. **Admission:** adults and children over 12, $2; children under 13, $1.

Maryland

JULIA A. PURNELL MUSEUM. See Art and History Museums.

Massachusetts

SALEM WITCH MUSEUM, WITCH DUNGEON MUSEUM, AND WITCH HISTORY MUSEUM. Three museums in Salem, Massachusetts—the Salem Witch Museum, Witch Dungeon Museum, and Witch History Museum—are devoted to the 1692 Salem trials in which fourteen women and six men were condemned to death as "witches"—nineteen being hanged and one tortured to death.

The Salem Witch Museum deals with the trials, the practice of witchcraft, and witch hunting. It features an audiovisual presentation on the trials and exhibits on witchcraft and witch perceptions. The Witch Dungeon Museum, housed in a nineteenth-century former church building, has a re-created dungeon in which accused witches were imprisoned and presents live reenactments of part of the trials. The Witch History Museum tells of the witch hysteria in a re-created Old Salem village, fifteen life-size scenes, and live presentations.

Salem also has the Witch House, a historic house where one of the trial judges lived and conducted some of the preliminary hearings, and the Salem Witch Trials Memorial, which has stone slabs in memory of the twenty victims (see Memorials to Women). Neighboring Danvers also has a Witchcraft Victims' Memorial, with a large granite sculpture and an eight-foot-high triptych with the names of 25 condemned witches, including five who died in jail (also see Memorials to Women). In addition, the Peabody Essex Museum in Salem contains the original documents and popular artworks of the trials.

Salem Witch Museum, 19 1/2 Washington Sq. North, Salem, MA 01970. **Phone:** 978/744-1692. **Fax:** 978/745-4414. **E-mail:** facts@salemwitchmuseum.com. **Website:** www. salemwitchmuseum.com. **Hours:** July-Labor Day—10-7 daily; remainder of year—10-5 daily; closed New Year's Day, Thanksgiving, and Christmas. **Admission:** adults, $6; seniors, $5.50; children, $4.

Witch Dungeon Museum, 16 Lynde St., Salem, MA 01970. **Phone:** 978/741-3570. **Website:** www.witchdungeon.com. **Hours:** Apr.-Nov.—10-5 daily; closed remainder of year. **Admission:** adults, $6; seniors, $5; children 4-13, $4; children under 4, free.

Witch History Museum, 197-201 Essex St., Salem, MA 01970. **Phone:** 978/741-7770. **Fax:** 978/741-1139. **Website:**www.witchhistorymuseum.com/. **Hours:** Apr.-Nov.—10-5 daily; closed remainder of year. **Admission:** adults and children over 13, $6; seniors, $5; children 4-13, $4; children under 4, free.

Michigan

ELLA SHARP MUSEUM. See Art and History Museums.

KEMPF HOUSE CENTER FOR LOCAL HISTORY. The 1853 Greek Revival–style home of Reuben Kempf and his wife, Pauline Kempf, music teachers who were leaders in the cultural life of the community, is the site of the Kempf House Center for Local History in Ann Arbor, Michigan. The contents focus on the background, possessions, and interests of a middle-class German pioneer family, as well as local history.

Kempf House Center for Local History, 312 S. Division St., Ann Arbor, MI 48104. **Phone:** 734/994-4898. **Hours:** Sept.-early June—1-4 Sun.; closed remainder of week and year. **Admission:** donation.

MICHIGAN WOMEN'S HISTORICAL CENTER AND HALL OF FAME. See Women's Museums, Galleries, and Halls of Fame.

ROCHESTER HILLS MUSEUM AT VAN HOOSEN FARM. See Historic Farms and Ranches.

ROSE HAWLEY MUSEUM. See Historic White Pine Village and Rose Hawley Museum in Re-created Pioneer Villages.

Minnesota

GIBBS FARM MUSEUM. See Historic Farms and Ranches.

LAURA INGALLS WILDER MUSEUM. See Museums Honoring Exceptional Women.

Mississippi

FLORENCE McLEOD HAZARD MUSEUM. The 1847 Blewett-Harrison-Lee Home in Columbus, Mississippi, was restored and converted into a historical society museum under the leadership of Florence McLeod Hazard, a community leader who also collected many of its historical contents. As a result, the Columbus and Lowndes County Historical Society named the museum for her. Among historical materials in the historic house are ca. 1833–1908 clothing, portraits, silver, furniture, china, glass, guns, medical instruments, diaries, and documents.

Florence McLeod Hazard Museum, Columbus and Lowndes County Historical Society, 316 7th St. N. Columbus, MS 39701 (postal address: 400 Main St., Columbus, MS 39701-4548). **Phone:** 662/327-8888. **Hours:** 10-4 Fri. and by appointment; closed Thanksgiving and Christmas. **Admission:** adults, $5; students and children, free.

Missouri

DOROTHEA B. HOOVER HISTORICAL MUSEUM. The early history of Joplin, Missouri, is presented at the Dorothea B. Hoover Historical Museum, named for a civic leader who was instrumental in founding the museum and the Joplin Historical Society. The museum, located in Schifferdecker Park, has exhibits of Victorian-era room settings, a miniature animated circus, antique dolls, and other historical materials from the late 1800s.

Dorothea B. Hoover Historical Museum, Joplin Historical Society, Schifferdecker Park, 4th St. and Schifferdecker Ave., PO Box 555, Joplin, MO 64802. **Phone:** 417/623-1180. **Fax:** 417/623-6393. **E-mail:** jopmusm@ipa.net. **Hours:** 9-4 Tues.-Sat., 1-4 Sun.; closed Mon., New Year's Day, Thanksgiving, and Christmas. **Admission:** free.

GENERAL SWEENY'S MUSEUM. General Sweeny's Museum—a privately operated historical military museum adjacent to Wilson's Creek National Battlefield, near Republic, Missouri—was founded in 1992 by Thomas P. Sweeney and his wife, Karen Sweeney. It contains more than 50 exhibits with weapons, uniforms, flags, photographs, and other materials from the Civil War in the West that have been collected by the Sweeneys. The museum is named for a relative, the one-armed General T. W. Sweeny, who played a key role in the Union Army (but spelled his name differently).

General Sweeny's Museum, 5228 S. State Hwy. ZZ, Republic, MO 65738. **Phone and Fax:** 417/732-1224. **E-mail:** tsweeney@altel.net. **Website:** www.civilwarmuseum.com. **Hours:** Mar.-Oct.—10-5 Wed.-Sun.; closed Mon.-Tues. and remainder of year. **Admission:** adults and children over 11, $3.50; seniors, $3; children 5-11, $2; children under 5, free.

LONGWELL MUSEUM. See Art and History Museums.

POWERS MUSEUM. At her death in 1981, Marian Powers Winchester left a bequest to the city of Carthage, Missouri, for the establishment and operation of a local history museum named for her parents,

Dr. Everett and Marian Wright Powers. Winchester, an active clubwoman and longtime secretary of Carthage's Red Cross chapter, spent much of her time in the 1970s making preparations for the museum and selecting the founding collection from her family's prized possessions. These and other local historical materials now tell the story of Carthage's past from the post–Civil War period to the twentieth century in changing exhibitions.

Powers Museum, 1617 W. Oak St., PO Box 593, Carthage, MO 64836. **Phone:** 417/358-2667. **Fax:** 417/359-9627. **E-mail:** info@powersmuseum.com. **Website:** www.powersmuseum.com. **Hours:** June-Oct.—10-5 Tues.-Sat., 1:30-5 Sun.; closed Mon.; remainder of year—11-4 Tues.-Sat.; closed Sun.-Mon., Thanksgiving, and mid-Dec.-Feb. **Admission:** free.

WOMEN'S INTERNATIONAL BOWLING CONGRESS HALL OF FAME. See Women's Museums, Galleries, and Halls of Fame.

Montana

H. EARL CLACK MEMORIAL MUSEUM. The historical collections of businessman H. Earl Clack and his wife, Margaret Turner Clack, are featured at the H. Earl Clack Memorial Museum—started in Havre, Montana, in 1964 by Eleanor Clack, a relative who became the first curator. The museum chronicles the history, archaeology, and geology of Hill County. Among the exhibits are materials on the Chippewa-Cree people, the Wahkpa Chu'gn Bison Kill Archaeological Site, and the 1879 Fort Assinniboine, once the largest frontier military post in Montana. Summer tours are also offered of the nearby fort's remaining buildings.

H. Earl Clack Memorial Museum, 306 3rd Ave., Havre, MT 59501 (postal address: 315 4th St., Havre, MT 59501). **Phone:** 406/265-4000. **Fax:** 406/265-7258. **E-mail:** mcgregord@nmcl.nmclites.edu. **Website:** www.theheritagecenter.com. **Hours:** June-Labor Day—10-6 daily; remainder of year—12-5 Tues.-Sat.; closed Sun.-Mon. and major holidays. **Admission:** adults, $4; students, $1; children under 6, free; fort tours—adults, $3; students, $1.50; children under 6, free.

MIRACLE OF AMERICA MUSEUM. Gil Mangels and his wife, Joanne Mangels, founded the Miracle of America Museum in Polson, Montana, in 1985—largely to illustrate the freedoms enjoyed in the United States, such as free enterprise, expression, religion, and firearms. The couple's museum is an unusual collection of artifacts, historic buildings, examples of ingenuity, and other materials. It has more than 100,000 objects that deal with pioneer, western, military, agricultural, nautical, business, and other aspects of history, as well as a pioneer village with over 26 buildings, including a sod log cabin, general store, blacksmith shop, barn, and saddle shop.

Miracle of America Museum, 58176 U.S. Hwy. 93, Polson, MT 59860. **Phone:** 406/888-6804. **E-mail:** museum@ cyberport.net. **Website:** www.cyberport.net/museum. **Hours:** June-Aug.—8-dusk daily; remainder of year—8-5 daily. **Admission:** adults and children over 12, $3; children 3-12, $1; children under 3, free.

Nebraska

ANNA BEMIS PALMER MUSEUM. Anna Bemis Palmer, a teacher, musician, and author in York, Nebraska, started a small historical museum in the community library in 1967 and then left a bequest for a larger facility, which was named in her honor. The Anna Bemis Palmer Museum, which is located in the York Community Center complex, has period rooms, artifacts, and exhibits on the county's history.

Anna Bemis Palmer Museum, 211 E. 7th St., York, NE 68467. **Phone:** 402/363-2630. **Fax:** 402/363-2601. **Hours:** 9-5 Mon.-Fri.; closed Sat.-Sun. and major holidays. **Admission:** free.

ARTHUR BOWRING SANDHILLS RANCH STATE HISTORICAL PARK. See Historic Farms and Ranches.

GREAT PLAINS BLACK MUSEUM. See Ethnic Museums.

MARI SANDOZ HIGH PLAINS HERITAGE CENTER. See Museums Honoring Exceptional Women.

MARI SANDOZ ROOM. See Museums Honoring Exceptional Women.

Nevada

NEVADA HISTORICAL SOCIETY. Nevada's oldest museum—the Nevada Historical Society—was founded in Reno in 1904, largely through the efforts of Jeanne Elizabeth Wier, chairman of the History Department at the University of Nevada, who served as the museum's director (then called secretary) for its first 40 years. The museum, which is part of the state's Department of Museums, Library, and Arts, has collections

and exhibits relating to Nevada's history, ranging from prehistoric Native American cultures to the twentieth century.

Nevada Historical Society, 1650 N. Virginia St., Reno, NV 89503. **Phone:** 775/688-1191. **Fax:** 775/688-2917. **Website:** www.clan.lib.nv.us/docs/museums/hist/soc.htm. **Hours:** 10-5 Mon.-Sat.; closed Sun. and major holidays. **Admission:** adults, $2; children under 18, free.

New Jersey

LONGSTREET FARM. See Historic Farms and Ranches.

New Mexico

EL RANCHO DE LAS GOLONDRINAS MUSEUM. See Historic Farms and Ranches.

New York

INTERNATIONAL WOMEN'S SPORTS HALL OF FAME. See Women's Museums, Galleries, and Halls of Fame.

LOWER EAST SIDE TENEMENT MUSEUM. Ruth J. Abram founded the Lower East Side Tenement Museum in New York City in 1988 and has served as its president and chief executive officer since. The museum, housed in an 1863 tenement building, tells the story of immigrants who settled on Manhattan's lower east side. All visits are by guided tours. Tours are also offered of the old tenement neighborhood.

Lower East Side Tenement Museum, 90 Orchard St., New York, NY 10002 (postal address: 66 Allen St., New York, NY 10002). **Phone:** 212/431-0233. **Fax:** 212/431-0402. **E-mail:** lestm@tenement.org. **Website:** www.tenement.org. **Hours:** 11-4 Tues.-Fri., 11-4:30 Sat.-Sun.; closed Mon., New Year's Day, Thanksgiving, and Christmas. **Admission:** adults, $9; seniors and students, $7; children under 6, free.

LUCY-DESI MUSEUM. See Museums Honoring Exceptional Women.

MARGARET REANEY MEMORIAL LIBRARY AND MUSEUM. See Library Museums and Exhibit Areas.

NATIONAL WOMEN'S HALL OF FAME. See Women's Museums, Galleries, and Halls of Fame.

The Strong Museum in Rochester, New York, is a hands-on history center created by the executors of the will of collector Margaret Woodbury Strong. It has more than 500,000 objects, most of which came from the founder's collection of dolls, toys, miniatures, dollhouses, games, and home furnishings. Courtesy Strong Museum, Rochester, New York.

STRONG MUSEUM. Margaret Woodbury Strong was a lifelong collector who amassed more than 300,000 objects in her large home in suburban Rochester, New York. Upon her death in 1969, the executors of her will could have dispersed the collection that chronicled popular taste in America, but decided instead to establish a museum in her name, build a 150,000-square-foot building to house the museum in downtown Rochester, and provide a substantial trust to help fund the operations.

The Strong Museum, which opened in 1982, became a major museum of American cultural history, with an annual attendance of 330,000. It is devoted to exploring and interpreting everyday life in the United States after 1820, to help residents and other visitors better understand themselves and each other. The museum now has more than 500,000 objects, including the nation's largest and most historically important collections of dolls, toys, home crafts, and souvenirs. It also features some of the most comprehensive and significant collections of home furnishings and advertising materials.

Strong was the only daughter of John and Alice Woodbury, who were early investors in the Eastman Kodak Company. She traveled extensively as a child and later in life, collecting dolls, toys, and a variety of decorative objects found in American homes. To house her collections, Strong added two gallery wings to her 32-room home and was constructing another wing and a lecture hall at the time of her death. The additions were part of a plan to eventually establish a museum,

but she never saw her dream through to completion. When she died, Strong was the largest individual shareholder of Eastman Kodak and left an estate of over $50 million, which had grown to more than $77 million by the time the will was settled.

Strong Museum, 1 Manhattan Sq., Rochester, NY 14607. **Phone:** 716/263-2701. **Fax:** 716/263-2493. **Website:** www.strongmuseum.org. **Hours:** 10-5 Mon.-Sat. (also to 8 p.m. Fri.), 12-5 Sun.; closed New Year's Day, Thanksgiving, and Christmas. **Admission:** adults, $6; seniors and students, $5; children 3-17, $4; children under 3, free.

North Dakota

DALE AND MARTHA HAWK MUSEUM. The Dale and Martha Hawk Museum near Wolford, North Dakota, is a storehouse of early farm and other machinery collected and restored by farmer Dale Hawk, with assistance from his wife, Martha Hawk. The museum's extensive collection of old tractors, plows, threshing machines, horse buggies, household appliances, automobiles, and other historical items is displayed in an 11-building complex that includes a schoolhouse, grocery, church, sheds, and the Hawks' former home. An annual farm and threshing show is held the second weekend in June.

Dale and Martha Hawk Museum, Rural Rte. 1, Box 19, Wolford, ND 58385. **Phone:** 701/583-2381. **E-mail:** baconec@stellarnet.com. **Website:** www.hawkmuseum.com. **Hours:** June-Oct.—8-7 daily; remainder of year—by appointment. **Admission:** adults and children over 11, $4; children under 12, free.

Ohio

ARMS FAMILY MUSEUM OF LOCAL HISTORY. The former home of realtor Wilford Arms and his wife, Olive Arms, is the site of the Arms Family Museum of Local History in Youngstown, Ohio. The Arts and Crafts–style mansion, called Greystone, was left to the Mahoning Valley Historical Society in Mrs. Arms's will when she died in 1960. It contains period rooms and historical exhibits about Youngstown and Mahoning Valley and has an archival library in the carriage house.

Arms Family Museum of Local History, Mahoning Valley Historical Society, 648 Wick Ave., Youngstown, OH 44502. **Phone:** 330/743-2589. **Fax:** 330/743-7210. **E-mail:** mvhs@mahoninghistory.org. **Hours:** 1-4 Tues.-Fri., 1:30-5 Sat.-Sun.; closed Mon. and major holidays. **Admission:** adults, $3; seniors and college students, $2; students under 18, $1.

INTERNATIONAL WOMEN'S AIR AND SPACE MU-SEUM. See Women's Museums, Galleries, and Halls of Fame.

LAKE COUNTY HISTORICAL SOCIETY. The Lake County Historical Society in Kirtland Hills, Ohio, is housed in the 1926 former home of Arthur Baldwin and his wife, Reba Williams, heiress to the Sherwin-Williams Paint fortune. In addition to the restored house with historical displays, the 543-acre site has an early 1800s log house, replicas of a one-room schoolhouse and a ca. 1400 Native American site, and hiking trails.

Lake County Historical Society, 8610 King Memorial Rd., Kirtland Hills, OH 44060. **Phone:** 440/255-8979. **Hours:** Apr.-Dec.—10-5 Tues.-Fri., 1-5 Sat.-Sun.; closed Mon. and remainder of year. **Admission:** donation.

MILAN HISTORICAL MUSEUM. The Edna Roe Newton Memorial Building, which houses items collected by Edna Newton and her husband, Bert Newton, in their travels throughout the world, is one of seven buildings at the Milan Historical Museum in Milan, Ohio. The complex includes four historic structures, a general store, and a doll and toy house.

Milan Historical Museum, 10 Edison Dr., PO Box 308, Milan, OH 44846. **Phone:** 419/499-2968. **Fax:** 419/499-9004. **E-mail:** museum@milanhist.org. **Website:** www.milanohio.com. **Hours:** Jan. and Apr.-Oct.—10-5 Tues.-Sat., 1-5 Sun.; closed Mon. and Labor Day weekend; remainder of year—by appointment. **Admission:** adults, $5; seniors, $4; children 6-12, $2; children under 6, free.

OHIO WOMEN'S HALL OF FAME. See Women's Museums, Galleries, and Halls of Fame.

RIPLEY MUSEUM. The Ripley Museum in Ripley, Ohio, is located in the former home of local historian Eliese Bambach Stivers and her father, County Judge Gottlieb Bambach. The house, which was given to Ripley Heritage, Inc., for a museum by Stivers's two daughters, contains artifacts and exhibits on local history.

Ripley Museum, 219 N. 2nd St., PO Box 176, Ripley, OH 45167. **Phone:** 937/392-4660. **Hours:** Apr.-mid-Dec.—10-4 Sat., 1-5 Sun.; other times by appointment. **Admission:** adults, $1; children, 75¢.

SUTLIFF MUSEUM. See Library Museums and Exhibit Areas.

TROY-HAYNER CULTURAL CENTER. The Troy-Hayner Cultural Center in Troy, Ohio, is housed in the ca. 1914 Norman-Romanesque Revival–style Mary Jane Hayner House. It contains memorabilia associated with the Hayner family and distillery, Mary Coleman Allen miniatures, historical and fine art photographs, architectural renderings and models, genealogical reference material, and changing holiday and traveling exhibitions.

Troy-Hayner Cultural Center, 301 W. Main St., Troy, OH 45373. **Phone:** 937/339-0457. **Fax:** 937/335-6373. **E-mail:** hayner@tdnpublishing.com. **Website:** www.tdn-net.com/hayner. **Hours:** 7-9 p.m. Mon, 9-5 and 7-9 Tues.-Thurs., 9-5 Fri.-Sat., 1-5 Sun.; closed major holidays. **Admission:** free.

Oklahoma

HARN HOMESTEAD AND 1889er MUSEUM. See Historic Farms and Ranches.

99s MUSEUM OF WOMEN PILOTS. See Women's Museums, Galleries, and Halls of Fame.

OVERSTREET-KERR HISTORICAL FARM. See Historic Farms and Ranches.

PAWNEE BILL RANCH SITE. See Historic Farms and Ranches.

PIONEER WOMAN MUSEUM. See Women's Museums, Galleries, and Halls of Fame.

WOOLAROC MUSEUM. See Art and History Museums.

Pennsylvania

AMY B. YERKES MUSEUM. The Amy B. Yerkes Museum in Hatboro, Pennsylvania, is named for a local schoolteacher who was also the first historian at the Hatboro Baptist Church, where the museum is located on the second floor. The museum, operated by the Millbrook Society, is devoted to local history, archaeology, and genealogy.

Amy B. Yerkes Museum, Millbrook Society, 32 N. York Rd., PO Box 506, Hatboro, PA 19040-0506. **Phone:** 215/675-0119. **E-mail:** millbrook@voicenet.com. **Website:** www.millbrooksociety.org. **Hours:** 7:30-10 p.m. Wed.; closed remainder of week. **Admission:** free.

DORETHA DIX MUSEUM. See Museums Honoring Exceptional Women.

HISTORIC JOHN BROWN MUSEUM. The farm where abolitionist John Brown lived in 1826–1835 is now the site of the Historic John Brown Museum in New Richmond, Pennsylvania. The original museum was founded in 1951 by Dr. Charles Olsen, a physician and collector of Civil War artifacts, but it operated for only a year before his death after a traffic accident. The 100-acre farm near Meadville was bought in 1980 from Dr. Olsen's estate by his grandson, Gary Coburn, whose wife, Donna Coburn, reopened the museum in a new location with additional collections in 2001.

Brown, a martyr in the antislavery movement who led a raid on a federal arsenal in 1849 and was executed, was a preacher, farmer, postmaster, and proprietor of a tannery in Crawford County before moving to Ohio. In addition to the museum, a cemetery with the graves of Brown's first wife, Dianthe Brown, and two of their children is located on the grounds, and the remains of Brown's tannery can be seen near the farm. A spring at the farm is where Brown proposed to Mary Ann Day, a 17-year-old housekeeper who became his second wife and bore thirteen of his twenty children.

The museum contains artifacts, photographs, and books related to Brown's life and times. Among the prized items are Dianthe Brown's purse, a gun from the Harpers Ferry arsenal raid, and an out-of-print edition of *The Life of Capt. John Brown* by James Redpath.

Historic John Brown Museum, 17620 John Brown Rd. (New Richmond, PA), Guys Mills, PA 16327. **Phone and Fax:** 814/967-2099. **E-mail:** coburn@toolcity.net. **Hours:** Apr.-Oct.—10-6 Tues.-Sun.; closed Mon.; remainder of year—by appointment. **Admission:** free.

MARIAN ANDERSON BIRTHPLACE AND MARIAN ANDERSON RESIDENCE/MUSEUM. See Museums Honoring Exceptional Women.

UNITED STATES FIELD HOCKEY ASSOCIATION HALL OF FAME. See Women's Museums, Galleries, and Halls of Fame.

Rhode Island

THE ASTORS' BEECHWOOD VICTORIAN LIVING HISTORY MUSEUM. See Historic House Museums.

South Carolina

RUTH DRAKE MUSEUM. The Belton City Museum in Belton, South Carolina, was renamed in 1987 for Ruth Drake, an elementary schoolteacher who emphasized history among her pupils and spearheaded the development of the museum. The Ruth Drake Museum, located in the historic Belton Depot building, traces local history and features such artifacts as early farm implements, textiles, and railroad materials.

Ruth Drake Museum, Belton Depot, 100 Main St., Belton, SC 29627 (postal address: 108 Carroll Lane, Belton, SC 29627). **Phone:** 864/338-7541. **Hours:** by appointment. **Admission:** free.

Tennessee

COAL MINER'S DAUGHTER MUSEUM. See Museums Honoring Exceptional Women.

DOLLY PARTON'S "RAGS TO RICHES" MUSEUM. See Museums Honoring Exceptional Women.

WOMEN'S BASKETBALL HALL OF FAME. See Women's Museums, Galleries, and Halls of Fame.

Texas

ANNIE RIGGS MEMORIAL MUSEUM. Annie Riggs came to Texas as a child in 1855, later married a sheriff and then a gunman, and became a rancher and eventually the owner of a hotel in Fort Stockton, Texas, from 1902 to 1931. In 1955, the 1899 Riggs Hotel building became the Annie Riggs Memorial Museum, which is devoted largely to the Old West.

The museum features Native American, cowboy, ranch, and other artifacts of the early days, as well as furnishings, textiles, religious items, and other historical materials. The museum is part of the Fort Stockton Historical Society, which also operates Historic Fort Stockton, featuring the remaining structures of an 1867–1886 frontier fort.

Annie Riggs Memorial Museum, Fort Stockton Historical Society, 301 S. Main St., Fort Stockton, TX 79735. **Phone:** 915/336-2167. **Fax:** 915/336-2402. **E-mail:** txrousse@aol.com. **Hours:** Memorial Day-Labor Day—10-6 Mon.-Sat., 1:30-6 Sun.; remainder of year—10-5 Mon.-Sat.; closed Sun., New Year's Day, Easter, Thanksgiving, and Christmas. **Admission:** adults, $2; seniors, $1.50; children 6-12, $1; children under 6, free.

BABE DIDRIKSON ZAHARIAS MUSEUM. See Museums Honoring Exceptional Women.

HERITAGE FARMSTEAD MUSEUM. See Historic Farms and Ranches.

KING RANCH MUSEUM. See Historic Farms and Ranches.

NITA STEWART HALEY MEMORIAL LIBRARY AND J. EVETTS HALEY HISTORY CENTER. See Library Museums and Exhibit Areas.

NATIONAL COWGIRL MUSEUM AND HALL OF FAME. See Women's Museums, Galleries, and Halls of Fame.

RANGERETTE SHOWCASE MUSEUM. See Women's Museums, Galleries, and Halls of Fame.

THE WOMEN'S MUSEUM: AN INSTITUTE FOR THE FUTURE. See Women's Museums, Galleries, and Halls of Fame.

Utah

WHEELER HISTORIC FARM. See Historic Farms and Ranches.

Vermont

ROKEBY MUSEUM. See Historic Farms and Ranches.

SHELBURNE MUSEUM. See Art and History Museums.

Virginia

ESTHER THOMAS ATKINSON MUSEUM. The Esther Thomas Atkinson Museum at Hampden-Sydney College in Hampden-Sydney, Virginia, is named for a woman who became concerned about the gradual loss of the college's history and began collecting memorabilia. Her efforts began a drive to collect, restore, and preserve objects reflecting the history of the college and resulted in a museum to house and display the materials. Atkinson came to the campus before 1916, stayed on as the wife of the college treasurer, and died on commencement day in 1994 at the age of 99. The museum was named for her in 1982.

Esther Thomas Atkinson Museum, Hampden-Sydney College, College Rd., PO Box 745, Hampden-Sydney, VA 23943. **Phone:** 804/223-6134. **Fax:** 804/223-6344. **E-mail:** lmastemaker@hsc.edu. **Website:** www.hsc.edu. **Hours:** June-Aug.—12:30-4:30 Wed. and Fri.; closed remainder of week; remainder of year—12:30-4:30 Mon.-Fri., by appointment Sat.-Sun.; closed major holidays and college breaks. **Admission:** free.

HISTORIC SMITHFIELD. See Historic House Museums.

MARY BALL WASHINGTON MUSEUM. The Mary Ball Washington Museum, a local history museum in a four-building complex in Lancaster, Virginia, is named for George Washington's mother, who was born nearby in Lancaster County. The 1800 Lancaster House contains Washington family memorabilia and historical materials pertaining to the area. The other historic structures include a 1797 clerk's office, with county artifacts; the 1823 old jail, which houses the archives and a historical library; and the 1900 Stewart-Blakemore Building, which holds genealogical materials.

Mary Ball Washington Museum, 8346 Mary Ball Rd., PO Box 97, Lancaster, VA 22503. **Phone:** 804/462-7280. **Fax:** 804/462-6107. **E-mail:** history@rivnet.net. **Website:** www.mbwn.org. **Hours:** 10-4 Thurs.-Sat., other times by appointment; closed Christmas to New Year's Day. **Admission:** $2 per person.

U.S. ARMY WOMEN'S MUSEUM. See Women's Museums, Galleries, and Halls of Fame.

Washington

WASHINGTON STATE CAPITAL MUSEUM. The Washington State Capital Museum in Olympia is housed in the 1920s Italian Renaissance Revival–style mansion that was the 32-room home of banker Clarence J. Lord and his wife, Elizabeth Lord. The Washington State Historical Society museum features exhibits on the history of the Washington territorial and state governments and the capital city of Olympia, and has pioneer herb and ethnobotanical gardens.

Washington State Capital Museum, 211 W. 21st Ave., Olympia, WA 98501. **Phone:** 360/753-2580. **Fax:** 360/586-8322. **E-mail:** dvalley@wshs.wa.gov. **Website:** www.wshs.com. **Hours:** 10-4 Tues.-Fri., 12-4 Sat.-Sun.; closed Mon. and state holidays. **Admission:** adults, $2; seniors, $1.75; children 6-18, $1; children under 6, free; families, $5.

West Virginia

WOMEN'S HISTORY MUSEUM. See Women's Museums, Galleries, and Halls of Fame.

Wisconsin

DR. KATE MUSEUM. See Museums Honoring Exceptional Women.

HOARD HISTORICAL MUSEUM. The Hoard Historical Museum in Fort Atkinson, Wisconsin, is located in the restored 1864 house of Frank Hoard and his wife, Luella Hoard. The house was donated by the Hoards' two children, and a daughter-in-law, Mary Cunningham Hoard, was instrumental in providing historical materials and funds for the museum.

The museum—operated jointly by the city and the local historical society—has sixteen exhibit rooms, with displays on such subjects as the Black Hawk War of 1832; Native American artifacts; Abraham Lincoln's connections with the area; and collections of pioneer tools, crafts, and quilts. The museum also has a Lincoln-era library, the 1841 home of Dwight and Almira Foster (the first frame house in the county), and the National Dairy Shrine Visitors' Center (located adjacent to the museum).

Hoard Historical Museum, 407 Merchants Ave., Fort Atkinson, WI 53538. **Phone:** 920/563-7769. **Fax:** 920/568-3203. **E-mail:** hartwick@hoardmuseum.org. **Website:** www.hoardmuseum.org. **Hours:** Memorial Day-Labor Day—9:30-4:30 Tues.-Sat., 11-3 Sun.; closed Mon.; remainder of year—9:30-3:30 Tues.-Sat.; closed Sun.-Mon. and first two weeks of Jan. **Admission:** free.

ROBERT AND ELIZABETH SOLEM MUSEUM. The Robert and Elizabeth Solem Museum (also known as the Lincoln Center) in Beloit, Wisconsin, is housed in the former Lincoln Junior High School building that was renovated in the late 1980s with funding largely from the local businessman and his wife. In addition to historical exhibits, the structure contains the Beloit Historical Society's library, archives, and offices.

Robert and Elizabeth Solem Museum, Beloit Historical Society, Lincoln Center, 845 Hackett St., Beloit, WI 53511. **Phone:** 608/365-7835. **Fax:** 608/365-5999. **E-mail:** beloiths@ticon.net. **Hours:** 9-4 Mon.-Fri.; closed Sat.-Sun. and major holidays. **Admission:** donation.

SWARTHOUT MEMORIAL MUSEUM. The Swarthout Memorial Museum in La Crosse, Wisconsin, was made possible by the bequests of Edith and Susan Swarthout, two sisters of a wealthy local family. They left funds for an addition to the community library to house a museum operated by the La Crosse County Historical Society.

Swarthout Memorial Museum, La Crosse County Historical Society, 112 S. 9th St., PO Box 1272, La Crosse, WI 54602. **Phone:** 608/782-1980. **Fax:** 608/793-1359. **Hours:** June-Aug.—10-5 Tues.-Fri., 1-5 Sat.; closed Sun.-Mon.; remainder of year—10-5 Tues.-Fri., 1-5 Sat.-Sun.; closed major holidays. **Admission:** free.

Wyoming

ANNA MILLER MUSEUM. The Anna Miller Museum, a local history museum housed in a 1930s National Guard cavalry stable in Newcastle, Wyoming, is named for a former county librarian and superintendent of schools who was a leader in the area's educational efforts.

The museum has exhibits on the early fur trade, exploration, settlement, Native Americans, and natural history. Three historic buildings have also been relocated to the site—the 1875 Jenny Stockade cabin, which served as a Cheyenne-Deadwood stage way station for approximately a decade; an 1898 country schoolhouse; and a turn-of-the-twentieth-century woman's homestead cabin.

Anna Miller Museum, 401 Delaware St., PO Box 698, Newcastle, WY 82701. **Phone:** 307/746-4188. **Fax:** 307/746-4629. **E-mail:** annamm@trib.com. **Hours:** June-Aug.—9-5 Mon.-Fri., 9-12 Sat.; closed Sun.; remainder of year—9-5 Mon.-Fri.; closed Sat.-Sun. and major holidays. **Admission:** free.

HISTORIC HOUSE MUSEUMS

See also Botanical Gardens and Arboretums; Historic Farms and Ranches; History Museums; Museums Founded and/or Operated by Women's Organizations; Other Historic Houses.

Alabama

BELLINGRATH GARDENS AND HOME. See Botanical Gardens and Arboretums.

IVY GREEN, BIRTHPLACE OF HELEN KELLER. See Museums Honoring Exceptional Women.

SCOTT AND ZELDA FITZGERALD MUSEUM. This museum is located in the house in Montgomery, Alabama, where F. Scott and Zelda Fitzgerald lived in the early 1930s while he was writing *Tender Is the Night* and she worked on the autobiographical *Save Me the Waltz*. The lives and works of the noted novelist and his author/artist wife are featured in exhibits, memorabilia, and a video presentation. Zelda was born and raised in Montgomery.

Scott and Zelda Fitzgerald Museum, 919 Felder Ave., Montgomery, AL 36106 (postal address: PO Box 64, Montgomery, AL 36101). **Phone:** 334/264-4222. **Hours:** 10-2 Wed.-Fri., 1-5 Sat.-Sun.; closed Mon.-Tues. **Admission:** donation.

WEEDEN HOUSE MUSEUM. See Museums Honoring Exceptional Women.

Arkansas

DECORATIVE ARTS MUSEUM. See Decorative Arts Museums.

California

ARDEN–THE HELENA MODJESKA HISTORIC HOUSE AND GARDENS. See Museums Honoring Exceptional Women.

BIDWELL MANSION STATE HISTORIC PARK. See Historic Parks and Sites.

FILOLI CENTER. Filoli Center, a 654-acre estate with a 41-room Georgian mansion and 17 acres of formal gardens in Woodside, California, was built in 1915–1917 for William B. Bourn II and his wife, Agnes Bourn, owners of the Empire Gold Mine in Grass Valley. The Bourns lived at the estate from 1917 to 1960, during a critical period in the growth of California.

Filoli Center, now part of the National Trust for Historic Preservation, is an outstanding example of an early-twentieth-century country estate. Its extensive garden is considered an exceptional private estate garden representing the golden age of American gardens. It also has carriage, tea, and greenhouses; a nature preserve; and the Bourn family cemetery.

Filoli Center, 86 Canada Rd., Woodside, CA 94062. **Phones:** 650/364-2880 and 650/364-8300. **Fax:** 650/366-7836. **E-mail:** filolifriend@earthlink.net. **Website:** www.filoli.org. **Hours:** mid-Feb.-Oct.—10-3:30 Tues.-Sat.; closed Sun.-Mon. and remainder of year. **Admission:** adults, $10; students, $5; children 7-12, $1; children under 7, free.

GAMBLE HOUSE. The Gamble House, a superb example of the turn-of-the-twentieth-century Arts and Crafts movement, was the home of David Gamble and his wife, Mary Gamble, in Pasadena, California. The 1908 house was designed for the Proctor and Gamble Company couple by brothers Charles and

Henry Greene, whose work had a great impact on the development of twentieth-century American architecture.

The house, which celebrates wood in articulated joinery, exposed structural timbers, and split shakes, has wide terraces, open sleeping porches, cross ventilation, and overhanging eaves. Its furniture, built-in cabinetry, paneling, wood carvings, rugs, lighting, leaded stained glass, accessories, and landscaping were also created in the spirit of the Arts and Crafts movement.

In 1966 the Gamble House was presented to the city of Pasadena and the University of Southern California by the heirs of Cecil and Louise Gamble. In addition to being a historic house with many of its original contents chosen by Mary Gamble (who lived in the house until 1929), it serves as an important teaching tool for students of architectural design and historic preservation.

Gamble House, 4 Westmoreland Pl., Pasadena, CA 91103-3593. **Phone:** 626/793-3334. **Fax:** 626/577-7547. **E-mail:** gamblehs@usc.edu. **Website:** www.gamblehouse.org. **Hours:** 12-3 Thurs.-Sun.; closed Mon.-Wed. and major holidays. **Admission:** Adults, $8; seniors and students, $5; children under 13, free.

GRACE HUDSON MUSEUM AND SUN HOUSE. See Museums Honoring Exceptional Women.

HOLLYHOCK HOUSE. Hollyhock House, its furniture, and the surrounding art park in Los Angeles were designed by noted architect Frank Lloyd Wright for philanthropist Louise "Aline" Barnsdall, an oil heiress. He undertook the commission in 1914, and the California Romanza–style house was built in 1919–1921. It was his first Los Angeles project.

Hollyhock House, named for Barnsdall's favorite flower, now interprets the 1920s, the lives of Barnsdall and Wright, Wright's architecture, and the history of Los Angeles. Also located at the site are gardens, the Barnsdall Art Center, the Children's Art Center, the Municipal Art Gallery, and the Gallery Theatre.

Hollyhock House, Barnsdall Art Park, 4800 Hollywood Blvd., Los Angeles, CA 90027. **Phone:** 213/485-4581. **Fax:** 213/485-8396. **E-mail:** cadmet@earthlink.net. **Hours:** 12-4 daily; closed New Year's Day, Thanksgiving, and Christmas. **Admission:** adults and children over 12, $2; seniors, $1.50; children under 13, free.

RANCHO LOS CERRITOS HISTORIC SITE. See Historic Farms and Ranches.

Winchester rifle heiress Sarah L. Winchester designed and built this 160-room mansion in San Jose, California, starting in 1884, with carpenters working on expansion and improvements 24 hours a day for 38 years. The house has come to be known as the Winchester Mystery House because of its many oddities. Courtesy Winchester Mystery House.

WINCHESTER MYSTERY HOUSE. In 1884 Sarah L. Winchester, a wealthy widow who was a Winchester rifle heiress, began building a $5.5 million Victorian mansion in San Jose, California, that occupied the lives of craftsmen until her death 38 years later. Because it was filled with so many unexplained oddities, the 160-room mansion came to be known as the Winchester Mystery House.

It is now possible to tour 110 of the 160 rooms and to see such bizarre construction as staircases that lead to nowhere, a window built into the floor, a chimney that rises four floors but stops before reaching the mansion's ceiling, and doors that open onto blank walls.

No one has been able to explain such mysteries or why Winchester kept carpenters working 24 hours a day for so many years. However, after the untimely deaths of her baby daughter and husband, Winchester was apparently convinced by a medium that continuous construction would appease the evil spirits of those killed by Winchester rifles—the so-called "gun that won the West"—and help her attain eternal life. Her $20 million inheritance from her husband—son of the rifle manufacturer—helped support the obsession until her death at the age of 82.

In addition to tours of the mansion, visitors can see the beautiful Victorian gardens that surround the huge structure and two museums—the Winchester Firearms Museum, with one of the larger Winchester rifle collections on the West Coast, and the Winchester Antique Products Museum, featuring a rare collection of early products once manufactured by the Winchester Products Company, a subsidiary of the Winchester Repeating Arms Company.

Winchester Mystery House, 525 S. Winchester Blvd., San Jose, CA 95128-2588. **Phone:** 408/247-2000. **Fax:** 408/247-2090. **Website:** www.winchestermysteryhouse.com. **Hours:** late Apr.-mid-June and early Sept.-mid-Oct.—9-5 Sun.-Thurs., 9-7 Fri.-Sat.; mid-June-early Sept.—9-7 daily; mid-Oct.-late Apr.—9-5 daily; closed Christmas. **Admission:** adults and children over 12, $15.95; seniors, $12.95; children 6-12, $9.95; children under 6, free.

WORKMAN AND TEMPLE FAMILY HOMESTEAD MUSEUM. See Historic Farms and Ranches.

Colorado

BACA HOUSE AND BLOOM HOUSE. The 1869 Baca House and 1882 Bloom House—restored homes of two prominent Santa Fe Trail–era families—are part of the Santa Fe Trail Museum in Trinidad, Colorado. The Baca House, a two-story territorial-style adobe home, was owned by Hispanic businessman, rancher, and community leader Felipe de Jesus Baca and his wife, Maria Delores Baca. The Bloom House, a three-story Victorian mansion, was the home of banker/cattle rancher Frank G. Bloom and his wife, Sarah Thatcher Bloom. The Santa Fe Trail Museum is part of the Trinidad History Museum, a Colorado Historical Society cultural complex that includes a historical museum, two historic houses, and two historic gardens at the houses.

Baca House and Bloom House, Santa Fe Trail Museum/Trinidad History Museum, 300 E. Main St., Trinidad, CO 81082. **Phone:** 719/846-7217. **Fax:** 719/846-6872. **Hours:** May-Sept.—10-4 daily; remainder of year—by appointment. **Admission:** adults, $5; seniors, $4.50; children 6-16, $2.50; children under 6, free.

GOLDA MEIR MUSEUM. See Museums Honoring Exceptional Women.

MOLLY BROWN HOUSE MUSEUM. See Museums Honoring Exceptional Women.

TABOR HOME. The 1877 frame house of silver king Horace A. W. Tabor and his first wife, Augusta Tabor, in Leadville, Colorado, was occupied by the couple until 1880, when they moved to Denver. The house was relocated from Harrison Avenue to its present site on Fifth Street in 1879 when the street became more commercial and residential property too expensive.

The Tabors entertained such visiting dignitaries as former president Ulysses S. Grant and his wife in the house. After the couple left for Denver, the house was sold to Augusta's sister, Mrs. Melvin Clark, who lived in the building for many years. The Tabors' marriage broke up over the "Baby Doe" affair, which became a national scandal. Tabor later divorced Augusta and married Elizabeth Doe. The city of Leadville now conducts tours of the house during the summer.

Tabor Home, 116 E. 5th St., Leadville, CO 80461 (contact Dept. of Administrative Services, City of Leadville, 800 Harrison Ave., Leadville, CO 80461). **Phone:** 719/486-0349. **Fax:** 719/486-1040. **Hours:** Memorial Day-Labor Day—groups of 10 or more by appointment only; closed remainder of year. **Admission:** free.

Connecticut

BUSH-HOLLEY HISTORIC SITE. The Bush-Holley Historic Site in Cos Cob, Connecticut, features the ca. 1730 Bush-Holley House, a national historic landmark and the center of Connecticut's first art colony. From 1890 to 1925, Josephine and Edward Holley ran a boardinghouse for over 200 artists and writers.

The artists and writers studied with such leading American Impressionists as John Henry Twachtman, J. Alden Weir, Theodore Robinson, and Childe Hassam, and interacted with such editors, critics, and authors as Lincoln Steffens and Willa Cather.

Guided tours are offered of eighteenth- and early-nineteenth-century Connecticut furniture and Impressionist art. A visitor center contains changing exhibitions, a sound and light show, and a hands-on history gallery.

Bush-Holley Historic Site, 39 Strickland Rd., Cos Cob, CT 06807. **Phone:** 203/869-6899. **Fax:** 203/861-9720. **Website:** www.hstg.org. **Hours:** Mar.-Dec.—12-4 Wed.-Sun.; closed Mon.-Tues.; Jan.-Feb.—12-4 Sat.-Sun.; closed remainder of week. **Admission:** adults, $6; seniors and students, $4; children under 12, free.

FLORENCE GRISWOLD MUSEUM. See Art and History Museums.

GERTRUDE JEKYLL GARDEN. See Botanical Gardens and Arboretums.

HARRIET BEECHER STOWE CENTER. See Museums Honoring Exceptional Women.

HILL-STEAD MUSEUM. See Art Museums.

PRUDENCE CRANDALL MUSEUM. The Prudence Crandall Museum in Canterbury, Connecticut, is the site of New England's first academy for African American girls. It was established in 1832 by Prudence Crandall, but was forced to close in 1834 after a mob attacked the school.

Crandall was a teacher who originally opened a private academy for local girls and boys in a ca. 1805 house on Canterbury Green in 1832. However, when a 20-year-old African American woman was admitted, Crandall lost much of her support and had to close the school. The following year, after conferring with William Lloyd Garrison and other abolitionists, she reopened the school for the purpose of instructing "young ladies and little misses of color."

In May 1833 the Connecticut General Assembly passed the infamous "Black Law" that made it illegal to establish any school to teach "colored persons who are not inhabitants of this State." Crandall was arrested and jailed overnight, and endured three court trials before the case was dismissed on a legal technicality in 1834.

During this period of turmoil, the students were harassed; the building was pelted with stones, eggs, and mud; and an unsuccessful attempt was made to set the school on fire. After a mob of local residents attacked the academy and broke many of its windows, Crandall feared for the safety of the students, closed the school, and left town with her husband, the Reverend Calvin Philleo. In 1886 the Connecticut Legislature granted Crandall $400 per year, which she received until her death in Kansas at the age of 87.

The state-operated museum has three period rooms and exhibits on Prudence Crandall, African American and women's history, and local history. Prudence Crandall Day is observed annually on the Saturday of Labor Day weekend with children's games, crafts demonstrations, and other entertainment.

Prudence Crandall Museum, State Hwys. 14 and 169, Canterbury Green, PO Box 58, Canterbury, CT 06331-0058. **Phone:** 860/546-9916. **Fax:** 860/546-7803. **E-mail:** crndll@snet.net. **Hours:** 10-4:30 Wed.-Sun.; closed Mon.-Tues. and mid-Dec.-Jan. **Admission:** adults, $2.50; seniors and children 6-17, $1.50; children under 6, free.

SARAH WHITMAN HOOKER HOMESTEAD. The Sarah Whitman Hooker Homestead in West Hartford, Connecticut, is called "a colonial New England treasure." It provides a glimpse of rural New England life as it was immediately following the American Revolution.

Sarah Whitman Hooker lived at the site in a 1715 Saltbox house purchased with her husband, Thomas Hart Hooker, in 1773. After her husband died of pneumonia when he went to defend Boston in 1775, she was ordered to house Tories in 1775–1776 by the Connecticut Committee for Public Safety. She continued to live in the house through the 1780s, and then married Captain Seth Collins and lived for another 62 years. Early in the nineteenth century, the house was remodeled from Saltbox to Georgian.

Today's restored colonial New England house has typical heavy hand-hewn beams and gunstock posts, the original exterior siding, and the initial brick noggin between the wall studs, which can be viewed through wall cutouts. The house also has an unplastered wall left open to reveal sawed and cut lath common to the period. The house features a collection of eighteenth-century and Federal-period furniture and transfer printed china, as well as many of the objects listed in Sarah Whitman Hooker's dowry.

Sarah Whitman Hooker Homestead, 1237 New Britain Ave., West Hartford, CT (postal address: Sarah Whitman Hooker Foundation, 11 Dodge Dr., West Hartford, CT 06107). **Phones:** 860/521-2455 and 800/475-1233. **E-mail:** fransson@ rh.edu. **Hours:** 1:30-3:30 Wed. and by appointment; closed Aug. and national holidays. **Admission:** $5 per person.

District of Columbia

HILLWOOD MUSEUM AND GARDENS. Hillwood Museum and Gardens in Washington, D.C., is the 25-acre former estate of Marjorie Merriweather Post, the prominent businesswoman, collector, and philanthropist who was the only child of Charles W. Post, founder of the Post Toasties cereal company that became General Foods.

She bought the 1923 Georgian-style mansion with its many gardens in 1955 after her divorce from Ambassador Joseph E. Davies (the third of her four husbands). She remodeled it extensively to make it more suitable for her collections and for entertaining. Mrs. Post was especially known for her collections of Russian and French art and decorative arts and her lavish garden parties.

The 40-room house contains collections of Russian paintings, icons, and decorative arts; eighteenth-century French furniture and porcelain; Native American artifacts; and memorabilia and furnishings assembled by Mrs. Post. The estate has rose gardens, a formal French garden, a Japanese garden, and a greenhouse, as well as a Friendship Walk, which commemorates over 100 of Mrs. Post's friends. All visits are by guided tour and require reservations.

Hillwood Museum and Gardens, 4155 Linnean Ave. N.W., Washington, DC 20008. **Phone:** 202/686-8500. **Fax:** 202/966-7846. **E-mail:** admin@hillwoodmuseum.org. **Website:** www.hillwoodmuseum.org. **Hours:** 9-5 Tues.-Sat. (also some Sun. and evenings); closed Sun.-Mon. and major holidays. **Admission (reservation deposits that usually become donations):** adults, $10; seniors, $8; students and children, $5; children under 6, free.

MARY McLEOD BETHUNE COUNCIL HOUSE NATIONAL HISTORIC SITE. See Museums Honoring Exceptional Women.

SEWALL-BELMONT HOUSE. See Museums Honoring Exceptional Women.

TUDOR PLACE HISTORIC HOUSE AND GARDEN. Tudor Place in Washington, D.C., was built in 1805–1816 by Martha Parke Custis Peter, granddaughter of Martha Washington, with an $8,000 legacy left by her step-grandfather, George Washington. The neoclassical house, with its circular domed portico, was intended as a monument to Washington as well as a home for Thomas and Martha Peter and their three daughters, Columbia, America, and Britannia.

Mrs. Peter lived there until her death in 1854. She willed the property to her daughter, Britannia W. Kennon, who lived for all but four of her 96 years at the house, and who catalogued over 800 Mount Vernon heirlooms inherited and purchased by her parents. The Mount Vernon objects are the largest and best-documented collection of Washington objects privately assembled.

Tudor Place was the home of one family for more than 180 years, covering six generations. A tour of the house tells the story of the Custis-Washington and Peters families. The house has more than 8,000 historical objects, changing exhibitions that usually relate to American domestic life in the nineteenth and twentieth centuries, and a beautiful five-acre garden.

Tudor Place Historic House and Garden, 1644 31st St. N.W., Washington, DC 20007 (postal address: 1605 32nd St. N.W., Washington, DC 20007). **Phone:** 202/965-0400. **Fax:** 202/965-0164. **E-mail:** erusch@tudorplace.org. **Website:** www.tudorplace.org. **Hours:** tours at 10, 11:30, 1, and 2:30 Tues.-Fri.; 10, 11, 12, 1, 2, and 3 Sat.; garden open Sun.; closed Mon., Jan., New Year's Day, Fourth of July, Thanksgiving, and Christmas. **Admission:** suggested donations—adults, $6; seniors, $5; children, $3.

Florida

BONNET HOUSE. Bonnet House, the whimsical 1920–1921 estate of artists Frederic Clay Bartlett and his third wife, Fortune Bartlett, in Fort Lauderdale, Florida, occupies 35 acres of a barrier island system in Fort Lauderdale, Florida. The unusual house has murals on the ceilings, faux marble on the walls and floors, and balustrades that are actually paintings. The Bartletts' eclectic collections include such items as antique china, turn-of-the-twentieth-century carousel animals, and shells and coral (housed in a separate museumlike building).

The estate also has Frederic Clay Bartlett's studio, examples of the Bartletts' artworks; extensive gardens; and such animals on the grounds as squirrel monkeys, raccoons, swans, wading birds, and an occasional manatee. Evelyn Bartlett, who lived in the house from their 1931 marriage until her death at the age of 109 in 1997, donated the property to the Florida Trust for Historic Preservation in 1983.

Bonnet House and Gardens, 900 N. Birch Rd., Fort Lauderdale, FL 33304. **Phone:** 954/563-5393. **Fax:** 954/561-4174. **E-mail:** dcunningham@bonnethouse.com. **Website:** www.bonnethouse.org. **Hours:** 10-3 Wed.-Fri., 12-4 Sat.-Sun.; closed Mon.-Tues., mid-Aug.-Sept., and major holidays. **Admission:** adults, $9; seniors, $8; children over 5, $7; children under 6, free.

JOHN AND MABLE RINGLING MUSEUM OF ART. See Art Museums.

MARIE SELBY BOTANICAL GARDENS. See Botanical Gardens and Arboretums.

MARJORIE KINNAN RAWLINGS HISTORIC STATE PARK. See Museums Honoring Exceptional Women.

Georgia

BULLOCH HALL. Bulloch Hall in Roswell, Georgia, was the childhood home of Martha "Mittie" Bulloch, the mother of President Theodore Roosevelt and grandmother of Eleanor Roosevelt, wife of President Franklin D. Roosevelt. The 1839 Greek Revival house has restored rooms featuring period furniture. Tours are given on the hour.

Bulloch Hall, 180 Bulloch Ave., PO Box 1309, Roswell, GA 30077. **Phone:** 770/992-1731. **Fax:** 770/587-1840. **Hours:** 10-3 Mon.-Sat., 1-3 Sun.; closed New Year's Day, Easter, Thanksgiving, and Christmas Eve and Day. **Admission:** adults, $5; children 6-16, $3; children under 6, free.

GERTRUDE HERBERT INSTITUTE OF ART. See Arts Centers.

JULIETTE LOW BIRTHPLACE. See Museums Honoring Exceptional Women.

MARGARET MITCHELL HOUSE AND MUSEUM. See Museums Honoring Exceptional Women.

OAK HILL AND THE MARTHA BERRY MUSEUM. An 1847 Georgian plantation mansion—known as Oak Hill—in Mount Berry, Georgia, was the home of Martha Berry, a cotton broker's daughter who began teaching local children in 1902 in a one-room log cabin that developed into Berry College. The historic building is now the site of the Martha Berry Museum and serves as a visitor center for the college. The museum contains period furnishings, china, silver, art, and memorabilia of Martha Berry and the college. Four exhibit rooms are devoted to Berry's life.

Oak Hill and the Martha Berry Museum, 24 Veterans Memorial Hwy., Rome, GA 30161 (postal address: PO Box 490189, Mount Berry, GA 30149-0189). **Phone:** 706/291-1883. **Fax:** 706/802-0902. **E-mail:** oakhill@roman.net. **Website:** www.berry.edu/oakhill/. **Hours:** 10-5 Mon.-Sat., 1-5 Sun.; closed major holidays. **Admission:** adults and children over 12, $5; children 6-12, $3; children under 6, free.

Hawaii

'IOLANI PALACE. See Museums Honoring Exceptional Women.

LYMAN HOUSE MEMORIAL MUSEUM. See History Museums.

Illinois

JANE ADDAMS HULL-HOUSE MUSEUM. See Museums Honoring Exceptional Women.

LINCOLN HOME NATIONAL HISTORIC SITE. See Historic Parks and Sites.

WILLARD HOUSE. See Museums Honoring Exceptional Women.

Iowa

ABBIE GARDNER STATE HISTORIC SITE. The Abbie Gardner State Historic Site in Arnolds Park, Iowa, features the log cabin where the "Spirit Lake Massacre" occurred in 1857, when a band of Wehpekute Dakota killed 36 settlers and abducted several others, including the 14-year-old Abbie Gardner. Gardner was orphaned during the raid and a captive for three months. She later returned to the cabin and ran it as a museum and tourist attraction. In addition to the restored cabin, a teepee, gravesite, and monument to the settlers who were killed are located on the grounds.

Abbie Gardner State Historic Site, 34 Monument Dr., PO Box 74, Arnolds Park, IA 51331. **Phone:** 712/332-7248. **Hours:** Memorial Day weekend-Labor Day—12-4 Mon.-Fri., 9-4 Sat.-Sun.; closed remainder of year. **Admission:** donation.

MAMIE DOUD EISENHOWER BIRTHPLACE. See Museums Honoring Exceptional Women.

MUSCATINE ART CENTER. See Art Museums.

NELSON PIONEER FARM MUSEUM. See Historic Farms and Ranches.

Kansas

ADAIR CABIN/JOHN BROWN MUSEUM STATE HISTORIC SITE. The log cabin in Osawatomie, Kansas, where radical abolitionist leader John Brown sometimes stayed, belonged to the Reverend Samuel Adair and his wife, Florella Adair, who was Brown's half-sister. The cabin, now part of the Adair Cabin/John Brown Museum State Historic Site, was a station on the Underground Railroad for fleeing slaves. It contains period furniture and an exhibit on Brown's efforts for the free-state cause in Kansas.

Adair Cabin/John Brown Museum State Historic Site, John Brown Memorial Park, PO Box 37, Osawatomie, KS 66064. **Phone:** 913/755-4384. **Fax:** 913/755-4164. **E-mail:** a_renick_bell@grapevine.net. **Website:** www.kshs.org. **Hours:** 11-5 Wed.-Sat., 1-5 Sun.; closed Mon.-Tues. and national holidays. **Admission:** free.

AMELIA EARHART BIRTHPLACE MUSEUM. See Museums Honoring Exceptional Women.

CARRY A. NATION HOME MEMORIAL. See Museums Honoring Exceptional Women.

GRINTER PLACE STATE HISTORIC SITE. Grinter Place State Historic Site in Kansas City, Kansas, features the ca. 1860 brick farmhouse of Moses Grinter and his Delaware Indian wife, Anna Marshall Grinter, who were married in about 1838 and first lived in a log cabin. Mr. Grinter ran a trading post and ferried travelers and the military across the Kaw River in the mid-nineteenth century, while his wife cared for the children, helped farm, raised poultry and livestock, and planted an apple orchard.

Mrs. Grinter was representative of the biracial women who lived between two cultures in Kansas. Born on the Delaware Reserve in Ohio, she was eleven years old when her family and tribe settled on the Kansas frontier. When the Delawares were removed to Oklahoma (then called Indian Territory) in 1866, she and nineteen other Delaware adults (along with their children) chose to give up their tribal status, become American citizens, and stay in Wyandotte County. The Delaware families who remained began purchasing more land and were eventually assimilated. Mrs. Grinter, who had ten children (five of whom lived to adulthood), lived at Grinter Place until her death in 1905. The restored house has period furniture, including several pieces from the Grinter family.

Grinter Place State Historic Site, 1420 S. 78th St., Kansas City, KS 66111-3208. **Phone:** 913/299-0373. **E-mail:** grinter @kshs.org. **Website:** www.kshs.org. **Hours:** 10-5 Wed.-Sat., 1-5 Sun.; closed Mon.-Tues. and state holidays. **Admission:** suggested donations—adults, $2; children, $1.

HILLSBORO HISTORICAL MUSEUM. See History Museums.

HOLLENBERG STATION STATE HISTORIC SITE. The Hollenberg Station State Historic Site near Hanover, Kansas, was a Pony Express stop operated by Gerat Hollenberg and his wife, Sophia Hollenberg. It is now the only unaltered 1860–1861 Pony Express station remaining at its original site.

The Hollenbergs' long frame structure served as their home and the site of their business activities. In addition to serving Pony Express riders carrying the mail to and from the West Coast, they sold draft animals, supplies, meals, and overnight lodging to travelers in immigrant wagons and stagecoaches along the Oregon-California Trail in the mid-nineteenth century. The building now has exhibits about the history of the Pony Express and Oregon-California Trail and changes in modes of transportation in the area over the years.

Hollenberg Station State Historic Site, 2889 23rd Rd., Hanover, KS 66945-9634. **Phone:** 785/337-2635. **Website:** www.histor.cc.ukans.edu/heritage/kshs/places/howlenbg. **Hours:** 10-5 Wed.-Sat., 1-5 Sun.; closed Mon.-Tues. and state holidays. **Admission:** donation.

MAHAFFIE STAGECOACH STOP AND FARM. See Historic Farms and Ranches.

SALTER MUSEUM. The 1884 two-story brick home of Susanna Medora Salter, the nation's first female mayor, houses the Salter Museum in Argonia, Kansas. Salter was elected in 1887, the year Kansas granted women the right to vote and hold municipal office. Salter was a 27-year-old Woman's Christian Temperance Union leader whose name had been placed on the ballot as a joke by anti-temperance pranksters. Much to everyone's surprise, she won with a two-thirds majority and served as an effective mayor. She decided not to run for reelection after giving birth to a son who died after eleven days. The museum contains nineteenth-century furnishings and tells the story of Salter.

Salter Museum, 22 W. Garfield St., PO Box 116, Argonia, KS 67004. **Phone:** 316/435-6376. **Hours:** by appointment. **Admission:** free.

Kentucky

MARY TODD LINCOLN HOUSE. See Museums Honoring Exceptional Women.

Louisiana

BEAUREGARD-KEYES HOUSE. See Museums Honoring Exceptional Women.

KATE CHOPIN HOUSE AND BAYOU FOLK MUSEUM. See Museums Honoring Exceptional Women.

LONGUE VUE HOUSE AND GARDENS. Longue Vue House and Gardens, a 1939–1942 Palladin-style mansion surrounded by eight acres of landscaped gardens and fountains in New Orleans, was the home of Edith Rosenwald Stern, daughter of the famed Sears Roebuck chairman and philanthropist Julius Rosenwald, and her cotton-broker husband, Edgar Bloom Stern.

Mrs. Stern, who married in 1921 and moved from Chicago to New Orleans, had a lifetime of community service. Her achievements included founding the New Orleans Nursery School (now Newcomb College Nursery School) and Metairie Country Day School to provide progressive education for her children and others, and helping establish the Voters' Registration League (now Voters Service) to ensure voting rights denied to African Americans because of political corruption.

Mrs. Stern oversaw the construction of the two-story Greek Revival home and gardens. The beautiful gardens were created by Ellen Biddle Shipman, considered the dean of American women landscape architects.

Longue Vue House and Gardens, 7 Bamboo Rd., New Orleans, LA 70124-1065. **Phone:** 504/488-5488. **Fax:** 504/486-7015. **E-mail:** lschmalz@longuevue.com. **Website:** www.longuevue.com. **Hours:** 10-4:30 Mon.-Sat., 1-5 Sun.; closed national holidays. **Admission:** adults, $7; seniors, $6; children 6-16, $3; children under 6, free.

MELROSE PLANTATION HOME COMPLEX. The Melrose Plantation Home Complex in Melrose, Louisiana, was owned by a freed African American woman slave at the turn of the nineteenth century and by another woman (and her husband) who entertained many writers and artists and made the plantation into a center of local arts and crafts a century later.

Marie Therese, whose last name is not known but who was called "Coin-Coin," was a slave who had ten children by the original French landowner, Claude Thomas Pierre Metoyer, as well as four earlier children by other men. Metoyer bought her freedom and left her and her sons 70 acres of the 13,000-acre plantation, where they raised cattle; grew tobacco, corn, and cotton; and constructed some buildings that still stand today. She then used the profits to obtain the freedom of her children.

However, Marie Therese's land later suffered from poor business and the Civil War, and it was eventually acquired by Cammie Garrett Henry and her husband, John Hamilton Henry, in 1898. Mrs. Henry was a patron of the arts who had many writers and artists as guests, converted two slave quarters into a weaving house and a bindery, added a writers' cabin, replanted and enlarged the gardens, and preserved many of the historic buildings. The latter included the ca. 1796 Yucca House, the original plantation home; and two structures moved from elsewhere—a ca. 1742 barn and the ca. 1780 Ghana House. The 12-acre site now has eight buildings with furnishings dating from 1796 to the early 1900s.

Melrose Plantation Home Complex, State Hwy. 119, General Delivery, Melrose, LA 71452 (postal address: PO Box 2248, Natchitoches, LA 71457). **Phone and Fax:** 318/379-0055.

E-mail: melrose@worldnet.net. **Hours:** July-Oct.—2-5 daily; remainder of year—12-4 daily; closed major holidays. **Admission:** adults, $6; students 13-17, $4; children 6-12, $3; children under 6, free.

Maine

ELIZABETH PERKINS HOUSE. The Elizabeth Perkins House in York, Maine, is one of the finest surviving examples of Colonial Revival architecture and interior design in New England that is open to the public on a regular basis.

The original one-room house at the site was built in 1686 by Timothy Yeales. A later owner added a two-story, four-room, Georgian-style house, incorporating part of the original structure, in approximately 1730. The property then changed hands a number of times until 1898, when Mary Sowles Perkins and her daughter, Elizabeth Perkins, purchased the house as a summer home. They made many additions and altered portions to accommodate their living and entertaining needs. After Mary Perkins died in 1929, Elizabeth decided that all further work would focus on creating a more "colonial" interior as a memorial to her mother. Upon her death in 1952, she bequeathed the house to the local historical society, and it has been preserved as it was at that time.

Elizabeth and Mary Perkins were the driving forces of the Colonial Revival movement in the York area, with Elizabeth being one of the founders of the predecessor organization of the Old York Historical Society, which now operates seven historic sites, including the Elizabeth Perkins House. The Perkins house features more than 20,000 American and European decorative and fine arts, mostly from the Colonial Revival period.

Elizabeth Perkins House, Sewall's Bridge, York, ME (postal address: Old York Historical Society, PO Box 312, York, ME 03909-0312). **Phone:** 207/363-4974. **Fax:** 207/363-4021. **E-mail:** oyhs@oldyork.org. **Website:** www.oldyork.org. **Hours:** June-mid-Oct.—1-5 Tues.-Fri.; closed Sat.-Mon., national holidays, and remainder of year. **Admission:** adults, $6; seniors, $5; children 6-16, $3; children under 6, free; families, $15.

NORDICA HOMESTEAD. See Museums Honoring Exceptional Women.

NORLANDS LIVING HISTORY CENTER. See History Museums.

OLD CONWAY HOMESTEAD AND MUSEUM. See Historic Farms and Ranches.

SARAH ORNE JEWETT HOUSE. See Museums Honoring Exceptional Women.

SAYWARD-WHEELER HOUSE. A ca. 1718 house overlooking the York River in York Harbor, Maine, was the childhood home of Sally Sayward Barrell Keating Wood, better known as Madame Wood, the state's first female novelist. Born in 1759, she lived there for three years and then moved back in 1778 when she married Richard Keating, who died five years later, leaving her with three small children. At that time she turned to writing.

Mrs. Keating became a celebrated conservative writer who married again in 1804—this time to General Abiel Wood, who died seven years later. The house now interprets the history of the family and the area and features Queen Anne and Chippendale furniture, family portraits, and eighteenth-century silver and china brought back as booty from an expedition against the French at Louisburg in 1745.

Sayward-Wheeler House, 9 Barrell Lane Ext., York Harbor, ME 03911 (postal address: Society for the Preservation of New England Antiquities, 141 Cambridge St., Boston, MA 02114). **Phone:** 617/227-3956. **Fax:** 617/227-9204. **E-mail:** ezopes@spnea.org. **Website:** www.spnea.org. **Phone:** 207/384-2454. **Fax:** 207/384-8182. **Hours:** June-Oct. 15—11-5 Sat.-Sun.; closed remainder of week and year. **Admission:** adults, $5; seniors, $4; children 6-12, $2; children under 6, free.

STANWOOD WILDLIFE SANCTUARY. See Nature and Wildlife Centers.

Maryland

CLARA BARTON NATIONAL HISTORIC SITE. See Museums Honoring Exceptional Women.

EVERGREEN HOUSE. Socialite and arts patron Alice Warder Garrett lived in the 1858 Evergreen House in Baltimore from 1920 until her death in 1952, when her will established the Evergreen House Foundation to ensure that her husband's wishes for the property—which he bequeathed to Johns Hopkins University in 1942 with life tenancy for his wife—were carried out. They wanted to keep the mansion "hospitably open to lovers of music, art, and beautiful things and to qualified and competent students and investigators who could make use of its collections ... "

The house was purchased in 1878 by John Work Garrett, president of the B&O Railroad, for his son, T. Harrison Garrett, who married Alice Whitridge. After Harrison drowned in a boating accident at the age of 39 and Alice died in 1920, their first-born son, also named John Work Garrett, inherited the property. In 1908 he married Alice Warder, whom he met in Berlin while serving as first secretary at the American Embassy (he later became ambassador to Italy). They moved into Evergreen House in 1920 and made many distinctive changes to the house, such as converting the gymnasium into a private theater, making the bowling alley into an exhibition area for their collection of Asian art, transforming the dining room into a reading room, and making the library into the central room of the house (they had over 30,000 books, with nearly 8,000 in the library).

Alice Warder Garrett was instrumental in making many of the house changes that can still be seen today. She also left her collection of paintings, which includes works by Picasso, Degas, Forain, Bonnard, Vuillard, Modigliani, and others. Among the other collections in the house are Japanese and Chinese decorative arts, Tiffany glass, sculpture and prints, and exquisite furniture. In addition to tours, Evergreen House is now the site of a concert series, special exhibitions, lectures, and symposia.

Evergreen House, Johns Hopkins University, 4545 N. Charles St., Baltimore, MD 21210. Phone: 410/516-0341. Fax: 410/516-0864. E-mail: ckelly@jhu.edu. Website: www. jhu.edu/historichouses. Hours: 10-4 Mon.-Fri., 1-4 Sat.-Sun.; closed major holidays and some university breaks. Admission: adults, $6; seniors and children, $5.

SOTTERLEY PLANTATION. The 1717 Colonial manor house of James Bowles and his wife, Rebecca Bowles, is featured at the Sotterley Plantation near Hollywood, Maryland. The house was restored in 1910 by lawyer Herbert Satterlee and Louisa Morgan Satterlee, daughter of financier J. P. Morgan, and was opened to the public in 1961 through a foundation established by the Satterlees' daughter, Mabel Satterlee Ingalls. The historic plantation also has a 1717 one-room schoolhouse building, a 1757 warehouse, 1830 slave cabins, and other early structures and formal gardens. The people and cultures of the Tidewater plantation are interpreted at the site.

Sotterley Plantation, 44300 Sotterley Rd., PO Box 67, Hollywood, MD 20636. Phones: 301/373-2280 and 800/671-0850. Fax: 301/373-8474. E-mail: sotterleyoffice@ mail.ameritel.net. Website: www.sotterley.com. Hours: grounds—10-4 Tues.-Sun.; house and ground tours—10-3 Tues.-Sun. in May-Oct.; closed Mon. and major holidays. Admission: grounds—$2; tour—adults and children over 6, $7; children under 7, free.

SURRATT HOUSE MUSEUM. The 1852 Surratt House in Clinton, Maryland, played a critical role in the events surrounding the President Abraham Lincoln assassination conspiracy. Mary Elizabeth Jenkins Surratt was the mistress of the house that also served as a tavern, public dining room, and hotel for travelers in what was called Surrattsville at the time. In 1854 the house also became the post office and polling place for the area, with Mr. Surratt serving as postmaster until his death in 1862.

In 1864 the Surratt family experienced financial difficulties, and Mrs. Surratt moved to Washington, D.C., opening a boardinghouse and renting out their country home. It was there that Mrs. Surratt, whose oldest and youngest sons served in the Confederate Army, was recruited by John Wilkes Booth into a plot to kidnap Lincoln, with the weapons and supplies being stored at the Surratt home in Maryland. When the kidnapping plot failed, Booth turned to assassination, stopping at the Surratt House to pick up the weapons and supplies. In the ensuing investigation, Mrs. Surratt was arrested, convicted, and hanged.

The two-story Surratt farm building has been restored and now serves as a historical museum that tells the story of Mrs. Surratt's involvement in the Lincoln conspiracy and her arrest, trial, conviction, and execution (she was the first woman executed by the federal government). The museum also contains some of the original furniture and decorative arts, as well as materials related to the Lincoln assassination, Civil War era, and mid-1800s life.

Surratt House Museum, 9118 Brandywine Rd., PO Box 427, Clinton, MD 20735. Phone: 301/868-1121. Fax: 301/868-8177. E-mail: laverge@radix.net. Website: www.surratt.org. Hours: 11-3 Thurs.-Sun.; closed Mon.-Wed., mid-Dec.-mid-Jan., and major holidays. Admission: adults, $3; seniors, $2; children 5-18, $1; children under 5, free.

Massachusetts

ABIGAIL ADAMS BIRTHPLACE. See Museums Honoring Exceptional Women.

ADAMS NATIONAL HISTORICAL PARK. See Historic Parks and Sites.

ALDEN HOUSE MUSEUM. The ca. 1653 Alden House in Duxbury, Massachusetts, was the last home of Pilgrims John and Priscilla Alden, who crossed the Atlantic on the *Mayflower*. Mrs. Alden was the matriarch of the Alden family, raising ten children on the property and having 68 grandchildren and at least 392 great-grandchildren.

John Alden and Priscilla Mullins arrived in Plimoth Colony on the *Mayflower* in 1620 and were married in about 1623. They moved to Duxbury in 1627, and tradition says that Alden House was built by Alden and his son Jonathan 26 years later. It is the only standing structure in which original Pilgrims are known to have lived.

The two-story house has eight rooms, four fireplaces, and period furniture, as well as some antique furnishings and artifacts. Among its other features are a powdered clam-and-oyster-shell ceiling in the main room and gunstock beams in the chambers.

Alden House Museum, 105 Alden St., Duxbury, MA 02332 (postal address: Alden Kindred of America, Inc., PO Box 2754, Duxbury, MA 02331). **Phone:** 781/934-9092. **Fax:** 781/934-9149. **E-mail:** director@alden.org. **Website:** www.alden.org. **Hours:** May 15-Oct.15—12-4 Mon.-Sat.; closed Sun. and remainder of year. **Admission:** adults, $4; seniors, $3; children 6-18, $2; children under 6, free.

CLARA BARTON BIRTHPLACE. See Museums Honoring Exceptional Women.

DICKINSON HOMESTEAD. See Museums Honoring Exceptional Women.

FAIRBANKS HOUSE. The ca. 1636 Fairbanks House, built for Jonathan Fairbanks and his wife, Grace Fairbanks, and their family in Dedham, Massachusetts, is the oldest surviving wood frame house in North America. The house, which has had later additions, contains furnishings and other objects belonging to various descendants in the Fairbanks family, who lived in the home continuously until 1904.

Fairbanks House, 511 East St., Dedham, MA 02026. **Phone:** 781/326-1170. **Fax:** 781/326-2147. **E-mail:** curator@fairbankshouse.org. **Website:** www.fairbankshouse.org. **Hours:** May-Oct—10-5 Tues.-Sat., 1-5 Sun.; closed Mon.

and remainder of year. **Admission:** adults and children over 12, $5; children 6-12, $2; children under 6, free.

GORE PLACE. The 1806 Gore Place in Waltham, Massachusetts, was the county seat of Governor Christopher Gore and his wife, Rebecca Amory Payne Gore, in the early nineteenth century. It was where the Gores entertained such leading citizens of their time as President James Monroe, Daniel Webster, John Trumbull, and the Marquis de Lafayette.

The 22-room mansion surrounded by 44 acres of gardens and landscaped grounds was planned by Mrs. Gore with a Paris architect. She also supervised much of the construction and played a key role in developing the interior decoration and landscape design. She lived in the house until her death in 1834. The mansion is now furnished to the period of the Gores' occupancy with paintings, furniture, silver, ceramics, textiles, books, and other objects from America, Europe, and Asia. In addition to the gardens and landscaping, the grounds include a 1793 carriage house, a ca. 1835 farm cottage, and a small farm with heritage breeds of animals.

Gore Place, 52 Gore St., Waltham, MA 02453. **Phone:** 781/894-2798. **Fax:** 781/894-5745. **E-mail:** info@goreplace.org. **Website:** www.goreplace.org. **Hours:** mid-Apr.-mid-Nov.—11-5 Tues.-Sat., 1-5 Sun.; other times by appointment; closed Mon. and national holidays. **Admission:** adults, $7; seniors and students, $6; children 5-12, $5; children under 5, free.

ISABELLA STEWART GARDNER MUSEUM. See Museums Honoring Exceptional Women.

MARIA MITCHELL BIRTHPLACE HOUSE. See Museums Honoring Exceptional Women.

MARY BAKER EDDY HISTORIC HOUSES. See Museums Honoring Exceptional Women.

THE MOUNT. See Museums Honoring Exceptional Women.

NICHOLS HOUSE MUSEUM. The Nichols House Museum, which offers a rare glimpse of life on Boston's historic Beacon Hill in the late nineteenth and early twentieth centuries, was the home of Rose Standish Nichols, a noted landscape architect and lifelong pacifist who was a founding member of the Women's International League for Peace and Freedom in 1915.

The 1804 four-story brick townhouse, which was Nichols's home for nearly 75 years, is filled with the furnishings she inherited, collected during her worldly travels, and left upon her death in 1960. They include ancestral portraits, Flemish tapestries, oriental rugs, European and Asian art, and works by sculptor Augustus Saint Gaudens.

Nichols House Museum, 55 Mount Vernon St., Boston, MA 02108. Phone: 617/227-6993. Fax: 617/723-8026. E-mail: nhm@channell.com. Hours: May-Oct.—12:15-4:15 Tues.-Sat.; remainder of year—12:15-4:15 Thurs.-Sat.; closed Sun., Jan., and major holidays. Admission: adults and children over 11, $5; children under 12, free.

ORCHARD HOUSE. See Museums Honoring Exceptional Women.

REBECCA NURSE HOMESTEAD. The Rebecca Nurse Homestead in Danvers, Massachusetts, was the 1678 home of Rebecca Nurse, who was hanged as a witch in the 1692 Salem witchcraft trials. The building later became the home of a 1775 Lexington-alarm minuteman. The 1672 Salem Village meeting house has also been reconstructed on the grounds. An exhibit in the barn describes the 1680s–1780s lifestyle on a farmstead, the witchcraft trials of 1692, and the Lexington alarm.

Rebecca Nurse Homestead, 149 Pine St., Danvers, MA 01023. Phone: 978/774-8799. Website: www.rebeccanurse.org. Hours: mid-June-mid-Oct.—1-4:30 Tues.-Sun.; closed Mon.; other times by appointment. Admission: adults and children over 15, $4; children under 16, $2.

SEDGWICK GARDENS AT LONG HILL RESERVATION. See Botanical Gardens and Arboretums.

WITCH DUNGEON MUSEUM. See History Museums.

THE WITCH HOUSE. See History Museums.

Michigan

CRANBROOK HOUSE AND GARDENS. Cranbrook House and Gardens—featuring the 1908 home, art, furniture, and gardens of newspaper publisher George G. Booth and his wife, Ellen Scripps Booth—are located at the innovative Cranbrook Educational Community complex they developed in Bloomfield Hills, Michigan. The educational community includes the Cranbrook Academy of Art, three schools, and

two museums—the Cranbrook Art Museum and Cranbrook Institute of Science (see Art Museums and Natural History Museums). The Booths' historic Arts and Crafts–style house was designed by Albert Kahn on 40 acres that include formal gardens, woodlands, fountains, sculpture, walks, and two lakes.

Cranbrook House and Gardens, 380 Lone Pine Rd., PO Box 801, Bloomfield Hills, MI 48303-0801. Phones: 248/645-3199 and 248/645-3000. Fax: 248/645-3151. Website: www.cranbrook.edu. Hours: house—June-Oct. tours: 11 and 1:15 Thurs. and 1:30 and 3 Sun.; gardens—May-Labor Day: 10-5 Mon.-Sat., 11-3 Sun.; Sept.: 11-3 Mon.-Sun.; Oct.: 11-3 Sat.-Sun.; both closed remainder of week and year. Admission: house and gardens—adults, $10; seniors, $8; gardens—adults, $5; seniors and students, $4; children under 5, free.

EDSEL AND ELEANOR FORD HOUSE. The 60-room mansion built in 1926–1929 in Grosse Pointe Shores, Michigan, by automobile executive Edsel Ford and his wife, Eleanor Ford, was designed by noted architect Albert Kahn and styled after houses in the Cotswold area west of London, England.

The house is located on 87 acres of gardens and grounds, which remain from the 125 acres originally given to Edsel by his father, Henry Ford, founder of the Ford Motor Company. Edsel first served as secretary of the automobile firm and then as president from 1921 to 1943.

The house remains essentially as it was originally. The decor and furnishings of the house reflect the Fords' lifelong love of art in many forms, with French and English period furniture, historic textiles, and paintings by such artists as Cézanne, Matisse, and Diego Rivera. Mrs. Ford, who lived in the house for 33 years after the death of Edsel in 1943, left the house to be used for the benefit of the public. Twenty of the rooms can be seen on guided tours.

Edsel and Eleanor Ford House, 1100 Lake Shore Rd., Grosse Pointe Shores, MI 48236. Phone: 313/884-4222. Fax: 313/884-5977. E-mail: info@fordhouse.org. Website: www.fordhouse.org. Hours: Apr.-Dec.—10-4 Tues.-Sat., 12-4 Sun.; remainder of year—12-4 Tues.-Sun.; closed Mon., a 2-week period in Jan. and Feb., New Year's Day, Thanksgiving, and Christmas. Admission: house—adults, $6; seniors, $5; children 6-12, $4; children under 6, free; grounds—free.

ELLA SHARP MUSEUM. See Art and History Museums.

KEMPF HOUSE CENTER FOR LOCAL HISTORY. See History Museums.

MEADOW BROOK HALL. Meadow Brook Hall, a historic house museum at Oakland University in Rochester, Michigan, is located in the late-1920s Tudor Revival–style mansion of Matilda Dodge Wilson, who donated her estate as the site of the university. She was the widow of automobile pioneer John Dodge and her second husband, Alfred Wilson, a Wisconsin lumber broker. The historic structure, which opened to the public in 1971, has 55,000 square feet of exhibits, a restaurant, gardens, and outbuildings. Among its collections are paintings, sculptures, prints, drawings, furniture, costumes, and textiles.

Meadow Brook Hall, Oakland University, Rochester, MI 48309-4401. **Phone:** 248/370-3140. **Fax:** 248/370-4301. **Website:** www.meadowbrookhall.org. **Hours:** guided tours— 1:30 Mon.-Sat., 1:30 and 3:30 Sun. (with additional tours in July-Aug.); closed Easter, Memorial Day, Fourth of July, Labor Day, Thanksgiving and the day after, and between Christmas and New Year's Day. **Admission:** adults, $8; seniors, $6; students and children 5-12, $4; children under 5, free.

ROCHESTER HILLS MUSEUM AT VAN HOOSEN FARM. See Historic Farms and Ranches.

Minnesota

JUDY GARLAND BIRTHPLACE HISTORIC HOUSE. See Museums Honoring Exceptional Women.

Mississippi

FLORENCE McLEOD HAZARD MUSEUM. See History Museums.

Missouri

BONNIEBROOK. See Museums Honoring Exceptional Women.

LAURA INGALLS WILDER HOME AND MUSEUM. See Museums Honoring Exceptional Women.

THORNHILL HISTORIC SITE. See Faust Park in Historic Parks and Sites.

Nebraska

BESS STREETER ALDRICH HOUSE. See Museums Honoring Exceptional Women.

WILLA CATHER STATE HISTORIC SITE. See Museums Honoring Exceptional Women.

New Hampshire

ANNIE E. WOODMAN INSTITUTE. See General Museums.

New Jersey

PERKINS CENTER FOR THE ARTS. See Arts Centers.

New Mexico

EL RANCHO DE LAS GOLONDRINAS MUSEUM. See Historic Farms and Ranches.

GEORGIA O'KEEFFE HOME AND STUDIO. See Museums Honoring Exceptional Women.

MABEL DODGE LUHAN HOUSE. Mabel Dodge was a celebrated patron of the arts who had a famous cultural salon in New York before moving to Taos, New Mexico, in 1918, marrying Taos Pueblo Indian Antonio Lujan (later Luhan) and becoming a prominent hostess promoting the Taos art colony.

In New York her home was a gathering place for such figures as John Reed, Margaret Sanger, Max Eastman, Lincoln Steffens, Walter Lippman, and Gertrude Stein. After moving to her handsome adobe house in Taos, she hosted such guests as D. H. Lawrence, Willa Cather, and Georgia O'Keeffe. She later wrote of her sometimes painful relationship with Lawrence and his wife, followed by a four-volume autobiography and several books about life and artists in Taos. The Luhan house is now a bed-and-breakfast and conference center that can be visited.

Mabel Dodge Luhan House, 240 Morada Lane, Taos, NM 87571. **Phone:** 505/751-9686. **Fax:** 505/737-0365. **E-mail:** mabel@mabeldodgeluhan.com. **Website:** www.mabeldodgeluhan.com. **Hours:** 8 a.m.-9 p.m. daily. **Admission:** free.

New York

ALICE AUSTEN HOUSE MUSEUM. See Museums Honoring Exceptional Women.

CLARK BOTANIC GARDEN. See Botanical Gardens and Arboretums.

ELEANOR ROOSEVELT NATIONAL HISTORIC SITE. See Museum Honoring Exceptional Women.

ELIZABETH CADY STANTON HOUSE. See Museums Honoring Exceptional Women.

HARRIET TUBMAN HOME. See Museums Honoring Exceptional Women.

HOME OF FRANKLIN D. ROOSEVELT NATIONAL HISTORIC SITE. See Historic Parks and Sites.

LOWER EAST SIDE TENEMENT MUSEUM. See History Museums.

MARCELLA SEMBRICH OPERA MUSEUM. See Museums Honoring Exceptional Women.

MORRIS-JUMEL MANSION. The ca. 1765 Morris-Jumel Mansion, where General George Washington and the British once had their Revolutionary War headquarters in New York City, was the home of the flamboyant and somewhat eccentric Eliza Jumel, who married political leader Aaron Burr in the historic house in 1833 after the death of her wealthy French wine-merchant husband. The brief, stormy marriage with Burr was followed by a separation and his death three years later.

Jumel, who lived in the mansion from 1810 until her death in 1865 at the age of 93, reportedly tricked Stephen Jumel into marrying her in 1804 after allegedly being his mistress for years. When Mr. Jumel learned that her stories of a noble upbringing were false, he became angry and distant. Later she transferred the title of his holdings to herself. A year after her husband died, she married Burr.

The majestic Georgian-Colonial mansion was originally built as a summer home by British Lieutenant Colonel Roger Morris, an aide-de-camp to General Edward Braddock during the French and Indian War who had married the wealthy Mary Philipse after the war. But in 1775 Morris, a Tory, fled to England. During the Revolutionary War, both American and British forces used the house as their headquarters. Washington made the mansion his temporary headquarters in 1776 while his Revolutionary Army retreated after the disastrous defeat on Long Island.

The house became a tavern after the Revolutionary War and was then purchased by Mr. Jumel in 1810. The socially ambitious Mrs. Jumel restored the house in the most magnificent style of the nineteenth century

and entertained lavishly. The mansion, one of the oldest surviving residential structures in Manhattan, now features Georgian, Federal, and French Empire furniture; some of Mrs. Jumel's clothing, Burr's desk table and trunk; and the second-floor rooms where Washington had his quarters.

Morris-Jumel Mansion, 65 Jumel Terrace, New York, NY 10032. **Phone:** 212/923-8008. **Fax:** 212/923-8947. **Hours:** 10-4 Wed.-Sun.; closed Mon.-Tues. and major holidays. **Admission:** adults, $3; seniors and student, $2; children under 10 with an adult, free.

NARCISSA PRENTISS HOUSE. See Museums Honoring Exceptional Women.

OLD WESTBURY GARDENS. See Botanical Gardens and Arboretums.

SAGAMORE HILL NATIONAL HISTORIC SITE. See Historic Parks and Sites.

SONNENBERG GARDENS AND MANSION. See Botanical Gardens and Arboretums.

SUSAN B. ANTHONY HOUSE. See Museums Honoring Exceptional Women.

North Carolina

BELLAMY MANSION MUSEUM OF HISTORY AND DESIGN ARTS. One of the best examples of antebellum architecture is the ca. 1861 Greek Revival home of Dr. John D. Bellamy, a prominent physician and planter, and his wife, Eliza Bellamy, in Wilmington, North Carolina. The 22-room mansion features Corinthian columns, white marble mantles, ornate cornice moldings, and early Victorian furniture.

The Bellamy family moved into the house on the eve of the Civil War, only to be displaced by the conflict. The mansion was used as a headquarters by Union officers in the area during the war. The Bellamys reclaimed the property in 1865, and it remained a family residence until 1946. It was restored and opened by the Historic Preservation Foundation of North Carolina in 1993 as the Bellamy Mansion Museum of History and Design Arts. In addition to interpreting the history and lifestyle of the Bellamy family, it features two gallery spaces with changing exhibitions on architectural history, historic preservation, and the design arts. The house also has its original slave quarters and re-created Victorian gardens.

Bellamy Mansion Museum of History and Design Arts, 503 Market St., PO Box 1176, Wilmington, NC 28402. **Phone:** 910/251-3700. **Fax:** 910/763-8154. **Website:** www.presnc.org. **Hours:** 10-5 Tues.-Sat., 1-5 Sun.; closed Mon. and major holidays. **Admission:** adults and children over 12, $6; children 6-12, $3; children under 6, free.

HISTORIC BATH STATE HISTORIC SITE. Three eighteenth- and nineteenth-century houses, a memorial garden, and a 1734 church are part of the Historic Bath State Historic Site in Bath, the oldest incorporated town in North Carolina, the colony's first official port of entry and the home of the pirate Blackbeard when he wasn't plundering in the Caribbean.

The restored historic houses are the 1751 Palmer-Marsh House, with its original colonial kitchen in the cellar; the 1790 Van Der Veer House, which contains exhibits on Bath's history; and the 1830 Bonner House, featuring period furniture. The Ruth McCloud Smith Memorial Garden is behind the Bonner House, and the historic St. Thomas Episcopal Church is believed to be the oldest church still functioning in the state.

The Palmer-Marsh House was built by port customs collector Michael Coutanche and his wife, Sarah Coutanche, and was later lived in by customs collector Robert Palmer and his wife, Margaret Palmer, and merchant Jonathan Marsh and his wife, Ann Bonner Marsh. The Van Der Veer House was the home of Mr. and Mrs. Jacob Van Der Veer, while the Bonner House was the summer residence of Joseph Bonner and his wife, Sallie Ann Bonner. The garden in memorial of Ruth McCloud Smith was added in the 1960s with funding from the Oscar Smith Foundation.

The Van Der Veer House is free to visitors, but the Palmer-Marsh and Bonner houses can be seen only as part of guided tours with a nominal admission.

Historic Bath State Historic Site, State Hwy. 92, PO Box 148, Bath, NC 27808. **Phone:** 252/923-3971. **Fax:** 252/923-0174. **E-mail:** historicbath@gotri-countynet.net. **Website:** www.ah.dcr.state.nc.us/sections/hs/bath/bath.htm. **Hours:** Apr.-Oct.—9-5 Mon.-Sat., 1-5 Sun.; remainder of year—10-4 Tues.-Sat., 1-4 Sun.; closed Mon., Thanksgiving, and Christmas Eve and Day. **Admission:** adults, $2; children, $1.

REYNOLDA HOUSE, MUSEUM OF AMERICAN ART. See Art Museums.

Ohio

ARMS FAMILY MUSEUM OF LOCAL HISTORY. See History Museums.

HARRIET TAYLOR UPTON HOUSE. The 1840 Harriet Taylor Upton House in Warren, Ohio, was the home of a leading suffrage activist from 1883 to 1931 and the headquarters of the National American Woman Suffrage Association in 1903–1905. Upton also served as treasurer of the association in 1895–1910. The house has been restored to its appearance at the turn of the twentieth century and features suffrage letters, books, and other materials; an exhibit on Upton's life; and period furniture, costumes, and textiles.

Harriet Taylor Upton House, 380 Mahoning Ave., Warren, OH 44483. **Phone:** 303/395-1840. **E-mail:** lanae1776@aol.com. **Hours:** by appointment. **Admission:** free.

LUCY HAYES HERITAGE CENTER. See Museums Honoring Exceptional Women.

TAFT MUSEUM OF ART. See Art Museums.

TROY-HAYNER CULTURAL CENTER. See History Museums.

WOLCOTT HOUSE MUSEUM COMPLEX. The Wolcott House Museum in Maumee, Ohio, is housed in the 1835 Federal-style mansion of merchant James Wolcott and his wife, Mary Wells Wolcott (Ahmahquauzah-quah), daughter of William Wells, the celebrated frontier scout and Indian agent, and Sweet Breeze (Wahmangopath), the daughter of Warrior Chief Little Turtle of the Miami Indians. The museum complex features Wolcott family heirlooms, Native American artifacts, period antiques, and a collection of other nineteenth- and early-twentieth-century historic buildings, including a ca. 1840 Greek Revival–style city house, ca. 1850 log cabin, ca. 1880 railroad depot, and ca. 1901 country church.

Wolcott House Museum Complex, 1031 River Rd., Maumee, OH 43537. **Phone:** 419/893-9602. **Fax:** 419/893-3108. **E-mail:** mvhs@accesstoledo.com. **Website:** www.maumee.org/wolcott/wolcott.htm. **Hours:** Apr.-Dec.—1-4:30 Wed.-Sun.; closed Mon.-Tues., Jan.-Mar., and major holidays. **Admission:** adults, $3.50; children 6-18, $1.50; children under 6, free.

Oklahoma

HARN HOMESTEAD AND 1889er MUSEUM. See Historic Farms and Ranches.

MATTIE BEAL PAYNE MANSION. Kansas telegraph operator Mattie Beal Payne—for whom the 1908 Mattie

Beal Payne Mansion in Lawton, Oklahoma, is named—drew number 2 in the land lottery that opened Lawton to development at the turn of the twentieth century. She later donated land for a school, church, parks, and housing. The Greek Revival–style house contains original Payne family objects and period pieces to show life in the early history of Lawton.

Mattie Beal Payne Mansion, 1006 S.W. 5th St., PO Box 311, Lawton, OK 73502. **Phone:** 580/357-3522. **Hours:** 2-4 2nd Sun. of month and by appointment. **Admission:** adults, $2; children, $1.

PAWNEE BILL RANCH SITE. See Historic Farms and Ranches.

Oregon

MAUDE KERNS ART CENTER. See Art Museums.

PITTOCK MANSION. The 16,000-square-foot chateauesque Pittock Mansion in Portland, Oregon, was the home of businessman Henry L. Pittock and his wife, civic leader Georgiana Martin Burton Pittock, from 1914 to 1919. During the late 1800s and early 1900s, the couple's lives and work paralleled the growth of Portland from a small Pacific Northwest town into a major metropolitan area.

Mr. Pittock, who traveled with a wagon train from Pennsylvania to Oregon in 1853, married the 15-year-old Georgiana in 1860. She had crossed the plains from Iowa to the Oregon Territory eight years earlier. Together they began 58 years of work, community service, and devotion to family (they had six children and fourteen grandchildren). He became a newspaper owner and builder of an empire in real estate, banking, railroads, steamboats, ranching, mining, and the pulp and paper industry. She served as a community leader dedicated to improving the lives of women and children by helping to found the Ladies Relief Society and its Children's Home and by working to further the Woman's Union and its Martha Washington Home for single working women, Boys and Girls Aid Society, Parry Center, Fruit and Flower Mission, Old People's Home, and Rose Festival.

The Pittocks began planning the mansion in 1909, but it was not completed until 1914. At the ages of 79 and 70, respectively, they moved into their new home in the heart of Portland. However, they lived in the mansion only a short time. She died in 1918, and he the following year. Members of the Pittock family continued to live in the house until 1958, when it was sold. The city of Portland later purchased and restored the estate and opened it as a community landmark in 1965.

Pittock Mansion, 3229 N.W. Pittock Dr., Portland, OR 97210. **Phone:** 503/823-3623. **Fax:** 503/823-3619. **E-mail:** pkdanc@ci.portland.or.us. **Website:** www.pittockmansion.com. **Hours:** 12-4 daily; closed Jan. and major holidays. **Admission:** adults, $5; seniors, $4.50; children 6-18, $2.50; children under 6, free.

PORTLAND MUSEUM OF ART (McLELLAN-Seat House). See Art Museums.

Pennsylvania

BETSY ROSS HOUSE. See Museums Honoring Exceptional Women.

JENNIE WADE HOUSE AND MUSEUM. The Jennie Wade House and Museum in Gettysburg, Pennsylvania, is named for the only civilian killed in the Battle of Gettysburg in the Civil War. The early 1800s structure was located between the Union and Confederate lines of the 1863 battle. Guided tours are offered of the house, which has its original furnishings and relates the story of Jennie Wade.

Jennie Wade House and Museum, 547 Baltimore St., Gettysburg, PA 17325. **Phones:** 717/334-4100 and 717/334-6294. **Fax:** 717/334-9100. **Hours:** June-Aug.—9-9 daily; Apr.-May and Sept.-Oct.—9- 7 daily; Mar. and Nov.—9-5 daily; closed Dec.-Feb. **Admission:** adults and children over 11, $5.75; children 6-11, $3.25; children under 6, free.

MARIAN ANDERSON BIRTHPLACE AND MARIAN ANDERSON RESIDENCE/MUSEUM. See Museums Honoring Exceptional Women.

PEARL S. BUCK HISTORIC SITE. See Museums Honoring Exceptional Women.

RACHEL CARSON HOMESTEAD. See Museums Honoring Exceptional Women.

TODD HOUSE. See Museums Honoring Exceptional Women.

South Carolina

AIKEN-RHETT HOUSE. The Aiken-Rhett House in Charleston, South Carolina, is an 1818 Greek Revival house that has survived virtually unaltered since 1858, when it was expanded and redecorated by Governor William Aiken Jr. and his wife, Harriet Lowndes Aiken.

The house was originally built by merchant John Robinson, who was forced to sell it after losing five ships at sea in 1825. It became the rental property of cotton merchant William Aiken Sr., who later served as president of the South Carolina Railroad. When he died in a carriage accident in 1831, his property was divided between his wife and his only son, William Aiken Jr. The son took possession of the property in 1833, and he and his new bride decided to make the house their primary residence. They made extensive renovations as Aiken became one of the state's wealthiest citizens and served in the state legislature, in Congress, and then as governor. Aiken family members continued to live in the house until the 1970s with only minimal alterations.

The house, now one of the historic houses operated by the Historic Charleston Foundation, features many items obtained during Aiken family trips to Europe, including crystal and bronze chandeliers, classical sculpture, and paintings. It also has such original outbuildings as kitchens, slave quarters, stables, privies, and cattle sheds.

Aiken-Rhett House, 48 Elizabeth St., Charleston, SC 29403 (contact: Historic Charleston Foundation, 40 E. Bay, PO Box 1120, Charleston, SC 29402). **Phone:** 843/723-1623. **Fax:** 843/577-2067. **Website:** www.historiccharleston.org. **Hours:** 10-5 Mon.-Sat., 2-5 Sun.; closed Thanksgiving and Christmas Eve and Day. **Admission:** adults and children over 6, $7; children under 7, free.

BROOKGREEN GARDENS. See Botanical Gardens and Arboretums.

South Dakota

PRAIRIE HOMESTEAD HISTORIC SITE. The 1909 sod dugout home of homesteaders Ed Brown and his wife, Alice Brown, can be seen at the Prairie Homestead Historic Site, near the east entrance to the Badlands National Park near Philip, South Dakota. The house is furnished much as it would have been when the Browns lived there.

Prairie Homestead Historic Site, Badlands Loop Hwy. 240, Philip, SD 57567. **Phone:** 605/433-5400. **Fax:** 605/433-5434. **E-mail:** klcrew@gwtc.net. **Website:** www.prairiehomestead. com. **Hours:** mid-May-mid-Oct.—6 a.m.-9 p.m. daily; Apr.

and Sept.—8-5 daily; closed remainder of year. **Admission:** adults, $4; seniors and children 11-17, $3.25; children under 11 with adult, free.

PYLE HOUSE MUSEUM. The Pyle House in Huron, South Dakota, was the home of two of the state's notable women—Mamie Shields Pyle and her daughter, Gladys Pyle. The 1894 Queen Anne house, built by Mamie's husband, John L. Pyle, who later became the state attorney general, is now a historic house museum.

Mamie Pyle was state chairperson of the women's suffrage movement and the first woman nominated in South Dakota as a presidential elector, and Gladys Pyle was the first woman elected to the South Dakota House of Representatives and the first woman from the state elected to the U.S. Congress (the Senate, in 1938). The Pyle House contains many of its original furnishings and family belongings.

Pyle House Museum, 376 Idaho Ave. S.E., Huron, SD 57350. **Phone:** 605/352-2528. **Hours:** 1-3:30 daily; closed Fourth of July, Thanksgiving, and Christmas. **Admission:** adults and children over 9, $1.50; children under 10, free.

SURVEYORS' HOUSE AND INGALLS HOME AND MUSEUM. See Museums Honoring Exceptional Women.

Rhode Island

THE ASTORS' BEECHWOOD VICTORIAN LIVING HISTORY MUSEUM. The Astors' Beechwood Victorian Living History Museum is housed in an 1857 mansion in Newport, Rhode Island, which was the summer home of Caroline Astor, creator of America's first social register. It is devoted to the lifestyle of the Victorian era and to the Astor family history.

The Astors' Beechwood Victorian Living History Museum, 580 Bellevue Ave., Newport, RI 02840. **Phone:** 401/846-3772. **Fax:** 401/849-6998. **E-mail:** linda@astors-beechwood.com. **Website:** www.astors-beechwood.com. **Hours:** mid-May-early Nov.—10-5 daily; Feb.-mid-May—10-4 Fri.-Sun.; closed Mon.-Thurs.; early Nov.-Dec. 2—varies; closed late Dec.-Jan. **Admission:** adults, $10; seniors and children, $8; students, $7.25; families, $30.

Tennessee

BELMONT MANSION. The Belmont Mansion, an 1853 Italian villa in Nashville, Tennessee, was built by the attractive Adelicia Acklen, one of the wealthiest women in America at the time. It still contains an exceptional collection of marble statues, gasoliers, and mirrors, and the largest collection of nineteenth-century cast-iron garden ornaments in the nation.

Acklen's life, while opulent, often experienced tragedy—premature death claimed her first fiancé, two husbands, and six of her ten children. In 1839 Adelicia Hayes married the wealthy businessman and planter Isaac Franklin, who left her an estate valued at $1 million when he died after seven years of marriage and four children (all of whom died by the age of eleven). After her second marriage to Joseph Acklen, in 1849, she built the mansion, with elaborate gardens, water tower, greenhouse, bowling alley, gazebos, art gallery, bear house, and zoo—which she opened to the public since there were no public parks. She had six children, but the twin daughters died of scarlet fever, and her husband died during the Civil War. Left with 2,800 bales of cotton during the war, she then outwitted Confederate and Union forces by going to Louisiana and negotiating the illegal sale of 2,800 bales of the family cotton to England for $960,000 in gold.

In 1867 Acklen married Dr. William Cheatham, a prominent Nashville physician, in a ceremony attended by 2,000 guests at the Belmont Mansion. When she started spending more time with her only surviving daughter, Pauline, in Washington, D.C., she sold the mansion in 1887—only to die later that year after contracting pneumonia while shopping in New York. Belmont Mansion became a women's school, then an academy and junior college for women, and is now part of Belmont University at the site.

Belmont Mansion, Belmont University, 1900 Belmont Blvd., Nashville, TN 37212-3757. Phone: 615/460-5459. Fax: 615/460-5688. E-mail: belmontmansion@mail.belmont.edu. Website: www.belmontmansion.com. Hours: June-Aug.—10-4 Mon.-Sat., 1-4 Sun.; remainder of year—10-4 Tues.-Sat.; closed Sun.-Mon. and major holidays. Admission: adults, $7; seniors, $6; children 6-12, $3; children under 6, free.

EDITH DAVIS GALLERY. See Art Galleries.

THE HERMITAGE, HOME OF PRESIDENT ANDREW JACKSON. See Other Women's Organizations.

HOUSTON MUSEUM OF DECORATIVE ARTS. See Decorative Arts Museums.

Texas

ANNIE RIGGS MEMORIAL MUSEUM. See History Museums.

AUSTIN MUSEUM OF ART-LAGUNA GLORIA. See Art Museums.

BAYOU BEND COLLECTION AND GARDENS. See Art Museums.

FLORENCE RANCH HOMESTEAD. See Historic Farms and Ranches.

HERITAGE FARMSTEAD MUSEUM. See Historic Farms and Ranches.

STILLMAN HOUSE MUSEUM. The 1851 Stillman House in Brownsville, Texas, was the home of city founder Charles Stillman and his wife, Elizabeth Goodrich Stillman, in the mid-nineteenth century.

Active with his father in the mercantile business in Matamoros, Mexico, Mr. Stillman became a prosperous ship owner, merchant, rancher, and land developer who moved north of the Rio Grande, bought acreage, and laid out the town site for Brownsville. In 1849 he married Elizabeth Goodrich from his boyhood hometown of Wethersfield, Connecticut. Two years later they moved into the Stillman House in the heart of the original town site. However, Mrs. Stillman and the two children born in Brownsville moved to New England in 1853, never to return. Mr. Stillman continued to live in Brownsville and visited the family in the summers, then moved to New York with his family in 1866.

The one-story historic house museum, which contains many of the Stillman family furnishings and personal belongings, provides a glimpse of the nineteenth-century lifestyle in Brownsville.

Stillman House Museum, 1305 E. Washington St., PO Box 846, Brownsville, TX 78522. Phone: 956/542-3929. Fax: 956/541-5524. Hours: 10-12 and 2-5 Mon.-Fri., 3-5 Sun.; closed Sat. and major holidays. Admission: adults and children over 12, $2; children under 13, 50¢.

VARNER-HOGG PLANTATION STATE HISTORICAL PARK. See Historic Parks and Sites.

WITTE MUSEUM. See General Museums.

Utah

MARY FIELDING SMITH HOME. The reconstructed 1850 adobe home of Mary Fielding Smith, an independent, strong-willed widow who came west with her six children in the initial Mormon migrations, is one of the attractions in Old Deseret Village at the This Is The Place Heritage Park in Salt Lake City.

Smith built the house with hired help, only to die the following year. But her family continued to live in the adobe, which was later destroyed by the winter elements. Among the other structures in the village is the restored John Gardiner Cabin, where the pioneer English immigrant and his wife, Harriet Gardiner, raised ten children. Old Deseret Village is a re-created pioneer village with restored and reconstructed buildings and costumed townspeople that represent Utah's past.

Mary Fielding Smith Home, Old Deseret Village, This Is The Place Heritage Park, 2601 E. Sunnyside Ave., Salt Lake City, UT 84108-1453. **Website:** www.thisistheplace.org. **Hours:** late May-early Sept.—10-5 Mon.-Sat.; closed Sun. and remainder of year. **Admission:** adults and children over 11, $6; seniors and children 3-11, $4; children under 3, free; families, $20.

WHEELER HISTORIC FARM. See Historic Farms and Ranches.

Vermont

HELEN DAY ART CENTER. See Arts Centers.

PARK-McCULLOUGH HOUSE. The 1865 Park-McCullough House in North Bennington, Vermont, was the Second Empire–style "summer cottage" of Trenor W. Park and his wife, Laura Hall Park, and was occupied by four generations of the Hall, Park, and McCullough families until 1965. The 35-room Victorian mansion was built on Hall family land by Mr. Park, a largely self-educated lawyer, after he had amassed a fortune in managing and selling the Mariposa gold mines in California.

Two of Vermont's governors—Hiland Hall, father of Laura Hall Park, and John G. McCullough, son-in-law of Trenor and Laura Park—once lived in the house, and every generation of the family played a significant role in public institutions of the area, including Bennington College, Bennington Battle Monument, Bennington Museum, the University of Vermont, and several libraries.

The three-story historic house remains essentially as it was originally built, with an Italianate central tower and such early technological innovations as a fresh-air heating and cooling system, gas lighting, indoor plumbing, and running water. The interior is an unspoiled representation of Victorian life, with much of the original family furnishings. The grounds also have a miniature version of the mansion that was converted from a doghouse into a playhouse, and a large carriage barn with horse-drawn carriages, buggies, and fire equipment as well as stalls, a tack room, and a metal-floored room for washing carriages.

Park-McCullough House, Park and West Sts., PO Box 388, North Bennington, VT 05257. **Phone:** 802/442-5441. **Fax:** 802/442-5442. **E-mail:** thehouse@sover.net. **Website:** www.parkmccullough.org. **Hours:** mid-May-mid-Oct.—10-3 daily (also open for Victorian Christmas); closed remainder of year. **Admission:** adults, $6; seniors, $5; children 12-17, $4; children under 12, free.

ROKEBY MUSEUM. See Historic Farms and Ranches.

Virginia

ANNE SPENCER MEMORIAL. See Museums Honoring Exceptional Women.

BELLE BOYD COTTAGE. Confederate spy Belle Boyd lived in this 1860s cottage in Front Royal, Virginia, while staying with her aunt and uncle for 18 months during the Civil War. She spied on Union soldiers and officers at the Fishback Hotel operated by her relatives, and helped Stonewall Jackson in the 1862 Battle of Front Royal.

Boyd began her spying career at the age of seventeen in Martinsburg, Virginia (later West Virginia), where she shot and killed a Union soldier who attempted to raise a Union flag over her house. She was exonerated of the charges and sent to Front Royal to stay with her aunt and uncle. While there, she lived in this small cottage behind the hotel, which now contains furniture, clothing, and other items of the period.

Belle Boyd Cottage, Warren Heritage Society, 101 Chester St., Front Royal, VA 22630. **Phone:** 540/636-1446. **Hours:** 10-3 Mon.-Fri.; Sat. by appointment; closed Sun., major holidays, and in bad weather. **Admission:** adults and children over 11, $2; children under 12, $1.

BELLE GROVE PLANTATION. The Belle Grove Plantation, located on a rise along the Great Wagon Road in the Shenandoah Valley near Middletown, Virginia, was originally the home of Major Isaac Hite Jr. and his wife, Nelly Conway Madison Hite, the sister of President James Madison. The plantation was named for Nelly's grandparents' home.

The Hites used limestone quarried on the property and design principles from Thomas Jefferson to build the elegant 1794–1797 home that was once the centerpiece of a 7,500-acre plantation. The house served as Union General Philip Sheridan's headquarters during the Civil War, and the Battle of Cedar Creek (which is reenacted every October) was fought on its grounds. The plantation also contains an overseer's house, a slave cemetery, a heritage orchard, and gardens.

Belle Grove Plantation, 336 Belle Grove Rd., PO Box 137, Middletown, VA 22645. Phone: 540/869-2028. Fax: 540/869-9638. E-mail: bellgro@shentel.net. Website: www.bellegrove.org. Hours: Apr.-Oct.—10-4 Mon.-Sat., 1-5 Sun.; also weekend tours in Nov., Christmas tours in Dec., and group tours by reservation throughout the year. Admission: adults and children over 12, $7; seniors, $6; children 6-12, $3; children under 6, free.

ELLANOR C. LAWRENCE PARK. See Historic Parks and Sites.

EVELYNTON PLANTATION. William Evelyn Byrd, a wealthy landowner, lawyer, and politician, named the Evelynton Plantation near Charles City, Virginia, for his daughter, Evelyn Byrd (legend says he hoped she would marry and live on the plantation, but she died unmarried at the age of 29). The plantation was purchased in 1847 by Edmund Ruffin, who is known as the "father of American agronomy." It was Ruffin who fired the first shot of the Civil War at Fort Sumter. During the war, the Battle of Evelynton Heights was fought at the plantation and all the buildings were burned. The current Georgian Revival–style plantation house, still owned by the Ruffin family, was built in 1935–1937.

Evelynton Plantation, 6701 John Tyler Hwy., Charles City, VA 23030. Phones: 804/829-5075 and 800/473-5075. Fax: 804/829-6903. E-mail: evelynton@aol.com. Hours: 9-5 daily; closed Thanksgiving and Christmas. Admission: adults, $9.50; seniors and military, $8.50; children over 5, $6; children under 6, free.

HISTORIC SMITHFIELD. The 1775 Smithfield Plantation—now known as Historic Smithfield—in Blacksburg, Virginia, was named by Revolutionary War Colonel William Preston, a noted surveyor and patriot, for his wife, Susanna Smith Preston. It was one of the earliest and largest estates west of the Blue Ridge

Mountains, and unlike plantation owners east of the mountains, the Prestons surrounded their house with a 14-foot-high stockade as protection from the Shawnees and later from their Tory neighbors during the Revolution.

In a society dominated by men, the plantation was operated for 40 years by a woman. Mrs. Preston was left a single mother with ten children at home after her husband's death, at a time when women were not allowed to even discuss business and politics in polite company. Under her management, Smithfield more than doubled in value before she died in 1823. The plantation remained in the Preston family until 1959, when Janie Preston Boulware Lamb, a great-great-granddaughter of Colonel and Mrs. Preston, gave Smithfield to the Association for the Preservation of Virginia Antiquities, which now operates the living history site.

The original frame house on the 1,900-acre estate was the birthplace of two Virginia governors and the home of a third. It contains furnishings from the Colonial and Federal periods and has a Colonial-style kitchen garden on the grounds. Guided tours by costumed interpreters are available, and family, Native American, and other artifacts are displayed in a Museum of Western Expansion.

Historic Smithfield, 1000 Smithfield Plantation Rd., Blacksburg, VA 24060. Phone: 540/231-3947. Fax: 540/231-3006. E-mail: smfd@vt.edu. Website: www.civic.bev.net/smithfield. Hours: Apr.-1st weekend in Dec.—1-5 Thurs.-Sun.; closed Mon.-Wed. and remainder of year. Admission: adults, $5; students over 12, $3; children 5-12, $2; children under 5, free.

KENMORE PLANTATION AND GARDENS. Kenmore Plantation and Gardens in Fredericksburg, Virginia, was the eighteenth-century home of Revolutionary War Colonel Fielding Lewis and his wife, Betty Washington Lewis, the only sister of George Washington. The early 1770s home is representative of a Tidewater mid-Georgian manor house. It has eighteenth-century decorative and fine arts, period furnishings, and ornamental plaster ceilings and overmantels, as well as a colonial kitchen, gardens, and Wilderness Walk on the grounds.

Kenmore Plantation and Gardens, 1201 Washington Ave., Fredericksburg, VA 22401-3747. Phone: 540-373-3381. Fax: 540/371-6066. E-mail: mailroom@kenmore.org. Website: www.kenmore.org. Hours: Mar.-Dec.—10-5 Mon.-Sat., 10-4 Sun.; closed New Year's Eve and Day, Thanksgiving, Christmas Eve and Day, and remainder of year. Admission: adults, $6; children 6-17, $3; children under 6, free.

MAGGIE L. WALKER NATIONAL HISTORIC SITE. See Museums Honoring Exceptional Women.

MARY BALL WASHINGTON MUSEUM. See History Museums.

MARY WASHINGTON HOUSE. See Museums Honoring Exceptional Women.

MOUNT VERNON ESTATE AND GARDENS. See Other Women's Organizations.

MAYMONT. Maymont is the 100-acre Victorian country estate with an 1893 mansion of businessman and civic leader James Dooley and his wife, Sallie May Dooley, in Richmond, Virginia. The estate represents the upper-class taste, material culture, domestic life, and design in the American Gilded Age at the turn of the twentieth century.

Maymont House contains much of the original furniture, decorative and fine arts, documents, and other belongings of the Dooleys. The grounds include Italian, Japanese, and herb gardens; an arboretum; a carriage house, with carriage collection; the Dooley mausoleum; and such more recent additions as a children's farm; a nature and visitor center, featuring a 20-foot waterfall; a river otter exhibit; and interactive galleries, habitats for Virginia wildlife; and carriage and tram rides.

Maymont, 1700 Hampton St., Richmond, VA 23220. Phone: 804/358-7166. Fax: 804/358-9994. E-mail: gplatt@ maymont.org. Website: www.maymont.org. Hours: 12-5 Tues.-Sun.; closed Mon. Admission: grounds—free; suggested house tour donation—$4; carriage rides—adults, $3; children, $2; tram rides—adults, $2; children, $1.

SHIRLEY PLANTATION. In 1613 Sir Thomas West received a grant of 8,000 acres from King James of England for what became Virginia's oldest plantation near Charles City. He named the land the Shirley Plantation for his wife, Lady Cessaeley Shirley, who never came to the colonies.

Owned by the Hill and Carter families since 1638, the plantation is said to be the nation's oldest continuously owned family business. Tobacco was originally the main crop, but the emphasis changed over the years, and corn, wheat, soybeans, cotton, and sheep are the main current products.

The present mansion, which was built in 1723, was the birthplace of Anne Hill Carter and the site of her marriage to "Light Horse" Harry Lee, an aide to General George Washington who later became the governor of Virginia and a congressman. Their son, Confederate General Robert E. Lee, was a frequent visitor to the Queen Anne House of Flemish blond brickwork, located on a bluff overlooking the James River. The mansion contains silver, furniture, and family portraits handed down through eleven generations of Hills and Carters, gardens, and such outbuildings as a two-story kitchen, laundry building, two barns, stable, smokehouse, root cellar, pump house, and dovecote.

Shirley Plantation, 501 Shirley Plantation Rd., Charles City, VA 23030. Phones: 804/820-5121 and 800/232-1613. Fax: 804/829-6322. E-mail: information@shirleyplantation.com. Website: www.shirleyplantation.com. Hours: 9-5 daily; closed Thanksgiving and Christmas. Admission: adults, $10; seniors and military, $9; children 6-18, $7; children under 6, free.

VIRGINIA HOUSE. Virginia House, an ancient English country house on a hillside overlooking the James River in Richmond, Virginia, was moved from England and reconstructed by Ambassador Alexander W. Weddell and his wife, Virginia Weddell, in the 1920s.

Transplanting the twelfth-century Priory of St. Sepulchre, which was to be demolished in Warwick, fulfilled the romantic vision of the newly married Weddells, who were about to build a Tudor home in a newly planned English-style village on the outskirts of Richmond in 1924. After reading about the proposed demolition sale in a newspaper announcement, they went to the site and decided to buy the structure and move it to Virginia—despite British outrage.

It took several ships to transport the 2,500 tons of stone and other materials from the priory to Virginia's shores, and from 1925 to 1928 to reconstruct the building. The Weddells also incorporated parts of two English manor houses in their country house. The west wing is a copy of the central portion of Sulgrave Manor, which was George Washington's ancestral home in Northamptonshire, and the east tower wing follows the lines of the Wormleighton gatehouse lodge, the ancestral home of Winston Churchill in Warwickshire. It took Mrs. Weddell, working with noted landscape architect Charles Gillette, twenty years to create the eight acres of picturesque gardens at Virginia House.

Mr. Weddell, a native of Richmond, was a consul general in India in 1923 when he met Virginia Chase Steedman, a wealthy midwestern widow. He was a confirmed bachelor of 47, and she a vivacious, middle-aged widow of a World War I munitions manufacturer. They found an instant rapport, and in a matter of months were married. Over the next 25 years of marriage, they became extraordinary collectors with a shared appreciation of art, poetry, beauty, history, travel, ancient objects, and fine living. With Mrs. Weddell at his side, Mr. Weddell rose to be ambassador to Argentina and Spain. In 1948, while the Weddells were traveling by train across America to the Southwest, another train ran into their Pullman coach in a blinding snowstorm, killing the couple and twelve other people. Upon their deaths, ownership of Virginia House was transferred to the Virginia Historical Society, as arranged earlier by the Weddells.

Virginia House, 4301 Sulgrave Rd., Richmond, VA 23221. **Phone:** 804/353-4251. **Fax:** 804/354-8247. **E-mail:** tracy@vahistorical.org. **Website:** www.vahistorical.org. **Hours:** 10-4 Fri.-Sat., 12:30-5 Sun.; closed Mon.-Thurs., New Year's Day, Fourth of July, Thanksgiving, and Christmas. **Admission:** adults, $4; seniors, $3; students and children, $2.

VIRGINIA QUILT MUSEUM (Warren-Sipe House). See Design, Textile, and Costume Museums.

WOODLAWN PLANTATION. The 1805 Georgian home of Major Lawrence Lewis and his wife, Nelly Parke Custis Lewis, granddaughter of George and Martha Washington, is located at the Woodlawn Plantation near Alexandria, Virginia. The land, which was originally part of Mount Vernon, was a wedding present to the couple.

The historic site, the first property acquired by the National Trust for Historic Preservation, interprets the lifestyle of the 1805–1833 plantation of the Lewis family and features collections relating to the Custis and Lewis families, George Washington, and textile and needle arts. It also has several outbuildings and reconstructed gardens. The 1940 Pope-Leighey House designed by Frank Lloyd Wright is also located on the property and can be toured.

Woodlawn Plantation, 900 Richmond Hwy., Alexandria, VA 22309. **Phone:** 703/780-4000. **Fax:** 703/780-8509. **E-mail:** woodlawn@nthp.org. **Website:** www.nthp.org/main/sites/woodlawn.htm. **Hours:** Mar.-Dec.—10-5 daily; closed Thanksgiving, Christmas, and remainder of year. **Admission:** adults, $6; seniors and children 6-18, $5; children under 6, free; combination ticket with Pope-Leighey House—adults, $10; seniors and children 6-18, $8; children under 6, free.

Washington

HULDA KLAGER LILAC GARDENS. See Botanical Gardens and Arboretums.

WASHINGTON STATE CAPITAL MUSEUM. See History Museums.

West Virginia

ANNA JARVIS BIRTHPLACE MUSEUM. Anna Jarvis, the founder of Mother's Day, was born in this 1854 Vernacular house in Webster, West Virginia, four miles south of Grafton, in 1864. The house also served as the temporary headquarters of Union General George B. McClellan in 1861 during the Civil War.

Jarvis's mother, Ann Marie Reeves Jarvis, provided nursing services and promoted better sanitation to save thousands of lives during the Civil War, and she continued to help heal wounds of the war years and bring families and communities together after the war. In 1907, two years after the death of her mother, Jarvis invited some friends to her home in Philadelphia to honor her mother for her great work during and after the Civil War. It was at that time that she proposed a national day of celebration in honor of mothers.

The following spring she wrote to the Andrews Methodist Church in Grafton, where her mother had taught Sunday school classes for twenty years, requesting that a Mother's Day service be held in her mother's honor. The service was held in 1908, and it was followed by the governor of West Virginia proclaiming the first Mother's Day in 1910 and Congress later passing a joint resolution signed by President Woodrow Wilson proclaiming the second Sunday in May as Mother's Day.

The Andrews Methodist Church is now the International Mother's Day Shrine, while the former Jarvis home houses the Anna Jarvis Birthplace Museum, which features Jarvis family materials and items donated in memory of mothers.

Anna Jarvis Birthplace Museum, Hwys. 119 and 250, Rural Rte. 2, Box 352, Grafton, WV 26354. **Phone:** 304/265-5549. **E-mail:** ajhouse26354@yahoo.com. **Website:** annajarvishouse.com. **Hours:** 10-4 Tues.-Sun.; closed Mon. **Admission:** adults, $4; seniors, $3; children over 12, $2; children under 13, free.

PEARL S. BUCK BIRTHPLACE MUSEUM. See Museums Honoring Exceptional Women.

Wisconsin

HOARD HISTORICAL MUSEUM. See History Museums.

LEIGH YAWKEY WOODSON ART MUSEUM. See Art Museums.

OCTAGON HOUSE. The Octagon House, an 1854 five-story, eight-sided brick house in Watertown, Wisconsin, was the home of Eliza Richards for 48 years. She continued to live in the house after the death of her husband, attorney John Richards, who designed and built the house, until she died at the age of 86. The Victorian house, one of the largest single-family residences of the pre–Civil War period in the region, had a spiral staircase, central heating, ventilating systems, and running water. It still contains much of the Richards family furniture and possessions.

Also located on the grounds is the building that housed the first kindergarten in the United States. It was founded in 1856 by Margarethe Meyer Schurz, wife of noted statesman Carl Schurz. The structure, which depicts an early class in session, was moved from downtown Watertown in 1956. Another building moved to the grounds is a late 1800s Plank Road Barn, originally along the Watertown-Milwaukee Plank Road a short distance east of the grounds. It was moved in the 1960s and now houses a collection of pioneer tools and farm implements.

Octagon House, 919 Charles St., Watertown, WI 53094. Phone: 920/261-2796. Hours: Memorial Day-Labor Day—10-4 daily; May until Memorial Day and day after Labor Day through Oct.—11-3 daily; closed remainder of year. Admission: adults, $4.50; seniors, $4; children 6-17, $2; children under 6, free.

OTHER HISTORIC HOUSES

Alabama

EDITH NEWMAN CULVER MEMORIAL MUSEUM. The Edith Newman Culver Memorial Museum, housed in an 1872 two-story frame house in Waterloo, Alabama, is named for a civic leader who donated the building to the city with her husband, businessman Ezra Lee Culver, to be developed as a museum and memorial to Mrs. Culver. She inherited the house from her grandfather, Joseph Marion Newman, an Ohio Union soldier who returned after the Civil War to start a sawmill, marry Sarah Long, and purchase the house in 1918. The museum contains nineteenth-century furnishings, clothing, and farm implements; Native American artifacts; and relics from the Civil War and later conflicts.

GORGAS HOUSE. Gorgas House, on the University of Alabama campus in Tuscaloosa, was originally built as a dining hall for students in 1829 and then became the home of university president Josiah Gorgas, his wife, Amelia Gayle Gorgas, and their family. It was the only building to survive the Civil War burning of the campus by federal troops in 1865. It became a historic house museum in 1954 and features a collection of eighteenth- and nineteenth-century Spanish silver.

SHOTGUN HOUSE. Shotgun House, the 1894–1914 home of washerwoman Vinie Fitzpatrick, is one of 50 nineteenth-century structures in Old Alabama Town, a living historic village in Montgomery. The collection of historic buildings ranges from pioneer to middle-class urban structures. Shotgun House is furnished and interpreted as the home of a late-nineteenth-century African American washerwoman.

Arkansas

MISS LAURA'S. An 1896 Victorian clapboard house, known as Miss Laura's, in Fort Smith, Arkansas, was a bordello operated by Laura Ziegler until 1911, when she sold the building to Berta Gale Dean, who owned the house until her death in 1948. After standing abandoned until 1963, the structure became a restaurant and social club and then was restored as the city's visitor center. It became the only brothel building on the National Register of Historic Places in 1973.

CARRY A. NATION HOUSE. The Carry A. Nation House, known as "Hatchet Hall," is a 14-room former boardinghouse in Eureka Springs, Arkansas, where the ax-wielding prohibitionist spent the last three years of her life. The historic house is now vacant, but visitors can see a collection of Carry Nation memorabilia at the nearby Eureka Springs Historical Museum (see also Carry A. Nation Home Memorial in Museums Honoring Exceptional Women).

California

CASTRO/BREEN ADOBE. The 1840 Castro/Breen Adobe at the San Juan Bautista State Historical Park in San Juan Bautista, California, was originally built to serve as the Mexican judicial and administrative headquarters for northern California. In 1848 it became the home of Patrick Breen, his wife, Margaret Breen, and their seven children. The Breens were surviving members of the ill-fated Donner emigrant party that was trapped in mountain snow in 1847, with only approximately half of the original party of 87 reaching California. The adobe has Breen family and early California artifacts and traces Spanish, Mexican, and American history in the region.

CLARKE HISTORICAL MUSEUM. See History Museums.

GEORGE WHITE AND ANNA GUNN MARSTON HOUSE. The George White and Anna Gunn Marston House, a shingled 1905 mansion, is San Diego's finest example of the Arts and Crafts movement at the turn of the twentieth century. The Craftsman house, an early example of the work of noted architects William Hubbard and Irving Gill, was built for the prominent merchant and civic leader George White Marston and his wife, Anna Gunn Marston. It was also the home of their daughter, Mary Marston, who moved in with her parents after the house was built and lived there for 82 years, until she died in 1987 at the age of 107, leaving the house to the city as a historic site. The house is now operated by the San Diego Historical Society.

NEWLAND HOUSE MUSEUM. The Newland House Museum is housed in the former 1897 Queen Anne home of farmer William Newland and his wife, Mary Juanita Newland, prominent pioneers and an important farming and business family, in Huntington Beach, California. It has period furnishings and relates the history of the Newland family and Huntington Beach.

SCOTTY'S CASTLE. Scotty's Castle is a 12,000-square-foot mansion built in the 1920s near Grapeville, California, for a wealthy Chicago couple, insurance executive Albert Johnson and his wife, Bessie Johnson, by a flamboyant character, Walter Scott. Scott convinced the Johnsons and others to invest in a gold mine in Death Valley, but no one ever saw the phantom mine or any of the gold it allegedly produced. Tours are offered of the castle, which has fine furnishings and art as well as numerous support buildings on its 1,500 acres.

Colorado

ASTOR HOUSE MUSEUM. The Astor House Museum in Golden, Colorado, is housed in an 1867 former hotel building that became a boardinghouse operated by Ida Goetze. It was originally built by Seth Lake, a Baptist deacon, to house legislators when Golden was the territorial capital of Colorado. After the capital moved to Denver, the hotel served other guests until it was purchased by Mrs. Goetze and converted into a boardinghouse. It was operated as a boardinghouse until the 1950s. The building was saved from demolition and from becoming a parking lot in 1972 by a voter ballot initiative, and has been restored as a turn-of-the-twentieth-century western Victorian hotel, with glimpses into the life and times of early Golden.

AUNTIE STONE CABIN. The Auntie Stone Cabin is an 1864 log structure from a frontier military fort in the courtyard of the Fort Collins Museum, a city-owned general museum in a 1904 former library building in Fort Collins, Colorado. The cabin was originally operated by Elizabeth "Auntie" Stone and her husband, Lewis Stone, as the officers' mess at the military outpost of Fort Collins. In 1866 the frontier town's first school was started by a niece in Auntie Stone's bedroom (her husband had died earlier that year). After the fort closed in 1867, Auntie Stone lived in and operated the cabin as an inn until 1873. She became Larimer County's first woman landowner and taxpayer, cofounded the first local gristmill and brick kiln, bought a larger hotel, worked for temperance and suffrage causes, loved to dance until age 86, and lived to be 94.

McGRAW MEMORIAL PARK. See Re-created Pioneer Villages.

ROSEMOUNT MUSEUM. Rosemount Museum in Pueblo, Colorado, is housed in a 37-room, 24,000-square-foot Richardsonian Romanesque Revival/Queen Anne mansion built in 1891–1893 for businessman John A. Thatcher and his wife, Margaret Henry Thatcher. Mrs. Thatcher lived in the house until her death in 1922. Nearly all the furnishings, wall and window treatments, decorative arts, and paintings are original to the house. A restaurant is located in the carriage house.

Connecticut

BATES-SCOFIELD HOMESTEAD. The ca. 1736 Saltbox home of John Bates and his wife, Mary Bates, is part of the Darien Historical Society in Darien, Connecticut. It emphasizes eighteenth-century culture and farm life in Middlesex Parish (renamed Darien in 1820) and contains early clothing, quilts, furnishings, diaries, and documents relating to the area. The society's offices, exhibits, and library are in a building adjoining the historic house.

BELLAMY-FERRIDAY HOUSE AND GARDEN. The 1754 Bellamy-Ferriday House and Garden in Bethlehem, Connecticut, was the home of the community's first minister, the Reverend Joseph Bellamy, and later the home of Caroline Woolsey Ferriday. It now interprets the early history and culture of Bethlehem and the history of women, with specific references to the life of Ferriday, who was dedicated to helping others. In addition to early furnishings and English and Dutch delft, the house contains a collection from Ferriday and her aunt, Eliza Woolsey, that highlights their experiences as nurses during the Civil War.

HOLLEY-WILLIAMS HOUSE MUSEUM. The roles, choices, and challenges of women in American history are among the topics presented at the Holley-Williams House Museum in Lakeville, Connecticut. Other subjects covered in the 1768 Federal/Classical Revival house include the Holley family's involvement in industry and politics and the nineteenth-century industrial era, the Civil War, and social reforms. The house was built by temperance leader John Milton Holley and his wife, Sally Porter Holley. Among their children were Alexander Hamilton Holley, who became governor of Connecticut in 1857, and Maria Holley Williams, to whom the house was left. Her granddaughter, Margaret Holley Williams, willed the house to the Salisbury Association to become a historic house museum when she died in 1971.

HOTCHKISS-FYLER HOUSE. The 1900 Hotchkiss-Fyler House in Torrington, Connecticut, is now part of the Torrington Historical Society. Once the home of politician Orsamus R. Fyler, it was left to the society—with two other buildings on the estate—

by Gertrude Hotchkiss upon her death in 1956. The Queen Anne/Chateauesque house, which is furnished as it was in 1956, is devoted to Hotchkiss family and Torrington history and contains collections of art glass, porcelain, Oriental carpets, paintings, and French Provincial–style furnishings.

JOHN AND MARY RIDER HOUSE. The ca. 1785 John and Mary Rider House in Danbury, Connecticut, was to be demolished for a gas station, but the Daughters of the American Revolution chapter and the local arts center saved it from destruction in the early 1940s. In 1942 the Danbury Museum and Historical Society was founded in the historic house, which served as the site of the museum and society until 1963. The house is still located on the museum grounds, along with several other historic buildings, but it is now devoted entirely to a collection of furniture, decorative items, and other historical materials of the Colonial period.

LOCKWOOD-MATHEWS MANSION MUSEUM. The 1868 Second Empire–style house of Civil War financier LeGrand Lockwood and his wife, Anna Louisa Benedict Lockwood, in Norwalk, Connecticut, tells about the everyday lives of the wealthy and their servants during the Victorian era. The partially restored 60-room chateau has stenciled walls, inlaid woodwork, a skylit rotunda, and Victorian furniture, as well as collections of nineteenth-century costumes, music boxes, decorative arts, and paintings.

MARTHA A. PARSONS HOUSE. The 1782 Martha A. Parsons House in Enfield, Connecticut, was built on land assigned for use by ministers. In 1800 it was purchased by John Ingraham, a retired sea captain, for his family. Ingraham decorated the front hall with the famous George Washington Memorial wallpaper that can still be seen in the house. Ingraham's granddaughter married Simeon Parsons, and they were the paternal grandparents of benefactor Martha A. Parsons, a businesswoman who left the family home to the Enfield Historical Society in her 1962 will. The house reveals one family's lifestyle of unpretentious simplicity and graciousness for over 180 years.

District of Columbia

OLD STONE HOUSE. The Old Stone House is a 1764–1765 pre–Revolutionary War building in the Georgetown area of the District of Columbia that was originally a one-room stone structure built by cabinet-maker Christopher Layman. After his death in 1765, Cassandra Chew, a neighbor, bought the house and added a kitchen in 1767 and then some rooms upstairs in the 1770s. The house remained in the family until the early 1800s. A series of businesses—including a tailor, clockmaker, printer, cobbler, glazier, and goldsmith—occupied the building until it was purchased by the National Park Service in 1950, restored, and opened to the public in 1960. Five rooms are furnished in the period, and a brick courtyard leads to a garden with fruit trees and seasonal plantings.

Florida

CLARA BARKLEY DOOR HOUSE, JULEE COTTAGE, LAVALLE HOUSE, AND LEAR-ROCHEBLAVE HOUSE. At least four historic houses involving women—Clara Barkley Door House, Julee Cottage, Lavalle House, and Lear-Rocheblave House—are part of the Historic Pensacola Village in one of the oldest historic districts in the Southeast—the Seville Historic District in Pensacola, Florida. The Clara Barkley Door House, a Greek Revival building furnished with antiques from the 1850s to the 1890s, was built in 1871 by the widow of a lumber tycoon. The 1805 Julee Cottage, now a museum classroom, is dedicated to the memory of Julee Paton, the legendary freedwoman of color who owned the cottage. The Lavalle House, an example of French Creole Colonial architecture, was built in 1805 during Florida's second Spanish period by Carlos Lavalle and Marianna Bonifay, a French widow who migrated from Santo Domingo during a slave revolt in the 1790s. The 1888 Lear-Rocheblave House, a two-story Folk Victorian structure, was constructed for merchant John Lear and his wife, Kate Lear, and was later owned for many years by the Benito Rocheblave family.

JESSIE PORTER HERITAGE HOUSE MUSEUM. The 1834 Greek Revival house and guest cottage where poet Robert Frost spent his winters are part of the Jessie Porter Heritage House Museum in Key West, Florida. The museum is named for Jessie Porter, founder of the Old Island Restoration Foundation, who lived in the house and spearheaded Key West's historic preservation efforts. The house museum contains much of the furniture, art, and other belongings of "Miss Jessie," as she was affectionately called, and relates her life and accomplishments and the history of Key West.

MAY-STRINGER HERITAGE MUSEUM. A four-story gabled house—originally built in 1856 and then expanded in 1880—was the home of socialite and civic leader Betty Lykes Stringer from 1880 to the early 1900s in Brooksville, Florida. Her family lived in the house until 1940, when her granddaughter, Betty Lykes Stringer Faircloth, sold it to the Hensley family. In 1981 the Hernando Historical Museum Association converted the house into the May-Stringer Heritage Museum, with furnished rooms and a re-created schoolroom depicting family and area history.

Georgia

HERITAGE HALL. Heritage Hall in Madison, Georgia, is housed in the 1833–1835 Jones-Turnell-Manley House. The Greek Revival home was built for Dr. Elijah Evans Jones and his family, was later sold to Steve Turnell, and remained a private residence until 1977. The last owner was philanthropist Sue Reid Walton Manley, known as "Madison's First Lady" for her support of churches, education, and the city. Susan Reid Manley Law, Manley's granddaughter, who was married in and inherited the house, donated the home to the Morgan County Historical Society in 1977. The restored house contains such items as period furniture, medical instruments, and the original windows with etchings made by the Jones family daughters with their engagement rings.

PLUM ORCHARD MANSION. Plum Orchard Mansion, an 1898 Georgian Revival mansion built by Lucy Coleman Carnegie for her son, George Lauder Carnegie, on the occasion of his marriage to Margaret Thaw, is located at the Cumberland Island National Seashore, near St. Mary's, Georgia. Mrs. Carnegie was the wife of Thomas Morrison Carnegie, brother and partner of steel magnate Andrew Carnegie. The mansion, which was donated to the National Park Foundation by Carnegie family members in 1971, is currently closed while undergoing exterior restoration.

SWAN HOUSE. Swan House is a 1928 Classical/Italianate home built for Edward Hamilton Inman and his wife, Emily Inman, who were one of Atlanta's leading families in the early twentieth century. It was designed by Philip Shutze, one of the South's premier classical architects. The house depicts the lifestyle of wealthy Atlantans in the 1920s to 1930s and features eighteenth- and nineteenth-century English furniture,

Chinese export porcelain, English and other European ceramics, and American and European paintings.

Hawaii

BAILEY HOUSE MUSEUM. Hawaiian royalty gave missionaries the land on which the Bailey House Museum in Wailuku, Maui, in Hawaii, was built. It was first used as a central Maui mission station, with schools for adults and children, and then became the Wailuku Female Seminary, with a boarding school from 1833 through 1849. After the seminary closed, missionary Edward Bailey (with his wife, Caroline Bailey) bought the property and continued to teach until his health failed. In the 1860s he attempted to support his family by growing and milling sugarcane. The site later became part of the Wailuku Sugar Plantation, and its managers lived there. When the entire property was purchased by Pundy Yokouchi in 1991, he gave Bailey House and its land to the Maui Historical Society. The house is now a museum with Hawaiian artifacts and crafts, paintings by Bailey, and furnishings and clothing from the earliest days of settlement on Maui.

LYMAN HOUSE MEMORIAL MUSEUM. The Lyman House Memorial Museum in Hilo, Hawaii, is adjacent to the 1839 missionary house built by the Reverend David Lyman and his wife, Sarah Joiner Lyman. They had seven children and boarded a number of island boys who attended their church school. Mrs. Lyman, who lived there until her death in 1885, schooled her children and operated a bed-and-breakfast for passing ship captains and dignitaries such as authors Mark Twain and Isabella Bird. The historic house, which has been restored to show missionary life in the mid-1800s, has many of the original furnishings, while the adjacent museum features exhibits about the history and natural history of Hawaii.

MISSION HOUSES MUSEUM. The Mission Houses Museum in Honolulu, Hawaii, features three historic structures—an 1821 New England Colonial house that was shipped around Cape Horn from Boston; the 1831 Chamberlain House, built of coral blocks as a home and storehouse; and the Printing House where the Hawaiian language was first printed. The site served as the headquarters for the Sandwich Islands Mission. It now shows the cultural interaction of Hawaiians, missionaries, and foreigners in the nineteenth century and displays 1820–1900 artifacts of Hawaiians and missionaries.

Idaho

MARY ANN CHAPMAN O'FARRELL HOUSE. An 1863 log cabin in Boise, Idaho, was the home of the Irish immigrant Mary Ann Chapman O'Farrell, who came west with her husband, John O'Farrell, who found gold in Colorado. She is remembered for her numerous good works, such as caring for seven orphans along with her own seven children, holding the first Catholic service in the cabin with two passing French missionaries, and later donating land for a church.

Illinois

BUTTERWORTH CENTER. Butterworth Center in Moline, Illinois, is housed in the former 1892 Queen Anne/Stick–style home of William Butterworth, the third president of Deere and Company, and his wife, Katherine Deere Butterworth, granddaughter of the company founder, John Deere. The center looks at the lives and interests of the Butterworths and the reasons behind the three alterations to the house. The house has period furniture and clothing and an eighteenth-century Italian ceiling painting.

CLARKE HOUSE MUSEUM. The restored 1836 Greek Revival home of Henry B. Clarke and his wife, Caroline P. Clarke, is the oldest surviving house in Chicago. The historic house museum shows how an early Chicago family lived in the 1840s–1850s boom-and-bust days of the city. It contains period rooms with early Victorian furniture, ceramics, glass, and decorative objects.

EMMA KUNZ HOUSE. A ca. 1830 brick house in Belleville, Illinois, known as the Emma Kunz House, is the oldest brick Greek Revival house in the state. It was built by brick contractor Conrad Bornman, who sold it to James Affleck and his wife, Ann Affleck, around 1835. It was then owned by several families before being purchased by fireman Henry Kunz in 1895. His family included a daughter, Emma Kunz, who lived there for 77 years before the house was given to the St. Clair County Historical Society. The house depicts the simpler lifestyle of early settlers in the 1830s.

GLESSNER HOUSE MUSEUM. The 1887 Richardsonian Romanesque residence of John J. Glessner and his wife, Frances M. Glessner, in Chicago interprets life in an upper-class Victorian urban home in the late nineteenth century. The historic house, designed by architect Henry Hobson Richardson, contains original family furnishings, including English arts and crafts.

HERITAGE HOUSE AND MUSEUM OF OKAWVILLE. The Heritage House and Museum of Okawville in Okawville, Illinois, includes three historic houses. They are the restored ca. 1869 Schlosser brick house, the last surviving Old World–style street house in Okawville, which was the home of cobbler Joseph Schlosser, his wife, Louise Schlosser, and their two sons; the largely restored 1888 Second Empire–style home of Dr. Robert C. Poos and his family, which is now a historic house museum; and the unrestored 1908 Schlosser Complex, the home of harness maker Frank Schlosser, his wife, laundress Sophia Schlosser, and their two daughters, Elsie and Stella, who ran a commercial laundry in a separate building on the property.

Indiana

GAAR HOUSE AND FARM MUSEUM. In 1876, threshing machine and steam engine manufacturer Abram Gaar and his wife, Agnes Gaar, built a remarkably advanced home on a country hillside overlooking Richmond, Indiana. The home—which contained central heating, indoor plumbing, gas, electricity, and an intercom system—was restored and opened to the public in the 1970s by the Gaars' great-granddaughter, Joanna Mikesell. Five generations of the Gaar family have lived in the historic house, now the site of the Gaar House and Farm Museum.

RUTHMERE. Ruthmere features the 1910 Beaux Arts–style home of Albert R. Beardsley, one of the founders of Miles Laboratories, and his wife, Elizabeth Beardsley, in Elkhart, Indiana. The house, which reflects the lifestyle of a wealthy midwestern business executive and his family, contains Louis XV Revival furniture, period decorative arts, Tiffany lamps, silk wall coverings, and sculptures by Auguste Rodin, William Ordway Partridge, Carducius Plantagenet Ream, and Camille Claudel. The estate also has gardens, a greenhouse/conservatory, a garage with antique cars, and a library of American decorative arts and domestic architecture.

Iowa

BEDSTEMOR'S HOUSE. Bedstemor's (Grandmother's) House, a 1908 historic house built by a Danish immi-grant for a grandmother, who lived in it for 30 years, is part of the Danish Immigrant Museum in Elk Horn, Iowa. The house, which reflects the architectural design preferences of Danish immigrant carpenters and builders in the area, illustrates how Danish settlers lived and kept alive many of their native customs and traditions.

CORNWALL RESTORED PIONEER HOME. The 1864–1867 Cornwall Restored Pioneer Home on the grounds of the Ringgold County Pioneer Center and Rural Life Museum in Ellston, Iowa, was the home of early settlers Elihue Cornwall and his wife, Emeline Cornwall. The house contains historical materials on the Cornwall family and early Ringgold County.

HARLAN-LINCOLN HOUSE. The 1876 Harlan-Lincoln House, located on the Iowa Wesleyan College campus in Mount Pleasant, Iowa, was the home of James Harlan, an early president of the college, a U.S. senator, and Secretary of the Interior, whose daughter, Mary Harlan, married Robert Todd Lincoln, son of President Abraham Lincoln and Mary Todd Lincoln. She spent many summers with her children at the house and owned it from 1895 to 1907, when she gave it to the college. The house, a museum since 1959, contains many Harlan and Lincoln family artifacts.

SALISBURY HOUSE. Salisbury House is a 42-room English manor in Des Moines, Iowa, built in 1923–1928 by cosmetics magnate Carl Weeks and his wife, Edith Van Slyke Weeks. The castlelike structure is modeled after the King's House in Salisbury, England, and reflects architecture from the Tudor, Gothic, and Carolean periods. The Weeks were lovers of the arts and great travelers and collectors. The mansion contains an eclectic collection of paintings by such artists as Thomas Lawrence, Anthony Van Dyck, and Joseph Stella; antique English furnishings; rugs and tapestries from Persia, China, and Europe; and over 3,000 books and documents, including rare works by Geoffrey Chaucer, Walt Whitman, and D. H. Lawrence.

Kentucky

AUGUSTA DILS YORK MANSION. The 1912 home of attorney James M. York and his wife, Augusta D. York, in Pikeville, Kentucky, tells about the family, the Appalachians, and the roles of Mr. York and Colonel John Dils Jr. in the Hatfield/McCoy feud (York was the attorney for the McCoys).

DINSMORE HOMESTEAD. James Dinsmore and his wife, Martha Dinsmore, purchased 700 acres close to the Ohio River near Burlington, Kentucky, in 1839; built a ca. 1842 Federal farmhouse; grew grapes, raised sheep, and used willows in basket making; and raised their three daughters, Isabella, Julia, and Susan. Isabella married and had a family of her own; Susan died in a boating accident at the age of fifteen, and Julia, a published poet, never married, inherited the farm in 1872 and operated it successfully for 54 years, until her death in 1926 at the age of 93. The homestead is now a living history museum, with nearly all the contents of the home and outbuildings still surviving.

FARMINGTON. Farmington is the nineteenth-century hemp plantation—with an 1816 Federal-style home—of John Speed and his wife, Lucy Speed, in Louisville, Kentucky. The 14-room house, based on a design by Thomas Jefferson, was the boyhood home of Joseph Speed, one of Abraham Lincoln's best friends, and Attorney General James Speed. Lincoln spent three weeks at the plantation in 1841. In addition to the historic house, the site has a carriage house, barn, summer kitchen, slave quarters, and a re-created nineteenth-century garden.

SARAH BUSH JOHNSTON LINCOLN MEMORIAL. A replica of the one-room log cabin lived in by Abraham Lincoln's stepmother, Sarah Bush Johnston Lincoln, with her three children before she married Lincoln's father, is a memorial to her in Elizabethtown, Kentucky. It traces the Bush family history and connection to the Lincoln story, and shows how area pioneers lived in the early 1800s.

Louisiana

MADAME JOHN'S LEGACY. Madame John's Legacy is a restored 1789 Creole cottage that is one of the last surviving examples of French Colonial architecture in the French Quarter of New Orleans. The two-story house, which has a solid masonry ground floor that was used for household work and storage and living quarters on the second floor (to protect it from frequent flooding), is named for a fictional woman whom writer George Washington Cable mentioned in one of his stories about the difficulties faced by Louisiana people of mixed racial heritage in the nineteenth century. The house had numerous owners before it was purchased in 1925 by Stella Hirsch Lemann. She rented it

to artists, who often produced images of the house for her in lieu of rent. In 1947 Lemann donated the historic house to the Louisiana State Museum. It now contains folk art and historical exhibits.

Maine

STANLEY MUSEUM. See History Museums.

Maryland

BARBARA FRITCHIE HOUSE. The Barbara Fritchie (also spelled Frietschie) House in Frederick, Maryland, is the rebuilt pre-1800 home of the 95-year-old woman who allegedly waved her Union flag as General Thomas "Stonewall" Jackson and his Confederate troops marched through the town in 1862 during the Civil War. The reputed incident inspired the "Barbara Fritchie" poem by John Greenleaf Whittier. The house was badly damaged by repeated flooding of a nearby creek and was torn down in 1868; it was then rebuilt in 1926, partly from materials salvaged from the original house. It contains many of Fritchie's furnishings and other belongings.

LILLIE CARROLL JACKSON MUSEUM. Lillie Carroll Jackson was a charismatic leader who was president of the Baltimore branch of the National Association for the Advancement of Colored people (NAACP) for 35 years, fought segregation in Maryland, and was instrumental in effecting passage of acts on civil rights (1957), voting rights (1965), and fair housing (1968). When she died in 1975, she left her home to serve as a museum.

MOUNT CLARE MANSION. The 1760 Georgian home of lawyer and plantation owner Charles Carroll and his wife, Margaret Tilghman Carroll, in Baltimore is devoted to their life and times in 1760–1817. The house features much of the Carrolls' furniture and decorative arts and their portrait collection, which includes the works of Charles Wilson Peale, John Hessalius, and Robert Feve.

Massachusetts

THE EVERGREENS. The Evergreens, an 1856 Italianate home in Amherst, Massachusetts, was a wedding present from attorney Edward Dickinson to his son, Austin Dickinson, and Susan Huntington Gilbert

Dickinson, the sister-in-law and close friend of poet Emily Dickinson. Mrs. Dickinson lived in the house until her death in 1913. Her daughter, Martha Dickinson Bianchi, was born there in 1865 and lived in the house until she died in 1943. The Evergreens, an exceptional example of a Victorian-period middle-class home, has remained almost completely intact, with original furnishings and decorative details throughout the house.

HINSDALE AND ANNA WILLIAMS HOUSE. The ca. 1749 house of Hinsdale and Anna Williams has been restored to its 1816–1838 appearance (when they lived there) at Historic Deerfield, a complex of fourteen historic structures from the eighteenth and nineteenth centuries, in Deerfield, Massachusetts. The Williams house, which was modernized during the Federal period, still has its ca. 1817 wallpaper, as well as period furniture, ceramics, and such household objects as a rotary cookstove and an early washing machine. Historic Deerfield also has the Flynt Center of Early New England Life, with changing exhibitions, and the Helen Geier Flynt Textile Museum, which has early coverlets, needlework, clothing, and textiles (see Design, Textile, and Costume Museums).

JULIA WOOD HOUSE. The Julia Wood House—formerly the ca. 1790 home of Dr. Francis Wicks—was renamed for its last resident when she left it to the Falmouth Historical Society in Falmouth, Massachusetts, in her 1932 will. The restored Federal/Georgian house shows how the house was used over time, with a focus on the 1812–1830 period. It has Colonial and Victorian rooms and collections of early textiles, medical instruments, dolls, and portraits of town leaders in 1812.

PARSONS HOUSE. The ca. 1730 Parsons House in Northampton, Massachusetts, stands on the 1654–1655 home lot of Cornet Joseph Parsons and his wife, Mary Bliss Parsons, who came to the area during the English settlement of the town. He was involved in the fur trade, while she stood trial and was acquitted of witchcraft in 1674–1675. The house, which is believed to have been built by the Parsons' grandson, Nathaniel, is now one of four historic structures that are part of Historic Northampton.

WISTARIAHURST MUSEUM. The Wistariahurst Museum in Holyoke, Massachusetts, is housed in the ca. 1868 mansion and carriage house of silk manufacturer William Skinner, his wife, Sarah Skinner, and their daughter, philanthropist Bell Skinner. The 26-room Colonial Revival/Beaux Arts/Victorian mansion, which had additions in 1914 and 1927, interprets the life and times of two generations of New England's industrial elite, along with generational changes and gender roles. It also has period furnishings and clothing, and Skinner company and family papers.

THE WITCH HOUSE. The 1642 home of Jonathan Corwin, one of the judges at the 1692 witchcraft trials in Salem, Massachusetts, was the site of some of the preliminary hearings that resulted in nineteen persons being hanged (including fourteen women) and one man being crushed to death in torture after being condemned as witches. Today, the city-owned restored structure is known as the "Witch House" and can be toured (see also Witch Museums in History Museums).

Michigan

HISTORIC WHITE PINE VILLAGE AND ROSE HAWLEY MUSEUM. See Re-created Pioneer Villages.

Minnesota

DOROTHY MOLTER MUSEUM. The Dorothy Molter Museum in Ely, Minnesota, occupies two cabins that belonged to the popular "Root Beer Lady" of Knife Lake, who was the last legal resident of the Boundary Waters Canoe Wilderness Area that forms the boundary with Canada. The lake was the waterway used by fur traders going to the Canadian Northwest nearly two centuries ago. Molter first came to Knife Lake in 1930 and then returned in 1934 to stay permanently to help operate a rustic resort, which was deeded to her in 1948. She received her nickname by making nearly 12,000 bottles of root beer annually to share with visitors. When the property was condemned and purchased by the U.S. Forest Service after passage of the Wilderness Act of 1975, she was granted a lifetime tenancy and stayed until her death in 1986. The following year, volunteers dismantled and moved much of the resort by dogsled and snowmobile to Moose Lake and then to Ely, and restored her cabin and one of the rental cabins as a museum in her memory.

Mississippi

MARTHA VICK HOUSE. The Martha Vick House is an 1830 Greek Revival mansion built for the spinster daughter of the founder of Vicksburg, Mississippi. This last remaining Vick family home contains late-eighteenth- and early-nineteenth-century antiques and a collection of post-Impressionist French paintings by Frederick Ragot, and tells the story of Martha Vick and the founding of Vicksburg.

Missouri

BECKY THATCHER HOUSE. The 1850s house in Hannibal, Missouri, was the home of Laura Hawkins, who was the model for Becky Thatcher in Mark Twain's *Adventures of Tom Sawyer*. It depicts early midwestern life and contains many of the furnishings belonging to Hawkins.

CHATILLON-DeMENIL MANSION. The story of the Chatillon-DeMenil Mansion in St. Louis goes back to 1848, when Odile DeLor, a widowed granddaughter of the French-born founder of a nearby village, bought several plots of land and married frontiersman Henri Chatillon. They built a two-story brick farmhouse with a wide veranda typical of Creole houses, and then sold it as a country retreat in 1856. Five years later, pharmacist Nicolas N. DeMenil and his wife, Emilie Sophie Chouteau, bought the Chatillon farmhouse and transformed it into a three-story mansion with a portico in the Greek Revival style. The first two floors have now been restored as they would have been when the DeMenils lived there, while the third contains memorabilia from the 1904 St. Louis World's Fair.

EDNA CUDDY MEMORIAL HOUSE. An 1882 Italianate house built for hardware businessman James P. Hamilton and his family in Bethany, Missouri, was purchased by Roberta C. Cuddy Koch and her husband, George Koch, and given to the Harrison County Historical Society in 1982 as a memorial to Mrs. Koch's mother, Edna Cuddy. The house, built of rare pink brick, depicts the heritage of Harrison County pioneers since 1845 and contains period furnishings.

Nevada

ELIZA ANN MIDDAUGH MOTT HOUSE. The reconstructed 1852 small log cabin in which Eliza Ann Middaugh Mott lived is part of the Mormon Station State Historic Park in Genoa, Nevada. Mott was the first white woman to live in Nevada's oldest white settlement. The original cabin, constructed from abandoned

wagon beds, burned in 1910. It was rebuilt as a small museum at the historic site where Mormons established a log stockade and trading post in 1851 for pioneers to rest before crossing the Sierra Nevada into California.

New Hampshire

ZIMMERMAN HOUSE. The 1950 Zimmerman House in Manchester, New Hampshire, was designed by Frank Lloyd Wright for Isadore J. Zimmerman and his wife, Lucille Zimmerman. It is one of Wright's small but elegant Usonian houses that contain furniture, textiles, and landscaping designed by the noted architect. The historic house is now owned by the Currier Gallery of Art.

New Mexico

ERNEST L. BLUMENSCHEIN HOME AND MUSEUM. The Ernest L. Blumenschein Home and Museum in Taos, New Mexico, is housed in the historic 1797 restored home of artists Ernest L. Blumenschein; his wife, Mary Greene Blumenschein; and their daughter, Helen Greene Blumenschein. Mr. Blumenschein was cofounder of the Taos Society of Artists that resulted in Taos becoming an art colony; Mrs. Blumenschein was a creative artist and jeweler; and their daughter was a printmaker and artist who was active in archaeological digs and histories of the area. The 11-room adobe house, built in the Spanish Colonial period and expanded by the Blumenscheins after their purchase in 1919, features the family's European and Spanish Colonial–style furnishings and representative artworks by the Blumenscheins and other Taos artists of the period.

KIT CARSON HOME AND MUSEUM. The Kit Carson Home and Museum in Taos, New Mexico, is named Christopher "Kit" Carson, the famous frontiersman, but it was actually more the home of his Spanish wife, Maria Josefa Jaramillo. He was away most of the time serving as a trapper, guide, military scout, Indian agent, and volunteer army officer in the Southwest during the Civil War. Carson bought the 1825 adobe home as a wedding present for his bride in 1843, and it remained their home until their deaths in 1868. The present structure contains a portion of the original home, with numerous artifacts and exhibits illustrating the lives of the Carson family, the character of frontier life in Taos, and the importance of Native American and Hispanic cultures in the history of northern New Mexico.

LA HACIENDA DE LOS MARTINEZ. La Hacienda de los Martinez—a restored fortresslike 1804 adobe complex in Taos, New Mexico—was the home and trading post of Don Antonio Severino Martinez, his wife, and their six children (including their eldest son, Padre Jose Antonio Martinez, who became a social reformer, fighting to preserve the Hispanic character of the Catholic Church in the territory, creating the first coeducational school in New Mexico, and bringing the first printing press to Taos). The hacienda, which consists of 21 rooms surrounding two courtyards, was the terminus for the Camino Real that connected Mexico City to northern New Mexico. Martinez and his family, who had extensive ranching and farming operations, later began trading goods brought by the Santa Fe Trail. The hacienda contains late Spanish Colonial furniture and exhibits on traditional crafts of the region, religious art, and Spanish Colonial life and culture.

MARY AUSTIN HOUSE. "Casa Querida" was the Santa Fe, New Mexico, home of novelist, short-story writer, and playwright Mary Hunter Austin. She settled in Santa Fe in 1924 and lived there until her death in 1934. She was known for her writings about nature and Native American life. Her first book, *The Land of Little Rain*, in 1903, was an immediate success. *A Woman of Genius*, published in 1912, is considered her best novel. She was active in movements to preserve Native American arts, crafts, and culture.

New York

ALICE T. MINER MUSEUM. The Alice T. Miner Museum in Chazy, New York, was founded in 1924 in a Colonial Revival–style building—constructed largely of stone from an 1810 limestone structure formerly at the site—by Alice T. Miner, with the assistance of her husband, William Miner, an industrialist and philanthropist who invented the tandem railroad coupling gear. The three-story, 15-room structure features the Alice T. Miner Colonial Collection, an eclectic assortment of paintings, decorative arts, furnishings, glassware, dolls, textiles, Native American artifacts, military items, and manuscripts—primarily from the eighteenth and nineteenth centuries.

HART-CLUETT MANSION. The Rensselaer County Historical Society in Troy, New York, is housed in the 1827 Hart-Cluett Mansion, where Richard and Betsey Hart, George and Amanda Cluett, and Caroline Cluett once resided. The historic house features nineteenth-century furnishings, fine and decorative arts, local industrial and agricultural artifacts, and other historical materials.

KINGSLAND HOMESTEAD. The ca. 1785 two-story house known as Kingsland Homestead in Flushing, New York, was built by Charles Doughty and his wife, Sarah Dusenbury Doughty. Doughty was a wealthy Quaker farmer believed to be the first person in Queens to free a slave. The house's name came from Captain Joseph King, an English sea captain, who married the Doughtys' daughter and inherited the house. The early farmhouse was originally located approximately a dozen blocks away, but it was moved to Weeping Beech Park—site of the nation's oldest weeping beech tree—in 1968, when it was threatened with demolition for a shopping center.

North Carolina

CHINQUA-PENN PLANTATION. The Chinqua-Penn Plantation in Reidsville, North Carolina, was built in 1925 by Thomas Jefferson Penn of the Penn/American Tobacco Company and his wife, Beatrice Schoellkopf Penn, to reflect their elaborate lifestyle of traveling, entertaining, and collecting worldly artifacts. The estate includes a 27-room Y-shaped country manor house, 22 acres of manicured lawns and gardens, pools, fountains, greenhouses, lodge houses, a Chinese pagoda replica, and a three-story clock tower at the entrance. The house contains such global collections as early tapestries, Egyptian winged-phoenix furnishings, ceramic artifacts, and Asian and religious art.

GERTRUDE SMITH HOUSE. The 1903 Gertrude Smith House in Mount Airy, North Carolina, was the home of Gertrude Gilmer Smith, an interior designer, for 78 years. She was married to merchant Jefferson Davis Smith and had seven children. When she died in 1981 at 90 years of age, she willed that the Victorian house be left as though it were still occupied by the Smith family.

LATIMER HOUSE. An Italianate-style Victorian home was built by businessman Zebulon Latimer and his bride, Elizabeth Savage Latimer, in 1852 when they married in Wilmington, North Carolina. It was the home of three generations of Latimers until 1963, when it was converted into a historic house museum and the home of the Lower Cape Fear Historical Society. The house now resembles its original appearance and features period furnishings, art, and portraits of the Latimer family.

North Dakota

CAMPBELL HOUSE. The 1879 Campbell House in Grand Forks, North Dakota, was the birthplace of Thomas D. Campbell Jr., who became known as America's "wheat king." Campbell, founder of the world's largest privately owned wheat farm, near Hardin, Montana, dedicated his boyhood home in 1918 in memory of his mother, Almira Campbell, and all pioneer women. The house, now part of the Grand Forks County Historical Society, displays the furnishings of pioneer family life.

CUSTER HOUSE. The reconstructed house where Lieutenant Colonel George Armstrong Custer and his wife, Libby Custer, lived in 1873–1876 can be seen at the Fort Abraham Lincoln State Park near Mandan, North Dakota. It is from this house at Cavalry Square on the park grounds that Custer set out for the 1876 Battle of the Little Bighorn, in which he and his troops were killed by Native Americans.

LUDWIG AND CHRISTINA WELK HOMESTEAD. The late 1800s sod house of Ludwig Welk and his wife, Christina Welk, near Strasburg, North Dakota, tells how German immigrants from Russia homesteaded, lived, and worked in the region at the turn of the twentieth century. The house was also the birthplace and childhood home of musician and entertainer Lawrence Welk.

Ohio

DOUGHERTY HOUSE. The Dougherty House—a branch of the Hardin County Historical Museums in Kenton, Ohio—is the former home of Frank Dougherty and his wife, Louella Dougherty. It has 1850–1900 period rooms and depicts Victorian domestic life in the county. Mr. Dougherty was an attorney, judge, and writer, and Mrs. Dougherty was a musician and composer.

FRANKLIN HOUSE. The 1907 modified Georgian house known as Franklin House in Chillicothe, Ohio, is dedicated to the pioneer women of Ross County and features clothing, furniture, decorative arts, and other historical items of the late nineteenth and early twentieth centuries. The house is named for Marianne Franklin, who made it her home from 1907 to 1971.

HARRIET BEECHER STOWE HOUSE. The Harriet Beecher Stowe House in Cincinnati was the 1830s home of Lyman Beecher, father of the author of *Uncle Tom's Cabin*. Harriet Beecher accompanied her father and sister, Catharine, when they came to Cincinnati from Connecticut in 1832. Harriet's father became president of the Lane Theological Seminary, and her sister founded the Western Female Institute, where Harriet taught. It was in Cincinnati that Harriet married Calvin E. Stowe, a teacher at Lane. She supplemented their income by writing stories for periodicals and published a collection, titled *The Mayflower*, in 1843. In 1850, when Mr. Stowe joined the faculty of Bowdoin College, the Stowes moved to Maine, where Harriet began writing a serial account of slavery for a journal that became the powerful novel *Uncle Tom's Cabin* in 1852. Although Harriet never lived in her father's house in Cincinnati, it has become a tribute to her and to her work. It also contains exhibits on the Beecher family, the abolitionist movement, and African American history. (See also Harriet Beecher Stowe Center in Museums Honoring Exceptional Women.)

LAKE COUNTY HISTORICAL SOCIETY. See History Museums.

MABEL HARTZELL HISTORICAL HOME. The Mabel Hartzell Historical Home, an 1867 Italianate house built by businessman Matthew Earley and his wife, Mary Earely, in Alliance, Ohio, is named for their adopted daughter, who donated the house to the Alliance Historical Society in 1954. She was a high school teacher who founded the historical society in 1939. The house has been restored to the 1880s period, with original furnishings.

MAC-O-CHEE CASTLE. The Mac-O-Chee Castle in West Liberty, Ohio, was built as a Gothic cottage by journalist, diplomat, and soldier Don Piatt and his wife, Louise Piatt, for the Shawnee people in the 1860s. In 1879, after Louise's death, Don and his second wife, Ella, expanded the house with a Flemish-inspired limestone front that wraps around the older section, and transformed the interior with designs inspired by Charles Eastlake and paintings by French artist Oliver Frey. Over the years the structure became a retreat for writers, artists, and politicians who were friends of the Piatt family. The Mac-O-Chee Castle is one of two buildings that constitute the Piatt Castles, with the other being the Mac-A-Cheek Castle, an 1871 limestone building with elaborate woodwork and intricately painted ceilings named in memory of Macachak, the Shawnee village located on the site 100 years earlier. It was the home of Don's brother, the brigadier general and farmer Abram Sanders Piatt. It now houses a collection of Native American tools, military artifacts, books, and family furnishings from the eighteenth to twentieth centuries.

MILAN HISTORICAL MUSEUM. See History Museums.

SHERMAN HOUSE MUSEUM. In 1810 a young Connecticut lawyer, Charles Sherman, moved to Lancaster, Ohio, to start a law practice. The following year he brought his wife, Mary Hoyt Sherman, and their infant son to the frontier and built a small frame house (which was later expanded).

It was here that their two famous sons were born— William Tecumseh Sherman, who became a Union general known for his army's Atlanta campaign and "march to the sea" during the Civil War, and John Sherman, who served as a congressman, U.S. senator, Secretary of the Treasury, and Secretary of State. Charles Sherman died in 1829, leaving his widow with eleven children. Relatives and friends came to the rescue of the Sherman family by taking some of the older children into their homes, including William and John. In 1844 Mary Sherman was persuaded by her sons Charles and John to move to Mansfield, Ohio, where she died in 1852. Her body was brought back to Lancaster to be buried beside her husband. The Sherman House has been restored and features Sherman family memorabilia, including a family album quilt.

Oklahoma

DRUMMOND HOME. The Drummond Home, a 1905 Victorian three-story house in Hominy, Oklahoma, reflects the lifestyle of Fred Drummond and his wife, Addie Drummond, who ran successful ranching and trading operations for many years. The house has been restored and contains most of its original furnishings, decorative arts, and other personal belongings.

HAR-BER VILLAGE. See Re-created Pioneer Villages.

MURRAY-LINDSAY MANSION. A renovated 1879 three-story stone and stucco mansion near Lindsay, Oklahoma, was the home of pioneer farmer and rancher Frank Murray, his Choctaw wife, Alzira McCaughey Murray, and their eight children. Because of Mrs. Murray's Native American heritage, the couple was able to acquire the 25,000 acres for farming and ranching. She lived in the house until her death in 1924. The mansion—restored to its 1902 appearance— still contains much of the family's furniture, paintings, clothing, and books.

MURRELL HOME. George M. Murrell, a mercantile businessman with Lewis Ross in the Cherokee Nation in Oklahoma in the mid-nineteenth century, was married to two of Ross's daughters—Minerva in 1834, and Amanda in 1857, after her sister died. They were nieces of Cherokee Chief John Ross. The ca. 1845 Murrell Home—called "Hunter's Home"—near Tahlequah was where Murrell and the sisters lived until the outbreak of the Civil War in 1861, when Murrell returned to Virginia with his family and enlisted in the Confederate Army. He was commissioned as a major, served in a support role in the Confederate capital of Richmond, and then purchased a sugar plantation in Louisiana after the war—never returning to live in his Oklahoma home, which was looted but not destroyed during the war. The Murrell Home, restored by the Oklahoma Historical Society, is now the only remaining antebellum plantation home in the state. It contains some original pieces and period furniture.

THOMAS-FOREMAN HOME. The 1898 Thomas-Foreman Home in Muskogee, Oklahoma, was the home of federal judge John R. Thomas, who was killed in a prison riot in 1914. His daughter, Carolyn, lived in the house from the time it was built until her death in 1967. She and her husband, lawyer Grant Foreman, became known for their writings about the life and plight of Native Americans in Indian Territory, which later became Oklahoma. The historic house, which contains the original furnishings and collections of the Thomas and Foreman families, is operated by the Oklahoma Historical Society.

Oregon

DIBBLE HOUSE. The 1859 Dibble House, the oldest house in Molalla, Oregon, was the home of Horace

Dibble, his wife, Julia Sturges Dibble, and their children. Mrs. Dibble lived in the New England Saltbox–style house until her death in 1904. The house has been furnished as a home of the 1800s period by the Molalla Area Historical Society, which also features the early Vonder Ahe farmhouse and stage stop, which was moved from between Portland and Salem to the Molalla museum complex.

Pennsylvania

CHARLOTTE ELIZABETH BATTLES MEMORIAL MUSEUM. The Battles family lived in this 1861 Vernacular farmhouse in Girard, Pennsylvania, for over 150 years. It is now a historical and agricultural museum named for Charlotte Elizabeth Battles, daughter of Rush S. and Charlotte Battles, the builders of the house. She lived on the site from 1864 to 1952. Also located on the Erie County Historical Society's 130-acre grounds are an 1857 farmhouse, 1867 church building, and 1893 bank museum.

DOROTHEA DIX MUSEUM. See Museums Honoring Exceptional Women.

GRAEME PARK. Graeme Park near Horsham, Pennsylvania, is the only surviving residence of a colonial Pennsylvania governor. The Georgian home was built in 1721 for Sir William Keith, who was removed from office after a conflict with founder William Penn's family. In 1739 the 1,200-acre estate was purchased as a summer residence by Dr. Thomas Graeme and his wife, Ann Diggs Keith, the governor's stepdaughter. Upon Dr. Graeme's death in 1772, the property was inherited by his only surviving child, Elizabeth Graeme, who is credited with hosting America's first literary gatherings. After an unhappy romance with Benjamin Franklin's son, William Franklin, she married Henry Hugh Fergusson, a Scottish immigrant, who served with the British during their Revolutionary War occupation of Philadelphia. When the British withdrew, Fergusson fled to England, never to return. In 1778 Graeme Park was seized by the colonial government as the property of a traitor, and its contents sold at a public auction. Elizabeth was able to regain title to the property in 1781, only to be forced to sell the land to her nephew, Dr. William Smith, a decade later because of mounting debts and ill health. After Elizabeth's death in 1801, the main section of the property, including the mansion, was sold to the Penrose family, wealthy Quaker farmers, who built their own house in

1810. In 1920 Welsh Strawbridge and his wife, Margaret Strawbridge, acquired the property, farmed, and raised thoroughbred horses. In 1958 the Strawbridges gave Graeme Park to the commonwealth, and it is now administered by the Pennsylvania Historical and Museum Commission. The mansion, which has changed little over the years, contains period furnishings, the writings and poetry of Elizabeth Graeme Fergusson, and the history of the historic house and the families that lived there.

WOODFORD MANSION. Naomi Wood, daughter of a wealthy Philadelphia merchant, was a collector of colonial furniture, decorative arts, and other antiques who left her collection in trust to be exhibited in a historic house to the public for educational purposes. After her death in 1926, the executors of her will selected the 1756 Woodford Mansion in Fairmont Park for restoration and displaying the collection. The mansion is one of the most elegant survivors of the early "country seats" built in the wooded countryside outside Philadelphia, now part of Fairmount Park. It was built by merchant and later judge William Coleman and his wife. After Coleman's death in 1769, it was owned by port comptroller Alexander Barclay, crown agent David Franks, and then the Parshall and Wharton Quaker families, until it was acquired by the city of Philadelphia in 1868. The mansion's parlor has been called one of the handsomest colonial rooms in America. Originally a one-story Georgian brick house, it was expanded to two stories in 1772. It also has a restored servants' house and a stable behind the house. Opened to the public in 1930, the mansion contains such items from Wood's collection as fine Pennsylvania Dutch ware and furniture, English delftware, Chinese export porcelain, silver, paintings, prints, and unusual clocks.

Rhode Island

BETSY WILLIAMS COTTAGE. The Betsy Williams Cottage in Roger Williams Park in Providence, Rhode Island, is a ca. 1782 Gambrel cottage built by the great-great-grandsons of Roger Williams, founder of Rhode Island, on land deeded to him by the Narragansett people. The historic cottage, now part of the Museum of Natural History, and the park were bequeathed to the city by Betsy Williams, a distant descendant of Roger Williams.

BELCOURT CASTLE. Belcourt Castle in Newport, Rhode Island, was built in 1891–1894 as the summer residence of Oliver H. P. Belmont and his wife, Alva Vanderbilt Belmont, the former wife of railroad millionaire William K. Vanderbilt. The French Louis XIII–style mansion, which became the home of the Tinney family, features furniture, art, and other treasures from 33 countries.

South Carolina

HANOVER HOUSE. Hanover House on the Clemson University campus in Clemson, South Carolina, was built in the Carolina low country, now Berkeley County, in 1716 by French Huguenots Paul de St. Julien and his wife, Mary Amy Ravenel. Their sixteen children were born at Hanover. The house was moved to Clemson and restored in 1941, after falling into ruin and being in the path of a hydroelectric plant development. The cypress timber house with brick triple-flue chimneys and French details was named for George Louis, elector of Hanover, who ascended the English throne as George I. He befriended French Huguenots when they fled religious persecution and immigrated to South Carolina by way of England in the late seventeenth century.

JENNINGS-BROWN HOUSE AND BENNETTSVILLE FEMALE ACADEMY. The Jennings-Brown House in Bennettsville, South Carolina, is an eight-room Saltbox house built by Dr. E. W. Jones, one of the town's earliest doctors, in 1826. It was purchased by Dr. and Mrs. J. Beaty Jennings in 1852, bought by Mrs. J. J. Brown in 1929, and then acquired by Dr. P. M. Kinney in 1969 and donated to Marlboro County for restoration as a historic house museum. In 1865, during the Union Army's march through Georgia and South Carolina, the house served as the headquarters for Major General Frank P. Blair, commander of the 17th Army Corps. The house has been restored as it was in 1852, with period furniture. Also located on the grounds is a two-room schoolhouse—site of the Bennettsville Female Academy—that was organized as a private school in 1830 to provide educational opportunities for girls. The school building, which operated between 1833 and 1881, is furnished to resemble a mid-nineteenth-century schoolroom.

South Dakota

PICKLER MANSION. The 20-room Pickler Mansion in Faulkton, South Dakota, started as a claim shanty in 1882 and evolved into a three-story Prairie Victorian home for lawyer John Pickler and his wife, Alice Alt Pickler, and their children. Mr. Pickler, a Union major in the Civil War, was active in land development as well as in law practice, and was elected to the South Dakota legislature and the U.S. House of Representatives. He and his wife also worked for women's suffrage, with Mrs. Pickler serving as president of the South Dakota Equal Suffrage Association. Suffrage leader Susan B. Anthony was a guest at the house in 1890, and Presidents Theodore Roosevelt and Grover Cleveland were visitors.

Tennessee

MABRY-HAZEN HOUSE. The 1858 Italianate home of railroad president Joseph Alexander Mabry and his wife, Laura Evelyn Churchwell Mabry, in Knoxville, Tennessee, still contains all its original furnishings and approximately 3,000 artifacts from the nineteenth century. The beautiful antebellum house served as the headquarters for both the Confederate and Union armies in the area during the Civil War. Mr. Mabry and his son's 1882 murder were documented in Mark Twain's book *Life on the Mississippi*. The Mabrys' daughter, Alice Evelyn, married wholesale grocer Rush Strong Hazen, and her family was the second generation to live in the house. Mr. Hazen was the benefactor of the mission school that was the subject of Catherine Marshall's book and television series, *Christy*. The house became a historic house museum through the efforts of the Hazens' daughter, Evelyn Montgomery Hazen, who lived in the house from 1899 to 1987. Her will formed a foundation to preserve the house and its collections.

Texas

DiLUE ROSE HARRIS HOUSE MUSEUM. The DiLue Rose Harris House Museum in Columbus, Texas, is housed in the 1858 Greek Revival–style home of a pioneer woman who was a writer of early memoirs of colonial life in Texas. The house contains early Texas primitive furniture and household items from the 1840–1880 period, some of which belonged to DiLue Rose Harris.

FULTON MANSION STATE HISTORIC SITE. The ca. 1877 French Second Empire–style mansion of George Ware Fulton and his wife, Harriet Gillette Smith Fulton, is the focus of the Fulton Mansion State Historic Site in Rockport, Texas. The Fultons were involved in the development of Rockport. The house has period furnishings, including some of the original furniture and examples of Mrs. Fulton's needlework.

GOVERNOR BILL AND VARA DANIEL HISTORIC VILLAGE. See Re-created Pioneer Villages.

HARRINGTON HOUSE HISTORIC HOME. The Neoclassical-style mansion built in 1914 by cattlemen John and Pat Landergin in Amarillo, Texas, became the home of philanthropists Don Harrington and his wife, Sybil Buckingham Harrington, who were leaders in the Texas oil and gas industry, in 1940. Some of the fine furnishings and appointments in the house are original, while others—including the decorative and fine arts—are from the Harringtons. Mrs. Harrington gave the house to the Panhandle-Plains Historical Society in 1983.

JANE LONG HOUSE. The Jane Long House, a ca. 1840 Greek Revival cottage in Richmond, Texas, originally sat on property owned by Long, a plantation owner known as the "mother of Texas" in the state's history. The house is also referred to as the Long-Smith Cottage, incorporating the name of its former resident Thomas Jefferson Smith, who participated in Texas's war of independence from Mexico in 1836. The historic house, now operated by the Fort Bend Museum Association, illustrates middle-class family life in Richmond in the 1860s.

MILLARD'S CROSSING HISTORIC VILLAGE. See Re-created Pioneer Villages.

MOODY MANSION MUSEUM. The 1895 Moody Mansion, a 31-room Richardsonian Romanesque house, is one of the so-called "Broadway Beauties" (the others being the 1859 Ashton Villa and the 1886 Bishop's Palace) in Galveston, Texas. The house, which was the home of William L. Moody, his wife, Libby Sheran Moody, and their family, is as it was in the 1911–1912 debutante season of the family's eldest child, Mary Elizabeth, with each public room in a different revival style. Their daughter, who became Mary Elizabeth Moody Northen, grew up in the house (1900–1915) and moved back after her father and her husband died in 1954. She lived there until 1983 and ran the family banking and insurance business until 1986. She also created an endowment to preserve the mansion, its furnishings, and

many objects and documents relating to the family, to Galveston, and to Texas.

W. H. STARK HOUSE. The 1894 W. H. Stark House in Orange, Texas, was the three-story, 15-room Victorian home of William H. Stark, one of the state's financial and industrial leaders; his wife, Miriam Lutcher Stark; and their only child, H. J. Lutcher Stark. Mr. Stark was successful in the lumber, oil, rice, insurance, and banking industries. The house, which has many gables, galleries, and a distinctive windowed turret, as well as its original furnishings, was occupied by the family until 1936. It now stands in the Stark-Lutcher complex, which consists of a museum, theater, church, and park in downtown Orange.

Vermont

FARRAR-MANSUR HOUSE. The ca. 1797 Farrar-Mansur House in Weston, Vermont, was built by Oliver Farrar and his wife, Polly Farrar, who were among the first settlers in the area. The Federal-style building served as a tavern and community gathering place, as well as their home. An old mill is also located on the property. The house gives a portrait of a newly settled Vermont village in the late eighteenth and early nineteenth centuries.

SHELBURNE MUSEUM. See Art and History Museums.

Virginia

JUNE TOLLIVER HOUSE. Big Stone Gap, Virginia, is located at the junction of three forks of the Powell River and was the setting for *The Trail of the Lonesome Pine*, by John Fox Jr. The 1890 June Tolliver House was the residence of Tolliver in the book.

OATLANDS. Oatlands is an 1804 mansion combining Federal and Greek Revival styles that was built on a 3,400-acre plantation near Leesburg, Virginia, by George Carter and his wife, Elizabeth Grayson Carter, and occupied by the family until 1897. In 1903 the property was purchased by William Corcoran Eustis and his wife, Edith Morton Eustis, and restored to its original state. Although only 261 acres remain of the original plantation, the grounds retain Carter's basic design of terraced formal gardens. The house now features the Eustis collection of American and French art and furnishings.

West Virginia

OGLEBAY INSTITUTE MANSION MUSEUM. The Oglebay Institute Mansion Museum is one of two museums—the other being the Oglebay Institute Glass Museum—at the former summer estate of Cleveland industrialist Earl W. Oglebay and his wife, Sallie Howell Oglebay, in Wheeling, West Virginia. The mansion museum is housed in the 1846 Greek Revival summer home of the Oglebays, who left the estate to the city of Wheeling. It features a dozen period rooms—focusing on Wheeling's earliest settlement through the Edwardian era—and collections of American furniture, china, silver, glass, pewter, textiles, and toys. The Oglebay Institute is West Virginia's oldest arts organization and operates an environmental education center, fine arts center, and theater/cinema in addition to the museums.

Wisconsin

LAURA INGALLS WILDER WAYSIDE. A replica of the cabin in which author Laura Ingalls Wilder was born in 1867 is located at the Laura Ingalls Wilder Wayside, a country park near Pepin, Wisconsin. The cabin is featured in Wilder's *Little House in the Big Woods*. (See also Laura Ingalls Wilder Home and Museum near Mansfield, Missouri; Laura Ingalls Wilder Museum in Walnut Grove, Minnesota; Surveyors' House and Ingalls Home and Museum in Burr Oak, Iowa; and Laura Ingalls Wilder Wayside near Pepin, Wisconsin, in Museums Honoring Exceptional Women.)

SHERRY-BUTT HOUSE. The 1870 Sherry-Butt House in Viroqua, Wisconsin, was originally the home of attorney Cyrus M. Butt, a lieutenant colonel in the Union Army during the Civil War; his wife, Margaret McAuley Butt; and their five children. The Butts left the Federal-style home to their daughter, Jane Butt, who sold it in 1947 to Orbec Sherry and his wife, Hilda Sherry, world-renowned breeders of Brown Swiss cattle. The house, now owned by the Vernon County Historical Society, contains most of the original Victorian furnishings, some of Butt's Civil War artifacts, and exhibits on the history and contributions of the Butt and Sherry families.

VILLA LOUIS HISTORIC SITE. The Villa Louis, an elegant Italianate mansion on St. Feriole Island in Prairie du Chien, Wisconsin, was saved and restored in the 1930s by two sisters, Violet Duosman Young and Virginia Duosman Bigalow, daughters of H. Louis Duosman, who built the house. The women located and returned many of the original furnishings and worked with the city of Prairie du Chien in establishing a museum in the stable. The site, which now includes other historic structures, two museums, and the reconstructed blockhouse of a frontier fort (Fort Crawford), later became the first historic site of the State Historical Society of Wisconsin.

Wyoming

ANNA MILLER MUSEUM. See History Museums.

HISTORIC FARMS AND RANCHES

See also Historic House Museums; History Museums; Other Historic Houses.

California

RANCHO LOS CERRITOS HISTORIC SITE. Women have played an important role in the history of the Rancho Los Cerritos Historic Site, which began as part of a huge 1784 Spanish land grant and today features an 1844 adobe home and grounds in Long Beach, California. The families that lived there helped transform southern California from its ranching beginnings into a modern urban society.

The site was originally a portion of the 300,000 acres in a land grant received by José Manuel Perez Nieto for his military service and to encourage settlement in the region. In 1790 the grant was reduced to 167,000 acres because of a dispute with the Mission San Gabriel. After

years of joint ownership, Nieto's lands were divided into six parcels among family members in 1834, with daughter Maria Manuel Antonia receiving 27,000 acres for the Rancho Los Cerritos.

John Temple purchased the property in 1843 and constructed the present two-story Monterey-style adobe the following year. He was a pioneer Los Angeles merchant who used the ranch as a country house and the headquarters for a large-scale cattle operation. He and his wife, Rafael Cota de Temple, utilized the ranch until 1866, when the ranch was sold to the firm of Flint, Bixby & Co. for sheep ranching. Jotham Bixby managed the ranch with his wife, Margaret Hathaway Bixby. They lived there until 1881, when they began selling off pieces of the land. In the process she became instrumental in the development of Long Beach, which was founded on part of the property in 1884, and was known as the "mother of Long Beach."

Two other women also trace their early years to the ranch. They were the Bixbys' daughter, Fanny Bixby Spencer, who became Long Beach's first police matron and later an anti–World War I pacifist, socialist, feminist, philanthropist, and writer, and Sarah Bixby Smith, a niece who wrote about growing up on the ranch and in early California in her 1925 memoir, *Adobe Days.*

From 1890 to 1927 the ranch adobe housed a succession of tenants and gradually fell into disrepair. In 1930 the house was renovated by a Bixby family member, and it was later sold to the city of Long Beach, which opened the site as a museum in 1955 on the history of the ranch and the surrounding area, emphasizing family life on a western sheep ranch in the 1870s.

Rancho Los Cerritos Historic Site, 4600 Virginia Rd., Long Beach, CA 90807. **Phone:** 562/570-1755. **Fax:** 562/570-1893. **Website:** www.ci.long-beach.ca.us/park/ranchlc.htm. **Hours:** 1-5 Wed.-Sun.; closed Mon.-Tues. and major holidays. **Admission:** free.

WORKMAN AND TEMPLE FAMILY HOMESTEAD MUSEUM. The Workman and Temple Family Homestead Museum, located on the remaining six acres of the once-large Rancho la Puenta in City of Industry, California, tells the story of two early prominent families and a century of southern California history, from 1830 to 1930.

The city-owned site has six restored historic structures, including a Victorian home constructed around an 1842 adobe by William and Nicolasa Workman, and the 1920s Spanish Colonial Revival–style home of the Workmans' grandson, Walter P. Temple Sr., and his wife, Laura. William Workman and Walter Temple were influential in the development of Los Angeles and the San Gabriel Valley. The other historic structures include a water tower, pump house, mausoleum, and glorieta (gazebo). Also located on the property are the ca. 1850 El Campo Santo Cemetery and a modern visitor center.

Workman and Temple Family Homestead Museum, 15414 W. Don Julian Rd., City of Industry, CA 91745. **Phone:** 626/968-8492. **Fax:** 626/968-2048. **E-mail:** info@homesteadmuseum.org. **Website:** www.homesteadmuseum.org. **Hours:** 1-4 Wed.-Sun.; closed Mon.-Tues. and major holidays. **Admission:** free.

Colorado

COZENS RANCH MUSEUM. The Cozens Ranch Museum, which features the 1874 homestead of Zane and Mary Cozens, is located between Winter Park and Fraser in the Colorado Rockies. The pioneering couple was among the first settlers in the Fraser Valley area. The ranch, which contains the restored 13-room ranch house and an 1876 stage stop and post office, has some of the original wallpaper, carpets, furnishings, and family photographs, as well as materials on the valley's early settlement and development, including the life of "Doc Susie," the frontier doctor Susan Anderson.

Cozens Ranch Museum, 77849 U.S. Hwy. 40, Winter Park, CO 80482 (contact: Grand County Historical Assn., PO Box 165, Hot Sulphur Springs, CO 80451). **Phone:** 970/726-5488. **Fax:** 970/725-0129. **E-mail:** gcha@rkymtnhi.com. **Website:** www.grandcountymuseum.com. **Hours:** Memorial Day-Labor Day—10-5 Mon.-Sat., 12-5 Sun.; remainder of year—11-4 Wed.-Sat., 12-4 Sun.; closed Mon.-Tues., New Year's Day, Thanksgiving, and Christmas. **Admission:** adults, $4; seniors, $4; children 6-18, $2; children under 6, free; families, $10.

GULLEY HOMESTEAD AND DeLANEY FARM. The Gully Homestead and DeLaney Farm in Aurora, Colorado, are two nineteenth-century homesteads operated as historic landmarks by the Aurora History Museum.

The Gully Homestead's 1870–1871 ranch house is the oldest surviving house in the Denver suburb of Aurora. The building was initially a one-room structure, constructed by John Gully and his wife, Elizabeth Gully. A front section was later added for a parlor, bedroom, and sleeping loft for their seven children. The house, stables, and corrals were moved from their original site to the 168-acre DeLaney Farm, where they can be toured as part of educational programs and special events.

The DeLaney Farm, homesteaded in the 1880s by the John DeLaney family, has a farmhouse, eleven outbuildings, and a large round barn considered to be the only surviving perfectly round barn in Colorado. The latter, built as a grain-storage silo and then converted into a two-story cow barn, houses an exhibit on farming in the area.

Gully Homestead, 200 S. Chambers Rd., and **DeLaney Farm,** 170 S. Chambers Rd., Aurora, CO 80012 (contact: Aurora History Museum, 15001 E. Alameda Dr., Aurora, CO 80012). **Phone:** 303/739-6660. **Fax:** 303/739-6657. **E-mail:** amain@ci.aurora.co.us. **Hours:** varies with programs and events. **Admission:** depends upon program or event.

MacGREGOR RANCH. When Muriel Lurilla MacGregor died in 1970, she thought her will provided for a trust and for the family's 3,000-acre ranch near Estes Park, Colorado, to become a pioneer living history center. Unfortunately, the will was not written as concisely as required, and the execution apparently was not handled properly. As a result, the Internal Revenue Service decided the ranch was not being operated as a trust, and assessed $1.6 million in inheritance taxes (which later grew to $2.7 million in federal and state taxes). This was followed by claims from distant relatives and attorneys.

As a result, part of the land was sold, including 400 acres to the National Park Service for the adjoining Rocky Mountain National Park. Eventually the matter was cleared up with the IRS and the state through negotiation and a few changes in the Muriel L. MacGregor Trust's charitable requirements. The National Park Service also assisted in preserving the ranch by providing a conservation easement.

The ranch, which was reduced to 1,221 acres, is now operated as a nonprofit living history museum by volunteers. The 1896 ranch house contains much of the original furniture and family possessions, and the ranch uses some of the early ranching and farming equipment and features cattle, horses, and educational programs.

MacGregor Ranch, MacGregor Lane (Devil's Gulch Rd.), PO Box 4675, Estes Park, CO 80517. **Phone:** 970/586-3717. **Hours:** Memorial Day-Labor Day—11-5 Tues.-Fri.; closed Sat.-Mon. and remainder of year. **Admission:** free.

Idaho

KIRKWOOD HISTORIC RANCH. The Kirkwood Historic Ranch in Hells Canyon National Recreation Area near Lewiston, Idaho, is unusual in that it can be reached only by water or air, since no roads lead to the wilderness ranch.

The first European Americans to settle in the area—which contains prehistoric pit houses and where the Nez Percé people lived when the Lewis and Clark Expedition passed through the Snake River country—were Dr. Jay W. Kirkwood, his wife, and a child. They built two cabins and then moved to Lewiston in 1885.

The land then passed through a number of owners before being acquired by Len Jordan and his family in the 1930s. They ran 3,000 sheep on 17,000 acres of range until 1941, when the family moved to Grangeville. Jordan went on to become governor of Idaho and a U.S. senator, while his wife, Grace Jordan, told of their years on the ranch in the book *Home Below Hells Canyon.* The Jordans' holdings were sold to Bud Wilson, who also ran sheep in the area with the help of ranch hand Dick Sterling and his wife, Bonnie Sterling, who worked as camp cook and wrote about their life in Hells Canyon in *The Sterling Years.*

In 1975 the ranch and surrounding area became the Hells Canyon National Recreation Area. Many of the early buildings can still be seen at the historic ranch site.

Kirkwood Historic Ranch, Snake River Rte., Lewiston, ID 83501. **Phone:** none at ranch, but 509/758-0616 at the Hells Canyon National Recreation Area office. **Hours:** varies. **Admission:** free.

Indiana

GAAR HOUSE AND FARM MUSEUM. See Other Historic Houses.

Iowa

NELSON PIONEER FARM MUSEUM. The Nelson Pioneer Farm Museum in Oskaloosa, Iowa, is located on land acquired by Daniel Nelson and his wife, Margaret Nelson, in 1844 and farmed by the Nelson family for 114 years. In 1958 the 310-acre farm was bequeathed to the Mahaska County Historical Society by Roy Nelson and Lillian Nelson for preservation as a memorial to their parents and grandparents.

In addition to the Nelsons' 1853 home, 1856 barn, and other outbuildings, the farm grounds also contain a number of other historic buildings, such as an 1844 log cabin, 1851 post office, 1861 schoolhouse, 1864 lumberyard office, 1868 church, and 1910 country store. A museum building has exhibits on Iowa history and quilts. Two Nelson-owned white mules that served in the U.S. Army during the Civil War are buried in a special plot near the museum.

Nelson Pioneer Farm Museum, Mahaska County Historical Society, 2294 Oxford Ave., PO Box 578, Oskaloosa, IA 52577. **Phone:** 515/672-2989. **Hours:** May-mid-Oct.—10-4:30 Tues.-Sat.; closed Sun. and remainder of year. **Admission:** adults, $4; children 5-16, $1; children under 5, free.

Kansas

MAHAFFIE STAGECOACH STOP AND FARM. The Mahaffie Stagecoach Stop and Farm in Olathe, Kansas, is a national historic landmark that was a stagecoach stop operated by James Beatty and Lucinda Mahaffie on the Santa Fe Trail from 1863 to 1869. It is the last authentic stagecoach stop remaining on the historic trail.

The Mahaffies lived on the 570-acre farm—of which 20 acres remain—from 1858 until 1886. Their 1865 two-story house, made of two-foot-thick native limestone, has a full cellar that was used as a kitchen and dining area for stagecoach passengers. Other historic structures on the property, now owned by the city, are a limestone icehouse and a wood-peg barn.

Mahaffie Stagecoach Stop and Farm, 1100 Kansas City Rd., Olathe, KS 66061. **Phone:** 913/782-6972. **Fax:** 913/397-5114. **E-mail:** mahaffie@unicom.net. **Website:** www.home.kc.rmi.net/mahaffie. **Hours:** 10-4 Mon.-Sat., 12-4 Sun.; closed Jan., Sat.-Sun. in Feb.-Mar., and major holidays. **Admission:** adults, $3; children 5-11, $1.75; children under 5, free.

Maine

OLD CONWAY HOMESTEAD AND MUSEUM. The Old Conway Homestead and Museum, operated by the Camden-Rockport Historical Society near Camden, Maine, features the eighteenth-century farmhouse of the Conway family and a history museum named in honor of Mary Meeker Cramer, the historical society's president who revitalized the society, organized its collections, and inspired the later founding of the museum.

The initial historic farmhouse was built by one of the town's first settlers about 1770 and was later expanded and modified by other owners. In 1807 Robert Thorndike Jr. and his wife, Sarah Chesbrook Thorndike, acquired the house and lived there until it was purchased by Frederick Conway and his wife, Julia Conway, in 1826. Members of the Conway family lived at the site until 1916. Mrs. Cramer bought the rundown property in 1961 and gave it to the historical society, which restored the house and furnished it with household items from the eighteenth and early nineteenth centuries. The house and its barn were opened to the public in 1962, with an early blacksmith shop and an 1820 maple-sugar house being moved to the grounds later. The house also has a re-created herb garden from the mid-1800s.

The Mary Meeker Cramer Museum, located in a separate building designed by her architect husband, Ambrose Cramer, was added in 1970. It houses period costumes, early glass, paintings, musical instruments, guns, sabers, quilts, ship models, and other collections from the historical society. Historic carriages, sleighs, and agricultural implements are also displayed in the barn.

Old Conway Homestead and Museum, U.S. Hwy. 1 and Conway Rd., Camden, ME 04843 (postal address: Camden-Rockport Historical Society, PO Box 747, Rockport, ME 04856). **Phone:** 207/236-2257. **E-mail:** chumuseum@mint.net. **Website:** www.mint.net/~chumuseum. **Hours:** July-Aug.—10-4 Tues.-Fri.; closed Sat.-Mon. and remainder of year. **Admission:** adults, $5; children 6-18, $3; children under 6, free.

Michigan

ROCHESTER HILLS MUSEUM AT VAN HOOSEN FARM. The Rochester Hills Museum at Van Hoosen Farm in Rochester Hills, Michigan, is a local history museum in an 1840 farmhouse that housed five generations of the Taylor-Van Hoosen families, including Dr. Bertha Van Hoosen, noted physician and surgeon, and Dr. Sarah Van Hoosen Jones, a dairy management specialist.

In 1823 Elisha Taylor led 60 family members from the state of New York to the territory of Michigan, where the family founded a log cabin community—Stoney Creek Village—which largely remains today as a reminder of the Taylor legacy.

The Taylors built the 1840 farmhouse in which the museum was founded in 1979. One of the Taylor children was Sarah Taylor, who married her childhood sweetheart, Joshua Van Hoosen, in 1854. Van Hoosen's successful gold prospecting in California enabled him to purchase the house and the Taylor farm, where the couple raised two daughters, Alice and Bertha. Alice taught Greek and Latin before marrying Joseph Jones, while Bertha had a 61-year medical career in which she developed an anesthesia for use during childbirth, the button-hole appendectomy, and the use of sterile conditions during surgery, and founded the American Medical Women's Association. Dr. Sarah Van Hoosen Jones, who was born to Joseph Comstock and Alice Van Hoosen Jones, became a premier breeder of Holstein cattle and excelled in dairy management on the family farm.

It was the Taylor-Van Hoosen women—Alice and Bertha, Sarah Taylor Van Hoosen, and Sarah Van Hoosen Jones—who transformed their small ancestral home into an expanded spacious house that now contains many of the family's heirlooms and acquisitions from world travels.

Rochester Hills Museum at Van Hoosen Farm, 1005 Van Hoosen Rd., Rochester Hills, MI 48306. **Phone:** 248/656-4663. **Fax:** 248/608-9198. **E-mail:** rhmuseum@

rochesterhills.org. Website: www.rochesterhills.org/museum. htm. **Hours:** 1-4 Wed.-Sat.; closed Sun.-Tues. and major holidays. **Admission:** adults, $3; seniors and students, $2; children under 3rd grade, free.

Minnesota

GIBBS FARM MUSEUM. The story of the Gibbs Farm Museum goes back to the 1830s, when five-year-old Jane DeBow was kidnapped by a missionary couple near Batavia, New York, and brought west to live among missionaries and the Dakota people near St. Paul, Minnesota.

The missionary couple, who became attached to the child after losing their own infant daughter, arrived at Fort Snelling in 1835 and then moved to Lake Harriet, where they lived in quarters built by other missionaries, surrounded by over 100 Dakota lodges and known as Cloud Man's Village.

Jane, who played with Dakota children, learned to speak their language, developed lifelong friendships with them, and acted as an interpreter later in life. She married Herman Gibbs, and in 1849 they bought the land on which the farm is located. The farm, which was the Gibbs family home for more than 100 years, is now a seven-acre living history museum operated by the Ramsey County Historical Society that depicts a prosperous farm of the late 1800s. Also located on the grounds are an 1870s one-room schoolhouse, replicas of a sod house and a Dakota village, and pioneer and Dakota gardens. Costumed interpreters conduct tours and perform quilting, baking, and other nineteenth-century demonstrations.

Gibbs Farm Museum, 2097 W. Larpenter Ave., St. Paul, MN 55113 (postal address: Ramsey County Historical Society, 323 Landmark Center, 75 W. 5th St., St. Paul, MN 55102). **Phone:** 651/646-8629. **Fax:** 651/659-0345. **Hours:** May-Oct.—10-4 Tues.-Fri. and Mon. holidays, 12-4 Sat.-Sun.; closed Mon. and remainder of year. **Admission:** adults, $3; seniors, $2.50; children 2-16, $1.50; children under 2, free.

Montana

GRANT-KOHRS RANCH NATIONAL HISTORIC SITE. The Grant-Kohrs Ranch National Historic Site near Deer Lodge, Montana, is located on a nineteenth-century frontier ranch that once grazed cattle on more than 10 million acres in four states and Canada.

Johnny Grant, a Canadian trapper, hunter, and mountain man, started the ranch in the late 1850s and built a herd of 2,000 cattle, mostly by trading along the Oregon Trail. In 1862 he and his wife, Quarra, a member of the Bannock people, moved the operation to the northern edge of the present town of Deer Lodge. In 1866 he sold the ranch to Conrad Kohrs, a German immigrant who was a butcher and already owned a sizable herd. Two years later Kohrs married Augusta Kruse, a 19-year-old woman of German ancestry who lived to be 96.

Under Kohrs' management, with his half-brother, John Bielenberg, as partner, the ranch grew rapidly. The cattle, which grazed throughout the region, improved substantially in quality through breeding with shorthorns and Herefords. The ranch increased to 25,000 acres, became a center for stock breeding, and shipped 8,000 to 10,000 cattle to market each year for a quarter of a century.

When homesteaders fenced in the range and it was no longer possible to move large herds across the plains in search of grass and water, Kohrs and Bielenberg sold off all but approximately 1,500 acres around the home ranch. It was this remaining land that a grandson, Conrad Kohrs Warren, and his wife, Nell Warren, managed until the ranch became a national historic site in 1972.

The site is now a working ranch with numerous historic structures, including the 1862 Grant ranch house, with an 1890 Kohrs brick wing; 1870 draft horse and oxen barns; 1875 buggy shed; 1880s thoroughbred barn and icehouse; and a bunkhouse and other early structures. The ranch also has a summer living history program.

Grant-Kohrs Ranch National Historic Site, 210 Missouri Ave., PO Box 790, Deer Lodge, MT 59722-0790. **Phone:** 406/846-2070. **Fax:** 406/846-3692. **E-mail:** darlene_koontz@nps.gov. **Website:** www.nps.gov/grko. **Hours:** May-Sept.—8-5:30 daily; remainder of year—9-4:30 daily; closed New Year's Day, Thanksgiving, and Christmas. **Admission:** adults and children over 16, $3; children under 17, free; free for all in Oct.-Apr.

Nebraska

ARTHUR BOWRING SANDHILLS RANCH STATE HISTORICAL PARK. The Arthur Bowring Sandhills Ranch State Historical Park near Merriman, Nebraska, is a 7,200-acre working cattle ranch and living history museum. The Bar 99 Ranch was established in 1894 by pioneering rancher Arthur Bowring and maintained by his second wife, U.S. Senator Eve Bowring, until her death in 1985. It contains many of the original buildings, including the ranch house, bunkhouse, barn, and other outbuildings, and a visitor center with exhibits on the Bowrings' lives and careers and the history, geology, and ranching of the Sandhills region.

Arthur Bowring Sandhills Ranch State Historical Park, State Hwy. 61, PO Box 38, Merriman, NE 69218. **Phone:** 308/684-3428. **Hours:** Memorial Day-Labor Day—8-5 daily; remainder of the year—8-5 Mon.-Fri.; closed Sat.-Sun. and major holidays. **Admission:** $2.50 per private vehicle.

HOMESTEAD NATIONAL MONUMENT OF AMERICA. The Homestead National Monument of America, located on the site of Daniel and Agnes Freeman's homestead near Beatrice, Nebraska, commemorates the lives and accomplishments of pioneering settlers and the changes brought by the Homestead Act of 1862.

Under the Homestead Act, more than 270 million acres—ten percent of the land in the United States—were given free to individuals who claimed 160 acres of surveyed government land, improved the plot with a dwelling and crops, and lived on the land for at least five years.

The site has a historic log cabin typical of those in eastern Nebraska, the original Freeman schoolhouse, trails that wind through the restored tallgrass prairie, and a visitor center with historical exhibits, farming implements, and a video on the history of homesteading and the park.

Homestead National Monument of America, 8523 W. State Hwy. 4, Rte. 3, Box 47, Beatrice, NE 68310-6743. **Phone:** 402/223-3514. **Fax:** 402/228-4231. **E-mail:** home_interpretation@nps.gov. **Website:** www.nps.gov/home. **Hours:** Memorial Day-Labor Day—8:30-5 daily; remainder of year—8:30-5 Mon.-Fri., 9-5 Sat.-Sun.; closed New Year's Day, Thanksgiving, and Christmas. **Admission:** free.

Nevada

PONDEROSA RANCH. The Ponderosa Ranch of the popular *Bonanza* television series has become a western theme park on the north shore of Lake Tahoe in Incline Village, Nevada. The 600-acre ranch was opened as a theme park in 1967 by Bill Anderson and his wife, Joyce Anderson, in partnership with three of the program's stars—Lorne Greene, Dan Blocker, and Michael Landon.

The television program, which featured Ben Cartwright and his three sons, Adam, Hoss, and Little Joe, was filmed at the ranch for 432 shows over thirteen years, beginning in 1959. The series was so popular that it was translated into twelve languages and presented in 86 countries.

The main attraction is still the Cartwright Ranch House, where guided tours are offered. The theme park also has a replica 1870s frontier town with a general store, saloon, church, bank, blacksmith shop, trading post, carriage house, and other structures, as well as a mystery mine, gold panning, museum, horseback and carriage rides, simulated gunfights, and other attractions.

Ponderosa Ranch, 100 Ponderosa Ranch Rd., Incline Village, NV 89451. **Phone:** 775/831-0691. **Fax:** 775/831-0113. **E-mail:** info@ponderosaranch.com. **Website:** www.ponderosaranch.com. **Hours:** mid-Apr.-Oct.—9:30-5 daily; closed remainder of year. **Admission:** adults and children over 11, $9.50; children 5-11, $5.50; children under 5, free.

New Jersey

LONGSTREET FARM. Longstreet Farm, founded in the late 1700s by Hendrick Longstreet and his wife, Williampe Longstreet, near present-day Holmdel, New Jersey, is now a living history museum that interprets the 1890s, when the couple's granddaughter, Mary Anne Longstreet, owned and operated the farm. It became part of the Monmouth County Park System in 1967, when Mary Holmes Duncan, a distant descendant, sold the farm.

The farm, which contains the 1794 Dutch barn, an expanded 1806 furnished farmhouse, and seventeen other restored historic structures, is an operating farm with live animals, interpretive walks, and demonstrations of sheep shearing, making apple cider, horseshoeing, cornhusking, grain threshing, and leatherwork.

Longstreet Farm, Holmdel Park, Longstreet Rd., Holmdel, NJ 07735 (postal address: Monmouth County Park System, Newmann Springs Rd., Lincroft, NJ 07738). **Phones:** 732/946-3758 and 732/842-4000. **Fax:** 732/946-0750. **E-mail:** info@monmouthcountyparks.com. **Website:** www.monmouthcountyparks.com. **Hours:** June-Labor Day—9-5 daily; remainder of year—10-4 daily; closed Christmas. **Admission:** free.

New Mexico

EL RANCHO DE LAS GOLONDRINAS MUSEUM. El Rancho de las Golondrinas (The Ranch of the Swallows) Museum near Santa Fe, New Mexico, was founded in the early 1700s, but it was not until 1972 that Y. A. Paloheimo and his wife, Leonora Curtin Paloheimo, restored the ranch and opened it as a living history museum and re-created Spanish Colonial village.

The ranch, once a stop on El Camino Real (The Royal Road) from Mexico City to early Santa Fe, depicts Spanish Colonial life in New Mexico. It features an eighteenth-century house with a defense tower, as well as a blacksmith shop, winery, wheelwright shop, country store, schoolhouse, gristmill, several water mills, and other historic buildings. The ranch is the site of spring, summer, harvest, and wine festivals.

El Rancho de las Golondrinas Museum, 334 Los Pinos Rd., Santa Fe, NM 87507. **Phone:** 505/471-2261. **Fax:** 505/471-5623. **E-mail:** erdlgolond@aol.com. **Website:** www.golondrinas.org. **Hours:** June-Sept.—10-4 Wed.-Sun.; Apr.-May and Oct.—by appointment; closed remainder of year. **Admission:** adults, $7; seniors and children 13-18, $5; children 5-12, $3; children under 5, free.

North Dakota

CROSS RANCH STATE PARK AND NATURE PRESERVE. The 1890s Cross Ranch is the site of the Cross Ranch State Park and the adjoining Cross Ranch Nature Preserve near Hensler and Center, North Dakota. The ranch was founded by A. D. Gaines, a Teddy Roosevelt enthusiast who bought Roosevelt's old brand— the Maltese Cross—when the president-to-be moved back to the East. Bob Levis and his wife, Gladys Levis, bought the Gaines Ranch in 1956 and renamed it the Cross Ranch in recognition of the brand. The Nature Conservatory purchased the ranch in 1978 and gave part of it for the park.

The 589-acre state park and the 6,000-acre nature preserve have Mandan village sites from the 1400s to the early 1800s. The park's visitor center features exhibits on Native Americans, pioneer settlers, and regional and natural history, while the preserve contains such historic buildings as the ranch house, foreman's house, bunkhouses, barn, shop, and support structures.

Cross Ranch State Park and Nature Preserve, County Rd. 1806, Hensler, ND (postal address: 1403 River Rd., Center, ND 58530-9445). **Phones:** 701/794-3731 and 701/794-8741. **Faxes:** 701/794-3262 and 701/794-3544. **E-mails:** crsp@state.nd.us and tncc-oss@westriv.com. **Websites:** www.nd.parks.com and www.tnc.org. **Park Hours:** Memorial Day-Labor Day—10-6 daily (also to 9 Fri.); remainder of year—varies. **Admission:** $4 per private vehicle. **Preserve Hours:** dawn-dusk daily. **Admission:** free.

DALE AND MARTHA HAWK MUSEUM. See History Museums.

Oklahoma

HARN HOMESTEAD AND 1889er MUSEUM. The Harn Homestead and 1889er Museum in Oklahoma City is located on a 10-acre tract that was part of the 1889 land run by settlers and others seeking 160 free acres on former Native American land. The site features the 1904 Queen Anne farmhouse built by William and Alice Harn; an exhibit barn; and four turn-of-the-twentieth-century buildings moved from elsewhere. The museum gives visitors a glimpse into the lives of the men and women who settled in frontier Oklahoma at the time.

Harn Homestead and 1889er Museum, 313 N.E. 16th St., Oklahoma City, OK 73104. **Phone:** 405/235-4058. **Fax:** 405/235-4041. **E-mail:** harnhomestead@yahoo.com. **Website:** www.connections.oklahoma.net/harn-homestead/index.html. **Hours:** 10-4 Tues.-Sat.; closed Sun.-Mon., 2 weeks in Aug., and major holidays. **Admission:** adults and children over 11, $4; children under 12, $2.

OVERSTREET-KERR HISTORICAL FARM. The 1895 Overstreet-Kerr Historical Farm near Keota, Oklahoma, was the home of ranchers T. G. Overstreet and his wife, Margaret Overstreet, and is now operated by the Kerr Center for Sustainable Agriculture. In addition to the farmhouse, the site has two barns, gardens, a carriage house, a smokehouse, and buildings for poultry and potatoes. The farm illustrates family life in the Indian Territory in 1871–1914.

Overstreet-Kerr Historical Farm, Overstreet-Kerr Rd. (off State Hwy. 595), Rte. 2, Box 693, Keota, OK 74941. **Phones:** 918/966-3282 and 918/966-3396. **Fax:** 918/966-3282. **E-mail:** okhfarm@crosstel.net. **Website:** www.kerrcenter.com. **Hours:** 10-4 Fri.-Sat.; closed Sun.-Thurs., Easter, Thanksgiving, and Christmas. **Admission:** $3 per person; children under 6, free.

PAWNEE BILL RANCH SITE. The Pawnee Bill Ranch Site near Pawnee, Oklahoma, features the restored 1910 home and outbuildings of Gordon W. Lillie, an army scout who became the owner of Pawnee Bill's Wild West Show, and his wife, Mary Lillie. The ranch house contains many of the original furnishings and personal belongings, while a museum building has a stagecoach and materials from the Wild West show and memorabilia from Pawnee Bill's travels and home life. Among the highlights of a summer Wild West show and festival are a reenactment of Custer's Last Stand, a stagecoach robbery, and trick riding and roping.

Pawnee Bill Ranch Site, 1141 Pawnee Bill Rd., Pawnee, OK 74058. **Phone:** 918/762-2513. **Fax:** 918/762-2514. **Hours:**

10-5 Tues.-Sat., 1-4 Sun.-Mon.; closed major holidays. **Admission:** free.

South Dakota

PRAIRIE HOMESTEAD HISTORIC SITE. See Historic House Museums.

Texas

FLORENCE RANCH HOMESTEAD. David Florence and his wife, Julia Florence, built the Florence Ranch Homestead in Mesquite, Texas, in 1871. The ranch house is now considered one of the best examples of late-nineteenth-century rural Texas architecture. The house has a gallery decorated with brackets and moldings in a gingerbread style, a limestone-lined root cellar, an inside spring-fed well, and a double-sided fireplace that separates the living room from the master bedroom. The house also has a family office, which contains a small historical museum and gift shop. The Florence family was known for breeding and exhibiting fine Percheron horses and Hampshire sheep.

Florence Ranch Homestead, Historic Mesquite Inc., 1474 Barnes Bridge Rd., PO Box 850137, Mesquite, TX 75185-0137. **Phone:** 972/216-6468. **Fax:** 972/216-8109. **E-mail:** charlene_orr@msn.com. **Hours:** 10-1 2nd Sat. of month and by appointment. **Admission:** free.

GEORGE RANCH HISTORICAL PARK. The George Ranch Historical Park, which occupies 470 acres of a 2,300-acre working ranch near Richmond, Texas, is the culmination of four generations of women.

The ranch was founded in the 1820s by Henry Jones and Nancy Stiles Jones, who had twelve children. It was passed on to one of the daughters, businesswoman Polly Ryon, who left the ranch to a granddaughter, Mamie Davis George. In 1945 Mamie and her husband, A. P. George, established a foundation to create and operate the historical park.

The historical park is a living history museum, where visitors can see such sights as cowboys working cattle, lye soap being made, and rope being twisted the old-fashioned way. The 1890s Victorian mansion and 1930s ranch house can also be toured. On the third Saturday of June, a rodeo and other festivities celebrate Juneteenth, which commemorates when slaves in Texas learned of their freedom.

George Ranch Historical Park, 10215 Farm Rd. 762, PO Box 1248, Richmond, TX 77406. **Phones:** 281/545-9212 and 281/343-0218. **Fax:** 218/343-9316. **Hours:** 9-5 daily; closed

New Year's Eve and Day, Thanksgiving, and Christmas Eve and Day. **Admission:** adults and children over 12, $7.50; seniors, $6.50; children 3-12, $4; children under 3, free.

HERITAGE FARMSTEAD MUSEUM. A stately 14-room farmhouse built by Hunter Farrell and his wife, Mary Alice Farrell, in Plano, Texas, in 1891 is the site of the Heritage Farmstead Museum, which depicts Blackland prairie life in the 1890–1920 period. In addition to the Victorian house, the museum has twelve outbuildings, nearly 5,000 artifacts of the period, gardens, live animals, a reconstructed one-room schoolhouse, and a Native American wickiup.

Heritage Farmstead Museum, 1900 W. 15th St., Plano, TX 75075. **Phone:** 972/881-0140. **Fax:** 972/422-6481. **E-mail:** museum@airmail.net. **Website:** www.heritagefarmstead. org. **Hours:** June-Aug.—10-1 Tues.-Fri., 1-4 Sat.-Sun.; closed Mon.; remainder of year—10-1 Thurs.-Fri., 1-4 Sat.-Sun.; closed Mon.-Wed. and major holidays. **Admission:** adults, $3.50; seniors and children 4-18, $2.50; military and children under 4, free.

KING RANCH MUSEUM. The 825,000-acre King Ranch near present-day Kingsville, Texas, began in 1853 when Captain Richard King purchased the 15,500-acre Santa Gertrudis land grant and stocked the ranch with longhorn cattle. Upon her husband's death, Henrietta King inherited the estate, along with a $500,000 debt. And it was under her leadership that the debt was cleared and the ranch grew rapidly.

The ranch continued to prosper after Robert J. Kleberg, legal counsel for the ranch, married the Kings' youngest daughter. King-Kleberg descendants now control the huge enterprise that includes cattle operations in other countries and is one of the largest ranches in the world.

The King Ranch developed the Santa Gertrudis and King Ranch Santa Cruz breeds of cattle, introduced purebred cattle in the nation, and produced the first registered American quarter horse. It is a national historic landmark and is recognized as the birthplace of the American ranching industry.

The ranch has a visitor center and a museum, as well as a saddle shop that still makes saddles, harnesses, and other leather products. The visitor center has exhibits and videos on the ranch's history and operations and offers guided ranch and nature tours, while the museum—located in the Henrietta Memorial Center—features videos on the ranch and main residence; saddles, guns, carriages, cars, and other artifacts;

and Toni Frissell's award-winning photographic essay on life at the King Ranch in the early 1940s.

King Ranch Visitor Center, State Hwy. 141, PO Box 1090, Kingsville, TX 78364-1090. **Phone:** 361/592-8055. **Fax:** 361/595-1344. **E-mail:** krvisitormgmt@interconnect.net. **Website:** www.king-ranch.com. **Hours:** 9-4 Mon.-Sat., 12-5 Sun.; closed New Year's Day, Easter, Thanksgiving, and Christmas Eve and Day. **Admission:** visitor center—free; tours—adults, $7; children 5-12, $2.50; children under 5, free.

King Ranch Museum, 405 N. 6th St., PO Box 1090, Kingsville, TX 78364-1090. **Phone:** 361/595-1881. **Fax:** 361/592-3247. **E-mail:** krmuseum@interconnect.net. **Website:** www.king-ranch.com. **Hours:** 10-4 Mon.-Sat., 1-5 Sun.; closed New Year's Day, Easter, Thanksgiving, and Christmas Eve and Day. **Admission:** adults, $4; children 5-12, $2.50; children under 5, free.

Utah

WHEELER HISTORIC FARM. An 1898 Victorian farmhouse—known as the "grand lady of South Cottonwood"—at the Wheeler Historic Farm near Salt Lake City was designed by Sariah Pixtou Wheeler, who lived on the farm with her husband, Henry Wheeler, and their children at the time. Salvaged adobe bricks from an earlier pioneer home at the site were incorporated into the new pressed brick walls.

The 75-acre living history dairy farm is now operated by the county as it was at the turn of the twentieth century. In addition to the historic farmhouse, the open-air museum has an early granary, barn, and icehouse; demonstrations of period rural skills and farming techniques; petting corral; nature preserve; wagon rides; and opportunities for visitors to help milk the cows, gather eggs, and feed the animals.

Wheeler Historic Farm, 6351 South 900 East, Salt Lake City, UT 84121. **Phone:** 801/264-2241. **Fax:** 801/264-2213.

Hours: Mar.-Oct.—9:30-5:30 daily; remainder of year—1-5:30 daily; closed major holidays. **Admission:** free.

Vermont

ROKEBY MUSEUM. The Rokeby Museum—which provides a record of two centuries of Vermont family life and agriculture—is located in Ferrisburgh on one of Champlain Valley's most prosperous farms. It was founded in the 1780s by Thomas Robinson and his wife, Jemima Robinson, young Quaker emigrants from Rhode Island.

Robinson women were important to each of the four generations to occupy the site. In addition to Jemima, Rachel Gilpin Robinson was an abolitionist involved in the Underground Railroad to assist slaves, and Anna Rachel Robinson Elmer and Mary Robinson Perkins were noted artists. The Rokeby farm is also the ancestral estate of Rowland Evans Robinson, who built a career first in art and then in literature.

Rokeby Museum tells the story of the Robinsons and the Vermont and New England social history from 1790s to 1961. It contains the ca. 1784 Robinson home with Federal-style additions and eight agricultural outbuildings. The house—which can be seen only as part of guided tours—contains many of the family's personal and domestic belongings, a large collection of art created by family members, and the family's library of books, pamphlets, and periodicals. Agricultural implements and artifacts relating to wool, butter, and fruit production are in the outbuildings.

Rokeby Museum, 4334 U.S. Hwy. 7, Ferrisburgh, VT 05456. **Phone:** 802/877-3406. **E-mail:** rokeby@globalnetisp.net. **Website:** www.rokeby.org. **Hours:** mid-May-mid-Oct.—house tours: 11, 12:30, and 2 Thurs.-Sun.; closed Mon.-Wed.; grounds and outbuildings open Tues.-Wed.; closed Thurs.-Mon. and remainder of year. **Admission:** adults, $6; seniors and students, $4; children under 13, $2.

HISTORIC OPERA HOUSES

California

AMARGOSA OPERA HOUSE. The Amargosa Opera House in Death Valley Junction, California, was created in 1968 by Marta Becket, who painted the building's sixteenth-century Spanish-style murals and still presents a unique program of ballet-pantomimes.

Exhibits on the opera house can be seen in the adjoining Amargosa Gallery.

Amargosa Opera House, State Hwys. 127 and 190, PO Box 8, Death Valley Junction, CA 92328. **Phone:** 760/852-4441. **Fax:** 760/852-4138. **E-mail:** amargosa@kaynet.com. **Website:** amargosaoperahouse.org. **Performance Hours:** Oct.-May—8:15 p.m.; visits by appointment; closed remainder of year. **Admission:** adults, $12; children under 12, $8.

Colorado

TABOR OPERA HOUSE AND MUSEUM. The lavish Tabor Opera House, opened in Leadville, Colorado, in 1879 by silver millionaire Horace A. W. Tabor, once featured Florence Ziegfield's showgirls, John Philip Sousa's marine band, Oscar Wilde's lectures, and the appearance of world boxing champion John L. Sullivan. But Tabor lost the building in the 1893 silver panic, and ownership passed through a number of owners before being saved by Florence Hollister, a 74-year-old retired schoolteacher, who bought the three-story structure in 1955 and then restored and opened it to visitors. When Hollister died in 1965, her heir, Evelyn E. Furman, made the opera house more museumlike.

Tabor Opera House and Museum, 308 Harrison Ave., Leadville, CO 80461 (postal address: 815 Harrison Ave., Leadville, CO 80461). **Phone:** 719/486-1147. **Hours:** Memorial Day weekend-Sept.—9-5:30 Sun.-Fri.; closed Sat. and remainder of year. **Admission:** adults, $4; children 6-12, $2; children under 6, free.

RE-CREATED PIONEER VILLAGES

See also History Museums.

Arizona

ROBSON'S MINING WORLD. See Mining Museums and Mines.

SHARLOT HALL MUSEUM. See Museums Honoring Exceptional Women.

California

EL PUEBLO DE LOS ANGELES HISTORIC MONUMENT. See Historic Parks and Sites.

Colorado

McGRAW MEMORIAL PARK. Helen McGraw Tatum, granddaughter of Edward and Blanche McGraw, who opened the first grocery in Bailey, Colorado, in the early 1870s, gave the land and an 1864 log cabin for the McGraw Memorial Park in the mountain community of Bailey in 1969. The re-created pioneer village now contains eight historic structures. In addition to the 1864 Entriken cabin, the only remaining building from the original town of Bailey, the site contains an 1865 wrought-iron bridge, 1898 one-room schoolhouse, early 1900s train wait station, 1925 summer camp log cabin, and an ore wagon, caboose, and storage building.

McGraw Memorial Park, Park County Historical Society, 39 County Rd. 68, PO Box 43, Bailey, CO 80421. **Phone:** 303/816-9384. **E-mail:** j.d.rankin@excite.com. **Hours:** by appointment. **Admission:** free.

Indiana

LOUIS H. AND LENA FIRN GROVER MUSEUM. See History Museums.

Kansas

HILLSBORO HISTORICAL MUSEUM. See History Museums.

Maine

NORLANDS LIVING HISTORY CENTER. See History Museums.

Maryland

HISTORIC ST. MARY'S CITY. See Margaret Brent Garden in Botanical Gardens and Arboretums.

Massachusetts

WITCH HISTORY MUSEUM. See History Museums.

Michigan

HISTORIC WHITE PINE VILLAGE AND ROSE HAWLEY MUSEUM. Rose Hawley was instrumental in the founding of the Mason County Historical Society, its museum, and the Historic White Pine Village, a re-created nineteenth-century village of 21 buildings with four museums, in Ludington, Michigan.

Hawley served as the first curator of the historical society's museum, which was named for her in 1968. The Rose Hawley Museum is now located at the society's Historic White Pine Village, of which she was the cofounder. Other museums at the pioneer village include the Maritime Museum, Abe Nelson Lumbering Museum, and Scottsville Clown Band's Museum of Music. Among the historic buildings at the site—many with early furnishings and artifacts—are a trapper's cabin, blacksmith shop, one-room schoolhouse, post office, courthouse, chapel, general store, hardware store, and farmhouse.

Historic White Pine Village, Mason County Historical Society, 1687 S. Lakeshore Dr., Ludington, MI 49431. Phone: 231/843-4808. Fax: 231/843-7089. E-mail: whitepine@ masoncounty.net. Website: www.historicwhitepinevillage. org. Hours: mid-Apr.-mid-Oct.—11-5 Tues.-Sat.; closed Sun.-Mon. and remainder of year. Admission: adults, $5; seniors, $4.50; children 6-18, $4; children under 6, free; families, $15.

Missouri

FAUST HISTORICAL VILLAGE. See Faust Park in Historic Parks and Sites.

Montana

HISTORIC VIRGINIA CITY AND NEVADA CITY. See Mining Museums and Mines.

MIRACLE OF AMERICA MUSEUM. See History Museums.

New Mexico

EL RANCHO DE LAS GOLONDRINAS MUSEUM. See Historic Farms and Ranches.

STEINS RAILROAD GHOST TOWN. Larry Link and his wife, Linda Link, have re-created an old western railroad town—called Steins Railroad Ghost Town—in Steins, near Roadforks and Lordsburg, in New Mexico. It has ten buildings and sixteen rooms filled with frontier artifacts and other historical materials dating from the 1800s.

The original town began as a stage stop in 1857, but the stage line was closed in 1861, after Apaches killed five aboard a stagecoach and the Civil War began. Steins came alive again in the 1880s, when the Southern Pacific Railroad built a work station there and the U.S. Army set up a heliograph station on Steins Peak to transmit information about the movements of Geronimo and then such outlaws as Apache Kid and Black Jack Ketchum. When the railroad work station

was closed following World War I, Steins became a ghost town.

The reconstructed town now functions like a living history museum. It has a restored hotel, bordello, and various adobe and stone structures; costumed interpreters; corrals with farm animals; and collections of early clothing, furniture, glass, tools, bottles, and other materials.

Steins Railroad Ghost Town, Interstate 10, Exit 3, PO Box 2185, Roadforks, NM 80045. Phone: 505/542-9791. Hours: Mar.-Oct.—9-7:30 daily; remainder of year—9-5 daily; closed Thanksgiving and Christmas. Admission: grounds—free; buildings—adults and children over 12, $2.50; children under 13, free.

North Dakota

DALE AND MARTHA HAWK MUSEUM. See History Museums.

Ohio

MILAN HISTORICAL MUSEUM. See History Museums.

Oklahoma

HAR-BER VILLAGE. One of the nation's largest re-created pioneer villages—with more than 100 buildings—was started in 1968 near Grove, Oklahoma, by Harvey Jones and his wife, Bernice Jones, who wanted to "preserve for future generations the way of life experienced by our forefathers who carved out of the wilderness this wonderful country we know and enjoy today."

The nineteenth-century village is located on 20 acres adjacent to a lake where the Springdale, Arkansas, couple has their summer home. The village began when Mr. Jones, who owned a large truck line, built a church for his wife from bricks that were handmade before the Civil War. The couple then relocated to the site such historic buildings as a one-room schoolhouse, bank, drugstore, barbershop, inn, courthouse, post office, doctor's and dentist's offices, and log cabins—the largest historic cabin collection in the Midwest.

The village also has replicas of such structures as a general store, a waterwheel, and the gallows used by "Hanging Judge" Isaac C. Parker, as well as numerous artifacts, including an early steam engine, hearse, farm machinery, pottery, glass, china, dresses, hats, shoes, firearms, military items, and Native American artifacts.

Har-Ber Village, 4404 W. 20th St., Grove, OK 74344. **Phone:** 918/786-3488. **Fax:** 918/787-6213. **E-mail:** harbervil@aol.com. **Website:** www.webh.com/grandlake/members/harber. **Hours:** Mar.-mid-Nov.—9-6 Mon.-Sat., 11-6 Sun.; closed remainder of year. **Admission:** free.

Oregon

COLLIER MEMORIAL STATE PARK AND LOGGING MUSEUM. See Historic Parks and Sites.

Texas

GOVERNOR BILL AND VARA DANIEL HISTORIC VILLAGE. The Governor Bill and Vara Daniel Historic Village—part of the Mayborn (formerly Strecker) Museum Complex at Baylor University in Waco, Texas—is named for a former governor of Guam and his wife, who were Texans.

The re-created pioneer village of 23 structures and more than 6,000 artifacts and other objects were donated by Bill Daniel, whose brother, Price Daniel, formerly was governor of Texas. The historic structures include a hotel, church, saloon, and cotton gin. The Mayborn complex's museum is a natural and cultural museum that also operates the Ollie Mae Moen Discovery Center, a downtown children's museum that is moving to the campus (see Children's Museums).

Governor Bill and Vara Daniel Historic Village, Mayborn Museum Complex, Baylor University, S. 4th St., PO Box 97154, Waco, TX 76798-7154. **Phone:** 254/710-1233. **Fax:** 254/710-1173. **E-mail:** calvin_smith@baylor.edu. **Website:** diogenes.baylor.edu/wwwproviders.strecker_museum/. **Hours:** 9-5 Mon.-Fri., 10-4 Sat.; closed Sun. and major holidays. **Admission:** free.

MILLARD'S CROSSING HISTORIC VILLAGE. Millard's Crossing Historic Village, a re-created pioneer village of fourteen original and reconstructed buildings in Nacogdoches, Texas, was founded in the 1970s by Lera Millard Thomas at a site where a railroad track once crossed the Millard family's property. The historic buildings on the 37-acre site range from an 1830s log house to a 1905 chapel and contain such nineteenth-century artifacts as butter churns, iron kettles, and pie safes from the collection of Thomas, daughter of Mr. and Mrs. Jesse Millard, the farm couple who owned the property at the time she was a child there.

Millard's Crossing Historic Village, 6020 North St., PO Box 634221, Nacogdoches, TX 75963. **Phone and Fax:** 936/564-6631. **Hours:** 9-4 Mon.-Sat., 1-4 Sun.; closed New Year's Day, Easter, Thanksgiving, and Christmas. **Admission:** adults, $4; students, $3; children under 12, $2.

Vermont

SHELBURNE MUSEUM. See Art and History Museums.

HISTORIC PARKS AND SITES

See also Historic Farms and Ranches; Historic House Museums; Historic Opera Houses; Memorials to Women; Mining Museums and Mines; Shrines to Women.

Arizona

HUBBELL TRADING POST NATIONAL HISTORIC SITE. The Hubbell Trading Post in Ganado, Arizona, was the first trading post on the Navajo Reservation. It was established in 1876 by John Lorenzo Hubbell, a trusted friend of the Navajo, who married Lina Rubi three years later, and whose family ran the trading post for over 60 years.

During this period Hubbell and his two sons—together or separately—owned 30 trading posts, two wholesale houses, several ranches and farms, business properties, and stage and freight lines in the region. When Hubbell died in 1930, he was buried with his wife and a Navajo friend on a hill overlooking the trading post. Dorothy S. Hubbell, who was married to the youngest son, was a teacher who became a Hubbell trader and carried on the family name and business after the other family members died.

In 1967 the Hubbell Trading Post became a national historic site operated by the National Park Service. The trading post looks much like it did at the turn of the twentieth century. It contains coffee, flour, sugar, calico, and canned goods in the trading area, and jewelry, rugs, blankets, baskets, saddles, saddlebags, bridles, paintings, and other materials in adjoining rooms. Visitors can also tour the adjacent Hubbell home and the nearby visitor center, which has exhibits and demonstrations of rug weaving and other indigenous arts and crafts.

Hubbell Trading Post National Historic Site, State Hwy. 264, PO Box 150, Ganado, AZ 86505. Phone: 520/755-3475. Fax: 520/755-3405. E-mail: hutr_ranger_activities_@nps.gov. Website: www.nps.gov/hutr/. Hours: May-Sept.—8-6 daily; remainder of year—8-5 daily; closed New Year's Day, Thanksgiving, and Christmas. Admission: free.

California

Horticulturist Kate O. Sessions was the first great benefactor of the world-famous Balboa Park in San Diego. She transformed the site from an arid, rocky expanse of chaparral and mulefat scrub into a botanical masterpiece at the turn of the twentieth century. This photo shows the Alcazar Garden, with the park's distinctive California Tower in the background. Courtesy Balboa Park and photographer Brett Shoaf/Artistic Visuals.

BALBOA PARK. Horticulturist Kate O. Sessions is known as the "mother of Balboa Park" in San Diego. She was the park's first great benefactor, transforming it from an arid, rocky expanse of chaparral and mulefat scrub into a botanical masterpiece.

In 1868, only two decades after the discovery of gold in California, San Diego civic leaders reserved the central city site for the 1,200-acre cultural and recreational park that has become one of the world's great urban parks. In 1892 Sessions received 30 acres of land for a private nursery. In return, she was to plant 100 trees a year in the park and 300 trees and other plants elsewhere in the city. For twelve years she planted exotic trees and shrubs that can still be seen at the park and in the city.

The park, originally called City Park, became Balboa Park in 1910, being renamed to honor Vasco Nuñez de Balboa, the first European explorer to sight the Pacific Ocean. It has been the site of two world expositions—the 1915–1916 Panama-California Exposition and the 1935–1936 California-Pacific International Exposition—and today is the home of such facilities as the world-famous San Diego Zoo, Old Globe Theatre, numerous museums, cultural and recreational facilities, and many distinctive Spanish Colonial–style buildings. The park also has a statue of Sessions.

Balboa Park, Visitors Center, House of Hospitality, 1349 El Prado, San Diego, CA 92101. Phone: 619/239-0512. E-mail: ali@balboapark.org. Website: www.balboapark.org. Hours: grounds—24 hours daily; visitors center—9-4 daily; closed New Year's Day and Christmas. Admission: park and visitors center—free; museums—vary, but one-week ticket to 13 museums, $30.

BIDWELL MANSION STATE HISTORIC PARK. The Bidwell Mansion, an 1868 Victorian Italian villa in Chico, California, was the home of General John Bidwell and his wife, Annie Ellicott Kennedy Bidwell, from the time of their marriage in 1868 until their deaths in 1900 and 1918, respectively.

Bidwell, who helped organize the first overland wagon train to Mexican-held California in 1841, struck it rich as a gold miner and became a major agricultural landowner (28,000 acres). He was a major in the Mexican-American War and became a brigadier general in the state militia during the Civil War. In 1864 he was elected to Congress, and he later ran unsuccessfully for governor and president. While in Washington, he met and fell in love with Annie Ellicott Kennedy, daughter of a socially prominent official. After their marriage she dedicated herself to helping the Meechoopda people who lived on the ranch, and worked with her husband to press for election reform, control of monopolies, Prohibition, and women's rights.

The Bidwell Mansion, which became part of the state park system in 1964, has been refurbished and restored to nearly its original appearance. A visitor center in the house contains exhibits on the life and times of the Bidwells and offers guided tours of the mansion.

Bidwell Mansion State Historic Park, 525 The Esplanade, Chico, CA 95926. Phone: 530/895-6144. Fax: 530/895-6699. E-mail: skend@parks.ca.gov. Website: www.cal-parks.ca.gov. Hours: 12-5 Mon.-Fri., 10-5 Sat.-Sun.; closed New Year's Day, Thanksgiving, and Christmas. Admission: adults, $1; children under 17, free.

EL PUEBLO DE LOS ANGELES HISTORIC MONUMENT. El Pueblo de Los Angeles Historic Monument is a 44-acre historic district and museum complex with 27 historic buildings near the site where Mexican and Spanish settlers established a farming community in 1781 that later became Los Angeles.

Although nothing remains of the original earth-and-willow huts, the historic area contains a wide range of nineteenth and early-twentieth-century structures (including four restored as museums) reflecting the heritage of the Hispanic and other ethnic groups that have lived there. The neighborhood was re-created largely through the efforts of Christine Sterling, who vowed in 1926 to restore the area and devoted the next 37 years to the effort. Sterling lived in the 1818 Avila Adobe, the oldest surviving home in the historic district and in Los Angeles, and died in 1963 at the age of 85.

Eleven of the historic buildings are open to the public, including the Avila Adobe. Other open structures include the 1818–1822 Our Lady Queen of Angels Catholic Church, 1858 Masonic Hall, 1884 Old Plaza Firehouse, and 1887 Sepulveda House, which serves as the area's visitor center. Other attractions in the historic district are the ca. 1825 Plaza, the former town square that was landscaped and given its circular form in the 1870s, and Olvera Street, a popular shopping street closed to vehicular traffic and made into a Mexican marketplace in 1930.

El Pueblo de Los Angeles Historic Monument, 125 Paseo de La Plaza, Suite 400, Los Angeles, CA 90012. **Phones:** 213/628-1274 and 213/680-2525. **Fax:** 213/485-8238. **E-mail:** plazala@aol.com. **Website:** cityofla.org/elp/. **Hours:** guided walking tours—10-1 Tues.-Sat.; Olvera Street marketplace—10-7 daily; Spulveda House and visitor center—10-3 Mon.-Sat.; Avila Adobe—9-4 daily; other historic buildings—usually 10-3 Tues.-Sun.; closed Thanksgiving and Christmas. **Admission:** free or donation.

RANCHO LOS CERRITOS HISTORIC SITE. See Historic Farms and Ranches.

Colorado

FOUR MILE HISTORIC PARK. Four Mile Historic Park is a living history museum that features the oldest building in metropolitan Denver—an 1859 structure that Mary Cawker, a 47-year-old widow with two children, ran as a stage stop and wayside inn in 1860–1864.

The house, originally built by two Branter brothers, was sold by Cawker to Levi and Millie Booth, who continued to operate the stage stop and wayside inn but then turned to farming after the railroad reached Denver in 1870. The Booths expanded the house and the 160-acre farm by 500 acres and became agricultural leaders in the state.

The historic house is now the centerpiece of an 11-acre park, which also includes its outbuildings and equipment. Costumed interpreters give guided tours and special events demonstrations of old-time skills and crafts. Horse-drawn rides are also offered when weather permits.

Four Mile Historic Park, 715 S. Forest St., Denver, CO 80222. **Phone:** 303/399-1859. **Fax:** 303/393-0788. **Hours:** Apr.-Sept.—12-4 Wed.-Fri.; 10-4 Sat.-Sun.; closed Mon.-Tues.; remainder of year—12-4 Sat.-Sun.; closed Mon.-Fri. **Admission:** adults, $3.50; seniors and children 6-15, $4; children under 6, free.

Connecticut

BUSH-HOLLEY HISTORIC SITE. See Historic House Museums.

ELIZABETH PARK ROSE GARDENS. See Botanical Gardens and Arboretums.

District of Columbia

MARY McLEOD BETHUNE COUNCIL HOUSE NATIONAL HISTORIC SITE. See Museums Honoring Exceptional Women.

Florida

MARJORIE KINNAN RAWLINGS HISTORIC STATE PARK. The Cracker-style farmhouse of Marjorie Kinnan Rawlings, author of the Pulitzer Prize–winning *The Yearling* and other popular books, is the centerpiece of the Marjorie Kinnan Rawlings State Historic Site in Cross Creek, Florida.

Rawlings came to the "half-wild, backwoods country" in 1928 with her husband, Charles Rawlings, and made a lifelong commitment to the place, growing oranges, cooking on a wood-burning stone, and writing her impressions of the land and her neighbors. She often sat on the wide veranda with her typewriter, writing the books that captured the beauty of Florida and the spirit of its people. She later divorced, remarried, and divided her time between St. Augustine and the Cross Creek retreat, where she continued to write until her death in 1953.

Marjorie Kinnan Rawlings Historic State Park, 19700 S. Country Rd. 325, Cross Creek, FL 32640 (postal address: Rte. 3, Box 92, Hawthorne, FL 32840). **Phone:** 352/466-3672. **Fax:** 352/466-4743. **Hours:** grounds—9-5 daily; house—Oct.-July (tours only): 10-4 Thurs.-Sun.; closed Mon.-Wed.;

Thanksgiving, and Christmas. **Admission:** grounds—free; house tours—adults and children over 12, $3; children 6-12, $2; children under 6, free.

PRESTON B. BIRD AND MARY HEINLEIN REDLAND FRUIT AND SPICE PARK. The Redland Fruit and Spice Park in Homestead, Florida, opened in 1944 and was renamed in 1982 for Preston B. Bird, the first commissioner of parks for the area, and Mary Heinlein, the first superintendent of the park. The 35-acre park has more than 500 species of fruit, nut, and spice trees from throughout the world. Among the other features are a banana grove and an herb and vegetable garden.

Preston B. Bird and Mary Heinlein Redland Fruit and Spice Park, 24801 S.W. 187th Ave., Homestead, FL 33031. **Phone:** 305/247-5727. **Fax:** 305/245-3369. **E-mail:** fsp@co. miamidade.fl.us. **Hours:** 10-5 daily; closed Christmas. **Admission:** adults and children over 12, $3.50; children 4-12, $1; children under 4, free.

ZORA NEALE HURSTON MEMORIAL PARK. The Zora Neale Hurston Memorial Park in the municipal complex in Eatonville, Florida, honors a local woman who became a best-selling author. She was born in Eatonville when it was the only incorporated African American town in the nation, at the turn of the twentieth century. She received literary acclaim in the 1930s and 1940s for such books as *Tell My Horse* and her autobiographical *Dust Tracks on a Road*, only to die in poverty when her fortunes plummeted.

Zora Neale Hurston Memorial Park, 11 People St., Eatonville, FL 32751. **Phone:** 407/623-1166. **Hours:** open 24 hours. **Admission:** free.

Idaho

JULIA DAVIS, ANN MORRISON, AND KATHRYN ALBERTSON PARKS. The city of Boise, Idaho, has three parks named for prominent local women—the Julia Davis Regional Park, Ann Morrison Park, and Kathryn Albertson Park.

The Julia Davis Regional Park in downtown Boise was the first. Forty-three acres were deeded to the city for a park in 1907 by Tom Davis, who owned thousands of agricultural acres in the name of his beloved wife, Julia. Known for her kindness and gracious hospitality, she died after becoming ill while assisting a traveler who may have had typhoid fever. The park, which has grown to 87 acres, is now the site of four museums and a zoo, rose garden, band shell, and playground.

The 153-acre Ann Morrison Park was developed and then given to the city in 1959 by the foundation named for her husband, Harry W. Morrison, founder of the Morrison-Knudsen Company, a major construction firm. Mrs. Morrison, who was active in civic affairs and traveled with her husband to construction sites throughout the world, died in 1957 from leukemia complications. The park has a reflecting pool, gardens, and recreational facilities.

The Kathryn Albertson Park was donated to the city by Joe and Kathryn Albertson in 1989. He was the founder of the Albertson supermarket chain, and the couple became known for their support of community and university activities. The park contains a wildlife sanctuary, fountain, and gazebos.

Julie Davis, Ann Morrison, and Kathryn Albertson Parks, Boise, ID (contact: Boise Parks and Recreation Dept., 1104 Royal Blvd., Boise, ID 83706). **Phone:** 208/384-4240. **Fax:** 208/384-4127. **E-mail:** parks&rec@cityofboise.org. **Website:** www.cityofboise.org/parks. **Hours:** open 24 hours daily. **Admission:** free.

NEZ PERCÉ NATIONAL HISTORICAL PARK. The Nez Percé National Historical Park—which extends for 1,500 miles over five states (Idaho, Montana, Oregon, Washington, and Wyoming)—has its headquarters and a visitor center at the site of the 1838 mission of the Reverend Henry H. Spalding and his wife, Eliza Spalding, near Spalding, Idaho.

The Spaldings came west with Dr. Marcus Whitman and his wife, Narcissa Prentiss Whitman, who established a mission near Walla Walla, Washington (see separate listing under Whitman Mission National Historic Site). They first opened a mission in Lapwai in 1836 to convert the Nez Percé people. But after two years the heat and mosquitoes drove the Spaldings to the nearby banks of the Clearwater River, where the Nez Percé National Historical Park is now headquartered and has a visitor center with artifacts and exhibits relating to the Lewis and Clark Expedition, the Nez Percé, battlefield sites, and the park.

The Spaldings planted Idaho's first orchard, introduced crop irrigation, brought the Northwest's first printing press to publish New Testament verses in Nez Percé translations, and built the first lumber mill, gristmill, and school in the region. None of the Spalding buildings remain at the site of the first mission, although a few of the army's Fort Lapwai structures—built in 1862 to prevent clashes between pioneers and Native Americans—have survived. At the second site, however, visitors can see the fireplace of the Spaldings' house, a Nez Percé tribal cemetery, the 1862 cabin of the Nez Percé Indian Agency, and the 1911 Watson's Store, which served settlers and Native Americans.

The Nez Percé National Park includes 28 sites throughout north central Idaho and ten sites in other states. Each site reflects the history and culture of the Nez Percé and their relationships with early explorers, missionaries, miners, settlers, and soldiers. The Nez Percé War of 1877 resulted after gold was found on the tribe's land, the reservation was reduced to one-tenth its original size, the army threatened to forcibly move dissenters to the smaller reservation, and eighteen settlers were killed by an angered group of young Native Americans after one of their fathers had been slain.

This led to a series of twenty running battles and skirmishes before the Nez Percé surrendered in Montana as they tried to flee to Canada later in the year. The Nez Percé National Historic Trail now marks much of the escape path used by the tribe. After the war the Nez Percé were relocated to Oklahoma for eight years before being allowed to return to the Pacific Northwest.

Nez Percé National Historical Park, State Hwy. 95, Rte. 1, Box 100, Spalding, ID 83540-9715. Phone: 208/843-2261. Fax: 208/843-2001. E-mail: bob_chenoweth@nps.gov. Website: www.nps.gov/nepe/. Hours: May-Sept.—8-5:30 daily; remainder of year—8-4:30 daily; closed New Year's Day, Thanksgiving, and Christmas. Admission: free.

Illinois

LINCOLN HOME NATIONAL HISTORIC SITE. The two-story home where Abraham Lincoln, his wife, Mary Todd Lincoln, and their family lived for seventeen years is part of the Lincoln Home National Historic Site in Springfield, Illinois (see also Mary Todd Lincoln House in Museums Honoring Exceptional Women).

The historic Greek Revival–style house—the only one that the Lincolns ever owned—was built in 1839, purchased in 1844, and later expanded several times to accommodate their growing family. Now restored and part of a four-block historic site, the house tells the story of President Lincoln's rise from humble origins to national prominence. It was in Springfield that he went from a small-town lawyer and local politician to a prominent attorney and political figure of national significance.

After the presidential election the Lincolns gave away or sold most of the furnishings and rented out the house. Robert Lincoln, their surviving son, donated the house to the people of Illinois in 1887, and the state turned it over to the federal government in 1972. It has

now been restored and filled with period furnishings to reflect the tastes of the Lincoln family. It also has a nearby visitor center, where tour tickets can be obtained.

Lincoln Home National Historic Site, 426 S. 7th St., Springfield, IL 62701 (postal address: 413 S. 8th St., Springfield, IL 62701-1905). Phone: 217/492-4241. Fax: 217/492-4673. E-mail: liho_superintendent@nps.gov. Website: www.nps.gov/liho. Hours: Apr.-Oct.—8-6 daily; remainder of year—8:30-5 daily; closed New Year's Day, Thanksgiving, and Christmas. Admission: free

Indiana

LOUIS H. AND LENA FIRN GROVER MUSEUM. See History Museums.

Iowa

ABBIE GARDNER STATE HISTORIC SITE. See Historic House Museums.

LAURA INGALLS WILDER PARK AND MUSEUM. See Museums Honoring Exceptional Women.

Kansas

ADAIR CABIN/JOHN BROWN MUSEUM STATE HISTORIC SITE. See Historic House Museums.

GRINTER PLACE STATE HISTORIC SITE. See Historic House Museums.

HILLSBORO HERITAGE PARK. The Hillsboro Heritage Park in Hillsboro, Kansas, features an 1876 Mennonite adobe house with attached barn and shed built by Peter Loewen and his wife, Anna Loewen, and occupied by the Loewen family and others until 1956, when it was moved to the present site and restored as a city museum. Other structures in the park are an 1886 one-room schoolhouse, another early house, and a replica of an 1876 windmill.

Hillsboro Heritage Park, 501 S. Ash St., Hillsboro, KS 67063. Phone: 316/947-3775. Hours: Mar.-Dec.—10-12 Tues.-Fri., 2-4 Sat.-Sun.; closed Mon., Jan.-Feb., Thanksgiving, and Christmas. Admission: adults, $2; children, $1.

HOLLENBERG STATION STATE HISTORIC SITE. See Historic House Museums.

Louisiana

LONGFELLOW EVANGELINE STATE HISTORIC SITE. The Longfellow Evangeline State Historic Site in St. Martinville, Louisiana, is a blend of legend and history. In legend the area was the meeting place of Longfellow's ill-fated lovers Evangeline and Gabriel, while in history it was a meeting place of exiled French aristocrats fleeing the French Revolution, and of Acadians of Nova Scotia seeking refuge after being expelled by the British.

In the late 1920s a local group wanted to build a monument to Longfellow and his much-loved poem *Evangeline*. The property was acquired and turned over to the state, which made it into one of the first state parks and then a historic site, which also covers Acadian history since Evangeline was described as Acadian.

The site has a ca. 1815 house built by Pierre Olivier du Clozel, a wealthy French Creole sugar planter; a re-created Acadian farmstead with a cabin, detached kitchen, barn, storage buildings, longhorn cattle, and crops; and an interpretive center. The Olivier house is furnished to depict how the family lived in the 1840s; the Acadian farmstead tells about the Acadians and how the *Evangeline* poem relates to them; and the interpretive center contains exhibits that compare the Creole and Acadian lifestyles.

Longfellow Evangeline State Historic Site, 1200 N. Main St., St. Martinville, LA 70582. **Phones:** 337/394-3754 and 888/677-2900. **Fax:** 337/394-3553. **E-mail:** longfellow@crt. state.la.us. **Website:** www.crt.state.la.us. **Hours:** 9-5 daily; closed New Year's Day, Thanksgiving, and Christmas. **Admission:** adults and children over 12, $2; seniors and children under 13, free.

Maryland

CLARA BARTON NATIONAL HISTORIC SITE. See Museums Honoring Exceptional Women.

Massachusetts

ADAMS NATIONAL HISTORICAL PARK. The Adams National Historical Park in Quincy, Massachusetts, commemorates the distinguished men and women of the Adams family who dedicated their lives to the development and service of the United States.

The 14-acre park consists of the birthplace of Presidents John Adams and John Quincy Adams; the 1731 "Old House," home to four generations of the Adams family; and the United First Parish Church, the final resting place of both presidents and their first ladies, Abigail and Louisa Catherine Adams. It also has a visitor center with exhibits, from which guided tours of the historic buildings begin.

In 1735 John Adams, the nation's second president, was born in the Saltbox house located only 75 feet away from the birthplace of his son, John Quincy Adams, who became the sixth president. It was in the latter house that John and his bride, Abigail, started their family, and he launched his career in law and politics (see also Abigail Adams Birthplace in Museums Honoring Exceptional Women).

The Old House, which was called "Peacefield Farm" by John and Abigail Adams, was the home of the Adams family from 1788 to 1927. It has more than 78,000 artifacts, a 14,000-volume library, an eighteenth-century-style garden, and an 1873 carriage house. The United First Parish Church, established in 1639 and built in 1828, is still an active parish. The two presidents and their wives are interred in the crypt beneath the sanctuary.

Both Abigail and Louisa Catherine Adams frequently spoke for women's rights and against slavery. Abigail was especially known for her "progressive ideas," for counseling and influencing her husband in politics and government, and for her extended correspondence during an important period of American history (her many letters were published later, in 1840).

Adams National Historical Park, 135 Adams St., PO Box 531, Quincy, MA 02169-0531. **Phone:** 617/773-1177. **Fax:** 617/471-9683. **E-mail:** adam_visitor_center@nps.gov. **Website:** www.nps.gov/adam. **Hours:** mid-May-mid-Nov.—9-5 daily; remainder of year—historic houses closed, but visitor center open 10-4 Tues.-Fri.; closed Sat.-Mon. and federal holidays. **Admission:** adults, $2; children under 17, free.

BORDERLAND STATE PARK. The Borderland State Park in North Easton, Massachusetts, features the fieldstone mansion and estate of artist and suffragist Blanche Ames and her husband, Oakes Ames, a noted Harvard University botanist. When married in 1900, Mr. Ames said, "you and I are forming a contract . . . we have an equal voice." She lobbied, organized, and campaigned for suffrage and birth control, and also provided illustrations for her husband's scholarly writings. She was later recognized for her portraits, many of which can be seen in the mansion with the family's furnishings and other possessions. A large bell on the lawn that the couple rang daily until suffrage was won is still being rung every day. The grounds, which have been increased to 1,800 acres, also offer hiking trails.

Borderland State Park, 257 Massapoag Ave., North Easton, MA 02356. Phone: 508/238-6566. Fax: 508/230-7193. Website: www.mass.gov/dcr/parks/southeast/bord.htm. Hours: May-Aug.—8-8 daily; remainder of year—varies from 8 to 5-7:30. Admission: free.

Michigan

ELLA SHARP MUSEUM. See Art and History Museums.

Missouri

FAUST PARK. Faust Park—which features the Thornhill Historic Site and the Faust Historical Village—in Chesterfield, Missouri, resulted from donations to St. Louis County by Leicester Faust and his wife, Mary Plant Faust, who became concerned that the state's oldest standing governor's home on their property might not be preserved.

The Thornhill Historic Site contains the estate of Governor Frederick Bates, which includes the 1819–1820 Federal-style Bates home, nine outbuildings, and 98 acres. The adjoining Faust Historical Village primarily spans the 1840–1888 period, but it also refers to the initial settlement of the county, beginning with Thornhill in 1818, and carries through to the twentieth-century Faust estate.

Among the historic buildings relocated to the park are a ca. 1817 house, 1848 log cabin, 1868 barn, ca. 1887 carriage house, and ca. 1889 smokehouse. The village also has period herb gardens, a reconstructed blacksmith shop, guided tours, and living history programs of blacksmithing, spinning, cooking, and log hewing. The annual attendance is around 650,000.

Faust Park (Thornhill Historic Site and Faust Historical Village), 15185 Olive Blvd., Chesterfield, MO 63017. Phone: 314/532-7298. Fax: 314/532-0640. E-mail: jim_foley@co.st.louis.mo.us. Website: www.st.louiscounty-parks.com. Hours: mid-May-Oct.—12-5 Sat.-Sun.; closed Mon.-Fri. and remainder of year. Admission: grounds—free; tours—adults, $2; children, $1.

VAN METER STATE PARK. The 983-acre Van Meter State Park near Miami, Missouri, is named for pioneers Abraham Van Meter and his wife, Elizabeth Van Meter, who settled in the area in the nineteenth century. The land was occupied by prehistoric tribes and then by the Missouri people until the late 1700s.

The Missouri people built a large village on the crest of one of the park's hills, known as the Pinnacles. They had their first contact with Europeans when French explorers Marquette and Jolliet passed through the area in 1673. The tribe had left the area by the end of the eighteenth century, following outbreaks of smallpox and other diseases that ravaged the village, which may once have had as many as 5,000 inhabitants.

The park contains the remains of a six-acre Missouri earthwork construction, known as the "old fort," as well as the burial grounds of the Woodland people, who pre-date the Missouri. Visitor center exhibits now trace the cultural and natural history of the park.

Van Meter State Park, State Hwy. 122, Rte. 1, Box 47, Miami, MO 65344. Phone: 660/886-7537. Fax: 660/886-7512. E-mail: vanmeter@murlin.com. Hours: park—8 a.m.-10 p.m. daily; visitor center—10-4 Thurs.-Mon.; closed Tues.-Wed., New Year's Day, Thanksgiving, and Christmas. Admission: free.

Montana

GRANT-KOHRS RANCH NATIONAL HISTORIC SITE. See Historic Farms and Ranches.

JEANNETTE RANKIN PARK. The nation's first congresswoman and its most celebrated pacifist and feminist is honored at the Jeannette Rankin Park in Missoula, Montana. The park is not far from where she grew up, and is on the same site where Meriwether Lewis of the Lewis and Clark Expedition once camped.

Rankin worked for the passage of suffrage and was elected to Congress in 1916. She became the only person to vote against entering World War I. She later said, "I felt at the time that the first woman [in Congress] should take the first stand, that the first time the first woman had a chance to say no to war she should say it." Rankin was defeated for reelection, but she regained the office and voted against the United States entering World War II in 1941. At the age of 88 in 1968, she also led the Jeannette Rankin Brigade on a march to the Capitol to protest the Vietnam War.

Jeannette Rankin Park, Madison St., Missoula, MT (contact: Parks and Recreation Dept., 100 Hickery St., Missoula, MT 59801). Phone: 406/721-7275. Fax: 406/523-2765. E-mail: jvanfossen@ci.missoula.mt.us. Website: www.ci.missoula.mt.us. Hours: 7 a.m.-11 p.m. daily. Admission: free.

Nebraska

HOMESTEAD NATIONAL MONUMENT OF AMERICA. See Historic Farms and Ranches.

WILLA CATHER STATE HISTORIC SITE. See Museums Honoring Exceptional Women.

New York

ELEANOR ROOSEVELT NATIONAL HISTORIC SITE. See Museums Honoring Exceptional Women.

HOME OF FRANKLIN D. ROOSEVELT NATIONAL HISTORIC SITE. The Home of Franklin D. Roosevelt National Historic Site near Hyde Park, New York, features the 1826 home and the graves of the nation's thirty-second president and his wife, Eleanor Roosevelt.

The house remains largely as it was when the president died in 1945, including the original furnishings, ancestral portraits, naval prints, and memorabilia. The 200-acre estate also has stables, icehouses, a walking trail, an information center, and a rose garden where the graves are marked by a plain white marble monument. The Franklin D. Roosevelt Library and Museum is also located on the grounds. In addition to a research library, it contains three galleries with family possessions and letters tracing the lives and careers of President and Mrs. Roosevelt, as well as photographs, documents, speeches, artworks, gifts from admirers and heads of state, and other historical materials.

Nearby is the Eleanor Roosevelt National Historic Site, located at "Val-Kill," which was Mrs. Roosevelt's home from 1945 until her death in 1962 (see Museums Honoring Exceptional Women).

Home of Franklin D. Roosevelt National Historic Site, U.S. Hwy. 9, 4097 Albany Post Rd., Hyde Park, NY 12538. **Phones:** 845/229-9115, 845/229-9116, and 845/229-2501. **Fax:** 845/229-0739. **E-mail:** rova_superintendent@nps.gov. **Website:** www.nps.gov/hofr. **Hours:** 9-5 daily; closed New Year's Day, Thanksgiving, and Christmas. **Admission:** adults, $10; children under 17, free; combination ticket with Eleanor Roosevelt National Historic Site, Franklin D. Roosevelt Library and Museum, and Vanderbilt Mansion National Historic Site, $18.

SAGAMORE HILL NATIONAL HISTORIC SITE. Sagamore Hill National Historic Site near Oyster Bay, New York, was the home of President Theodore Roosevelt and his wife, Edith Roosevelt. The 1885 Queen Anne house, which served as the "summer White House" during the twenty-sixth president's administration in 1901–1909, contains the personal and household effects of the Roosevelt family, including furniture, trophies, and memorabilia. The nearby Old Orchard

Museum has exhibits and audiovisual programs on Roosevelt's career and family life.

Sagamore Hill National Historic Site, 20 Sagamore Hill Rd., Oyster Bay, NY 11771-1899. **Phones:** 516/922-4788 and 516/922-4447. **Fax:** 516/922-4792. **Website:** www.nps.gov/sahi. **Hours:** grounds—9:30-dusk daily; house—Memorial Day-day before Columbus Day: 9:30-5 daily; remainder of year: 9:30-4 daily; closed New Year's Day, Thanksgiving, and Christmas. **Admission:** adults, $5; children under 17, free.

WOMEN'S RIGHTS NATIONAL HISTORICAL PARK. See Women's Museums, Galleries, and Halls of Fame.

North Carolina

HISTORIC BATH STATE HISTORIC SITE. See Historic House Museums.

North Dakota

CROSS RANCH STATE PARK AND NATURE PRESERVE. See Historic Farms and Ranches.

Ohio

ANNIE OAKLEY MEMORIAL PARK. The Annie Oakley Memorial Park in Greenville, Ohio, honors Phoebe Ann Moses, the Wild West sharpshooter who went by the name of Annie Oakley. She grew up in Greenville with her widowed mother and helped pay off their house's mortgage with her earnings from hunting, and later achieved fame for her shooting exploits while touring with the Buffalo Bill Wild West Show. The park features a life-size bronze statue of Oakley, who is buried in Brock Cemetery in Greenville.

Annie Oakley Memorial Park, Broadway, Washington St., and Martin St., Greenville, OH (contact: Greenville Parks and Recreation Dept., Room 240, 100 Public Sq., Greenville, OH 45331). **Phone:** 937/548-1314. **Fax:** 937/548-4491. **Hours:** open 24 hours. **Admission:** free.

FIRST LADIES NATIONAL HISTORIC SITE. See Women's Museums, Galleries, and Halls of Fame.

Oklahoma

ARTHUR BOWRING SANDHILLS RANCH STATE HISTORICAL PARK. See Historic Farms and Ranches.

Oregon

COLLIER MEMORIAL STATE PARK AND LOGGING MU-SEUM. The Collier Memorial State Park and Logging Museum near Chiloquin, Oregon, was established with a gift of 146 acres to the state in 1945 by Alfred and Andrew Collier as a memorial to their parents, Charles and Janet Collier. The museum, which began two years later, features the Collier brothers' donated collection of antique logging equipment that shows the evolution of logging equipment from the use of oxen and axes to trucks and chain saws.

The park now has a re-created pioneer village and one of the nation's largest collections of early logging equipment. The pioneer village consists of twelve historic buildings moved from elsewhere and filled with artifacts, while the logging equipment includes many types of saws, axes, and other small tools; donkey steam engines; skidding and moving equipment; wagons and carts; trucks and tractors; and a steam locomotive and other railroad equipment.

Collier Memorial State Park and Logging Museum, 46000 U.S. Hwy. 97 North, Chiloquin, OR 97624. **Phone:** 541/783-2471. **Fax:** 541/783-2707. **Website:** www.prd.state.or.us. **Hours:** park—open 24 hours; museum—Apr.-Oct.: 8-8 daily; remainder of year: 8-4 daily. **Admission:** free.

Rhode Island

HANNAH ROBINSON PARK. Local legend holds that a young girl named Hannah Robinson sat on a large rock and cried over a tortured love affair at the site of a state park now named for her near South Kingstown, Rhode Island. The park—also known as Sad Rock, Crying Rock, and Meditation Rock—features the rock and a 100-foot tower that offers spectacular views of Narragansett Bay and the Rhode Island shoreline.

Hannah Robinson Park, U.S. Hwy. 1 and State Hwy. 138 South Kingstown, RI (contact: South Kingstown Chamber of Commerce, 328 Main St., PO Box 289, Wakefield, RI 02880-0289). **Phone:** 401/783-2801. **Fax:** 401/789-3120. **E-mail:** skcc@netsense.net.skchamber.com. **Phone:** 401/884-2010. **Website:** riparks.com. **Hours:** dawn-dusk daily. **Admission:** free.

South Dakota

PRAIRIE HOMESTEAD HISTORIC SITE. See Historic House Museums.

Texas

GEORGE RANCH HISTORICAL PARK. See Historic Farms and Ranches.

OLD FORT PARKER STATE HISTORIC SITE. Old Fort Parker State Historic Site is a re-created fort between Groesbeck and Mexia, Texas, that honors the Parker family and other pioneers who settled in the area in the 1830s. It is best known, however, in connection with the story of Cynthia Ann Parker, who was taken into captivity by the Comanche people in 1836.

Baptist elder John Parker and three of his sons built the original fort in 1833–1834 on a Mexican land grant to protect the nearby homesteads. Several hundred Comanches overran the fort in a surprise attack in 1836, killing five members of the Parker family and capturing five persons, including nine-year-old Cynthia Ann Parker.

Cynthia Ann grew up among the Comanches, married Chief Peta Nacona, and lived with the tribe until she was rescued by the Texas Rangers with her two-year-old daughter, Prairie Flower, 24 years later. She was also the mother of two others, including Quanah Parker, the last great Comanche chief. Cynthia Ann was never able to readjust to Anglo-American society, and died in 1864, four years after her rescue and six months after her daughter died. Chief Quanah Parker later reburied her remains at the Post Oak Mission cemetery near his home in Cache, Oklahoma, and was interred next to her when he died. However, they and 700 other Comanches buried at the mission were moved to Fort Sill in Oklahoma in 1957 so that the military could build proving grounds for guided missiles at the site.

Fort Parker was reconstructed twice—in 1936 and 1967. It has an upright split cedar stockade, two two-story blockhouses, and six log cabins where the families of the Parker brothers and other members of the pioneer group lived in 1834–1836 before moving to Fort Houston near present-day Palestine. The fort also has a museum/visitor center with pioneer and Comanche artifacts and exhibits on the history of the fort and Cynthia Ann Parker.

Old Fort Parker State Historic Site, Park Rd., Rte. 3, Box 746, Groesbeck, TX 76642. **Phone:** 254/724-5253. **Fax:** 254/729-3501. **E-mail:** ketron2@aol.com. **Hours:** 9-5 daily; closed New Year's Day and Christmas. **Admission:** adults, $2; children 6-11, $1; children under 6, free.

VARNER-HOGG PLANTATION STATE HISTORICAL PARK. The Varner-Hogg Plantation State Historical

Park in West Columbia, Texas, was the site of socialite Ima Hogg's estate and country home. It became a state park in 1958. The land was originally obtained by Martin Varner in an 1824 land grant. He was one of the 300 American colonists that Stephen F. Austin—known as the "father of Texas"—brought to the area, where the first capital of the Republic of Texas was established in 1836.

Miss Hogg was the daughter of former Governor James Stephen Hogg, who purchased the property in 1901. She lived in the restored ca. 1835 Colonial-style home, which is now the park museum and interprets the 1835–1850 plantation period in Texas, the Civil War, cattle ranching, and the area's political and multicultural history. Her principal home—a Latin Colonial–style mansion in Houston—has become the Bayou Bend Collection and Gardens, a branch of the Museum of Fine Arts, featuring more than 4,800 artworks and eight formal gardens (see separate listing in Art Museums).

Varner-Hogg Plantation State Historical Park, 1702 N. 13th St., PO Box 696, West Columbia, TX 77486. Phone: 979/345-4656. Fax: 979/345-4412. E-mail: varner-hogg@computron. net. Website: www.tpwd.state.tx.us. Hours: 9-4:30 Wed.-Sat., 1-4:30 Sun.; closed Mon.-Tues. Admission: adults, $4; children over 5, $2; children under 6, free.

Vermont

MOLLY STARK STATE PARK. Molly Stark State Park, between Wilmington and Marlboro, Vermont, is named for Elizabeth Page "Molly" Stark, a Revolutionary War heroine. She was the wife of Colonel John Stark and cared for her husband's wounded compatriots in their home. She is also known for riding wildly after her husband to deliver his uniforms after he rushed away without them upon hearing that the British had invaded Boston harbor.

Molly Stark State Park, 705 State Hwy. 9, Wilmington, VT 05363 (contact: Vermont Agency of Natural Resources, Dept. of Forests, Parks, and Recreation, 103 S. Main St., Bldg. 10 South, Waterbury, VT 05671). Phone: 802/241-3650. Fax: 802/244-1481. Website: www.vt.stateparks.com. Hours: May-mid-Oct.—9-dusk daily; closed remainder of year. Admission: adults and children over 13, $2; children 4-13, $1.50; children under 4, free.

Virginia

ELLANOR C. LAWRENCE PARK. Ellanor C. Lawrence lived in a renovated 1780 house on a 640-acre site near Chantilly, Virginia, from 1935 to 1969—and then gave the property to the Fairfax County Park Authority for use as a park, which was named for her. The park's Walney Visitor Center contains exhibits on David and Ellanor Lawrence; James and Carolyn Machen, whose family built the house and lived on the property from 1843 to 1913; prehistoric peoples who lived in the county; the Civil War; tobacco farming; live animals; and other subjects.

Ellanor C. Lawrence Park, Walney Visitor Center, 5040 Walney Rd., Chantilly, VA 20151-2306. Phone: 703/631-0013. Fax: 703/378-2535. E-mail: charles.smith@co.fairfax.va.us. Website: www.fairfax.va.us/parks/ecl. Hours: Mar.-Dec.— 9-5 Mon. and Wed.-Fri., 12-5 Sat.-Sun.; closed Tues., Thanksgiving, and Christmas; Jan.-Feb.—12-5 Wed.-Mon.; closed Tues. and New Year's Day. Admission: free.

MAGGIE L. WALKER NATIONAL HISTORIC SITE. See Museums Honoring Exceptional Women.

Washington

ESTHER SHORT PARK. The Esther Short Park in Vancouver, Washington, honors the founder of the city who defied British authorities of the Hudson's Bay Company—who did not want any American settlers—when she and her husband arrived in 1845 and refused to leave. She later laid out the frontier town and then donated this block-square park to the public in 1855. The park features a heroic bronze statue of a pioneer woman with a rifle and three children clutching her skirt—symbolic of the efforts of Esther Short to protect her home and ten children.

Esther Short Park, 800 Columbia St., Vancouver, WA (contact: Vancouver-Clark Parks and Recreation Dept., 603 W. Evergreen Blvd., Vancouver, WA 98660). Phone: 360/696-8171. Fax: 360/696-8009. Website: www.ci.vancouver.wa.us. Hours: open 24 hours. Admission: free.

SACAJAWEA STATE PARK. Sacajawea State Park, at the confluence of the Snake and Columbia rivers near Pasco, Washington, is named for the Shoshone woman who was an interpreter and guide for the Lewis and Clark Expedition that explored the Louisiana Purchase and the land beyond to the Pacific Ocean in 1803–1806.

Sacajawea, the sole woman in the expedition, was captured by the Mandan and traded to Toussaint Charbonneau, a French-Canadian trapper, who had been living among the Native Americans. He married her in 1804, and then joined the Lewis and Clark Expedition when it arrived among the Mandan near present-day

Bismarck, North Dakota. Charbonneau was hired as an interpreter, and Sacajawea was allowed to accompany the party and gave birth to a baby boy along the way.

In 1805 the expedition made its first contact with Sacajawea's Shoshones. She helped the party obtain horses through the goodwill of her brother, who had become chief of the Lemhi. Charbonneau and Sacajawea then enabled the party to communicate with various other tribes of the Plains and the Northwest and to complete the return journey. Sacajawea is believed to have died in 1812 at Fort Manuel near Omaha, but there is some question as to where she is buried.

The park has an interpretive center with exhibits on the expedition, Native American culture in the area, and stone and bone tools of the early Columbia Plateau peoples.

Sacajawea State Park, 2503 Sacajawea Park Rd., Pasco, WA 99301. Phone: 509/545-2361. Hours: park—Mar.-Oct.: dawn-dusk daily; closed remainder of year; interpretive center—Apr.-Sept.: 1-5 Fri.-Tues.; closed remainder of week and year. **Admission:** free.

WHITMAN MISSION NATIONAL HISTORIC SITE. The 1836 Waiilatpu mission established by Dr. Marcus Whitman and his wife, Narcissa Prentiss Whitman, is memorialized at the Whitman Mission National Historic Site near Walla Walla, Washington. The mission served the Cayuse, Walla Walla, and Umatilla peoples until 1847, when the Whitmans were killed in a Cayuse uprising during a measles epidemic.

Whitman was a young medical doctor from western New York who hoped to combine his new medical skills with his religious zeal to convert native peoples in the Oregon Territory. After he learned that the American Board of Commissioners of Foreign Missions frowned on bachelors, he met and married another ardent single applicant, Narcissa Prentiss. The Whitmans then joined the Reverend Henry Spalding and Eliza Spalding, another young missionary couple, on their way to

Oregon. However, they argued along the trail and decided to establish separate missions about 100 miles apart—the Whitmans at Waiilatpu and the Spaldings at Lapwai, Idaho, near present-day Lewiston (see separate listing under Nez Percé National Historical Park).

The Whitman mission achieved moderate success through the mid-1840s, but the white settlers who followed brought diseases that were deadly to people without immunity. As a result, the Cayuse tribe was among those nearly decimated by a measles epidemic in 1847. In November, angry Cayuse men broke into the mission, burned the buildings, killed Marcus and Narcissa Whitman and eleven others, and took 48 men, women, and children as captives.

Since becoming a historic site, the area has been excavated and the sites of early buildings outlined. A trail now takes visitors to the building sites, restored millpond, apple orchard, irrigation ditch, grave area, memorial shaft, and a portion of the old Oregon Trail. Exhibits on the Whitman story and the missionary era in the Pacific Northwest are presented in a visitor center, and demonstrations are given during summer weekends of such pioneer crafts as butter churning, candle dipping, and wool dyeing, and Native American skills like cornhusk finger weaving, tulle mat construction, and cooking.

Whitman Mission National Historic Site, 328 Whitman Mission Rd., Rte. 2, Box 247, Walla Walla, WA 99362-9699. **Phone:** 509/522-6360. **Fax:** 509/522-6355. **E-mail:** whmi_interpretation@ nps.gov. **Website:** www.nps.gov/whmi. **Hours:** June-Aug.—8-6 daily; remainder of year—8-4:30 daily; closed New Year's Day, Thanksgiving, and Christmas. **Admission:** adults, $3; children under 17, free; families, $5.

Wisconsin

VILLA LOUIS HISTORIC SITE. See Other Historic Houses.

Science-based Museums and Facilities

NATURAL HISTORY MUSEUMS

See also Botanical Gardens and Arboretums; Cultural Art and History Museums; Earth Sciences Museums; Nature and Wildlife Centers; Science and Technology Centers.

Arizona

MUSEUM OF NORTHERN ARIZONA. See General Museums.

Arkansas

ARKANSAS MUSEUM OF SCIENCE AND HISTORY. Bernie Babcock was a young Arkansas widow who crusaded for Prohibition and suffrage and worked as a journalist, poet, and author (eventually publishing 26 novels). She was disturbed that Arkansans were being criticized for lacking cultural centers and set out to correct the impression by starting a museum.

The result was the Arkansas Museum of Science and History, which she almost single-handedly established in Little Rock in 1927. Babcock, who was the first woman from Arkansas to be listed in *Who's Who in America*, became curator of the museum and served until she was 85. She died in 1962 at the age of 94.

The city-operated museum—now also known as the Museum of Discovery—contains collections and exhibits of birds, mammals, reptiles, invertebrates, plants, Native American artifacts, pioneer items, and South American and African anthropological objects, and serves more than 110,000 visitors annually.

Arkansas Museum of Science and History, 500 E. Markham St., Little Rock, AR 72201. **Phone:** 501/396-7050. **Fax:** 501/396-7054. **E-mail:** amod@aristotle.net. **Website:** www.amod.org. **Hours:** 9-5 Mon.-Sat. (also 9 a.m.-9 p.m. 1st Fri. of month), 1-6 Sun.; closed New Year's Day, Thanksgiving, and Christmas. **Admission:** adults, $5.95; seniors, $5; children 3-12, $5.50; children under 3, free.

California

MUSEUM OF VERTEBRATE ZOOLOGY AND MUSEUM OF PALEONTOLOGY. Annie Montague Alexander was a wealthy naturalist who founded and endowed two museums at the University of California at Berkeley—the Museum of Vertebrate Zoology in 1908 and the Museum of Paleontology in 1921—and had more than fifteen fossil, plant, and mammal species named for her.

Alexander, the daughter of a successful sugarcane planter in Hawaii, was an intrepid and persistent explorer and collector who uncovered rare fossils and tens of thousands of specimens of mammals, birds, amphibians, and plants—and gave many of them to the museums. She celebrated her eightieth birthday in 1947 by going on a three-month collecting trip to Baja, in what turned out to be her last expedition. She died three years later, after a stroke.

The Museum of Vertebrate Zoology and the Museum of Paleontology are primarily teaching and research institutions. The former features collections of amphibians, reptiles, birds, mammals, and other aspects of natural history, while the latter contains fossil vertebrates, invertebrates, plants, mollusk shells, foraminifera, vertebrate skeletal elements, marine sediments, protists, amber, and sedimentary rock samples.

Museum of Vertebrate Zoology, University of California, Berkeley, 3101 Valley Life Sciences Bldg., Berkeley, CA 94720-3160. **Phone:** 510/642-3567. **Fax:** 510/643-8238. **E-mail:** mvquery@uclink.berkeley.edu. **Website:** www.mip.berkeley.edu/mvz/. **Hours:** open by appointment only to research scientists, students, and agency personnel. **Admission:** free.

Museum of Paleontology, University of California, Berkeley, 1101 Valley Life Sciences Bldg., Berkeley, CA 94720-4780.

Phone: 510/642-1821. Fax: 510/642-1822. E-mail: webmaster@ucmpl.berkeley.edu. Website: www.ucmp. berkeley.edu. Hours: 8-5 Mon.-Fri. (also to 10 p.m. Mon.-Thurs.), 10-5 Sat., 1-10 Sun.; hours vary in summer and on some holidays; closed major holidays. Admission: free.

Connecticut

CONNECTICUT AUDUBON BIRDCRAFT MUSEUM. See Nature and Wildlife Centers.

Florida

SOUTH FLORIDA MUSEUM OF NATURAL HISTORY. The South Florida Museum of Natural History in Dania Beach was originally named the Graves Museum of Archaeology and Natural History, in honor of Ottalie Graves, who spearheaded the museum's founding and provided funds for its establishment in nearby Fort Lauderdale in the 1980s. The museum's name was changed in 2001 after a move to larger facilities in Dania Beach.

The museum's collections include Tequesta Indian ceramics, shell bone materials and burials, dinosaur materials, Florida minerals and crystals, archaeological materials, Egyptian artifacts, and pre-Columbian and African tribal art. Among the other exhibits are displays on Pleistocene mammals, evolution, and replicas of an Egyptian tomb and a Turkish Mugla house.

South Florida Museum of Natural History, 481 S. Federal Hwy., Dania Beach, FL 33004. Phone: 954/925-7770. Fax: 954/925-7064. E-mail: dig-it@sfmuseumnh.org. Website: sfmuseumnh.org. Hours: 10-4 Tues.-Fri., 10-6 Sat., 12-6 Sun., closed Mon. and most major holidays. Admission: adults, $9.95; seniors and students, $7; children 4-12, $6; children under 4, free.

Hawaii

BISHOP MUSEUM. See Archaeology, Anthropology, and Ethnology Museums.

Illinois

BURPEE MUSEUM OF NATURAL HISTORY. The Burpee Museum of Natural History in Rockford, Illinois, was founded in 1942 by undertaker Harry Burpee and his wife, Della Burpee, who also established the Harry and Della Burpee Art Gallery, which became the Rockford Art Museum (see Art Museums). The museum, housed in two Victorian-era mansions linked by a contemporary three-story gallery, has collections and exhibits pertaining to animals, birds, plants, minerals, fossils, rocks, archaeology, and Native Americans. One of its featured attractions is a full-size *Tyrannosaurus rex* skeleton.

Burpee Museum of Natural History, 737 N. Main St., Rockford, IL 61103. Phone: 815/965-3433. Fax: 815/965-2703. E-mail: wsburpee@aol.com. Hours: 10-5 Tues.-Sat., 12-5 Sun; closed Mon. and national holidays. Admission: adults, $4; children 3-18, $3; children under 3 and Wed. admission free.

PEGGY NOTEBAERT NATURE MUSEUM. Peggy Notebaert Nature Museum is the name of the Chicago Academy of Sciences' new museum—named for the wife of a board member who made a major donation in honor of the couple's thirtieth wedding anniversary. The academy's original museum, founded in 1857, was replaced by the new museum building in 1999. It has more than 250,000 specimens—mostly from the turn of the twentieth century—and exhibits related to midwestern flora, fauna, and waterways, including a large butterfly section.

Peggy Notebaert Nature Museum, Chicago Academy of Sciences, 2430 N. Cannon Dr., Chicago, IL 60614. Phone: 773/755-5100. Fax: 773/755-5188. E-mail: cas@chias.org. Website: www.chias.org. Hours: 9-4:30 Mon.-Fri.; 10-5 Sat.-Sun.; closed New Year's Day, Thanksgiving, and Christmas. Admission: adults, $6; seniors and children 3-17, $4; children under 3, free.

Maryland

CARRIE WEEDOM SCIENCE CENTER. The Carrie Weedom Science Center in Galesville, Maryland, is named for a science teacher who worked in the building when it was an elementary school. Founded in 1988, the science center, which has natural science collections, exhibits, and programs, serves as a field-trip laboratory for Anne Arundel County public schools.

Carrie Weedom Science Center, 911 Galesville Rd., Galesville, MD 20765. Phone: 410/222-1625. Fax: 410/867-0588. Hours: 9-3 Mon.-Fri. (limited to county public school students); closed Sat.-Sun. and school holidays and breaks. Admission: free.

Michigan

CRANBROOK INSTITUTE OF SCIENCE. The Cranbrook Institute of Science in Bloomfield Hills, Michigan, is a natural history and physical sciences museum founded in 1932 by newspaper publisher George Booth and his wife, Ellen Scripps Booth, as part of the Cranbrook

Educational Community, which also contains an art academy, three schools, and the Cranbrook Art Museum (see Art Museums). The Booths' 1908 historic home and gardens—known as Cranbrook House and Gardens—are also on the grounds (see Historic House Museums).

The Cranbrook Institute of Science has more than 150,000 artifacts and specimens in its collections, including one of the finest mineralogy collections in the world. The institute presents permanent and changing exhibits and programs and conducts research in natural history and science. It also has a planetarium, observatory, herbarium, and nature center.

Cranbrook Institute of Science, 39221 N. Woodward Ave., PO Box 801, Bloomfield Hills, MI 48303-0801. **Phone:** 248/645-3204. **Fax:** 248/345-3050. **Website:** www.cranbrook.edu/institute/. **Hours:** 10-5 daily (also to 10 p.m. Fri.); closed New Year's Day, Fourth of July, Thanksgiving, and Christmas. **Admission:** adults, $7; seniors, students, and children 3-17, $4; children under 3, free.

Mississippi

MISSISSIPPI MUSEUM OF NATURAL SCIENCE. The Mississippi Museum of Natural Science in Jackson is a memorial to founder Frances A. "Fannye" Cook, who also was instrumental in starting the parent Mississippi Department of Wildlife, Fisheries, and Parks.

Cook began a campaign in 1926 to protect the state's vanishing wildlife after two years of drought and fire. She conducted annual animal censuses, worked to create the state's game and fish commission, and served as director and curator of the predecessor Wildlife Museum, founded in 1933, for 25 years. In 1964 the Mississippi Legislature passed a resolution commending her life, and the Mississippi Game and Fish Commission renamed the museum the State Wildlife Museum, the Fannye A. Cook Memorial. A statue of her now stands in the museum, which later became the Mississippi Museum of Natural History.

The museum has collections of botany, herpetology, ichthyology, invertebrates, mammalogy, ornithology, and paleontology, with an emphasis on Mississippi materials. The exhibits feature dioramas and aquariums depicting Mississippi habitats.

Mississippi Museum of Natural Science, 2148 Riverside Dr., Jackson, MS 39202. **Phone:** 601/354-7303. **Fax:** 601/354-7227. **Website:** www.mdwft.state.ms.us/museum. **Hours:** 8-5 Mon.-Fri., 9-5 Sat., 1-5 Sun.; closed Mon., New Year's Day, Fourth of July, Thanksgiving, and Christmas.

Admission: adults, $4; seniors, $4; children 3-18, $2; children under 3, free.

Nevada

MARJORIE BARRICK MUSEUM OF NATURAL HISTORY. The Marjorie Barrick Museum of Natural History at the University of Nevada, Las Vegas, was founded in 1967 with funds from a former showgirl who married and became a community philanthropist. The museum, which focuses on the natural history of southern Nevada and the Mojave Desert, has invertebrate and vertebrate fossils, fish, geological and herpetological specimens, archaeological findings, and a botanical garden.

Marjorie Barrick Museum of Natural History, University of Nevada, Las Vegas, 4505 Maryland Pkwy., Las Vegas, NV 89154-4012. **Phone:** 702/895-3381. **Fax:** 702/895-3094. **Website:** hrcweb.lv-hrc.nevada.edu/mbm/index/html. **Hours:** 8-4:45 Mon.-Fri., 10-2 Sat.; closed Sun. and national holidays. **Admission:** free.

New Mexico

RUTH HALL MUSEUM OF PALEONTOLOGY. The Ruth Hall Museum of Paleontology is named for an amateur paleontologist and wife of the first permanent director of the Presbyterian Church's Ghost Ranch Conference Center near Abiquiu, New Mexico, where the museum adjoins the Florence Hawley Ellis Museum of Anthropology (see Archaeology, Anthropology, and Ethnology Museums). Ghost Ranch is the home of the *Coelophysis* state fossil and the location of fossil materials from the Triassic Age.

Ruth Hall Museum of Paleontology, Ghost Ranch Conference Center, U.S. Hwy. 84, HC 77, Box 11, Abiquiu, NM 87510. **Phone:** 505/685-4333, Ext. 118. **Fax:** 505/685-4519. **Website:** www.newmexico-ghostranch.org. **Hours:** 9-12 and 1-5 Tues.-Sat. (also 1-5 Sun. in summer); closed Sun.-Mon., Easter, Thanksgiving, and last two weeks of Dec. **Admission:** suggested donations—adults, $2; seniors and children, $1.

Texas

WITTE MUSEUM. See General Museums.

Virginia

LORA ROBINS GALLERY OF DESIGN FROM NATURE. Lora McGlasson Robins donated her collection and funds to establish the Lora Robins Gallery of Design from Nature in 1977 at the University of Richmond in Richmond, Virginia. The gallery's collections and displays consist largely of minerals, fossils, seashells, and gemstones, with cultural arts and artifacts from around the world. The gallery moved into an expanded 25,000-square-foot facility in 1989.

Lora Robins Gallery of Design from Nature, Richmond Way, University of Richmond, Richmond, VA 23173. **Phone:** 804/289-8276. **Fax:** 804/287-6467. **E-mail:** museums@richmond.edu. **Website:** www.richmond.edu/cultural/museums/index.html. **Hours:** 11-5 Tues.-Fri., 1-5 Sat.-Sun.; closed Mon. and university holidays and breaks. **Admission:** free.

Wyoming

DRAPER MUSEUM OF NATURAL HISTORY. The newest of the five museums at the Buffalo Bill Historical Center in Cody, Wyoming, is the Draper Museum of Natural History, a 37,000-square-foot wing named for trustee and benefactor Nancy-Carroll

Draper. The $17 million museum, which opened in 2002, explores human interaction with the natural world, leading visitors down an interpretive trail through the sights and sounds of the greater Yellowstone ecosystem.

The umbrella historical center began in a log cabin in 1917 with the Buffalo Bill Museum, which moved to its present site in 1969. Other facilities located at the multifaceted complex are the Whitney Gallery of Western Art (see Art Museums), Plains Indian Museum, Cody Firearms Museum, and McCracken Research Library.

Draper Museum of Natural History, Buffalo Bill Historical Center, 720 Sheridan Ave., Cody, WY 82414. **Phone:** 307/587-4771. **Fax:** 307/587-5714. **E-mail:** thomb@bbhc.org. **Website:** www.bbhc.org. **Hours:** Apr.—10-5 daily; May—8 a.m.-8 p.m. daily; June-mid-Sept.—7 a.m.-8 p.m.; mid-Sept.-Oct.—8-5 daily; Nov.-Mar.—10-3 Tues.-Sun.; closed Mon. **Admission:** adults, $10; college students, $6; children 6-17, $4; children under 6, free.

ARCHAEOLOGY, ANTHROPOLOGY, AND ETHNOLOGY MUSEUMS

See also Cultural Art and History Museums; Natural History Museums.

Arizona

HEARD MUSEUM. See Cultural Art and History Museums.

California

ANTELOPE VALLEY INDIAN MUSEUM. See Cultural Art and History Museums.

PHOEBE A. HEARST MUSEUM OF ANTHROPOLOGY. Phoebe Apperson Hearst, the wife of Senator George Hearst and mother of newspaper publisher William Randolph Hearst, was a patron of the sciences, arts, and social causes at the turn of the twentieth century. One of her projects was a new anthropology museum founded in 1901 at the University of California, Berkeley—supporting systematic collecting by archaeologists and ethnologists principally in ancient Egypt, pre-Columbian Peru, and California.

Because of her early role, the name of the museum—which had become the Lowie Museum of Anthropology—was changed to the Phoebe A. Hearst Museum of Anthropology in 1991. The artifacts collected from expeditions Hearst sponsored within

California and to Egypt, Peru, Guatemala, and the Mediterranean still form the nucleus of the museum's collections, which have grown from 230,000 to approximately 3.8 million objects. Later, major collections were acquired from the peoples of the Arctic, Africa, and Oceania—and now nearly every past and present culture is represented. The museum's research collections are considered among the finest in North America.

Phoebe A. Hearst Museum of Anthropology, University of California, Berkeley, 103 Kroeber Hall, Berkeley, CA 94720-3712. **Phone:** 510/642-3682. **Fax:** 510/642-6271. **E-mail:** pahma@uclink.berkeley.edu. **Website:** www.qal.berkeley.edu/~hearst. **Hours:** 10-4:30 Wed.-Sun.; closed Mon.-Tues. and university holidays. **Admission:** adults and children over 10, $2; seniors, $1; children under 11, 50¢.

Hawaii

BISHOP MUSEUM. The Bishop Museum, Hawaii's oldest, largest, and most popular museum, was founded in Honolulu in 1889 by Charles Reed Bishop as a memorial to his late wife, Princess Bernice Pauahi Bishop,

The Hawaiian Hall, a Victorian masterpiece built in 1898–1903, is still the premier gallery at the Bishop Museum in Honolulu. The museum was founded in 1899 by banker Charles Reed Bishop in memory of his wife, Princess Bernice Pauahi Bishop, the last living direct descendant of Kamehameha, unifier of the Hawaiian Kingdom. Courtesy Bishop Museum.

the last direct descendant of the royal Kamehameha family. She was the heir apparent to the kingdom of Hawaii (before it became a state), but she declined to take the throne so she could devote herself to the cause of educating Hawaiian children.

The museum, which has an annual attendance of 450,000, was originally established to house a large collection of Hawaiian artifacts and royal family heirlooms of the princess. It has since become a center of cultural and natural history in the Pacific, with over 1 million artifacts and 2 million plant and animal specimens. It has one of the finest collections of feather caps, helmets, kahilis (royal standards), and other Hawaiian cultural and artistic works.

The 1891 Hawaiian Hall, one of the museum's three main buildings, features exhibits and artifacts on the history of the Hawaiian and Pacific Island peoples, as well as the region's natural history and royal treasures.

The museum also operates the Hawaii Maritime Center, which covers the maritime history of the islands, and the 15-acre Amy B. H. Greenwell Ethnobotanical Gardens on the island of Hawaii (see Botanical Gardens and Arboretums).

Bishop Museum, 1525 Bernice St., Honolulu, HI 96817-0916. **Phone:** 808/847-3511. **Fax:** 808/841-8968. **E-mail:** webmaster@bishopmuseum.org. **Website:** www. bishopmuseum.org. **Hours:** 9-5 daily; closed Christmas. **Admission:** resident adults and children over 12, $7.95; nonresident adults and children over 12, $14.95; resident seniors and children 4-12, $6.95; nonresident seniors and children 4-12, $11.95; children under 4, free.

Illinois

MITCHELL MUSEUM OF THE AMERICAN INDIAN. See Cultural Art and History Museums.

SCHINGOETHE CENTER FOR NATIVE AMERICAN CULTURES. See Cultural Art and History Museums.

SPURLOCK MUSEUM. See Cultural Art and History Museums.

Kansas

MARTIN AND OSA JOHNSON SAFARI MUSEUM. See Museums Honoring Exceptional Women.

Maine

HUDSON MUSEUM. The Hudson Museum, which explores the cultures of the world at the University of Maine in Orono, was founded in 1986 with a donation from alumnus J. Russell Hudson in memory of his wife, Caroline Doane Hudson. Located in the Maine Center for the Arts, the museum contains archaeological collections and exhibits from the Americas and Europe, and ethnographic materials from Oceania, Africa, Asia, the Arctic, and the Americas.

Hudson Museum, University of Maine, 5476 Maine Center for the Arts, Orono, ME 04469-5746. **Phone:** 207/581-1901. **Fax:** 207/581-1950. **E-mail:** hudsonmuseum@umit. maine.edu. **Website:** www.umaine.edu/hudsonmuseum/. **Hours:** 9-4 Tues.-Fri., 11-4 Sat.-Sun.; closed Mon. and university holidays. **Admission:** free.

Mississippi

LOIS DOWDLE COBB MUSEUM OF ARCHAEOLOGY. The Lois Dowdle Cobb Museum of Archaeology at Mississippi State University is named for the wife of agricultural newspaper publisher Cully Cobb, an alumnus who also funded the Cobb Institute of Archaeology. The museum, founded as part of the archaeological institute in 1972, has collections and exhibits pertaining to archaeological materials from the Middle East and the southeastern United States.

Lois Dowdle Cobb Museum of Archaeology, Mississippi State University, Cobb Institute of Archaeology, Barr Ave. and Lee Blvd., PO Box AR, Mississippi State University, MS 39762. **Phone:** 662/325-3826. **Fax:** 662/325-3826. **E-mail:** jdsl@ra.msstate.edu. **Website:** www.cob.msstate.edu. **Hours:** 1-4 Mon.-Fri.; closed Sat.-Sun. and university holidays and breaks. **Admission:** free.

New Mexico

FLORENCE HAWLEY ELLIS MUSEUM OF ANTHROPOLOGY. The Florence Hawley Ellis Museum of Anthropology at the Presbyterian Church's Ghost Ranch Conference Center near Abiquiu, New Mexico, is named for the professor emeritus of anthropology at the University of New Mexico. The museum has an exhibit on Ellis's work in southwestern anthropology and archaeology, as well as displays on prehistoric and modern peoples of the area. The museum adjoins the Ruth Hall Museum of Paleontology (see Natural History Museums).

Florence Hawley Ellis Museum of Anthropology, Ghost Ranch Conference Center, U.S. Hwy. 84, HC 77, Box 11, Abiquiu, NM 87510. **Phone:** 505/685-4333, Ext. 118. **Fax:** 505/685-4519. **Website:** www.newmexico-ghostranch.org. **Hours:** 9-12 and 1-5 Tues.-Sat. (also 1-5 Sun. in summer); closed Sun.-Mon., Easter, Thanksgiving, and last 2 weeks of Dec. **Admission:** suggested donations—adults, $2; seniors and children, $1.

WHEELWRIGHT MUSEUM OF THE AMERICAN INDIAN. See Cultural Art and History Museums.

Oklahoma

ATALOA LODGE MUSEUM. See Cultural Art and History Museums.

SCIENCE AND TECHNOLOGY MUSEUMS

See also Earth Sciences Museums; Natural History Museums; Mining Museums and Mines; Nature and Wildlife Centers.

District of Columbia

MARIAN KOSHLAND SCIENCE MUSEUM. The National Academy of Sciences in Washington, D.C., received a gift of approximately $30 million in 1998 to develop and operate a new public science museum. The funds came from academy member Daniel E. Koshland, professor of biochemistry at the University of California, Berkeley, with the museum being named in memory of his wife, Marian Koshland, a distinguished immunologist and academy member who had died the previous year. The Koshland Science Museum, which opened in 2004 in the new National Research Center building in Washington, is devoted to explaining how science works and examining scientific and technological controversies and trends.

Marian Koshland Science Museum, 6th and E Sts., Washington, D.C. (postal address: 500 5th St., Washington, DC 20001). Phone: 202/334-1201. Fax: 202/334-1548. E-mail: ksm@nas.edu. Website: www.koshlandmuseum.org. Hours: 10-6 Wed.-Mon.; closed Tues., New Year's Day, Thanksgiving, and Christmas. Admission: adults, $5; seniors and children 5-18, $3; children under 5, free.

Massachusetts

MARGARET HUTCHINSON COMPTON GALLERY. The Margaret Hutchinson Compton Gallery, named for a former faculty member, is a branch science and technology exhibitions gallery that is part of the MIT Museum at the Massachusetts Institute of Technology in Cambridge.

Margaret Hutchinson Compton Gallery, MIT Museum, 77 Massachusetts Ave., Bldg. 10, Massachusetts Institute of Technology, Cambridge, MA (postal address: MIT Museum, 265 Massachusetts Ave., Cambridge, MA 02139-4307). Phone: 617/253-4444. Fax: 617/253-8994. E-mail: museum@mit.edu. Website: www.mit.edu/museum. Hours: 9-5 Mon.-Fri.; closed Sat.-Sun. and major holidays. Admission: free.

Michigan

CRANBROOK INSTITUTE OF SCIENCE. See Natural History Museums.

IMPRESSION 5 SCIENCE CENTER. The Impression 5 Science Center was founded in Lansing, Michigan, in 1972 by Marilynne Eichinger, who wanted to fill a cultural need in the community. The hands-on science and technology center emphasizes the five senses. It started in Eichinger's basement and is now housed in a renovated century-old building. It offers interactive energy, biology, physics, medical, and other exhibits, educational programs, workshops, camp-ins, summer camp, and teacher programs.

Impression 5 Science Center, 200 Museum Dr., Lansing, MI 48933. Phone: 517/485-8116. Fax: 517/485-8125. Website: www.impression5.org. Hours: 10-5 Mon.-Sat.; closed Sun., 1st week in Sept., and major holidays. Admission: adults, $4.50; seniors and children 3-17, $3; children under 3, free.

Pennsylvania

ESTHER M. KLEIN ART GALLERY. See Art Galleries.

Texas

WITTE MUSEUM. See General Museums.

EARTH SCIENCES MUSEUMS

See also Natural History Museums; Science and Technology Museums.

Florida

GILLESPIE MUSEUM OF MINERALS. Paving contractor Thomas B. Gillespie and his wife, Nellie Gillespie, of Palatka, Florida, were fascinated when they saw an unusually beautiful exhibit of minerals while visiting Seattle in the 1930s. As a result, they became interested in the earth sciences and began collecting minerals, with the assistance of noted mineralogists Arthur Montgomery and Edwin Over. After almost three decades of collecting, the couple donated their collection and provided an acquisition fund to Stetson University in DeLand, Florida, for the Gillespie Museum of Minerals. In addition to an outstanding collection of mineral specimens, the museum illustrates and interprets other aspects of earth sciences.

Gillespie Museum of Minerals, Stetson University, 234 E. Michigan Ave., DeLand, FL 32720 (postal ad-

dress: 421 N. Woodland Blvd., Unit 8403, DeLand, FL 32720). Phone: 386/822-7330. Fax: 386/822-7328. E-mail: hvanter@stetson.edu. Website: www.gillespiemuseum.stetson.edu. Hours: June-July—10-3 Tues.-Fri.; closed Sat.-Mon.; remainder of year—9-4 Mon.-Fri.; closed Sat.-Sun., major holidays, and when university not in session. Admission: suggested donations: adults, $2; students and children, $1.

Nebraska

ELEANOR BARBOUR COOK MUSEUM OF GEOLOGY. The Eleanor Barbour Cook Museum of Geology at Chadron State College in Chadron, Nebraska, is named for the college's first geology professor, who was the prime mover in developing the institution's museum and rock, mineral, and fossil collections. Cook, who became professor in 1924, collected many of the institution's original specimens with her father, E. H. Barbour, who was the founder of the University of Nebraska State Museum, and her rancher husband, Harold Cook.

Eleanor Barbour Cook Museum of Geology, Chadron State College, Math and Science Bldg., 1000 Main St., Chadron, NE 69337-2690. **Phone:** 308/432-6377. **Fax:** 308/432-6434. **E-mail:** mleite@csc.edu. **Website:** www.cscms.csc.edu. **Hours:** 8-4:30 Mon.-Fri.; closed Sat.-Sun., June-Aug., major holidays, and when college not in session. **Admission:** donation.

Texas

A. M. AND ALMA FIEDLER MEMORIAL MUSEUM.
The A. M. and Alma Fiedler Memorial Museum at Texas Lutheran University in Sequin was the fulfillment of the dream of an educator (who became a Lutheran minister), his wife, and their daughter, Professor Evelyn Fiedler Streng, who initiated and became director of the museum. Fiedler collected rocks, minerals, arrowheads, guns, and other objects most of his adult life. After both he and his wife died in 1971, their only daughter used their modest estate to establish the museum and supplemented the collection with her own specimens. In addition to the objects on exhibit, the museum has an outdoor rock garden.

A. M. and Alma Fiedler Memorial Museum, Texas Lutheran University, 1000 W. Court St., Sequin, TX 78155. **Phone:** 830/372-8000. **Fax:** 830/372-8188. **Website:** www.tlu.edu. **Hours:** 1-5 Mon.-Fri., other times by appointment; closed major holidays and when university not in session. **Admission:** free.

Wyoming

TATE GEOLOGICAL MUSEUM.
The Tate Geological Museum at Casper College in Casper, Wyoming, was established in 1988 by geologist Marion Tate and his wife, Inez Tate, who moved from Oklahoma to Casper's oil fields in 1940. The museum contains collections and exhibits of Wyoming's paleontological and mineralogical heritage.

Tate Geological Museum, Casper College, 125 College Dr., Casper, WY 82601. **Phone:** 307/268-2447. **Fax:** 307/268-2514. **Website:** www.dc.whecn.edu/tate/webpage.htm. **Hours:** 9-4 Mon.-Fri., 10-3 Sat.; closed Sun. and major holidays. **Admission:** free.

MINING MUSEUMS AND MINES

Arizona

ROBSON'S MINING WORLD.
Robson's Mining World is a re-created turn-of-the-twentieth-century mining town established by Charles Robson and his wife, Jeri Robson, at the site of a once prosperous Arizona mining community in the Harcuvar Mountains, 27 miles northwest of Wickenburg.

The town has 40 original and reconstructed buildings, including old miners' cabins, a grocery, and a rebuilt three-story boardinghouse that has become a 24-room hotel. Most have period artifacts collected by the Robsons on their visits to Arizona's many mining and ghost towns. Among the site's highlights are one of the world's largest collections of early mining equipment, a 20,000-pound collection of minerals, Native American artifacts, and a trail leading to nearby prehistoric petroglyphs.

Robson's Mining World, U.S. Hwy. 71, PO Box 3465, Wickenburg, AZ 85358. **Phone:** 520/685-2609. **Fax:** 520/685-2343. **Website:** www.wickenburgchamber.com. **Hours:** Oct.-May—10-4 Mon.-Fri., 8-6 Sat.-Sun.; closed remainder of year. **Tour Admission:** adults, $5; seniors, $4.50; children under 10, free.

Colorado

MATCHLESS MINE MUSEUM.
The Matchless Mine in Leadville, Colorado, boomed during its fourteen years of operation, and Horace A. W. Tabor never lost faith in the mine, even after the bottom dropped out of the silver market in the panic of 1893. On his deathbed he told his second wife, Elizabeth "Baby Doe" Tabor, to "hang on to the Matchless. It will make millions again."

Baby Doe moved to a cabin at the mining site and struggled and starved for nearly 36 years in the hope of striking it rich again, but the mine never recovered. Her vigil ended in 1935, when her 83-year-old frozen body was found in the cabin. Much of the mining machinery was later removed and the property vandalized before the Leadville Assembly, Inc., a nonprofit group, restored the cabin and opened the property to the public. The site now offers guided tours of the furnished cabin, which contains some personal items, and the site itself, which still has the mine shaft, hoist, hoist house, blacksmith shop, and other mining equipment and tools.

Matchless Mine Museum, E. 7th St., Leadville, CO (postal address: 3940 State Hwy. 91, Leadville, CO 80461). **Phone:** 719/486-1899. **E-mail:** marvidson@amigo.net. **Website:** www.leadvilleco.com. **Hours:** June-Aug.—9-4:45 Tues.-Sun.; closed Mon. and remainder of year. **Admission:** adults and children over 12, $4; children 6-12, $1; children under 6, free.

MOLLY KATHLEEN MINE. Guided tours are offered of the 1891 Molly Kathleen Mine, a gold mine started after Molly Kathleen Gortner found gold while hiking near Cripple Creek, Colorado. She was one of the first women to register a mining claim in her own name. The mine closed in 1961, but tours began in the 1930s while the mine was still operating. Today, tourists ride the "skip" (a caged elevator) down 1,000 feet to the tenth level of the mine, where a guide explains how gold was mined at the turn of the twentieth century.

Molly Kathleen Mine, State Hwy. 67, PO Box 339, Cripple Creek, CO 80813. **Phones:** 719/689-2465 and 719/689-2466. **Hours:** May-Oct.—9-5 daily; closed remainder of year. **Admission:** adults and children over 11, $10; children 3-11, $5; children under 3, free.

Montana

HISTORIC VIRGINIA CITY AND NEVADA CITY. In 1853, six prospectors discovered gold along Alder Creek in Montana's southwest corner. This led to the founding of two mining boomtowns—Virginia City and nearby Nevada City—and to the greatest placer gold rush in Montana history.

Within a year, approximately 10,000 gold seekers and others had poured into Virginia City and what later became Nevada City. After the boom, the two adjoining mining towns gradually became virtual ghost towns. By 1945, plans were being made to tear down what remained and sell it for firewood. That's when Charles and Sue Bovey, a ranching couple from Great Falls with a great interest in history, decided to buy

up much of Virginia City and restore the business district. They did the same with Nevada City in the 1950s. Their enthusiasm was contagious, and others joined in the restorations and even opened businesses. Today, Virginia City is considered one of the best-preserved nineteenth-century gold rush towns in the American West, and the two old mining towns have become popular tourist sites, with even some year-round residents.

The Boveys worked at restoration until their deaths. Their heirs then maintained the twin towns until 1997, when the properties were sold to the state. Of the 237 remaining structures in Virginia City, 50 are original structures from the 1860s and 1870s. Nevada City has about 200 historic buildings, but only twelve are originals—most of the others were relocated from elsewhere and are now part of the outdoor Nevada City Museum, which has 105 buildings. Both towns have wooden boardwalks, simulated gunfights, and special western events during the summer season.

Historic Virginia City and Nevada City (contact: Virginia City Chamber of Commerce, Wallace St., PO Box 218, Virginia City, MT 59755). **Phones:** 406/843-5555 and 800/829-2969. **E-mail:** townofvc@3rivers.net. **Website:** www.virginiacitychamber.com.

South Dakota

WADE'S GOLD MILL AND MINING MUSEUM. Wade's Gold Mill and Mining Museum is a family-run placer gold mine and mill and a museum of historic Black Hills mining equipment near Hill City, South Dakota. The milling process—which can be observed in tours—was started at the site in 1979 by Les Wade and his wife, Idella Wade, who designed and built the gold mill. The mining museum has a simulated mine tunnel and such historic equipment as mining locomotives, winches, stamp mills, pumps, carts, drills, 110-year-old cradle, small placer mill, and elevator cage, as well as a blacksmith shop and assay office.

Wade's Gold Mill and Mining Museum, 12401 Deerfield Rd., PO Box 312, Hill City, SD 57745. **Phone:** 605/574-2680. **E-mail:** rlwade@earthlink.net. **Website:** www.home.earthlink.net/~r/wade/. **Hours:** Memorial Day-Labor Day—9-6 daily. **Admission:** adults and children over 11, $8; children 6-11, $4; children under 6, free.

NATURE AND WILDLIFE CENTERS

See also Botanical Gardens and Arboretums; Natural History Museums.

California

EFFIE YEAW NATURE CENTER. The Effie Yeaw Nature Center, created at the edge of Ancil Hoffman Park in Carmichael, California, in 1976, is named for a teacher who was the leading spirit in a movement to understand and protect the Sacramento area's natural environment. During the 1950s and 1960s, she personified the increasing concern to preserve heritage trees and plant seedlings and to cultivate an awareness of streams and diverse forms of plant and animal life. The nature center, a unit of the Sacramento County park system, has a 77-acre nature preserve and presents changing exhibits on the natural and cultural history of the Sacramento region, as well as environmental education programs.

Effie Yeaw Nature Center, 6700 Tarshes Dr., PO Box 579, Carmichael, CA 95609-0579. **Phone:** 916/489-4918. **Fax:** 914/489-4983. **E-mail:** swittorff@sacparks.org. **Website:** www.effieyeaw.org. **Hours:** Mar.-Oct.—9-5 daily; remainder of year—9:30-4 daily; closed New Year's Day, Thanksgiving, and Christmas. **Admission:** free.

FILOLI CENTER. See Historic House Museums.

Connecticut

CONNECTICUT AUDUBON BIRDCRAFT MUSEUM. Mabel Osgood Wright, a pioneer in the American conservation movement and one of the founders of the Connecticut Audubon Society, established the Connecticut Audubon Birdcraft Museum in Fairfield in 1914 while serving as founding society president. She planned the museum's buildings, sanctuary layout, exhibits, and programs until her death in 1934. The museum was named after her best-selling 1895 field guide to birds.

The museum, which has a 5.2-acre songbird sanctuary (the nation's first private bird sanctuary), contains dioramas of birds and wildlife, mounts of Connecticut birds, duck-stamp prints, and an herbarium. The Connecticut Audubon Society also operates three environmental centers and a statewide network of nineteen sanctuaries, preserving 2,200 acres of open space.

Connecticut Audubon Birdcraft Museum, 314 Unquowa Rd., Fairfield, CT 06430. **Phone:** 203/259-0416. **Fax:** 203/259-1344. **E-mail:** birdcraft@snet.net. **Website:** www.birdcraft.org. **Hours:** 10-5 Tues.-Fri.; 12-5 Sat.-Sun.; closed Mon. and major holidays. **Admission:** adults and children over 12, $2; children under 13, $1.

LUTZ CHILDREN'S MUSEUM. See Children's Museums.

Florida

KATHARINE ORDWAY PRESERVE. The Katharine Ordway Preserve near Putnam Hall, Florida, is named for one of the founders of the Goodhill Foundation, which provided the gift to purchase the property and endow an eminent scholar chair in ecosystem conservation at the University of Florida. The preserve and the Swisher Memorial Sanctuary, both managed by the Florida Museum of Natural History at the university in Gainesville, are contiguous properties that form a 9,500-acre ecological preserve and research and teaching area, 41 miles from the campus.

The Florida Museum of Natural History is the largest collection-based natural history museum in the Southeast. It has two principal facilities on the Gainesville campus—Powell Hall, a 55,000-square-foot education and exhibit center, and Dickinson Hall, a 100,000-square-foot research and collections storage facility with more than 25 million specimens and artifacts.

Katharine Ordway Preserve, near State Hwys. 26 and 100, Putnam, FL (contact: Ordway Preserve, Dept. of Wildlife, Ecology, and Conservation, University of Florida, PO Box 110430, Gainesville, FL 32611). **Phone:** 352/846-0576. **Fax:** 352/475-2848. **E-mail:** coates@mail.ifas.ufl.edu. **Website:** www.ordway.ufl.edu. **Hours:** by appointment. **Admission:** free.

MARIE SELBY BOTANICAL GARDENS. See Botanical Gardens and Arboretums.

Indiana

MARY GRAY BIRD SANCTUARY. In the 1940s, Congressman Finley Gray and his wife, Alice Greene Gray, gave the Indiana Audubon Society land for a bird sanctuary near Connersville, Indiana, as a memorial for their daughter, Mary Gray. Mrs. Gray donated the first 260 acres in 1943, followed by a gift of 400 acres from

Mr. Gray in 1947. The society purchased the remaining acres later for the 700-acre bird sanctuary, which has more than six miles of marked trails and picnicking facilities.

Mary Gray Bird Sanctuary, 3499 Bird Sanctuary Rd., Connersville, IN 47331. **Phone:** 765/825-9788. **Website:** www.indianaaudubon.org. **Hours:** dawn-dusk daily. **Admission:** free.

Iowa

DOROTHY PECAUT NATURE CENTER. The Loess Ridge Nature Center in Stone State Park near Sioux City, Iowa, was renamed in 1997 in memory of Dorothy Pecaut, a local community leader, following a commemorative gift from family, friends, and the Woodbury County Conservation Board. The center is devoted largely to the Loess Hills area, formed by wind-blown soil thousands of years ago, and contains exhibits on a "walk-under" prairie, natural history dioramas, a 400-gallon aquarium, and a "hands-on" discovery area with furs, antlers, fossils, and artifacts.

Dorothy Pecaut Nature Center, 4500 Sioux River Rd., Sioux City, IA 51109-1657. **Phone:** 712/258-0838. **Fax:** 712/258-1261. **E-mail:** dchapman@siouxcity.org. **Website:** www.woodburyparks.com. **Hours:** 9-5 Tues.-Sat. (also to 8 p.m. Tues. and Thurs. in summer); 1-5 Sun.; closed Mon., New Year's Day, Thanksgiving, and Christmas Eve and Day. **Admission:** free.

Louisiana

CAROLINE DORMAN NATURE PRESERVE. Caroline Dorman, who is said to have been the first woman employed in forestry in the United States, left her 154-acre estate with its wild garden and woods to become the Caroline Dorman Nature Preserve near Natchitoches, Louisiana, when she died in 1971. She played a crucial role in the establishment of the 600,000-acre Kisatchie National Forest and loved the pine forests and native plants of Louisiana. The site of the nature preserve—called Briarwood—was settled in 1860 by Dorman's grandparents. Dorman's will set up a foundation for the preserve, which also contains her log home and a reconstructed cabin in which she did her writing and artwork.

Caroline Dorman Nature Preserve, State Hwy. 9, PO Box 226, Natchitoches, LA 71458. **Phone:** 318/576-3379. **E-mail:** briarwood@ce-tel.net. **Hours:** Mar.-May and Nov.—9-5 Sat.,

12-5 Sun.; closed Mon.-Fri.; remainder of year—by appointment. **Admission:** $5 per person; children under 8, free.

Maine

JOSEPHINE NEWMAN SANCTUARY. The Josephine Newman Sanctuary in Georgetown, Maine, is named for its donor, who left the 119-acre property to the Maine Audubon Society in her will in 1968. The sanctuary, which is rich in animal life in upland and shoreline habitats, includes tidal mudflats, marshes, a forest, and walking trails.

Josephine Newman Sanctuary, off State Hwy. 127, Georgetown, ME (postal address: Maine Audubon Society, 20 Gilsland Farm Rd., Falmouth, ME 04105-2100). **Phone:** 207/781-2330. **Fax:** 207/781-6185. **E-mail:** bsavage@ maineaudubon. org. **Website:** www.maineaudubon.org. **Hours:** dawn-dusk daily. **Admission:** free.

RACHEL CARSON NATIONAL WILDLIFE REFUGE. The Coastal Maine National Wildlife Refuge near Wells, Maine, was renamed the Rachel Carson National Wildlife Refuge as a living memorial for the renowned marine biologist and science writer in 1970. Carson, whose ecological classic *Silent Spring* (1962) changed the way Americans looked at nature, spent her summers and conducted many of her studies along the coast at and near the refuge until her death in 1964.

Carson came to Maine for the first time in 1946, as an aquatic biologist and editor for the U.S. Fish and Wildlife Service. She was working on a series of conservation pamphlets highlighting the work of the federal agency's refuges along the Atlantic flyway. In 1952, after her study of the ocean, she built a cottage on an estuary of the Sheepscot River on Southport Island. In addition to *Silent Spring*, which warned of the dangerous consequences of the widespread misuse of pesticides, she wrote the first of her three-part biography of the ocean, *Under the Sea-Wind*, in 1941; the international best-seller *The Sea Around Us* in 1951; and *The Edge of the Sea*, large parts of which were written at the cottage, in 1955.

The refuge, which covers approximately 5,000 acres of estuarine salt marshes and upland habitats, is a haven for migratory and resident wildlife and has an interpretive nature trail and exhibits on the history and features of the refuge. The Maine chapter of the Nature Conservancy, which Carson helped establish, also has a Rachel Carson Salt Pond Preserve near New Harbor, Maine.

Rachel Carson National Wildlife Refuge, 321 Port Rd., Wells, ME 04090. **Phone:** 207/646-9226. **Fax:** 207/646-6554. E-mail: fwsrw_rcnwr@fws.gov. **Hours:** 8-4:30 Mon.-Fri. (also 10-2 Sat.-Sun. in summer); closed federal holidays. **Admission:** free.

STANWOOD WILDLIFE SANCTUARY. The 130-acre Stanwood Wildlife Sanctuary in Ellsworth, Maine, is where Cordelia J. Stanwood, pioneer ornithologist, photographer, and nature writer, lived and worked. After her death in 1958, the wildlife sanctuary and a nonprofit foundation were named in her honor. The sanctuary still contains the Cape Cod–style frame house—called Birdsacre—in which she was born and lived the last 50 years of her life, photographing and writing about birds and other wildlife in the surrounding forest.

Stanwood Wildlife Sanctuary, 289 High St., PO Box 485, Ellsworth, ME 04605. **Phone:** 207/667-8460. **Hours:** sanctuary—dawn-dusk daily; nature center—10-4 daily; house museum—mid-June-mid-Oct.: 1-4 Mon., Wed., and Fri.; closed remainder of week and year, Fourth of July, and Labor Day. **Admission:** sanctuary and nature center—free; house museum—adults, $2.50; children, 50¢.

Massachusetts

GERTRUDE M. BOYDEN WILDLIFE AND NATURE REFUGE. The Gertrude M. Boyden Wildlife and Nature Refuge in Taunton, Massachusetts, was established in 1968 with the purchase of the Laura Thomas estate by the city's Conservation Commission. It was named for the commission's first chairperson, who initiated plans to utilize the site along the Three Mile River for public enjoyment. The refuge, which has grown from fourteen to 50 acres through subsequent acquisitions and donations, has many varieties of birds, animals, and plants; nature trails; a wetlands boardwalk; a covered bridge; and a log cabin built in memory of Arthur Cleveland Bent, author of *Life Histories of American Birds*, whose favorite bird-watching site was the Boyden refuge.

Gertrude M. Boyden Wildlife and Nature Refuge, 1298 Cohannet St., Box 247, Taunton, MA 02780-0247. **Phone:** 508/821-1676. **Fax:** 508/821-1665. **Hours:** 9-dusk daily. **Admission:** free.

Michigan

CRANBROOK INSTITUTE OF SCIENCE. See Natural History Museums.

Minnesota

ELOISE BUTLER WILDFLOWER GARDEN AND BIRD SANCTUARY. See Botanical Gardens and Arboretums.

New Jersey

CORA HARTSHORN ARBORETUM. See Botanical Gardens and Arboretums.

New York

MINNA ANTHONY COMMON NATURE CENTER. The nature center at Wellesley Island State Park near Fineview, New York, is named for Minna Anthony Common, a teacher, naturalist, and summer resident who developed a nature trail and observed and catalogued the island's wildlife and geology. The 600-acre wildlife sanctuary has eight miles of trails, a butterfly house, and a nature center with exhibits on the island's wildlife, geology, and Common's work.

Minna Anthony Common Nature Center, Wellesley Island State Park, 44927 Cross Island Rd., Fineview, NY 13640. **Phone:** 315/482-2479. **Fax:** 315/482-2785. **Hours:** mid-June-Aug.—8 a.m.-7 p.m. Mon.-Sat., 9 a.m.-7 p.m. Sun.; remainder of year—8-4:30 Mon.-Sat., 9-5 Sun.; closed New Year's Day, Easter, Thanksgiving, and Christmas. **Admission:** nature center—free; park—$5 per private vehicle from Memorial Day to Labor Day, free remainder of year.

South Carolina

BROOKGREEN GARDENS. See Botanical Gardens and Arboretums.

Texas

LADY BIRD JOHNSON WILDFLOWER CENTER. See Botanical Gardens and Arboretums.

Virginia

MAYMONT. See Historic House Museums.

Washington

CATHERINE MONTGOMERY INTERPRETIVE CENTER. See Botanical Gardens and Arboretums.

BOTANICAL GARDENS AND ARBORETUMS

See also Natural History Museums; Nature and Wildlife Centers.

Alabama

BELLINGRATH GARDENS AND HOME. The Bellingrath Gardens and Home in Theodore, Alabama, were created by soft drink executive Walter Bellingrath and his wife, Bessie Mae Morse Bellingrath, who spent many years observing and studying outstanding European and American landscapes to develop their gardens. The 900-acre estate, which opened to the public in 1932, has 65 acres of landscaped gardens surrounding the mansion, which feature more than 2,000 rosebushes, as well as camellias, daffodils, azaleas, lilies, chrysanthemums, poinsettias, and other plants. The brick and wrought-iron home contains Mrs. Bellingrath's collection of antique furniture, china, silver, crystal, Oriental rugs, and European porcelain. Cruises of the nearby River of Birds also are offered in February through November.

Bellingrath Gardens and Home, 12401 Bellingrath Gardens Rd., Theodore, AL 36582. **Phone:** 334/973-2217. **Fax:** 334/973-0540. **E-mail:** bellingrath@juno.com. **Website:** www.bellingrath.org/gardens/. **Hours:** home—9-4 daily; gardens—8-5 daily; cruise—10-4 daily. **Admission:** gardens—adults $8.50; seniors and military, $7.65; children 5-12, $5; children under 5, free; cruise and gardens—adults, $15.75; children 5-12, $10; children under 5, free; cruise, gardens, and home—adults, $24; children 5-12, $15; children under 5, free.

IVY GREEN, BIRTHPLACE OF HELEN KELLER. See Museums Honoring Exceptional Women.

California

ALICE KECK PARK MEMORIAL GARDEN. The Alice Keck Park Memorial Garden in Santa Barbara, California, is named for the oil heiress who bought a former hotel site that became a community garden in 1975 and gave it to the city. The 4.5-acre botanical garden has native ground covers, trees, shrubs, and flowers.

Alice Keck Park Memorial Garden, 1500 Santa Barbara St., Santa Barbara, CA 93101 (contact: Santa Barbara Parks and Recreation Dept., 620 Lagoon St., PO Box 1990, Santa Barbara, CA 93102-1990). **Phone:** 805/564-5418. **Fax:** 805/564-5499. **Website:** xbparksandrecreation.com. **Hours:** open 24 hours. **Admission:** free.

ARDEN-THE HELENA MODJESKA HISTORIC HOUSE AND GARDENS. See Museums Honoring Exceptional Women.

EFFIE YEAW NATURE CENTER. See Nature and Wildlife Centers.

FILOLI CENTER. See Historic House Museums.

HOLLYHOCK HOUSE. See Historic House Museums.

MILDRED E. MATHIAS BOTANICAL GARDEN. The Mildred E. Mathias Botanical Garden was established as the Botanical Garden at the University of California at Los Angeles in 1930 to provide a convenient teaching facility for academic classes. In 1979 the garden was renamed to honor Dr. Mathias for her distinguished contributions to horticulture and her dedication to UCLA. The eight-acre garden, which emphasizes subtropical and tropical plants that can be grown outdoors, has approximately 4,000 plant species in 225 families.

Mildred E. Mathias Botanical Garden, University of California at Los Angeles, Dept. of Biology Bldg., Box 951606, Los Angeles, CA 90095-1606. **Phones:** 310/825-3620 and 310/825-1260. **Fax:** 310/206-3987. **Website:** www.lifesci.ucla.edu/botgard. **Hours:** 8-5 Mon.-Fri., 8-4 Sat.-Sun.; closed university holidays. **Admission:** free.

STRYBING ARBORETUM AND BOTANICAL GARDENS. The Strybing Arboretum and Botanical Gardens in San Francisco's Golden Gate Park is named for donor Helen Strybing. The 55-acre arboretum and botanical gardens, founded in 1937, has more than 7,000 varieties of plants from around the world and an annual attendance of over 800,000 visitors. Among its features are a fragrance garden, primitive plant garden, Japanese moon-viewing garden, redwood grove, and cloud forest. Free 45-minute tours are offered at 1:30 p.m. weekdays and 10:30 a.m. weekends.

Strybing Arboretum and Botanical Gardens, 9th Ave. and Lincoln Way, Golden Gate Park, San Francisco, CA 94122. **Phone:** 415/661-1316. **Fax:** 415/661-3539. **E-mail:**

bphcrl@ix.netcom.com. **Website:** www.strybing.org. **Hours:** 8-4:30 Mon.-Fri., 10-5 Sat.-Sun. and holidays. **Admission:** free.

UCLA HANNAH CARTER JAPANESE GARDEN. The UCLA Hannah Carter Japanese Garden, an adjunct to teaching programs at the University of California at Los Angeles, was created in Bel Air in 1961 by Mr. and Mrs. Gordon Guiberson in memory of Mr. Guiberson's mother, Ethel L. Guiberson, organizer of the Beverly Hills Garden Club. It was later purchased and donated to the university in 1965 by Edward W. Carter, a department store head and chairman of the Board of Regents, and named for his wife. In addition to many plants, trees, stones, and water basins, the two-acre garden has an impressive gate, five-tiered pagoda, shrine, and teahouse.

UCLA Hannah Carter Japanese Garden, 10619 Bellagio Rd., Los Angeles, CA (postal address: 10920 Wilshire Blvd., Suite 1520, Los Angeles, CA 90024). **Phone:** 310/825-4574. **Fax:** 310/974-8208. **Website:** www.japanesegarden.ucla.edu. **Hours:** 10-3 Tues.-Wed., Fri., and 1st Sun. of month by reservation; closed Mon., Thurs., Sat., other Suns., and university holidays. **Admission:** free.

WINCHESTER MYSTERY HOUSE. See Historic House Museums.

Colorado

BACA HOUSE AND BLOOM HOUSE. See Historic House Museums.

BETTY FORD ALPINE GARDENS. The Betty Ford Alpine Gardens in Vail, Colorado, comprises the highest public alpine garden in the world. It is named for the wife of former president Gerald R. Ford in appreciation of her many contributions to the Vail Valley in the Colorado Rockies. The 1.5-acre garden, located in Ford Park and adjacent to the Gerald R. Ford Amphitheater, features nearly 500 varieties of alpine and subalpine plans in four microclimates and displays an additional 1,500 varieties of plants in a perennial garden.

Betty Ford Alpine Gardens, Vail Alpine Garden Foundation, 183 Gore Creek Dr., Vail, CO 81657. **Phone:** 970/476-0103. **Fax:** 970/476-1685. **Website:** www.bettyfordalpinegardens. org. **Hours:** dawn-dusk daily. **Admission:** free.

Connecticut

BELLAMY-FERRIDAY HOUSE AND GARDEN. See Other Historic Houses.

ELIZABETH PARK ROSE GARDENS. Elizabeth Park and its rose gardens in West Hartford, Connecticut, are named for Elizabeth Pond, who bequeathed the property to the city. More than 15,000 plants of 750 varieties of roses can be seen at the gardens.

Elizabeth Park Rose Gardens, 915 Prospect Ave., West Hartford, CT 06119 (postal address: 150 Wallbridge Rd., West Hartford, CT 06119). **Phone:** 860/722-6514. **Hours:** park—dawn-dusk daily; greenhouses—8-3 Mon.-Fri.; closed Sat.-Sun. **Admission:** free.

GERTRUDE JEKYLL GARDEN. The Gertrude Jekyll Garden—named for the 1843–1932 English landscape architect known for her informal garden style marked by a rhythmic use of color and form—is located at the Glebe House Museum in Woodbury, Connecticut. The ca. 1750 Glebe House, called the birthplace of American Episcopacy, contains eighteenth-century prints, paintings, and documents relating to Samuel Seabury, the first bishop of the Episcopal church in America.

Gertrude Jekyll Garden, Glebe House Museum, Hollow Rd., PO Box 245, Woodbury, CT 06798. **Phone:** 203/263-2855. **Fax:** 203/263-6726. **E-mail:** ghmgjg@wtco.net. **Hours:** 1-4 Wed.-Sun.; closed Mon.-Tues.; remainder of year—by appointment. **Admission:** adults, $5; children, $2.

HILL-STEAD MUSEUM. See Art Museums.

District of Columbia

ENID A. HAUPT, KATHRINE DULIN FOLGER, AND MARY LIVINGSTON RIPLEY GARDENS. The Smithsonian Institution has three gardens named for women near the Smithsonian Castle in Washington, D.C. They are the Enid A. Haupt Garden, Kathrine Dulin Folger Rose Garden, and Mary Livingston Ripley Garden.

The four-acre Enid A. Haupt Garden, between the Freer Gallery of Art and the Arts and Industries Building, is named for its donor. It is a ground-level garden atop a three-story building that lies beneath it, and blends Victorian and modern motifs and features a Victorian embroidery parterre.

The Kathrine Dulin Folger Rose Garden, at the east end of the castle, contains roses and other plants that bloom year-round. It is also named for its founder.

The Mary Livingston Ripley Garden, located between the Arts and Industries Building and the Hirshhorn Museum and Sculpture Garden, has more than 200 varieties of plants. It was the inspiration of the wife of S. Dillon Ripley while he was director of the Smithsonian. In 1978 Mrs. Ripley convinced the Women's Committee of the Smithsonian Associates, which she founded in 1966, to support the garden. In 1988 the committee recognized Mrs. Ripley by naming the garden for her.

Enid A. Haupt Garden, Kathrine Dulin Folger Rose Garden, and Mary Livingston Ripley Garden, Smithsonian Institution, Horticulture Services Div., Arts and Industries Bldg., Room 2282, 900 Jefferson Dr. S.W., Washington, DC 20560-0420. **Phone:** 202/357-1926. **Fax:** 202/786-2026. **Website:** www.si.edu/horticulture. **Hours:** May-Oct.—7 a.m.-8 a.m. daily; remainder of year—7-5 daily; tours—mid-Apr.-Sept.—once a week (varies with gardens and days—check garden entrances for tour signs). **Admission:** free.

HILLWOOD MUSEUM AND GARDENS. See Historic House Museums.

OLD STONE HOUSE. See Other Historic Houses.

TUDOR PLACE HISTORIC HOUSE AND GARDEN. See Historic House Museums.

Florida

BONNET HOUSE. See Historic House Museums.

CUMMER MUSEUM OF ART AND GARDENS. See Art Museums.

JOHN AND MABLE RINGLING MUSEUM OF ART. See Art Museums.

MARIE SELBY BOTANICAL GARDENS. The Marie Selby Botanical Gardens in Sarasota, Florida, was left for the enjoyment of the public in the 1971 will of Marie Selby, widow of oil executive William Selby, cofounder of Texaco. The gardens are located on the grounds of the Selbys' 1921 Spanish-style home, where Mrs. Selby created the gardens with roses, banyans, and plants native to Florida.

The original seven acres, expanded to nearly thirteen acres with the addition of the adjoining Christy-Payne mansion (which has become the Gardens' museum), overlook Sarasota Bay and the Hudson Bayou. They feature more than 8,000 epiphytes and various other plants, seven greenhouses with over 20,000 plants, an herbarium with approximately 60,000 mounted and acquired specimens, a butterfly garden, orchid and bromeliad identification centers, a collection of botanical art, and a learning center. Nearby are the Stark Botanical Research Center and the Baywalk Sanctuary, which has an elevated boardwalk that winds through a mangrove swamp.

Marie Selby Botanical Gardens, 811 S. Palm Ave., Sarasota, FL 34236. **Phone:** 941/366-5731. **Fax:** 941/366-9807. **Website:** www.selby.org. **Hours:** 10-5 daily; closed Christmas. **Admission:** adults and children over 11, $8; children 6-11, $4; children under 6, free.

PRESTON B. BIRD AND MARY HEINLEIN REDLAND FRUIT AND SPICE PARK. See Historic Parks and Sites.

Georgia

JACQUELINE CASEY HUDGENS CENTER FOR THE ARTS. See Arts Centers.

Hawaii

AMY B. H. GREENWELL ETHNOBOTANICAL GARDENS. Amy B. H. Greenwell was a member of a western Hawaii family that started ranching in Kona in the mid-nineteenth century. She joined museum archaeologists and botanists in their fieldwork and wrote many scholarly and popular articles on botany and ethnobotany. When she died in 1974, she left her garden property near Captain Cook, Hawaii, to the Bishop Museum (see Archaeology, Anthropology, and Ethnology Museums).

The Amy B. H. Greenwell Ethnobotanical Gardens is a 15-acre garden landscaped to reflect the plant life of the area in the era before 1779, when Captain James Cook, the English mariner and explorer, sailed into Kealakekua Bay. The gardens' focus is on traditional Hawaiian culture and the plants that support it. It has five principal sections—archaeology preserve, agricultural zone, coastal zone, lowland dry forest, and upland forest.

Amy B. H. Greenwell Ethnobotanical Gardens, Bishop Museum, State Hwy. 11, PO Box 1053, Captain Cook, HI 96704. **Phone:** 808/323-3318. **Fax:** 808/323-2394. **Website:**

www.bishop.hawaii.org/bishop/greenwell/. **Hours:** 8:30-5 Mon.-Fri.; closed Sun. **Admission:** suggested donation—$4.

QUEEN KAPIOLANI HIBISCUS GARDEN. The Queen Kapiolani Hibiscus Garden in Honolulu, Hawaii, honors the consort of King Kalakaua, who ruled the Hawaiian Islands in the mid-nineteenth century. The garden, near the Honolulu Zoo, features varieties of hibiscus and other tropical flowering plants as well as Kahuna stones, which are said to guard the blossoms from pickers and to have healing powers for Hawaiians.

Queen Kapiolani Hibiscus Garden, Paki and Monsarrat Aves., Honolulu, HI (contact: Honolulu Parks and Recreation Dept., Horticultural Services, 3902 Paki Ave., Honolulu, HI 96815). **Phone:** 808/971-7151. **Fax:** 8008/971-7160. **Hours:** open 24 hours. **Admission:** free.

Indiana

RUTHMERE. See Other Historic Houses.

Kentucky

FARMINGTON. See Other Historic Houses.

MARY TODD LINCOLN HOUSE. See Museums Honoring Exceptional Women.

Louisiana

BEAUREGARD-KEYES HOUSE. See Museums Honoring Exceptional Women.

LONGUE VUE HOUSE AND GARDENS. See Historic House Museums.

Maryland

HELEN AVALYNNE TAWES GARDEN. The Helen Avalynne Tawes Garden is nestled amid state government office buildings in Annapolis, Maryland. It is named in honor of Helen Avalynne Tawes, a popular former first lady of Maryland. She and Governor J. Millard Tawes were the state's gracious hosts in 1959–1967. The complex of state buildings is named for the governor. Various geographic areas of the state are featured in the five-acre garden, including a western Maryland forest, a streamside environment, and an eastern shore peninsula. In addition, it has a barrier-free garden with

ponds; plants of varied textures, tastes, and fragrances; and many cultivated plantings.

Helen Avalynne Tawes Garden, 580 Taylor Ave., Annapolis, MD 21401 (postal address: Tawes State Office Bldg. E-3, Annapolis, MD 21401). **Phone:** 410/260-8189. **Fax:** 410/260-8191. **E-mail:** dmyers@dnr.state.md.us. **Website:** www.dnr.state.md.us/publiclands/tawesgarden.html. **Hours:** dawn-dusk daily. **Admission:** free.

MARGARET BRENT GARDEN. The Margaret Brent Garden—named for the nation's first suffragist and Maryland's first female landowner—is part of Historic St. Mary's City, an outdoor living history museum in St. Mary's City, Maryland. The garden features a gazebo and bas-relief in commemoration of her achievements.

Brent, who arrived from England in 1638 and received the first land grant to a woman in Maryland, began her historic stand for women's rights ten years later. She startled the colony's General Assembly by asking to be admitted as a member and demanded two votes—one as an attorney and another as a landowner. She was turned down. But she continued to buy land, became the largest landowner in the colony, and hauled the men of Maryland's first capital city into court for any misdealings. She was in court 124 times in eight years—and won every case.

Historic St. Mary's City has exhibits, living history and craft demonstrations, educational programs, and such re-created historic structures as the 1676 State House, a seventeenth-century inn, a 1633 ship, and a seventeenth-century plantation and outbuildings.

Margaret Brent Garden, Historic St. Mary's City, State Hwy. 5, PO Box 39, St. Mary's City, MD 20686. **Phone:** 240/895-4960. **Fax:** 240/895-4968. **Website:** www.stmaryscity.org. **Hours:** mid-Mar.-mid-Sept.—10-5 Wed.-Sat.; mid-Sept.-Nov.—10-5 Tues.-Sun.; closed remainder of year and Thanksgiving. **Admission:** mid-Mar.-mid-Sept.—adults, $7.50; seniors, $6; children 6-12, $3.50; children under 6, free; mid-Sept.-Nov.—adults, $5; seniors, $4; children 6-12, $2; children under 6, free.

SOTTERLEY PLANTATION. See Historic House Museums.

Massachusetts

DICKINSON HOMESTEAD. See Museums Honoring Exceptional Women.

GORE PLACE. See Historic House Museums.

THE MOUNT. See Museums Honoring Exceptional Women.

SEDGWICK GARDENS AT LONG HILL RESERVATION. The Sedgwick Gardens at Long Hill Reservation near Beverly, Massachusetts, features the former summer estate of Ellery and Marjorie Sedgwick, who built their mansion in 1921 and modeled it after a Charleston home of the early 1800s. The surrounding formal gardens, fields, woods, and wetlands have over 1,500 varieties of trees, shrubs, and flowers. The Sedgwick house and gardens occupy only about six of the 114 acres of the nature preserve.

Sedgwick Gardens at Long Hill Reservation, 572 Essex St., Beverly, MA 01915. **Phone:** 978/921-1944. **Fax:** 978/921-1948. **Website:** www.thetrustees.org. **Hours:** grounds—8-dusk daily; house—by appointment. **Admission:** grounds—donation; house and grounds tour—$5 per person.

Michigan

ANNA SCRIPPS WHITCOMB CONSERVATORY. The Anna Scripps Whitcomb Conservatory, a landmark on Belle Isle in Detroit since 1904, was dedicated in 1955 to a civic leader who "contributed generously to the cultural life of the city" and gave many orchids to the city's collection. The conservatory is divided into a dome area with large palms and other trees; a south wing devoted to tropical fruit, other plants of economic importance, and flowering plants; a north wing housing the cacti and succulent collection and ferns; and a show house with a continuous display of blooming plants throughout the year.

Anna Scripps Whitcomb Conservatory, Belle Isle Greenhouse, Detroit, MI 48207. **Phone:** 313/852-4064. **Fax:** 313/852-4074. **E-mail:** jjustus@rec.ci.detroit.mi.us. **Website:** www.bibsociety.org. **Hours:** 10-5 daily. **Admission:** adults and children over 12, $2; seniors and children 2-12, $1; children under 2, free.

CRANBROOK HOUSE AND GARDENS. See Historic House Museums.

EDSEL AND ELEANOR FORD HOUSE. See Historic House Museums.

LEILA ARBORETUM. Philanthropist Leila Post Montgomery, widow of cereal pioneer C. W. Post, bought the site of a former country club in 1922 and gave it to the city of Battle Creek, Michigan, to be developed as a park and arboretum. The 72-acre tract of ornamental trees and shrubs, designed by landscape architect T. Clifton Shepherd, is known for its mature conifers and perennial demonstration beds.

Leila Arboretum, W. Michigan Ave. at 20th St., Battle Creek, MI 49017 (postal address: 928 W. Michigan Ave., Battle Creek, MI 49017). **Phone:** 616/969-0270. **Fax:** 616/969-0616. **E-mail:** bcgreen@voyager.net. **Hours:** dawn-dusk daily. **Admission:** free.

MATTHAEI BOTANICAL GARDENS. The University of Michigan's Matthaei Gardens are named for Frederick C. Matthaei Sr. and his wife, Malora Matthaei, whose gifts made the development of the Dixboro Road site near Ann Arbor possible. The gardens evolved from the nineteenth-century medicinal plantings of Asa Gray, the university's first professor and botanist. The gardens were formally organized in 1907 and were then expanded to include agricultural field plots and research greenhouses. By 1915 the gardens required even more space, and that is when the Matthaeis' contributions made it possible to move off the campus to the 265-acre southeast site. In addition to extensive gardens, the site now has a conservatory with tropical, warm-temperature, and desert plants; nature trails; natural habitats; and an education center.

Matthaei Botanical Gardens, University of Michigan, 1800 N. Dixboro Rd., Ann Arbor, MI 48105-9741. **Phone:** 734/998-7061. **Fax:** 734/998-6205. **Website:** www.lsa.umich.edu/mbg. **Hours:** 10-4:30 daily; closed New Year's Day, Thanksgiving, and Christmas. **Admission:** grounds—free; conservatory—adults, $3; children 5-18, $1; children under 5, free.

MEADOW BROOK HALL. See Historic House Museums.

NICHOLS ARBORETUM. The 123-acre Nichols Arboretum at the University of Michigan in Ann Arbor began in 1907 with a 27.5-acre gift from Esther Nichols and her husband, Walter Nichols. The arboretum—consisting of glacially carved terrain varying from steep ravines to rolling hills and prairie—serves as an education and research facility for the university and city schools.

Nichols Arboretum, University of Michigan, 1610 Washington Heights, Ann Arbor, MI 48104-1700. **Phone:** 734/998-9540. **Fax:** 734/998-9536. **E-mail:** arb@umich.edu. **Hours:** dawn-dusk daily. **Admission:** free.

Minnesota

ELOISE BUTLER WILDFLOWER GARDEN AND BIRD SANCTUARY. The Eloise Butler Wildflower Garden and Bird Sanctuary in Wirth Park in Minneapolis is named for an inspired botanist who founded and tended the 15-acre wildflower garden and bird sanctuary—believed to be the nation's oldest public wildflower garden.

Founded in 1907, the garden has winding trails through many rare and endangered species of wildflowers. To keep visitors from trampling the flowers, Butler was given police powers by the park board—and proudly wore the police star. After she died in 1933, her ashes were scattered over the grounds, where a plaque informs nature lovers that "her protective spirit lingers" over the wildflower garden and bird sanctuary.

Eloise Butler Wildflower Garden and Bird Sanctuary, Wirth Park, Wirth Pkwy. and Glenwood Ave., Minneapolis, MN (contact: Minneapolis Park and Recreation Board, 3800 Bryant Ave. South, Minneapolis, MN 55409-1029). **Phones:** 612/370-4903 and 612/370-4900. **Fax:** 612/370-4801. **E-mail:** marylynn.1.pulscher@ci.minneapolis.mn.us. **Website:** www.minneapolisparks.org. **Hours:** Apr.-mid-Oct.—garden: 7:30-dusk daily; Martha Crone Shelter: 10-dusk Mon.-Sat., 12-dusk Sun.; closed remainder of year. **Admission:** free.

Nevada

MARJORIE BARRICK MUSEUM OF NATURAL HISTORY. See Natural History Museums.

New Hampshire

ZIMMERMAN HOUSE. See Other Historic Houses.

New Jersey

CORA HARTSHORN ARBORETUM. The Cora Hartshorn Arboretum in Short Hills, New Jersey, was created in 1962 through a bequest from Cora Hartshorn to Millburn Township. The arboretum has 16.5 acres of woodlands with hiking trails and a nature center containing exhibits, live animals, and natural history specimens.

Cora Hartshorn Arboretum, 324 Forest Dr., Short Hills, NJ 07078. **Phone:** 973/376-3587. **Fax:** 973/379-5059. **E-mail:** hartshornarboretum@worldnet.att.net. **Website:** www.hartshornarboretum.com. **Hours:** Sept.-May—

9-3:30 Mon.-Thurs., 9:30-11:30 Sat.; bldgs. closed Fri., Sun., and remainder of year, but grounds and gardens open. **Admission:** free.

New York

ALICE AUSTEN HOUSE MUSEUM. See Museums Honoring Exceptional Women.

CLARK BOTANIC GARDEN. The Clark Botanic Garden in Albertson, New York, is named for Fanny Dwight Clark. The 12-acre estate, which includes the garden, house, and three ponds, was left to the Brooklyn Botanic Garden in 1966 by Clark's husband, lawyer Granville Clark, in her memory. The property was later sold to the town of North Hempstead.

Clark Botanic Garden, 193 I. U. Willets Rd., Albertson, NY 11507. **Phones:** 516/484-8600 and 516/484-2208. **Fax:** 516/625-3718. **Hours:** 10-4:30 daily. **Admission:** free.

ELEANOR ROOSEVELT NATIONAL HISTORIC SITE. See Museums Honoring Exceptional Women.

NEW YORK BOTANICAL GARDEN. The New York Botanical Garden in the Bronx, New York, was founded at the suggestion of Elizabeth Britton, a botanist and moss expert who was inspired while visiting the Royal Botanic Gardens at Kew, England. It was largely through her support and encouragement and that of her botanist husband, Nathaniel Lord Britton, that the 250-acre garden was incorporated in 1891. He later became the garden's first director.

Elizabeth Britton, whose expertise was bryology, became honorary curator of mosses at the garden in 1912, and many varieties of mosses were named in her honor. Numerous other women have made significant contributions to the New York Botanical Garden, one of the largest botanical gardens in the world. Among the facilities named for women are the Enid A. Haupt Conservatory, Peggy Rockefeller Rose Garden, Jane Watson Irwin Perennial Garden, and Ruth Rea Howell Family Garden.

The New York Botanical Garden has comprehensive tree and shrub collections, specialized garden and conservatory collections of tropical and subtropical plants, 6.5 million herbarium specimens, native woodlands, horticultural exhibits, educational programs, laboratories, a 260,000-volume library, and over 1 million nonbook items, consisting of botanical art, photographs, manuscripts, architectural plans, seed and nursery catalogs, and other materials.

New York Botanical Garden, 200th St. and Kazimiroff Blvd., Bronx, NY 10458. **Phone:** 718/817-8700. **Fax:** 718/220-6504. **E-mail:** pubrel@nybg.org. **Website:** www.nybg.org. **Hours:** grounds—Apr.-Oct.: 10-6 Tues.-Sun.; Nov.-Mar.: 10-4 Tues.-Sun.; conservatory and children's, rock, and native plant gardens—hours vary; closed Mon., Thanksgiving, and Christmas. **Admission:** grounds—adults, $3; seniors and students, $2; children 2-12, $1; children under 2, free; free on Wed. and 10-12 Sat.; conservatory—adults, $3.50; seniors and students, $2.50; children 2-12, $2; children under 2, free; children's garden—adults, $3; seniors and students, $2; children 2-12, $1; children under 2, free; rock and native plant gardens—adults, $1; seniors, students, and children 2-12, 50¢; children under 2, free; combination tickets—adults, $10; seniors and students, $7.50; children 2-12, $4.50; children under 2, free.

OLD WESTBURY GARDENS. The Old Westbury Gardens—featuring a 1906 Charles II–style mansion on 173 acres of formal gardens, landscaped grounds, woodlands, ponds, and lakes in Old Westbury, New York—is located at the former home of John S. and Margarita Grace Phipps. Phipps built the estate for his wife, who was instrumental in planning the gardens. The historic site, which is listed in the National Register of Historic Places, has 25 acres of gardens with roses, lilacs, rhododendrons, boxwood, and other plants. Seven original buildings are located on the grounds, including the Westbury House and greenhouses. The house is furnished with fine English antiques and decorative arts from the nearly 50 years of the Phipps family's residence. The site was opened to the public in 1959.

Old Westbury Gardens, 71 Old Westbury Rd., PO Box 430, Old Westbury, NY 11568. **Phone:** 516/333-0048. **Fax:** 516/333-6807. **Website:** www.oldwestburygardens.org. **Hours:** late Apr.-mid-Dec.—10-5 Wed.-Mon.; closed Tues. and remainder of year. **Admission:** gardens—adults, $8; seniors, $6; children 6-12, $3; children under 6, free; house and gardens—adults, $10; seniors, $8; children 6-12, $6; children under 6, free.

SONNENBERG GARDENS AND MANSION. The Sonnenberg Gardens and Mansion at the former summer home of Mary Clark Thompson and her banker husband, Frederick Ferris Thompson, in Canandaigua, New York, feature 50 acres of Victorian gardens and a collection of period furniture and furnishings. Mrs. Thompson was a major benefactor in the community, Vassar College, and the National Academy of Sciences, where she established an honors program in geology and paleontology.

Sonnenberg Gardens and Mansion, 151 Charlotte St., Canandaigua, NY 14424. **Phone:** 716/394-4922. **Fax:** 716/394-2192. **E-mail:** congard@eznet.net. **Website:** www .sonnenberg.org. **Hours:** May-mid-Oct.—9:30-5:30 daily; closed remainder of year. **Admission:** adults, $8.50; seniors, $6.50; children 6-16, $2.50; children under 6, free.

North Carolina

BELLAMY MANSION MUSEUM OF HISTORY AND DESIGN ARTS. See Historic House Museums.

HISTORIC BATH STATE HISTORIC SITE (Ruth McCloud Smith Memorial Garden). See Historic House Museums.

REYNOLDA GARDENS OF WAKE FOREST UNIVERSITY. The 129 acres now known as Reynolda Gardens of Wake Forest University in Winston-Salem, North Carolina, were originally part of the 1,067-acre estate of Richard Joshua Reynolds, founder of the R. J. Reynolds Tobacco Company, and his wife, Katharine Smith Reynolds.

The estate included more than 350 acres of farmland and a formal garden of 4 acres—both developed under the direction of Mrs. Reynolds. After Mr. Reynolds died in 1917 and Mrs. Reynolds Johnson (who had remarried) passed away in 1924, trustees supervised estate operations until the mid-1930s, when the Reynolds's daughter, Mary Reynolds Babcock, and her husband, Charles, became owners of Reynolda. It was the Mary Reynolds Babcock Foundation that donated the formal gardens, greenhouses, and 125 acres of woodlands, fields, and wetlands to Wake Forest University in a series of gifts in 1958, 1961, and 1962.

Reynolda Gardens now consists of 129 acres of formal and nature plantings, with approximately 4.5 acres devoted to formal gardens featuring boxwood, annual, and perennial beds. The site also has three other gardens (roses; vegetables, fruits, and flowers; and fields and woodlands) and a 1913 conservatory with a variety of tropical plants. The Reynolds mansion, which features a collection of American art, is located on an adjoining 20 acres and is operated separately by a nonprofit organization (see Art Museums).

Reynolda Gardens of Wake Forest University, 100 Reynolda Village, Winston-Salem, NC 27106. **Phone:** 336/758-5593. **Fax:** 336/758-4132. **E-mail:** gardens@wfu.edu. **Website:** www.wfu.edu/gardens/. **Hours:** gardens—dawn-dusk daily; greenhouses—9-4 Mon.-Fri., 10-4 Sun.; closed Sat. **Admission:** free.

The 129 acres known as Reynolda Gardens surround Reynolda House, Museum of American Art, in Winston-Salem, North Carolina. The gardens and the house were part of the 1,067-acre estate of Richard J. Reynolds and his wife, Katharine Smith Reynolds, in the early twentieth century. Courtesy Reynolda House, Museum of American Art, and photographer Ken Bennett, Wake Forest University.

Ohio

TAFT MUSEUM OF ART. See Art Museums.

Pennsylvania

MORRIS ARBORETUM OF THE UNIVERSITY OF PENN-SYLVANIA. The Morris Arboretum of the University of Pennsylvania in Philadelphia is the legacy of John T. and Lydia Morris, a brother and sister from an iron manufacturing family who began developing their Chestnut Hill estate—known as Compton—in the tradition of English landscape gardens in 1887.

The 92-acre facility, which became part of the university in 1932, has natural woodlands, meadows, landscaped gardens, a mature collection of trees, winding paths, outdoor sculpture, natural and constructed water attractions, and historic structures, including a log cabin once used by Lydia Morris as a pastoral retreat, which has become an interpretive pavilion. It is an interdisciplinary resource center, a living museum with over 3,500 types of trees and shrubs, and a plant science education and research center. It also has a 74-acre satellite site.

The Rose Garden is one of the attractions at the Morris Arboretum of the University of Pennsylvania in Philadelphia. The site began in 1887 as the summer home of John and Lydia Morris, brother and sister; became part of the university in 1932; and is considered one of the best remaining examples of a Victorian eclectic garden. Courtesy Morris Arboretum of the University of Pennsylvania and photographer Paul W. Meyer.

Morris Arboretum of the University of Pennsylvania, 100 Northwestern Ave., Philadelphia, PA 19118-2697 (postal address: 9414 Meadowbrook Ave., Philadelphia, PA 19118). **Phone:** 215/247-5777. **Fax:** 215/248-4439. **E-mail:** kms@pobox.upenn.edu. **Website:** www.upenn.edu/morris.

Hours: Apr.-Oct.—10-4 Mon.-Fri., 10-5 Sat.-Sun.; remainder of year—10-4 daily; closed Thanksgiving and Christmas through New Year's Day. **Admission:** adults, $6; seniors, $5; students, $4; children under 6, free.

South Carolina

BROOKGREEN GARDENS. Brookgreen Gardens, which features more than 2,000 species of indigenous and exotic plants and trees and over 500 nineteenth-century and contemporary sculptures, was created in the 1930s near Murrells Inlet, South Carolina, by railroad heir Archer M. Huntington and his sculptor wife, Anna Hyatt Huntington. The gardens, considered among the most beautiful in the South, are located on the site of a mid-1700s rice and indigo plantation and have six large millstones once used for hulling rice in the area.

Moss-hung oak trees, dogwoods, azaleas, and other trees and plants can be seen on the grounds, while the statuary is concentrated in a sculpture gallery around a pool and fountain. The site also has a wildlife park with an aviary, cypress swamp, nature trails, and picnic area. Scenic pontoon tours of the creeks and former rich fields are offered.

Brookgreen Gardens, 1931 Brookgreen Gardens Dr., Murrells Inlet, SC 29576 (postal address: PO Box 3368, Pawleys Island, SC 29585-3368). **Phones:** 843/235-6000 and 800/849-1931. **Fax:** 843/237-1014. **E-mail:** info@brookgreen.org. **Website:** www.brookgreen.org. **Hours:** 9:30-5 daily; closed Christmas. **Admission:** adults and children over 12, $8.50; children 6-12, $4; children under 6, free.

Tennessee

DIXON GALLERY AND GARDENS. See Art Museums.

Texas

AUSTIN MUSEUM OF ART-LAGUNA GLORIA. See Art Museums.

BAYOU BEND COLLECTION AND GARDENS. See Art Museums.

GLADYS PORTER ZOO. See Zoos.

LADY BIRD JOHNSON WILDFLOWER CENTER. The Lady Bird Johnson Wildflower Center in Austin, Texas, honors Claudia Alta Taylor Johnson (better known as Lady Bird Johnson), wife of Lyndon Baines Johnson, thirty-sixth president of the United States. The 42-acre botanical garden and nature center features plants from the American Southwest and northern Mexico. The facility is dedicated to furthering education about the environmental necessity, economic value, and natural beauty of native plants. In addition to a nature center, it has 23 theme gardens, courtyards, nature trails, observation tower, visitors' gallery with exhibits, children's house, library, and cafe.

Lady Bird Johnson Wildflower Center, 4801 La Crosse Ave., Austin, TX 78739. **Phone:** 512/292-4200. **Fax:** 512/292-4627. **E-mail:** wildflower@wildflower.org. **Website:** www.wildflower.org. **Hours:** grounds—Apr.—9-5:30 daily; remainder of year—9-5:30 Tues.-Sun.; closed Mon. and major holidays; visitors' gallery—9-4 Tues.-Sat.; 1-4 Sun.; closed Mon. and major holidays. **Admission:** adults, $5; seniors and students, $4; children under 6, free.

Virginia

BELLE GROVE PLANTATION. See Historic House Museums.

HISTORIC SMITHFIELD. See Historic House Museums.

KENMORE PLANTATION AND GARDENS. See Historic House Museums.

MAYMONT. See Historic House Museums.

SHIRLEY PLANTATION. See Historic House Museums.

VIRGINIA HOUSE. See Historic House Museums.

WOODLAWN PLANTATION. See Historic House Museums.

Washington

CATHERINE MONTGOMERY INTERPRETIVE CENTER. The Catherine Montgomery Interpretive Center in the Federation Forest State Park near Enumclaw, Washington, is named for its donor, who wanted to preserve and interpret the forests of the Pacific Northwest. Opened in 1963, the center has collections and exhibits of natural specimens located in the park. It is also the starting point for trails throughout the park.

Catherine Montgomery Interpretive Center, Federation Forest State Park, 49201 State Hwy. 410, Enumclaw, WA 98022. **Phone:** 360/663-2207. **Fax:** 360/663-0172. **Hours:** Memorial Day-Labor Day—9-4 daily; other times by appointment. **Admission:** free.

HULDA KLAGER LILAC GARDENS. The Hulda Klager Lilac Gardens in Woodland, Washington, is located at the former estate of noted hybridizer Hulda Klager, known for her work with lilacs. In addition to lilacs, which bloom for approximately three weeks, from mid-April to mid-May, the gardens contain a variety of other plants, shrubs, and trees. Tours of Klager's 1889 Victorian farmhouse are also offered during the lilac season.

Hulda Klager Lilac Gardens, 115 S. Pekin Rd., PO Box 828, Woodland, WA 98674. **Phone:** 360/225-8996. **Website:** www.lilacgardens.com. **Hours:** gardens—dawn-dusk daily; house—10-4 from mid-Apr. to mid-May; closed remainder of year. **Admission:** suggested donation—adults and children over 12, $2; children under 13, free.

WASHINGTON STATE CAPITAL MUSEUM. See History Museums.

Wisconsin

LEIGH YAWKEY WOODSON ART MUSEUM. See Art Museums.

PAINE ART CENTER AND GARDENS. See Art Museums.

PLANETARIUMS

See also Natural History Museums; Science and Technology Museums.

Michigan

CRANBROOK INSTITUTE OF SCIENCE. See Natural History Museums.

Montana

RUTH AND VERNON TAYLOR PLANETARIUM. Ruth and Vernon Taylor Planetarium at the Museum of the Rockies at Montana State University in Bozeman is named for its benefactors. Astronomy, multimedia, and laser shows are presented in the 100-seat planetarium with the Digistar computer graphics projection system. The museum is a regional history and natural history museum.

Ruth and Vernon Taylor Planetarium, Museum of the Rockies, Montana State University, 600 W. Kagy Blvd., Bozeman, MT 59717-0272. **Phone:** 406/994-5283. **Fax:** 406/994-2682. **Website:** www.montana.edu/wwwmor/. **Hours:** day after Labor Day-day before Memorial Day—9-5 Mon.-Sat., 12:30-5 Sun.; closed New Year's Day, Thanksgiving, and Christmas; Memorial Day-Labor Day—8 a.m.-8 p.m. **Admission:** museum—adults, $7; students and children 5-18, $4; children under 5, free; planetarium—$3; laser shows—$5; combination tickets—adults, $9; students and children 5-18, $6.50; children under 5, free.

New Hampshire

CHRISTA McAULIFFE PLANETARIUM. See Museums Honoring Exceptional Women.

Texas

MARIAN BLAKEMORE PLANETARIUM. The Marian Blakemore Planetarium at the Museum of the Southwest in Midland, Texas, is named for the wife of its donor, Bill Blakemore. The planetarium presents sky shows at the complex, which also includes the museum's home in a historic 1934 mansion and the Fredda Turner Durham Children's Museum (see Children's Museums).

Marian Blakemore Planetarium, Museum of the Southwest, 1705 W. Missouri Ave., Midland, TX 79701-6516. **Phone:** 915/683-2882. **Fax:** 915/570-7077. **Website:** www.museumsw.org. **Hours:** July—8 p.m. Fri.; Aug.-June—also by appointment; closed major holidays. **Admission:** adults, $3; children, $2.

Utah

SARAH SUMMERHAYS PLANETARIUM. The Sarah Summerhays Planetarium at Brigham Young University in Provo, Utah, was funded in 1955 by a family and named in honor of its grandmother. The small 65-seat facility was built as a laboratory to support astronomy classes and to present weekly public sky shows. It was closed in 2001 and was scheduled to be replaced by a new, larger planetarium in 2005.

Sarah Summerhays Planetarium, Brigham Young University, Dept. of Physics and Astronomy, Eyririg Science Center, Provo, UT 84602. **Phone:** 801/378-3849. **Hours and Admission:** closed, but will reopen as a new facility with a different name.

AQUARIUMS

California

MONTEREY BAY AQUARIUM. The Monterey Bay Aquarium, one of the world's largest and most popular aquatic public education and research facilities in Monterey, California, was made possible by a $50 million gift from David Packard, cofounder and former chairman of the Hewlett-Packard Company, and his wife, Lucile Packard.

The aquarium, which opened in 1984 on the former site of Cannery Row's largest and last cannery to close in 1972, was first proposed by four marine biologists from Stanford University's Hopkins Marine Station in Pacific Grove in 1977. A group of marine scientists, local residents, and members of the David and Lucile Packard Foundation of Los Altos formed the Monterey Aquarium Foundation the following year to pursue the project. The abandoned Hovden Cannery was demolished in 1980, and the construction of the aquarium followed.

The Monterey Bay Aquarium has more than 500 species of marine life in over 100 galleries, exhibits, and tanks that focus on such topics as the kelp forest, sea lions and otters, marine life, habitats, and the canning industry of Monterey Bay. It also has guided tours, educational programs, and research facilities. The aquarium attracts more than 1.8 million visitors each year.

Monterey Bay Aquarium, 886 Cannery Row, Monterey, CA 93940. **Phones:** 831/648-4888 and 831/648-4800. **Fax:** 831/648-4810. **E-mail:** executiveasst@mbayaq.org. **Website:** www.montereybayaquarium.org. **Hours:** Memorial Day weekend-Labor Day and holidays—9:30-6 daily; remainder of year—10-6 daily; closed Christmas. **Admission:** adults, $17.95; seniors and students 13-18, $14.95; disabled and children 3-12, $7.95; children under 3, free.

The Monterey Bay Aquarium, which began in Monterey, California, in the 1970s with funding from David and Lucile Packard's foundation, has become one of the largest and most popular aquariums in the world. This is the entrance hall of the aquarium, which features more than 500 species of marine life in over 100 galleries and exhibits. Courtesy Monterey Bay Aquarium.

Colorado

COLORADO'S OCEAN JOURNEY. Colorado's Ocean Journey—the first major aquatic facility in the Rocky Mountain region—was conceived in 1991 by Bill Fleming and his wife, Judy Peterson-Fleming, who sought to create a major aquarium in Denver in a land-locked state. The $93 million facility opened in 1999 but went into bankruptcy in 2002, when attendance fell below projections and bondholders foreclosed on a remaining $57 million debt. In 2003, Landry's Restaurants, Inc., of Houston, Texas, purchased the aquarium for $13.6 million, and the company is now in the process of reorganizing and expanding the site. The 106,515-square-foot aquarium has five major exhibits designed to inspire visitors "to discover, explore, enjoy, and protect our aquatic world." It features two water journeys—from Colorado to Mexico's Sea of Cortez, and from an Indonesian rain forest to the Pacific Ocean—as well as major exhibits on the Sea of Cortez and the depths of the Pacific, a sea otter cove, and sixteen focus areas.

Colorado's Ocean Journey, 700 Water St., Denver, CO 80211. **Phone:** 303/561-4450. **Fax:** 303/561-4465. **Website:** www.oceanjourney.org. **Hours:** Memorial Day weekend-Labor Day and some holidays—10-6 daily; remainder of year—10-5 daily; closed Christmas. **Admission:** adults, $14.95; seniors and children 13-17, $12.95; children 4-11, $6.95; children under 4, free.

Texas

GLADYS PORTER ZOO. See Zoos.

ZOOS

See also Natural History Museums; Nature and Wildlife Centers.

New York

ROSAMOND GIFFORD ZOO AT BURNET PARK. The Rosamond Gifford Zoo at Burnet Park in Syracuse, New York, is named for a local philanthropist whose foundation established a significant endowment for the zoo. Founded in 1914, the county zoo covers 45 acres and has collections of mammals, amphibians, reptiles, birds, and fish.

Rosamond Gifford Zoo at Burnet Park, 1 Conservation Pl., Syracuse, NY 13204. **Phone:** 315/435-8512. **Fax:** 315/435-8517. **E-mail:** bpzoo@emi.com. **Website:** www.rosamondgiffordzoo.org. **Hours:** 10-4:30 daily; closed New Year's Day, Thanksgiving, and Christmas. **Admission:** adults, $5; seniors, $3; children 5-14, $2; children under 5, free.

Texas

ELLEN TROUT ZOO. The Ellen Trout Zoo in Lufkin, Texas, is named in memory of the mother of industrialist Walter W. Trout, who founded the zoo in 1967. The 20-acre zoo has a variety of vertebrate animals, including mammals, amphibians, reptiles, and birds.

Ellen Trout Zoo, 402 Zoo Circle, Lufkin, TX 75904. **Phone:** 936/633-0399. **Fax:** 936/633-0311. **E-mail:** ghenley@ellentroutzoo.com. **Website:** www.ellentroutzoo.

The Gladys Porter Zoo in Brownsville, Texas, is named for its founder, shown here with a baby orangutan and some young admirers when the zoo opened in 1971. The zoo now has over 1,500 animals in approximately 400 species. Courtesy Gladys Porter Zoo.

com. **Hours:** Sept.-May—9-5 daily; June-Aug.—9-6 daily. **Admission:** adults and children over 11, $2; children 4-11, $1; children under 4, free.

GLADYS PORTER ZOO. Civic leader and philanthropist Gladys Porter was the founder and first president of the zoo named for her in Brownsville, Texas. Porter, who was the daughter of Earl C. Sams, longtime president and later chairman of the JCPenney Company, was involved in planning, constructing, and stocking the zoo, which was given to the city by the Earl C. Sams Foundation.

The 31-acre Gladys Porter Zoo, which opened in 1971 and now serves 350,000 visitors annually, has more than 1,600 animal specimens representing approximately 400 species, as well as an aquarium and botanical garden with over 250 species and subspecies of tropical and neotropical plants. The zoo is laid out in four major geographical areas—Tropical America, Indo-Australia, Asia, and Africa. It also has such non-geographical areas as a small animals section, including nursery; herpetarium and aquatic wing; free-flight aviary; bear grottoes; sea lions exhibit; and Mexican canyon replica with macaws, crested caracaras, and king vultures.

Gladys Porter Zoo, 500 Ringgold St., Brownsville, TX 78520. **Phone:** 956/546-7187. **Fax:** 956/546-4940. **E-mail:** admin@gpz.org. **Website:** www.gpz.org. **Hours:** late Oct.-early Apr.—9-5 Mon.-Fri., 9-5:30 Sat.-Sun.; early Apr.-late Oct.—9-6 Mon.-Fri., 9-6:30 Sat.-Sun. **Admission:** adults, $6.50; seniors, $5; children 2-13, $3.25; children under 2, free.

Other Types of Museums and Sites

CHILDREN'S MUSEUMS

See also Museums Founded and/or Operated by Women's Organizations.

California

LORI BROCK CHILDREN'S DISCOVERY CENTER. The Lori Brock Children's Discovery Center, which is part of the Kern County Museum in Bakersfield, California, is named for the daughter of John Brock Sr., a local department store owner who funded the children's museum in her memory. Opened in 1976, the museum grew out of a Junior League project called Young Adventurers. It has participatory thematic exhibits, hobby workshops, arts festivals, drama programs, and other educational programs. The Kern County Museum is an outdoor museum with several museums and nearly 50 historic buildings.

Lori Brock Children's Discovery Center, Kern County Museum, 3801 Chester Ave., Bakersfield, CA 93301. **Phone:** 661/852-5000. **Fax:** 661/322-6415. **E-mail:** caenriquez@kern. org. **Website:** www.kcmuseum.org. **Hours:** 8-5 Mon.-Fri., 10-5 Sat., 12-5 Sun.; closed Thanksgiving and Christmas. **Admission:** adults, $5; seniors, $4; children 3-12, $3; children under 3, free.

RANDALL MUSEUM. The Randall Museum in San Francisco originally opened in 1937 as the Junior Recreation Museum, and in 1951—when a new building to house the museum was dedicated—it was renamed in honor of Josephine D. Randall, the city's first woman superintendent of recreation and parks. The hands-on museum, operated by the San Francisco Recreation and Parks Department, has exhibits, nature study, arts and crafts, clubs, and field trips, primarily for 9- to 12-year-olds, but some activities also serve younger children and adults.

Randall Museum, 199 Museum Way, San Francisco, CA 94114. **Phone:** 415/554-9600. **Fax:** 415/554-9609. **E-mail:** info@randallmuseum.org. **Website:** www.randall.mus.ca.us. **Hours:** 10-5 Tues.-Sat.; closed Sun.-Mon. and major holidays. **Admission:** free.

Colorado

COLLAGE CHILDREN'S MUSEUM. The founding of the Collage Children's Museum in Boulder, Colorado, in 1989 was spearheaded by two mothers of young children—Jane Oniki and Wendy Daniels. The storefront museum, for children from preschool through third grade, sought to foster children's curiosity about their world, primarily through hands-on experiences that would enhance their knowledge about the arts and sciences, diverse cultures, and uses of technology. The museum closed in 2003 due to lack of funds.

Collage Children's Museum, 2065 30th St., PO Box 2209, Boulder, CO 80306. **Phone:** 303/440-0053. **Fax:** 303/443-8040. **E-mail:** ngeyer@collagemuseum.org. **Website:** www.bcn.boulder.co.us/arts/collage. Now closed.

SANGRE DE CRISTO ARTS CENTER (Buell Children's Museum). See Arts Centers.

WOW! CHILDREN'S MUSEUM. The WOW! Children's Museum in Lafayette, Colorado, was founded in 1996 by Lisa Atallah and her husband, Dario Atallah, to provide a hands-on educational center for young children and to encourage parents to spend more time with their children. Lisa Atallah is now the director, and Dario Atallah helps with the bookkeeping. The nonprofit museum, which serves children from ages 1 through 11, has interactive exhibits on dinosaurs, a pirate ship, a grocery store, and other subjects. The museum moved from Louisville to the Old Firehouse in the adjoining city of Lafayette in 2004.

WOW! Children's Museum, 110 N. Harrison St., Lafayette, CO 80026. **Phone:** 303/604-2424. **Fax:** 303/666-8376. **Website:** www.wowmuseum.com. **Hours:** 9-6 Mon.-Thurs, 10-6 Fri.-Sat.; closed Sun. and major holidays. **Admission:** adults, free; children 15 months-12 years, $6.50.

Connecticut

LUTZ CHILDREN'S MUSEUM. The Lutz Children's Museum in Manchester, Connecticut, was founded in 1953 by Hazel Lutz, a school art supervisor, with the assistance of the Manchester Parent-Teacher Association. Under Lutz's leadership, the museum initially developed school loan kits that brought historical and other real teaching objects into the classrooms. The museum now occupies a former elementary school building and has participatory exhibits, educational programs, an outdoor playscape, and a 53-acre nature center.

Lutz Children's Museum, 247 S. Main St., Manchester, CT 06040. **Phone:** 860/649-2838. **Hours:** 10-2 Mon., 12-5 Tues.-Wed., 9:30-5 Thurs.-Fri., 12-5 Sat.-Sun.; closed major holidays. **Admission:** adults and children, $3; children under 1, free.

Georgia

JACQUELINE CASEY HUDGENS CENTER FOR THE ARTS (Children's Art Museum). See Arts Centers.

Illinois

KOHL CHILDREN'S MUSEUM. Dolores Kohl of the Kohl Educational Foundation founded the Kohl Children's Museum in Wilmette, Illinois, in 1985—based largely on the interactive learning activities carried out in the United States and Israel by the Kohl Teacher Centers since 1974. The museum features hands-on exhibits and activities to further the understanding of basic life skills, science, the arts, and world cultures.

Kohl Children's Museum, 165 Green Bay Rd., Wilmette, IL 60091. **Phone:** 847/256-6056. **Fax:** 847/256-2921. **E-mail:** sturner165@aol.com. **Website:** www.kohlchildrensmuseum. org. **Hours:** 9-12 Mon., 9-5 Tues.-Sat., 12-5 Sun.; closed major holidays. **Admission:** adults and children, $5; seniors, $3.50.

Indiana

CHILDREN'S MUSEUM OF INDIANAPOLIS. The Children's Museum of Indianapolis was established in 1925 through the efforts of Mrs. John N. Carey, after she became enthused by a visit to the nation's first children's museum—the Brooklyn Children's Museum. She was able to generate interest among other civic-minded women in the community, and in cooperation with the Progressive Teachers Association, she opened a small children's museum in a carriage house.

The Indianapolis museum is now the largest and most popular children's museum, occupying 365,000 square feet and having an annual attendance of 1 million. It has 10 exhibit halls, with displays ranging from prehistory and history to natural history, physical sciences, art, toys, railroading, and peoples of the world. The museum also has an operating turn-of-the-twentieth-century carousel, preschool playscape, planetarium, 350-seat theater, large-screen domed theater, resource center with over 800 loan exhibits, 50,000-square-foot outdoor park, and 180-acre outdoor preserve at another site.

The Children's Museum of Indianapolis, which was begun in the 1920s by women, consists of the museum building and the CineDome (at right), a five-story theater with a domed screen. The Indiana museum is the nation's largest children's museum. Courtesy Children's Museum of Indianapolis.

Children's Museum of Indianapolis, 300 N. Meridian St., PO Box 3000, Indianapolis, IN 46206-3000. **Phone:** 317/334-4000. **Fax:** 317/921-4122. **E-mail:** tcmi@childrensmuseum.org. **Website:** www.childrensmuseum.org. **Hours:** Mar.-Labor Day—10-5 daily (also to 8 p.m. first Thurs. of month); closed Mon. remainder of year, Easter, Thanksgiving, and Christmas. **Admission:** adults, $8; seniors, $7; children 2-17, $3.50; children under 2, free; also free after 5 p.m. first Thurs. of month.

HANNAH LINDAHL CHILDREN'S MUSEUM. The Hannah Lindahl Children's Museum, operated by the public school district in Mishawaka, Indiana, was founded in 1946 by elementary education director Hannah Lindahl and civic leader Carol Eberhart Hiller to supplement the school curricula. The 6,000-square-foot museum has exhibits on local history, natural history, ethnic culture of Mishawaka, fire safety, and other subjects. It also has a Japanese house and gardens, one-room schoolhouse, general store, dental office, two-room furnished house, and a ca. 1800 Mishawaka village.

Hannah Lindahl Children's Museum, 1402 S. Main St., Mishawaka, IN 46544. **Phone:** 219/254-4540. **Fax:** 219/254-4585. **E-mail:** hlindahl@michianatoday.com. **Website:** www.hlcm.org. **Hours:** Sept.-May—9-4 Tues.-Fri., 10-2 1st and 2nd Sat. of month; June—10-2 Tues.-Thurs.; closed July-Aug. and school holidays and breaks. **Admission:** local school classes, free; adults and children over 5, $1; children 3-5, 50¢; children under 3, free.

Kansas

DEANNA ROSE CHILDREN'S FARMSTEAD. The Deanna Rose Children's Farmstead was founded by the city of Overland Park, Kansas, in 1976, and was renamed in 1985 in memory of the city's first police officer killed in the line of duty. The farmstead has a miniature barn and silo and such full-size buildings as an early 1900s schoolhouse, church, and windmill. It functions as a young children's petting zoo, featuring such barnyard animals and fowl as sheep, goats, pigs, rabbits, chickens, ducks, and turkeys. The farmstead also has a birds of prey exhibit with eagles, hawks, and owls.

Deanna Rose Children's Farmstead, 13800 Switzer Rd., Overland Park, KS 66210. **Phone:** 913/897-2360. **Website:** www.deannarosefarmstead.com. **Hours:** Apr.-day before Memorial Day weekend—9-5 daily; Memorial Day weekend-Labor Day—9-8 daily; day after Labor Day-Oct.—9-5 daily; closed remainder of year. **Admission:** free.

Massachusetts

CHILDREN'S MUSEUM IN DARTMOUTH. The Children's Museum in Dartmouth, which is housed in a 1930s two-story barn in South Dartmouth, Massachusetts, was founded in 1952 by a group of women who wanted to stimulate children's interest in the arts, natural sciences, and humanities. Originally a small natural-science center, it was destroyed in a fire in 1965 and again in 1982. It reopened at a dairy farm complex in 1983 as a more comprehensive children's museum. The museum now has natural history, Native American, agricultural, art, and other collections; hands-on exhibits; live animals; and 60 acres with trails.

Children's Museum in Dartmouth, 276 Gulf Rd., South Dartmouth, MA. **Phone:** 508/993-3361. **Fax:** 508/993-3332. **E-mail:** darmuse@meganet.net. **Website:** www.dartmouthmuseum.com. **Hours:** 10-5 Tues.-Fri., 10-4 Sat., 11-3 Sun.; closed Mon. and major holidays. **Admission:** adults and children, $3.75.

Minnesota

JUDY GARLAND CHILDREN'S MUSEUM. See Museums Honoring Exceptional Women.

MINNESOTA CHILDREN'S MUSEUM. Three mothers of small children who were intrigued by children's museums in other cities established the children's museum in the Twin Cities area of Minnesota in 1979. They were Marialice Harwood, Suzanne Payne, and Kay Donaldson of suburban Kenwood. The museum, which opened in 1981 in a former cold-storage building in Itasca, is now the Minnesota Children's Museum in a new building in St. Paul. The museum has six galleries—on such subjects as how things work, different cultures, and Minnesota habitats—for children 6 months through 10 years of age.

Minnesota Children's Museum, 10 W. 7th St., St. Paul, MN 55102. **Phone:** 651/225-6001. **Fax:** 651/225-6006. **E-mail:** mcm@mcm.org. **Website:** www.mcm.org. **Hours:** 9-5 Tues.-Sun. (also to 8 p.m. Thurs.); closed Mon., Thanksgiving, and Christmas; Memorial Day-Labor Day—also 9-5 Mon.; **Admission:** adults and children over 2, $5.95; seniors and children 1 and 2, $3.95; children under 1, free.

Missouri

THE MAGIC HOUSE, ST. LOUIS CHILDREN'S MUSEUM. Jody Newman and Barbie Freund, two young women who recognized the need for a children's participatory museum, spent three years raising the funds, overseeing the renovation of a 1901 Victorian mansion, and developing the exhibits for what became the Magic House in St. Louis in 1979. The children's museum now has over 170 hands-on exhibits, numerous educational programs, and an annual attendance of over 370,000.

The Magic House, St. Louis Children's Museum, 516 S. Kirkwood Rd., St. Louis, MO 63122. Phones: 314/822-8900 and 314/822-8905. Fax: 314/822-8930. E-mail: beth@magichouse.org. Website: www.magichouse.com. Hours: Memorial Day-Labor Day—9:30-5:30 Mon.-Sat. (also to 9 p.m. Fri.), 11-5:30 Sun.; remainder of year—12-5:30 Tues.-Fri., 9:30-5:30 Sat., 11-5:30 Sun.; closed Mon., New Year's Day, Easter, Thanksgiving, and Christmas. Admission: adults and children, $6; children under 2, free.

New York

BROOKLYN CHILDREN'S MUSEUM. The Brooklyn Children's Museum, the world's first children's museum, was established in 1899 as a branch of the Brooklyn Museum in a Victorian mansion. The objective was to have an educational center that would stimulate a child's power of observation and instruct and delight young children. Anna Billings Gallup, who was appointed museum curator in 1902 and served until 1937, helped transform these goals into reality.

Gallup made children feel that the museum was created for them—and that they could touch and manipulate the exhibits, which was unusual at the time. The exhibits demonstrated principles and relationships, and sometimes used live animals as well as stuffed ones. Clubs were formed with children having similar interests, relationships were developed with teachers and teacher-training institutions, and loan collections were made available to schools.

The Brooklyn Children's Museum, which has undergone numerous changes over the years, now occupies a partly underground high-tech building with four levels leading to an exterior courtyard. It has collections in ethnology, natural history, and folk crafts, and places emphasis on art, science, and cultural interactions.

Brooklyn Children's Museum, 145 Brooklyn Ave., Brooklyn, NY 11213. Phones: 718/735-4400 and 718/735-4402. Fax: 718/604-7442. Website: www.brooklynkids.org. Hours: June-Aug.—12-5 Mon. and Wed.-Thurs., 12-6:30 Fri., 10-5 Sat.-Sun.; closed Tues.; remainder of year—2-5 Wed.-Fri., 10-5 Sat.-Sun., holidays, and school vacations; closed Mon.-Tues. Suggested Admission: $4.

CHILDREN'S MUSEUM OF MANHATTAN. The Children's Museum of Manhattan in New York City evolved from a neighborhood educational and arts center conceived in 1972 by Bette Korman. It opened in 1973 as G.A.M.E. (Growth through Art and Museum Experience) in two basement storefronts and served as a cultural resource center that united school and museum programs.

As the idea caught on and more space was needed, G.A.M.E. moved into a renovated nineteenth-century courthouse in 1979, changed its name to the Manhattan Laboratory Museum, and expanded its programs to serve the entire metropolitan area. In 1985 it became the Children's Museum of Manhattan. Now located in a former elementary school building, the museum has participatory exhibits, arts studios, literacy programs, and environmental, media, performing arts, early childhood, and adventure centers.

Children's Museum of Manhattan, Tisch Bldg., 212 W. 83rd St., New York, NY 10024. Phone: 212/721-1223. Fax: 212/721-1127. E-mail: mail@cmom.org. Website: www.cmom.org. Hours: mid-June-early Sept.—10-5 Tues.-Sun.; closed Mon.; remainder of year—10-5 Wed.-Sun.; open Mon.-Tues. only for school and outreach groups; closed New Year's Day, Thanksgiving, and Christmas. Admission: adults and children, $6; seniors, $3.

Oklahoma

JASMINE MORAN CHILDREN'S MUSEUM. The Jasmine Moran Children's Museum—a hands-on museum in the form of a child-size town in Seminole, Oklahoma—is named for the wife of the donor, oilman Melvin Moran. The museum, founded in 1993, has a miniature courthouse, hospital, grocery, fire station, television studio, and other community settings, where children can dress and assume such roles as firefighter, dentist, and grocer. It also has such other attractions as model trains and airplanes, a dollhouse, Native American artifacts, a computer exhibit, and a historic fire truck, car, and caboose.

Jasmine Moran Children's Museum, 1714 W. State Hwy. 9, Seminole, OK 74868. Phone: 405/382-0950. Fax: 405/382-3707. Website: www.jasminemoran.mus.ok.us/museum. Hours: 10-5 Tues.-Sat., 1-5 Sun.; closed Mon., first 2 weeks in Sept., and major holidays. Admission: adults and children over 2, $6; seniors, $5; children under 3, free.

Pennsylvania

PLEASE TOUCH MUSEUM. Portia Hamilton Sperr, a Montessori educator, was the founder and first director of the Please Touch Museum in Philadelphia. The museum, which began in 1976, serves children through eight years of age and has multidisciplinary exhibits in the arts, sciences, and humanities. Among the exhibit settings are a simulated supermarket, television studio, barnyard, science park, bus, boat, and an "Alice's Adventures in Wonderland" mock-up.

Please Touch Museum, 210 N. 21st St., Philadelphia, PA 19103. **Phone:** 215/963-0667. **Fax:** 215/963-0424. **E-mail:** ceo@pleasetouchmuseum.org. **Website:** www. pleasetouchmuseum.org. **Hours:** July-Labor Day—9-5 daily; remainder of year—9-4:30 daily; closed New Year's Day, Thanksgiving, and Christmas. **Admission:** adults and children, $8.95; children under 1, free.

Texas

FREDDA TURNER DURHAM CHILDREN'S MUSEUM. The Fredda Turner Durham Children's Museum, at the Museum of the Southwest in Midland, Texas, is named for its donor. The children's museum was added to the Museum of the Southwest complex in 1990. The complex also includes the 1934 Turner family mansion, where the museum is housed, and the Marian Blakemore Planetarium (see Planetariums).

Fredda Turner Durham Children's Museum, Museum of the Southwest, 1705 W. Missouri Ave., Midland, TX 79701-6516. **Phone:** 915/683-2882. **Fax:** 915/570-7077. **Website:** www.museum.org. **Hours:** 10-5 Tues.-Sat., 2-5 Sun.; closed Mon. and major holidays. **Admission:** free.

OLLIE MAE MOEN DISCOVERY CENTER. Ollie Mae Moen of Waco, Texas, was an active parent, collector, and firm believer in "hands-on" education for children. In 1962 she convinced the local Parent Teacher Association to start the Youth Cultural Center, which she directed for nearly two decades. After Moen retired in 1982, the Strecker Museum at Baylor University assumed responsibility for the center. In 1994 the center was renamed in her honor as the Ollie Mae Moen Discovery Center, a museum for children.

The center—which has had many temporary homes during its history—finally received a permanent home in 2002. It moved from its downtown warehouse site and was incorporated into the Strecker Museum's new building—called the Harry and Anna Jeanes Discovery Center—on the Baylor campus. The museum com-

plex's name was changed to the Mayborn Museum Complex. The children's museum became the Children's World section in the complex and features an exhibit/program area called Mrs. Moen's Neighborhood.

Ollie Mae Moen Discovery Center, Strecker Museum, Baylor University, 220 S. 4th St., PO Box 97154, Waco, TX 76798-7154. **Phone:** 254/710-1233. **Fax:** 254/710-1173. **E-mail:** jill_barrow@baylor.edu. **Hours:** 9-5 Mon.-Fri.; 104 Sat.; closed Sun. and national holidays. **Admission:** free.

Washington

PAUL H. KARSHNER MEMORIAL MUSEUM. The Paul H. Karshner Memorial Museum, a children's history teaching museum that is part of the public school system in Puyallup, Washington, was established in 1930 by Warner and Ella Karshner in honor of their young son, who died of polio. The museum, housed in a 1920s school building, was founded primarily to strengthen visual education. The Karshners originally donated more than 10,000 artifacts, which have been expanded over the years, with an emphasis on local history, natural history, major Native American groups, and cultures from around the world.

Paul H. Karshner Memorial Museum, 309 4th St. N.E., Puyallup, WA 98372. **Phone:** 253/841-8748. **Fax:** 253/840-8950. **E-mail:** reckerson@puyallup.k12.wa.us. **Hours:** Labor Day-mid-June—9-3 Mon.-Fri.; closed Sat.-Sun., national holidays, and remainder of year. **Admission:** free.

Wisconsin

BETTY BRINN CHILDREN'S MUSEUM. The Betty Brinn Children's Museum, which serves children ages 10 and under in the Milwaukee area, was founded in 1995 and named for a supportive businesswoman. The museum uses hands-on exhibits and programming to stimulate learning in a fun environment. Children can pick apples from an orchard, perform in a television studio, crawl through a giant human ear, create their own works of art, and play different job roles in the community.

Betty Brinn Children's Museum, 929 E. Wisconsin Ave., Milwaukee, WI 53202. **Phone:** 414/291-0888. **Fax:** 414/291-0906. **E-mail:** kadam@bbcmkids.org. **Website:** www.vvcmkids.org. **Hours:** June-Aug.: 9-5 Mon.-Sat., 12-5 Sun.; remainder of year—9-5 Tues.-Sat., 12-5 Sun.; closed Mon., New Year's Day, Fourth of July, Thanksgiving, and Christmas. **Admission:** adults and children, $4; children under 1, free.

DOLL, TOY, AND MINIATURE MUSEUMS

Arizona

ARIZONA DOLL AND TOY MUSEUM. Antique dolls and toys from around the world are featured at the Arizona Doll and Toy Museum, founded in Phoenix in 1987 by Inez McCrary, director and curator. The museum has five rooms of exhibits, including a 1912 schoolroom with dolls as students and a miniature hat shop and dry goods store with tiny hats, accessories, bolts of materials, laces, and working scissors.

Arizona Doll and Toy Museum, Heritage Square, 602 E. Adams St., Phoenix, AZ 85004. **Phone:** 602/253-9337. **Fax:** 480/948-7973. **E-mail:** azdollntoy@aol.com. **Hours:** 10-4 Tues.-Sat., 12-4 Sun.; closed Mon., Aug., and major holidays. **Admission:** adults and children over 12, $2.50; seniors, $2; children under 13, $1.

California

HELEN MOE ANTIQUE DOLL MUSEUM. The Helen Moe Antique Doll Museum in Paso Robles, California, has more than 800 antique dolls, including a 1540 doll that belonged to Edward VI, son of King Henry VIII of England, and room settings depicting the early 1900s. The museum was founded in the 1960s.

Helen Moe Antique Doll Museum, 88 Wellsona Rd., Paso Robles, CA 93446. **Phone:** 805/239-4556. **Hours:** by appointment. **Admission:** adults and children over 11, $2; children under 12, free.

District of Columbia

WASHINGTON DOLLS' HOUSE AND TOY MUSEUM. The Washington Dolls' House and Toy Museum in Washington, D.C., began in 1975 when Flora Gill Jacobs's collection of dollhouses, dolls, antique toys, and miniature items began to overflow her home. Most of the objects are from the nineteenth century, and several date from the eighteenth century.

Jacobs bought her first dollhouse in 1945 while researching material for *A History of Doll Houses.* She eventually acquired more than 100 furnished miniature houses, shops, stables, schools, and churches, as well as many antique dolls, toys, games, and miniature items such as pewter plates, copper pots, earthenware bowls, teacups, clocks, and books. The museum also has a 20-seat Edwardian tearoom for parties.

Washington Dolls' House and Toy Museum, 5236 44th St. N.W., Washington, DC 20015. **Phones:** 202/363-6400 and 202/244-0024. **Fax:** 202/237-1659. **E-mail:** dollshousetoymuseum.com. **Hours:** 10-5 Tues.-Sat., 12-5 Sun.; closed Mon., New Year's Day, Thanksgiving, and Christmas. **Admission:** adults and children over 11, $4; seniors, $3; children under 12, $2.

Georgia

MARY MILLER DOLL MUSEUM. Mary Miller was the founder and benefactor of the Mary Miller Doll Museum in Brunswick, Georgia, which features more than 3,500 dolls in period costumes representing approximately 90 countries. The museum, founded in 1976, also contains dollhouses and miniature vehicles.

Mary Miller Doll Museum, 209-11 Gloucester St., Brunswick, GA 31520. **Phone and Fax:** 912/267-7569. **E-mail:** dollmuseum@thebest.net. **Hours:** 10-4:30 Mon.-Fri.; closed Sat.-Sun., New Year's Day, Easter, Thanksgiving, and Christmas. **Admission:** adults, $4; students, $3; students, $3; children under 5, free.

Louisiana

ENCHANTED MANSION, A DOLL MUSEUM. Rosemary Sedberry founded the Enchanted Mansion, a Doll Museum in Baton Rouge, Louisiana, in 1995 to display her collection of over 2,000 dolls. Another feature of the museum is a life-size Victorian dollhouse.

Enchanted Mansion, A Doll Museum, 190 Lee Dr., Baton Rouge, LA 70808. **Phone:** 225/769-0005. **Fax:** 225/766-6822. **E-mail:** temansion@bellsouth.net. **Website:** www.angelfire.com/laa/. **Hours:** 10-5 Mon. and Wed.-Sat., 1-4 Sun.; closed Tues., Easter, Thanksgiving, and Christmas. **Admission:** adults and children over 14, $4.50; seniors, $3.50; children 2-14, $2; children under 2, free.

Missouri

SOCIETY OF MEMORIES DOLL MUSEUM. The Society of Memories Doll Museum in St. Joseph, Missouri, was started in 1968 with dolls purchased at an auction from the collection of Orel Andrews. Since then, the museum's collection has been increased to approximately 1,000 dolls and toys. The museum is housed in a restored 1871 former church building.

Society of Memories Doll Museum, 1115 S. 12th St., St. Joseph, MO 64503. **Phone:** 816/233-1420. **Hours:**

May-Sept.—11:30-4:30 Tues.-Sat., 1-4 Sun.; closed Mon.; Apr. and Oct.—11:30-4:30 Sat., 1-4 Sun.; closed Mon.-Fri. and remainder of year. **Admission:** adults and children over 12, $2; seniors, $1.50; children 5-12, 75¢; children under 5, free.

TOY AND MINIATURE MUSEUM OF KANSAS CITY. The Toy and Miniature Museum of Kansas City was opened in 1982 by two collectors, Mary Harris Francis and Barbara Marshall. The museum, housed in the 24-room 1911 Tureman-McCune Mansion, on the University of Missouri–Kansas City campus, features more than 100 furnished dollhouses and room settings, nineteenth- and twentieth-century toys, and transportation miniatures.

Toy and Miniature Museum of Kansas City, 5235 Oak St., Kansas City, MO 64112. **Phone:** 816/333-9328. **Fax:** 816/333-2055. **E-mail:** toynmin@swbell.net. **Website:** www.umkc.edu/tmm. **Hours:** 10-4 Wed.-Sat., 1-4 Sun.; closed Mon.-Tues., major holidays and two weeks after Labor Day. **Admission:** adults, $4; seniors and students over 12, $3.50; children 3-12, $2; children under 3, free.

Montana

HOUSE OF A THOUSAND DOLLS. The House of a Thousand Dolls in Loma, Montana, was founded in 1978 by Marion Britton, who still operates the museum, which contains approximately 1,000 dolls and toys from 1830 to the present.

House of a Thousand Dolls, 106 1st St., PO Box 136, Loma, MT 59460. **Phone:** 406/739-4338. **Hours:** by appointment. **Admission:** adults and children over 11, $1; children 6-11, 50¢; children under 6, free.

YESTERDAY'S PLAYTHINGS MUSEUM. The doll, toy, and other collections of two women have been the highlights of Yesterday's Playthings Museum, one of four museums at the Old Prison Museums in Deer Lodge, Montana. The museum was started in 1986 by the Powell County Museum and Arts Foundation with the loan of Genevieve Hostetter's antique collection. When she died, the collection was returned to her family and was replaced by Harriet Free's collection, which features dolls she made. Other museums in the territorial prison complex include the Old Montana Prison Museum, Frontier Montana Museum, and Montana Auto Museum.

Yesterday's Playthings Museum, 1106 Deer Lodge, MT 59722. **Phone:** 406/846-1480. **Fax:** 406/846-3156. **E-mail:** oldprisonmuseums@in-tch.com. **Website:** www.

montanaprisonmuseums.com. **Hours:** 9-5 mid-May-Sept.; closed remainder of year. **Admission** (includes all 4 museums in the prison complex): adults, $9; seniors, $8; children 10-15, $5; children under 10, free.

New Hampshire

MUSEUM OF CHILDHOOD. More than 5,000 dolls and toys—some dating from the mid-1800s—collected by two sisters, Marjorie G. Banks and Elizabeth B. MacRury, in their travels, are featured at the Museum of Childhood in Wakefield, New Hampshire. The museum—called a Museum of Memories—has 12 rooms of dolls, dollhouses, toys, music boxes, children's books, and other historical items, including an 1890s one-room school, child's room, and kitchen.

Museum of Childhood, 2784 Wakefield Rd., Wakefield, NH 03872. **Phone:** 603/522-8073. **Hours:** Memorial Day-Labor Day—11-4 Wed.-Mon.; closed Tues. and remainder of year. **Admission:** adults and children over 9, $3; children under 10, $1.25.

PAULINE E. GLIDDEN TOY MUSEUM. Pauline E. Glidden purchased and renovated an 1810 house adjacent to the Ashland (New Hampshire) Historical Society in 1991 to house her lifetime collection of toys—and then gave the house and the collection to the society. The collection includes more than 2,000 antique toys, as well as dolls, miniature china, appliances, and furniture; children's books, prints, and games; and other such materials.

Pauline E. Glidden Toy Museum, Ashland Historical Society, Pleasant St., PO Box 175, Ashland, NH 03217. **Phone:** 603/968-7289. **Hours:** July-Labor Day—1-4 Wed.-Sat.; closed Sun.-Tues. and remainder of year. **Admission:** adults and children over 12, $1; children under 13, free.

New York

VICTORIAN DOLL MUSEUM. While still in high school, Linda Greenfield started an antique-doll restoration and repair service in 1967 in North Chili, a suburb of Rochester, New York. Three years later she founded the Victorian Doll Museum, which now has over 3,000 bisque, china, wax, tin, and vinyl dolls, as well as toys, a puppet theater, circus, and miniature Noah's Ark. The museum and doll hospital are located in the same building but are operated by Greenfield separately.

Victorian Doll Museum, 4332 Buffalo Rd., North Chili, NY 14514. **Phone:** 716/247-0130. **Hours:** Feb.-Dec.—10-4:30

Tues.-Sat.; closed Sun.-Mon., Jan., and major holidays. Admission: adults and children over 12, $2.50; children 5-12, $1.50; children under 5, free.

North Carolina

ANGELA PETERSON DOLL AND MINIATURE MUSEUM. The Angela Peterson Doll and Miniature Museum in High Point, North Carolina, features more than 1,700 dolls and miniatures—most of which were from Peterson's original collection. The dolls and miniatures represent a wide range of styles and periods.

Angela Peterson Doll and Miniature Museum, 101 W. Green Dr., High Point, NC 27260. **Phone:** 336/885-3655. **Hours:** 10-4:30 Mon.-Fri., 9-4:30 Sat., 1-4:30 Sun.; closed Mon. in Nov.-Mar. **Admission:** adults, $4; seniors, $3.50; children 6-15, $2.50; children 3-5, $1; children under 3, free.

Ohio

BARBARA BARBE DOLL MUSEUM. More than 3,000 dolls are displayed at the Barbara Barbe Doll Museum in Barnesville, Ohio. They include early bisque dolls, tin heads, wax dolls, hard plastics, and vinyls, as well as contemporary models.

Barbara Barbe Doll Museum, 211 Chestnut St., Barnesville, OH 43713. **Phones:** 740/425-1760 and 740/425-2301. **Hours:** May-Sept.—1-4 Wed.-Sun.; closed Mon.-Tues. and remainder of year. **Admission:** adults and children over 12, $2; children 6-12, $1; children under 6, free.

MILAN HISTORICAL MUSEUM. See History Museums.

Oklahoma

ELIZA CRUCE HALL DOLL COLLECTION. The Eliza Cruce Hall Doll Collection is featured in the children's section of the Ardmore Public Library in Ardmore, Oklahoma. It contains more than 300 dolls, some dating to the early 1700s.

Eliza Cruce Hall Doll Collection, Ardmore Public Library, 320 E. St. N.W., Ardmore, OK 73401. **Phone:** 580/233-8290. **Hours:** 10-8:30 Mon.-Thurs., 10-4 Fri.-Sat.; closed Sun. and major holidays. **Admission:** free.

IDA DENNIE WILLIS MUSEUM OF MINIATURES, DOLLS, AND TOYS. For over 30 years, Ida Dennie Willis collected dolls, dollhouses, toys, and miniatures. They are now part of the Ida Dennie Willis Museum of Miniatures, Dolls, and Toys, housed in a renovated 1910 Tudor mansion in Tulsa, Oklahoma. Among the

more than 2,000 dolls are collections of Native American and other ethnic dolls.

Ida Dennie Willis Museum of Miniatures, Dolls, and Toys, 628 N. Country Club Dr., Tulsa, OK 74127. **Phone:** 918/584-6654. **Hours:** 11-4:30 Wed.-Sat.; closed Sun.-Tues. and major holidays. **Admission:** adults, $3.50; seniors and children 12-17, $3; children under 12, $2.50.

Oregon

DOLLY WARES DOLL MUSEUM. Dorothy Smith, who began restoring and repairing antique dolls in 1940, opened the Dolly Wares Doll Museum in Florence, Oregon, in 1970. The museum now features a collection of over 3,000 dolls, ranging from a crude pre-Columbian clay doll to some of the present-day European glamour dolls.

Dolly Wares Doll Museum, 3620 U.S. Hwy. 101, Florence, OR 97439. **Phone:** 541/997-3391. **Hours:** 10-5 Tues.-Sun.; closed Mon., New Year's Day, Thanksgiving, and Christmas. **Admission:** adults and children over 12, $5; children 6-12, $3; children under 6, free.

Pennsylvania

MARY MERRITT DOLL MUSEUM. In addition to over 3,500 dolls, the Mary Merritt Doll Museum in Douglassville, Pennsylvania, has more than 40 miniature period rooms and a full-size replica of a ca. 1850 Philadelphia toy shop. It is considered one of the nation's most comprehensive doll museums.

Mary Merritt Doll Museum, 843 Ben Franklin Hwy., Douglassville, PA 19518. **Phone:** 610/385-3809. **E-mail:** dollmuseum@merritts.com. **Hours:** 10-4:30 Mon. and Wed.-Sat., 1-5 Sun.; closed Tues. and major holidays. **Admission:** adults and children over 12, $3; children 5-12, $1.50; children under 5, free.

South Dakota

ENCHANTED WORLD DOLL MUSEUM. Eunice and Reese Sheldon started collecting dolls in the 1930s, and in 1977 they established the Enchanted World Doll Museum in Mitchell, South Dakota. The museum, operated by an endowed foundation, has nearly 5,000 antique, rare, character, and contemporary dolls, and such miniature items as dishes, furniture, buggies, and dollhouses.

Enchanted World Doll Museum, 615 N. Main St., Mitchell, SD 57301. **Phone:** 605/996-9896. **Fax:** 605/996-0210. **Hours:**

June-Sept.—8-8 daily; Mar.-May and Oct.-Dec.—9-5 Mon.-Sat., 1-5 Sun.; closed Jan.-Feb. and major holidays. **Admission:** adults, $3.50; seniors, $3; children 6-18, $1.25; children under 6, free.

Texas

FRANKS ANTIQUE DOLL MUSEUM. The Franks Antique Doll Museum, which contains over 2,000 dolls from the 1700s to the present, was founded in Marshall, Texas, in 1960 by Clara Franks, who still operates the museum on the grounds of the 1894 Hochwald Home. The museum also has toys and such miniatures as furniture, dishes, and buggies.

Franks Antique Doll Museum, 211 W. Grand Ave., Marshall, TX 75670 (postal address: 410 N. Grove St., Marshall, TX 75670). **Phones:** 903/935-3065 and 903/935-3070. **Hours:** by appointment. **Admission:** adults and children over 12, $5; children 7-12, $2.50; children under 7, free.

Utah

McCURDY HISTORICAL DOLL MUSEUM. Shirley Paxman founded the McCurdy Historical Doll Museum in 1978 in Provo, Utah, and named it for Laura Christensen McCurdy, who provided the first 800 of the museum's more than 3,000 dolls. McCurdy, who was a teacher, collected and used the original dolls in her instructional programs. The museum's dolls are grouped in such historical themes as women of the Bible, folk dresses of the world, Native American dolls, and first ladies of America. The museum, located in a restored 1893 carriage house, also has antique toys and games.

McCurdy Historical Doll Museum, 246 North 100 East, Provo, UT 84606. **Phone and Fax:** 801/377-9935. **Hours:** 1-5

Tues.-Sat.; closed Sun.-Mon. **Admission:** adults and children over 11, $2; children 3-11, $1; children under 3, free.

Washington

ROSALIE WHYEL MUSEUM OF DOLL ART. Doll collector Rosalie Whyel had strong feelings about treating doll creation as an art and appealing primarily to adults when she founded the Rosalie Whyel Museum of Doll Art in Bellevue, Washington, in 1989. As a result, the museum has a collection of over 4,000 dolls that emphasizes the history of dolls from prehistoric to contemporary times, a library of doll research and identification, and a costume history center, as well as photographs, books, workshops, lectures, study clubs, and other educational programs. The museum also has a selection of toys, miniatures, and games, and a history of toys and toymakers center.

Rosalie Whyel Museum of Doll Art, 1116 108th Ave. N.E., Bellevue, WA 98004. **Phone:** 425/455-1116. **Fax:** 425/455-4793. **E-mail:** dollart@dollart.com. **Website:** www.dollart.com/dollart. **Hours:** 10-5 Mon.-Sat., 1-5 Sun.; closed major holidays. **Admission:** adults, $7; seniors, $6; children 5-17, $5; children under 5, free.

Wisconsin

DOLL MUSEUM. The Doll Museum in Appleton, Wisconsin, features more than 1,500 dolls from Amelia Bubolz's collection that date from the 1850s to the present. The museum, located in the Children's Museum wing of the Avenue Mall in downtown Appleton, has over 3,000 dolls, toys, miniatures, and dollhouses—including contributions from Bubolz's daughter, Mildren Ruglano.

Doll Museum, 100 W. College Ave., Appleton, WI 54911. **Phone:** 920/734-3226. **Hours:** 10-5 Tues.-Sat., 12-5 Sun.; closed Mon. and major holidays. **Admission:** free.

ETHNIC MUSEUMS

See also Cultural Art and History Museums; History Museums.

Arizona

SYLVIA PLOTKIN JUDAICA MUSEUM. The Sylvia Plotkin Judaica Museum, housed in the Temple Beth Israel in Scottsdale, Arizona, is named for the wife of a rabbi who was instrumental in the museum's founding in 1966. The museum is devoted to Jewish religious ceremonial, archaeological, and arts objects from 1600

to the present, as well as the story of pioneer Jews in Arizona from 1850 to 1920.

Sylvia Plotkin Judaica Museum, 10460 N. 56th St., Scottsdale, AZ 85253. **Phone:** 480/951-0323. **Fax:** 480/951-7150. **E-mail:** museum@templebethisrael.org. **Website:** www.templebethisrael.org. **Hours:** June-Aug.—10-3 Tues.-Thurs.; closed Fri.-Mon.; remainder of year—10-3

Tues.-Thurs. and Sun.; closed Mon., Fri.-Sat., and national and Jewish holidays. **Admission:** $3 suggested donation.

Colorado

BLACK AMERICAN WEST MUSEUM AND HERITAGE CENTER. The Black American West Museum and Heritage Center in Denver is housed in the former home and office of Dr. Justina L. Ford, Colorado's first African American female licensed physician. The Victorian house was scheduled for demolition in 1983, but was saved from the wrecking ball, relocated to its present site, and restored for use by the museum.

Dr. Ford, who was called the "lady doctor," specialized in gynecology, obstetrics, and pediatrics and delivered more than 7,000 babies of varied ethnic backgrounds and from all walks of life. She began her practice in 1902 but was denied hospital privileges for many years. As a result, she became known for her home delivery practice.

The three-story museum, which was founded in 1971 by Paul W. Stewart, a barber turned historian, contains artifacts, photographs, and other historical materials on African Americans in fur trading, homesteading, mining, cattle raising, military service, and other areas in the American West. It has become one of the most comprehensive sources of historical materials about African Americans in the early West.

Black American West Museum and Heritage Center, 3091 California St., Denver, CO 80205. **Phone:** 303/292-2566. **Fax:** 303/892-1981. **E-mail:** bawmhc@aol.com. **Website:** www.coax.net/people/lwf/bawmus.htm. **Hours:** May-Sept.—10-5 daily; remainder of year—10-2 Wed.-Fri., 10-5 Sat.-Sun.; closed Mon.-Tues. and major holidays. **Admission:** adults, $6; seniors, $5.50; children 5-12, $4; children under 5, free.

Connecticut

PRUDENCE CRANDALL MUSEUM. See Historic House Museums.

District of Columbia

LILLIAN AND ALBERT SMALL JEWISH MUSEUM. Longtime Washington residents Lillian and Albert Small donated a major portion of the funds for the restoration of the 1876 Old Adas Israel Synagogue— the first structure built in the District of Columbia as a Jewish house of worship—for use as a museum and headquarters for the Jewish Historical Society of Greater Washington. When the museum opened in 1975, it was named for them. The museum contains artifacts documenting the history of the Jewish people and the origins and historical development of customs, beliefs, and activities practiced by Jews in the greater Washington area.

Lillian and Albert Small Jewish Museum, 701 3rd St. N.W., Washington, DC 20001. **Phone:** 202/789-0900. **Fax:** 202/789-0485. **Hours:** 12-4 Sun.-Thurs.; closed Mon., Fri.-Sat., and major Jewish holidays. **Admission:** free.

MARY McLEOD BETHUNE COUNCIL HOUSE NATIONAL HISTORIC SITE. See Museums Honoring Exceptional Women.

Florida

ZORA NEALE HURSTON MEMORIAL PARK. See Historic Parks and Sites.

Georgia

LUCY CRAFT LANEY MUSEUM OF BLACK HISTORY. The Lucy Craft Laney Museum of Black History in Augusta, Georgia, is named for an educator who devoted her life to providing African American children with a good education. She started in a church basement but soon was overseeing a private school with more than 1,000 young African American students. One of her students was Mary McLeod Bethune, who became the nation's premier African American educator. The museum focuses on the history and contributions of African Americans in the Augusta and central Savannah River areas.

Lucy Craft Laney Museum of Black History, 1116 Phillips St., Augusta, GA 30901. **Phone:** 706/724-3576. **E-mail:** lcltherise.net. **Website:** www.lucycraftlaneymuseum.com. **Hours:** 9-5 Tues.-Sat.; closed Sun.-Mon. **Admission:** adults, $2; students and children 6-17, 75¢; children under 6, free.

TUBMAN AFRICAN-AMERICAN MUSEUM. The Tubman African-American Museum—named for Harriet Tubman, a former slave who became a leader of the Underground Railroad—is devoted to the history, art, and culture of African Americans. Tubman, who served as an army nurse, cook, and spy during the Civil War, helped an estimated 300 fugitive slaves to freedom. The museum serves as a cultural and community center in Macon, Georgia.

Tubman African-American Museum, 340 Walnut St., PO Box 6671, Macon, GA 31208. **Phone:** 912/743-8544. **Fax:** 912/743-9063. **E-mail:** tubman@mindspring.com. **Website:** www.tubmanmuseum.com. **Hours:** 9-5 Mon.-Fri., 10-5 Sat., 2-5 Sun.; closed New Year's Day, Fourth of July, Thanksgiving, and Christmas. **Admission:** adults, $3; children, $2.

Illinois

DuSABLE MUSEUM OF AFRICAN-AMERICAN HISTORY. The DuSable Museum of African-American History in Chicago began in the home of artist Margaret Burroughs and her husband, Charles Burroughs, in 1961. Mrs. Burroughs and five others started the museum because they believed the public should have a better understanding of African American history, art, culture, and contributions to the nation and world.

The museum, which now occupies a renovated and expanded facility in Washington Park, is named for Jean Batiste Pointe DuSable, a black Haitian trader who was the first settler in Chicago. Under the initial direction of artist Margaret Burroughs, the museum became a center of a wide range of cultural activities celebrating the experiences and achievements of African Americans.

DuSable Museum of African-American History, 740 E. 56th Pl., Chicago, IL 60637. **Phone:** 773/947-0600. **Fax:** 773/947-0677. **E-mail:** awright@dusablemuseum.org. **Website:** www.dusablemuseum.org. **Hours:** 10-5 Mon.-Sat., 12-5 Sun.; closed major holidays. **Admission:** adults, $3; seniors and students, $2; children 6-12, $1; children under 6, free; Sun. admission free.

Kentucky

HARRIET BEECHER STOWE SLAVERY TO FREEDOM MUSEUM. The Harriet Beecher Stowe Slavery to Freedom Museum in Washington, Kentucky, is named for the abolitionist author of *Uncle Tom's Cabin*. It contains exhibits of slave documents and shackles, various editions of *Uncle Tom's Cabin*, books written by and about Stowe, and photographs of Stowe and her family.

Harriet Beecher Stowe Slavery to Freedom Museum, PO Box 184, Washington, KY 41096. **Phone:** 606/759-4860. **Hours:** Mar.-Dec.—11-4:30 daily; closed remainder of year. **Admission:** $1 per person.

Louisiana

MELROSE PLANTATION HOME COMPLEX. See Historic House Museums.

Maryland

JANE L. AND ROBERT H. WEINER JUDAIC MUSEUM. The Jane L. and Robert H. Weiner Judaic Museum in Rockville, Maryland, is named for the former executive director of the Jewish Community Center of Greater Washington and his wife, who made a major donation to the founding of the museum in 1969. The museum is devoted to the history, ethnology, archaeology, and art of Judaica.

Jane L. and Robert H. Weiner Judaic Museum, 6125 Montrose Rd., Rockville, MD 20852. **Phones:** 301/881-0100 and 301/230-3711. **Fax:** 301/881-5512. **Hours:** 11-5 Mon.-Thurs. (also 7:30-9:30 p.m. Tues. and Thurs.), 2-5 Sun.; closed Fri.-Sat. and national and Jewish holidays.

Nebraska

GREAT PLAINS BLACK MUSEUM. The Great Plains Black Museum in Omaha, Nebraska, was founded in 1975 by Berta Calloway, who still serves as the director. The museum features exhibits on African American settlers, cowboys, women, and other aspects of Great Plains history, and has a library and repository of materials on African American history in the region.

Great Plains Black Museum, 2213 Lake St., Omaha, NE 68110. **Phone:** 402/345-2212. **Fax:** 402/345-2256. **Hours:** 10-2 Tues.-Sat., other times by appointment. **Admission:** free.

LENTZ CENTER FOR ASIAN CULTURE. See Cultural Art and History Museums.

New York

HARRIET TUBMAN HOME. See Museums Honoring Exceptional Women.

HERBERT AND EILEEN BERNARD MUSEUM. The Herbert and Eileen Bernard Museum, a Judaica museum at the Congregation Emanu-El of the City of New York, was made possible by a gift from an active board member and his wife to create the space in the community building of the 1929 synagogue. It contains liturgical items, historical documents, art, photographs pertaining to the congregation, and objects from other Jewish communities throughout the United States, Europe, North Africa, and the Near East.

Herbert and Eileen Bernard Museum, Congregation Emanu-El of the City of New York, 1 E. 65th St., New York, NY 10021. **Phone:** 212/744-1400. **Fax:** 212/570-0826. **E-mail:** info@emanuelnyc.org. **Website:** www. emanuelnyc.org. **Hours:** 10-4:30 Sun.-Thurs., 10-4 Fri., 1-4:30 Sat. **Admission:** free.

North Carolina

CHARLOTTE HAWKINS BROWN MEMORIAL STATE HISTORIC SITE. See Museums Honoring Exceptional Women.

MATTYE REED AFRICAN HERITAGE CENTER. The Mattye Reed African Heritage Center at North Carolina Agricultural and Technical State University in Greensboro was started in 1968 by the wife of a faculty member who had an extensive collection of African arts and crafts. More than 30 African nations, New Guinea, and Haiti are represented in the museum's collections and exhibits.

Mattye Reed African Heritage Center, North Carolina A. and T. University, Greensboro, NC 27411. **Phone:** 336/334-3209. **Fax:** 336/334-4378. **Hours:** 10-5 Mon.-Sat., 2-5 Sun.; closed major holidays. **Admission:** free.

Tennessee

CHATTANOOGA AFRICAN MUSEUM/BESSIE SMITH HALL. See Museums Honoring Exceptional Women.

Virginia

ANNE SPENCER MEMORIAL. See Museums Honoring Exceptional Women.

LOIS E. WOODS MUSEUM. John S. Woods began collecting African and African American art and memorabilia as a child. He was encouraged by his mother, Lois E. Woods, who later also contributed to the collection with her husband. In 1996 the family established the Lois E. Woods Museum to house the collection at Norfolk State University in Norfolk, Virginia, with John S. Woods serving as the museum director.

Lois E. Woods Museum, Norfolk State University, 3401 Corfew Ave., Norfolk, VA 23504 (postal address: 300 Park Ave., Norfolk, VA 23504). **Phone:** 757/823-2006. **Fax:** 757/823-2005. **E-mail:** j.s.woods@nsu.edu. **Website:** www.nsu.edu/recourses/woods/index.htm. **Hours:** 9-5 Mon.-Fri., other times by appointment; closed major holidays. **Admission:** free.

MAGGIE L. WALKER NATIONAL HISTORIC SITE. See Museum Honoring Exceptional Women.

GENERAL MUSEUMS

See also Art and History Museums; Cultural Art and History Museums; Historic House Museums; History Museums; Natural History Museums.

Arizona

MUSEUM OF NORTHERN ARIZONA. The Museum of Northern Arizona, a general museum in Flagstaff that features the natural and cultural history of the region, was founded in 1928 by Dr. Harold S. Colton and his wife, Mary-Russell Ferrell Colton.

Mrs. Colton, an accomplished artist, became curator of art and ethnology at the museum and was largely responsible for reviving the artistry of Hopi jewelry makers by inaugurating the annual Hopi Craftsman Exhibition in 1930 and proposing a new style of silversmithing—the overlay technique—which stimulated a new generation of craftsmen while preserving ancient traditions.

The museum's galleries and changing exhibitions explore the geology, anthropology, biology, history, and fine arts of the region, featuring many of the institution's more than 5 million specimens and artifacts. The 1929 Colton House, a 5,000-square-foot Spanish Colonial Revival–style home constructed by Hopi craftsmen, is now used as the Historic Colton House Retreat Center, a residential facility for museum guests, seminars, and receptions.

Museum of Northern Arizona, 3101 N. Fort Valley Rd., Flagstaff, AZ 86001. **Phone:** 520/774-5213. **Fax:** 520/799-1527. **E-mail:** info@musnaz.org. **Website:** www.musnaz.org. **Hours:** 9-5 daily; closed New Year's Day, Thanksgiving, and Christmas. **Admission:** adults, $5; seniors, $4; students, $3; children 7-17, $2; children under 7, free.

New Hampshire

ANNIE E. WOODMAN INSTITUTE. The Annie E. Woodman Institute, a general museum in Dover, New Hampshire, was founded in 1916 as a result of a bequest by a prominent local woman. In addition to funds for the facility, she left 200 artifacts, which are displayed with a variety of other historical and natural materials in three historic houses on the grounds—ca. 1675 Old Garrison House, ca. 1813 U.S. Senator John P. Hale Home, and ca. 1818 Woodman Home.

Annie E. Woodman Institute, 182 Central Ave., PO Box 146, Dover, NH 03821-0146. **Phone:** 603/742-1038. **Hours:** Apr.-Nov.—12:30-4:30 Wed.-Sun.; closed Mon.-Tues., Jan.-Mar., and major holidays; Dec.—12-4:30 Sat.-Sun.; closed remainder of week and holidays. **Admission:** adults, $3; seniors, $2; children 14-18, $1; children under 14, free.

Texas

WITTE MUSEUM. The multifaceted Witte Museum in San Antonio, Texas, was founded in 1926 by Ellen S. Quillan, a local schoolteacher and botanist who served as its director for 34 years. It was named in memory of the parents of businessman and benefactor Alfred G. Witte. The museum began with a natural history collection and gradually expanded into history and other fields of science and humanities. It has a hands-on science center, motion-based flight simulator, and collections and exhibits of dinosaurs, mummies, handmade furniture, ecology, birds, and rock art. In addition, the museum grounds contain a courtyard garden, three historic houses (from 1745, 1835, and 1841), and two reconstructed frontier log cabins.

Witte Museum, 3801 Broadway, San Antonio, TX 78209-6396. **Phone:** 210/357-1900. **Fax:** 210/357-1882. **E-mail:** witte@wittemuseum.org. **Website:** www.wittemuseum.org. **Hours:** June-Aug.—10-6 Mon.-Sat. (also to 9 p.m. Tues.), 12-6 Sun.; remainder of year—10-5 Mon.-Sat. (also to 9 p.m. Tues.), 12-5 Sun.; closed Thanksgiving and Christmas Eve and Day. **Admission:** adults, $5.95; seniors, $4.95; children 4-11, $3.95; children under 4, free.

LIBRARY MUSEUMS AND EXHIBIT AREAS

Georgia

ELLEN PAYNE ODOM GENEALOGY LIBRARY. Ellen Payne Odom, an educator and library board member in Moultrie, Georgia, left a $1 million bequest to establish a genealogy and local history library in her name. The Ellen Payne Odom Genealogy Library—located in the Moultrie/Colquitt County Library building—now houses the archives of 107 Scottish clans, genealogical materials about families who entered the country on the eastern seaboard and migrated west, and historical exhibits about the region.

Ellen Payne Odom Genealogy Library, 204 5th St. S.E., PO Box 2828, Moultrie, GA 31768. **Phone:** 229/985-6540. **Fax:** 229/985-0936. **Hours:** 8:30-5:30 Mon.-Sat.; closed Sun., first week in Apr., and major holidays. **Admission:** free.

Louisiana

ELIZABETH BASS COLLECTION ON WOMEN AND MEDICINE. See Women's Museums, Galleries, and Halls of Fame.

Maine

MARGARET CHASE SMITH LIBRARY. See Museums Honoring Exceptional Women.

Maryland

EVERGREEN HOUSE. See Historic House Museums.

Massachusetts

ARTHUR AND ELIZABETH SCHLESINGER LIBRARY. See Women's Museums, Galleries, and Halls of Fame.

STERLING AND FRANCINE CLARK ART INSTITUTE. See Art Museums.

New York

MARGARET REANEY MEMORIAL LIBRARY AND MUSEUM. The Margaret Reaney Memorial Library and Museum in St. Johnsville, New York, was founded in 1909 by textile mill owner Joseph H. Reaney in memory of his mother. The museum portion of the name was added in 1936 when the building was expanded. The library has approximately 25,000 books and historical displays that include period rooms, Civil War items, paintings, bronze sculptures, and farm and trade tools.

Margaret Reaney Memorial Library and Museum, 19 Kingsbury Ave., St. Johnsville, NY 13452. **Phone and**

Fax: 518/568-7822. E-mail: mrml@telenet.net. Website: www2.telenet.net/community/mrla/stjo. Hours: 9-5 Mon.-Wed. and Fri. (also 6:30-8:30 p.m. Mon. and Fri.), 1-5 Thurs., 9:30-12 Sat.; closed Sun. and major holidays. Admission: free.

Ohio

SUTLIFF MUSEUM. The Sutliff Museum, housed on the second floor of the Warren-Trumbull County Public Library in Warren, Ohio, resulted from the 1955 will of civic leader Phebe T. Sutliff, library board president and former president of Rockford College. She left the bulk of her estate and many furnishings of her family home to the library association for the purpose of establishing a museum in honor of her parents, attorney Levi Sutliff and Phebe Sutliff. Established in 1971, the museum depicts life in the area in the 1800–1900 Victorian period.

Sutliff Museum, Warren-Trumbull County Public Library, 444 Mahoning Ave. N.W., Warren, OH 44483. **Phone:** 330/399-8807, Ext. 121. **Website:** www.wtcpl.lib.oh.us. **Hours:** 2-4 Wed.-Sat.; other times by appointment; closed major holidays. **Admission:** free.

WAGNALLS MEMORIAL. The funds and incentive to establish the Wagnalls Memorial, dedicated to Adam Willis Wagnalls, cofounder of the Funk and Wagnalls publishing house in 1877, were provided by Wagnalls' daughter, Mabel Wagnalls Jones. The library and community center, founded in 1924 in Lithopolis, Ohio, contain paintings of John Ward Dunsmore, poems of Edwin Markham, and historical materials pertaining to the Wagnalls family and the publishing company.

Wagnalls Memorial, 150 E. Columbus St., PO Box 217, Lithopolis, OH 43136-0217. **Phone:** 614/833-4767. **Fax:** 614/837-0781. **E-mail:** jneff@wagnalls.org. **Website:** www.wagnalls.org. **Hours:** 9-9 Mon.-Fri., 9-5 Sat.; closed Sun. and major holidays. **Admission:** free.

Oklahoma

ELIZA CRUCE HALL DOLL COLLECTION (Ardmore Public Library). See Doll, Toy, and Miniature Museums.

Pennsylvania

HUNT INSTITUTE FOR BOTANICAL DOCUMENTATION. The Hunt Institute for Botanical Documentation, a research division of Carnegie Mellon University in Pittsburgh, was founded in 1961 by philanthropists Roy

A. and Rachel Hunt. It is housed in the Hunt Library building, also donated by the Hunts.

The institute was originally named for Mrs. Hunt—the Rachel McMasters Miller Hunt Botanical Library. She had rich collections of botanical literature, art, and archival materials and was determined that they not only be preserved, but also be actively curated and used productively in the service of science and scholarship. However, by 1971 the institution's research and service activities had become so diversified—including exhibitions—that the name was changed.

The institute now acquires and conserves collections of books, plant images, manuscript materials, and portraits; compiles authoritative data files; produces publications; and provides other information services to assist current research in botanical systematics, history, and biography and to meet the reference needs of biologists, historians, conservationists, librarians, bibliographers, and the general public.

Among the collections are more than 25,000 library volumes; over 30,000 botanical watercolors, drawings, and original prints from the Renaissance to the present; and letters, private papers, illustrations, and data on thousands of botanists, horticulturists, and others in related fields.

Hunt Institute for Botanical Documentation, Carnegie Mellon University, Hunt Library, Pittsburgh, PA 15213-3890. **Phone:** 412/268-2434. **Fax:** 412/268-5677. **Website:** www.huntbot.andrew.cmu.edu. **Hours:** 8:30-12 and 1-5 Mon.-Fri.; closed Sat.-Sun. and major holidays. **Admission:** free.

Rhode Island

ANNMARY BROWN MEMORIAL. See Art Museums.

Texas

ARMSTRONG BROWNING LIBRARY. One of the largest collections of books, manuscripts, and artifacts relating to poets Robert and Elizabeth Barrett Browning is at the Armstrong Browning Library at Baylor University in Waco, Texas.

In 1918 Dr. A. J. Armstrong, chairman of the English Department, gave his extensive Browning collection to the university. The collection was kept in the Browning Room of Carroll Library until 1951, when an elegant Italian Renaissance–style building was dedicated as the Armstrong Browning Library.

Robert Browning became one of the great British poets of the Victorian age, although Elizabeth Barrett was more widely known before their 1846 marriage because she was more extensively published. She is chiefly known today for *Sonnets from the Portuguese*, love poems to her husband, and for her role as a spokeswoman for women writers, as evidenced in *Aurora Leigh*.

Armstrong Browning Library, Baylor University, 8th and Speight Sts., PO Box 97152, Waco, TX 76798-7152. **Phone:** 254/710-3566. **Fax:** 254/710-3552. **E-mail:** rita_patteson@ baylor.edu. **Website:** www.baylor.edu/library/libdepts/abl/ abl.html. **Hours:** 9-5 Mon.-Fri., 9-12 Sat.; closed 1st two weeks of Aug., and university holidays. **Admission:** free.

NITA STEWART HALEY MEMORIAL LIBRARY AND J. EVETTS HALEY HISTORY CENTER. The Nita Stewart Haley Memorial Library and J. Evetts Haley History Center in Midland, Texas, began in 1971 when Mr. Haley, a leading range-country historian, established the library in memory of his wife, who had helped him assemble his large historical collections over the years. In 1976, when a new building was completed, the history center was founded and was added to the name.

The library has more than 30,000 volumes, while the history center features the research and collections of J. Evetts Haley and has more than 10,000 items on all facets of early western life, especially cowboys and the range-cattle industry. Both are devoted largely to Texas and the Southwest. Among the collections and exhibits are Native American baskets and blankets, early maps, the original 1722 Alamo mission bell, cowboy gear, western paintings and bronzes, glassware, and historical photographs.

Nita Stewart Haley Memorial Library and J. Evetts Haley History Center, 1805 W. Indiana Ave., Midland, TX 79701. **Phone:** 915/682-5785. **Fax:** 915/685-3512. **Website:** www.haleylibrary.com. **Hours:** 9-5 Mon.-Fri.; closed Sat.-Sun. and major holidays. **Admission:** free.

Wisconsin

SWARTHOUT MEMORIAL MUSEUM. See History Museums.

OTHER MUSEUMS

Arizona

THE BEAD MUSEUM. The Bead Museum—which collects and displays beads, beadwork, and beaded artifacts from throughout the world—was founded in Glendale, Arizona, in 1984 by interiors shop proprietor Gabrielle Liese, who became the founding director at the age of 70 (she retired at 86 but is still active at the museum). The museum contains ancient and ethnic beads and other objects of personal adornment from Africa, Asia, Europe, Middle East, Oceania, and North and South America.

The Bead Museum, 5754 W. Glenn Dr., Glendale, AZ 85301. **Phone:** 623/931-2731. **Fax:** 623/930-8561. **E-mail:** info@ beadmuseumaz.org. **Website:** www.beadmuseumaz.org. **Hours:** 9-5 Mon.-Sat.; 11-4 Sun.; closed major holidays. **Admission:** adults and children over 12, $3; children under 13, free.

Connecticut

THE NUT MUSEUM. Nut collector Elizabeth Tashjian founded the Nut Museum in Old Lyme, Connecticut, in 1972. She still devotes three rooms of her 18-room mansion to the museum, and asks visitors to pay one nut (any variety) as part of the admission.

Miss Tashjian, known as the "Nut Lady," fell in love with nuts as a child. She was so impressed by the beauty of a nut when she cracked it open that she decided to sketch it rather than eat it. Ever since, she has been collecting, painting, and sculpting nuts.

The museum's main room is decorated with acorn cornices and features nuts from many countries, nut masks, and paintings by Miss Tashjian. It also has a display of nutcrackers, a 35-pound Coco de Mer nut (said to be the world's largest nut), and a double coconut from the Seychelles islands. Among the museum's other objects are jewelry made from beechnuts, spoons from walnuts, tiny scenes from hickory shells, and toy furniture from a variety of nuts.

The Nut Museum, 303 Ferry Rd., Old Lyme, CT 06371. **Phone:** 860/434-7636. **Website:** www.roadsideamerica.com/ nut. **Hours:** by appointment. **Admission:** one nut and $3.

Florida

BAILEY-MATTHEWS SHELL MUSEUM. The Bailey-Matthews Shell Museum on the southwest Florida island of Sanibel began in 1986 with a $10,000 bequest from local shell collector Charlene McMurphy and opened in 1995 after two brothers—longtime resident

Samuel Bailey (and his wife, Frances Bailey) and John Bailey of Jacksonville—donated eight acres for the site of the museum in 1990 in memory of their parents, Frank P. Bailey and Annie Mead Matthews. The museum features collections and exhibits about shells and shell-making mollusks. The islands of Sanibel and Captiva are considered among the Western Hemisphere's best shell-collecting areas.

Bailey-Matthews Shell Museum, 3075 Sanibel-Captiva Rd., PO Box 1580, Sanibel, FL 39457. **Phone:** 941/395-2233. **Fax:** 941/395-6706. **E-mail:** shell@shellmuseum.org. **Website:** www.shellmuseum.org. **Hours:** 10-4 Tues.-Sun.; closed Mon. and major holidays. **Admission:** adults, $5; children 8-16, $3; children under 8, free.

Illinois

COOKIE JAR MUSEUM. More than 2,000 cookie jars of all descriptions are displayed at the Cookie Jar Museum, founded in the 1970s and still operated by Lucille Hodges-Bromberek in Lemont, Illinois. The cookie jars range in style from Mickey Mouse and Porky Pig to Raggedy Ann and Wedgwood cookie jars from the United States, Europe, and Asia.

Cookie Jar Museum, 111 Stephen St., Lemont, IL 60439. **Phone:** 630/257-5012. **Hours:** 10-3 daily. **Admission:** adults, $2; children, 50 ¢.

Iowa

MARY SHELLEY RAILROAD MUSEUM. The Mary Shelley Railroad Museum in Boone, Iowa, is named for a pioneer woman who saved a passenger train from derailment in 1881 when a flood damaged a trestle over a river near her farmhouse. She ran and crawled across the bridge to a nearby depot in time to stop the train. Founded in 1976, the Boone County Historical Society's museum is located in an 1860s depot and features artifacts relating to Shelley's life, railroad memorabilia, a working telegraph system, and a rail passenger car on an adjacent track.

Mary Shelley Railroad Museum, 1198 232nd St., Boone, IA 50036 (postal address: Boone County Historical Center, 602 Story St., Boone, IA 50036). **Phone:** 515/432-1907. **E-mail:** bchs@opencominc.com. **Hours:** by appointment. **Admission:** donation.

Michigan

MARGARET DOW TOWSLEY SPORTS MUSEUM. The Margaret Dow Towsley Sports Museum, which honors athletes and teams in 21 varsity sports at the University of Michigan in Ann Arbor, is named for its donor. The museum, which opened in 1991 in Schembechler Hall, contains photographs, memorabilia, trophies, murals, films, and interactive exhibits on the history, teams, players, games, and other aspects of sports at the university.

Margaret Dow Towsley Sports Museum, University of Michigan, Schembechler Hall, 1200 S. State St., Ann Arbor, MI 48109-2201. **Phone:** 734/763-4422. **Hours:** 11-4 Mon.-Fri. (also 6-8 p.m. Fri. for home hockey games); closed Sat.-Sun. and university holidays. **Admission:** free.

New Hampshire

CARPENTER MUSEUM OF ANTIQUE OUTBOARD MOTORS. Civil engineer Lawrence C. Carpenter and his wife, Ann-Marie Carpenter, founded the Carpenter Museum of Antique Outboard Motors to house their collection of outboard motors and marine-related objects in 1976. The couple, now retired, has approximately 100 early outboard motors on display in the museum on their ca. 1830 farm near Belmont and Gilmanton, New Hampshire.

Carpenter Museum of Antique Outboard Motors, Province Rd., Belmont, NH (postal address: PO Box 459, Gilmanton, NH 03237-0459). **Phone and Fax:** 603/524-7611. **E-mail:** amc@cyberportal.net. **Hours:** by appointment. **Admission:** free.

New York

NATIONAL MUSEUM OF DANCE. The National Museum of Dance and its Dance Hall of Fame were founded in Saratoga Springs, New York, in 1986 with the financial support of philanthropist Marylou Whitney and her entrepreneurial husband, Cornelius Vanderbilt Whitney. In recognition of their support, the hall of fame was named the Mr. and Mrs. Cornelius Vanderbilt Whitney Hall of Fame.

The museum, the nation's only one devoted exclusively to dance, covers all forms of professional dance, including ballet, Broadway, modern jazz, tap, and ethnic dance. Open only during the summer tourist season, the museum contains artifacts, memorabilia, costumes, props, photographs, videos, and films—many of which are related to the dancers and choreographers enshrined in the hall of fame. Of the hall's 30 inductees, thirteen are women. The honorees include such dance figures as Isadora Duncan, Katherine Durham, Martha Graham, and Ruth St. Denis.

National Museum of Dance and Dance Hall of Fame, 99 S. Broadway, Saratoga Springs, NY 12866. Phone: 518/584-2225. Fax: 518/584-4515. E-mail: info@dancemuseum.org. Website: www.dancemuseum.org. Hours: Memorial Day weekend-Oct.—10-5 Tues.-Sun.; closed Mon. Admission: adults, $5; seniors and students, $4; children under 13, $2.

Oregon

COLLIER MEMORIAL STATE PARK AND LOGGING MUSEUM. See Historic Parks and Sites.

South Dakota

WALL DRUG STORE. In 1931 Theodore Hustead and his wife, Dorothy Hustead, bought the only drugstore in Wall, South Dakota. When business didn't change much in five years, Mrs. Hustead suggested that they put signs along the highway in the dusty Dakota prairie to offer free ice water to thirsty travelers. Much to their surprise, business boomed—and Wall Drug Store gradually expanded into the largest and most unusual drugstore in the world. It is now much more than a pharmacy, covering an entire city block and becoming one of the leading tourist attractions in the American West.

Wall Drug Store now has an Apothecary Shoppe and Pharmacy Museum, based largely on the original drugstore and featuring a wide range of pharmaceutical artifacts. In addition, visitors can see pioneer and Native American artifacts, more than 1,500 historical photographs, an art gallery with 210 original works, and life-size carvings of many early western historical figures in the family-run, museumlike tourist complex.

Wall Drug Store, 510 Main St., PO Box 401, Wall, SD 57790. Phone: 605/279-2175. Fax: 605/279-2699. E-mail: walldrug@gwtc.net. Website: www.walldrug.com. Hours: Memorial Day-Labor Day—6 a.m.-10 p.m. daily; remainder of year—6:30 a.m.-6 p.m. daily; closed New Year's Day, Easter, Thanksgiving, and Christmas. Admission: free.

MUSEUMS FOUNDED AND/OR OPERATED BY WOMEN'S ORGANIZATIONS

Many museums are founded and/or operated by chapters of such national women's organizations as the Junior League, Daughters of the American Revolution, and Colonial Dames of America, and by such state and regional bodies as the Daughters of Utah Pioneers, Daughters of the Republic of Texas, and Daughters of Hawaii. Others often result from the efforts of local groups like women's clubs, auxiliary organizations, and special-interest groups.

These museums are rarely devoted specifically to the history or contributions of women. Rather, they are usually general history, art, science, or children's museums established to meet community educational and cultural needs and/or to preserve historic houses of significance. In some cases the women's organizations merely provide start-up assistance, while in other instances they help fund and/or actually operate the facilities. Some representative examples follow.

JUNIOR LEAGUE

The Junior League—which has 296 chapters and is committed to promoting volunteerism, improving communities, and developing the potential of women—is best known for its volunteer projects. One of the most common projects is to establish or assist with the founding of a community museum, or to provide some form of support for an ongoing museum. Most of the museum projects are children's museums, but the Junior League has also helped start science centers, save historic houses, and/or fund children's discovery galleries in art and other museums, examples of which follow.

Children's Museums

CHICAGO CHILDREN'S MUSEUM. The Chicago Children's Museum, which has 56,000 square feet of exhibits on Navy Pier in Chicago, was founded in 1982 with Junior League support as the Express-Ways Children's Museum, using 2,500 square feet of space on the fourth floor of the Chicago Public Library Cultural Center.

CHILDREN'S MUSEUM OF HISTORY, NATURAL HISTORY, AND SCIENCE AT UTICA, NEW YORK. The Children's Museum in Utica, New York, was founded in 1963 by the Junior League as a Discovery Room at the Utica Public Library. It outgrew three sites before moving into its present five-story building in 1980, expanding its offerings and name and becoming part of the New York State museum system.

CHILDREN'S MUSEUM OF DENVER. The Junior League of Denver collaborated with the Denver Art Museum in the 1940s in presenting children's museum programs, which resulted in the founding of the Children's Museum of Denver in 1973. The cultural project served as a prototype for many similar children's museum programs. The children's museum, which occupies a 24,000-square-foot building, now focuses largely on hands-on learning opportunities for newborns and children to the age of eight.

CHILDREN'S MUSEUM OF MAINE. The Junior League of Portland, Maine, started the Children's Museum of Maine in two rooms of a vacant school building in Cape Elizabeth in 1977. It is now operated by a nonprofit board in a modified four-story historic business building in Portland.

COBB COUNTY YOUTH MUSEUM. The Junior League of Marietta, Georgia, raised the funds, purchased the land, and built the building that houses the Cobb County Youth Museum, which was founded in 1964 and opened in 1970. The museum is now supported by county and city school funds.

NEW BRITAIN YOUTH MUSEUM. The Service League of New Britain (now the Junior League) founded the Children's Museum (which later changed its name to New Britain Youth Museum) in New Britain, Connecticut, in 1956. It began in the basement of the Hawley Memorial Children's Library with natural history and cultural artifacts and moved into a new two-story building in 1975 (with the Junior League funding a hands-on Discovery Room).

OMAHA CHILDREN'S MUSEUM. The Omaha Children's Museum in Nebraska was started in 1975 by the Junior League and a group of local educators. It began

as a program of traveling exhibits and art activities and evolved into a 60,000-square-foot children's museum with participatory exhibits in the arts, sciences, and humanities.

PITTSBURGH CHILDREN'S MUSEUM. The Pittsburgh Children's Museum was founded in 1980 with Junior League support in the basement of a ca. 1897 post office building. It initially occupied only 5,900 square feet of the building, but by 1985 it had taken over the remainder of the 22,000-square-foot historic structure.

Science and Art Centers

AUDUBON LOUISIANA NATURE CENTER. The Junior League of New Orleans played an important role in starting a children's area in 1980 at the Audubon Louisiana Park and Zoological Garden, which evolved into the present Audubon Louisiana Nature Center. The League was part of the original exploration/steering committee, assisted with the funding, and provided board members and volunteers. The center is now devoted to Louisiana natural history and general science.

CHARLOTTE NATURE MUSEUM AND DISCOVERY PLACE. The Charlotte Nature Museum in Charlotte, North Carolina, began in a frame house in 1947 as the Charlotte Children's Nature Museum with the support of the Junior League. In 1951 the Junior League helped raise the funds for a 7,000-square-foot building on a 31-acre wooded site donated by the Lions Club. A downtown science and technology center—called Discovery Place—was added in 1981, and the two sites were called the Science Museums of Charlotte for several decades before being separated administratively.

DISCOVERY CENTER MUSEUM. The Discovery Center Museum, a children's science museum in Riverfront Museum Park in Rockford, Illinois, was established in 1980 by the Junior League and the Rockford Council for Arts and Sciences. The Junior League provided funds, leadership, planning, and programming assistance in the early years, but now helps only with specific projects from time to time.

DISCOVERY CENTER OF THE SOUTHERN TIER. The Discovery Center of the Southern Tier in Binghamton, New York, was founded in 1983 through the combined efforts of the Junior League and a group of parents. The League provided seed money, assisted with a capital fund drive, and helped obtain municipal, county, and state funding.

JUNIOR MUSEUM. The Junior Museum in Troy, New York, was started in 1954 by the Junior League in the basement of the Rensselaer County Historical Society. It relocated to a Victorian house four years later and then to a renovated 1904 firehouse in 1975, and it now features history, art, and science exhibits for children.

LIVING ARTS AND SCIENCE CENTER. In 1965 the Junior League in Lexington, Kentucky, spearheaded a movement to establish a children's art and science center. The Living Arts and Science Center opened three years later but was forced to close in February 1980 due to lack of funds. After a public outcry and a fund-raising drive, it reopened in August 1980 and is now affiliated with the Lexington Arts and Cultural Council.

LORI BROCK CHILDREN'S DISCOVERY CENTER. See Children's Museums.

LOUISIANA ARTS AND SCIENCE CENTER. The Louisiana Arts and Science Center in Baton Rouge began in 1960 as a children's museum in three rooms of the Old State Capitol building funded with $7,000 from the Junior League. The museum, now housed in a renovated and expanded former railroad depot, features American and European paintings and sculpture, crafts, graphics, drawings, photographs, and science and space exhibits. The Junior League sponsors an annual exhibition of children's-book illustrations by award-winning artists.

MIAMI MUSEUM OF SCIENCE. The Junior League of Miami, Florida, opened the Junior Museum of Miami in 1950 in a small frame house downtown. The Miami Museum of Science, with extensive natural history collections and exhibits, hands-on science and technology displays, and a walk-in wildlife center with birds, insects, and reptiles, grew out of the modest beginnings.

MILTON J. RUBENSTEIN MUSEUM OF SCIENCE AND TECHNOLOGY. The Milton J. Rubenstein Museum of Science and Technology in Syracuse, New York, was founded as the Discovery Center in 1976. The concept was initially developed by a coalition of three local groups—the Junior League, National Council of Jewish Women, and Technology Club. The museum was originally planned as a children's museum, but the Technology Club, composed of engineers, convinced the planning group that it should be a science and technology museum and serve the entire community. As part of its efforts, the Junior League underwrote the director's position for a year and circulated an exhibit on the plans to shopping malls and other places to promote the 1981 opening. The museum later moved to the former Armory Building and was renamed for a major benefactor.

MUSEUM OF DISCOVERY AND SCIENCE. The Museum of Discovery and Science in Fort Lauderdale, Florida, began as a youth museum called the Discovery Center in 1976. The Junior League provided the impetus for the project, and shared with the city and National Park Service in covering the cost of renovating a historic building as the site. The museum is now a science center in a new building with exhibits and more than 50,000 specimens and artifacts related to ecology, health, physical sciences, and space.

SOUTH FLORIDA SCIENCE MUSEUM. The South Florida Science Museum in West Palm Beach, Florida, was started by the Junior League in 1959 as a children's museum called the Junior Museum of West Palm Beach. In 1964 it became the Science Museum and Planetarium of Palm Beach County, and in 1985 the South Florida Science Museum, to better reflect its regional natural history focus. It now has collections and exhibits on paleontology, archaeology, astronomy, geology, and conchology, and such facilities as a discovery room, planetarium, and aquarium.

WHITAKER CENTER FOR SCIENCE AND THE ARTS. In 1977 the Junior League in Harrisburg, Pennsylvania, began a movement to establish a hands-on science center. The League sponsored a pilot project, called Sensorama, in the William Penn Memorial Museum in 1979. The success of the exhibit resulted in business and community leaders joining the effort to create such a museum, which became the Museum of Scientific Discovery in 1982, with physical, natural, and life science exhibits. The name was later changed to the Whitaker Center for Science and the Arts, as its offerings and support broadened.

Historic Houses and History Museums

BLUCHER FAMILY MUSEUM AND SIDBURY HOUSE. The Blucher Family Museum in Corpus Christi, Texas, is housed in an 1880 Neoclassical home that was one of three historic buildings on two acres donated to the local Junior League in 1990. The mansion, built by civil engineer and surveyor Charles Blucher, was given to the League by Blucher's heirs and contains furnishings, letters, and artifacts of the prominent family. The Junior League also restored the 1893 Sidbury House as a bicentennial gift to the city and opened it as a historic house museum in 1978. The structure is thought to be the last example of High Victorian architecture in Corpus Christi. Originally one of the stately homes that once lined the bluff overlooking the city, the house was moved in the late 1920s to Old Irishtown, near the ship channel.

CHARLES GATES DAWES HOUSE. The Junior League of Evanston, Illinois, was instrumental in restoring the 1894 former home of Vice President and Nobel Laureate Charles G. Dawes. Dawes left the palatial 28-room Chateauesque mansion to Northwestern University in the hope that the Evanston Historical Society would make it into a museum. It became a historic house museum with the assistance of the Junior League, which contributed $5,000 to the restoration, helped underwrite the salary of the museum director and the renovation of the kitchen and clubrooms, trained the museum guides, assisted with the programming, and now shares the office space with the historical society.

JOHN H. STEVENS HOUSE. The 1850 John H. Stevens House—said to be the birthplace of Minneapolis—was restored with the assistance of the Junior League. The five-room frame house was moved to a city park in 1896, with thousands of children helping to pull the structure to the site. Years of neglect followed until 1980, when the city asked for help from the Junior League, which raised $300,000 and contributed 35,000 volunteer hours to the restoration. The historic house was later moved to another location in the park—and was again towed by children, in a reenactment of the previous move 80 years earlier.

KELTON HOUSE MUSEUM AND GARDEN. The Kelton House Museum and Garden in Columbus, Ohio, is operated by the local Junior League. The 1852 Italianate house with Greek Revival features, a carriage house, and gardens was home to three generations of the Fernando Kelton family and was a stop on the Underground Railroad for fugitive slaves. The museum provides insight into life in urban Columbus in 1850–1900, the Civil War, and the Underground Railroad, and contains Kelton family records, Victorian furniture

and decorative arts, and materials on women's suffrage efforts. The Junior League maintains its headquarters in an outbuilding on the property.

PIONEER HERITAGE CENTER. The Pioneer Heritage Center, which features the folklife and history of northwestern Louisiana and the nineteenth-century Red River region, began in 1970 as a joint project of the Junior League and Louisiana State University at Shreveport. It has six examples of southern vernacular architecture and collections of early quilts, clothing, and other historical materials of the tristate region.

TALLAHASSEE MUSEUM OF HISTORY AND NATURAL SCIENCE. The Tallahassee Junior Museum—which evolved into the Tallahassee Museum of History and Natural Science—was founded in the Florida capital city in 1957 by the Junior League and the Association for Childhood Education, a teachers' group, with additional support from the National Foundation for Junior Museums. The children's museum opened in a donated house in 1958 and then moved to a 50-acre site in 1962. A number of historic buildings were also moved to the grounds, and an 1880s pioneer farm was re-created as the facility became a museum with history, natural science, and other collections and exhibits.

TAYLOR-GRADY HOUSE AND ARNOCROFT. The Junior League of Athens, Georgia, manages two historic house museums—the 1840s Taylor-Grady House, built by cotton planter and merchant Robert Taylor and later lived in by newspaper editor Henry Grady, and Arnocroft, the home of Eugenia Arnold Blount Friend, one of the founding members in 1935 of the Junior Assembly (which became the Junior League), who bequeathed the house and its furnishings to the League. The Taylor-Grady House, a Greek Revival home owned by Athens-Clarke County, was restored by the Junior League in the 1960s, beginning the historic preservation movement in Athens, and now also serves as the League's headquarters.

Children's Discovery Rooms

ART INSTITUTE OF CHICAGO. A children's discovery room—called the Junior Museum—was opened at the Art Institute of Chicago in 1964 after several years of planning by the institute's Women's Board and the Junior League of Chicago. The Junior Museum, a division of the art museum's education department, featured several galleries, a library, and support areas and was designed to introduce art to children in contexts they can understand.

BREVARD MUSEUM OF HISTORY AND SCIENCE. The Discovery Room at Brevard Museum of History and Science in Cocoa, Florida, was started by the Junior League of Cocoa-Titusville in 1980. The League, which initially staffed the room with volunteers, has continued to provide support for the multisensory facility, which contains discovery boxes, natural history collections, an aquarium, a beehive, a microscope, videotapes, and books.

CHARLOTTE MUSEUM OF HISTORY. The Hands-on History Room in the new home of the Charlotte Museum of History in Charlotte, North Carolina, was made possible by a $75,000 gift from the city's Junior League in 1999. The room provides participatory educational experiences in history for school-age children.

CUMBERLAND SCIENCE MUSEUM. The Curiosity Corner is a Junior League children's project that opened in 1981 at the Cumberland Science Museum in Nashville, Tennessee. The project resulted in a natural history and science participatory area for tactile exploration by young children at the museum, which began in 1944 as the Nashville Children's Museum and evolved into a science and technology museum.

DALLAS MUSEUM OF ART. The Junior League of Dallas was instrumental in the creation and funding of the Gateway Gallery, an art-oriented discovery area for children, at the Dallas Museum of Art in 1984. The 8,500-square-foot space included orientation areas, exhibit spaces, two studios, and a multimedia library.

GREENSBORO CHILDREN'S MUSEUM. The Junior League of Greensboro, North Carolina, provided $75,000 and volunteer support for the Early Childhood Exhibit at the newly opened Greensboro Children's Museum in 1999. The discovery room features hands-on exhibits for children 12 and under in a "kid-friendly" environment. Junior League members also provide support to the museum staff in the exhibit, a parent/educator resource room, and toddler programming.

MILWAUKEE PUBLIC MUSEUM. The Milwaukee Public Museum, a natural and human history museum, has had hands-on children's areas since 1965, beginning with the Youth Center, which evolved into the Dis-

covery Center. The children's program was expanded in 1975 to include participatory activities for families through the Touch-Me-Do program. In 1977 the Junior League opened Musement Park, an area for children four to seven years of age, which the Friends of the Museum took over in 1980.

MONMOUTH MUSEUM. Monmouth Museum, a general museum in Lincroft, New Jersey, developed the Junior Gallery for young children in 1978 with the assistance of the Junior League. The Junior Gallery, featuring participatory exhibits, traveling trunks, and teacher workshops, was refined over the years and eventually expanded into the Becker Children's Wing.

PHOENIX ART MUSEUM. A Junior Museum, sponsored and funded by the Junior League of Phoenix, was opened in 1965 at the Phoenix Art Museum in Arizona. The Junior League's support continued until 1972, when sponsorship was assumed by the Art Museum League. The Junior Museum featured exhibitions and programs designed to increase children's understanding of art. A Junior Gallery was also added, and both the children's museum and gallery later developed into the current Artworks Gallery, designed for children.

SAN ANTONIO MUSEUM OF ART. The basic elements of art, with an emphasis on children's participation, was the thrust of the Start Gallery, which was funded by the Junior League and opened in 1982 at the San Antonio Museum of Art in Texas. The League is still involved, providing docents for children's and other educational programs.

SCIENCE CENTER OF IOWA. The Junior League of Des Moines initiated a Discovery Room project in 1980 at the Des Moines Science Center, which later became the Science Center of Iowa. It became a cooperative effort between the League and the science center staff, opening in 1982 with an emphasis on interactive learning through experimentation.

TACOMA ART MUSEUM. A Children's Gallery, originally maintained by the Junior League, was incorporated into the Tacoma Art Museum when a former bank building was converted into the new home of the Tacoma, Washington, museum in 1971. It became the site of themed exhibitions, displays of art by schoolchildren, hands-on experiences, and multimedia programs.

DAUGHTERS OF THE AMERICAN REVOLUTION

The National Society of the Daughters of the American Revolution (DAR) has a museum at its headquarters complex in Washington, D.C., and many of its state societies and local chapters restore and/or operate historic houses and other buildings of historic significance around the nation. In addition to several hundred historic structures, a few also have DAR historical museums at other sites. Among the representative branches, historic buildings, and museums are the following.

Museums

DAUGHTERS OF THE AMERICAN REVOLUTION MUSEUM. The Daughters of the American Revolution Museum, housed in the 1904 Memorial Continental Hall in Washington, D.C., is devoted to history and the decorative arts. Established at the time of the founding of the DAR in 1890, the museum has 33 American period rooms, Revolutionary War artifacts, and decorative arts made or used in America in the preindustrial period. Its collections include quilts, coverlets, needlework, costumes, ceramics, glass, silver, pewter, furniture, paintings, miniatures, toys, dolls, and musical instruments.

DAR MEMORIAL MUSEUM. The DAR Memorial Museum—containing historical furnishings, clothing, documents, books, and other materials collected by the local chapter of the Daughters of the American Revolution—is one of four museumlike rooms at the Ponca City Cultural Center, located in the 1916 former home of oilman and former governor E. W. Marland in Ponca City, Oklahoma.

DAR MUSEUM/FIRST LADIES OF TEXAS HISTORIC COSTUMES COLLECTION. The DAR Museum/First Ladies of Texas Historic Costumes Collection at the Texas Woman's University in Denton features the inaugural ball gowns of the wives of the presidents of the Republic of Texas and the governors of the state. The museum, started by the Texas Society of the DAR, also contains gowns worn by the wives of Presidents Dwight D. Eisenhower and Lyndon B. Johnson and Vice President John Nance Garner.

FAITH TRUMBULL CHAPTER DAR MUSEUM. The Faith Trumbull DAR Chapter in Norwich, Connecticut, has a historical museum with collections of early furniture, clothing, quilts, local portraits, and other histori-

cal materials. The collections are housed in two historic houses—the 1750 Nathaniel Backus House and 1818 Rockwell House—on the museum grounds.

Historic Houses and Other Buildings

BUCCLEUCH MANSION. The Buccleuch Mansion, a 1739 three-story Georgian house in New Brunswick, New Jersey, was the home of Anthony Walton White, a brigadier general under George Washington during the Revolutionary War. Located at the site of the 1776 fortifications, it was occupied by the British during the war. The Jersey Blue Chapter of the DAR restored and now maintains and staffs the historic structure, which is owned by the city in Buccleuch Park. The mansion features period rooms from the eighteenth century to the late Victorian period; DuFors wallpaper; some original furniture; collections of spinning wheels, carders, metal dress patterns, costumes, textiles, and toys; and displays on the American Revolution, White, and life in early New Brunswick.

DAR JOHN STRONG MANSION MUSEUM. The Vermont State Society of the Daughters of the American Revolution owns and operates the DAR John Strong Mansion Museum in Addison. The 1795–1796 Federal mansion, the home of an early Addison resident, was built to replace the family's residence, which had been burned by Native American and Tory forces. Five generations of the Strong family have occupied the house. It was purchased by the DAR state society in 1934 and now contains period furnishings and exhibits that tell the story of a colonial family's life in the northern wilderness.

DAR ROBERT NEWELL HOUSE AND DAR PIONEER MOTHERS' MEMORIAL CABIN. The DAR Robert Newell House and DAR Pioneer Mothers' Memorial Cabin, located in the Champoeg State Heritage Area near St. Paul, Oregon, are operated by the Oregon State Society of the Daughters of the American Revolution. The Newell House is a reconstruction of an 1852 home, which contains Native American artifacts, gowns of the wives of Oregon governors, and an antique quilt collection. The 1931 cabin is a memorial to pioneer mothers and features pioneer artifacts. An 1850 Butteville jail, a frontier schoolhouse, and a visitor center are also located on the park grounds, where the first provisional government in the Pacific Northwest was located in 1843.

MADAM BRETT HOMESTEAD. The Madam Brett Homestead in Beacon, New York, features the ca. 1709 Dutch Colonial home of Catheryna Rombout Brett, the first woman settler and a successful businesswoman, Native American trader, and benefactor. It has the furnishings of seven generations of Brett descendants and contains displays referring to Revolutionary War events, including visits by George Washington and the Marquis of Lafayette. The site is administered by the Melzingah Chapter of the Daughters of the American Revolution.

OLD EXCHANGE AND PROVOST DUNGEON. The Old Exchange Building in Charleston, South Carolina, was built by the British for the prosperous port in 1771, and was then used to imprison prominent patriots during the American Revolution. It is also where South Carolina ratified the Constitution in 1788, and where George Washington was entertained in 1791. In 1913 the South Carolina Society of the Daughters of the American Revolution acquired the building, which is now leased and operated by the state as a historical museum. The exchange and customshouse is devoted to early events in the history of the city and nation and contains such collections as colonial artifacts, early postal materials, Civil War art, and materials related to the history of the pirates of the Carolinas.

RICHARDS-DAR HOUSE MUSEUM. The 1860 Richards House in Mobile, Alabama, is operated by the city and the local chapter of the Daughters of the American Revolution. The Italianate-style house shows how a prosperous merchant of the period lived in Mobile.

ROSALIE HOUSE MUSEUM. The Rosalie House Museum, owned and operated by the Mississippi State Society of the DAR, is an 1820–1823 Federal-style mansion in Natchez. It was originally built for Peter and Eliza Little, who sold it to the Andrew Wilson family in 1857. The DAR state society purchased the historic house from two Wilson granddaughters in 1938. It now contains much of the Wilson furnishings and the gardens restored by the state society.

SCHUYLER-HAMILTON HOUSE. The 1760 Schuyler-Hamilton House in Morristown, New Jersey, was the 1765–1821 home of Dr. Jabez Campfield, who was George Washington's chief physician and surgeon when the Continental Army was stationed near Morristown. However, the house, now owned and operated by the Morristown Chapter of the Daughters of the American Revolution, is named for Betsy Schuyler and Alexander Hamilton, who never lived in the house. Displays tell of their courtship while Schuyler was visiting and Hamilton was an aide to Washington. The historic house also has 1775–1810 period furnishings, American Revolution documents, and early china, silver, paintings, maps, newspapers, and books.

COLONIAL DAMES OF AMERICA

Eighty-two historic houses and other buildings are owned and/or operated—including 40 in collaboration with various preservation groups—by state societies and local chapters of the National Society of the Colonial Dames of America. They range from colonial and frontier homes to hotels and other historic sites, including the following examples.

BURGWIN-WRIGHT MUSEUM HOUSE. John Burgwin, a planter, merchant, and treasurer of the colony of Carolina, and his wife, Margaret Haynes Burgwin, built a townhouse—using an abandoned city jail and dungeon as the foundation—in Wilmington, North Carolina, in 1770. The Colonial house was occupied by Lord Charles Cornwallis as his headquarters in 1781, shortly before his defeat and surrender at Yorktown.

The North Carolina Society of the Colonial Dames of America bought the house in 1937 and opened it as a museum in 1950. The house has been restored and now features eighteenth- and early-nineteenth-century furnishings, a separate kitchen building, a courtyard, and gardens.

HOTEL de PARIS MUSEUM. The Hotel de Paris was opened in the mining town of Georgetown, Colorado, in 1875 by Louis Dupuy, a Frenchman who sought to have a luxurious hostelry and restaurant similar to the Normandy inns of his homeland. It quickly became one of the most elegant places to stay and dine in the Old West. It was the site of the famous "millionaires' dinner" in 1879, when nine mining, railroad, and financial tycoons (with combined assets of more than

$200 million) joined Dupuy for dinner. Dupuy died in 1900, but the hotel continued to operate until the 1940s. The Colorado branch of the Colonial Dames of America purchased the old hotel in 1954 and restored it to its 1875–1900 splendor with most of its original furnishings.

McALLISTER HOUSE MUSEUM. In 1873, Civil War General William Jackson Palmer brought a young Army major, Henry McAllister, to the frontier town of Colorado Springs, Colorado, to head the development of Palmer's dream of an "idyllic community" at the foot of Pikes Peak. McAllister and his wife, Elizabeth, built a Gothic Downing brick and stone cottage with 20-inch walls and a roof anchored into the masonry with iron rods to withstand the worst of elements in an area buffeted by high winds. In 1961 it became a historic house museum and was restored with late Victorian furnishings by the Colorado Society of the Colonial Dames of America.

MOUNT VERNON HOTEL MUSEUM AND GARDEN. The Mount Vernon Hotel Museum and Garden in New York City was built in 1799 as a carriage house on the country estate of Colonel William Stephens Smith, aide-de-camp to George Washington and hus-

band of Abigail Adams Smith, daughter of President John Adams and his wife, Abigail. The huge estate mansion was destroyed by fire in 1826, after which the carriage house was converted into the Mount Vernon Hotel. The Colonial Dames of America purchased the building in 1924, restored it to the 1826–1833 period of the hotel, and opened it to the public in 1939 as the Abigail Adams Smith Museum (later changed to its present name).

NEILL-COCHRAN MUSEUM HOUSE. The 1855 Neill-Cochran House in Austin, Texas, is a historic house museum operated by the Colonial Dames of America in Texas. It features the furnishings of the 1855–1878 period.

WILTON HOUSE MUSEUM. The Virginia Society of the Colonial Dames of America owns and manages the Wilton House Museum in Richmond. The 1753 Georgian-style brick mansion, home of William Randolph III, was saved by the Colonial Dames in 1933. It was dismantled, reassembled, and restored at a new site, and was used as the state society's headquarters by 1935. Open for tours since 1952, it has changing exhibitions and exceptional collections of eighteenth- and nineteenth-century silver, porcelain, and furniture.

STATE AND REGIONAL WOMEN'S ORGANIZATIONS

Women's organizations have been established in some states and regions to preserve historic buildings and sites and/or to interpret the history and artifacts of pioneers in history museums. The largest such group is the Mormon-oriented Daughters of Utah Pioneers, which was founded in 1901 and now operates such facilities at 105 sites—85 in Utah and twenty in surrounding states. Among the other similar but smaller organizations are the Daughters of Hawaii and Daughters of the Republic of Texas. Some examples of each follow.

Daughters of Utah Pioneers

PIONEER MEMORIAL MUSEUM. The Pioneer Memorial Museum in Salt Lake City is the oldest and largest of the Daughters of Utah Pioneers museums. It contains the most extensive collection of artifacts and memorabilia from the time Mormon settlers entered the Valley of the Great Salt Lake in 1847 until the joining of

the transcontinental railroads at Promontory, Utah, in 1869. It also has other historical objects from the community. The museum, located in a replica of the old Salt Lake Theater and an adjacent carriage house, also serves as the headquarters for the International Society of Daughters of Utah Pioneers.

CACHE COUNTY DAUGHTERS OF UTAH PIONEERS MUSEUM. The Cache County Daughter of Utah Pioneers Museum, located in the chamber of commerce building in Logan, Utah, features pioneer artifacts, a collection of early musical instruments, and wood drying, carding, and spinning demonstrations.

DAUGHTERS OF UTAH PIONEERS MUSEUM. Artifacts and memorabilia from the 1847–1870 pioneer days are featured at the Daughters of Utah Pioneers Museum, also known as the McQuarrie Memorial Museum and operated by the local chapter of the Daughters of Utah Pioneers in St. George, Utah. The museum was erected in 1938–1939 with funding from Hortense McQuarrie Odlum and was later expanded by a cousin, Ferol McQuarrie Kincade. It contains clothing, relics, portraits, manuscripts, and histories of early settlers.

WEBER COUNTY DAUGHTERS OF UTAH PIONEERS MUSEUM AND MILES GOODYEAR CABIN. The Weber County Daughters of Utah Pioneers Museum and Miles Goodyear Cabin in Ogden, Utah, contain period rooms, pioneer artifacts and memorabilia, and the first Anglo home in Utah. The period rooms include a pioneer parlor, kitchen, and bedroom, while the collections feature early carpenter tools, clothing, household utensils, furniture, farm equipment, musical instruments, and items belonging to Mormon leader Brigham Young. The 1845 log cabin, which has been relocated to the grounds, was built by mountain man Miles Goodyear and was originally used as a trading post and way station, and then as a home.

Daughters of Hawaii

HULIHEE PALACE. The Hulihee Palace in Kailu-Kona, Hawaii, was the ca. 1838 vacation residence of Hawaiian royalty in the nineteenth century. The palace was built by John Adams Kuakini, the second governor of the island, who lived there until his death in 1844. It was restored to the 1874–1891 Kalakaua period and was opened to the public in 1927 by the Daughters of Hawaii. It contains Hawaiian royalty clothing, jewelry, tapa, featherwork, quilts, furniture, and portraits. The site is one of three surviving palaces at which Hawaiian royalty lived before Hawaii became a state.

QUEEN EMMA SUMMER PALACE. The Daughters of Hawaii prevented the razing of Hanaiakamalama, now known as Queen Emma Summer Palace, in Nuuanu Valley near Honolulu; restored it to become a historic house museum; and maintain and operate the facility on lease from the state of Hawaii. The six-room building was the summer home of Queen Emma and her husband, King Kamehameha IV, who reigned in Hawaii in 1854–1863. The queen became known for her efforts to overcome epidemics of smallpox, measles, and whooping cough by raising funds to build Hawaii's first public hospital in 1860 (now the 506-bed Queen's Medical Center). The summer palace contains the household furnishings and personal effects of Queen Emma and her family, as well as period pieces, portraits, photographs, and Hawaiian artifacts.

Daughters of the Republic of Texas

THE ALAMO. The Alamo, that historic site of the 1836 battle with Mexican forces that inspired the rallying cry "Remember the Alamo," has been maintained and operated in San Antonio since 1905 by the Daughters of the Republic of Texas. The Alamo, founded in 1718 as a Spanish mission, is where 189 Texans—including frontiersmen James Bowie and Davy Crockett—held out for thirteen days before losing their lives to nearly 4,000 Mexican soldiers commanded by General Antonio López de Santa Anna. The heroic stand gave General Sam Houston time to organize his troops and defeat Santa Anna's forces in the Battle of San Jacinto 46 days later, giving birth to the Republic of Texas. The site later served as a U.S. Army quartermaster's depot. Nearly 3 million visitors now walk through the two original buildings dating to the mission period and the 1836 battle—Alamo Church, which has become a shrine to Alamo heroes, and Long Barrack, housing a museum that shows a film on the history of the site. Exhibits on Alamo archaeology and Texas history are presented at the Alamo Gift Museum, and an outdoor display, called the Wall of History, allows the public to stroll along porcelain panels depicting the Alamo's history.

OTHER WOMEN'S ORGANIZATIONS

Other women's organizations—such as women's and garden clubs, medical auxiliaries, and branches of the American Association of University Women and the National Woman's Relief Corps of the Grand Army of the Republic—have founded and/or operated museums, historic houses, and other museumlike facilities. They include such sites as the following.

BRAZOS VALLEY MUSEUM OF NATURAL HISTORY. The Brazos Valley Museum of Natural History in Bryan, Texas, was started as the Junior Museum of Natural History in 1961 by the local chapter of the American Association of University Women. It broadened its audience and scope to become the Brazos Valley Museum in 1983. It is now organized as an independent nonprofit and features collections and exhibits on local history as well as minerals, gems, fossils, plants, birds, mammals, and insects.

CHILDREN'S MUSEUM OF OAK RIDGE. The Children's Museum of Oak Ridge in Tennessee began in 1973 as a project of the local Senior Girl Scouts. Located in a former elementary school building, the museum is oriented toward Appalachia, but also has other ethnic and historical materials. Among the collections and exhibits are Appalachian primitives and folk art, Cherokee artifacts, Japanese and other foreign dolls, Liberian artifacts, and coal mining, costume, natural history, and local history materials.

CM2—CHILDREN'S MUSEUM 2ND GENERATION. The Portland children's museum in Oregon, called CM2—Children's Museum 2nd Generation—was started in 1949 by the American Association of University Women chapter and the city's Bureau of Parks and Recreation. It began in a pioneer home, moved to a building near downtown, and is currently located in Washington Park. The museum, now an independent nonprofit, was founded as an art-based activities center and gradually added hands-on natural and cultural history collections and exhibits.

CHILDREN'S MUSEUM OF INDIANAPOLIS. See Children's Museums.

FOUNDERS' MEMORIAL GARDEN. The Founders' Memorial Garden in Athens, Georgia, was started in the late 1800s by the Ladies Garden Club of Athens, which later became the Garden Club of Georgia. A sunken formal garden serves as a memorial to the twelve members of the original group, who founded the nation's first garden club.

GRAND ARMY OF THE REPUBLIC MEMORIAL MUSEUM. The Grand Army of the Republic Memorial Museum, a memorial to the Union veterans of the Civil War in Springfield, Illinois, was founded by the National Woman's Relief Corps of the Grand Army of the Republic. The G.A.R. was established in 1866 to help veterans and their families, obtain pension increases, and preserve the memory of fallen comrades, while the Woman's Relief Corps was started in 1883 to assist in the effort. The museum contains Civil War artifacts and documents, Matthew Brady photographs, a flag from Ford Theater at the time Abraham Lincoln was

shot, and photographs of past G.A.R. commanders and National Woman's Relief Corps presidents.

THE HEALTH ADVENTURE. The Health Adventure in Asheville, North Carolina, was founded as a children's health museum in 1968 by the Medical Auxiliary of Buncombe County, which raised the funds, designed the exhibits, and staffed the original museum. Now an independent nonprofit, the museum has grown from a one-room display into a 20,000-square-foot health and science facility dedicated to improving health awareness, promoting wellness lifestyles, and increasing science literacy through exhibits and programs.

THE HERMITAGE, HOME OF PRESIDENT ANDREW JACKSON. The Ladies Hermitage Association operates the Hermitage, Home of President Andrew Jackson (and his wife, Rachel Jackson) in Hermitage, Tennessee. It has a trust deed from the state of Tennessee. Jackson purchased the 625-acre property in 1804, built the Federal-style mansion in 1821 (which was partially burned in an 1834 fire), and restored and remodeled the structure in Greek Revival style in 1836. Jackson died in 1845 and is buried with his wife in a tomb behind the garden. The site also contains several early 1800s cabins; an 1823 church; the 1836 Tulip Grove mansion where Jackson's nephew confidant and secretary, Andrew Jackson Donelson, lived with his wife, Emily; and a museum and visitor center featuring Jackson family items.

LUTZ CHILDREN'S MUSEUM. See Children's Museums.

MORTON HOUSE MUSEUM. The Morton House Museum—also known as the Josephine Morton Memorial Home—is owned and operated by the Benton Harbor-St. Joseph Federation of Women's Clubs in Michigan. The 1849 farmhouse, which became a historic house museum in 1966, was the home of four generations of the Morton family, which was instrumental in the founding, growth, and governing of the Lake Michigan port city. It was given to the women's federation for educational purposes by descendants in memorial of Mrs. Morton, wife of Henry Morton. The house features period rooms and a costumes collection.

MOUNT VERNON ESTATE AND GARDENS. Mount Vernon, the historic Virginia home of George and Martha Washington that overlooks the Potomac River near Washington, D.C., was purchased in 1858 by the Mount Vernon Ladies Association, which still owns and operates the mansion and its 500 acres. The association was founded in 1853 by Ann Pamela Cunningham for the purpose of recruiting women across the country to raise funds to preserve Mount Vernon as a national shrine. In addition to touring the house, visitors can see Washington's tomb, gardens, a museum, and more than a dozen restored outbuildings, including the stables, greenhouse, kitchen, slave quarters, and a 16-sided barn. The association is raising $85 million for three new buildings—an orientation center, a museum, and an education center—and expanded educational programming.

OLD CHEYENNE COUNTY JAIL MUSEUM. A group of business and professional women in Cheyenne Wells, Colorado, formed the Eastern Colorado Historical Society in 1961 for the purpose of creating what became the Old Cheyenne County Jail Museum in an 1894–1961 jail building. The museum consists of three rooms that were originally the jailer's quarters, the jail section (which included the sheriff's office, men's cells, and a women's cell), and a second-floor observation room overlooking the men's cells.

OLLIE MAE MOEN DISCOVERY CENTER. See Children's Museums.

PIONEER DAUGHTERS MUSEUM. The Pioneer Daughters Museum, operated by the Lake Region Pioneer Daughters, is located at the Fort Totten State Historic Site, administered by the State Historical Society of North Dakota, at Fort Totten. The historic site has seventeen buildings from the 1868–1890 frontier military post and succeeding 1891–1959 Native American school. The history museum occupies the former hospital building.

SHELDON MUSEUM AND CULTURAL CENTER. The Sheldon Museum and Cultural Center in Haines, Alaska, was founded in 1975 by the Haines Women's Club with the assistance of the two daughters of Steve Sheldon, whose collections are featured in the museum. The daughters, Elisabeth S. Hakkinen and Harriet S. Barkken, were members of the club and spearheaded the museum effort. Their father began a lifelong collecting passion in 1893 and dreamed of eventually starting a regional history museum. The Sheldon Museum now interprets the history and blending of diverse cultures in the Chilkat Valley region.

TEKAKWITHA FINE ARTS CENTER. The Tekakwitha Fine Arts Center in Sisseton, South Dakota, is operated by the Missionary Oblates of Mary Immaculate. Housed in the former dormitory of the Tekakwitha Indian Children's Home, it features the creative works of 47 Native Americans of the Lake Traverse Dakota Sioux Reservation.

Selected Bibliography

Abernathy, Francis Edward, ed. *Legendary Ladies of Texas.* Denton, TX: University of North Texas, 1994.

Aikman, Duncan. *Calamity Jane and the Lady Wildcats.* Lincoln, NE: University of Nebraska Press, 1987.

Allen, Opal Sweazea. *Narcissa Whitman.* Portland, OR: Binfords & Mort, 1959.

American Women Writers. 2d ed. 4 vols. Farmington Hills, MI: St. James Press, 2000.

American Women Writers: A Critical Reference Guide from Colonial Times to the Present. Farmington Hills, MI: St. James Press, 2000.

Anderson, William. *Laura Ingalls Wilder: A Biography.* New York: Harper Collins Publishers, 1992.

Anthony, Carl Sferrazza. *First Ladies: The Saga of the Presidents' Wives and Their Power, 1961–1990.* New York: Quill/William Morrow and Co., 1991.

Armitage, Susan, and Elizabeth Jameson, eds. *The Women's West.* Norman, OK: University of Oklahoma Press, 1987.

Augur, Helen. *Anne Hutchinson: An American Jezebel.* New York: Brentano, 1930.

Baker, Jean H. *Mary Todd Lincoln: A Biography.* New York: W. W. Norton & Co., 1987.

Banning, Evelyn I. *Helen Hunt Jackson.* New York: Vanguard Press, 1973.

Barber, Elizabeth Wayland. *Women's Work: The First 20,000 Years—Women, Cloth, and Society in Early Times.* New York: W. W. Norton & Co., 1994.

Barzman, Sol. *The First Ladies.* New York: Cowles Book Co., 1970.

Baxandall, Rosalyn, and Linda Gordon. *America's Working Women: A Documentary History.* New York: W. W. Norton & Co., 1995.

Beach, Cora, ed. *Women of Wyoming.* Casper, WY: S. E. Boyer & Co., 1927.

Bernikow, Louise. *The American Women's Almanac: An Inspiring and Irreverent Women's History.* New York: Berkeley Books, 1997.

Biddle, Gertrude Bosler, and Sarah Dickinson Lowrie. *Notable Women of Pennsylvania.* Philadelphia: University of Pennsylvania Press, 1942.

Blair, Fredrika. *Isadora: Portrait of the Artist as a Woman.* New York: Quill/William Morrow and Co., 1986.

Blair, Karen. *The Clubwoman as Feminist: True Womanhood Redefined, 1868–1914.* New York: Holmes and Meier, 1980.

Blair, Karen J., ed. *Women in Pacific Northwest History: An Anthology.* Seattle: University of Washington Press, 1990.

Bluemel, Elinor. *Florence Sabin: Colorado Woman of the Century.* Boulder, CO: University of Colorado Press, 1959.

Bodie, Idella. *South Carolina Women.* Orangeburg, SC: Sandlapper Publishing, 1978.

Bonta, Marcia Myers. *Women in the Field: America's Pioneering Women Naturalists.* College Station, TX: Texas A&M University Press, 1991.

Boulding, Elise. *The Underside of History: A View of Women Through Time.* Vols. I and II. Newbury Park, CA: Sage Publications, 1992.

Bradford, Sarah. *The Historic Biography of America's Joan of Arc, Harriet Tubman: The Moses of Her People.* Bedford, MA: Applewood Books, 1993.

Brooks, Geraldine. *Dames and Daughters of Colonial Days.* New York: Crowell, 1900.

Brooks-Pizmany, Kathleen. *United States Women in Aviation, 1919–1929.* Washington, DC: Smithsonian Institution Press, 1991.

Brooks, Van Wyck. *Helen Keller.* New York: E. P. Dutton, 1956.

Brown, Dee. *The Great Tamers: Women of the Old Wild West.* Lincoln, NE: University of Nebraska Press, 1958.

Brown, E. K. *Willa Cather.* New York: Alfred A. Knopf, 1953.

Bundles, A'Lelia Perry. *Madam C. J. Walker: Entrepreneur.* New York: Chelsea House Publishers, 1991.

Burke, John. *The Legend of Baby Doe: The Life and Times of the Silver Queen of the West.* Lincoln: NE: University of Nebraska Press, 1974.

———. *Winged Legend: The Story of Amelia Earhart.* New York: G. P. Putnam's Sons, 1970.

Burstyn, Joan N., ed. *Past and Promise: Lives of New Jersey Women.* Metuchen, NJ: Scarecrow Press, 1990.

Bushman, Claudia L., ed. *Mormon Sisters: Women in Early Utah.* Logan, UT: Utah State University Press, 1997.

Cameron, Mabel Ward, ed. *Biographical Cyclopedia of American Women.* New York: Halvord Publishing Co., 1924.

Canfield, Gae Whitney. *Sarah Winnemucca of the Northern Plains.* Norman, OK: University of Oklahoma Press, 1983.

Carrington, Evelyn M. *Women in Early Texas.* Austin, TX: Texas State Historical Association, 1994.

Carter, Morris. *Isabella Stewart Gardner and Fenway Court.* Boston: Isabella Stewart Gardner Museum, 1925.

Cayleff, Susan E. *Babe: The Life and Legend of Babe Didrikson Zaharias*. Urbana and Chicago: University of Illinois Press, 1995.

Chester, Laura, and Sharon Barba, eds. *Rising Tides: Twentieth-Century American Women Poets*. New York: Washington Square Press, 1973.

Christensen, Karen, Allen Guttman, and Gertrud Pfister, eds. *International Encyclopedia of Women and Sports*. Farmington Hills, MI: Macmillan Reference USA, 2001.

Clarke, Robert. *Ellen Swallow: The Woman Who Founded Ecology*. Chicago: Follett Publishing, 1973.

Coburn, Carol K., and Martha Smith. *Spirited Lives: How Nuns Shaped Catholic Culture and American Life*. Chapel Hill, NC: University of North Carolina Press, 1999.

Cole, Doris. *From Tipi to Skyscraper: A History of Women in Architecture*. Boston: MIT Press, 1973.

Conant, Roger. *Mercer's Belles: The Journal of a Reporter*. Pullman, WA: Washington State University Press, 1992.

Contemporary Women Artists. Farmington Hills, MI: St. James Press, 1999.

Contemporary Women Poets. Farmington Hills, MI: St. James Press, 1998.

Cook, Blanche Wiesen. *Eleanor Roosevelt*. Vols. I and II. New York: Viking, 1992 and 1999.

Cooper, Courtney Ryley. *Annie Oakley*. New York: Duffield & Co., 1927.

Corbett, Katharine T. *In Her Place: A Guide to St. Louis Women's History*. St. Louis: Missouri Historical Society, 1999.

Cordier, Mary Hurlbut. *Schoolwomen of the Prairies and Plains: Personal Narratives from Iowa, Kansas, and Nebraska, 1860s to the 1920s*. Albuquerque: University of New Mexico Press, 1992.

Cornell, Virginia. *Doc Susie: The True Story of a Country Physician in the Colorado Rockies*. Carpinteria, CA: Manifest Publications, 1991.

Cott, Nancy F., gen. ed. *The Young Oxford History of Women in the United States*. Vols. I–XI. New York: Oxford University Press, 1995.

———, ed. *No Small Courage: A History of Women in the United States*. New York: Oxford University Press, 2000.

Covey, Alan, ed. *A Century of Women*. Atlanta: TBS Books, 1994.

Crawford, Ann Fears, and Crystal Sasse Ragsdale. *Women in Texas*. Austin, TX: State House Press, 1992.

Cutrer, Emily Fourmy. *The Art of the Woman: The Life and Work of Elisabet Ney*. Lincoln, NE: University of Nebraska Press, 1988.

Dains, Mary K. *Show Me Missouri Women*. Kirksville, MO: Thomas Jefferson University Press, 1989.

Davis, Curtis Carroll, ed. *Belle Boyd in Camp and Prison*. South Brunswick, NJ: Thomas Yoseloff, 1968.

DeMille, Agnes. *Martha: The Life and Work of Martha Graham*. New York: Random House, 1991.

Directory of Historical Organizations in the United States and Canada. 15th ed. Walnut Creek, CA: AltaMira Press, 2002.

Douglas, Deborah G. *United States Women in Aviation, 1940–1985*. Washington, DC: Smithsonian Institution Press, 1991.

Douglas, Emily Taft. *Margaret Sanger: Pioneer of the Future*. New York: Holt, Rinehart & Winston, 1970.

Downing, Sybil, and Jane Valentine Barker. *Florence Rena Sabin: Pioneer Scientist*. Boulder, CO: Pruett Publishing Co., 1981.

Downs, Fane, and Nancy Baker Jones, eds. *Women and Texas History: Selected Essays*. Austin, TX: Texas State Historical Association, 1993.

Drinnon, Richard. *Rebel in Paradise: A Biography of Emma Goldman*. New York, Bantam Books, 1973.

Dublin, Thomas. *Transforming Women's Work: New England Lives in the Industrial Revolution*. Ithaca, NY: Cornell University Press, 1994.

DuBois, Ellen Carol, and Vicki L. Ruiz. *Unequal Sisters: A Multi-Cultural Reader in U.S. Women's History*. New York: Routledge, 2000.

Dubrow, Gail Lee, and Jennifer B. Gordon, eds. *Restoring Women's History Though Historic Preservation*. Baltimore: Johns Hopkins University Press, 2003.

Duniway, Abigail Scott. *Path Breaking*. New York: Schocken Books, 1971.

Edmonson, Catherine M. *Extraordinary Women: Women Who Changed History*. Holbrook, MA: Adams Media Corp., 1999.

Enkelis, Liane, and Karen Olsen. *On Our Own Terms: Portraits of Women Business Leaders*. San Francisco: Berrett-Koehler Publishers, 1995.

Evans, Sarah. *Born for Liberty: A History of Women in America*. New York: Oxford University Press, 1997.

Faderman, Lillian. *To Believe in Women*. New York: Houghton Mifflin Co., 1999.

Farley, Ronnie. *Women of the Native Struggle: Portraits and Testimony of Native American Women*. New York: Orion Books, 1993.

Farnham, Christie Anne, ed. *Women of the American South: A Multicultural Reader*. New York: New York University Press, 1997.

Ferris, Jeri. *Native American Doctor: The Story of Susan LaFlesche Picotte*. Minneapolis: Carolrhoda Books, Inc., 1991.

Fetherling, Dale. *Mother Jones: The Miners' Angel*. Carbondale, IL: Southern Illinois University Press, 1974.

Fields, Leslie Leyland. *The Entangling Net: Alaska's Commercial Fishing Women Tell Their Lives*. Urbana and Chicago: University of Illinois Press, 1997.

Fink, Augusta. *I-Mary: A Biography of Mary Austin*. Tucson: University of Arizona Press, 1983.

Foote, Cheryl J. *Women of the New Mexico Frontier, 1846–1912*. Boulder, CO: University Press of Colorado, 1990.

Fortune, Jan, and Jean Burton. *Elisabet Ney.* New York: Alfred A. Knopf, 1943.

Fox, Mary Virginia. *The Story of Women Who Shaped the West.* Chicago: Children's Press, 1991.

Frost-Knappman, Elizabeth, and Kathryn Cullen-DuPont. *Women's Rights on Trial.* Farmington Hills, MI: Gale, 1997.

Gavin, Lettie. *American Women in World War I: They Also Served.* Boulder, CO: University Press of Colorado, 1997.

Gibson, Arrell Morgan. *The Santa Fe and Taos Colonies: Age of the Muses, 1900–1942.* Norman, OK: University of Oklahoma Press, 1983.

Giddings, Paula. *When and Where I Enter: The Impact of Black Women on Race and Sex in America.* New York: Morrow, 1984.

Ginzberg, Lori D. *Women and the Work of Benevolence: Morality, Politics, and Class in the 19th-Century United States.* New Haven, CT: Yale University Press, 1990.

Glaser, Jane R., and Artemis A. Zenetou, eds. *Gender Perspectives: Essays on Women in Museums.* Washington, DC: Smithsonian Institution Press, 1994.

Goodwin, Maud Wilder. *Dolley Madison.* New York: Charles Scribner and Sons, 1896.

Gornick, Vivian. *Women in Science: Portraits from a World in Transition.* New York: Simon & Schuster, 1983.

Graham, Katharine. *Personal History.* New York: Alfred A. Knopf, Inc., 1997.

Gridley, Marion E. *American Indian Women.* New York: Hawthorn, 1974.

Hacker, Margaret Schmidt. *Cynthia Ann Parker: The Life and the Legend.* El Paso, TX: Texas Western Press, 1990.

Hail, Barbara A., ed. *Gifts of Pride and Love: Kowa and Comanche Cradles.* Providence, RI: Brown University, Haffenreffer Museum of Anthropology, 2000.

Hanft, Ethel W. *Remarkable Iowa Women.* Muscatine, IA: River Bend Publishing, 1983.

Harris, Theodore F. *Pearl S. Buck.* New York: John Day Co., 1969.

Havighurst, Walter. *Annie Oakley of the Wild West.* Lincoln, NE: University of Nebraska Press, 1954.

Hayden, Dolores. *The Power of Place: Urban Landscapes as Public History.* Cambridge, MA: MIT Press. 1995.

Head, Judith. *America's Daughters: 400 Years of American Women.* Los Angeles: Perspective Publishing, 1999.

Heinemann, Sue. *Timelines of American Women's History.* New York: Roundtable Press/Perigee, 1996.

Herrman, Dorothy. *Anne Morrow Lindbergh: A Gift of Life.* New York: Penguin Books, 1993.

Hillstorm, Laurie Collier, ed. *Contemporary Women Artists.* Farmington Hills, MI: St. James Press, 2000.

Hine, Darlene Clark, Rosalyn Terborg-Penn, and Elsa B. Brown, eds. *Black Women in America: An Historical Encyclopedia.* Bloomington, IN: Indiana University Press, 1994.

Hine, Darlene Clark, and Kathleen Thompson. *A Shining Thread of Hope: The History of Black Women in America.* New York: Broadway Books, 1998.

Holm, Jeanne. *Women in the Military: An Unfinished Revolution.* Novato, CA: Presidio Press, 1992.

Howard, Harold P. *Sacajawea.* Norman, OK: University of Oklahoma Press, 1971.

Hudson, Linda S. *Mistress of Manifest Destiny: A Biography of Jane McManus Storm Cazneau, 1807–1878.* Austin, TX: Texas State Historical Association, 2001.

Hymowitz, Carol, and Michaele Weissman. *A History of Women in America.* New York: Bantam Books, 1978.

Jackson, Grace. *Cynthia Ann Parker.* San Antonio, TX: Naylor Co., 1959.

James, Edward T., Janet Wilson, and Paul S. Boyer, eds. *Notable American Women 1607–1950: A Biographical Dictionary.* Cambridge, MA: Belknap Press, 1971.

Jeffrey, Julie R. *Converting the West: A Biography of Narcissa Whitman.* Norman, OK: University of Oklahoma Press, 1991.

Jensen, Joan M. *One Foot on the Rockies: Women and Creativity in the Modern American West.* Albuquerque: University of New Mexico Press, 1995.

Jensen, Joan M., and Darlis A. Miller. *New Mexico Women: Intercultural Perspectives.* Albuquerque: University of New Mexico Press, 1986.

Johnson, Anne Janette. *Great Women in Sports.* Detroit: Visible Ink Press, 1996.

Johnson, Gerald. *Mount Vernon: The Story of a Shrine.* New York: Random House, 1953.

Jones, Katherine M., ed. *Heroines of Dixie: Spring of High Hopes.* New York: Ballantine Books, 1974.

Jordan, Teresa. *Cowgirls: Women of the American West—An Oral History.* New York: Anchor Press, 1982.

Josephson, Hannah. *Jeannette Rankin, First Lady in Congress.* New York: Bobbs-Merrill, 1974.

Juster, Norton. *A Woman's Place: Yesterday's Women in Rural America.* Golden, CO: Fulcrum Publishing, 1996.

Kallir, Otto, ed. *Grandma Moses, American Primitive.* New York: Dryden Press, 1946.

Kasper, Shirl. *Annie Oakley.* Norman, OK: University of Oklahoma Press, 1992.

Katz, Jane, ed. *Messengers of the Wind: Native American Women Tell Their Life Stories.* New York: Ballantine Books, 1995.

Katz, William Loren. *Black Women of the Old West.* New York: Ethrac Publications, Inc., 1995.

Kaufman, Polly Welts. *Women Teachers on the Frontier.* New Haven, CT: Yale University Press, 1984.

Kaufman, Polly Welts, and Katharine T. Corbett, eds. *Her Past Around Us: Interpreting Sites for Women's History.* Malabar, FL: Krieger Publishing Co., 2003.

Keil, Sally Van Wagen. *Those Wonderful Women in Their Flying Machines.* New York: Rawson, Wade, 1979.

Kerber, Linda K., and Jane Sherron DeHart. *Women's America: Refocusing the Past.* New York: Oxford University Press, 1999.

Klapthor, Margaret Brown. *The First Ladies*. Washington, DC: White House Historical Association, 1975.

Klein, Laura F., and Lillian A. Ackerman, eds. *Women and Power in Native North America*. Norman, OK: University of Oklahoma Press, 1995.

Kofalk, Harriet. *No Women Tenderfoot: Florence Merriam Bailey, Pioneer Naturalist*. College Station, TX: Texas A&M University Press, 1989.

Kraft, Betsy Harvey. *Mother Jones: One Woman's Fight for Labor*. New York: Clarion Books, 1995.

Lanigan, Esther F. *Mary Austin: Song of a Maverick*. Tucson: University of Arizona Press, 1989.

Lanker, Brian. *I Dream a World: Portraits of Black Women Who Changed America*. New York: Stewart, Tabori & Chang, 1989.

Lash, Joseph. *Eleanor and Franklin*. New York: W. W. Norton & Co., 1971.

LeCompte, Mary Lou. *Cowgirls of the Rodeo: Pioneer Professional Athletes*. Urbana and Chicago: University of Illinois Press, 1993.

Ledbetter, Suzann. *Nellie Cashman: Prospector and Trailblazer*. El Paso, TX: Texas Western Press, 1993.

Leider, Emily Wortis. *California's Daughter: Gertrude Atherton and Her Times*. Stanford, CA: Stanford University Press, 1991.

Lewis, Vickie. *Side-by-Side: A Photographic History of American Women in War*. New York: Stewart, Tabori & Chang, 1999.

Lisle, Laurie. *Portrait of an Artist: A Biography of Georgia O'Keeffe*. New York: Seaview Books, 1980.

Love, Barbara, and Frances Love Froidevaux. *Lady's Choice: Ethel Waxman's Journals and Letters, 1905–1910*. Albuquerque: University of New Mexico, 1993.

Luchetti, Cathy, and Carol Olwell. *Women of the West*. Berkeley, CA: Antelope Island Press, 1982.

Lunardini, Christine. *What Every American Should Know About Women's History: 200 Events that Shaped Our Destiny*. Holbrook, MA: Bob Adams, Inc., 1994.

Lutz, Alma. *Susan B. Anthony: Rebel, Crusader, Humanitarian*. Boston: Beacon Press, 1959.

———. *Emma Willard, Daughter of Democracy*. Boston: Houghton Mifflin, 1929.

Lynn, Elizabeth A. *Babe Didrikson Zaharias*. New York: Chelsea House Publishers, 1989.

MacDonald, Anne L. *Female Ingenuity: Women and Invention in America*. New York: Ballantine Books, 1992.

Mankiller, Wilma, and Michael Wallis. *Mankiller: A Chief and Her People*. New York: St. Martin's Press, 1993.

Marriot, Alice. *Maria: The Potter of San Ildefonso*. Norman, OK: University of Oklahoma Press, 1948.

Mathes, Valerie Sherer. *Helen Hunt Jackson and Her Indian Reform Legacy*. Austin, TX: University of Texas Press, 1990.

McCarthy, Kathleen D. *Women's Culture: American Philanthropy and Art, 1830–1930*. Chicago: University of Chicago Press, 1991.

McHenry, Robert, ed. *Famous American Women: A Biographical Dictionary from Colonial Times to the Present*. New York: Dover Publications, 1980.

McQuiston, Liz. *Suffragettes to She-Devils: Women's Liberation and Beyond*. London: Phaidon Press, Ltd., 1997.

Merrill, Christopher, and Ellen Bradbury, eds. *From the Faraway Nearby: Georgia O'Keeffe as Icon*. Albuquerque: University of New Mexico Press, 1998.

Milford, Nancy. *Zelda*. New York: Harper & Row, 1970.

Miller, Kristie. *Ruth Hanna McCormick: A Life in Politics, 1880–1944*. Albuquerque: University of New Mexico Press, 1992.

Miller, Page Putnam, ed. *Reclaiming the Past: Landmarks of Women's History*. Bloomington, IN: Indiana University Press, 1992.

Morris, Juddi. *The Harvey Girls: The Women Who Civilized the West*. New York: Walker & Co., 1994.

Moynihan, Ruth B., Cynthia Russett, and Laurie Crumpacker, eds. *Second to None: A Documentary History of American Women*. Vols. I and II. Lincoln, NE: University of Nebraska Press, 1990 and 1993.

Murphy, Claire Rudolf, and Jane G. Haigh. *Gold Rush Women*. Seattle: Alaska Northwest Books, 1997.

Murphy, Lucy Eldersveld, and Wendy Hamand Venet, eds. *Midwestern Women: Work, Community and Leadership at the Crossroads*. Bloomington, IN: Indiana University Press, 1997.

Nakano, Mei T. *Japanese American Women: Three Generations 1890–1990*. Berkeley, CA: Mina Press Publishing, 1990.

National Museum of Women in the Arts. New York: Harry N. Abrams, Inc., 1987.

Nemeh, Kathy, ed. *American Men & Women of Science*. 21st ed. Vol. I. Farmington Hills, MI: Gale, 2002.

Nielsen, Waldemar A. *The Golden Donors*. New York: Truman Talley Books/E. P. Dutton, 1985.

Nelson, Nancy Owen, ed. *Private Voices, Public Lives: Women Speak on the Literary Life*. Denton, TX: University of North Texas Press, 1995.

Niethammer, Carolyn. *Daughters of the Earth: The Lives and Legends of American Indian Women*. New York: Macmillan Publishing Co., 1977.

Oakes, Claudia M. *United States Women in Aviation, 1930–1939*. Washington, DC: Smithsonian Institution Press, 1991.

O'Brien, Mary Barnmeyer. *Jeannette Rankin 1880–1973: Bright Star in the Big Sky*. Helena, MT: Falcon Press Publishing Co., 1995.

The Official Museum Directory, 2002. 32nd ed. New Providence, NJ: National Register Publishing, 2002.

Okihiro, Gary Y. *Margins and Mainstreams: Asians in American History and Culture*. Seattle: University of Washington Press, 1994.

Olsen, Kirstin. *Chronology of Women's History*. Westport, CT: Greenwood Press, 1994.

100 Most Important Women of the 20th Century. Des Moines: Meredith Corp., 1998.

O'Neill, William. *The Woman Movement.* New York: Quadrangle, 1971.

Parezo, Nancy J., ed. *Hidden Scholars: Women Anthropologists and the Native American Southwest.* Albuquerque: University of New Mexico Press, 1993.

Parton, Mary Field, ed. *The Autobiography of Mother Jones.* Chicago: Charles H. Kerr Publishing Co., 1974.

Pascoe, Peggy. *Relations of Rescue: The Search for Female Moral Authority in the American West, 1874–1939.* New York: Oxford University Press, 1990.

Passet, Joanne E. *Cultural Crusaders: Women Librarians in the American West, 1900–1917.* Albuquerque: University of New Mexico Press, 1994.

Patterson-Black, Sheryll, and Gene Patterson-Black. *Western Women in History and Literature.* Crawford, NE: Cottonwood Press, 1978.

Peavy, Linda, and Ursula Smith. *Frontier Women.* New York: Barnes & Noble, Inc., 1996.

Penson-Ward, Betty. *Idaho Women in History.* Boise, ID: Legendary Publishing Co., 1991.

Peterson, Susan. *The Living Tradition of Maria Martinez.* Tokyo: Kodansha International, Ltd., 1977.

Phillips, Catherine Coffin. *Jessie Benton Frémont: A Woman Who Made History.* Lincoln, NE: University of Nebraska Press, 1995.

Polk, Milbry, and Mary Tiegreen. *Women of Discovery: A Celebration of Intrepid Women Who Explored the World.* New York: Clarkson Potter Publishers, 2001.

Proffitt, Pamela, ed. *Notable Women Scientists.* Farmington Hills, MI: Gale, 2000.

Prominent Women of the 20th Century. 4 vols. Farmington Hills, MI: UXL, 1996.

Rasmussen, Linda, Lorna Rasmussen, Candace Savage, and Anne Wheeler. *A Harvest to Reap: A History of Prairie Women.* Lincoln, NE: University of Nebraska Press, 1976.

Ravage, John W. *Black Pioneers: Images of the Black Experience on the North American Frontier.* Salt Lake City: University of Utah Press, 1997.

Read, Phyllis J., and Bernard L. Witlieb. *The Book of Women's Firsts.* New York: Random House, Inc., 1992.

Rennert, Richard, ed. *Profiles of Great Black Americans: Female Leaders.* New York: Chelsea House Publishers, 1994.

Reese, Linda Williams. *Women of Oklahoma, 1890–1920.* Norman, OK: University of Oklahoma Press, 1997.

Richey, Elinor. *Eminent Women of the West.* Berkeley, CA: Howell-North Books, 1975.

Ridenhower, Marilyn, and Audrey Brigl Zins. *Women of North Dakota.* Bismarck, ND: Department of Public Instruction, 1990.

Riley, Glenda. *Inventing the American Woman: A Perspective on Women's History.* Vols. I and II. Arlington Heights, IL: Harlan Davidson, Inc., 1995.

_____. *The Life and Legend of Annie Oakley.* Norman, OK: University of Oklahoma Press, 1994.

Rittenhouse, Mignon. *The Amazing Nellie Bly.* New York: E. P. Dutton, 1956.

Roach, Joyce Gibson. *The Cowgirls.* Denton, TX: University of North Texas Press, 1990.

Robbins, Phyllis. *Maude Adams: An Intimate Portrait.* New York: G. P. Putnam's Sons, 1956.

Robertson, Janet. *The Magnificent Mountain Women: Adventures in the Colorado Rockies.* Lincoln, NE: University of Nebraska Press, 1990.

Robinson, Lillian S. *Modern Women Writers.* Farmington Hills, MI: St. James Press, 1997.

Robinson, Roxana. *Georgia O'Keeffe: A Life.* New York: Harper Collins Publishers, 1989.

Rogers, Lou. *Tar Heel Women.* Raleigh, NC: Warren Publishing Co., 1949.

Ross, Ishbell. *The President's Wife: Mary Todd Lincoln.* New York: G. P. Putnam's Sons, 1973.

_____. *Charmers and Cranks: Twelve Famous American Women Who Defied the Conventions.* New York: Harper & Row, 1965.

Rossiter, Margaret W. *Women Scientists in America: Struggles and Strategies to 1940.* Baltimore: Johns Hopkins University Press, 1982.

Rudnick, Lois Palken. *Mabel Dodge Luhan: New Woman, New World.* Albuquerque: University of New Mexico Press, 1984.

Ruiz, Vicki L. *From Out of the Shadows: Mexican Women in Twentieth-Century America.* New York: Oxford University Press, 1998.

Sanders, Marion K. *Dorothy Thompson: A Legend in Her Time.* Boston: Houghton Mifflin, 1973.

Schackel, Sandra. *Social Housekeeping: Women Shaping Public Policy in New Mexico, 1920–1940.* Albuquerque: University of New Mexico Press, 1992.

Schlegell, Abbie, and Joan M. Fisher, eds. *Women as Donors, Women as Philanthropists.* San Francisco: Jossey-Bass, Inc., 1993.

Scott, Ann Firor. *Natural Allies: Women's Associations in American History.* Chicago: University of Illinois Press, 1992.

Seagraves, Ann. *Daughters of the West.* Hayden, OH: Wesanne Publications, 1996.

Seller, Maxine Schwartz. *Immigrant Women.* New York: State University of New York Press, 1994.

Sherr, Lynn. *Failure Is Impossible: Susan B. Anthony in Her Own Words.* New York: Times Books/Random House, Inc., 1995.

Sherr, Lynn, and Jurate Kazickas. *Susan B. Anthony Slept Here: A Guide to American Women's Landmarks.* New York: Times Books/Random House, Inc., 1994.

Shirley, Gayle C. *More than Petticoats: Remarkable Montana Women.* Helena, MT: Falcon Press Publishing Co., 1996.

Sicherman, Barbara, and Carol Hurd Green, eds. *Notable American Women: The Modern Period.* Cambridge, MA: Belknap Press, 1980.

Simkins, Francis B., and James Welch Patton. *The Women of the Confederacy.* Richmond, VA: Garrett & Massie, 1936.

Smith, Jean K. *Those Intriguing Indomitable Vermont Women.* Montpelier, VT: Vermont State Division, American Association of University Women, 1980.

Smith, Jessie Carney, ed. *Notable Black American Women.* Vols. I and II. Farmington Hills, MI: Gale, 1992 and 1996.

Snodgrass, Mary Ellen, ed. *Celebrating Women's History: A Women's History Month Reference Book.* Farmington Hills, MI: Gale, 1996.

Stanton, Elizabeth Cady. *Eighty Years and More.* New York: Schocken, 1971.

Stauffer, Helen Winter. *Maria Sandoz: Story Catcher of the Plains.* Lincoln, NE: University of Nebraska Press, 1982.

Sterling, Dorothy, ed. *We Are Sisters: Black Women in the Nineteenth Century.* New York, W. W. Norton & Co., 1984.

Sullivan, George. *The Day the Women Got to Vote: A Photo History of the Women's Rights Movement.* New York: Scholastic, Inc., 1994.

Telgen, Diane, and Jim Kamp, eds. *Notable Hispanic American Women.* Vols. I and II. Farmington Hills, MI: Gale, 1993 and 1998.

Terborg-Penn, Rosalyn. *African American Women in the Struggle for the Vote, 1850–1920.* Bloomington, IN: Indiana University Press, 1998.

Thompson, Ray. *Betsy Ross: Last of Philadelphia's Free Quakers.* Fort Washington, PA: Bicentennial Press, 1974.

Tinling, Marion. *Women Remembered: A Guide to Landmarks of Women's History in the United States.* Westport, CT: Greenwood Press, 1986.

Trenton, Patricia, ed. *Independent Spirits: Women Painters of the American West, 1890–1945.* Los Angeles: University of California Press, 1995.

Tucker, Cynthia Grant. *Prophetic Sisterhood: Liberal Women Ministers of the Frontier, 1880–1930.* Bloomington, IN: Indiana University Press, 1994.

Walker, Patricia Chambers, and Thomas Graham. *Directory of Historic House Museums in the United States.* Walnut Creek, CA: AltaMira Press, 2000.

Ward, Jean M., and Elaine A. Maveety, eds. *Pacific Northwest Women 1815–1925: Lives, Memories, and Writings.* Corvallis, OR: Oregon State University Press, 1995.

Warner, Carolyn. *The Last Word: A Treasury of Women's Quotes.* Englewood Cliffs, NJ: Prentice Hall, 1992.

Watkins, Bonnie, and Nina Rothchild. *In the Company of Women: Voices from the Women's Movement.* St. Paul, MN: Minnesota Historical Society Press, 1996.

We Remember: Women Born at the Turn of the Century Tell the Stories of Their Lives. New York: William Morrow & Co., 1999.

Weatherford, Doris. *American Women's History: An A to Z of People, Organizations, Issues, and Events.* New York: Prentice Hall General Reference, 1994.

Webster's Dictionary of American Women. New York: Smithmark Publishers, 1996.

Weimann, Jeanne Madeline. *The Fair Women: The Story of the Women's Building, World's Columbian Exposition, Chicago 1893.* Chicago: Academy Chicago, 1981.

Western Writers of America. *The Women Who Made the West: The Stories of the Unsung Heroes of the American Frontier.* New York: Doubleday, 1980.

Whitacre, Christine. *Molly Brown: Denver's Unsinkable Lady.* Denver: Historic Denver, Inc., 1984.

Whitley, Colleen, ed. *Worth Their Salt: Notable But Often Unnoted Women of Utah.* Logan, UT: Utah State University Press, 1996.

Winegarten, Ruthe. *Black Texas Women: 150 Years of Trial and Triumph.* Austin, TX: University of Texas Press, 1995.

Witt, Linda, Karen M. Paget, and Glenna Matthews. *Running As a Woman in American Politics.* New York: The Free Press/Macmillan, Inc., 1994.

Women Filmmakers & Their Films. Farmington Hills, MI: St. James Press, 1998.

Women's Firsts. Farmington Hills, MI: Gale, 1997.

Women in World History. 17 vols. Farmington Hills, MI: Gale/Yorkin Publications, 1999–2003.

Woodress, James. *Willa Cather: A Literary Life.* Lincoln, NE: University of Nebraska Press, 1987.

Woodward, Grace Steele. *Pocahontas.* Norman, OK: University of Oklahoma Press, 1969.

Yellin, Jean Fagan. *Women & Sisters: The Antislavery Feminists in American Culture.* New Haven, CT: Yale University Press, 1989.

Yung, Judy. *Chinese Women of America: A Pictorial History.* Seattle: University of Washington Press, 1986.

Zanjani, Sally. *A Mine of Her Own: Women Prospectors in the American West, 1850–1950.* Lincoln, NE: University of Nebraska Press, 1997.

Zeinert, Karen. *Those Incredible Women of World War II.* Brookfield, CT: Millbrook Press, 1994.

Zucker, Barbara Fleisher. *Children's Museums, Zoos, and Discovery Rooms: An International Reference Guide.* Westport, CT: Greenwood Press, 1987.

Indexes

Founders, Donors, and Honorees

Butterworth, Katherine Deere, 170
Byrd, Evelyn, 163

Cabrini, St. Frances, 69–71
Cahalan, Mary A., 57
Calloway, Berta, 7, 238
Cameron, Louise Wells, 92–92
Campbell, Almira, 176
Cantor, Iris, 74–75, 106
Carey, Mrs. John N., 229–30
Carlson, Edna, 112
Carnegie, Lucy Coleman, 169
Carnell, Julia Shaw Patterson, 7, 93
Carpenter, Ann-Marie, 243
Carroll, Margaret Tilghman, 172
Carson, Rachel, 48
Carter, Elizabeth Grayson, 180
Carter, Hannah, 216
Carter, Mrs. Edward W., 216
Cartan, Barbara Sesnon, 102
Catalini, Susan Dimock, 104
Caten, Emma, 90
Cather, Willa, 41
Cawker, Mary, 194
Cenci, Beatrice, 63
Chatilon, Odile DeLor, 174
Chew, Cassandra, 168–69
Chopin, Kate, 34
Chouteau, Emile Sophie, 174
Christlieb, Elizabeth B., 87
Clack, Margaret Turner, 138
Clark, Fanny Dwight, 220
Clark, Francine, 84–85
Clark, Kate Freeman, 85–86
Clarke, Caroline P., 170
Clarke, Cecile, 7, 133
Cluett, Amanda, 175
Cluett, Caroline, 175
Cobb, Lois Dowdle, 208
Coburn, Donna, 142
Cogswell, Alice, 58
Coit, Lillie Hitchcock, 57
Coker, Cecelia, 110–11
Collier, Janet, 200
Collins, Maribeth, 94
Colonial Dames of America, 2, 244, 250–51
Colton, Mary-Russell Ferrell, 239
Comer, Isabel Anderson, 127
Common, Minna Anthony, 214
Compton, Margaret Hutchinson, 209
Conway, Julia, 184
Cook, Eleanor Barbour, 209–10
Cook, Frances A. "Fannye," 205
Copeland, Helen E., 107
Cornell, Harriet W., 78, 128

Cornwall, Emeline, 171
Couanche, Sarah, 158
Cozens, Mary, 182
Crabtree, Lotta, 57
Cramer, Mary Meeker, 184
Crandall, Prudence, 147
Crossman, Kathleen, 112
Crow, Margaret, 98
Cuddy, Edna, 174
Cullis, Irene, 109
Culver, Edith Newman, 166
Cummer, Ninah May Holden, 78
Custer, Libby, 176

Daniel, Vara, 192
Daniels, Myra Janco, 79
Daniels, Wendy, 228
Dare, Virginia, 64
Daughters of Hawaii, 2, 244, 252
Daughters of the American Revolution (DAR), 2, 55, 61,
    168, 244, 249–50
Daughters of the Republic of Texas, 2, 252
Daughters of Utah Pioneers, 2, 66, 244, 251–52
Davis, Alice Brown, 25
Davis, Edith, 111
Davis, Emily, 109
Davis, Julia, 195
Davis, Nellie Stratton, 107
Davis, Sarah, 59
Davis, Susan G., 136
Davis, Varina "Winnie," 65
Day, Helen, 114
Day, Katherine Seymour, 29
Dean, Berta Gale, 166
Degenhart, Elizabeth, 6, 116
Degenstein, Lore, 110
Delano, Jane, 56
DeLany, Mrs. John, 182
Del Rio, Delores, 59–60
de Menil, Dominique, 50–51
de Saisset, Isabel, 127
de Temple, Rafael Cota, 181–82
Dibble, Julia Sturges, 177–78
Dickinson, Emily, 9, 36
Dickinson, Susan Huntington Gilbert, 172–73
Didrikson, Babe. See Zaharias, Mildred "Babe" Didrikson
Dimock, Susan Whitney, 104
Dinsmore, Julia, 172
Dinsmore, Martha, 172
Dix, Doretha, 47
Dixon, Margaret Oates, 96
Dodge, Nancy, 88
Donaldson, Kay, 230
Dooley, Sallie May, 164
Door, Clara Barkley, 169

Subject

About the Authors

Victor J. Danilov has been a leader in the museum field for more than a quarter of a century—as a museum director, president of museum organizations, founder and director of a university training program for museum administrators, and author of numerous articles and books on museums. He was president and director of Chicago's Museum of Science and Industry, the nation's first and largest interactive science and technology museum, for fifteen years. During that period, he also served as first chairman of Chicago's arts council for eight years. Danilov was a founder and president of the Association of Science-Technology Centers, the Science Museum Exhibit Collaborative, and the Museum Film Network; chairman of the International Council of Museums' International Committee of Science and Technology Museums; and a member of the American Association of Museums Council.

Following Danilov's retirement in Chicago in 1987, he served as adjunct professor and started and directed the Museum Management Program, a short summer course for museum directors and other senior administrators, at the University of Colorado in Boulder until a second retirement in 2004. In the 1990s, he also was involved in the Colorado-based Women of the West Museum, which was founded by his wife, Toni Dewey, and later was merged into the Autry Museum of Western Heritage (now the Museum of the American West) in Los Angeles.

He has written several hundred professional articles and has written or edited 23 books, mostly in the museum field. They include books on science, corporate, university/college, hall of fame, sports, and western museums and historic sites, as well as a manual on museum career and training programs and museum and gallery guidebooks on Colorado and the Chicago area.

Danilov holds degrees from Pennsylvania State University, Northwestern University, and the University of Colorado, and has received numerous honors from professional and community organizations, governments, and universities.

Susan Armitage is Claudius O. and Mary W. Johnson Distinguished Professor of History and director of the Center for Columbia River History at Washington State University, where she has been a member of the faculty since 1978. She teaches history and has also served as director of women's studies, director of American studies, and editor of *Frontiers: A Journal of Women Studies*. Well known for her work in western women's history, she is coeditor (with Elizabeth Jameson) of *The Women's West* (1987) and *Writing the Range* (1997), as well as numerous articles.